# Experiencing
# Intercultural
# Communication

# Experiencing Intercultural Communication

## *An Introduction*

Sixth Edition

Judith N. Martin
*Arizona State University*

Thomas K. Nakayama
*Northeastern University*

EXPERIENCING INTERCULTURAL COMMUNICATION: AN INTRODUCTION, SIXTH EDITION

Published by McGraw-Hill Education, 2 Penn Plaza, New York, NY 10121. Copyright © 2018 by McGraw-Hill Education. All rights reserved. Printed in the United States of America. Previous editions © 2014 and 2011. No part of this publication may be reproduced or distributed in any form or by any means, or stored in a database or retrieval system, without the prior written consent of McGraw-Hill Education, including, but not limited to, in any network or other electronic storage or transmission, or broadcast for distance learning.

Some ancillaries, including electronic and print components, may not be available to customers outside the United States.

This book is printed on acid-free paper.

1 2 3 4 5 6 7 8 9 LCR 21 20 19 18 17

ISBN        978-1-259-87056-9
MHID        1-259-87056-1

Chief Product Officer, SVP Products & Markets: *G. Scott Virkler*
Vice President, General Manager, Products & Markets: *Michael Ryan*
Vice President, Content Design & Delivery: *Betsy Whalen*
Managing Director: *David Patterson*
Brand Manager: *Penina Braffman*
Director, Product Development: *Meghan Campbell*
Product Developer: *Jamie Laferrera*
Marketing Manager: *Meredith Leo*
Director, Content Design & Delivery: *Terri Schiesl*
Program Manager: *Jennifer Shekleton*
Content Project Managers: *Lisa Bruflodt, Samantha Donisi-Hamm*
Buyer: *Laura M. Fuller*
Content Licensing Specialist: *DeAnna Dausener*
Cover Image: *Shutterstock/Nicolas Economou; Shutterstock/Tyler Olson;* © *McGraw-Hill Education/John Flournoy*
Compositor: *MPS Limited*
Printer: *LSC Communications*

All credits appearing on page or at the end of the book are considered to be an extension of the copyright page

**Library of Congress Cataloging-in-Publication Data**

Cataloging-in-Publication Data has been requested from the Library of Congress.

The Internet addresses listed in the text were accurate at the time of publication. The inclusion of a website does not indicate an endorsement by the authors or McGraw-Hill Education, and McGraw-Hill Education does not guarantee the accuracy of the information presented at these sites.

mheducation.com/highered

# Brief Contents

# ● Contents

# Preface

As the once powerful Chinese economy slows down, what economic changes will ensue around the world? What changes will happen in Europe after the departure of the United Kingdom from the European Union? Economic inequality, the disparity between the rich and the poor in the United States, is higher than ever and highest of all industrialized countries. These economic issues may drive the shape and character of intercultural contact in the future—because businesses drive what types and which cultures are more and less likely to come into contact.

Changes in governmental systems seem to happen at a rapid rate. In the aftermath of the Arab Spring, governments all over the Middle East—Libya, Egypt, Iraq, Tunisia, etc.—seem fragile or almost nonexistent. Rising regional identities may lead to new nations (e.g., Flanders, Catalonia, Scotland). Is a Palestinian state a future possibility, and how might it change the Middle East? As these changes and others appear on the horizon, how will intercultural conflict be managed? What role does intercultural communication play in these disputes?

Natural disasters may also affect intercultural communication. Climate change may bring about significant changes that require us to work with others around the world. Droughts, earthquakes, hurricanes, typhoons, tsunamis, and other natural disasters may increase the need for intercultural cooperation to help those in need.

The rising use of social media presents new intercultural issues; social media enable both better intercultural understanding as well as negative attacks on various cultural groups. The photo of the body of a tiny Syrian child washed up on a beach in Greece went viral on social media and garnered much sympathy for the plight of refugees fleeing war and tragedy in the Middle East. On the other hand, social media have been used to broadcast beheadings of journalists and others by the Islamic State and to recruit new members around the world.

They are not alone in using social media to heighten intercultural tensions. How we use and misuse social media leaves a trail that can build bridges to other cultures or reinforce walls between them.

What role can intercultural communication play in the changing world that we all live in? How can we use our intercultural skills to help enrich our lives and the lives of those around us? What should intercultural communication scholars be focusing on? What are the best ways to better understand intercultural communication in this dynamic world? As the world changes, how important is it for us to understand the past? Should we focus on culture-specific information? Or should we strive to develop more universal rules? How can anyone understand every culture around the world? Or every language? We wrote this book to shed light on these and many other questions about intercultural communication.

As in our earlier books, we have tried to use information from a variety of approaches, drawing from social psychological approaches as well as from ethnographic studies and more recent critical media studies. However, the emphasis in this book is on the practical, experiential nature of intercultural communication. We still acknowledge that there are no easy answers to many intercultural situations. However, we attempt to give solid, practical guidelines, while noting the complexity of the task facing the student of intercultural communication.

## FEATURES OF THE BOOK

This book addresses the core issues and concerns of intercultural communication by introducing a group of general skills in Chapter 1 and emphasizing the concepts and the skills of communicating interculturally throughout the text. This textbook

- Includes a balanced treatment of skills and theory. The skills focus is framed by the presentation of the conceptual aspects of culture and communication. Each chapter has a section called "Building Intercultural Skills" that provides guidelines for improving the reader's intercultural communication.

- Provides a framework for understanding intercultural communication, focusing on four building blocks (culture, communication, context, and power) and four barriers (ethnocentrism, stereotyping, prejudice, and discrimination).

- Focuses on personal experiences by including students' narratives and the authors' personal experiences highlighted throughout the text.

- Presents the material in a student-friendly way. There are four types of thoughtful and fun bits of information in the margin provided for students' interest. This edition contains new updated examples and websites:

 "What Do You Think?" includes information and questions that challenge students to think about their own culture and communication styles.

 "Surf's Up!" suggests websites that students can visit for more information about culture and communication.

 "Pop Culture Spotlight" presents examples of culture and communication from today's popular culture.

 "Info Bites" provides fun facts and figures that illustrate issues related to intercultural communication.

- Includes separate chapters on history and identity, with sections on Whiteness and assisting European American students in exploring their own cultural issues.

- Focuses on popular culture, both in a separate chapter and in examples woven throughout the book.

- Discusses important role of communication technologies in intercultural encounters in various contexts.

- Applies concepts to real-life contexts; the book includes four chapters on how intercultural communication works in everyday settings in tourism, business, education, and health.

## NEW TO THE SIXTH EDITION

This edition includes updated material addressing recent challenges of intercultural communication, including increased worldwide religious and ethnic conflict, the enormous numbers of migrants fleeing intercultural conflict and economic challenges, the impact of political context on intercultural encounters, and technological challenges. For example, Chapter 1 includes a discussion of how security concerns translated to anti-immigrant/refugee attitudes and legislation and their impacts on intercultural communication. In Chapter 8, we extended our discussion of ongoing religious and racial tensions in the United States and overseas, and added new material on peacebuilding efforts and "skilled disagreement" strategies as responses to protracted intercultural conflicts.

We also recognize the continuing importance of political issues in intercultural contexts. For example, Chapter 2 includes a discussion of the slow reaction to finding lead in Flint Michigan drinking water; in Chapter 4, Canada's welcoming stance to refugees, as part of its national identity; and in Chapter 13, the impact of various communication strategies about the Zika virus.

To continue to recognize the increasing role technology plays in intercultural communication, in Chapter 1 we acknowledge the increasing role, both negative and positive, of social media in intercultural encounters. Chapter 5 includes a discussion of the impact of machine translation on intercultural communication. Chapters 10 and 11 include new material on the role of social media in tourist and business contexts, and social media examples are interwoven throughout the other chapters.

## OVERVIEW OF THE BOOK

The first chapter focuses on the changing dynamics of social life and global conditions that provide a rationale for the study of intercultural communication, suggesting that intercultural learning is not just transformative for the individual, but also benefits the larger society and other cultural groups in our increasingly interdependent world. In this edition, we have updated statistics and examples as well as provided expanded discussions on the impact of income wealth and income inequality in the United States as well as the negative and positive impacts of social media on intercultural communication.

Chapter 2 outlines a framework for the book and identifies four building blocks of intercultural communication—culture, communication, context, and power, as well as four attitudinal and behavioral barriers to effective intercultural communication: ethnocentrism, stereotyping, prejudice, and discrimination. In this edition, we discuss the most recent addition to the Hofstede value framework (indulgence vs. restraint) as well as examples of cultural resistance through social media (e.g., #blacklivesmatter) and also provide updated examples of anti-immigrant prejudice and discrimination.

Chapter 3 focuses on helping students see the importance of history in understanding contemporary intercultural communication issues and a discussion of how postcolonial histories intertwine with today's practices of outsourcing and global business. This edition provides updated examples of the use of history for contemporary situations and underscores the ways that intercultural relationships can be impacted.

Chapter 4 discusses issues of identity and intercultural communication. In this chapter we address a number of identities (gender, age, race, and ethnicity [including White identity], physical ability, religion, class, national and regional identity). We also discuss issues of multicultural identity—people who live on the borders—and issues of crossing borders and cultural shock and adaptation. This edition includes a discussion of Canada's welcoming refugees and how it ties to Canadian identity, as well as new examples of popular culture products and their impact on various cultural identities.

Chapter 5 addresses verbal issues in intercultural communication, describing cultural variations in language and communication style, attitudes toward speaking, writing and silences, as well as issues of power and language. This edition includes an expanded discussion of how social media influences cultural differences in communication style, as well as a discussion of the impact of machine translation on intercultural encounters, and new material in code-switching.

Chapter 6 focuses on the role of nonverbal behavior in intercultural interaction, describing universal and culture-specific aspects of nonverbal communication, and the ways nonverbal behavior can provide a basis for stereotyping and prejudice. This chapter also addresses cultural space and its dynamic, changing nature, and a discussion of cyberspace as cultural space. This edition includes recent research questioning the universality of facial expressions, and an expanded discussion focusing on micro-aggression—nonverbal expression of bias and prejudice.

Chapter 7 addresses popular culture and intercultural communication. We define pop culture and discuss the ways in which pop culture forms our images of culture groups and the ways in which we consume (or resist) popular culture products. This edition includes updated popular culture examples, including Beyoncé's new music video, "Formation," in the current context of concern over policing and race relations.

Chapter 8 discusses the role of culture and conflict. The chapter identifies characteristics of intercultural conflict, describes both personal and social/political aspects of conflict, and examines the role of religion in intercultural conflict and the ways conflict management varies from culture to culture. This edition includes an updated discussion of the role economic conditions and social inequities play in intercultural conflict and peacebuilding efforts in protracted intercultural conflict situations.

Chapter 9 focuses on intercultural relationships in everyday life. It identifies the challenges and benefits of intercultural relationships, examining how relationships may differ across cultures and exploring a variety of relationship types: friendship, gay, dating, and marriage relationships. In this edition, we updated the status of same-sex marriages and included a discussion of transgender friendships.

Chapters 10 through 13 focus on intercultural communication in specific contexts. Chapter 10 addresses issues of intercultural communication in the tourism industry, exploring various ways in which hosts and tourists may interact, the ways varying cultural norms may affect tourist encounters, language issues and communication style, and the sometimes-complex attitudes of hosts toward tourists. In this edition, we include discussions of the impacts of the recent economic downturn, political instability, terrorist attacks, health risks, and environmental disasters (earthquakes, hurricanes) on touristic encounters; new material on hosts' attitude toward tourism; and the role of social media on tourism.

Chapter 11 focuses on intercultural communication in business contexts, identifying several communication challenges (work-related values, differences in management styles, language issues, and affirmative action) in both domestic and international contexts, and the social and political contexts of business. We also provide a discussion of how power relations affect intercultural business encounters—both interpersonal relationships and larger system impacts. This edition includes new material on workplace diversity issues as well as the impact of globalization, immigration, terrorist attacks, and intercultural communication in business contexts.

Chapter 12 explores intercultural communication and education, discussing different kinds of educational experiences (e.g., study abroad, culture-specific settings) and communication challenges (e.g., varying roles for teachers and students, grading, and power); addressing social concerns and the role of culture in admissions, affirmative action, and standardized tests; and examining the challenges of educating immigrants. We also explore minority serving institutions as well as  gender issues, including campus rape.

Chapter 13 addresses intercultural communication and health care, focusing on intercultural barriers to effective health care, the historical treatment of cultural groups, and the ways power dynamics, religious beliefs, and language barriers influence communication in health care settings. It also includes a discussion on alternative and complementary medicine as other ways of thinking about health care. This edition provides information on the communication strategies in response to the Zika virus as well as issues with vaccines and updated information on the Affordable Care Act (Obamacare).

## connect®

*The sixth edition of Experiencing Intercultural Communication: An Introduction is now available online with Connect, McGraw-Hill Education's integrated assignment and assessment platform. Connect also offers SmartBook for the new edition, which is the first adaptive reading experience proven to improve grades and help students study more effectively. All of the title's website and ancillary content is also available through Connect, including:*

- *A full Test Bank of multiple choice questions that test students on central concepts and ideas in each chapter.*

- *An Instructor's Manual for each chapter with full chapter outlines, sample test questions, and discussion topics.*

- *Lecture Slides for instructor use in class.*

©Getty Images/iStockphoto

## McGraw-Hill Connect®
## Learn Without Limits

Connect is a teaching and learning platform that is proven to deliver better results for students and instructors.

Connect empowers students by continually adapting to deliver precisely what they need, when they need it, and how they need it, so your class time is more engaging and effective.

### Connect's Impact on Retention Rates, Pass Rates, and Average Exam Scores

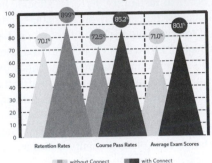

without Connect    with Connect

**73% of instructors who use Connect require it; instructor satisfaction increases by 28% when Connect is required.**

Using **Connect** improves retention rates by **19.8%**, passing rates by **12.7%**, and exam scores by **9.1%**.

# Analytics

## Connect Insight®

Connect Insight is Connect's new one-of-a-kind visual analytics dashboard—now available for both instructors and students—that provides at-a-glance information regarding student performance, which is immediately actionable. By presenting assignment, assessment, and topical performance results together with a time metric that is easily visible for aggregate or individual results, Connect Insight gives the user the ability to take a just-in-time approach to teaching and learning, which was never before available. Connect Insight presents data that empowers students and helps instructors improve class performance in a way that is efficient and effective.

### Impact on Final Course Grade Distribution

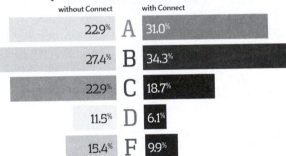

without Connect    with Connect

| without Connect | Grade | with Connect |
| --- | --- | --- |
| 22.9% | A | 31.0% |
| 27.4% | B | 34.3% |
| 22.9% | C | 18.7% |
| 11.5% | D | 6.1% |
| 15.4% | F | 9.9% |

Students can view their results for any **Connect** course.

# Mobile

Connect's new, intuitive mobile interface gives students and instructors flexible and convenient, anytime–anywhere access to all components of the Connect platform.

# Adaptive

More students earn **A's** and **B's** when they use McGraw-Hill Education **Adaptive** products.

## SmartBook®

Proven to help students improve grades and study more efficiently, SmartBook contains the same content within the print book, but actively tailors that content to the needs of the individual. SmartBook's adaptive technology provides precise, personalized instruction on what the student should do next, guiding the student to master and remember key concepts, targeting gaps in knowledge and offering customized feedback, and driving the student toward comprehension and retention of the subject matter. Available on tablets, SmartBook puts learning at the student's fingertips—anywhere, anytime.

Over **8 billion questions** have been answered, making McGraw-Hill Education products more intelligent, reliable, and precise.

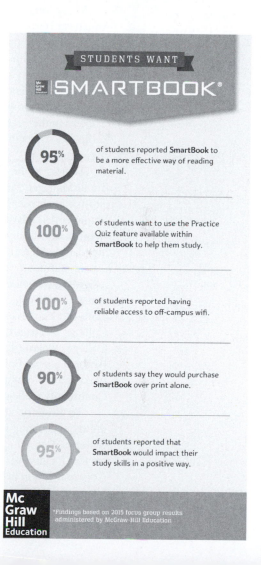

## ACKNOWLEDGMENTS

As always, we owe a great deal to our colleagues in the Hugh Downs School of Human Communication, College of Liberal Arts and Sciences, at Arizona State University as well as to our colleagues outside our school. Our colleagues at ASU helped us work though our ideas and shared insights from their lives and the lives of their students. Our students have contributed a great deal to this book; they willingly shared examples and stories from their own lives and enthusiastically supported this project.

Special thanks go to our graduate editorial assistants Maggie Williams at Northeastern University and Gladys Muasya, Arizona State University, who found new margin material for us, worked competently, creatively, and with extreme good nature under tight deadlines.

Many other Communication colleagues contributed, including Professor Anneliese Harper (Scottsdale Community College) who gave us the idea of writing this book by pointing out the need for more context-specific and experientially based materials in the intercultural communication curriculum. Professor Shelley Smith (University of Minnesota–Duluth), Professor Dawn Braithwaite (University of Nebraska), and Professor Denis Leclerc (Thunderbird School of Global Management) provided us with resources and suggestions for framing the "contexts" chapters in the first edition. Thanks also to Robert Barr, M.D., of the Mecklenburg Radiology Associates in Charlotte, North Carolina, for the helpful tips on health communication.

Thanks to the fine team at McGraw-Hill who make it all happen. Thanks to Brand Manager, Jamie Laferrera, who skillfully guided us through the McGraw-Hill publishing process. We also want to acknowledge the fine work of Production Manager Lisa Bruflodt and Marketing Manager, Meredith Leo; and Editorial Coordinator, Jasmine Staton. Finally, thanks to the **ansr**source developmental editing team led by Anne Sheroff and Poornima H.

In addition, we want to thank the reviewers and readers, whose thoughtful and insightful comments led to careful revisions and a much-improved manuscript: Amie D. Kincaid, University of Illinois–Springfield; Cheryl L. Nicholas, Penn State–Berks; Kevin C. Lee, Darton College; Marilyn Brimo, Mt. Hood Community College; Michael Lenaghan, Miami Dade College; Tracey Powers, Central Arizona College; Celeste Lacroix, College of Charleston; Cheryl L. Nicholas, Penn State Berks; Thomas Damp, Central New Mexico Community College; Karen Krumrey-Fulks, Lane Community College; Racheal Ruble, Iowa State; Puvana Ganesan, Mesa Community College; and Elizabeth Catanese, Community College of Philadelphia.

To those friends and colleagues who enrich our lives and our scholarship by helping us understand what it means to live interculturally, we are grateful: Dr. Amalia Villegas, Laura Laguna, Cruzita and Aurelio Mori, Lucia Madril and family, many of the faculty, staff, and participants at the Summer Institute for Intercultural Communication in Portland, Oregon, and Jean-Louis Sauvage (Université de Mons-Hainaut). Finally, we thank our partners, Ronald S. Chaldu and David L. Karbonski, for hanging in there with us once again!

# About the Authors

**Judith Martin** grew up in Mennonite communities, primarily in Delaware and Pennsylvania. She has studied at the Université de Grenoble in France and has taught in Algeria. She received her doctorate from the Pennsylvania State University. By background and training, she is a social scientist who has focused on intercultural communication on an interpersonal level and has studied how people's communication is affected as they move or sojourn between international locations. More recently, she has studied how people's cultural backgrounds influence their online communication. She has taught at the State University of New York at Oswego, the University of Minnesota, the University of New Mexico, and Arizona State University. She enjoys gardening, reading murder mysteries, traveling, and hanging out with her large extended family.

**Tom Nakayama** grew up mainly in Georgia, at a time when the Asian American presence was much less than it is now. He has studied at the Université de Paris and various universities in the United States. He received his doctorate from the University of Iowa. By background and training, he is a critical rhetorician who views intercultural communication in a social context. Prior to Northeastern University, he has taught at California State University at San Bernardino, Arizona State University, the University of Iowa, and the Université de Mons-Hainaut (now the Université de Mons). He has guest lectured at many institutions, including the University of Maine, Centre Universitaire (Luxembourg), University of Southern California, University of Georgia, Centre National de la Recherche Scientifique (Paris), and the École des hautes études commerciales du nord (Lille). He loves the changes of seasons in New England, traveling, and playing trivia.

© kristian sekulic/Getty Images RF

## CHAPTER ONE

# Studying Intercultural Communication

## CHAPTER OUTLINE

## STUDY OBJECTIVES

*After reading this chapter, you should be able to:*

1. Describe the peace imperative for studying intercultural communication.

2. Identify and describe the economic and technological imperatives for studying intercultural communication.

3. Describe how the changing demographics in the United States and the changing worldwide immigration patterns affect intercultural communication.

4. Explain how studying intercultural communication can lead to increased self-understanding.

5. Understand the difference between a universalistic and relativist approach to the study of ethics and intercultural communication.

6. Identify and describe characteristics of an ethical student of culture.

## KEY TERMS

| | |
|---|---|
| assimilable | heterogeneous |
| class structure | immigration |
| cosmopolitans | *maquiladoras* |
| cross-cultural trainers | melting pot metaphor |
| demographics | relativist position |
| diversity | self-awareness |
| enclaves | self-reflexivity |
| ethics | universalist position |
| globalization | |

*A child born today will be faced as an adult, almost daily, with problems of a global interdependent nature, be it peace, food, the quality of life, inflation, or scarcity of resources. He/she will be both an actor and a beneficiary or a victim in the total world fabric, and may rightly ask: "Why was I not warned? Why was I not better educated? Why did my teachers not tell me about these problems and indicate my behavior as a member of an interdependent human race?"*

—*Robert Muller*[1]

This quote from Robert Muller, known as "the father of global education" is as relevant today as it was 30 years ago and underscores the importance of learning about our interdependent world. In addition to peace, food, the economy, and the quality of life identified by Muller, climate change, terrorism, conflicts around the globe require working across cultural differences to find solutions to these complex problems. For example, religious and ethnic conflicts in the Middle East and Africa, territorial tensions in Asia over strategic island claimed by more than one country (China, Japan, Vietnam, the Philippines, South Korea) as well as the worldwide refugee problem with millions of migrants streaming into Europe into already fragile economies, for example, Greece and Eastern European countries. In addition, the once powerful Chinese economy is now struggling, leading to nervousness of U.S. investors and a volatile stock market.[2] On the more positive side, global interconnectedness also brings us the World Cup, the Olympics, as well as global cooperation in dealing with health challenges like the Ebola and Zika outbreaks. The personal impact of this global interconnectedness has been extensive. Although the recession in the United States is technically over, wages here are stagnant and the promises of the American Dream seem illusive for many—particularly for minority households whose financial resources remain at a fraction of White households. Perhaps your parents or someone you know lost their jobs, or their houses in the economic downtown. Perhaps you worry about how you'll pay off your college debt or whether you'll ever be able to own a home or achieve economic independence. Let's consider how the economic conditions and world tensions are affecting intercultural relations. Let's start at home, in the United States where some adult children, many saddled with large college debt, are still living at home and according to a recent report, even though there have been positive economic trends, there has been no increase in the number of young adults establishing their own household. In fact, the number is no higher in 2015 than it was before the recession.[3] As one 20 something said "I can't foresee a future where we're going to buy a house. . . It'll be 10 to 15 years, and by that time, we'll be too old to have children. I don't know how people afford to have children these days."[4]

This intergenerational living arrangement, common in many parts of the world, presents challenges to independent minded children (and parents) in the United States and requires (intercultural) communication skills—listening to each other openly and respectfully. Some even say it's a good thing—that parents and children get to spend extra time with each other that they wouldn't be able to do in other circumstances.[5]

The global economic slowdown has had enormous consequences for intercultural relations in the fledging European Union (EU). As you probably know, European countries have experienced the crisis differently but are economically interdependent. The northern countries of Germany, Finland, Sweden, and Denmark have implemented austerity measures and have relatively healthy economies, which are being dragged down by the economically weak southern countries of Greece, Spain, and Italy. The resulting tensions over economic issues and the recent refugee crisis are fueling old stereotypes. Germans (even some politicians) are calling Greeks work-shy, rule-bending, and recklessly extravagant while they see themselves as hard-working, law-abiding people who live within their means. On the other hand, Greeks make fun of German frugality and some are even invoking the old "Germans as Nazis" stereotype.[6]

The challenges of increased immigration and economic tensions in Europe and the resulting fears of security are present in the United States as well. After the devastating terror attacks in Paris and San Bernardino in 2015, security concerns translated to anti-immigrant/refugee attitudes and legislation. One poll found that 53 percent of U.S. Americans didn't want to accept any Syrian refugees at all and about 50 percent said immigrants are a burden because they take jobs, housing, and health care.[7] While some feel that these are reasonable attitudes and policies, others feel that it paves the way for increased prejudice and discrimination against foreigners, particularly those from the Middle East and Latin America.

So what does all this mean for intercultural communication? While these close economic connections highlight our global economy, these relationships also point to the large numbers of people who communicate every day with people from around the world. Some of this communication is face-to-face with international students, business travelers, tourists, migrants, and others. Some of this communication is online through the Internet, texting, or other communication media.

Economics are one important force, but there are many other reasons that people come into intercultural contact. Wars or other violent conflicts drive some people to leave their homelands to seek a safer place to live. Natural disasters can drive people to other areas where they can rebuild their lives. Some people seek a better life somewhere else, or are driven by their own curiosity to seek out and visit other parts of the world. People often fall in love and build families in another country. Can you think of other reasons that drive people to interact across cultural differences?

What do you as a student of intercultural communication need to learn to understand the complexities of intercultural interaction? And how can learning about intercultural communication benefit you?

It is easy to become overwhelmed by that complexity. However, not knowing everything that you would like to know is very much a part of the learning process, and this inability to know everything is what makes intercultural communication experiences so exciting. Rather than being discouraged by everything that you cannot know, think of all the things you can learn from intercultural communication experiences. This book will introduce you to some of the basic concepts and guidelines for thinking about intercultural interaction. You can also learn a lot of intercultural communication by listening to other people's experiences, but intercultural communication is a lifelong project and we hope you will continue your journey long after you read this textbook.

Why is it important to focus on intercultural communication and to strive to become better at this complex form of interaction? There are many reasons why you might want to learn more about intercultural communication. Perhaps you want to better serve a diverse clientele in your chosen occupation; perhaps members of your extended family are from different races or religions, or have physical abilities that you would like to understand better. Perhaps you want to better understand the culturally diverse colleagues in your workplace. Or perhaps you want to learn more about the people you come into contact with through the Internet, or to learn more about the countries and cultures that are in the daily news: Iraq, racial tensions on university campuses, hate crimes in cities large and small. In this chapter we discuss the following imperatives—reasons to study intercultural communication: peace, economic, technological, demographic, self-awareness, and ethical. Perhaps one or more will apply to your situation.

## THE PEACE IMPERATIVE

**What Do You Think?**

A group of prominent Canadian international figures have called for a "Department of Peace" or "Ministries of Peace" that would promote and utilize nonviolent methods of resolving conflicts around the world. What do you think would be the major functions of a Department of Peace? What kind of person is capable of becoming a Minister of Peace?

The key issue is this: Can individuals of different genders, ages, ethnicities, races, languages, and religions peacefully coexist on the planet? According to the Center for Systemic Peace, while conflict between national powers has decreased, societal wars (conflict between groups within a country) have increased. The current trend is toward longer, more intra-national protracted conflicts where military or material support is supplied by foreign powers—fighting "proxy wars"—to warring groups (http://www.systemicpeace.org/vlibrary/GlobalReport2014.pdf). For example, consider the religious strife between Shia and Sunni Muslims throughout the Middle East and between Kurds and government forces in Iraq and Turkey, the conflict between insurgent rebel groups and the government in Syria—with Russia and the United States backing different factions; the various groups in Libya where there is no central government at the moment, and woven throughout this region, conflict with the Islamic State of Iraq and the Levant (ISIL). There are also the conflicts between the government and various drug cartels in Mexico, and the Boko Haram and Christian–Muslim conflicts in Nigeria.

Some of the conflicts have roots in past foreign policies. The rise of the Islamic State of Iraq and Syria (ISIS) has been linked to the U.S. invasion of Iraq in 2003 and the strength of the Taliban related to the U.S. policies in twice promising to help Afghanistan people (against Soviet aggression in late 1980s and against the Taliban

© Abid Katib/Getty Images

People are often caught in devastating consequences of conflicts they neither started nor chose. In this photo, victims of the Gaza conflict search through the rubble of buildings destroyed by war. While communication skills cannot solve all political conflicts, they are vital in dealing with intercultural strife.

in 2003) and both times withdrawing military and infrastructure building support, both times leaving Afghan people at the mercy of the Taliban. Still other conflicts are tied to the tremendous influence of U.S. technology and media which may be celebrated by some and as a cause of resistance by others. For example, the massive influence of U.S. pop culture is seen by some as inhibiting the development of other nations' indigenous popular culture products and forcing U.S. values on them, which sometimes leads to resentment and conflict.[8]

Some conflicts have to do with economic disparities and legacies of oppression, seen in the racial and ethnic tensions in U.S. neighborhoods and recent conflicts between law enforcement and some Black communities. There are also tensions regarding what some people perceive as racist symbolism of the Cleveland Indians, a U.S. major league baseball team, and the Washington Redskins, a U.S. professional football team.

Communication scholar Benjamin Broome has worked with many conflict areas, including in Cyprus with Greeks and Turk Cypriots (once the most heavily fortified border in the world) and also Native American groups in the United States. He emphasizes that one cannot focus only on the interpersonal level or the societal level, but all levels. He proposes an approach of peacebuilding which is not just the absence of conflict, but an effort to stop all forms of violence and promote transformative ways to deal with conflict, including strategies that address personal, relational, and structural (organizational, economic conditions, etc.) elements of conflict. According to Broome, communication, especially facilitated dialogue, plays a key role in the peacebuilding process.[9] We need to remember that individuals

**Surf's Up!**

How global is the news you get each day? Think about the lead stories in the newspapers that you read, the news stories in the blogs and Internet sites you visit, the news programs you watch, and the news stories you hear on the radio. Is the news primarily about local or international events? For daily news on international events, check out www.PBS.org /frontlineworld/ and compare the stories to other U.S. news sites.

often are born into and are caught up in conflicts that they neither started nor chose and are impacted by larger societal forces. We will explore further approaches to dealing with conflict in Chapter 8.

## THE ECONOMIC IMPERATIVE

You may want to know more about intercultural communication because you foresee tremendous changes in the workplace in the coming years. This is one important reason to know about other cultures and communication patterns. In addition, knowing about intercultural communication is strategically important for U.S. businesses in the emerging transnational economy. As noted by writer Carol Hymowitz of the *Wall Street Journal*, "If companies are going to sell products and services globally, then they will need a rich mix of employees with varied perspectives and experiences. They will need top executives who understand different countries and cultures."[10]

### The Workplace

Given the growing cultural diversity in the United States, businesses necessarily must be more attentive to diversity issues. As the workforce becomes more diverse, many businesses are seeking to capitalize on these differences: "Once organizations learn to adopt an inclusive orientation in dealing with their members, this will also have a positive impact on how they look at their customer base, how they develop products and assess business opportunities, and how they relate to their communities."[11] Benefiting from cultural differences in the workplace involves not only working with diverse employees and employers but also seeing new business markets, developing new products for differing cultural contexts, and marketing products in culturally appropriate and effective ways. From this perspective, diversity is a potentially powerful economic tool for business organizations. We will discuss diversity issues further in Chapter 11.

### The Global Economy

Businesses all around the world are continually expanding into overseas markets in a process of **globalization.** This recent trend is shown dramatically in the report of a journalist who asked a Dell computer manager where his laptop is made. The answer? It was codesigned by engineers in Texas and Taiwan; the microprocessor was made in one of Intel's factories in the Philippines, Costa Rica, Malaysia, or China; the memory came from factories in Korea, Germany, Taiwan, or Japan. Other components (keyboard, hard-disk drive, batteries, etc.) were made by Japanese, Taiwanese, Irish, Israeli, or British firms with factories mainly in Asia; and finally, the laptop was assembled in Taiwan.[12]

What is the ultimate impact of globalization on the average person? Some economists defend it, saying that the losses are always offset by the gains in consumer prices but many workers who have lost jobs in the recent past and seen wages stagnate aren't so sure. There are many blue collar industrial jobs that have been lost to overseas in the past 10 years but one recent study concludes that as many as

**Surf's Up!**

Do you know the proper procedure for exchanging business cards in Japan? Did you know that even though meetings run late in Brazil, it is considered rude to exit before the gathering ends? Did you know you should never give a clock as gift to a Chinese, it represents death? Globalization has changed the face of business. The manner by which we conduct business in the United States is often very different from other countries. What should you know about different cultural practices to become an international business
*(continued)*

© Pixtal/AGE Fotostock RF

Multicultural work environments are becoming increasingly common in the twenty-first century. In many of these situations, working in small groups is especially important. Given this trend, workers need to learn to deal with cultural differences.

14 million white-collar jobs are also vulnerable to being outsourced offshore—jobs in information technology, accounting, architecture, advanced engineering design, news reporting, stock analysis, and medical and legal services—jobs that generate the bulk of tax revenues that fund our education, health, infrastructure, and social security systems. In fact, the Department of Labor reminds us that the track record for the re-employment of displaced U.S. workers is not good, that more than one in three workers who are displaced remains unemployed, and many of those who are lucky enough to find jobs take major pay cuts.[13]

The world economy has been volatile and seemingly shrinking in recent years. The economic powerhouse, China, has seen disastrous economic trends with a plummeting stock market, housing crises, and a manufacturing slowdown, and its slowest growth since 1990. The worry now and the evidence seems to support it that a slowing China also lowers growth in other countries.[14]

The point is that to compete effectively in this shrinking global market, Americans must understand how business is conducted in other countries and how to negotiate deals that are advantageous to the U.S. economy.[15] However, they are not always willing to take the time and effort to do this. For example, eBay, the successful American Ecommerce giant copied its American model to China and got completely destroyed by local competitor *Taobao*. Why? Because *Taobao* understood that in China, shopping was a social experience and people like talking and even haggling with sellers and building relationships with them. *Taobao* had a chat feature that allowed customers to easily talk to sellers.[16] Stories abound of U.S. marketing slogans that were inaccurately translated, like Pepsi's "Come alive with Pepsi Generation" (which was translated into Chinese as "Pepsi brings your ancestors back from the grave"), or General Motors marketing the Nova in South America (*no va* is Spanish for "no go").[17] In contrast, Starbucks' recent decision to change its logo

**Surf's Up! (cont.)**

traveler? Check out www.buzzle.com /chapters/travel-and -tourism_business -and-executive-travel _etiquette-and-related -issues.asp for information on conducting business in other countries. Check out the following link for information on conducting business in other countries: http:// www.forbes.com/sites /susanadams/2012 /06/15/business -etiquette-tips-for -international-travel /#409041f86755

International trade is one of the driving forces in interactions between cultures. However, as shown by these people protesting at the G-20 meeting in Brisbane, Australia, in November 2014, there is some concern that growing poverty and inequality resulting from globalization may lead to increased intercultural conflict.

© Daniel Munoz/Getty Images

when it entered the Asian markets seems to be successful. Starbucks decided to drop the Starbucks name and the word "coffee" from its logo, giving it a more rounded appearance, which seems to appeal to collectivist consumers—found in China and other Asian countries.[18]

In addition, there are other considerations in understanding the global market. Moving operations overseas to take advantage of lower labor costs has far-reaching implications for corporations. One example is the ***maquiladoras***—foreign-owned plants that use domestic labor—just across the U.S.–Mexican border. The U.S. companies that relocate their plants there benefit from lower labor costs and lack of environmental and other business regulations, while Mexican laborers benefit from the jobs. But there is a cost in terms of environmental hazards. Because Mexico has less stringent air and water pollution regulations than the United States, many of these *maquiladoras* have a negative environmental impact on the Mexican side of the border. Because the two nations are economically and environmentally interdependent, they share the economic and environmental impact. Thus, these contexts present intercultural challenges for Mexicans and Americans alike.

To help bridge the cultural gap, many companies employ **cross-cultural trainers,** who assist people going abroad by giving them information about and strategies for dealing with cultural differences; such trainers report that Japanese and other business personnel often spend years in the United States studying English and learning about the country before they decide to build a factory or invest money here. By contrast, many U.S. companies provide little or no training before sending their workers overseas and expect business deals to be completed very quickly. They seem to have little regard for cultural idiosyncrasies, which can cause ill will and mistrust, enhance negative stereotypes, and result in lost business opportunities.

In the future, global economic development will create even more demand for intercultural communication. Economic exchanges will drive intercultural interactions. This development will create not only more jobs but also more consumers to purchase goods from around the world—and to travel in that world.

## THE TECHNOLOGICAL IMPERATIVE

Communication technology is a constant. We are linked by technology to events in the most remote parts of the world and also to people that we may never meet face-to-face. In any given day you may text message or snapchat with friends about evening plans, post a Facebook message to a relative stationed overseas, participate in a discussion board for one of your courses, send an e-mail message to your professor and use Google Hangout for a virtual team project in an online course. It's possible not only to communicate with other people but also to develop complex relationships with them through such technology.

### Technology and Human Communication

The extent of global connection and communication through social network sites is staggering. For example, Facebook was the first to surpass 1 billion monthly active users. These networks are often available in multiple languages and enable users to connect with friends or people across geographical, political, or economic borders. About 2 billion people now use social network sites Facebook, Instagram, and Tumblr in the United States, VK in the United Kingdom, and Qzone and Renren in China.[19] By some accounts, people spend more time on social networking sites (SNSs) like Facebook than any other online activity, and 80 percent of Facebook users are outside the United States and Canada.[20] The effect of social media like Facebook and Twitter have far-reaching consequences, and it is important to understand that these technologies can have positive and negative impacts on intercultural encounters. For example, by using Twitter and Facebook, people were able to receive up-to-the-minute information and connect with friends and family in the immediate aftermath of the devastating Japanese tsunami in January 2011.[21] Syrians, Egyptians, and Libyans were able to broadcast to the world—through text and videos—minute-by-minute reports of the progress and challenges of their fight for democracy against their repressive governments.[22]

On the other hand, you may feel like you're too dependent on social media and suffer from FOMO (Fear of Missing Out), checking your phone many times a day to see if you have messages or if there are new posts to Facebook that you have to see. An even worse impact of social media is the vicious trolls and nasty posts. For example, there was a multitude of vicious racist tweets posted in reaction to the crowning of the first Indian American as Miss America.[23] Or consider the videos of brutal beheadings of U.S. journalists and others posted by Islamic State militants that shocked and appalled millions as well as their skillful use of social media to persuade and enlist recruits all around the world. These media videos and messages illustrate the far-reaching negative potential of

**Surf's Up!**

Social media is not just for socializing. Remember the poignant photo of the little three-year-old Syrian boy whose body (still dressed in his red shirt, blue shorts, and velcro shoes) washed up on a Turkish beach? His family was fleeing the Syrian civil war and their boat capsized. The photo went viral on social media when a Human Rights Watch staff member shared it on Twitter. It is just one example of the tremendous power of social media in drawing world attention to human events (and tragedies) in faraway places. Read more about the impact of this photo on http://www.pbs.org/newshour/rundown/photo-dead-syrian-refugee-boy-puts-face-crisis-rooted-numbers/.

communication technologies and some media sites Facebook and Twitter have increased their efforts to thwart Islamic State's use of their platforms for recruitment and propaganda.

Some media experts worry that all the connectivity has not necessarily strengthened our relationships. Sometimes, in face-to-face encounters, we are not really present because we are checking our mobile phones for text messages or searching for information on our smartphones. One expert terms this the "absent presence."[24] Another suggests that technology gives us control over our relationships and makes it easy for us to communicate when and how we wish, so that we often choose technologies, like texting or voice-mail messages, that actually distance us from each other.[25]

That said, more and more people around the world are using technology to communicate with each other. Consider these statistics

- Mobile phone use in Africa has grown from 1 percent in 2000 to more than 54 percent today and people in South Africa and Nigeria have the same level of cellphone ownership as in America.[26]

- The number of Internet users in Africa grew at seven times the global average, clocking more than 3,600 percent growth between 2000 and 2015, to 330 million users, according to data from Internet World Statistics (Internetstats.com).

What does this have to do with intercultural communication? Through high-tech communication, we come into contact with people who are very different from ourselves, often in ways we don't understand. The people we talk to on e-mail networks and blogs may speak languages different from our own, come from different countries, be of different ethnic backgrounds, and have had many different life experiences.

Technology has increased the frequency with which many people encounter multilingual situations; they must decide which language will be used. Contrast this situation with the everyday lives of people 100 years ago, in which they rarely communicated with people outside their own villages, much less people speaking different languages. Digital translation apps like Google Translate, Universal Translator, iTranslate can facilitate communication for travelers and business people and others in everyday intercultural encounters. Of course the use of some languages is privileged over others on the Internet. As experts note, if you want to do business online, it's more than likely going to be in English, the FIGS languages (French, Italian, German, Spanish), the CJK languages (Chinese, Japanese, Korean), and "the main languages of former colonial empires" (Dutch, Russian, Portuguese).

In addition to language and translation issues, online communication across cultures can present other challenges. For example, some online communication (e.g., e-mail, text messages, tweets) filters out important nonverbal cues. When we are talking to individuals face-to-face we use nonverbal information to help us interpret what they are really saying—tone of voice, facial expressions, gestures, and so on. The absence of these cues in some online communication makes communication more difficult and can lead to misunderstandings, especially when communicating across cultures. One of our colleagues discovered in working in several virtual team

## Pop Culture Spotlight

The movie *Metropolis* (1927) was a futuristic film set in 2020, with dazzling neo-architecture revealing a world where progress has gone too far. It has everything that people are scared about the future—from robots taking over jobs and revolts by unemployed rebels to an industrialist's scheme to rule the world and the creation of a cyborg, the doomsday machine. *Metropolis* also predicts the accelerating global dominance of visual technology for communication and the mounting preoccupation of present and future popular culture.

- Do you think what the movie predicted has come true?
- How has communication technology changed the global landscape politically and economically in the past century?

*(continued)*

projects that her colleagues in some countries (e.g., India) tend to deliver part of their message with silence or nonverbal signs and prefer to communicate face-to-face. With this knowledge, she now uses Skype more to communicate with some team members rather than e-mail. One of our students, Lydia, described the challenges of online intercultural communication:

> My last year of college my roommate was from Taiwan and we became good friends. When she went back home in June, we decided to stay friends through Facebook and Skype. I find it much more difficult to communicate with her online because she doesn't always understand what I was writing and I couldn't repeat my sentences like I could if I were speaking to her, and the same applied to her. Skyping is definitely a lot easier, so we usually keep in touch this way.

**Pop Culture Spotlight (cont.)**

• In what ways have new media technologies improved intercultural relations worldwide? In what ways have they hindered intergroup relations?

Social media and other interactive media also give us the opportunity to stay in contact with people who are very similar to ourselves, with family members, friends, and others who share common interests. We can also turn to online groups for support and community. For example, international students can stay in touch with their local communities, keep up with what's going on at home, and receive emotional support during difficult time of cultural adaptation. Immigrants can stay in touch with friends and family at home or other immigrants from their country who are living all over the world. Similarly, discussion forums provide virtual communities of support for cultural minorities (e.g., emptyclosets.com, a discussion forum for gay, lesbian, bisexual, transgender people).

However, the social media can also provide a venue for like-minded people to promote prejudice and hatred. The number of websites that promote hatred against Americans, Muslims, Jews, gays, and people of non-European ancestry has increased exponentially to more than 30,000 and experts point out that young people are especially vulnerable to racist online flash games, jokes, and general hate-filled information on social media.[27] One of the issues of interest to those who study intercultural communication is the "digital divide" that exists between those who have access to technologies like the Internet and those who do not.

Studies show that in the United States the people most likely to have access to and use the Internet are young or middle age, have a college degree or are students, and have a comfortable income.[28] Race and ethnicity doesn't seem to play a role, if we compare similar levels of education and income. While the digital divide is shrinking, there are still some inequities, mostly related to income, urban–rural location, and physical ability.[29] In addition, those Americans (mostly poor and some ethnic minorities) who have only a smartphone for online access at home have challenges. They are more likely than other users to encounter data-cap limits on smartphone service, frequently have to cancel or suspend service due to financial constraints, and face challenges when it comes to important tasks such as filling out job applications and writing (and reading) documents.[30]

Even larger inequalities exist outside the United States. In many countries (Asia, Africa, and Middle East), only a fraction of the population has access to computers and the Internet, for example, Internet access in Africa is 29 percent compared to the worldwide average of about 50 percent.[31]

These inequities have enormous implications for intercultural communication. In the global information society, information is an important commodity. Everybody needs it to function. This ability is especially important in an increasingly "networked" society. It is easy to see how without these skills and knowledge one can feel marginalized and disconnected from the center of society.[32]

## THE DEMOGRAPHIC IMPERATIVE

**Demographics** refers to the general characteristics of a given population. As shown by the 2000 and 2010 U.S. Census data, the demographics of the United States are changing dramatically during your lifetime—the next 50 years. The workforce that you enter will differ significantly from the one that your parents entered. These changes come from two sources: changing demographics within the United States and changing immigration patterns.

### Changing U.S. Demographics

According to the U.S. Population Reference Bureau, the nation's Hispanic and Asian populations are expected to triple by 2050, while non-Hispanic Whites are expected to grow more slowly to represent about one-half of the nation's population. People of Hispanic origin (who may be of any race) will increase from 36 million to 103 million. The Asian population is projected to triple, from 11 million to 33 million. The Black population is projected to grow from 36 million to 61 million in 2050, an increase of 71 percent. That change will increase Blacks' share of the nation's population from 13 percent in 2000 to 15 percent in 2050.

The population representing "all other races"—a category that includes American Indians, Alaska Natives, Hawaiian and other Pacific Islanders, as well as those who indicated two or more races on census forms—is also expected to triple between 2000 and 2050, growing from 7 million to about 22 million.[33]

Another interesting projection involves the "multiracial" category, partly due to the increasing numbers of interracial couples.[34] The 2000 Census was the first that allowed persons to categorize themselves as being of "two or more races"— 2.4 percent of respondents did just that, and this number is projected to increase. The most recent statistics released from the 2010 Census shows that the projections for increasing diversity are right on target—reflecting dramatic changes in the ethnic and racial makeup of the United States. In fact, the nation is moving a step closer to a demographic milestone in which no group commands a majority, already true in 317 counties in four states (California, Hawaii, New Mexico, and Texas) and the District of Columbia with Nevada, Arizona, Florida, Georgia, and Maryland approaching this milestone. As you can see, the states with the most diverse populations tend to be in the southern and western regions of the United States. These statistics show rather dramatically that where you live determines to some extent how many opportunities you have to interact with people who are different from you ethnically or racially.[35] Overall, the integration of new workers with the current ones will provide both opportunities and challenges for American businesses, as well as for the country as a whole.

**Surf's Up!**

How diverse is your school? Go to http://colleges.usnews.rankingsandreviews.com/best-colleges/rankings/national-universities/campus-ethnic-diversity and see the ethnic diversity rankings for many colleges and universities. The diversity ranking is a number from 0 to 1, the closer a school's number is to 1, the more diverse the student population. How important was it to you to study with people of different racial and ethnic backgrounds? How does diversity of a student body impact learning about intercultural communication?

## Changing Immigration Patterns

The second source of demographic change is **immigration.** There are two contradictory faces to the story of immigration in the United States. The United States often is described as a nation of immigrants, but it is also a nation that established itself by subjugating the original inhabitants of the land and that prospered economically while forcibly importing millions of Africans to perform slave labor. It is important to recognize the many different experiences that people have had in the United States so that we can better understand what it means to be a U.S. American. We cannot simply think of ourselves as a nation of immigrants if we want to better understand contemporary U.S. society.

Current patterns of immigration are having a significant effect on the social landscape, as the foreign born population continues to rise as a percentage of the total population, up from almost 5 percent in 1970 to more than 12 percent in 2013. However, this is still lower than it was during the great migrations of the 1800s and 1900s when most Europeans came to the United States. According to the U.S. Census Bureau, the vast majority of today's immigrants now come from Latin America (52 percent) and Asia (25 percent). These immigrants also tend to settle in particular areas of the country. They are more likely to live in the western part of the United States and more likely to live in the central locations of metropolitan areas, adding to the diversity of these areas. These immigration changes, along with increasing domestic diversity clearly show that the United States is becoming more **heterogeneous** (diverse).[36]

These demographic changes present many opportunities and challenges for students of intercultural communication and for society. Tensions among different racial and ethnic groups, as well as fear on the part of politically dominant groups, must be acknowledged. However, intercultural conflict is not necessarily a consequence of **diversity.** As we'll see in Chapter 9, intercultural encounters in certain types of conditions can lead to very positive outcomes, including reduced prejudice and positive intergroup relationships. Diverse college campuses, for example, can provide opportunities for the type of intercultural contact in which intercultural friendships can flourish—opportunities for extensive contact in a variety of formal and informal settings that promote communication and foster relationship development.[37] In fact, not surprisingly, the more diverse a campus is, the more likely students are to develop intercultural friendships—these friendships provide opportunities to expand our horizons linguistically, politically, and socially.[38] We often profit from being exposed to different ways of doing things and incorporate these customs into our own lifestyles.

*Historical Overview*   To get a better sense of the sociocultural situation in the United States today, let's take a look at our history. As mentioned, the United States has always been a nation of immigrants. When Europeans began arriving on the shores of the New World, an estimated 8 to 10 million Native Americans were already living here. The outcome of the encounters between these groups—the colonizing Europeans and the native peoples—is well known. By 1940, the Native American population of the United States had been reduced to an estimated 250,000.

**Pop Culture Spotlight**

Check out the following movies that tell stories of how immigrants survive in new environments. Compare the experiences of early immigrants to America (*Far and Away*) to more recent (*In America*). Compare the experiences of immigrants to the United States with immigrants to England (*Dirty Pretty Things*).

*A Better Life* (2011). The poignant story of a Mexican immigrant gardener trying to keep his son away from gangs and other bad influences in their East L.A. neighborhood and set up his own landscape business. A realistic portrayal of the ups and downs of immigrant life.

How does the immigration experience vary, depending on the historical context and country? What things stay the same?

Today, there are about 2.5 million American Indians, from 542 recognized tribes, living in the United States.[39]

African Americans are a special case in the history of U.S. immigration because they were brought to this country involuntarily. Some Europeans and Asians also arrived in the country as indentured or contract labor. However, by the middle of the seventeenth century this system of indenture was stopped because it was not economically viable for farmers and did not solve the problem of chronic labor shortage.[40] Landowners needed captive workers who could neither escape servitude nor become competitors. The answer was slavery. Native Americans were not a good choice, given that they could always escape back to their own lands, but Africans were. In fact, Europeans and Africans were already in the slave business, and so America became a prime market. The slave trade lasted about 350 years, during which time 9 to 10 million Africans reached the Americas (the vast majority died in the brutal overseas passage).[41] As James Baldwin has suggested, slavery is what makes U.S. history and current interracial relations different from those in Europe.[42]

Historically, slavery presented a moral dilemma for many Whites, but today a common response is to ignore history. Many Whites say that because not all Whites owned slaves we should simply forget it and move on. For most African Americans, however, this is unacceptable. Rather, as Cornel West, a professor of Afro-American studies and the philosophy of religion at Harvard University, suggests, we should begin by acknowledging the historical flaws in American society and recognizing the historical consequences of slavery.[43] It is interesting to note that there are several Holocaust museums in the United States, but only recently has there been official national recognition of the horrors of slavery—with the Smithsonian National Museum of African American History and Culture which opened in Fall 2016. A second museum, Whitney Plantation on 2000 acres in Wallace Louisiana, was refurbished by real estate magnate John Cummings at his own expense of $8 million and is dedicated to telling the story of slavery. The site has the requisite 220-year-old genteel and beautifully furnished "big house" but also restored tiny slave cabins, a slave jail, blacksmith shop, and a number of memorials to the slaves who lived, worked, and died there.[44]

Relationships between residents and immigrants—between old-timers and new-comers—often have been contentious. In the nineteenth century, Native Americans sometimes were caught in the middle of U.S. and European rivalries. During the War of 1812, for example, Indian allies of the British were severely punished by the United States when the war ended. In 1832, the U.S. Congress recognized Native Americans' right to self-government, but an 1871 congressional act prohibited treaties between the U.S. government and Indian tribes. In 1887, Congress passed the Dawes Severalty Act, terminating Native Americans' special relationship with the U.S. government and paving the way for the removal of Native Americans from their land.

As waves of immigrants continued to roll in from Europe, the more firmly established European—mainly English—immigrants tried to protect their way of life, language, and culture. James Banks has identified various conflicts throughout the nation's history, many of which were not uniquely American but were imported from Europe.[45] In 1729, for example, an English mob prevented a group of Irish immigrants from landing in Boston. A few years later, another mob destroyed a new Scotch-Irish Presbyterian church in Worcester, Massachusetts. Subsequently, as immigrants from northern and western Europe came to dominate American culture, immigrants from southern, central, and eastern Europe were expected to assimilate into the so-called mainstream culture—to jump into the "melting pot" and come out "American."

In the late nineteenth and early twentieth centuries, an anti-immigrant, nativistic movement promoted violence against newer immigrants. For example, in 1885, 28 Chinese were killed in an anti-Chinese riot in Wyoming; in 1891, a White mob attacked a Chinese community in Los Angeles and killed 19 people; in 1891, 11 Italian Americans were lynched in New Orleans.

The anti-immigrant, nativistic sentiment was well supported at the government level as well. In 1882, Congress passed the Chinese Exclusion Act, officially prohibiting Chinese from immigrating to this country. In 1924, the Johnson-Reed Act and the Oriental Exclusion Act established strict quotas on immigration and completely barred the immigration of Asians. According to Ronald Takaki, these 1924 laws "provided for immigration based on nationality quotas: the number of immigrants to be admitted annually was limited to 2 percent of the foreign-born individuals of each nationality residing in the United States in 1890."[46] The underlying rationale was that economic and political opportunities should be reserved for Whites, native-born Americans or not. Thus, the dominance of Whites in the United States is not simply the result of more Europeans wanting to come here; the U.S. government designed our society in this way.[47]

**Info Bites**

Could the slave trade be the first organization in world history? The United Nations Educational, Scientific and Cultural Organization (UNESCO) holds a project called the Slave Trade, launched in 1994 with the goal of maintaining a commitment to peace, historical truth, intercultural dialogue, and human rights and development. UNESCO cultural programs aim to improve global intercultural dialogues.

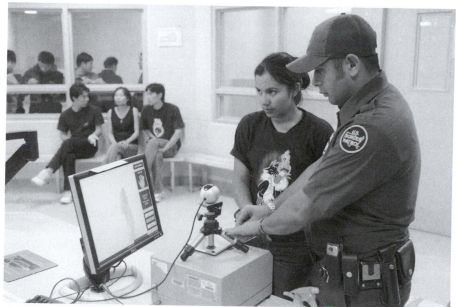

© Atomic/Alamy Photos

An immigration officer in San Ysidro, California, compares an immigrant's fingerprints against those shown on a green card. Immigration, especially from Asia and Latin America, will only serve to increase the intercultural experiences of many U.S. Americans.

**Pop Culture Spotlight**

If you haven't seen it yet, check out Spike Lee's movie *Chi-Raq*, described by IMDB as a modern day adaptation of an ancient Greek play—set against the backdrop of gang violence in Chicago. Some felt the film didn't tell the story of real Chicagoans living with everyday gang violence, that it made light of tragedy and brought negative publicity to Chicago. Lee's response was a reference to the old saying "I gotta laugh to keep from crying." What do you think? When is it ok to use humor in pop culture when focusing on tragic cultural encounters (e.g., gang violence)?

By the 1930s, immigrants from southern and eastern Europe were considered **assimilable,** or able to become members of White American society, and the concept of race assumed new meaning. All of the so-called White races were now considered one, so racial hostilities were directed toward members of non-White ethnic groups, such as Asian Americans, Native Americans, and Mexican Americans; this bias was particularly devastating for African Americans.[48] In the growing but sometimes fragile economy of the first half of the twentieth century, only White workers were assured a place. White immigrants may have earned relatively low wages, but they were paid additional "psychological" wages in the form of better schools, increased access to public facilities, and more public deference.

Economic conditions make a big difference in attitudes toward foreign workers and immigration policies. Thus, during the Great Depression of the 1930s, Mexicans and Mexican Americans were forced to return to Mexico to free up jobs for White Americans. When prosperity returned in the 1940s, Mexicans were welcomed back as a source of cheap labor. In recent years, many businesses as well as the government favored a "guest worker program" with Mexico—which would allow Mexican workers to temporarily reside in the United States. In fact, this occurs all over the world. North African workers are alternately welcomed and rejected in France, depending on the condition of the French economy and the need for imported labor. The resulting discontent and marginalization of these immigrants were seen in the weeks of rioting in French cities in the fall of 2005 and 2007 and the riots that occurred in London in 2011. In France, it was primarily the children and grandchildren of North African immigrants; in London, many are children and grandchildren of Caribbean and African immigrants. The rioting in both England and France started with those from poor neighborhoods. *The Economist* suggests that in France "[a] much greater contributor than Islam to the malaise in the suburbs is the lack of jobs" and that in London, soaring property prices push the middle class into "ever-edgier" neighborhoods.[49] Guest workers from Turkey have been subjected to similar uncertainties in Germany. Indian workers in Kenya, Chinese immigrants in Malaysia, and many other workers toiling outside their native lands have suffered from the vagaries of fluctuating economies and inconsistent immigration policies.

***The Current Situation***    Ethnic and race relations in the United States are impacted by specific events and the economic climate. For example, Hispanic–Black relations were at a low in 2013 after George Zimmerman was acquitted in the killing of unarmed Black teenager Trayvon Martin, sparking a national debate over the nature of racism in the United States. The media described Zimmerman, whose father is a White American and whose mother is Peruvian, as both White and Hispanic (http://www.latintimes.com/articles/6341/20130715/george-zimmerman-white-race-peruvian-black-gladys.htm). Similarly, relations between Hispanics and Whites were affected negatively over the contentious debates about immigration, and Whites and Blacks relations have suffered as a result of the many Black unarmed young men killed by White police. The racial divide is clear: 86 percent of Blacks say more needs to be done to achieve racial equality, compared to 53 percent of Whites; however a growing number of Americans, across all demographic groups, say that racism in society is a big problem—50 percent of Americans polled agreed in 2016, up from 33 percent in 2010.[50]

Some of the conflict may be due to the economic disparity that exists among these different groups. To understand this disparity we need to look at issues of economic class. Most Americans are reluctant to admit that a **class structure** exists, let alone admit how difficult it is to move up in this structure. But the fact is that most people live their lives in the same economic class into which they were born. In addition, the U.S. cultural myth that anyone can move up the class structure through hard work, known as the Horatio Alger myth, is not benign. Rather, it reinforces middle- and upper-class beliefs in their own superiority and perpetuates a false hope among members of the working class that they can get ahead. And there are just enough success stories—for example, celebrity Oprah Winfrey, former President Bill Clinton, rapper Eminem, singer and songwriter Dolly Parton, Wendy's founder Dave Thomas—of impressive upward mobility to perpetuate the myth.

Studies have shown that U.S. Americans seriously underestimate the gap between the rich and not rich. The reality is strikingly grim. The top 20 percent of U.S. households own more than 84 percent of the wealth, and the bottom 40 percent combine for a mere 0.3 percent (that's right, not 3 percent, but 0.3 percent). Most of the recent growth after the recession is going to a tiny segment: 95 percent of the gains have gone to the richest 1 percent of people, whose share of overall income is once again close to its highest level in a century. The most unequal country in the rich world is thus becoming even more so.[51] The Walton family, for example, has more wealth than 42 percent of American families combined, and the nation's official poverty rate in 2014 was 14.8 percent, which means there were 46.7 million people in poverty. The difference between CEO pay and unskilled worker is 354-1. Fifty years ago, it was 20-1. While many Americans acknowledge this gap between rich and poor, very few see it as a serious issue (one study reports only 5 percent). These two studies imply that our apathy about inequality may be due to rose-colored misperceptions.[52]

A real consequence of this gap and the number of working poor is lowered economic growth in the nation and less equality of opportunity for the next generation. There are real material consequences. For example, the gap in test scores between rich and poor children is 30 to 40 percent wider than it was 25 years ago, suggesting that rich youngsters are benefiting more than ever from their economic and social advantages. Measures of social mobility between generations, already lower than in much of Europe, have stagnated.[53]

This widening gap is partly due to the loss of stable industrial jobs as companies move to cheaper labor markets within the United States and abroad, and slow recovery from the recession with wages remaining low. Class and demographic issues also play a role, with racial and ethnic minorities typically hardest hit by economic downturns. The impact of the downturn on household net worth of Whites, Black, and Hispanic families is dramatic. [Net worth is defined as what you have if you subtract your debt from what you own.] According to a recent Pew Research Center analysis of government data, the wealth of White households was 13 times the median wealth of Black households in 2013, compared with eight times the wealth in 2010.

**Pop Culture Spotlight**

The film *Spanglish* (2004) features the life of a Mexican immigrant mother and daughter in the United States. The mother is hired to care for the children of a wealthy White family, eventually asked to sacrifice the care of her own daughter in order to spend more time with her employers' children. It shows the current debates over multiculturalism and immigration policies. The interactions between a White family and the immigrant family present the complexity of intercultural communication. However, both sides do their best to adapt to each other in spite of language barriers and cultural differences.

**What Do You Think?**

Information about others often helps us to see ourselves in a different way. According to the architectural website, *archdaily.com*, of the 10 tallest buildings in the world in 2015, only one was in the United States (432 Park Avenue in New York City); the majority are in China, several in Russia and the Middle East (Dubai, Saudi Arabia, the United Arab Emirates). According to *smsglobal.com*, the country with the most cell phones per capita in 2015 was the United Kingdom with 64 percent penetration (the United States is second with 57 percent). The country with the fastest Internet connection in 2015 was South Korea (22.2 average Mbps). The United States was number 17 (*business .com*). Do these facts surprise you or make you think about the United States in a different way?

The wealth of White households is now more than 10 times the wealth of Hispanic households, compared with nine times the wealth in 2010.[54] Changing these differences will not be easy, but how will they influence our intercultural interaction?

Increasingly diverse groups mostly come in contact during the day in schools, businesses, and hospitals, but they bring different languages, histories, and economic backgrounds to these encounters. This presents a challenge for our society and for us as individuals to look beyond the Hollywood stereotypes, to be aware of this diversity, and to apply what we know about intercultural communication. Perhaps the first step is to realize that the **melting pot metaphor**—in which all immigrants enter and blend into American society—probably was never viable. That is, not all immigrants could be assimilated into the United States in the same way.

The legacy of the tensions over immigration remains today. With a stagnant economy, stalled wages, and fears about terrorist attacks, many U.S. Americans are not in favor of additional immigration; they see immigrants as additional competition for jobs. One area where this debate has taken place is over the immigration of highly skilled workers. These workers are typically given H-1B visas to work in the United States. Yet with a flagging economy and unfavorable immigration laws, highly skilled workers may not choose to remain in the United States. As Commerce Secretary Penny Pritzker said.

"These individuals are American families in waiting," "Many tire of waiting for green cards and leave the country to work for our competition . . . we have to do more to retain and attract world-class talent to the United States."[55]

What impact will changes in immigration make to our society? How will the loss of highly skilled workers impact our ability to recover economically and technologically? And how will these changes impact how we interact with others?

Fortunately, most individuals are able to negotiate day-to-day activities in schools, businesses, and other settings in spite of cultural differences. Diversity can even be a positive force. Demographic diversity in the United States has provided us with tremendous linguistic richness and culinary variety, has given us the resources to meet new social challenges, and has created domestic and international business opportunities.

## THE SELF-AWARENESS IMPERATIVE

One of the most important reasons for studying intercultural communication is to gain an awareness of one's own cultural identity and background. This **self-awareness** is one of the least obvious reasons. Peter Adler, a noted social psychologist, observes that the study of intercultural communication begins as a journey into another culture and reality and ends as a journey into one's own culture.[56]

Examples from the authors' own lives come to mind. Judith's earliest experiences in public school made her realize that not everyone wore "coverings" and "bonnets" and "cape dresses," the clothing worn by the females in her Amish/ Mennonite family. She realized that her family was different from most of the others she came in contact with. Years later, when she was teaching high school in Algeria, a Muslim country, she realized something about her own religious identity as a Protestant. December 25 came and went, and she taught classes with no mention of

Christmas. Judith had never thought about how special the celebration of Christmas was or how important the holiday was to her. She recognized on a personal level the uniqueness of this particular cultural practice.

When Tom, who is of Japanese descent, first started elementary school, he attended a White school in the segregated American South. By the time he reached the fourth grade, schools were integrated, and some African American students were intrigued by his very straight black hair. At that point, he recognized a connection between himself and the Black students, and he began to develop a kernel of self-awareness about his identity. Living in an increasingly diverse world, we can take the opportunity to learn more about our own cultural backgrounds and identities and about how we are similar to and different from the people we interact with. However, it is important to recognize intercultural learning is not always easy or comfortable. What you learn depends on your social and economic position in society. Self-awareness through intercultural contact for someone from a racial or minority group may mean learning to be wary and not surprised at subtle slights by members of the dominant majority—and reminders of their place in society. For example, an African American colleague has remarked that she notices some White cashiers avoid touching her hand when they return her change.

If you are White and middle class, intercultural learning may mean an enhanced awareness of your privilege. A White colleague tells of feeling uncomfortable staying in a Jamaican resort, being served by Blacks whose ancestors were brought there as slaves by European colonizers. On the one hand, it is a privilege that allows travelers like our colleague to experience new cultures and places. On the other hand, one might wonder if we, through this type of travel, are reproducing those same historical postcolonial economic patterns.

Self-awareness, then, that comes through intercultural learning may involve an increased awareness of being caught up in political, economic, and historical systems not of our own making.

## THE ETHICAL IMPERATIVE

Living in an intercultural world presents challenging ethical issues that can be addressed by the study of intercultural communication. **Ethics** may be thought of as principles of conduct that help govern the behavior of individuals and groups. These principles often arise from communities' views on what is good and bad behavior. Cultural values tell us what is "good" and what "ought" to be.

### Ethical Judgments and Cultural Values

Ethical judgments focus more on the degrees of rightness and wrongness in human behavior than do cultural values.[57]

Some judgments are stated very explicitly. For example, the Ten Commandments teach that it is wrong to steal, tell a lie, commit murder, and so on. Many Americans are taught the "Golden Rule"—do unto others as you would have them do unto you. Laws often reflect the cultural values of dominant groups. For instance, in the past, many states had miscegenation laws prohibiting interracial marriage.

**Surf's Up!**

Did you know that in China, bribery is called "gray money," and is often accepted as a form of payment to low-paid government officials? Visit the website of Transparency International (www.transparency.org/), a global organization that monitors and tracks various bribery practices in businesses around the world.

Contemporary debates about legalizing same-sex marriage reflect the role of cultural values in laws. Many other identifiable principles arise from our cultural experience that may be less explicit—for example, that people should be treated equally and that they should work hard.

Several issues come to mind in any discussion of ethics in intercultural communication. For example, what happens when two ethical systems collide? While the desire to contribute to the development of a better society by doing the right thing can be an important motivation, it is not always easy to know what is "right" in more specific situations in intercultural communication. Ethical principles are often culture-bound, and intercultural conflicts arise from varying notions of what constitutes ethical behavior.

Another ethical dilemma involves standards of conducting business in multinational corporations. The U.S. Congress and the Securities and Exchange Commission consider it unethical for corporations to make payments to government officials of other countries to promote trade. Essentially, such payment smacks of bribery. However, in many countries, such as China, government officials are paid in this informal way instead of being supported by taxes. What is ethical behavior for personnel in multinational subsidiaries?

This book stresses the relativity of cultural behavior; no cultural pattern is inherently right or wrong. Is there any universality in ethics? Are any cultural behaviors always right or always wrong?

The answers depend on one's perspective.[58] According to the **universalist position,** we need to identify those rules that apply across cultures. A universalist might try, for example, to identify acts and conditions that most societies think of as wrong, such as murder, treason, and theft. Someone who takes an extreme universalist position would insist that cultural differences are only superficial, that fundamental notions of right and wrong are universal. Some religions take universal positions—for example, that the Ten Commandments are a universal code of behavior. But Christian groups often disagree about the universality of the Bible. For example, are the teachings of the New Testament mainly guidelines for the Christians of Jesus's time, or can they be applied to Christians in the twenty-first century? These are difficult issues for many people searching for ethical guidelines.

By contrast, according to the **relativist position,** any cultural behavior can be judged only within the cultural context in which it occurs. This means that only a community can truly judge the ethics of its members. Intercultural scholar William S. Howell explains the relativist position:

> Ethical principles in action operate contingently. Circumstances and people exert powerful influences. . . . The environment, the situation, the timing of an interaction, human relationships—all affect the way ethical standards are applied. Operationally, ethics are a function of context. . . . All moral choices flow from the perceptions of the decision maker, and those perceptions are produced by unique experiences in one person's life, in the context in which the choices are made.[59]

These are not easy issues, and philosophers and anthropologists have struggled to develop ethical guidelines that are universally applicable but that also reflect the tremendous cultural variability in the world.

**Info Bites**

In London, it is unlawful to kiss in a movie theater. It is taboo, or forbidden, for Greenland Eskimos to mention their own names. Donald Duck comic books were banned from libraries in Finland because authorities felt that it wasn't good to show children a hero who ran around without pants on.
(Source: *It Is Illegal to Quack Like a Duck and Other Freaky Laws*, by Barbara Seuling and Gwen Seuling, 1988, New York: Penguin Group [U.S.A.])

Scholar David W. Kale has proposed a universal code of ethics for intercultural communicators. This code is based on a universal belief in the sanctity of the human spirit and the desirability of peace.[60] While we may wish to assume that universal ethical principles exist, we must be careful not to assume that our ethical principles are shared by others. When we encounter other ethical principles in various situations, it is often difficult to know if we are imposing our ethical principles on others and whether we should. There are no easy answers to these ethical dilemmas.

Like David Kale, philosopher Kwame Appiah agrees that there are, and should be, values such as tolerance that are universal. He discusses how the misplaced belief of "my values are the only right ones" can lead to intolerance, cruelty, and even murder by both Christians and Muslim fundamentalists (e.g., bombings of abortion clinics or other buildings). He addresses the difficult question of how we can maintain universal values and still respect cultural distinctness. His answer is that we must all become **cosmopolitans**—citizens of the world—taking seriously the value of not just human life, but particular human life, never forgetting that each human being has responsibilities to every other.[61]

The study of intercultural communication should not only provide insights into cultural patterns but also help us address these ethical issues involved in intercultural interaction. Appiah and other contemporary scholars stress the importance of dialogue and "conversations across differences," suggesting that as part of coordinating our lives with each other as world citizens, we critique existing norms together and arrive at more acceptable ethical standards.[62] First, we should be able to judge what is ethical and unethical behavior given variations in cultural priorities. Second, we should be able to identify guidelines for ethical behavior in intercultural contexts where ethics clash.

Another ethical issue concerns the application of intercultural communication scholarship. Everett Kleinjans, an international educator, stresses that intercultural education differs from some other kinds of education: Although all education may be potentially transformative, learning as a result of intercultural contact is particularly so in that it deals with fundamental aspects of human behavior.[63] Learning about intercultural communication sometimes calls into question the very core of our assumptive framework and challenges existing beliefs, values, and patterns of behavior.

## Becoming an Ethical Student of Culture

Part of learning about intercultural communication is learning about cultural patterns and identities—your own and those of others. Four skills are important here: practicing self-reflexivity, learning about others, listening to the voices of others, and developing a sense of social justice.

*Practicing Self-Reflexivity*  **Self-reflexivity** refers to the process by which we "look in the mirror" to see ourselves. In studying intercultural communication, you must understand yourself and your position in society. When you learn about other cultures and cultural practices, you often learn much about yourself as well. And the

**What Do You Think?**

How do people learn about indigenous cultures? The Alaska Native Knowledge Network (ANKN, www.ankn.uaf.edu/index.html) serves as a resource for compiling and exchanging information concerning the Alaska native knowledge systems and their ways of knowing. They try to preserve and understand the experiences of Alaska natives.

What do you know about the aborigines of Australia, Maori of New Zealand, Saami of Scandinavia, and native Indians and Hawaiians of America? How might you learn about them?

knowledge that you gain from experience is an important way to learn about intercultural communication. Intercultural experiences teach you much about how you react and interact in different cultural contexts and help you evaluate situations and deal with uncertainty. Self-reflection about your intercultural experiences will go a long way toward helping you learn about intercultural communication. When you consider ethical issues in intercultural communication, you need to recognize the strengths and limitations of your own intercultural experiences. Many immigrants have observed that they never felt so much like someone of their nationality until they left their homeland. As part of the process of self-reflexivity, when you gain more intercultural experiences, your views on ethics may change. For example, you may have thought that arranged marriages were misguided and unethical until you gained more experience with people in successful arranged marriages, which have very low divorce rates in comparison with traditional "romantic" marriages.

Many cultural attitudes and ideas are instilled in you and are difficult to unravel and identify. Discovering who you are is never a simple matter; rather, it is an ongoing process that can never fully capture the ever-emerging person. Not only do you grow older, but your intercultural experiences change who you are and who you think you are. When Judith compares her intercultural experiences in France and in Mexico, she notes that, while the two experiences were similar, her own reactions to these intercultural encounters differed markedly because she was younger and less settled into her identity when she went to France.

It is also important to reflect on your place in society. By knowing what social categories—groups defined by society—you fill and what the implications of those categories are, you will be in a better position to understand how to communicate. For example, your status as a male or female may influence how certain messages are interpreted as sexual harassment. Or your identification as a member of some groups may allow you to use certain words and humor, but using other words or telling some jokes may get you in trouble. Many Belgians, for example, are well aware that French sometimes tell *blagues belges*, or jokes about Belgians. Yet if the same joke is told by a Belgian, it has a different tenor. It is important to recognize which social categories you belong to, as well as which ones you are perceived by others as belonging to, as it influences how your message may be interpreted.

***Learning about Others***    It is important to remember that the study of cultures is actually the study of other people. Never lose sight of the humanity of the topic of study. Try not to observe people as if they are zoo animals. Remember that you are studying real people who have real lives, and your conclusions about them may have very real consequences for them and for you.

When Tom was growing up, he was surprised to hear from an older woman that the first time she saw a Japanese or Chinese person was in the circus when she was a little girl. Judith remembers feeling uneasy watching White tourists at the Navajo Nation fair in Window Rock, Arizona, intrusively videotaping the Navajo dancers during their religious ceremonies. In each case, people who were different were viewed and treated as if their cultural practices were for the display and entertainment of others and there was no real attempt to understand them or their culture.

**Surf's Up!**

Do you know

• How many Turks are in different countries?
• Which countries tested with the highest IQs?
• Which countries have legal gay marriages, radar detectors, and synthetic marijuana?

For plenty of interesting stats and to graphically compare nations side-by-side, visit www.nationmaster .com/index.php. How can learning this type of information help you be a more effective intercultural communicator?

Cultural studies scholar Linda Alcoff discusses the ethical issue involved when students of culture try to describe cultural patterns of others.[64] She acknowledges the difficulty of speaking "for" and "about" people from different cultures. Instead, she claims, students of culture should try to speak "with" and "to" people. Rather than merely describe other people from afar, it's better to listen to and engage them in a dialogue about their cultural realities.

**Listening to the Voices of Others**   We learn much from real-life experiences. Hearing about the experiences of people who are different from you can lead to different ways of viewing the world. Many differences—based on race, gender, sexual orientation, nationality, ethnicity, age, and so on—deeply affect the everyday lives of people. Listening carefully as people relate their experiences and their knowledge helps us learn about other cultures. What we mean by listening here involves more than face-to-face encounters with others. It may mean listening to the voices of others through websites or movies or blogs (see "What Do You Think" on the previous page, "Surf's Up" on this page, and "Pop Culture Spotlight" on the following page).

Communication scholars Starosta and Chen suggest that a focus on mutual listening, instead of talking, forms the core of successful intercultural understanding. They suggest that good intercultural listeners are receptive to "life stories" from a wide range of culturally different individuals, as a way of understanding and explaining the world around them. These listening skills are built on a foundation of openness, curiosity, and empathy.[65]

Japanese scholar Ishii suggests that the very core of intercultural communication is listening. The effective intercultural communicator, sensitive to the other person, listens *carefully* before speaking. He or she hears the message from the other person, considers it, then reconsiders it, trying on different possible interpretations—trying to understand the speaker's possible intent. When the listener believes she has understood the point being made, she may respond, always in a nonthreatening manner.[66] The point here is that we can only really understand another person when we have listened to him or her carefully.

**Developing a Sense of Social Justice**   A final ethical issue involves the responsibility that comes with the acquisition of intercultural knowledge and insights. What constitutes ethical and unethical applications of intercultural knowledge? One questionable practice concerns people who study intercultural communication in order to proselytize others without their consent. For example, some religious organizations conduct Bible study sessions on college campuses for international students under the guise of English conversation lessons. Another questionable practice involves cross-cultural consultants who misrepresent or exaggerate their ability to deal with complex issues of prejudice and racism in brief, one-shot training sessions. Another way of looking at ethical responsibility suggests that intercultural learning is not just transformative for the individual, but should also benefit the larger society and other cultural groups in the increasingly interdependent world. The first step in working for social justice is acknowledging that oppression and inequities exist. As we have tried to point out, cultural differences are not just interesting and fascinating; they exist within a hierarchy where some are privileged and set the rules for others.

**Pop Culture Spotlight**

*The Constant Gardener* (2005) is about Justin Quale, a low-level British diplomat in Kenya, and his wife Tessa, an activist with a keen interest in issues of poverty and social justice. They fight against a giant multinational pharmaceutical company that is using AIDS patients in Kenya's slums to test dangerous drugs with known harmful side effects. This movie deals with issues of environment, corruption, and poverty. Do these types of movies encourage viewers to work for social justice in global contexts? Do you think they present realistic portrayals of life in Africa? Or do they just perpetuate the old European colonial stereotypes where the "poor" Africans must depend on the white Europeans to "save" them? How might movies like this influence intercultural encounters between Africans and British or Americans?

For example, how could you apply intercultural communication concepts in situations where gay and lesbian young people are the targets of bullying? Statistics show that these adolescents get bullied two to three times more than their heterosexual peers, and it often occurs through social media like Facebook and Twitter, where there is a large audience and relative anonymity.[67] Why does this happen? What can be done to reduce harassment of this particular cultural group?

In the following chapters, you will learn about the causes and patterns of conflict between various cultural groups, the origins and expressions of prejudice and discrimination, as well as strategies for reducing conflict and discrimination. Consider the homeless—another cultural group rarely mentioned by cultural communication scholars—often the target of prejudice and violence. Perhaps increased knowledge about this group and ethical application of intercultural communication principles could lead to better understanding of these individuals and ultimately to less discrimination and prejudice. After working as an advocate for homeless people in Denver, one communication scholar, Professor Phil Tompkins, describes the link between communication skills and social justice. He defines social justice as the "process of communicating, inspiring, advocating, organizing, and working with others of similar and diverse organizational affiliations to help all people gain respect and participate fully in society in a way that benefits the community as well as the individual."[68] This definition has three important components: (1) communication is central; (2) the outcome of social justice must be beneficial to society, not just the individuals involved; and (3) respect for and participation by all is important. We hope that as you read the following chapters, you will agree with us that learning about intercultural communication also involves ethical application of that knowledge.

As you learn about yourself and others as cultural beings, as you come to understand the larger economic, political, and historical contexts in which interaction occurs, is there an ethical obligation to continue learning? Can popular culture products, like films. play a part in motivating others to work for social justice? (See "Pop Culture Spotlight" on the previous page.) We believe that as members of an increasingly interdependent global community, intercultural communication students have a responsibility to educate themselves, not just about interesting cultural differences, but also about intercultural conflicts, the impacts of stereotyping and prejudice, and the larger systems that can oppress and deny basic human rights—and to apply this knowledge to the communities in which they live and interact.

## SUMMARY

In this chapter, we identified six reasons for studying intercultural communication: the peace imperative, the economic imperative, the technological imperative, the demographic imperative, the self-awareness imperative, and the ethical imperative. Perhaps you can think of some other reasons. We stressed that the situations in which intercultural communication takes place are complex and challenging.

## BUILDING INTERCULTURAL SKILLS

So what are the skills necessary to communicate effectively across cultures? It isn't easy to come up with specific suggestions that will always work in every situation. Communication is much too complex. However, we can identify several general skills that can be applied to the various aspects of intercultural communication covered in this book: (1) understanding cultural identity and history, (2) improving verbal and nonverbal communication, (3) understanding the role of popular culture in intercultural communication, and (4) building relationships and resolving conflicts.

Throughout the book, we'll focus on cultivating and improving the following communication skills:

1. Become more conscious of your communication. This may sound simple, but how often do you really think about your communication and whether it is working? Much of your communication, including intercultural communication, occurs at an unconscious level. A first step in improving your intercultural communication is to become aware of the messages you send and receive, both verbal and nonverbal, in both face-to-face and mediated contexts (Facebook, Twitter, text messaging). Do you communicate differently face-to-face or online? You can't really work on improving your communication until you become aware of it on a conscious level.

2. Become more aware of others' communication. Understanding other people's communication requires the important intercultural skill of empathy—knowing where someone else is coming from, or "walking in his or her shoes." This is no easy task, especially in online communication, but by doing things such as improving your observational skills and learning how to build better intercultural relations you can accomplish it.

3. Expand your own intercultural communication repertoire. This involves experimenting with different ways of looking at the world and of communicating, verbally and nonverbally, both face-to-face and online. Building this skill may require that you step outside your communication comfort zone and look at things in a different light. It may require that you question ideas and assumptions you've not thought about before. All this is part of expanding your communication options.

4. Become more flexible in your communication. Closely related to the previous skill—and perhaps the most important one—this involves avoiding what has been called "hardening of the categories."

5. Be an advocate for others. This is something that isn't often included in lists of communication skills. To improve intercultural communication among groups, however, everybody's voice must be heard. Improving relations among groups of people—whether based on ethnicity, race, gender, physical ability, or whatever difference—is not just about improving individual communication skills; it is also about forming coalitions with others.

It is important to remember that becoming a better intercultural communicator is not achieved quickly but rather is a lifelong process. In each of the following chapters, we invite you to take up the challenge of continuing to build these skills.

## ACTIVITIES

1. *Intercultural encounters:* Describe and analyze your first intercultural encounter with someone of a different age, ethnicity, race, religion, and so on.

   a. Describe the encounter. What made it "intercultural"?

   b. How did you react to the encounter? Was it a positive experience? A negative experience?

   c. What did you learn from the experience? Based on this experience, identify some characteristics that may be important for successful intercultural communication.

2. *Intercultural imperatives:* There are many reasons to study intercultural communication, including the six discussed in this chapter. What other imperatives can you identify?

3. *Household products:* Look at the products in your home. How many different countries do they come from? How might your purchases increase intercultural contact?

## ENDNOTES

1. Muller, R. (1982). *New Genesis. Shaping a Global Spirituality.* New York, NY: Doubleday, p. 6.
2. Walker, A. (2016, January 7). China share turmoil: How it affects the rest of the world. *bbc.com.* Retrieved April 17, 2016, from http://www.bbc.com/news/business-34040679.
3. Fry, R. (2015, July 29). More millennials living with family despite improved job market. Pew Report. Retrieved April 17, 2016, from http://www.pewsocialtrends.org/2015/07/29/more-millennials-living-with-family-despite-improved-job-market/.
4. Wagner, J. (2015, October 27). Why millennials love Bernie Sanders, and why that may not be enough. *washingtonpost.com.* Retrieved April 17, 2016, from https://www.washingtonpost.com/politics/in-bernie-sanders-anxious-millennials-find-a-candidate-who-speaks-to-them/2015/10/27/923d0b74-66cc-11e5-9223-70cb36460919_story.html.
5. Fry, R. (2015, July 29). More millennials living with family despite improved job market. Pew Report. Retrieved April 17, 2016, from http://www.pewsocialtrends.org/2015/07/29/more-millennials-living-with-family-despite-improved-job-market/.
6. Stevis, M., & Thomas, A. (2015, July 4). Greek, German tensions turn to open resentment as referendum looms. wsj.com. Retrieved April 17, 2016, from http://www.wsj.com/articles/greek-german-tensions-turn-to-open-resentment-1436004768.
7. Desilver, D. (2015, November 19). U.S. public seldom has welcomed refugees into country. Pew Research Reports. Retrieved March 8, 2016, from http://www.pewresearch.org/fact-tank/2015/11/19/u-s-public-seldom-has-welcomed-refugees-into-country/; Krogstad, J. M. (2015, September 24). What Americans, Europeans think of immigrants. Pew Research Center. Retrieved March 8, 2015, from http://www.pewresearch.org/fact-tank/2015/09/24/what-americans-europeans-think-of-immigrants/.
8. Delgado, F. (2002). Mass-mediated communication and intercultural conflict. In J. N. Martin, T. K. Nakayama, & L. A. Flores (Eds.), *Readings in intercultural communication* (pp. 351–360). Boston, MA: McGraw-Hill.
9. Broome, B. J. (2013). Building cultures of peace: The role of intergroup dialogue. In J. G. Oetzel & S. Ting-Toomey (Eds.), *Sage handbook of conflict communication: Integrating theory, research, and practice* (2nd ed., pp. 737–762). Los Angeles, CA: Sage; Broome, B. J., & Collier, M. J. (2012). Culture, communication, and peacebuilding: A reflexive multi-dimensional contextual framework. *Journal of International & Intercultural Communication, 5*(4), 245–269.
10. Hymowitz, C. (2005, November 14). The new diversity. *The Wall Street Journal,* p. R1.

11. Pacelle, M. (2003, June 12). U.S. banks vie for big postwar roles—Financial reconstruction may include J. P. Morgan, Citigroup, Bank of America. The *Wall Street Journal (Europe)*, p. A3.

12. Friedman, T. L. (2005). *The world is flat: A brief history of the twenty-first century*. New York, NY: Farrar, Straus & Giroux.

13. Roberts, P. C. (2014). The offshore outsourcing of American jobs: A greater threat than terrorism. *Globalresearch.ca*. Retrieved March 8, from http://www.globalresearch.ca/the-offshore-outsourcing-of-american-jobs-a-greater-threat-than-terrorism/18725.

14. Beech, H. (2016, March 7). As China's NPC meets, here are four danger signs to watch for in the nation's economy. *Time.com*. Retrieved March 7, 2016, from http://time.com/4249299/china-economy-npc-national-peoples-congress/; Worstall, T. (2015, January 20). The really bad news about China's economic slowdown. *Forbes.com*. Retrieved March 8, 2016, from http://www.forbes.com/sites/timworstall/2015/01/20/the-really-bad-news-about-chinas-economic-slowdown-and-growth-targets-miss/#47c2c95e7d40.

15. Varner, I., & Beamer, L. (2010). *Intercultural communication in the global workplace,* 5th ed. Boston, MA: McGraw-Hill.

16. Custer, C. (2015, May 20). The 3 biggest reasons foreign companies fail in China. *techinasia.com*. Retrieved April 4, 2016, from https://www.techinasia.com/3-biggest-reasons-foreign-companies-fail-china.

17. Branding so much more than a name (2011). *Strategic Direction, 27*(3), 6–8.

18. Walsh, M. F., Winterich, K. P., & Mittal, V. (2010). Do logo redesigns help or hurt your brand? The role of brand commitment. *Journal of Product & Brand Management, 19*(2), 76–84.

19. Statista (2016, January). Leading social networks worldwide as of January 2016. *statista.com*. Retrieved April 17, 2016, from http://www.statista.com/statistics/272014/global-social-networks-ranked-by-number-of-users/.

20. Hampton, K. N., Goulet, L. S., Rainie, L. & Purcell, K. (2011). Social networking sites and our lives. Pew Internet & American Life Project. Retrieved May 8, 2012, from http://www.pewinternet.org/Reports/2011/Technology-and-social-networks.aspx; http://newsroom.fb.com/content/default.aspx?NewsAreaId=22.

21. Smith, A. (2010, August 11). Home broadband 2010. Pew Internet & American Life Project. Retrieved April 29, 2011, from http://www.pewinternet.org/~/media//Files/Reports/2010/Home%20broadband%202010.pdf

22. Griffin, G. (2011, April 20). Egypt's uprising: Tracking the social media factor. *PBS Newshour*. Retrieved May 7, 2012, from http://www.pbs.org/newshour/updates/middle_east/jan-june11/revsocial_04-19.html.

23. Cisneros, J. D., & Nakayama, T. K. (2015). New media, old racisms: Twitter, Miss America, and cultural logics of race. *Journal of International & Intercultural Communication, 8*(2), 108–127.

24. Gergen, K. J. (2002). The challenge of absent-presence. In J. Katz & M. Aakhus (Eds.), *Perpetual contact: Mobile communication, private talk, public performance* (pp. 223–227). Cambridge, UK: Cambridge University Press.

25. Turkle, S. (2011). *Alone together: Why we expect more from technology and less from each other*. New York, NY: Basic Books.

26. Winsor, M. (2015, April 15). African cell phone use: Sub-Saharan Africa sees surge in mobile ownership, study finds. *International Business Time*. Retrieved March 8, 2016, from http://www.ibtimes.com/african-cell-phone-use-sub-saharan-africa-sees-surge-mobile-ownership-study-finds-1883449; Macharia, J. (2014, April). Internet access is no longer a luxury. *africarenewal magazine*. Retrieved April 17, 2016, http://www.un.org/africarenewal/magazine/april-2014/internet-access-no-longer-luxury.

27. Simon Wiesenthal Center 2014 Report on Digital terrorism and hate. Retrieved April 17, 2016, from http://www.wiesenthal.com/site/apps/nlnet/content.aspx?c=lsKWLbPJLnF&b=8776547&ct=13928897.

28. Rainie, L. (2015, September 22). Digital divide 2015. Pew Research Presentation. Retrieved March 8, 2016, from http://www.pewinternet.org/2015/09/22/digital-divides-2015/.

29. Wei, L. (2012). Number matters: The multimodality of Internet use as an indicator of the digital inequalities. *Journal of Computer-Mediated Communication, 17*, 303–318.

30. Horrigan, J., & Duggan, M. (2015, December 15). Home broadband 2015. Pew Research Report. Retrieved March 8, 2016, from http://www.pewinternet.org/files/2015/12/Broadband-adoption-full.pdf.

31. Internet usage statistics for Africa. (2015, November 15). Retrieved March 8, 2016, from http://www.internetworldstats.com/stats1.htm.

32. van Dijk, J. (2004). Divides in succession: Possession, skills, and use of new media for societal participation. In E. P. Bucy & J. E. Newhagen (Eds.), *Media access: Social and psychological dimensions of new technology use* (pp. 233–254). Mahwah, NJ: Erlbaum; Rojas, V., Straubhaar, J., Roychowdhury, D., & Okur, O. (2004). Communities, cultural capital, and the digital divide. In Bucy & Newhagen, pp. 107–130.

33. Scommegna, P. (2003). U.S. growing bigger, older and more diverse. Population Reference Bureau website, http://www.prb.org/.

34. Jayson, S. (2012, April, 26). Census shows big jump in interracial couples. *USAToday.com*. Retrieved July 2, 2012, from http://www.usatoday.com/news/nation/story/2012-04-24/census-interracial-couples/54531706/1.

35. Kayne, E. (2013, June 13). White majority in U.S. gone by 2043. NBCNews.com. Retrieved March 6, 2015, from http://usnews.nbcnews.com/_news/2013/06/13/18934111-census-white-majority-in-us-gone-by-2043?lite; Teixeira, R., Frey, W. H., & Griffin, R. (2015, February 24). 10 big trends that are transforming America. *Center for American Progress.com*. Retrieved March 8, 2016, from https://www.americanprogress.org/issues/progressive-movement/report/2015/02/24/107261/states-of-change/.

36. Zong, J., & Batalova, J. (2015, February 26). Frequently requested statistics on immigrants and immigration in the United States. Migration Policy Institute. Retrieved March 8, 2016, from http://www.migrationpolicy.org/article/frequently-requested-statistics-immigrants-and-immigration-united-states.

37. Fischer, M. J. (2008). Does campus diversity promote friendship diversity? A look at interracial friendships in college. *Social Science Quarterly, 89*(3), 631–655.

38. Gurin, P., Nagda, B. A., & Lopez, G. E. (2004). Benefits of diversity in education for democratic citizenship. *Journal of Social Issues, 60*(1), 17–34.

39. U.S. Bureau of the Census website, http://www.census.gov/prod/2002pubs/c2kbr01-15.pdf. The American Indian and Alaskan Native Population: 2000.

40. Webster, Y. O. (1992). *The racialization of America*. New York, NY: St. Martin's Press.

41. Curtin, P. D. (1969). *The Atlantic slave trade: A census*. Madison, WI: University of Wisconsin Press.

42. Baldwin, J. (1955). *Notes of a native son*. Boston, MA: Beacon Press.

43. West, C. (1993). *Race matters*. Boston, MA: Beacon Press.

44. Amsden, D. (2015, February 26). Building the first slavery museum in America. *nytimes.com*. Retrieved April 17, 2016, from http://www.nytimes.com/2015/03/01/magazine/building-the-first-slave-museum-in-america.html?_r=0.

45. Banks, J. (1991). *Teaching strategies for ethnic studies*. Needham, MA: Allyn & Bacon.

46. Takaki, R. (1989). *Strangers from a different shore*. New York, NY: Penguin Books, p. 209.

47. Roediger, D. R. (2005). *Working toward Whiteness: How America's immigrants became White*. New York, NY: Basic Books.

48. Roediger, D. R. (1991). *The wages of Whiteness: Race and the making of the American working class*. New York, NY: Verso.

49. After the riots: The knees jerk. (2011, August 20). The *Economist, 400*(8747), pp. 13–14; Rennie, D. (2011, August 2011). Bagehot: The transportation option. The *Economist, 400*(8747), p. 54.

50. Jones, J. M. (2013, July 13). Americans rate ethnic relations positively: View black-Hispanic relations least positively. *gallup.com*. Retrieved April 20, 2016, from http://www.gallup.com/poll/163535/americans-rate-racial-ethnic-relations-positively.aspx; Drake, B. (2016, January 18). 5 facts about race in America. Pew Research Center. Retrieved April 20, 2016, from http://www.pewresearch.org/fact-tank/2016/01/18/5-facts-about-race-in-america/.

51. Growing apart. (2013, September 21). *Economist.com*. Retrieved March 8, 2016, from http://www.economist.com/news/leaders/21586578-americas-income-inequality-growing-again-time-cut-subsidies-rich-and-invest.

52. Fitz, N. (2015, March 31). Economic inequality: It's far worse than you think. *Scientificamerica.com*. Retrieved March 8, 2015, from http://www.scientificamerican.com/article/economic-inequality-it-s-far-worse-than-you-think/.

53. Growing apart. (2013, September 21). *Economist.com*. Retrieved March 8, 2016, from http://www .economist.com/news/leaders/21586578-americas-income-inequality-growing-again-time-cut -subsidies-rich-and-invest.

54. Kochhar, R., & Fry, R. (2014, December 12). Wealth inequality has widened along racial, ethnic lines since end of Great Recession. Pew Research Center. Retrieved on March 8, 2014, from http:// www.pewresearch.org/fact-tank/2014/12/12/racial-wealth-gaps-great-recession/.

55. Wadhwa, V. (2009, March 2). Why skilled immigrants are leaving the U.S. *BusinessWeek*. Retrieved March 2, 2009 from http://www.businessweek.com/technology/content/feb2009 /tc20090228_990934.htm

56. Adler, P. S. (1975). The transition experience: An alternative view of culture shock. *Journal of Humanistic Psychology, 15*, 13–23.

57. Johannesen, R. L. (1990). *Ethics in human communication* (3rd ed.). Prospect Heights, IL: Waveland Press.

58. Evanoff, R. J. (2004). Universalist, relativist, and constructivist approaches to intercultural ethics. *International Journal of Intercultural Relations, 28*, 439–458.

59. Howell, W. S. (1982). *The empathic communicator*. Belmont, CA: Wadsworth.

60. Kale, D. W. (1994). Peace as an ethic for intercultural communication. In L. Samovar & R. E. Porter (Eds.), *Intercultural communication: A reader* (7th ed., pp. 435–441). Belmont, CA: Wadsworth.

61. Appiah, K. A. (2006). *Cosmopolitanism: Ethics in a world of strangers*. New York, NY: Norton.

62. Appiah (2006); Evanoff (2004); Kidder, R. M. (2006, April 4). Values for citizens of a flat world. *Christian Science Monitor*, p. 17.

63. Kleinjans, E. (1975). A question of ethics. *International Education and Cultural Exchange, 10*, 20–25.

64. Alcoff, L. (1991/1992). The problem of speaking for others. *Cultural Critique, 20*, 5–32.

65. Starosta, W. J., & Chen, G.-M. (2005). Intercultural listening: Collected reflections, collated refractions. In W. J. Starosta & G.-M. Chen (Eds.), *Taking stock in intercultural communication: Where to now?* (pp. 274–285). Washington, DC: National Communication Association.

66. Ishii, S. (1984). *Enryo-sasshi* communication: A key to understanding Japanese interpersonal relations. *Cross Currents, 11*, 49–58.

67. Berlan, E. D., Corliss, H. L., Field, A. E., Goodman, E. & Austin, S. B. (2010). Sexual orientation and bullying among adolescents in the Growing Up Today study. *Journal of Adolescent Health, 46*(4), 366–371.

68. Tompkins, P. K. (2009). *Who is my neighbor? Communicating and organizing to end homelessness*. Boulder, CO: Paradigm Publishers.

© kristian sekulic/Getty Images RF

## CHAPTER TWO

# Intercultural Communication

## BUILDING BLOCKS AND BARRIERS

**STUDY OBJECTIVES**

*After reading this chapter, you should be able to:*

1. Define culture.

2. Define communication.

3. Discuss the relationship between culture and communication.

4. Describe the role that context and power play in intercultural interactions.

5. Identify and define ethnocentrism.

6. Identify and describe stereotyping.

7. Identify and describe prejudice.

8. Identify and describe discrimination.

9. Explain the ways in which ethnocentrism, stereotyping, prejudice, and discrimination act as barriers to effective intercultural communication.

**KEY TERMS**

color-blind approach
communication
context
culture
discrimination
embodied ethnocentrism
ethnocentrism
hate speech
individualism
indulgence versus restraint
intercultural communication
long-term versus
   short-term orientation
masculinity/femininity
perceptions
power
power distance
prejudice
stereotypes
uncertainty avoidance
values
worldview

Every year for 30 years, Kraków, Poland, has hosted the *International Festival of Jewish Culture*. Jews and Gentiles from around the world come together to celebrate Jewish cultural traditions of music, dance, theatre, arts, and cuisine.

**Surf's Up!**

If you would like more information about this fascinating festival, visit http://www.jewishfestival.pl/, the official website of the International Jewish Festival of Krakow, where you can see the program, read about the various events of the festival, and watch live streaming music.

You can also taste Chorba soup and other Jewish specialties, or listen to lectures by international holocaust and Jewish history experts. It all takes place in the cellars, cafes and synagogues of the Kazimierz district, once an epicenter of Jewish life in Eastern Europe. The grand finale is the open air concert on aptly named Szeroka street (wide street) where Klezmer bands and musicians from around the world are guaranteed to leave you humming Yiddish.[1]

What is interesting about this intercultural event is that there are few Jews currently living in Kraków. While it *was* once a Jewish cultural epicenter, it now hosts the largest Jewish cemetery in the world because most of the Jews of Kraków were slaughtered by Nazis in World War II. Most were first forced into the crowded ghetto of Podgórze, across the river, and then killed there or in death camps. It is estimated that 85 percent of Polish Jews (about 3 million) were killed, and the district of Kazimierz became a ghost town. Only a few hundred Jews live in Kraków today.

The festival was started by Janusz Makuch, who is not Jewish. As he describes it, in his late 20s he wanted to "discover the traces of the past, the vast richness of culture in Krakow." "The Jewish people gave Poland a tremendous culture—we lived together for so many years. . . . There was a huge gap and something had to be done to close it and bring back what had been missing and I had this crazy idea . . . to organize a Jewish festival."[2]

He was afraid no one would come, and he was proven wrong. Thousands have been coming every year for 10 days in midsummer to remember, but also to look beyond the trauma, to life celebration. An interesting unintended result is that the once run-down Kazimierz area is being revitalized. Jews are returning to live there.[3]

While this event represents intercultural interaction on a global and national scale, intercultural interactions are also a part of your everyday life—from your encounters with diverse groups of students in your classes, to your interactions with your parents (from a different generational culture!), as well as your interaction with friends of opposite genders and sexual orientations.

Groups of people everywhere are coming together, sometimes with enormous differences in cultural backgrounds, beliefs, lifestyles, economic resources, and religions. This illustrates that intercultural communication does not happen in a vacuum. History, economics, and politics play an important role in how various people and groups react when they encounter each other in specific contexts and engage in intercultural communication. What are some of the specific building blocks and barriers of intercultural communication? The answer to that question is the focus of this chapter.

**Intercultural communication** occurs when people of different cultural backgrounds interact, but this definition seems simplistic and redundant. To properly define intercultural communication, it's necessary to understand the two root words—*culture* and *communication*—that represent the first two building blocks. In addition, communication always happens in a particular situation or context,

In today's global world, groups of people everywhere come together, sometimes with enormous differences in cultural backgrounds, beliefs, lifestyles, economic resources, and religions—like these people participating in the Toureg dance performance at the annual Festival in the Desert in Essakane, Mali. Unfortunately, this festival is now suspended due to political unrest in Mali.

© Janet Kimber/The Image Bank/Getty Images

**What Do You Think?**

Rank-order the following in terms of their importance in defining "American culture": hamburgers, movies, corn, apple pie, pizza, baseball, hot dogs, milkshakes, french fries, and big cars. Did you know that only three of those things actually are indigenous to the United States (corn, baseball, milkshakes), while the other seven are from Europe? What does this say about the ideas and values of U.S. culture?

our third building block. Our fourth building block concerns the element of power, something that is part of every intercultural interaction. We first define and describe culture and communication and then discuss how these two interact with issues of context and power to form our understanding of intercultural communication.

## BUILDING BLOCK 1: CULTURE

Culture is often considered the core concept in intercultural communication. One characteristic of culture is that we may not think about it very much. Trying to understand one's own culture is like trying to explain to a fish that it lives in water. Often, we cannot identify our own cultural backgrounds and assumptions until we encounter people from other cultures, which gives us a frame of reference. For example, consider our student, Ann, who participated in a study-abroad program in Mexico. She told us that she thought it was strange that many young Mexicans lived with their parents even after they had graduated from college and were working. Gradually, she recognized that

Mexicans tend to have a stronger sense of family responsibilities between children and parents than Americans do. Thus, young people often live at home and contribute to the family income. Older parents rarely go to retirement communities, but are cared for within the family. While volunteering in a senior citizens' home, Ann was impressed by how few people lived in the facility.

Culture has been defined in many ways. For some people, it means the opera or classical music, but for the purposes of this book, we define **culture** as learned patterns of perception, values, and behaviors, shared by a group of people, that are dynamic and heterogeneous. Culture also involves our emotions and feelings. Let's look at what this definition actually means.

## Culture Is Learned

First, culture is learned. While all human beings share some universal habits and tendencies—we all eat, sleep, seek shelter, and share some motivations to be loved and to protect ourselves—these are not aspects of culture. Rather, culture is the unique way we have learned to eat, sleep, and seek shelter because we are American or Japanese, male or female, and so on. For example, most Americans eat holding a fork in one hand, but when they use a knife, they shift the fork to their other hand. Europeans think this is clumsy; they simply eat with fork in one hand and knife in the other. While Americans and Japanese share a need to be loved, Americans tend to express feelings of love more overtly, whereas Japanese are taught to be more restrained. When we are born, we don't know how to be a male or female, American or Mexican, and so on; we are taught. We have to learn how to eat, walk, talk, and love like other members of our cultural groups—and we usually do so slowly and subconsciously, through a process of socialization. Think of how young children learn to be male or female. Young boys imitate their fathers and other grown men, while young girls learn to talk and act like their mothers and other women. The same is true for other groups we belong to. For example, an American child adopted by a Finnish family will embrace Finnish cultural values; likewise, a Korean child raised by a German family will exhibit German cultural values.

When we move into new cultures, we learn new cultural patterns. For example, when Chinese students first arrive in the United States they are surprised to see car drivers motioning with their hand to pedestrians to let them pass first. In China, this gesture is used only when a person gets frustrated or irritated at another person! Gradually Chinese students learn the meaning of this gesture—that the driver is actually being polite—and then use it themselves when driving.

## Culture Involves Perception and Values

What do cultural groups learn and share? First, they share **perceptions,** or ways of looking at the world. Culture is sometimes described as a sort of lens through which we view the world. All the information we receive in a given day passes through this perceptual lens. The process of perception is composed of three phases: selection, organization, and interpretation. Our cultural experiences influence every phase of the perception process and ultimately determine how we make sense of the world and how we respond to the people, places, and things in it. During the *selection* process, we are only able to

© BananaStock/PunchStock RF

Many cultural groups value family relationships, but how and how often families interact may depend on the particular cultural norms. How often does your extended family get together and what are the expectations for the interaction?

**What Do You Think?**

What kind of cultural values are embraced by children in multiracial families, such as singer Alisha Keys, who has a Jamaican father and Irish Italian mother? What about the Hollywood movie star Keanu Reeves, who is "Eurasian," being White, Chinese, and Hawaiian? He was born in Lebanon and grew up in Canada and America. With such family backgrounds, might multiracial kids be more interculturally competent?

give attention to a small fraction of all the information available to our senses. What we choose to pay attention to is based upon features of stimuli (size, intensity, etc.) as well as what we perceive to be important and relevant to us. In the *organization* phase we categorize the information into recognizable groups. Last in the perception process is *interpretation*, the ways in which we assign meaning to the information we have organized.[4]

Consider the following scenario: Towanda and Matthew are walking across campus discussing a problem that Matthew is having with his sociology course project. In the distance another group of students wearing deerskin clothing, soft moccasins, and carrying feathers is walking toward an open area of campus. Matthew is engrossed in his thoughts and does not even perceive the group of students, and even when he notices them he does not perceive them as Towanda does. Towanda grew up close to the Dineh nation and organizes the perception of these individuals into a known cognitive category and says, "The American Indian student group is practicing for their dance competition. I have a friend in the competition; let's go watch the practice." She selected, organized, and interpreted the sights and sounds of the students because of her familiarity with them. Matthew, on the other hand, does not see them at first, and then he notices but does not interpret any special meaning. This scenario shows how individuals may be exposed to the same stimuli, but because of differences in cultural backgrounds (age, gender, race, ethnicity, nationality) may select, organize, and interpret things very differently. Each cultural group has a different "prescription" for its "lenses." The difficulty is in trying to understand our own cultural perceptions—like trying to look at our own glasses without taking them off.

The perception process is laden with opportunities for us to compare ourselves and our culture to others. Later in the chapter, we'll show that categorization and interpretation processes *can* lead to overgeneralizations, stereotypes, and prejudice, which can have negative consequences.

Another metaphor for culture is a computer program in that culture, in a sense, serves as a "program of the mind" that every individual carries within himself or herself. These programs of the mind, or patterns of thinking, feeling, and potential acting, work just like computer software. That is, they tell people (subconsciously) how to walk, talk, eat, dance, socialize, and otherwise conduct their lives.[5]

## Culture Involves Feelings

Culture is experienced not only as perceptions and values but also as feelings. When we are in our own cultural surroundings we *feel* a sense of familiarity and a certain level of comfort in the space, behavior, and actions of others. We might characterize this feeling as a kind of **embodied ethnocentrism,** which is normal.[6] (Later on we'll discuss the negative side of ethnocentrism.) This aspect of culture has implications for understanding adaptation to other cultural norms and spaces. The stronger your identification with a particular space or cultural situation, the more difficult it might be to change spaces without experiencing a lot of discomfort—actual psychological and physiological changes. For example, dining in a formal Japanese restaurant, with flat tables, rice-paper walls, silence, and low light, would probably give U.S. Americans a feeling of mild unfamiliarity, compared to experiences in most U.S. restaurants. However, experiencing new cultural situations on a daily basis can give a stronger *feeling* of disorientation. (We'll discuss this more when we talk about culture shock in Chapter 10.)

U.S. students studying in France described their feelings in coping with the French language. Their self-esteem dropped and they became very self-conscious. Their whole bodies were entrenched in this effort of trying to communicate in French; it was a laborious and involved process that was connected to all aspects of themselves—a feeling of being out of their cultural comfort zone.[7] We should not underestimate the importance of culture in providing us a feeling of familiarity and comfort.

## Culture Is Shared

Another important part of our definition of culture is that cultural patterns are shared. The idea of a culture implies a group of people. These cultural patterns of perceptions and beliefs are developed through interactions with different groups of individuals—at home, in the neighborhood, at school, in youth groups, at college, and so on. Culture becomes a group experience because it is shared with people who live in and experience the same social environments. Our perceptions are similar to those of other individuals who belong to the same cultural groups. In class, the authors sometimes put students in same-gender groups to highlight how many men share many similar perceptions about being male and similar

**What Do You Think?**

The cause of the crash of Asiana Airlines Boeing 777 at San Francisco International Airport in July 2013 may have been partly related to cultural values (e.g., power distance). The plane crashed on landing, killing 3 passengers and injuring nearly 200. Analysis of the crash placed part of the blame on pilot confusion about the automatic throttle. However, some experts suggested that a contributing factor may have been Korea's emphasis on authoritarian structure and strong respect for age seniority, in play during pilot training. That is, co-pilots are not encouraged to challenge senior pilots, nor ever speak out of turn and civilian pilots defer to military-trained pilots. The pilot that day was a veteran pilot but new to the 777 and a training captain was in the right seat watching his performance.

*(continued)*

**What Do You Think? (cont.)**
The pilot reported that he did not immediately move to abort the landing when he should have because he felt that only the instructor pilot had that authority. How might other cultural values affect cockpit communication? (Source: Asiana airlines crash caused by pilot error and confusion, investigators say. (2014, June 24). *theguardian.com.* Retrieved April 21, 2016, from http://www .theguardian.com /world/2014/jun/24 /asiana-crash-san -francsico-controls -investigation-pilot).

attitudes toward women; the same seems to hold true for women. For example, men sometimes share a perception that women have power in social situations. Women sometimes share a perception that men think badly of women who go out with a lot of guys. Some older people sometimes see no use for smartphones or social media; young people couldn't live without them. Another pattern of shared perception is evident in surveys of global attitudes toward U.S. popular culture. The majority of people surveyed in European countries say they like American music, movies, and television (Spain [79 percent], Italy [74 percent], and France [72 percent]), while U.S. popular culture gets generally poor reviews in the majority of Muslim nations surveyed, especially Pakistan, where 78 percent dislike it.[8]

Our membership in cultural groups ranges from involuntary to voluntary. Many of the cultural groups we belong to—specifically, those based on age, race, gender, physical ability, sexual orientation, and family membership—are involuntary associations over which we have little choice. We belong to other cultural groups— those based on professions, political associations, and hobbies—that are voluntary associations. And some groups may be involuntary at the beginning of our lives (those based on religion, nationality, or socioeconomic status) but become voluntary associations later on. Some experts argue that involuntary memberships, like gender or race, are more consequential than voluntary ones in impacting on our communication. People often respond to us on the basis of physical characteristics that define these identities, which can, as we'll see later in the chapter, lead to stereotyping and prejudice.[9]

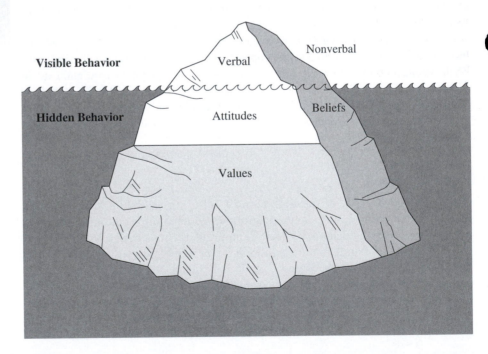

The visible and hidden layers of culture.

## Culture Is Expressed as Behavior

Our cultural lens or computer program influences not only our perceptions and beliefs but also our behaviors. For example, Ann's belief in (or lens on) the importance of individual independence, or individualism, is reflected in her behavior. She was expected to become increasingly independent when growing up and to be on her own after college, and she was socialized to make her own decisions about dating, marriage, and career. By contrast, the young people she met in Mexico were socialized to the cultural value of collectivism. They were expected to be more responsible for caring for other family members and to take their wishes into consideration in marriage and career decisions.

It is important to understand that we belong to many different cultural groups and that these groups collectively help determine our perceptions, beliefs, and behavior. These patterns endure over time and are passed on from person to person. Therefore, just as Ann was socialized to be individualistic, she'll probably pass on these same beliefs and behaviors to her own children.

## Culture Is Dynamic and Heterogeneous

**Surf's Up!**

If culture is sometimes about making spaces to resist the dominant culture, Native American cultures are good examples of this. A website that seeks to further this resistance is On This Date in North American Indian History (http://americanindian .net). What happened on today's date?

Another crucial feature of culture is that it is dynamic, or changing, and can often be a source of conflict among different groups.[10] It is important to recognize that cultural patterns are not rigid and homogeneous but are dynamic and heterogeneous. A good example of cultural heterogeneity is the varying opinions among Latinos/as regarding U.S. immigration policies. People sometimes assume that Latinos are all sympathetic to other Latino immigrants, even those who are undocumented. However, a recent study found that Latinos are divided over issues of illegal immigration. A small majority (53 percent) says illegal immigrants should pay a fine but not be departed, a small minority (13 percent) says they should be deported, and a larger minority (28 percent) says they should not be punished. It's important to remember that members of cultural groups do not all think or behave in the same way.[11] Sometimes there is conflict over cultural patterns and meanings. For example, who gets to define what "Native American" means? The government has one definition: a person who has proven Native American ancestry and is enrolled in a particular tribe. But some people feel that a Native American can be anyone who follows Native American cultural and spiritual traditions and practices.

Table 2.1 shows some cultural behaviors that are widely shared in some cultures around the world. Note that these are shared, collective cultural behaviors, rather than individual characteristics.

Viewing culture as dynamic is particularly important for understanding the struggles of various groups—Native Americans, Asian Americans and Pacific Islanders, African Americans, Latinos/as, women, gays and lesbians, working-class people, and so on—as they try to negotiate their relationships and ensure their well-being within U.S. society. By studying the communication that arises from these ongoing struggles, we can better understand several intercultural concerns. Consider, for example, the debates surrounding the DREAM Act (Development, Relief, and Education for Alien Minors Act) and President Obama's decree that stopped deportation procedures for undocumented youth (sometimes called DREAMers) as long as they meet certain criteria (e.g., are enrolled in school or serving in the military,

## Pop Culture Spotlight

The Japanese movie *Shall We Dance* (1996) is about a successful but unhappy Japanese accountant who finds the missing passion in his life when he begins to secretly take ballroom dance lessons. When the movie was released in the United States, in order for the movie to make sense to American audiences, a voiceover had to be added explaining that, in Japan, married couples rarely said "I love you" or held hands in public and that dancing together in public (e.g., ballroom dancing) was "beyond embarrassing" and viewed with suspicion.

What would you have thought if this information was not provided? Would you have thought it absurd that ballroom dancing was taboo? Do you think that more movies should have voiceovers explaining unfamiliar cultural details?

**TABLE 2.1  Interesting Cultural Behaviors**

**Thailand:** Thai people greet each other with a wai greeting—hold your hands together at the chest like a prayer and give a light bow.

**Kenya:** Pointing with an index finger is very insulting. Use the whole hand.

**China:** Use both hands when passing a gift or food.

**Germany:** Germans often bang their fists on the table to show their appreciation at the end of a meeting.

**Japan:** When you are offered a gift, you must first refuse it once, modestly and serenely. Then you should accept it using both hands.

**Israel:** When Israelis invite someone to their home, it is an important gesture. It is appropriate to bring a book as a gift.

**Spain:** After a meal, you must place your utensils together on the plate. Otherwise, your Spanish host would think that you were not satisfied.

**French Polynesia:** It is not necessary to tip. People usually give small gifts instead.

*Source:* Adapted from Mancini. Selling Destinations, 5E. © 2010 Delmar Learning, a part of Cengage Learning, Inc. Reproduced by permission. www.cengage.com/permissions

are younger than 30, and came to the United States before the age of 16). The controversies concerning these and other propositions illustrate the concerns of many different cultural groups. Those in favor of the act think that these students should not be punished because their parents came here illegally, that it's a good investment for America because these college-educated adults will ultimately contribute to our society and to the tax base. Others think that allowing these youth to stay in the United States sends the wrong message, is rewarding illegal actions, and may encourage others to pursue the path of illegal immigration.

Seeing culture as dynamic and heterogeneous opens up new ways of thinking about intercultural communication. After all, the people from a particular culture are not identical, and any culture has many intercultural struggles. For instance, when we speak of Chinese culture or French culture, we ignore the diversity that resides in that culture. That "Chinese culture" may refer to the mainland Chinese; or to the inhabitants of the island of Taiwan, who speak Taiwanese or Mandarin; or to the Chinese from Hong Kong, who speak Cantonese. The label "Chinese" thus obscures incredible diversity. Similarly, "French culture" could refer to the "Pieds Noirs" (North Africans of French descent), or to Vietnamese of French descent, or to the Bretons, who live in northwestern France and speak their own language.

Yet, cultures are not heterogeneous in the same way everywhere. How sexuality, race, gender, and class function in other cultures is not necessarily the same as or even similar to how they do in the United States. For example, there are poor people in most nations. The poor in the United States are often viewed with disdain, as people to be avoided; in many European countries, by contrast, the poor are seen as a part of society, to be helped by government programs. Likewise, gender issues are not framed the same way in all countries. In the United States, gender equality is defined in terms of equal pay and career opportunities. In some Middle Eastern countries, women may be seen to have equality because they have tremendous power within the home and family but less influence in public arenas. In short, by viewing any culture as heterogeneous, we can understand the complexities of that culture and become more sensitive to how people in that culture live.

## BUILDING BLOCK 2: COMMUNICATION

Communication, our second building block, is also complex and may be defined in many ways. For our purposes we define **communication** as a symbolic process whereby meaning is shared and negotiated. In other words, communication occurs whenever someone attributes meaning to another's words or actions. In addition, communication is dynamic, may be unintentional, and is receiver-oriented. Let's look more closely at what this means.

First, communication is symbolic. That is, the words we speak and the gestures we make have no meaning in themselves; rather, they achieve significance only because people agree, at least to some extent, on their meaning. When we use symbols, such as words or gestures, to communicate, we assume that the other person shares our symbol system. If we tell someone to "sit down," we assume that the individual knows what these two words (symbols) mean. Also, these symbolic meanings are conveyed both verbally and nonverbally. Thousands of nonverbal behaviors—gestures, postures, eye movements, facial expressions, and so on—involve shared meaning.

Think about the symbolic meaning of some clothing. Why is it that many people value Ralph Lauren clothing more than clothes from JCPenney? It has to do with the symbolic meaning associated with the clothing, rather than anything intrinsically special about the clothing. Sometimes we mistakenly assume that the other person shares our symbol systems. When Jenny, a Canadian, moved to the United States as a child, she knew Canadian money and American money did not look alike, but thought they at least would be called the same things. She was very confused when she found out that in the United States, one-dollar bills or coins were not called Loonies and two-dollar bills or coins not called Toonies. In America, she couldn't even find a two-dollar bill or coin!

People also disagree over the meaning of powerful verbal and nonverbal symbols—like the flag and the national anthem. Consider the recent controversy over the removal of the Confederate flag from the South Carolina Statehouse. Obviously, the flag has tremendous symbolic meaning for many people. For some Whites, the flag symbolizes the rich legacy of the South and the gallant fight in the Civil War. For some African Americans, the same flag is a negative reminder of slavery, oppression, segregation, and prejudice. Consider also the lawsuit regarding the placement of a prayer in a Rhode Island high school. The eight-foot high prayer was papered onto the auditorium wall in 1963. In 2012, a federal judge ruled that the prayer's presence was unconstitutional because it violated the principle of government neutrality in religion. The subsequent uproar in the community showed the power of this particular symbol for many people—on both sides. Those supporting its presence posted hateful messages and even death threats on Twitter

**Info Bites**

In 2015, the top five Internet languages were English, Chinese, Spanish, Arabic, and Portuguese. In 2015, the top five countries with the highest Internet usage were China, India, the United States, Brazil, and Japan. Think about the differences in online communication and the influence it brings to our daily communication. Do you visit websites in a language other than your own? (Source: http://www .internetworldstats.com /top20.htm)

An important U.S. value revolves around keeping busy and achieving things in life. Unlike people in many cultures, most Americans prefer to work longer hours for extra money rather than work less and have more time to spend with family and friends.

© Corbis RF

to the student who first proposed its removal. The student, who is not a Christian, defended her proposal saying that the prayer always made her feel unwelcome, like she didn't belong there.[12]

Second, communication is a process involving several components: people who are communicating, a message that is being communicated (verbal or nonverbal), a channel through which the communication takes place, and a context. People communicating can be thought of as senders and receivers—they are sending and receiving messages. However, communication does not involve tossing "message balls" back and forth, such that one person sends a single message and the other person receives it. Rather, it is more akin to clicking on a website and being bombarded by many different messages at once.

Third, communication involves sharing and negotiating meaning. People have to agree on the meaning of a particular message, but to make things more complicated, each message often has more than one meaning. For example, the message "I love you" may mean, "I want to have sex with you tonight," "I feel guilty about what I did last night without you," "I need you to do me a favor," "I have a good time when I'm with you," or "I want to spend the rest of my life with you." When we communicate, we assume that the other person takes the meaning that we intend. But for individuals from different cultural backgrounds and experiences, this assumption may be wrong and may lead to misunderstanding and a lack of shared meaning. Often, we have to try harder in intercultural communication to make sure that meaning is truly shared.

Fourth, communication is dynamic. This means that communication is not a single event but is ongoing, so that communicators are at once both senders and receivers. For example, when a teacher walks into the classroom, even before she starts speaking, communication messages are flying all around. The students are looking at her and interpreting her nonverbal messages: Do her attire, her bearing, her facial expressions, and her eye movements suggest that she will be a good teacher? A hard teacher? Someone who is easy to talk with? The teacher in turn is interpreting the nonverbal messages of the students: Are they too quiet? Do they look interested? Disruptive? When we are communicating with another person, we take in messages through our senses of sight, smell, and hearing—and these messages do not happen one at a time, but rather simultaneously. When we are communicating, we are creating, maintaining, or sharing meaning. This implies that people are actively involved in the communication process. Technically, then, one person cannot communicate alone—talking to yourself while washing your car in the driveway does not qualify as communication.

Fifth, communication does not have to be intentional. Some of the most important (and sometimes disastrous) communication occurs without the sender knowing a particular message has been sent. During business negotiations, an American businessman in Saudi Arabia sat across from his Saudi host showing the soles of his feet (an insult in Saudi society), inquired about the health of his wife (an inappropriate topic), and turned down the offer of tea (a rude act). Because of this triple insult, the business deal was never completed, although no insult was intended. The American returned home wondering what went wrong.

Finally, communication is receiver-oriented. Ultimately, it is the person who assigns meaning who determines the outcome of the communication situation. That is, the Saudi businessman who misinterpreted the American's messages determined the outcome of the interaction—he never signed the contract. It didn't matter that the American didn't intend this outcome. Similarly, if someone interprets your messages as prejudicial or sexist or negative, those interpretations have much more influence over future interactions than does your intended meaning. What can you do when people interpret your communication in ways you don't intend? First, you need to realize that there is a possibility, particularly in intercultural encounters, that you will be misunderstood. To check whether others are understanding you, you can paraphrase or ask questions ("What did you think I meant?"), or you can observe closely to see if others are giving nonverbal cues that they are misinterpreting your messages. We'll address this issue of how to communicate more effectively throughout this textbook.

## CULTURE AND COMMUNICATION

### Communication, Cultural Worldviews, and Values

As already noted, culture influences communication. All cultural groups influence the ways in which their members experience and perceive the world. Members of a culture create a worldview, which, in turn, influences communication. For Judith, growing

**Surf's Up!**

Learn more about the disability culture and how it exemplifies the five elements of this textbook's definition of culture at www .disabilityculture. org. To learn the characteristics of the American deaf culture, go to www.deafculture .com. Think about whether the disability culture is a full-fledged culture and how it is similar to or different from an ethnic culture.

**What Do You Think?**

The book *Communication Ethics and Universal Values* points out some of the fundamental ethical principles across cultures; for example, justice, reciprocity, and human dignity. Based on their different cultures, the authors propose additional ethical principles—truth, respect for another person's dignity, and no harm to the innocent. Do you think it is possible for the world to move into the next century with a more universal value system?

(SOURCE: *Communication Ethics and Universal Values*, by C. Clifford and M. Traber [Eds.], 1997, Thousand Oaks, CA: Sage)

up in an Amish/Mennonite culture meant that she thought war was absolutely wrong. Tom, growing up in an Asian American, academic family, did not share that particular perception but learned other values.

**Values,** you will recall, have to do with what is judged to be good or bad, or right or wrong. They are deeply felt beliefs that are shared by a cultural group and that reflect a perception of what ought to be, not what is. Equality, for example, is a value shared by many people in the United States. It is a belief that all humans are created equal, even though we acknowledge that in reality there are many disparities, such as in talent, looks, and access to material goods. Collectively, the values of a cultural group represent a **worldview,** a particular way of looking at the world. Table 2.2 highlights some interesting cultural patterns from around the world. How do these cultural patterns reflect cultural values? Let's look more closely at specific conceptions of values.

*Kluckhohn and Strodtbeck's Value Orientation*   To more fully explain the concept of values, two anthropologists, Fred Strodtbeck and Florence Kluckhohn, studied how the cultural values of Hispanics, Native Americans, and European Americans differ.[13] They suggested that members of all cultural groups must answer these important questions:

- What is human nature?
- What is the relationship between humans and nature?
- What is the relationship between humans?
- What is the preferred personality?
- What is the orientation toward time?

**TABLE 2.2  More Interesting Cultural Patterns**

**Great Britain:** Business appointments must be made well in advance, and honorary titles are always used.

**Jordan:** People are proud of their Arab heritage and are tremendously hospitable to their guests.

**Fiji:** When talking with a Fijian, crossed arms is a sign of respect.

**Singapore:** Punctuality for meetings is expected.

**Egypt:** Building trust is the most important aspect of any relationship. Visitors should be prepared to engage in extended conversation and coffee before starting a meeting.

**Thailand:** Don't pause on the doorsill of a house. Thais believe that a spirit lives here.

**Mexico:** "Mañana" (putting off a task until tomorrow) is a prevalent norm. This does not indicate Mexicans are lazy, but shows that their pace is more relaxed than in other places.

**Tahiti:** It is polite to taste a little bit of every food offered with your fingers in a Tahitian's home.

*Source:* Adapted from Mancini. Selling Destinations, 5E. © 2010 Delmar Learning, a part of Cengage Learning, Inc. Reproduced by permission. www.cengage.com/permissions

There are three possible responses to each question, and each cultural group has one or possibly two preferred responses. The range of answers to these questions is shown in Table 2.3. It is important to remember that value orientations are deeply held beliefs about the way the world should be, and not necessarily the way it is. These questions and responses help us understand broad cultural differences among various cultural groups—national groups, ethnic groups, and groups based on gender, class, and so on.

*The Nature of Human Nature*   As shown in Table 2.3, there are three "solutions." The solution to the issue of human nature is related to dominant religious and legal practices. One solution is a belief in the basic goodness of human nature. Legal systems in a society holding this orientation would emphasize rehabilitating those who violate the law; jails would be seen as places to train violators to rejoin society as contributing citizens. Some religions, such as Buddhism and Confucianism, focus on the perceived natural goodness of humans.

A second solution involves a combination of goodness and evil in human nature. We could argue that many groups within the United States hold to this orientation and that there has been a shift in this value orientation in the past 50 years. In terms of religious beliefs, there is less emphasis on the fundamental evil of humanity than in, say, colonial America. However, with regard to the criminal justice system, there seems to be an increasing emphasis on incarceration and punishment ("three strikes" legislation) and less talk about rehabilitation and reform. The United States currently has a higher proportion of citizens incarcerated than any other Western nation.

According to a third solution, humans are essentially evil. Societies holding to this orientation would more likely punish criminals than rehabilitate them. For example, the strict laws and codes of Islam seem to reflect this orientation toward human nature, as do some forms of Christianity. While he lived in Belgium, Tom

### Surf's Up!

Could it be possible for people in various countries to develop a similar system of cultural values? See what efforts UNESCO is making through its Universal Ethics Project (unesdoc.unesco.org /images/0011/001176 /117622eo.pdf). The website notes, "In a multipolar world of heightened individualism and a possibly unprecedented splintering of perceptions, it is more than ever necessary to look for the acknowledgment, or rather the emergence of a common substratum of values which would make economically, ecologically, socially and culturally viable coexistence possible on a world-scale."

**TABLE 2.3  Value Orientation**

|  | RANGE OF VALUES | | |
|---|---|---|---|
| Human nature | Basically good | Mixture of good and evil | Basically evil |
| Relationship between Humans and Nature | Humans dominate | Harmony between the two | Nature dominates |
| Relationships between Humans | Individual | Group-oriented | Collateral |
| Preferred Personality | "Doing": stress on action | "Growing": stress on spiritual growth | "Being": stress on who you are |
| Time Orientation | Future-oriented | Present-oriented | Past-oriented |

*Source:* Adapted from *Variations in Value Orientations,* by F. Kluckhohn and F. Strodtbeck, 1961, Chicago: Row & Peterson.

was particularly struck by the images of punishment and torture on display in the Counts of Flanders Castle in Ghent. He often wondered if he would better understand these cultural practices if he accepted the Christian view of humanity as essentially evil and born with sin.

*The Relationship between Humans and Nature*    In most of U.S. society, humans seem to dominate nature. For example, clouds are seeded in an attempt to bring rain. Rivers are rerouted and dammed to make way for human settlement, to form lakes for recreation, and to provide power. Conception is controlled by drugs and birth control devices. Of course, not everyone in the United States agrees that humans should dominate nature. Conflicts between environmentalists and land developers often center on disagreements over this value orientation. For example, there is an ongoing debate in Arizona between astronomers who want to build more telescopes on Mount Lemon (near Tucson) for scientific exploration and environmentalists who want to block construction in order to protect a rare species of squirrel.

By contrast, in a society that emphasizes the domination of nature over humans, families may be more accepting of the number of children that are born naturally. There is less intervention in processes of nature and fewer attempts to control what is seen as the natural order. An example might be people who live in floodplains; they often face floods and devastation, but they accept that relationship with nature. The same can be said of some people in the United States who keep repairing homes built too close to flooding rivers.

Many Native American groups, and also the Japanese, believe in the value of humans living in harmony with nature, rather than one dominating the other. Some Native Americans even consider living animals to be their brothers or sisters. In this value orientation, nature is respected and plays an important role in the spiritual and religious life of the community. Thus, for example, a hawk may be considered a messenger that guides humans in decision making and brings messages from God. And some societies, including many Arab cultural groups, emphasize aspects of both harmony with and domination of nature.

*The Relationship between Humans*    As the example of Ann and her Mexican friends showed, some cultural groups value individualism, while others are more group-oriented and value collectivism. (See "What Do You Think?" where our Kenyan students describe how this value is expressed in their communities.) **Individualism**, a key European American (and Canadian and Australian) value, places importance on the individual rather than the family or work team or other group. By contrast, people from more collectivist societies—such as those of Central and South America, many Arab groups, and the Amish and some Chicano and Native American communities in the United States—place a great deal of importance on extended families. For example, many collectivists believe that after children leave home they should still be in frequent contact with parents. This family bond extends even to in-laws. In some collectivist countries, like China, when you marry, you are expected to call your spouse's parents "mom" and "dad" and respect them as if they were your own parents. This stands in

**What Do You Think?**

Our Kenyan students provided these examples of how collectivism works in their communities. How easy would it be for you to embrace this value and participate in these activities?

- If you are undertaking an activity that requires a lot of human labor (e.g., building a terrace, molding bricks), you may request help from your neighbors. And you would be expected to provide food for the workers. Failure to respond to a neighbor's request for help would be viewed negatively.
- Most people live in extended families. Children are expected to live with parents until they marry and sometimes after they marry.
- Children in the village belong to everyone. If they come to your house while you're eating, you give them food. If they misbehave, you discipline them as a parent, with no repercussion.

contrast to many people's attitudes in the United States. A Yugoslav student comments:

> When I told my friends that my grandmother from Yugoslavia was going to visit my family for a couple of months, the only person who thought that was great was my Chinese friend. All my other (American) friends felt bad for my mother because she had to deal with her mother-in-law for a couple of months.

Some collectivist cultural groups share a collateral value, a connection to ancestors even after they are no longer living. While relatives may be dead, they are believed to influence present-day relationships and family relationships continue. During the *Dia de los Muertos* (Day of the Dead) celebrations at the beginning of November, many Mexicans and Mexican American families visit the gravesites of deceased relatives and communicate concerns and events of the past year, often through humorous stories, remembering and honoring family members who have died. The Vietnamese similarly revere their departed ancestors. As scholar Lana Lebozec describes it:

> They believe that those souls will never be destroyed and their ancestors will continue to watch over them; so, unless they give due respect to the dead, through the offering of foods and paper money, during the special family events, such as births, weddings, funerals, anniversaries, etc., their lives will be unfavorably influenced. . . . On the anniversary of the ancestor's death, everyone in the family is expected to be present . . . through family offerings, the ancestors are kept informed of any events of the family.[14]

Values may also be related to economic class or rural/urban distinctions. In the United States, for example, working-class people may be more collectively oriented than members of the middle or upper classes, given that working-class people reportedly give a higher percentage of their time and money to helping others.

These cultural values may influence how people communicate. For example, people who value individualism tend to value more direct forms of communication and conflict resolution. People in collectivist societies may employ less direct communication and more avoidance-style conflict resolution. For example, a Japanese student describes how her less direct Japanese style conflicts sometimes with the more direct U.S. communication style:

> When I was talking with an American friend, he pointed out that I nodded too much during our conversations and didn't respond to him verbally. That's because when Japanese listen, they nod a lot to show that they are paying attention and being good listeners. My American friend told me that during conversations, Americans would rather ask questions, respond verbally, and say something instead of nodding quietly to show that they're listening. Even though I know it, it is hard for me to change my behavior.

It is important to remember that people may belong to cultural groups that hold contradictory values. For example, most work contexts in the United States require highly individualistic behavior, which may conflict with a more collectivist family/ethnic background. Some workers may find it hard to live with these competing values. For example, Phyllencia, a Navajo student, told us that she often feels a conflict between her more family-oriented life at home and the individualistic life expected of college students. She's expected to return home to participate in family and community activities; but she feels torn because she knows she'll be penalized for missing classes and not submitting schoolwork. Many students like Phyllencia, who live "between" two cultures, struggle to meet the demands of both cultures—meeting as many family and cultural obligations as possible while still succeeding in the academic and work worlds. This bicultural existence is akin to swinging on a trapeze. We'll talk more about bicultural identities in Chapter 4.

*The Preferred Personality*    The most common form of activity in the United States seems to involve a "doing" orientation. Thus, being productive and keeping busy are highly valued in many contexts—for example, in the workplace, most employees have to document what they "do" (number of sales made, number of clients seen, and so on). The highest status is usually given to those who "do" (sports figures, performers, physicians, lawyers) rather than those who mostly "think" (philosophers, priests, scholars).

By contrast, a "growing" orientation places importance on the spiritual aspects of life. This orientation seems to be less common than the other two; the main practitioners are Zen Buddhists. Some societies, such as Japan, are said to combine a doing and a growing orientation, emphasizing both action and spiritual growing.

A final orientation revolves around "being." In this process of self-actualization, "peak experiences," in which the individual is fused with the experience, are most important. This orientation can be found in Central and South America, and in Greek and Spanish cultural groups. For example, one of our Spanish students told us that his mother worked for an American company in Spain. The company was behind in production and asked the employees to work overtime, offering a good bonus as an incentive. The company was surprised when all the employees turned it down, saying they would rather have their usual five weeks of summer vacation than the additional money. This illustrates a being value orientation, whereby it is more important to spend time interacting with family and friends than to work (doing) for financial gain.

*The Orientation to Time*    Most U.S. cultural communities—particularly European American and middle-class ones—seem to emphasize the future. This is evident in practices such as depositing money in retirement accounts that can be recovered only in the distant future and having appointment books that can reach several years into the future. A seeming contradiction is the heavy debt load carried by many Americans, indicating a lack of planning and a desire to live in the present. Perhaps this reflects a sense of optimism about the future, an assumption that things will get better—the future will be "new and improved!" This same optimism about the future can also be seen in the relative lack of concern about saving "historical" buildings

This school, attended by Ulysses S. Grant in the early 1800s, was demolished several years ago. The lack of concern for saving "historical" buildings and areas reflects a U.S. American value system that emphasizes newness and innovation rather than preservation of the old.

© AP Photo/Lexington Herald-Leader, David Perry

and areas. Many old buildings in the United States have been destroyed and replaced with newer—and sometimes less well constructed—buildings, whereas in Europe and South America buildings are constantly being refurbished.

Other societies (Spain, Greece, Mexico) seem to emphasize the importance of the present, recognizing the value of living in the here and now, and the potential of the current moment. Many European societies (France, Germany, Belgium) and Asian societies (Japan, Korea, Indonesia) place a relatively strong emphasis on the past, believing that history has something to contribute to an understanding of contemporary life. And some cultures emphasize the present but also recognize the importance of the past. When Judith was in language school in Mexico, her professors would always answer questions about contemporary society with a story about history. For instance, there were regional elections going on at the time. If students asked about the implications of the campaign platform of one of the candidates, the professors would always answer by describing what had happened in the region 50 or 100 years earlier.

***Hofstede's Value Dimensions***   Dutch social psychologist Geert Hofstede and his associates have identified several additional cultural values that help us understand cultural differences: (1) power distance, (2) masculinity/femininity, (3) uncertainty avoidance, (4) long-term versus short-term orientation to life, and (5) indulgence/restraint orientation.[15] (See Table 2.4.) These values also affect communication.

**Power distance** refers to the extent to which less powerful members of institutions and organizations within a country expect and accept that power is distributed unequally. Societies that value low power distance (Denmark, Israel, New Zealand)

**Info Bites**

Different cultures have different sayings that often reflect their particular values. For example, an Italian proverb says "A closed mouth catches no flies." A Chinese saying goes "A man may dig his grave with his teeth." One Spanish proverb is "Who knows most speaks least." These sayings reflect cultural views on the relative importance of speaking or not speaking. (SOURCE: *Brain Candy Quotations* [www.corsinet .com/braincandy/proverb .html])

### TABLE 2.4 Hofstede Value Orientations

| | |
|---|---|
| **Power Distance** | |
| Low power distance | High power distance |
| Less hierarchy better | More hierarchy better |
| **Femininity/Masculinity** | |
| Femininity | Masculinity |
| Fewer gender-specific roles | More gender-specific roles |
| Value quality of life, support for unfortunate | Value achievement, ambition, acquisition of material goods |
| **Uncertainty Avoidance** | |
| Low uncertainty avoidance | High uncertainty avoidance |
| Dislike rules, accept dissent | More extensive rules, limit dissent |
| Less formality | More formality |
| **Long-Term/Short-Term Orientation** | |
| Short-term orientation | Long-term orientation |
| Truth over virtue | Virtue over truth |
| Prefer quick results | Value perseverance and tenacity |
| **Indulgence/Restraint** | |
| Indulgent | Restraint |
| Relatively free gratification of needs related to enjoying life and having fun | Suppression and regulation of needs related to enjoying life and having fun |
| Freedom of speech over maintaining order | Maintaining order over freedom of speech |

*Source:* Adapted from *Cultures and Organizations: Software of the Mind,* 3rd ed., by G. Hofstede, G. J. Hofstede, and M. Minkov, 2010. Boston: McGraw-Hill.

## Pop Culture Spotlight

Do we learn our values through children's stories? Think of what Kluckhohn and Strodtbeck and Hofstede might say about your favorite characters from the universes of Winnie the Pooh, Bugs Bunny, Mickey Mouse, Scooby Doo, Sesame Street, the Muppets, Marvel superheroes, Teenage Mutant Ninja Turtles, and even the Teletubbies, Pokémon, and the Power Rangers.

believe that less hierarchy is better and that power should be used only for legitimate purposes. For example, in organizational settings in the United States, the best bosses are those who play down power differences by telling subordinates to call them by their first names, by accepting subordinates' suggestions as important and worthwhile, and so on. By contrast, in societies that value large power distance (Mexico, the Philippines, India), boss–subordinate relationships and decision-making processes are more formalized. Thus, bosses are expected to provide answers and to give orders. For example, an American working in India got into trouble when he tried to use an egalitarian approach and let the workers decide how to sequence their work. The workers thought he was insincere and incompetent because he didn't act the way a boss should act in India and failed to emphasize the status difference between himself and his subordinates. One of our students, Sang Won, described the positive and negative aspects of high power distance value as demonstrated in the educational settings in his country of South Korea. One way this value is expressed is in the high respect students have for teachers there. Korean students would never eat or talk during class, out of respect for their teachers. However, he goes on to explain the negative aspect of being so respectful: "Sometimes, students do not speak up and say their opinion out of respect for the teacher. Consequently, teachers have to teach them how to speak up for their opinions."

The **masculinity/femininity** dimension refers to (1) the degree to which gender-specific roles are valued and (2) the degree to which a cultural group values "masculine" (achievement, ambition, acquisition of material goods) or "feminine" (quality of life, service to others, nurturance) values. People in Japan, Austria, and Mexico seem to prefer a masculine orientation, expressing a general preference for gender-specific roles. In these countries, certain roles (wage-earner) should be filled by men, and other roles (homemaker, teacher) by women. By contrast, many people in northern Europe (Denmark, Norway, Sweden, the Netherlands) seem to prefer a feminine orientation, reflecting more gender equality and a stronger belief in the importance of quality of life for all. In the United States, we tend to prefer gender-specific roles, though not as rigid as in Japan, Austria, or Mexico; but we also tend toward a masculine orientation, with a high value placed on competition and acquisition.

**Uncertainty avoidance** describes the degree to which people feel threatened by ambiguous situations and try to ensure certainty by establishing more structure. Relatively weak uncertainty-avoidance societies (Great Britain, Sweden, Ireland, Hong Kong, the United States) share a preference for a reduction of rules and an acceptance of dissent, as well as an increased willingness to take risks. By contrast, strong uncertainty-avoidance societies (Greece, Portugal, Japan) usually prefer more extensive rules and regulations in organizational settings and more consensus concerning goals.

Hofstede acknowledged and adopted the **long-term** (Confucian) **versus short-term orientation** to life, which originally was identified by a group of Asian researchers.[16] This value has to do with a society's search for virtue versus truth. Societies with a short-term orientation (the United States, Canada, Great Britain, the Philippines, Nigeria) are concerned with "possessing" the truth (reflected in Western religions like Judaism, Christianity, and Islam). The emphasis is on quick results in endeavors, and social pressure exists to "keep up with the Joneses" even if it means overspending. Societies with a long-term orientation (China, Hong Kong, Taiwan, Japan, South Korea, Brazil, India) are more concerned with virtue (reflected in Eastern religions like Confucianism, Hinduism, Buddhism, and Shintoism). The emphasis is on perseverance and tenacity in whatever is attempted regardless of how long it takes, as well as on thrift.

Based on recent research by Michael Minkov, one of Hofstede's associates, there is now an additional value dimension, **indulgence versus restraint**. This dimension is related to the *subjective* feelings of happiness. That is, people may not actually *be* happy or healthy but they report that they *feel* happier and healthier. National cultures that are categorized as more indulgent (Mexico, Nigeria, Sweden, Australia) tend to allow relatively free gratification of needs related to enjoying life and having fun. They report that having lots of friends is important (e.g., Facebook), they participate actively in sports, and there is less moral regulation. Societies that emphasize restraint (Russia, Egypt and other Islamic countries, China, India) tend to suppress gratification of needs and regulate it by means of strict social norms. Having many friends is reportedly less important in these cultures, there is more watching of sports, but less participation, and a strong work ethic. Countries with a predominant indulgence orientation emphasize freedom of speech over maintaining order; countries with a more restraint orientation tend to value maintaining order over allowing freedom of speech.

Intercultural conflicts often result from differences in value orientations. For example, past-oriented people may feel strongly that it is important to consider how things were done in the past. For them, the past and tradition hold answers. Values often conflict in international assistance projects, such as fertilizing crops or improving infrastructures, in which future-oriented individuals (such as many Americans) may show a lack of respect for traditional ways of doing things. For another example, individualist-oriented people often value direct confrontation to solve problems, while collectivists prefer more nonconfrontative ways. One American student talks about her experience with her roommate:

> One of my college roommates is a girl from South America. I can recall one incident when she was upset with me and instead of confronting me about the problem, she left a note hanging on our bedroom door. It was so irritating to me that she would do that. The girl was very nonconfrontational. She never told me when she was upset. She probably thought it was better for our relationships if we didn't have confrontation; however, from my individualistic upbringing, I didn't see it that way!

Conflicts may be even more complex when power differentials are factored in. Often, certain values are privileged over others. For example, most U.S. workplaces reward extremely individualistic relationships and "doing" behaviors at the expense of more collaborative, but equally productive, efforts. Individual employees frequently are recognized for achieving the most sales or issuing the most reports, but awards rarely are given for being a good team member or for helping someone else achieve a departmental goal.

**What Do You Think?**

How many holidays can you name for other cultures? Which culture celebrates "namedays"? Which culture celebrates the Quinceañera when a girl enters womanhood? Which culture celebrates *Summerfest?* How does this knowledge about other cultures help us better communicate with their people?

***Limitations of Value Frameworks***    While identifying cultural values helps us understand broad cultural differences, it is important to remember that not everyone in a given society holds the dominant value. We shouldn't merely reduce individuals to stereotypes based on these value orientations. After all, not all Amish or Japanese are group-oriented, and not all Americans and Australians are individualistic. While people in small rural communities may be more collectively oriented, or more willing to help their neighbors, we cannot say that all people in big cities ignore those around them. While Danish people as a cultural group score high on the "feminine" value scale, reflecting a strong belief in nurturing and providing a high quality of life for others, many Danes currently hold strong anti-immigrant attitudes.

One of the problems with these and similar cultural frameworks is that they tend to "essentialize" people. In other words, people tend to assume that a particular group characteristic is the essential characteristic of given group members at all times and in all contexts. But this ignores the heterogeneity within any population. For example, one could characterize the current debate about health care in the United States as a struggle between "masculine" and "feminine" value orientations. Some people believe that each person should be able to take care of himself or herself and should be responsible for paying for his or her own medical care. Others, representing a more feminine position, believe that everyone should sacrifice a little for the good of the whole, that everyone should be assured equal access to health care and hospitalization.

Value heterogeneity may be particularly noticeable in a society that is undergoing rapid change. Japan, for example, was defeated militarily and was in economic ruin only 50 years ago. It now has one of the world's strongest economies. This rapid social and economic change influenced traditional values. While many of the older folk in Japan hold to the traditional values of collectivism, giving undying loyalty to their companies and elders, this is not so true of the younger generation. They are moving toward more individualism, showing less loyalty to their families and companies—causing somewhat of a rift between the generations in contemporary Japanese society.[17] This could be compared to the way that the hippie generation of the 1960s altered some of the traditional values held by previous generations.

Although people may differ with respect to specific value orientations, they may hold other value orientations in common. For example, individuals may hold different views on the importance of individual or group loyalty but share a deep belief in the goodness of human nature and in certain religious observances. While these group-related values tend to be relatively consistent, people are dynamic, and their behavior varies contextually. That is, people may be more or less individualistic or group-oriented depending on the context. For example, both Judith and Tom find that they are more individualistic (more competitive, more self-oriented) in work settings than in family settings.

In this sense, there are no easy lists of behaviors that are key to "successful" intercultural interaction. Instead, it's important to understand the contexts when interacting with Asian Americans, or persons with disabilities, or men or women, for that matter. A trip to the library or Internet research on a particular group may be helpful, but always remember that exceptions can and do occur. The value orientations discussed here are general guidelines, not rigid rules, to help you in your intercultural communication. Your own learning and behavior and experience with others will make a difference in your intercultural experiences.

## Communication and Cultural Rituals and Rules

Even as culture influences communication, communication influences and reinforces culture. This means that the way we communicate in cultural contexts often strengthens our sense of cultural identity. For example, participating in communication rituals such as prayers in a church or synagogue may strengthen our religious identity and sense of belonging to a religious community. Participating in a daily communication greeting ritual ("Hi, how are you?" "Fine, and you?") may strengthen our sense of who we are in our friendship networks.

Many White middle-class (mostly women) participate in a communication ritual that is aimed at solving personal problems and affirming participants' identities. It is initiated when people sit down and acknowledge the problem ("We need to talk"), and one usually describes the problem (e.g., trouble in a relationship, or dilemma regarding a course of action or decision). Together they explore possible options and negotiate potential solutions. The ultimate cultural purpose is that it dramatizes common cultural problems, provides a preferred social context for the venting of problems, and promotes a sense of community identity.[18]

Similarly, patterns of talk about drinking alcohol help shape and reinforce notions of masculinity and gender identity among U.S. college students. Specifically, communication expert David Engstrom studied the way college students talk about drinking and found that in order to be seen as a competent communicator in some college communities, male students portray drinking as a normal behavior and follow several communication rules, including (1) refer to alcoholic consumption in a very abstract way, never say exactly how much was drunk (e.g., "I *partied* hard," "At least you got to have fun") and others should not ask specifically how much was consumed, and (2) refer to alcohol positively and as a normal behavior (one should not make negative statements about alcohol consumption—even when there is clearly an alcohol-related tragedy, but rather search for other explanations). Behavior that seemed out of the ordinary or excessive would be normalized and excused by "normal" alcoholic consumption. This excuse was used even *when students were not drinking* as a way to downplay unacceptable behavior (e.g., urinating in public, exhibiting aggressive behavior toward women). Engstrom suggested that by following these communication rules, male students can get "off the hook" for questionable behaviors, and also maintain and reinforce a cultural identity of masculinity.[19]

There are other examples of how people's communication behavior reinforces their cultural identity and worldviews. For example, in many White working-class communities in the United States, men express their gender roles in many contexts by engaging in conversation with their peers, but not with women or children.[20]

Other examples can be seen in online communication. A recent study compared Korean and American online personal profiles and found that Koreans were less likely to reveal personal information and more likely to present themselves rather indirectly, through visual means (e.g., graphics) and links to their interests. Americans were more likely to present personal information about themselves, directly through personal stories. These differences show how each cultural group expressed and reinforced their cultural identity, the more individualistic, direct Americans, and the more collectivistic, indirect Koreans.[21]

### Communication and Resistance to the Dominant Culture

Another way to look at culture and communication is to think about how people may use their own space to resist the dominant culture. Similarly, workers can find ways to resist the authority structure of management in many ways, some subtle (e.g., work slowdowns, posting negative information about their employer or organization on

Facebook or YouTube) and some more obvious (e.g., whistle-blowing, boycotting). For example, in Fall 2015, University of Missouri football team refused to play football as a protest against the administration's lack of response to racist incidents on campus, at a potential cost of more than $1 million if the team forfeited the game.[22]

Social media has dramatically increased the efficiency of resistance. The Black Lives Matter movement started as a Facebook post and then a tweet #blacklivesmatter, after the murder of Trayvon Martin and Michael Brown by White police officers. The resistance movement gathered momentum as hundreds of protesters from around the country converged on Ferguson, Missouri (home of Michael Brown) in 2014 and then thousands joined, showing up at scenes of police action against unarmed Black youth, political rallies and other meetings, communicating their nonviolent resistance. Another example of resistance to dominant culture is students who sign their advisers' names on course registration forms, thereby circumventing the university bureaucracy. Or students can pay attention to their mobile devices in the classroom, carry on conversations through instant messages, read Facebook buzzfeeds, Twitter feeds, or engage in other "distracting" behaviors—thus weakening the professor's power over them.[23] In all these ways of resisting the dominant cultural systems, people find means to meet their needs and struggle to make relationships and contexts more equitable.

## BUILDING BLOCK 3: CONTEXT

A third building block of intercultural communication is **context**—the physical, social, or virtual situation in which communication occurs. For example, communication may occur in a classroom, a bar, a church, or online and people communicate differently depending on the context. You probably communicate differently when hanging out with friends than when talking with your instructor and other students in a classroom. Intercultural communication may be more or less challenging online or face-to-face. For example, communicating via a phone conversation can be more challenging than talking face-to-face when there are language barriers. On the other hand, communicating online through Facebook posts or e-mail maybe easier than face-to-face context when language barriers are involved. Perhaps you can think of other examples of how an online context affects intercultural communication.

The same context may call for different behavior in different cultures. For example, one American student went to Scotland with his father to play golf—in celebration of his high school graduation. He loved to play golf and because Scotland is the birthplace of golf, he was very excited about the trip. When he and his father arrived at the golf club, they were dressed in golf hats and golf spikes, ready to start playing. To their surprise they received no assistance and were eventually asked to leave the building, although they had not yet played the course. Finally they realized that in Scotland, it is rude and unacceptable to wear golf hats or spikes in the clubhouse.

Context may consist of the physical, social, political, and historical structures in which the communication occurs. Consider the controversy over the Calvin Klein underwear ads that use adolescents as models. The controversy takes place in a social context that says that pedophilia is perverse or immoral. This means that any communication that encourages or feeds that behavior or perspective, including advertising, is deemed wrong by the majority of residents. However, pedophilia has not been considered wrong in all societies in all periods of history. To really understand the Calvin Klein ads, we have to know something about the current attitudes toward and meanings attached to pedophilia wherever the ads are displayed.

The political context in which communication occurs includes those forces that attempt to change or retain existing social structures and relations. For example, to understand the acts of protesters who throw blood or red paint on people who wear fur coats, we must consider the political context. In this case, the political context would be the ongoing informal debates about animal rights and animals farmed for their fur. In other countries or in other times, the protesters' communicative act would not make sense or would be interpreted in other ways.

We also need to examine the historical context of communication. For instance, African Americans and Whites in the United States might have more trouble communicating with one another than Whites and Blacks in Europe because the legacy of slavery influences these interactions even today.

## BUILDING BLOCK 4: POWER

**Power** is always present when we communicate with each other although it is not always evident or obvious. We often think of communication between individuals as being between equals, but this is rarely the case. In every society, a social hierarchy exists that gives some groups more power and privilege than others. The groups with the most power determine, to a great extent, the communication system of the entire society. This is certainly true in intercultural communication. For example, straight people often have more power than gays or lesbians, males more power than females, and nondisabled people more power than those with disabilities. Those in power, consciously or unconsciously, create and maintain communication systems that reflect, reinforce, and promote their own ways of thinking and communicating.

There are two types of group-related power. The first involves membership in involuntary groups based on age, ethnicity, gender, physical ability, race, and sexual orientation and is more permanent in nature. The second involves membership in more voluntary groups based on educational background, geographic location, marital status, and socioeconomic status and is more changeable. The key point is that the dominant communication systems ultimately impede others who do not have the same ways of communicating. Arguably, the communication style most valued in college classrooms is a traditional White, middle-class male style—with emphasis on competition (the first person who raises a hand gets to speak)—a style that is not as comfortable for many women and members of minority groups. By contrast, the call-and-response style of African Americans is not the norm in corporate boardrooms or classrooms. However, some hip-hop cultural norms, such as baggy jeans worn low and caps worn backward, have entered American youth culture.

Power also comes from social institutions and the roles people occupy in those institutions. A college is such an institution. For example, in the classroom, there

### Pop Culture Spotlight

Words have meaning only through our agreement as to that meaning. In the movie *Mean Girls*, teenager Gretchen tries to use the word "fetch" for "cool." When Regina, another teenager, says that she loves another girl's bracelet, Gretchen says, "So fetch!" Regina asks, "What is fetch?" Caught off-guard, Gretchen makes up the word's origin: "Oh, it's like slang, from . . . England." How hip are you? Can you list other examples of words used by teens that seem to mean something only because they say they do?

is temporary inequality, with the instructor having more power. He or she sets the course requirements, gives grades, and determines who speaks. In this case, the power rests not with the individual instructor but with the role that he or she is enacting.

Power is not a simple one-way proposition but is dynamic. Students in a classroom, for example, are not powerless; they may assert and negotiate their power. After all, one cannot be a teacher without students. Also, the typical power relationship between instructor and student often is not perpetuated beyond the classroom. There are, however, also issues of power in broader societal contexts. For example, in contemporary society, cosmetics companies have a vested interest in a particular image of female beauty that involves purchasing and using makeup. Advertising encourages women to feel compelled to participate in this cultural definition. But what happens if a woman decides not to buy into this definition? Regardless of her reasons for not participating, other people are likely to interpret her behavior in ways that may not match her own motivation. What her unadorned face communicates is understood against a backdrop of society's definitions—that is, the backdrop developed by the cosmetics industry.

Power in this sense should be thought of in broad terms. Dominant cultural groups attempt to perpetuate their positions of privilege in many ways. For example, one might speculate that the delay in recognizing and finding solutions to the lead in drinking water in Flint Michigan in 2016 was because its population is mostly Black and about 40 percent poor (http://www.cnn.com/2016/01/26/us/flint-michigan-water-crisis-race-poverty/). It is hard to imagine the same thing happening in a White, affluent area. Subordinate groups can resist this domination in many ways, too. For example, cultural groups can use political and legal means to maintain or resist domination. But these are not the only means of invoking power relations. Groups can negotiate their various relations to culture through economic boycotts, strikes, and sit-ins. An example of a group that used these tactics to negotiate their relations to more powerful groups is the recent Black Lives Matter movement described earlier. Through their actions they protested the inequality and racism of policing practices and the treatment of many unarmed Black men killed by White police officers. Individuals can subscribe or not subscribe to specific magazines or newspapers, change TV channels, write letters to government officials, or take other action to influence power relations. For example, the European clothing distributor Benetton launched an "unhate" ad campaign showing computer-altered images of President Obama kissing Chinese leader Hu Jintao and Pope Benedict XVI kissing an Egyptian imam (religious leader).

Power is complex, especially in relation to institutions or the social structure. Some inequities, such as those involving gender, class, or race, are more rigid than those resulting from temporary roles like student or teacher. The power relations between student and teacher, for example, are more complex if the teacher is a woman challenged by male students. In short, we really can't understand intercultural communication without considering the power dynamics in the interaction.

## BARRIERS TO INTERCULTURAL COMMUNICATION

### Ethnocentrism

**Ethnocentrism** is the belief that one's own cultural group—usually equated with nationality—is superior to all other cultural groups. Believing that one's own country and culture are good is not bad in itself. After all, it is necessary to believe in one's country and group in order to pass along the values that are seen as important. One interesting place to see ethnocentrism is in world maps produced in different places. Most show their own country and culture centered in the middle of the world. One Chinese teaching assistant reported:

> When I asked my students to draw a world map in one intercultural communication class, we were all amazed to see that everybody started from different places. American students started from the map of the United States, Mexican students started from Mexico, and Chinese students started from China. Students are often confused about the locations of other countries or continents, partly because on the maps they are familiar with their own countries are always in the middle!

But ethnocentrism can also be extreme, to the point that one cannot believe that another culture's values are equally good or worthy. Ethnocentrism becomes a barrier when it prevents people from even trying to see another's point of view, through another's "prescription lens."

It can be very difficult to see our own ethnocentrism. Often, we see it best when we spend extended time in another cultural group. One of our students, Sara, described her realization of her own ethnocentrism:

Intercultural communication may involve groups whose members differ in terms of gender, age, ethnicity, and physical ability, among other things.

© Stockbroker/SuperStock RF

When I was 22 years old, I joined the Peace Corps and lived for two years in a remote, rural part of West Africa. I experienced first-hand a culture that was so entirely different from my own and yet had its own sensible, internal logic, that the complacency and arrogance of my U.S. American ethnocentrism was shaken to its core. I came to realize not only that other societies had valid worldviews and important wisdom but that it would take a special kind of attention to take in and understand these other ways of seeing the world.

Learning to see her own ethnocentrism helped Sara to be more receptive to learning about other cultures and to be more curious about other people's ways of living and experiencing the world. However, is it ever okay to be ethnocentric? In 2015, U.S. soldiers stationed in Afghanistan reported that members of the U.S. backed Afghan militia were sexually abusing boys they had brought to the base. The soldiers were told by their superiors to "look the other way" and not interfere—because it was their culture. Those soldiers who did intervene were reprimanded, and some were even expelled from the Army. This illustration shows that avoiding ethnocentrism can be complex and can involve moral/ethical dilemmas.[24]

## Stereotyping

Another barrier to intercultural communication is stereotypes, which develop as part of our everyday thought processes. In order to make sense out of the overwhelming amount of information we receive every day, we categorize and generalize from this information. **Stereotypes** "are widely held beliefs about a group of people" and are a form of generalization—a way of categorizing and processing information we receive about others in our daily life. For example, Tom and Judith hold some generalizations about students. We assume that students don't want to study too much but that they want to know what will be on the tests we give. These generalizations, or mental short-cuts, help us know how to interact with students. However, generalizations become potentially harmful stereotypes when they are held rigidly. Thus, if we thought that all students were lazy or unwilling to study on their own, and we interacted with students based on this belief, we would hold a negative stereotype. A Korean student encountered negative stereotypes while shopping with his wife:

> My wife and I went to a shopping mall to buy some cosmetics. After comparing several products, my wife decided to buy a brand which is kind of expensive. When she went to pay for the cosmetic, the salesclerk saw our Asian faces and we also probably looked like students. She said, "You can't buy this. This is over one hundred dollars." We bought the lotion but did not want to return to her counter again. She communicated her negative stereotypes of Asian people and especially Asian students—as being very poor.

Stereotypes also may be positive. For example, some people hold the stereotype that all attractive people are also smart and socially skilled. Even positive stereotypes can cause problems for those stereotyped. Attractive individuals may feel excessive pressure to fit the stereotype that they are competent at something they're not, or they may be hired on the basis of their appearance and then find out they cannot do the job.

**Surf's Up!**

Discriminatory practices often go unnoticed by those who are responsible for them. We tend to perceive ourselves as fair, good-hearted human beings, unaware that there are hidden biases ingrained in us based on our cultural upbringing or socialization. Our cultural biases may be based on such factors as religion, race, class, gender, sexual orientation, age, disability, or even body image. Test yourself to explore your hidden biases, and reflect on what you can do to fight hate and prejudice in society (http://www.tolerance.org /hiddenbias).

Why do we hold stereotypes? One reason is that stereotypes help us know what to expect from and how to react to others. However, stereotypes, once adopted, are not easily discarded. In fact, people tend to remember information that supports a stereotype and to not retain information that contradicts the stereotype.

We pick up stereotypes in different ways. The media, for example, tend to portray cultural groups in stereotypic ways—for example, older people as needing help, or Asian Americans or African Americans as followers or background figures for Whites or women as needing men in order to be happy. Sometimes stereotypes persist because the media choose to not pass along information that would contradict stereotypes. Consider the many recent stereotypes about Muslim people and their religion of Islam. Western portrayals of Islam often omit the fact that Judaism, Christianity, and Islam are closely related—called "the three sisters of Abrahamic religions" by theologians. All three religions are monotheistic and absolutists (in contrast to the Asian religions that have many gods and are more relative in their dictates about right and wrong). Both Islam and Christianity accept Jesus as the messiah, accept the virgin birth, and recognize Jesus's sacred mission on earth—in contrast to Judaism. However in other aspects, Islam and Judaism are closer; for example, they emphasize a God of justice rather than love, hold to dietary laws, and require male circumcision.

Other stereotypes portray Muslims as sexist and violent. The stereotype of Muslim women in Western media is usually drawn from a small minority of Muslim societies and does not represent the vast majority of Muslim people. The media neglect to tell us about the millions of Muslims who live mundane lives, loving their spouses and children, doing ordinary (or heroic) activities. The media also neglect to tell us that when Canada had its first female prime minister, three different Muslim countries already had female prime ministers and one also had a woman leader of the opposition. Pakistan, Turkey, Malawi, Brazil, and Bangladesh have had women as chief executives, whereas the United States, France, nor Russia have had a woman president.

Recent studies show that the old racist stereotypes of African Americans are still alive and well—in reality TV, of all places. A recent analysis of 10 reality shows, including *Survivor* and *The Apprentice,* revealed that every show had a least one African American participant who fit a stereotype. Male stereotypes were a Sambo (fun-loving buffoon, foolish ladies man), Uncle Tom (generous, selfless, and kind), and coon (unreliable, crazy, and lazy), and Black females fit three other stereotypes: the angry Black woman, hoochie mama (uneducated, with little social status and sex is her primary commodity), and chicken head (sexual hang-ups, no inhibition, high risk, dangerous sexual behaviors). What is so important about stereotypes on reality TV is that people tend to believe that these "characters" are real—especially if those who watch these shows have little access to African Americans in everyday life.[25]

Similarly, old American Indian stereotypes show up on programs like *Saturday Night Live*, *Chappelle's Show*, *Family Guy*, and *South Park*. Another research study found that all the episodes with Native American characters portray the natives as inferior to whites, as stupid or slow—in the way they talk (e.g., on *Chappelle's*

*Show,* Native man uses stunted speech) and/or in their "supposed humor" that tries to be funny but is not (e.g., Indian comedians in *Family Guy* and *South Park* scenes in casino comedy clubs). The shows consistently make fun of Indian traditions and motifs (e.g., the *Family Guy* bathroom attendant character named "Watches You Pee").[26]

We may learn stereotypes in our family. As one young man reported:

> So I grew up with my dad particularly being really racist—he didn't really say much about any other group except Black people. The N word was a common word in my family. I knew there was the black side of town, there was the black neighborhood, and then the rest was white, and that's what I grew up in . . . but we never had any personal interactions with anybody from the black neighborhood.[27]

Stereotypes can also develop out of negative experiences. If we have unpleasant contact with certain people, we may generalize that unpleasantness to include all members of that particular group, whatever group characteristic we focus on (race, gender, sexual orientation).

Because stereotypes often operate at an unconscious level and are so persistent, people have to work consciously at rejecting them. This process involves two steps: (1) recognizing the negative stereotypes (we all have them; see "Surf's Up on page 57 for suggestion on how to uncover your own implicit biases), and (2) obtaining individual information that can counteract the stereotype. For another student, Jenni, an experience working at a homeless shelter helped break some stereotypes. She was amazed at the strength and adaptability of the children who lived there—and then realized that she must have expected something negative. She also realized "that it doesn't matter what race you are, you could end up being down on your luck or homeless. It really broke a stereotype for me personally. As much as I hate to admit it, I always thought of homeless people as lazy and usually not white."

Just as parents can perpetuate stereotypes, they can also help break them. Armstrong Williams, a *Los Angeles Times* reporter, recounts how his father resisted the impulse to stereotype:

> My father told us that the men who burned down our farm were not three white men. They were individuals with jealousy and hatred in their hearts. He implored us not to label or stereotype anyone based on the color of their skin.[28]

## Prejudice

**Prejudice** is a negative attitude toward a cultural group based on little or no experience. It is a prejudgment of sorts. Whereas stereotypes tell us what a group is like, prejudice tells us how we are likely to feel about that group. Why are people prejudiced? One answer might be that prejudice fills some social functions.[29]

One such function is the adjustment function, whereby people hold certain prejudices because it may lead to social rewards. People want to be accepted and liked by their cultural groups, and if they need to reject members of another group to do so,

**Surf's Up!**

There are many barriers to intercultural communication, including cultural stereotypes and misconceptions. Did you know that Muslim women leaders include presidents (Indonesia, Kosovo), prime ministers (Bangladesh, Turkey, Senegal), as well as soldiers (female Peshmerga fighters, Emirati fighter pilots) and that not all Muslim women are required to wear the headscarf or burqa? To check out other misconceptions about Islam and Muslims, visit http:// www.teenvogue .com/story/islam-and -muslim-american -misconceptions. Do you believe that these misconceptions can lead to prejudice and discrimination?

then prejudice serves a certain function. Another function is the ego-defensive function, whereby people may hold certain prejudices because they don't want to admit certain things about themselves. For example, an instructor who does not feel successful as a teacher may find it easier to blame students and hold prejudices against them than to admit shortcomings as a teacher. Finally, people hold some prejudices because they help reinforce certain beliefs or values—the value-expressive function. For example, part of belonging to some religious groups might require holding certain prejudices against other religious groups. Our student Ron's family belonged to an evangelical Protestant church. When he was growing up, his parents made disparaging remarks about the Catholic religion. In his family, part of being a good church member meant being prejudiced against Catholics.

Prejudice may also arise from a personal need to feel positive about one's own group and negative about others, or from perceived or real threats.[30] These may be genuine threats that challenge a group's existence or economic/political power, or symbolic threats in the form of intergroup value conflicts and the accompanying anxieties.[31] For example, one of our students from a multicultural family told us about the prejudice that his mother experienced. His mother is a middle-aged White woman and his father is Latino. When his mom was running for superior court judge in a predominantly Hispanic county, she encountered much prejudice because the Latino/a population generally thinks that White officials are not sensitive to the needs of minority populations. They didn't want to vote for a White woman judge since they saw her as a source of the problems facing their people. In addition, prejudice can flourish where there are cultural differences, language barriers, and limited opportunity for extended interaction. This is probably the case for interactions between one group of immigrants—Montagnards—and residents of North Carolina. The Montagnards come from the Central Highlands of Vietnam and fought with the United States against the Vietnam government in 1960. After the war ended, they were persecuted by the Vietnamese for helping the United States and many fled the country and settled in the United States, some in North Carolina. They report that they find it very difficult to make friends and form relationships with U.S. Americans—the cultural differences seemed insurmountable and they have limited opportunities to interact with Americans. From their point of view Americans are too busy, life is too hurried and stressful, and no one has time to talk. Nobody just drops by unannounced to see their friends—a common and cherished tradition within their Montagnard community. They feel targeted by indifference at best and prejudice and racism at worst, and think they are often mistaken for Mexicans and that "Americans don't seem to like Mexicans."[32]

It is also helpful to think about in different kinds of prejudice. The most blatant prejudice is easy to see but is less common today. It is more difficult, however, to pinpoint less obvious forms of prejudice. For example, "tokenism" is a kind of prejudice shown by people who do not want to admit they are prejudiced. They go out of their way to engage in unimportant but positive intergroup behaviors—showing support for diversity programs or making statements like "I'm not prejudiced" to persuade themselves and others that they are not prejudiced. "Arms-length" prejudice is when people engage in friendly, positive behavior toward members of another group in public and semiformal situations (casual friendships at work, interactions in large social gatherings or at lectures) but avoid closer contact (dating, attending intimate social gatherings).[33]

These subtle yet real forms of prejudice often go hand-in-hand with a **color-blind approach** to intercultural relations. Many of us were taught that the best way to improve race relations was to not notice color, as comments from two students show:

> The message I got from teachers at the school and other people was that the way not to be racist was to just pretend that you don't see any differences between people. And so everyone had feelings about race, but no-body talked, there was no place to talk about those things. And you only have to treat everybody as an individual and everything will be fine.[34]

Many experts think that this approach is counterproductive to the improvement of U.S. race relations—for many reasons. First, it's not possible. We do notice color in the United States and our race and ethnicity is often an important part of our identities. Clarence Page, an African American journalist, remarks: "Too much has been made of the virtue of 'colorblindness.' I don't want Americans to be blind to my color as long as color continues to make a profound difference in determining life chances and opportunities. Nor do I wish to see so significant a part of my identity denied."[35]

Second, a color-blind approach discourages any meaningful conversations about race relations—in our families, schools, churches, and synagogues. Psychologist Beverly Tatum illustrates how some White children learn this at an early age:

> A young child asks his mother why the man in the grocery store is so dark. Instead of answering, his mother tells him to be quiet, which tells the child it's not OK to discuss differences.[36]

Third, a color-blind approach allows people to ignore, deny, disregard, and therefore continue to support (actively or passively) the status quo—existence of racial inequalities.[37] It allows blame to be placed on the minorities of lagging economically behind Whites. If discrimination is over, then Blacks' plight is because of their cultural deficiencies (laziness, lack of good values, etc).[38]

Ignoring race and not discussing it will not make problems disappear; as a Yale Law School professor cautions: "to not notice race is to miss one of the central ways in which power, position, and material well-being are distributed in our society."[39]

Like stereotypes, prejudice, once established, is very difficult to undo. Because it operates at a subconscious level (we often aren't really aware of our prejudice), there has to be a very explicit motivation to change our ways of thinking. But it can be tackled. Take the case of Lewiston Maine, where 4,000 Somali refugees settled in this small French Canadian Catholic all White city almost 20 years ago. (The state of Maine is 92 percent White). It was rough going. The residents saw the refugees as competing for already scarce jobs, the residents' lack

**Info Bites**

A recent report revealed that temporary employment agencies in California show significant preference for White applicants over African Americans in undercover paired tests. For example, the White job applicants were more likely than African American applicants to be

- Offered a temporary or permanent job.
- Granted an interview.
- Offered a job with a higher salary or for a longer duration.
- Offered a job more quickly.
- Offered coaching on how to present themselves.

To read the full report, visit http://www.docstoc.com/docs/2975674/Racial-Preferences-The-Treatment-of-White-and-African-American-Job.

of experience with diversity probably reinforced their prejudice, and there were a number of racists incidents directed at the refugees. Over the years, the economy has improved, unemployment is about average for the state, the crime rate is lowest of Maine's cities, and the initial culture clash between Somali refugees and residents has subsided somewhat. However, some residents insist that town leaders need to explicitly confront issues of prejudice and racism, and in 2015 a series of community discussions on race relations was held after a group of high school students put up a poster in their school (#blackLivesMatter) to raise awareness about racial injustices. They were told to take it down, that it was divisive. The story made the national news, the school reversed its decision, and the result was community discussions. One resident commended the students, noting that young people are our future: "they are connecting across racial lines and having the types of discussions among themselves that many of us who are much older won't even dare to have with our family, friends or even ourselves. Social change is often guided by the young."[40]

### Discrimination

The behavior that results from stereotyping or prejudice—overt actions to exclude, avoid, or distance oneself from other groups—is called **discrimination**. Discrimination may be based on racism or any of the other "isms" related to belonging to a cultural group (sexism, ageism, elitism). One way of thinking about discrimination is that power plus prejudice equals "ism." That is, if one belongs to a more powerful group and holds prejudices toward another, less powerful group, resulting actions toward members of that group are based on an "ism" and so can be called discrimination.

Discrimination may range from very subtle nonverbal (lack of eye contact, exclusion of someone from a conversation), to verbal insults and exclusion from job or other economic opportunities, to physical violence. For example, there were two recent incidents in the U.S. Midwest where White people physically attacked others because they were speaking in a foreign language and not English. In Wisconsin, a White man was arrested after he punched two men he believed were speaking Spanish—even though it turns out they were speaking Hebrew, not Spanish. A White diner at a Coon Rapids Minnesota restaurant injured another customer by smashing a mug of beer across her face because the other diner was speaking a language other than English.[41]

The connection between prejudice and extreme discrimination is closer than you might think. The famous psychologist Gordon Allport showed how, when no one speaks out initially, prejudice against a group of people can develop into scapegoating, which, in turn, can escalate into systematic elimination, or genocide, of a people.[42] This kind of ethnic cleansing has been seen recently in the former Yugoslavia and in Rwanda and Darfur, as well as in Nazi Germany in the 1930s and 1940s. He makes a powerful case for why it is important to speak up whenever we see prejudice or discrimination. **Hate speech** is a particular form of verbal communication that can lead to (or reflect) prejudice and discrimination.

It is legally defined as speech that is "intended to degrade, intimidate, or incite violence or prejudicial action against a person or group of people based on their group membership: race, gender, age, ethnicity, nationality, religion, sexual orientation, gender identity, disability, language ability, moral or political views, socioeconomic class, occupation or appearance (such as height, weight, and hair color), mental capacity and any other distinction-liability."[43]

There has been an attempt by some organizations, like universities and colleges, to ban hate speech based on the assumption that such speech is the first point on Allport's scale, which measures prejudice in a society, and that it ultimately leads to illegal actions (discrimination) against certain groups. Other groups, like the ACLU, assert that forbidding certain types of speech is not the way to go on campuses, "where all views are entitled to be heard, explored, supported or refuted." They counter that "when hate is out in the open, people can see the problem. Then they can organize effectively to counter bad attitudes, possibly change them, and forge solidarity against the forces of intolerance."[44]

Discrimination may be interpersonal, collective, and/or institutional. In recent years, interpersonal racism seems to be much more subtle and indirect but still persistent. Institutionalized or collective discrimination—whereby individuals are systematically denied equal participation or rights in informal and formal ways—also persists. Sometimes institutional discrimination is rather blatant. Consider, for example, the case of Novartis pharmaceutical company, long considered one of the best places to work for mothers. Novartis was found guilty of discriminating against female employees, paying them less than their male counterparts and denying them promotions.[45] Sometimes it is less blatant and only revealed after systematic study. For an example, see the "Info Bites" describing a systematic pattern of institutional discrimination against African American high school students.[46]

Some discrimination is based on religion. One group that faces more discrimination in the United States than any other major religious group is Muslims. For example, just after the December 2015 attacks in San Bernardino, California (where husband and wife terrorists shot and killed 14 people at a Public Health holiday party), the Equal Employment Opportunity Commission quickly issued a statement urging employers to be particularly mindful of instances of harassment, intimidation, or discrimination in the workplace against individuals who are or are perceived to be Muslim or Middle Eastern. At the same time, a local American-Arab Anti-Discrimination Committee in Michigan received more than a dozen reports of workplace discrimination, ranging from nasty comments to Muslim workers about "wackos and your people" to other incidents like a Muslim medical receptionist who said she was fired from her job because she wore a head covering to work. It is a fact that hate crimes targeting Muslims, their mosques, and businesses have tripled in 2015.[47]

A frequent example of discrimination occurs in the hiring process. Because of this, some minority applicants "whiten" their resumes. That is, they alter their names to sound white (Greg Kelly or Emily Walsh instead of Jamal Jackson or Lakisha Washington) and also tweak some resume information so that employers can't

**Info Bites**

According to a recent government study of 72,000 high schools, African American students are arrested much more frequently than Whites in these schools and there is also a racial gap in student suspensions and expulsions as well. As one government official said, "The sad fact is that minority students across America face much harsher discipline than non-minorities—even within the same school. This is especially important because, according to experts, a first-time arrest doubles the chances a student will drop out and first-time court appearance quadruples them." (Source: St. George, S. (2012, March 5). Federal data show racial gaps in school arrest. *Washingtonpost.com*. Retrieved April 25, 2016, from https://www.washingtonpost.com/national/federal-data-show-racial-gaps-in-school-arrests/2012/03/01/gIQApbjvtR_story.html).

identify their race. In a recent study, researchers wanted to find if employers who say they are committed to diversity actually practice their stated policy. They created two sets of resumes. One set was "whitened"; and the other set of resumes were left as is. The researchers randomly sent the resumes in response to 1,600 job postings in 16 U.S. cities. They found that the whitened resumes were twice as likely to get callbacks, and the most troubling finding, according to the researchers was that the resumes got the same responses for employers who *said* they were pro-diversity (in job postings) and the ones that didn't mention it. The researchers conclude that "the statements that employers are putting out there aren't really tied to any real change in the discriminatory practices." These examples show how easily stereotypes about religion and race can lead to discrimination.[48]

It is particularly important that young people understand and actively work to eradicate prejudice, racism, and discrimination. Much of the prejudice is more subtle—though still pervasive—than in earlier generations. At the same time, there has been a rise in violent racial acts committed by young White men. Finally, because of the changing U.S. demographics, young people will have more contact with diverse groups of people than did their parents and grandparents; they will likely have more impact on changing attitudes than older generations.[49]

## SUMMARY

In this chapter, we identified and described the four building blocks of intercultural communication: culture, communication, context, and power. Culture can be viewed as learned, shared perceptions and values involving emotions, expressed as behaviors, that are dynamic and heterogeneous. Communication is a symbolic process whereby meaning is shared and negotiated. In addition, communication is dynamic, may be unintentional, and is receiver-oriented. The relationship between culture and communication is complex because (1) culture influences communication, (2) communication reinforces culture, and (3) communication is a way of resisting the dominant culture.

The context—the physical and virtual setting in which communication occurs, or the larger political, societal, and historical environment—affects that communication. The fourth building block, power, is pervasive and plays an enormous, though often hidden, role in intercultural communication interactions. Power relationships—determined largely by social institutions and roles—influence communication.

We also identified attitudinal and behavioral barriers to intercultural communication. Ethnocentrism is the belief that one's own culture is superior to all others. Stereotyping is the process of rigidly categorizing others; stereotypes may be negative or positive. Prejudice is the negative prejudging of others on the basis of little or no experience. Attitudes like stereotyping and prejudice may lead to behavioral barriers such as discrimination.

Now that we have laid the foundation of our approach to intercultural communication, the next step is to examine the role of history in intercultural communication.

## BUILDING INTERCULTURAL SKILLS

1. Become more conscious of the identity groups you belong to, both voluntary and involuntary. Which are most important to you? Also become more conscious of the cultural values of your family. What sayings did your mother and father repeat to you ("Just because so-and-so does something doesn't mean you have to do it too!")? Which values were emphasized and communicated in your family? How do you think these values influenced the way you perceive other cultural groups? How did they influence your communication with others who are different from you?

2. Become more aware of your own communication in intercultural encounters. Think about the message you are sending, verbally and nonverbally. Think about your tone of voice, your posture, your gestures, and your eye contact. Are you sending the messages you want to send?

3. Notice how diverse your friends are. Do you have friends from different age groups? From different ethnic groups? Do you have friends with disabilities? Of both genders? From different socioeconomic classes? Whose first language is not English? Think about why you have or don't have diverse friends and what you can learn from seeing the world through their "prescription lenses."

4. Become more knowledgeable about different cultures by reading local ethnic news websites and blogs and seeing foreign films.

5. Notice how different cultural groups are portrayed in the media. If there are people of color or other minority groups represented, what roles do they play? Major roles? Background? Comic relief?

6. When speaking about other groups, try to use tentative words that don't reflect generalizations—like "generally," or "many times," or "it seems to me," or "in my experience."

7. Practice speaking up when someone tells a joke that is hurtful toward another group. A simple "What do you mean by that?" or "Why is that funny?" or "I really don't think that's very funny" can prod the joketeller into thinking twice about telling racist or sexist jokes around you.

## ACTIVITIES

1. *Cultural values:* Look for advertisements in popular websites and magazines. Analyze the ads to see if you can identify the societal values that they appeal to.

2. *Cultural groups and communication:* Identify the various cultural groups you belong to, both voluntary and involuntary. Choose two of these groups, and think about each group and your membership in that group. Then try to describe how belonging to that group influences your perceptions. For example, how is your worldview influenced by belonging to your family? By being a female or male? By being Asian American, or White, or an international student? Finally, describe how your communication with others is influenced by your membership in these two groups.

## ENDNOTES

1.  Kraków Jewish Culture Festival (2012). *Joobili Timely Travel.com.* Retrieved April 20, 2016, from http://joobili.com/krakow_jewish_culture_festival_cracow_11197/

2.  Grossman, D. (2012, March 30). Founder promotes Kraków Jewish festival. *The Canadian Jewish News.* Retrieved July 2, 2012, from http://www.cjnews.com/node/89645

3.  Noworól, A., & Skalski, K. (2010). *Contemporary understanding of revitalization in Poland.* Kraków Poland: Jagiellonian University (*Uniwersytet Jagielloúski*), Institute of Public Affairs (*Instytut Spraw Publicznych*). Retrieved July 2, 2012, from http://149.156.173.214/pliki/e-monografie /monografia-3.pdf

4.  Bennett, M. J. (2013). *Basic concepts intercultural communication: Paradigms, principles, & practices* (2nd ed.). Boston, MA: Nicholas Brealey.

5.  Hofstede, G., Hofstede, G. J., & Minkov, M. (2010). *Cultures and organizations: Software of the mind* (Revised and Expanded Third Edition). Boston, MA: McGraw-Hill.

6.  Bennett, M. J., & Castiglioni, I. (2004). Embodied ethnocentrism and the feeling of culture. In D. Landis, J. M. Bennett, & M. J. Bennett (Eds.), *Handbook of intercultural training* (3rd ed., pp. 249–265). Thousand Oaks, CA: Sage.

7.  Kristjánsdóttir, E. S. (2009). U.S. American student sojourners' lived experience in France: Phenomenological inquiry of cross-cultural adaptation. *Howard Journal of Communications, 20*(2).

8.  Global opinion of Obama slips, international policies faulted. Pew Research Center, Global Attitudes Project Report. Retrieved April 21, 2016, from http://www.pewglobal.org/files/2012/06/PewGlobal -Attitudes-U.S.-Image-Report-FINAL-June-13-20123.pdf.

9.  Allen, B. J. (2011). *Difference matters: Communicating social identity* (2nd ed.). Long Grove, IL: Waveland Press.

10. Hall, S. (1992). Cultural studies and its theoretical legacies. In L. Grossberg, C. Nelson, & P. Treichler (Eds.), *Cultural studies* (pp. 277–294). New York, NY: Routledge.

11. Lopez, M. H., Morin, R., & Taylor, P. (2010, October 28). Illegal immigration backlash worries, divides Latinos. Pew Hispanic Center Report. Retrieved May 26, 2012, from http://www .pewhispanic.org/files/reports/128.pdf.

12. Goodnough, A. (2012, January 27). Student faces town's wrath in protest against a prayer. The *New York Times.* Retrieved May 8, 2012, from http://www.nytimes.com/2012/01/27/us/rhode-island -city-enraged-over-school-prayer-lawsuit.html?_r=1.

13. Kluckhohn, F., & Strodtbeck, F. (1961). *Variations in value orientations.* Chicago, IL: Row, Peterson.

14. Lebozec, L. (2001, October 6). *Vietnam: The extended family.* Retrieved October 4, 2008, from http://www.suite101.com/article.cfm/vietnam/81880.

15. Hofstede, G., Hofstede, G. J., & Minkov, M. (2010). *Cultures and organizations: Software of the mind* (Revised and Expanded Third Edition). Boston, MA: McGraw-Hill. Note that Hofstede's research can be criticized. He conducted his initial research only in countries where IBM subsidiaries were located, ignoring many African and Middle Eastern countries in developing his value framework. In addition, his masculine/feminine orientation has been criticized for its stereotypical definitions of masculinity and femininity.

16. Chinese Culture Connection. (1987). Chinese values and the search for culture-free dimensions of culture. *Journal of Cross-Cultural Psychology, 18,* 143–164.

17. Matsumoto, D. (2002). *The new Japan: Debunking seven cultural stereotypes.* Yarmouth, ME: Intercultural Press.

18. Katriel, T., & Philipsen, G. (1990). What we need is communication: "Communication" as a cultural category in some American speech. In Carbaugh, pp. 77–94.

19. Engstrom, C. L. (2012). "Yes . . ., But I Was Drunk": Alcohol references and the (re)production of masculinity on a college campus. *Communication Quarterly, 60*(3), 403–423.

20. Philipsen, G. (1990). Speaking like a man in "Teamsterville": Culture patterns of role enactment in an urban neighborhood. In Carbaugh, pp. 11–12.

21. Kim, H., & Papacharissi, Z. (2003). Cross cultural differences in online self-presentation: A content analysis of personal Korean and U.S. home pages. *Asian Journal of Communication, 13,* 100–119.

22.  Tracy, M., & Southall, A. (2015, November 8). Black football players lend heft to protests at Missouri. *nytimes.com*. Retrieved April 21, 2016, from http://www.nytimes.com/2015/11/09/us /missouri-football-players-boycott-in-protest-of-university-president.html?_r=0.

23.  Cheong, P. H., Shuter, R., & Suwinyattichaiporn, T. (2016). Managing student digital distractions and hyperconnectivity: Communication strategies and challenges for professorial authority. *Communication Education, 65*(3), 272–289.

24.  Goldstein, J. (2015, September). U.S. soldiers told to ignore sexual abuse of boys by Afghan allies. *nytimes.com*. Retrieved April 22, 2016, from http://www.nytimes.com/2015/09/21/world/asia/us -soldiers-told-to-ignore-afghan-allies-abuse-of-boys.html.

25.  Tyree, T. (2011). African American stereotypes in reality television. *Howard Journal of Communications, 22*(4), 394–413.

26.  Lacroix, C. C. (2011). High stakes stereotypes: The emergence of the "Casino Indian" trope in television depictions of contemporary Native Americans. *Howard Journal of Communications, 22*(1), 1–23.

27.  Chesler, M. A., Peet, M., & Sevig, T. (2003). Blinded by Whiteness: The development of White college students' racial awareness. In A. W. Doane & E. Bonilla-Silva (Eds.), *White out: The continuing significance of racism* (pp. 215–230). New York, NY: Routledge.

28.  Mazel, E. (1998). *And don't call me racist: A treasury of quotes on the past, present and future of the color line in America* (p. 81). Lexington, MA: Argonaut Press.

29.  Brislin, R. (1999). *Understanding culture's influence on behavior* (2nd ed.). Belmont, CA: Wadsworth.

30.  Hecht, M. L. (1998). Introduction. In M. L. Hecht (Ed.), *Communicating prejudice* (pp. 3–23). Thousand Oaks, CA: Sage.

31.  Zhang, Q. (2015). Perceived intergroup stereotypes, threats, and emotions toward Asian Americans. *Howard Journal of Communications, 26*(2), 115–131.

32.  Kinefuchi, E. (2011). Finding home in migration: Montagnard refugees and post-migration identity. *Journal of International and Intercultural Communication, 3*(3), 240.

33.  Brislin (1999).

34.  Chesler, Peet, & Sevig (2003), p. 223.

35.  Mazel (1998), p. 127.

36.  Mazel (1998), p. 130.

37.  Simpson, J. L. (2008). The color-blind double bind. *Communication Theory, 18*(1), 139–159.

38.  Gallagher, C. A. (2003). Playing the White ethnic card: Using ethnic identity to deny racial discrimination. In Doane & Bonilla-Silva, pp. 145–158.

39.  Mazel (1998), p. 126.

40.  Gibney (2015, November 9). Maine's Somalis could be its saviors. *bloombergview.com*. Retrieved April 22, 2016, from http://www.bloombergview.com/articles/2015-11-09/maine-s-somalis-could -be-its-saviors; Stewart-Bouley, S. (2014, December 13). Fighting the fight for racial justice in Maine. *blackgirlinmaine.com*. Retrieved April 22, 2016, from http://blackgirlinmaine.com/current -events/fighting-the-fight-for-racial-justice-in-maine-i-salute-these-brave-young-people/.

41.  Terrero, N. (2013, October 28). Wisconsin man arrested for punching two males for speaking Spanish. *nbclatino.com*. Retrieved April 22, 2016, from http://nbclatino.com/2013/10/28/wisconsin -man-arrested-for-punching-two-males-for-speaking-spanish/; Zamora, K. (2015, November 4). Coon Rapids Applebee customer charged. *startribune.com*. Retrieved April 22, 2016, from http:// www.startribune.com/coon-rapids-applebee-s-customer-charged-with-attacking-woman-for-not -speaking-english/340442261/.

42.  Allport, G. (1970). *The nature of prejudice*. Reading, MA: Addison-Wesley.

43.  Hate speech on campus (1994, December 31). American Civil Liberties Union website. Retrieved October 4, 2008, from http://www.aclu.org/studentsrights/expression/12808pub19941231.html

44.  Hate speech on campus. (1994).

45.  Friedman, E. (2012, May 18). Jury finds Novartis liable for female employee discrimination complaints. *ABC News.com*. Retrieved July 2, 2012, from http://abcnews.go.com/Business /novartis-pharmaceuticals-corp-found-guilty-gender-discrimination/story?id=10678178# .T_JArrXLyTU.

46.  St. George, S. (2012, March 5). Federal data show racial gaps in school arrest. *Washingtonpost.com.* Retrieved May 12, 2012, from http://www.washingtonpost.com/national/federal-data-show-racial -gaps-in-school-arrests/2012/03/01/gIQApbjvtR_story.html.

47.  Baldas, T. (2015, December 27). Workplace bias complaints pour in from Michigan Muslims. *religionnews.com.* Retrieved April 22, 2016, from http://religionnews.com/2015/12/27/workplace-bias -complaints-pour-in-from-michigan-muslims/; Yang, J. R. (2015, December 23). EEOC issues a state- ment to address workplace discrimination against individuals who are or are perceived to be Muslim or Middle Eastern. *www.eeoc.gov.* Retrieved April 22, 2016, from https://www.eeoc.gov/eeoc/newsroom /release/12-13-15.cfm; Siemaszko, C. (2015, December 20). Hate attacks on Muslims in U.S. spike after recent acts of terrorism. *nbcnews.com.* Retrieved March 8, 2016, from http://www.nbcnews.com /news/us-news/hate-attacks-muslims-u-s-spike-after-recent-acts-terrorism-n482456.

48.  Lam, B. (2016, March 23). When resumes are made "whiter" to please potential employers. *theatlantic.com.* Retrieved April 22, 2016, from http://www.startribune.com/coon-rapids-applebee -s-customer-charged-with-attacking-woman-for-not-speaking-english.

49.  McKinney, K. D., & Feagin, J. R. (2003). Diverse perspectives on doing anti-racism: The younger generation. In A. W. Doane & E. Bonilla-Silva (Eds.), *White Out: The continuing significance of racism* (pp. 233–253). New York, NY: Routledge.

© kristian sekulic/Getty Images RF

## CHAPTER THREE

# History and Intercultural Communication

## CHAPTER OUTLINE

### From History to Histories
*Political, Intellectual, and Social Histories*
*Family Histories*
*National Histories*
*Cultural Group Histories*
*The Power of Other Histories*

### History and Identity
*Histories as Stories*
*Nonmainstream Histories*

### Intercultural Communication and History
*Historical Legacies*

### Summary

### Building Intercultural Skills

### Activities

### Endnotes

## STUDY OBJECTIVES

*After reading this chapter, you should be able to:*

1. Understand the role of history in intercultural communication interactions. Describe some of the histories that influence our communication.

2. Explain the importance of "nonmainstream" histories and their relation to cultural identities. Explain why it is necessary to recover nonmainstream histories.

3. Understand the role of narratives in understanding various histories.

4. Understand the importance of history in contemporary intercultural relations.

5. Explain how diasporic histories influence intercultural interactions.

6. Explain how we can negotiate histories in interactions.

## KEY TERMS

colonial histories
cultural group histories
diaspora
diasporic histories
ethnic histories
family histories
gender histories
grand narrative
*Homo narrans*
intellectual histories

national histories
political histories
postcolonialism
racial histories
religious histories
sexual orientation
  histories
social histories
socioeconomic class
  histories

In an April 23, 2012 press release, the White House announced that President Barack Obama would be posthumously giving Jan Karski the Presidential Medal of Freedom. President Obama said:

> We must tell our children about how this evil was allowed to happen—because so many people succumbed to their darkest instincts; because so many others stood silent. But let us also tell our children about the Righteous Among the Nations. Among them was Jan Karski—a young Polish Catholic—who witnessed Jews being put on cattle cars, who saw the killings, and who told the truth, all the way to President Roosevelt himself. Jan Karski passed away more than a decade ago. But today, I'm proud to announce that this spring I will honor him with America's highest civilian honor—the Presidential Medal of Freedom.[1]

On May 29, 2012 when the award was made, President Obama said:

> Fluent in four languages, possessed of a photographic memory, Jan served as a courier for the Polish resistance during the darkest days of World War II. Before one trip across enemy lines, resistance fighters told him that Jews were being murdered on a massive scale, and smuggled him into the Warsaw Ghetto and a *Polish death camp* to see for himself. Jan took that information to President Franklin Roosevelt, giving one of the first accounts of the Holocaust and imploring to the world to take action.[2]

After President Obama's laudatory remarks on all the recipients of the Presidential Medal of Freedom, an immediate uproar ensued over the use of the term, "Polish death camp." The Polish prime minister, Donald Tusk, explained: "When someone says 'Polish death camps,' it's as if there were no Nazis, no German responsibility, as if there was no Hitler. That is why our Polish sensitivity in these situations is so much more than just simply a feeling of national pride."[3] In his analysis of the speech, David Frum more directly explains that "the camps were German, German, German: ordered into being by Germans, designed by Germans, fulfilling a German plan of murder." And he concludes: "The medal to Karski was to be part of the process of laying painful memories to rest. It was intended too to strengthen the U.S.-Polish relations that the Obama administration had frayed in pursuit of its "reset" with Russia. Instead, this administration bungled everything: past, present and future."[4] In response, the White House amended the posted speech with: "*Note—the language in asterisks below is historically inaccurate. It should instead have been: 'Nazi death camps in German occupied Poland.' We regret the error."[5]

How we communicate about the past can have tremendous impacts on contemporary and future intercultural relations.

It is not always immediately apparent what history has to do with culture, communication, or intercultural communication. In this chapter, we hope to show you the significance of history in forming cultural identities and in forming intercultural interactions.

The history that we know and our feelings about that history are strongly influenced by our culture. When people from differing cultural backgrounds encounter one another, these differences can form hidden barriers to communication. However,

**Info Bites**

Currently, numerous states and cities trace their names to Native American tribes and languages, such as Massachusetts, Nebraska, and Tallahassee. Native American names are used on some vehicles, such as the Dodge Dakota or Jeep Cherokee. There are many other ways that Native American names and words are invoked in the contemporary United States. On the one hand, it recognizes the larger history of the land and the people who lived before the Europeans arrived. On the other hand, how much does it lead contemporary U.S. Americans to understand this history, these peoples, and cultures?

people often overlook this set of dynamics in intercultural communication. Although we typically think of "history" as something contained in history books, an awareness of history is important in understanding intercultural interaction.

History, of course, spans a long, long time. Many events have happened in the past that have created differences among cultural groups and then maintained those differences. It is not always easy to look back and deal with some of these events. Some people ask, "Why do we have to dwell on the past? Can't we all move on?" Other people say that it is impossible to understand them without understanding the history of their cultural group. These different viewpoints certainly can affect the intercultural communication among these people.

On a larger scale, we can see how history influences intercultural interaction in many different contexts. For example, Australia used to have what is often called a "White Australia" policy that guided their immigration restrictions. Australian immigration policy restricted non-Europeans from immigrating until the last of the racial restrictions was lifted in the 1970s.[6] When you imagine an "Australian" today, what do you envision? There are historical reasons why Australia is populated largely by people with European origins. History helps us understand why Australia looks the way it does today. The legacy of White Australia, and attempts to move toward "Multicultural Australia," laid the groundwork for cultural conflict between whites and ethnic minorities that flared up in December 2005. The important point here is that we do not escape history because decisions made in the past continue to influence us today.

How we view the past directly influences how we view ourselves and others even here in the United States. Think about where you are from and what that might signify. What does it mean to be a midwesterner? A southerner? A New Englander? How do you know what these other regional identities mean, given that people's identities are rooted in different histories? In fact, this is the main theme of this chapter—that history is an important element in the experience of intercultural communication.

As you will see, culture and cultural identities are intimately tied to history, as they have no meaning without history. Yet there is no single version of history; the past has been recorded in many different ways. For example, your family has its own version of its history. Is it important to you to feel positively about who your forebears were and where they came from? We often feel a strong need to identify in positive ways with our past even if we are not interested in history. The stories of the past, accurate or inaccurate, help us understand why our families live where they do, why they own or lost land there, and so on. It helps us understand who we are and why we live and communicate in the ways we do.

In this chapter, we discuss the various histories that provide the contexts in which we communicate: political, intellectual, social, family, national, and cultural group. We then describe how these histories are intertwined with our various identities, based on gender, sexual orientation, ethnicity, race, and so on. Two identities have strong historical bases—diasporic and colonial. We pay particular attention to the role of narrating our personal histories. Finally, we explore how history influences intercultural communication. Throughout this chapter, you should think about the importance of history in constructing your own identity and how the relationship between the past and the present helps us understand different identities for others in different cultural groups.

## FROM HISTORY TO HISTORIES

Many different kinds of history influence our understanding of who we are—as individuals, as family members, as members of cultural groups, as citizens of a nation. These histories necessarily overlap and influence one another. For example, think about the history of your family. How has your family history been influenced by your family's membership in certain cultural groups but not others? How has members' nationality been an important part of this history? How does your family history tie into the larger story of U.S. history? Identifying the various historical contexts is the first step in understanding how history affects communication.

### Political, Intellectual, and Social Histories

Some people view "history" as only that information contained in documented events. When these types of history focus on political events, we call them **political histories.** Political histories are often the type of history taught in history courses. In these histories we learn about the past through politicians, such as Roman, Chinese, and other emperors, monarchs, as well as presidents and their decisions that helped shape the past. For example, the development of presidential libraries and the study of U.S. presidents focuses our understanding of U.S. history from the political history of the nation. With this focus on history, our attention is drawn to the political history as a way to understand how the United States came to be. When they focus on the transmission and development of ideas or ways of thinking, we call them **intellectual histories.** An intellectual history might trace the development of ideas about the unconscious or democracy. A focus on the history of capitalism points to the ideas that gave rise to this way of viewing the world. While the free exchange of goods for monetary gain had long been practiced, the term "capitalism" did not emerge until the nineteenth century. An intellectual history would follow the discussions over the definition of "capitalism" and different conceptions of it from Adam Smith's *The Wealth of Nations* to Max Weber's *The Protestant Ethic and the Spirit of Capitalism*. Many of the key concepts in capitalism, such as production, consumption, the invisible hand of the market, and other terms, would be traced to their contemporary usage and ideas today as people and governments try to correct the current economic situation. We could trace these ideas to their current expression by U.S. Federal Reserve Chairman Janet Yellen and U.S. Secretary of the Treasury Jack Lew, as they struggle with how much government intervention to recommend as they deal with averting a financial crisis. And when they provide insight into the everyday life experiences of various groups in the past, we call them **social histories.** Social histories tell us about how we understand the past, but from a focus on the everyday lives of people. In contrast to political or intellectual history, social history draws our attention to the ways that people understood the world in the past. For example, social historians might focus on why eighteenth-century French people massacred cats[7] and how they understood the need to do so.

## What Do You Think?

Did you know that Albert Einstein's wife was also a promising physicist? Before meeting Einstein, Mileva Maric was on the track to becoming a scientist of her own accord. She was the fifth woman to attend the ETH, an honored technical institute in Heidelberg, Germany, where she would later meet a younger Albert Einstein. The two were married in 1903 and thus began Einstein's most successful years as a theorist. Their divorce in 1919 marked the end of Einstein's most productive years. Is this mere coincidence? Historians now debate whether Mileva contributed to Albert's theories. How might we think of the history of science differently if we knew that Mileva contributed to Einstein's theories? Why must we consider the gendered dynamics of histories?

This way of organizing and thinking about history may seem more manageable than the broad notion of history as "everything that has happened before now." But many different kinds of history influence our views and knowledge about the past, and many historical events never get documented. For example, the strict laws that forbade teaching slaves in the United States to read kept many of their stories from being documented. The lack of a written record, of course, does not mean that the people did not exist, that their experiences do not matter, or that their history has no bearing on us. To consider such absent histories requires that we think in more complex ways about the past and the ways it influences the present and the future.

## Family Histories

**Family histories** occur at the same time as other histories but on a more personal level. Often, they are not written down but are passed along orally from one generation to the next. Perhaps surprisingly, some people do not know which countries or cities their families emigrated from, or what tribes they belonged to, or where they lived in the United States. But other people place great emphasis on knowing that, say, their ancestors arrived on the *Mayflower*, or migrated to Utah with Brigham Young, or survived the Holocaust. Many of these family histories are deeply intertwined with ethnic group histories and religious histories, but the family histories identify the family's actual participation in these events. A key issue is whether it is possible or even desirable to escape from the history of one's family.

Sometimes, family histories shed some light on well-known figures. In his autobiography, *Dreams from My Father*, Obama recounts his family's history from his mother's family in Kansas and their migration to Hawaii to his father's Kenyan family and his connection to them. Although he did not have much contact with his father's family until after his father passed away, Obama's visit to Kenya thrust him back into that part of his family history. More recently, on a visit to Ireland, Obama went to the town where his forebearer, Falmouth Kearney, a shoemaker, lived before immigrating to the United States in 1850.[8] His family history is one of immigration and migration that is one part of U.S. history.

Michelle Obama's family reflects a very different family history that is entwined in another part of the nation's story: slavery. The *New York Times* traced her family history and found "the more complete map of Mrs. Obama's ancestors—including the slave mother, white father and their biracial son, Dolphus T. Shields—for the first time fully connects the first African-American first lady to the history of slavery, tracing their five-generation journey from bondage to a front-row seat to the presidency."[9] Think about how these family histories inform us and the Obamas about their past, as well as their place in the United States and in the world.

One of our students told us that his family immigrated to the United States from Warsaw, Poland, right before World War II. Because of their experiences there and the perceived anti-Jewish sentiment in Poland, his grandparents immediately quit speaking Polish upon arrival in the United States. Because of this family history, our student today does not speak Polish, as his parents and grandparents did not want to maintain that language in the family. Family histories can be very helpful in explaining who you are.

**Info Bites**

George Washington never chopped down that cherry tree, and he didn't really use wooden dentures. Abe Lincoln had a high-pitched, squeaky voice, and his Gettysburg Address was generally considered an embarrassment when he delivered it. How much of what you think you know about history is real, and how much is fiction? The more interesting question is, How can you be sure of the difference?

## National Histories

Obviously, the **national histories** of nations—its great events and figures—are important to the people of that nation. U.S. national history typically begins with the arrival of Europeans in North America. U.S. citizens are expected to recognize the great events and the so-called great people (mostly men of European ancestry) who were influential in the development of the country. Thus, students are told stories, verging on myths, that give life to these events and people. For example, they learn about the Founding Fathers—George Washington, Benjamin Franklin, Thomas Jefferson, James Madison, and so on. They learn about Patrick Henry's "Give me liberty or give me death" speech, although the text of the speech was collected by a biographer who "pieced together twelve hundred words from scattered fragments that earwitnesses remembered from twenty years before."[10] And they learn about George Washington chopping down a cherry tree and then confessing his guilt, and about Abraham Lincoln helping to bind the nation's wounds with his stirring Gettysburg Address.

Yet, as you probably already know, traditionally, U.S. history textbooks "leave out anything that might reflect badly upon our national character."[11] They are written for White Americans. In his review of textbooks, James Loewen points to the importance of studying Native American Indian history since it "is the antidote to the pious ethnocentrism of American exceptionalism, the notion that European Americans are God's chosen people. Indian history reveals that the United States and its predecessor British colonies have wrought great harm in the world. We must not forget this—not to wallow in our wrongdoing, but to understand and to learn, that we might not wreak harm again."[12]

National history gives us a shared notion of who we are and solidifies our sense of nationhood. Although we may not personally fit into the national narrative, we are expected to know this particular telling of U.S. history so we can understand the many references used in communication. For example, when people talk about the "13 colonies," we are expected to know that the speaker is not referring to colonies in Africa or Asia. National history simply represents one way of constructing cultural discourses and cultural identities.

Yet U.S. students do not often learn much about the histories of other nations and cultures unless they are studying their languages. As any student of another language knows, it is part of the curriculum to study not only the grammar and vocabulary of the language but also the culture and history of the people who speak that language. Table 3.1 shows some of the name changes that places have undergone. Understanding the history of these places would help you understand why their names have changed.

Judith and Tom both studied French. Because we learned a great deal about French history, we were taught the French national narrative. The French have their own national history, centering on the evolution of France from a monarchy, to a dictatorship, to a republic. For example, French people know that they live in the Cinquième République (or Fifth Republic), and they know what this means

**TABLE 3.1 Dynamic Country Names**

| PRESENT NAME | PREVIOUS NAME |
|---|---|
| Belize | British Honduras |
| Cambodia | Kampuchea Republic |
| Czechia | Czech Republic |
| Ethiopia | Abyssinia |
| Ghana | Gold Coast |
| Indonesia | Dutch East Indies |
| Iran | Persia |
| Mali | French Sudan |
| Myanmar | Burma |
| Sri Lanka | Ceylon |
| Taiwan | Formosa |
| Thailand | Siam |

**Surf's Up!**

How do we investigate historical events such as parades, performances, political rallies, and protests? Moreover, how do we study these histories without actually participating in the events? The Hemispheric Institute, a group committed to making the political and social activities of the Americas accessible to publics, is working to answer these questions by electronically archiving key documents, videos, sound recordings, and photos of such events in Central, North, and South America. To view Cuban dance or to watch Tepeyac Television Service, a television project created by Mexican immigrant workers in New York City, go to http://hemi.nyu.edu/.

within the grand narrative of French history. This history helps French citizens comprehend what it means to be French, as well as their country's relationships with other nations.

## Cultural Group Histories

Although people may share a single national history, each cultural group within the nation may have its own history. The history may be hidden, but it also is related to the national history. These **cultural group histories** help us understand the identity of the group.

Consider, for example, the expulsion in the 1750s of many French-speaking Acadians from eastern Canada and their migration to Louisiana. These historical events are central to understanding the cultural traits of the Cajuns. For example, the popular saying "Laissez les bons temps roulez!" (Let the good times roll!) is spoken in French because of this history. The forced removal in 1838 of the Cherokees from their former nation, New Echota (located mostly in Georgia), to settlements in what eventually became the state of Oklahoma resulted in the death of one-fifth of the Cherokee population. This event, known as the Trail of Tears, explains much about the Cherokee Nation, including the split between the eastern and western Cherokees. The northward migration of African Americans in the early twentieth century helps us understand the settlement patterns and working conditions in northern cities like Cleveland, Detroit, Chicago, and New York. These cultural histories are not typically included in our national history, but they are important in the development of group identities, family histories, and the contemporary lives of individual members of these cocultures.

Mount Vernon, near Alexandria, Virginia, has been designated a National Historic Landmark, as it was the former plantation of George Washington, the first president. Visitors can see the house, the grounds, and the slave quarters. What cultural myths do we tell ourselves about George Washington? What function do these myths lay in the national identity of Americans?

Photographs in the Carol M. Highsmith Archive, Library of Congress, Prints and Photographs Division

In this sense, history represents the many stories we tell about the past, rather than one ongoing story on a singular time continuum. Certainly, the events of families, cultural groups, and nations are related; even world events are related. Ignorance of the histories of other groups makes intercultural communication more difficult and fraught with potential misunderstandings.

### The Power of Other Histories

The past is very complex and people have attempted to understand history in a way that helps make sense of this complexity. In order to do so, many cultures developed what is called a **"grand narrative"** to explain the past and, in part, the future. By telling a particular story about the past, the grand narrative brings coherence to everything that has happened before now. Some Christians, for example, believe in a more traditional narrative about the past that begins with Adam and Eve. All history and all events are guided by our relationship with God. For Enlightenment historians, reliance on human reason and rational thought, society would progress morally, ethically, socially into the future. For Marxist historians, the past is explained by economics and class differences. There are many other ways to understand the past. And we can read the story of the past through any of these lenses to make sense of everything that has happened.

Many U.S. Americans were taught a particular grand narrative in which the founding fathers built a great nation that is based upon key principles, such as equality and freedom. The destiny of the nation was to move further west and expand into a great nation. The celebration of "American exceptionalism" and the upward trajectory of the United States, economically, socially, and geographically, is the grand narrative of this country. This grand narrative gives U.S. Americans a particular identity that is important to their notion of what it means to be an "American."

Since then, many other stories have arisen that have challenged the grand narrative. The traditional grand narrative left out many stories of the United States that did not demonstrate the values of equality and freedom. These other narratives have not necessarily displaced the grand narrative as much as they have created a more complex picture of the past. There are now many competing stories of the past.[13]

In place of the grand narrative are revised and restored histories that had been suppressed, hidden, or erased. The cultural movements that make this shift possible empower other cultural identities and enable the rewriting of the history of U.S. colonialism, slavery, immigration laws, and so on. Recovering various histories is necessary to rethinking what some cultural identities mean. It also helps us rethink the dominant cultural identity—what it means to be an "American."

Regardless of whether we choose to recognize the foundations for many of our differences, these inequalities influence how we think about others and how we interact. They also influence how we think about ourselves—our identities. These are important aspects of intercultural communication. It may seem daunting to confront the history of the world, and, indeed, there are many histories of the world. Nevertheless, the more you know, the better you will be positioned to engage in successful intercultural interactions.

## HISTORY AND IDENTITY

In the previous chapter, we saw how individual identities develop. Here, we discuss the development of cultural identities, which is strongly influenced by history.

### Histories as Stories

Faced with these many levels of history, you might wonder how we make sense of them in our everyday lives. Although it might be tempting to ignore them all and just pretend to be "ourselves," this belies the substantial influence that history has on our own identities.

According to communication scholar Walter Fisher, telling stories is fundamental to the human experience.[14] Instead of referring to humans as *Homo sapiens*, Fisher prefers to call them **Homo narrans**, because that label underscores the importance of narratives in human life. Histories are stories we use to make sense

**Surf's Up!**

Visit the History Channel website (www .historychannel.com/). What happened today in history?

**What Do You Think?**

In 2015, the South Side of Chicago was chosen to be the site of the Obama Presidential Center which will host the Obama Presidential Library, as well as a museum and other programs. The center will be affiliated with the University of Chicago. How do presidential libraries function to establish a president's legacy and understanding of our national history?

of who we are and who we think others are. However, it is important to recognize that a strong cultural element sometimes encourages us to try to forget history. As French writer Jean Baudrillard observes, "America was created in the hope of escaping from history, of building a utopia sheltered from history. . . . [It] has in part succeeded in that project, a project it is still pursuing today."[15]

The desire to escape history is significant in what it tells us about how our own culture negotiates its relation to the past and how we view the relation of other nations and cultures to their pasts. By ignoring history, we sometimes come to wrongheaded conclusions about others that reinforce particular stereotypes—for example, that "everybody loves Americans" in spite of many historical reasons they would not. The paradox is that we really cannot escape history even if we fail to recognize it or try to suppress it.

### Nonmainstream Histories

For people whose histories are hidden from the mainstream, speaking out is an important step in the construction of personal and cultural identities. Telling our personal narratives offers us an entry into history and an opportunity to reconcile with the events of history. These stories help us understand how others negotiated the cultural attitudes of the past that have relevance for the present. Here, we identify some kinds of history that have the most influence on intercultural interaction.

*Religious Histories*    Different religious groups have had very different experiences throughout history. **Religious histories** emphasize the role of religions in understanding the past. In the wake of recent terrorist attacks around the world, the conflation of Islam with terrorism is becoming more commonplace. Some people have tried to distinguish between the religion and some people's use of the religion to justify their own behaviors and actions. For example, when President Obama spoke at the 2015 National Prayer Breakfast, he tried to show how people can use religion for their own purposes: "And lest we get on our high horse and think this is unique to some other place, remember that during the Crusades and the Inquisition, people committed terrible deeds in the name of Christ. In our home country, slavery and Jim Crow all too often was justified in the name of Christ." In the ensuing controversy, it became clear that some Christians were uncomfortable seeing how people have used Christianity to justify a range of actions taken in the past.[16]

For Jewish people, remembering the Holocaust is crucial to their identity. Since the Holocaust, survivors and others have insisted on the importance of "never forget" as a way to have the Holocaust make a difference in the contemporary world. Jeff Jacoby, a journalist whose father survived the Holocaust, ponders the future of the "never forget" movement and speculates that:

> It was always inevitable that the enormity of the Holocaust would recede in public awareness. [. . .] Accounts of what was done in Treblinka did not prevent mass murder in Cambodia or Bosnia or Rwanda. Holocaust remembrance has not inoculated human beings against treating other human beings with

© 123RF

When Brigham Young, who led the Mormons to Utah, first crossed the Wasatch Mountains and saw the Salt Lake Valley, he proclaimed, "This is the place." Today, a state park and monument mark "the place." This historic site is a significant part of Mormon identity.

brutality. [. . .] I have always taken the Holocaust personally, and always will. But the world, I know, will not. Eventually, everything is forgotten. Even the worst crime in history.[17]

In an effort to keeping the memory of the Holocaust alive, people have built monuments and museums, and captured the oral histories and voices of survivors and worked to document as much as possible. But like other horrors in the past, will the Holocaust also become just another event in history books? What does that mean about how history shapes our present and future?

Mormons also have experienced a turbulent history. In the early nineteenth century, Mormons were not welcomed in many U.S. communities, moving from New York to Ohio to Illinois, where they founded the town of Nauvoo (Hebrew for "beautiful place"). After the murder of Mormon leader Joseph Smith in 1844, however, Brigham Young decided to take the Mormons west, on what today is known as the Mormon Trek. Eventually, after crossing the pass into the Salt Lake Basin, Young is purported to have claimed, "This is the place!" Without understanding this history, you may not understand why so many Mormons today live in Salt Lake City and elsewhere in Utah.

Religious histories are never isolated; rather, they crisscross other cultural trajectories. Thus, we may feel placed in the role of victim or victimizer by historical events, or even both roles at the same time. Consider, for example, the position of German American Mennonites during World War II. They were punished as pacifists and yet also were seen as aggressors by Jewish Americans. It is often important to see the various ways that these histories make religious differences significant.

**Pop Culture Spotlight**

*The Man in the High Castle* is a television series produced by Amazon. It debuted in 2015 and portrays life in 1962 in a world where the United States and its allies lost World War II. How does a TV series like this influence how you view the 1960s, racism, gender roles, as well as the Axis powers? This television series has been very successful. Why are people interested in watching this kind of alternative history that never happened?

**Info Bites**

The influence of gender history may be reflected in the differential pay rates for men and women. Traditionally, female occupations tended to pay less than male occupations, for example, nurses vs. doctors. As occupations and the workplace became less gendered, "equal pay for equal work" became an important issue across the workplace. For example, the U.S. professional women soccer players claim that, despite performing better than the men, the women are paid less. In 2016, U.S. women's professional soccer players filed a lawsuit claiming that they are underpaid relative to the U.S. men's professional soccer players. How can we overcome a history of differential value placed on men's and women's work?.

*Gender Histories*   Feminist scholars have long insisted that much of the history of women has been obliterated, marginalized, or erased. **Gender histories** emphasize the importance of gender in understanding the past, particularly the role of women. These histories are important in understanding how we live today, but they are often ignored. Historian Mei Nakano notes:

> The history of women, told by women, is a recent phenomenon. It has called for a fundamental reevaluation of assumptions and principles that govern traditional history. It challenges us to have a more inclusive view of history, not merely the chronicling of events of the past, not dominated by the record of men marching forward through time, their paths strewn with the detritus of war and politics and industry and labor.[18]

Although contemporary scholars are very much interested in women's history, they find it difficult to write that history due to the historical restrictions on women's access to public forums, public documents, and public records. For example, in the United States, women did not obtain the right to vote until 1920, so their participation in the nation's political history was restricted. And the attainment of women's suffrage has not followed the same pattern around the world, as the history of gender has been different in other cultures. For example, in 1893, New Zealand became the first nation to grant women the right to vote. Some nations recognized women's right to vote early in the twentieth century, such as Poland (1918), Mongolia (1924), Turkey (1930), Thailand (1932), Brazil (1934), and France (1944); others were slower to do so, such as Switzerland (1971), Jordan (1974), Iraq (1980), Liechtenstein (1984), Samoa (1990), and Saudi Arabia (2015). A number of countries have also had female leaders, including Argentina, Brazil, Germany, India, Pakistan, and Thailand. Women have played significant roles throughout history, even if it is difficult to recover that history.

It is important to note that contemporary life continues to be influenced by gender histories. Traditionally, many women were encouraged to focus on the home and on domestic concerns. Even today, many women in dual-career couples feel tremendous pressure to do the bulk of the housework, reflecting the influence of the past on the present. However, many people are working to overcome these historical legacies.

*Sexual Orientation Histories*   Interest in the history of sexuality is a fairly recent phenomenon that is beginning to challenge the ways that we think about the past. **Sexual orientation histories** emphasize the significance of sexuality in understanding the past and the present, yet these histories are often overlooked or silenced. If we do not listen to or cannot hear the voices of others, we will miss important historical lessons and create enormous misunderstandings about who we are. For example, Martin Duberman notes that "until recently the official image of the typical American was hysterically suburban: Anglo-Saxon, monogamous, heterosexual parents pair-bonded with two children and two cars—an image as narrow and propagandist as the smiling workers of China saluting the rice fields."[19] To correct this narrow view of the past, he wrote a partial history of gays and lesbians in the United States.

The late Guy Hocquenghem, a gay French philosopher, lamented the letting go of the past because that made it difficult to avoid the lessons of history. He once observed: "I am struck by the ignorance among gay people about the past—no, more even than ignorance: the 'will to forget' the German gay holocaust. . . . But we aren't even the only ones who remember, we don't remember! So we find ourselves beginning at zero in each generation."[20]

How we think and what we know about the past contribute to building and maintaining communities and cultural identities. For example, stories of the treatment of gays and lesbians during World War II promote a common history and influence intercultural communication among gays and lesbians in France, Germany, the Netherlands, and other nations. Today, a monument in Amsterdam marks that history, helping to ensure that we remember that gays and lesbians were victims of the Nazi Holocaust as well.

Because these histories are so closely tied to our identities, many U.S. Americans were upset when they read about one historian's book that suggested that Abraham Lincoln may have engaged in same-sex activities.[21] As an important figure in U.S. history, the notion that president Lincoln may have engaged in homosexual relationships challenged many U.S. Americans' idea about their national identity. A writer for the *Christian Post* dismisses the book, noting that "a group of homosexual advocates has been ransacking history, looking for traces of homosexuality in major historical figures. Their agenda is clear—to argue for the normalization of homosexuality by suggesting that some of history's most preeminent figures were actually closeted (or not so closeted) homosexuals."[22] In contrast, commentator Andrew Sullivan chimes in: "The truth about Lincoln—his unusual sexuality, his comfort with male-male love and sex—is not a truth today's Republican leaders want to hear."[23] While we can never know for certain about Lincoln's complete sexual history, it is important to think about what difference it makes whether or not he did engage in homosexual relationships. It is also important to remember that our contemporary rigid categories of "homosexual" and "heterosexual" did not exist in Lincoln's era, so to identify him by these categories does not make sense.

**What Do You Think?**

Although exact numbers are difficult to get, ISIS, Iran, and some other countries have executed men accused of being gay. Some are stoned to death, others shot in the head and others thrown from high-rise buildings. Despite human rights concerns raised in other countries, some people justify these executions based on their religious beliefs. Think about how gays are treated in other countries. How has a country's history influenced, how gay men are regarded, and what rights they might have?

*Racial and Ethnic Histories*    People from nonmainstream cultural groups often struggle to retain their histories. Theirs are not the histories that everyone learns about in school, yet these histories are vital to understanding how others perceive us, and why. Mainstream history has neither the time nor the space to include all **ethnic** and **racial histories,** which focus on the significance of race and ethnicity in understanding the past. Sometimes, the histories of such cultural groups seem to question, and even undermine, the celebratory nature of a national history.

The history of lynching in the United States reflects the brutality and horrific character of racism. Yet this history continues to return and its use in contemporary situations can be quite offensive. For example, in 2016, a Joe's Crab Shack in Minnesota was criticized for using a lynching photo as part of its table décor: "The picture, which showed a large group of white people at the public hanging of a black man, was labeled 'Hanging at Groesbeck, Texas on April 12th 1895.' All I said was 'I don't like the gumbo!' said a joking speech bubble coming from the executioner's stand."[24] The restaurant has since apologized and removed the lynching photo. Some customers were upset that this man's death was used in a humorous way that was disrespectful and ignored the horrific racial history of lynching in the United States.

The injustices done by any nation are often swept under the carpet. For example, in her book *The Rape of Nanking,* Iris Chang attempts to recover the history of the atrocities that occurred in the 1937 Japanese attack on Nanking, China—what she calls the "forgotten holocaust."[25] The millions killed in Kampuchea (Cambodia) after the Vietnam War, as well as the millions of Africans killed by European colonists in Africa and South America, are all reminders of the silencing of these histories. For example, the Royal Museum of Central Africa has little to say about the atrocities committed by the Belgians in the Congo.

In the United States, other histories have also been overlooked. In an attempt to bring attention to an understanding of the internment of Japanese Americans during World War II, former English professor John Tateishi collected the stories of some of the internees. He notes at the outset of his book that it "makes no attempt to be a definitive academic history of Japanese American internment. Rather it tries to present for the first time in human and personal terms the experience of the only group of American citizens ever to be confined in concentration camps in the United States."[26]

Although this collection of oral histories is not an academic history, it offers valuable insights into the experience of many Japanese Americans. Because this historical event demonstrates the fragility of the constitutional system and its guarantees in the face of rampant prejudice, it is not often discussed as a significant event in U.S. history. For Japanese Americans, however, it has been the most defining event in the development of their communities.

When Tom's parents meet other Japanese Americans of their generation, they are often asked, "What camp were you in?" This question makes little sense outside its historical context. We can see how this question is embedded in understanding a particular moment in history, a moment that is not widely understood. In the aftermath of that experience of internment, the use of that history as a marker has been important in maintaining cultural identity.

*Diasporic Histories* The international relationships that many racial and ethnic groups have with others who share their heritage and history often are overlooked in intercultural communication. These international ties may have been created by transnational migrations, slavery, religious crusades, or other historical events and forces. Because most people do not think about the diverse ways that people have connections to other nations and cultures, we consider these histories to be hidden. In his book *The Black Atlantic,* scholar Paul Gilroy emphasizes that, to understand the identities, cultures, and experiences of African descendants in Britain and the United States, we must examine the connections between Africa, North America, and Europe.[27]

**What Do You Think?**

What kind of history classes should be required in college? Should you take Western Civilization, or should you have the option of learning the history of other regions of the world? What might be the arguments on both sides?

Courtesy Library of Congress Prints and Photograph Division (LC-DIG-fsac-1a35014)

These women are in a U.S. internment camp for people of Japanese ancestry that the U.S. government established during World War II. How might the incarceration of people based upon their ancestry influence the cultural identity of this group? Could this history be repeated again in the United States in the future? Do many contemporary U.S. Americans know this history?

A massive migration, often caused by war, famine, enslavement, or persecution, that results in the dispersal of a unified group is called a **diaspora.** A cultural group (or even an individual) that flees its homeland is likely to bring along some old customs and practices to its new homeland. In fact, diasporic migrations often cause people to cling more strongly to their group's identity. Over the years, though, people become acculturated to some degree in their new homelands.

Consider, for example, the dispersal of eastern European Jews who migrated during or after World War II to the United States, Australia, Argentina, Israel, and other parts of the world. They brought with them their Jewish culture and their eastern European culture. But they also adopted new cultural patterns as they became U.S. Americans, Argentinians, Israelis, and so on. Imagine the communication differences among these people that have evolved over time. Imagine the differences between these groups and the dominant culture of their new homelands.

**Diasporic histories** help us understand the important cultural connections among people affected by diasporas and other transnational migrations. Yet we must be careful to distinguish between the ways that these connections are helpful or hurtful to intercultural communication. For example, some cultures tend to regard negatively those who have left the homeland. Many Japanese tend to look down on Japanese Canadians, Japanese Americans, Japanese Brazilians, Japanese Mexicans, and Japanese Peruvians. By contrast, the Irish tend not to look down on Irish Americans or Irish Canadians. Of course, we must remember as well that many other intervening factors might influence diasporic relationships on an interpersonal level.

**Info Bites**

The Supreme Court of India has decided to take another look at the decision that upholds a law instituted during the colonial period that criminalizes same-sex activities. This law was instituted in 1860 when India was a colony of the United Kingdom. What other legacies of the colonial era continue to influence everyday life in India and other former colonies?

*Colonial Histories*    As you probably know from history, many nations did not confine themselves within their own borders. Due to overpopulation, limited resources, notions of grandeur, or other factors, many people in recent centuries left their homelands to colonize other lands. It is important to recognize these **colonial histories,** which emphasize the important role of colonialism in understanding the past and its influence on the present, so we can better understand the dynamics of intercultural communication today.

Let's look at the significance of colonialism in determining language. Three of the most important colonizers were Britain, France, and Spain. As a result of colonialism, English is spoken in Canada, Australia, New Zealand, Belize, Nigeria, South Africa, India, Pakistan, Bangladesh, Zimbabwe, Hong Kong, Singapore, and the United States, among other places. French is spoken in Canada, Senegal, Tahiti, Haiti, Benin, Côte d'Ivoire, Niger, Rwanda, Mali, Chad, and the Central African Republic, among other places. And Spanish is spoken in most of the Western Hemisphere, from Mexico to Chile and Argentina, including Cuba, Venezuela, Colombia, and Panama.

Many foreign language textbooks proudly display maps that show the many places around the world where that language is commonly spoken. But the maps don't reveal why those languages are widely spoken in those regions, and they don't reveal the legacies of colonialism in those regions. For example, the United Kingdom maintains close relations with many of its former colonies through the Commonwealth of Nations—an intergovernmental organization of 53 nations, including Britain and mostly comprised of its former colonies. The queen of England is also the queen of Canada, Australia, New Zealand, and the Bahamas.

Other languages have been spread through colonialism, including Portuguese in Brazil, Macao, and Angola; Dutch in Angola, Suriname, and Mozambique; and a related Dutch language, Afrikaans, in South Africa. Russian is spoken in the break-away republics of Kazakhstan, Azerbaijan, and Tajikistan. But many nations have reclaimed their own languages in an effort to resist the influences of colonialism. For example, Arabic is spoken in Algeria, and Vietnamese is spoken in Vietnam; at one time, French was widely spoken in both countries. Today, in the newly independent Latvia, the ability to speak Latvian is a requirement for citizenship.

The reality is, we do not freely choose the languages we speak. Rather, we must learn the languages of the societies into which we are born. Judith and Tom, for example, both speak English, although their ancestors came to the United States from non-English-speaking countries. We did not choose to learn English among all of the languages of the world. Although we don't resent our native tongue, we recognize why many individuals might resent a language imposed on them. Think about the historical forces that led you to speak some language(s) and not others. Understanding history is crucial to understanding the linguistic worlds we inhabit.

The imposition of language is but one aspect of cultural invasion. Much colonial history is a history of oppression and brutality. To cast off the legacy, many people have looked toward **postcolonialism**—an intellectual, political, and cultural movement that calls for the independence of colonized states and for liberation from colonialist ways of thinking. Postcolonialism is a movement with many different emphases. In struggling with a colonial past, people have devised many ways of confronting that past. Because postcolonialism comes from the critical approach to intercultural communication, "it theorizes not just colonial conditions but why those conditions are what they are, and how they can be undone and redone."[28] It is not simply the study of colonialism, but the study of how we might deal with that past and its aftermath, which may include the ongoing use of the colonial language, culture, and religion. For example, many companies are locating parts of their businesses in India because of the widespread use of English as a former British colony. How should people in India deal with the ongoing dominance of English, the colonizer's language, but also the language of business?

As another example, Hispanics or Latinos/as share a common history of colonization by Spain, whether their families trace their origins to Mexico, Puerto Rico, Cuba, and so on. Although Spain is no longer in political control of these lands, how do those who live in the legacy of this history deal with that history? In what ways does it remain important, as a part of this cultural identity, to embrace the colonizer's language (Spanish)? The colonizer's religion (Catholicism)? And are there other aspects of Spanish culture that continue to be reproduced over and over again? Postcolonialism is not simply a call to make a clean break from that colonial past, but "to examine the violent actions and erasures of colonialism."[29] In this case, that interrogation might even mean reconsidering the category "Hispanic" that incorporates a wide range of groups that share a Spanish colonial history, but do not share other histories that constitute their cultures.

*Socioeconomic Class Histories*   Many U.S. Americans prefer to ignore class differences, but socioeconomic class has been a significant factor in the way people experienced the past. **Socioeconomic class histories** focus on the role of class in understanding these experiences. While we often overlook the importance of socioeconomic class as a factor in history, socioeconomic class helps explain why many people have immigrated to the United States. The poverty in nineteenth-century Ireland did much to fuel the flight of the Irish to the United States, so that today there are more Irish Americans than Irish.

Yet it is not always the socioeconomically disadvantaged who immigrate. After the Russian Revolution in 1917, a large number of fairly wealthy Russians moved to Paris. Similarly, after the Cuban Revolution in 1959, a large number of fairly wealthy Cubans fled Cuba. Today, the United States and some other countries offer permanent residency to foreign investors who bring a substantial investment to their country. In the United States, it is called the EB-5 Immigrant Investor Program, which ensures that socioeconomic class will continue to inspire some migrations.

The point here is that these socioeconomic class distinctions often are overlooked in understanding the historical migrations and acculturation of groups around the world. The kinds of locations these migrants settled and the employment they found often were marked by the kinds of capital—cultural and financial—that they were or were not able to bring with them.

**What Do You Think?**

Recently, debates over income inequality have overtaken concerns about poverty in the United States, but this issue is not unique to the United States as many other countries have seen a similar phenomenon of a disparate portion of wealth going to the top 1 percent. Economists track this disparity with the Gini coefficient. Different cultures have different amounts of tolerance for inequality. What do you think are the consequences of continuing to increase income inequality? For an overview of this phenomenon worldwide, see http://www.economist.com/node/21564414.

## Pop Culture Spotlight

Films based upon historical events are often quite popular, which explains the continued production of them. In 2015, some of these films included *Suffragette*, a film about the women who pushed for the right to vote, *The 33*, a film about the real-life mine collapse that trapped 33 miners, and *Spotlight*, which won the Academy Award's best picture award, focused on the journalists who uncovered the Catholic priest abuse in Boston. In 2016, *Free State of Jones* was released which retold the story of Newton Knight who led a group in Mississippi against the Confederacy, *Patriots Day*, a film that focused on the Boston Marathon bombing, and *Hacksaw Ridge*, the story of Desmond Doss, the first contentious objector to receive the Medal of Honor. Why do we enjoy seeing these historical films? How does it change, how we think about the past?

## INTERCULTURAL COMMUNICATION AND HISTORY

So far, we have examined some interesting ways of thinking about the past and of viewing history. We are often uncomfortable in dealing with the past because we do not know how we should feel about or deal with many of the ugly things that have happened. Think, for example, about the history of the indigenous peoples in the United States. Native peoples throughout most of the United States were exterminated or removed to settlements in other regions, and many states now have few Native Americans and few, if any, reservations. The current residents had nothing to do with the events in their state's history, but they are the beneficiaries through the ownership of farms and other land. So, although contemporary U.S. Americans are not in a position of fault, they are, through these benefits, in a position of responsibility. In *Writing the Disaster*, Maurice Blanchot makes this important distinction between the position of fault and the position of responsibility.[30] Dealing with this past is not easy, but it is even more problematic simply to ignore it, because ignoring the past erases other cultural identities by pretending that we are all the same.

Our lives are entangled in the web of history from which there is no escape, only denial and silence. How should this influence the ways we think about intercultural communication? What does all of this have to do with intercultural interaction? There are various ways that we might think about history and intercultural communication. First, we can think about the ways that history helps us understand who we are—with all of our identities—and how we may feel constrained by those identities. Second, we can examine how various histories are negotiated in intercultural interaction.

Think about how history has determined, for example, what languages you do and do not speak. Many U.S. Americans no longer speak the language(s) of their forebears. Yet, languages may be an attraction or a repellent in intercultural interactions. Many U.S. Americans, for example, enjoy traveling to Britain, Australia, and Canada, where English is spoken. Many U.S. Americans also are hesitant to travel to non-English-speaking countries because of language differences, and popular movies may reinforce these fears.

Also consider what your identity positions mean to you. How do you feel about being an "American," if this is your national identity? How might non-Americans feel about Americans based on their historical knowledge of what U.S. Americans have and have not done to them and for them? Why do some people dislike U.S. Americans? Can you offer the same reflexive analyses of your other identities?

It is important to recognize that your identities—as a member of a racial or ethnic group, a nationality, a socioeconomic class, and so on—do not have the same meanings for you as they might for someone with differing identities. If you are "White," how might your racial identity have a different meaning for you than for someone who is not White? Is there a history to "Whiteness" that gives it different meanings for different groups of people? Conversely, what their identities mean to you may not be the same as what they mean for them. For example, your notion of "Polish" or

© Jeff Swensen/Getty Images

Not all history is hidden. Here we see an anniversary memorial service at the crash site of Flight 93—held on September 11, 2008. How might this commemoration help us, as U.S. Americans, think about our past?

"German" or other identities across history can create intercultural communication difficulties. How we communicate about the past can create enormous differences in how the past is used in the present and future, as well as impact contemporary cultural identities, as we saw at the beginning of this chapter for President Obama.

Second, how can we balance the past and the present in our everyday intercultural interactions? Initially, it is important to recognize that each of us brings our histories (some known, some hidden) to interactions. We can try to evaluate the role that history plays for those with whom we interact. (Many tourist guidebooks offer a brief history of other countries to help tourists prepare for their trip there.)

Also, we should understand the role that histories play in our identities, in what we bring to the interaction. Communication scholar Marsha Houston says there are three things that White people who want to be her friends should never say: "I don't notice you're black," "You're not like the others," and "I know how you feel." In her opinion, each of these denies or rejects a part of her identity that is deeply rooted in history.[31]

Sometimes, it is unwise to ask people where they are "really from." Such questions assume that they cannot be from where they said they were, due to racial characteristics or other apparent features. Although she was born and raised in New York City, Geeta Kothari is often asked where she is from. She writes:

> "Where are you from?" The bartender asks this as I get up from my table. It's quiet at the Bloomfield Bridge Tavern, home of the best pirogies in Pittsburgh. . . . The man has no reason to ask me that question. We are not having a conversation, I am not his friend. Out of the blue, having said no other words to me, he

feels that it is okay for him, a white man, to ask me where I am from. The only context for this question is my skin color and his need to classify me. I am sure he doesn't expect me to say New York. I look different, therefore it's assumed that I must be from somewhere, somewhere that isn't here, America. It would never occur to him to ask my boyfriend, who is white—and Canadian—where he's from.[32]

Although it may seem innocent to ask her where she is from, the question implies differences based on racial characteristics between those assumed to be "American" and those assumed to be from somewhere else. Recognizing a person's history and its link to his or her identity, as well as your own historical blinders and assumptions, is a first step toward establishing intercultural relationships.

### Historical Legacies

Given these different histories—histories that we have been exposed to and histories that we have remained hidden from us—what are the consequences of this past? How have they changed how we live, who we are, and what we hope for the future? We have already discussed how these different histories influence what languages we speak and what languages we do not speak.

At the outset of this chapter, we began with a look at President Obama's use of the term "Polish death camp" and the harm that it caused to U.S.–Polish relations. How does calling it "Polish death camps" shape how we view the past? What was Poland's role in the Holocaust? Were Polish people simply victims of the Germans? Or did some Polish people collaborate with the Germans? Did other Polish people resist the Germans in various ways?

What do you know about the history of the concentration camps in Poland and other European countries? How should we think about and communicate about this history? Notably, "over the past two decades Poland has become a place where the nation's past, in particular its relationship to the more than three million Polish Jews who were murdered in the Holocaust, is debated more vigorously by politicians, intellectuals and ordinary people."[33] For Poland, this history is very relevant to their cultural identity, their understanding of themselves, and their place in the world.

Yet, Poland is also attempting to deal with this past in more legalistic ways as well. "In February [2016] Patryk Jaki, the deputy minister for justice, proposed banning the phrase 'Polish death camps' on pain of a fine or three years' imprisonment."[34] Do you think that this is a good move for Poland to make? Or will it create more problems than it solves by absolving any Polish participation in the camps?

The question of how we deal with the past is never far away, particularly when the past is not really past. We are always working on our relationships with the past, because the past shapes our present and future. In a context of fear about terrorism, some politicians have referenced the U.S. internment of Americans of Japanese descent in World War II. This historical touchstone is used as a guide to future action. In 2016, Governor Jay Inslee of Washington State argued that the U.S. should

© 123RF

Jan Karski is today widely recognized for his work with the Polish resistance movement during World War II. He is widely credited with informing the United States and allies about the atrocities occurring in Auschwitz-Birkenau. There are statues honoring him in Israel, Poland, and the United States. How is this history important to understanding what happened in Poland in World War II, as well as the current situation of Poles, Jews, Germans, and Americans today?

continue to take and settle Syrian refugees. He felt that the example of the U.S. internment camps point to the kinds of mistakes made by treating people differently based on their ethnicity. At the same time, the mayor of Roanoke, VA, David Bower, said that President Franklin Roosevelt felt compelled to [sic] sequester Japanese foreign nationals after the bombing of Pearl Harbor, and it appers that the threat of harm to America from [the Islamic State] now is just as real.[35]

In both cases, the past is a reference for future action. While Mayor Bowers later apologized, the internment continues to play a role in how we discuss how to deal with refugees.

Donald Trump has spoken about the refugee situation and on MSNBC's "Morning Joe" show, he referred to FDR's actions as a "respected president, a highly respected president."

Host Joe Scarborough asked: "You certainly aren't proposing internment camps, are you?"

"I am not proposing that," Trump said, moving back to Roosevelt's presidential proclamations. "It was tough stuff, but it wasn't internment. We're not talking about the Japanese internment camps. No, not at all. But we have to get our head around a very serious problem, and it's getting worse."[36]

Although Trump did not embrace the use of internment camps for refugees or for Muslims, the discussion about the internment camps places the past in the present. The past is never past.

Despite his use of the term "Japanese internment camps," these camps were not built or created by Japan or the Japanese government. These camps were instituted and operated by the U.S. government. Does it protect our view of the United States to call them "Japanese internment camps" instead of "American internment camps"? Again, how should we communicate about this past?

What is important to understand is that the past is not simply over; rather, we should consider all of the ways that the past has constructed how we live in the present and what we think should happen in the future. These are all influences in intercultural interaction and how we think about ourselves and others.

## SUMMARY

In this chapter, we explored some of the dimensions of history in intercultural communication. Multiple histories are important for empowering different cultural identities. These include political, intellectual, social, family, national, religious, and cultural group histories.

History is constructed through narrative. Our understanding of the events that occur comes to us through our "telling" of the events. Histories that typically are not conveyed in a widespread manner are considered to be hidden. These include histories based on gender, sexual orientation, race and ethnicity, migration, colonialism, and socioeconomic class. All kinds of histories contribute to the success or failure of intercultural interaction.

We also looked at how history plays a role in intercultural interaction. The key is to balance the past and the present in intercultural encounters. As the controversy over the relationship between the United States and Poland shows, history certainly plays a central role in intercultural conflict.

## BUILDING INTERCULTURAL SKILLS

1. Reflect on the limitations of your understanding of the past and how some of those histories have been marketed to you. What kinds of history would you want to include in a tourist guidebook for non-Americans who are visiting your state? What would you not include? Why? Whose histories would you include? Think about how history might shape people's understanding of a destination and what they want to see.

2. Think about how some of these histories are important to different people in different ways. Some tourist destinations are marketed based on their historical importance. How might you connect this history with what you expect to see, say, in Tombstone, Arizona; at the Magnolia Plantation in South Carolina; or in Williamsburg, Virginia? Why might some people want to visit the old slave auction block in Fayetteville, North Carolina, or German concentration camps, such as Auschwitz in Poland or Dachau in Germany?

3. Reflect on the history of your family. In what ways does this history connect you with members of some cultural groups and distance you from members of other cultural groups? How has your family history determined your culture— what language(s) you speak, what foods you eat, what holidays you celebrate, and so on?

4. Understand the relationship between identity and history. How does history help you understand who you are? Which kinds of history are most important in your identity? National? Family? Sexual orientation?

5. Develop sensitivity to other people's histories. Aside from "Where are you from?" what questions might strangers ask that can be irritating to some people? Should you know about how history has shaped other cultural group identities? Think about how their histories are intertwined with your histories.

## ACTIVITIES

1. *Family history:* Talk to members of your own family to see how they feel about your family's history. Find out, for example, how the family history influences the way they think about who they are. Do they wish they knew more about your family? What things has your family continued to do that your forebears probably also did? Do you eat some of the same foods? Practice the same religion? Celebrate birthdays or weddings in the same way? Often, the continuity between past and present is taken for granted.

2. *Cultural group history:* Individually or in groups, choose a cultural group in the United States that is unfamiliar to you. Study the history of this group, answering the following questions:

   a. What is the historical relationship between this group and other groups (particularly the dominant cultural groups)?

   b. What are some significant events in the group's history?

   c. Are there any historical incidents of discrimination?

   d. What are common stereotypes about the group, and how did they originate?

   e. Who are important leaders and heroes of the group?

   f. What are some notable achievements of the group?

   g. In what ways does the history of this group influence the identity of group members today?

## ENDNOTES

1.  The White House. (2012, April 23). President Obama announces Jan Karski as a recipient of the presidential medal of freedom. Retrieved from https://www.whitehouse.gov/the-press-office/2012/04 /23/president-obama-announces-jan-karski-recipient-presidential-medal-freedo.

2.  President Obama. (2012, May 29). Remarks by the president at presidential medal of freedom ceremony. The White House Office of the Press Secretary. Retrieved from https://www.whitehouse .gov/the-press-office/2012/05/29/remarks-president-presidential-medal-freedom-ceremony.

3.  Tusk, D. quoted in Landler, M. (2012, May 30). Polish premier denounces Obama for referring to a 'Polish death camp.' *New York Times*. Retrieved April 16, 2016, from http://www.nytimes .com/2012/05/31/world/europe/poland-bristles-as-obama-says-polish-death-camps.html.

4.  Frum, D. (2012, May 30). It wasn't a "gaffe." *The Daily Beast*. Retrieved April 16, 2016, from: http://www.thedailybeast.com/articles/2012/05/30/poland-insult.html.

5.  President Obama. (2012, May 29). Remarks by the President at Presidential Medal of Freedom Ceremony. The White House Office of the Press Secretary. https://www.whitehouse.gov/the -press-office/2012/05/29/remarks-president-presidential-medal-freedom-ceremony.

6.  Department of Immigration & Multicultural & Indigenous Affairs, Public Affairs Section, Fact Sheet No. 8. *Abolition of the "White Australia" Policy*, November 6, 2002. Retrieved from http:// www.immi.gov.au/facts/08abolition.htm.

7.  Darnton, R. (1985). *The Great Cat Massacre and other episodes in French cultural history*. New York, NY: Vintage.

8.  Mason, J., & Halpin, P. (2011, May 23). Obama visits family roots in Ireland. *Reuters*. Retrieved May 30, 2011, from http://www.reuters.com/article/2011/05/23/us-obama-ireland -idUSTRE74M09F20110523.

9.  Swarns, R. L., & Kantor, J. (2009, October 7). In First Lady's roots, a complex path from slavery. *New York Times*. Retrieved May 30, 2011, from http://www.nytimes.com/2009/10/08/us /politics/08genealogy.html?_r=3.

10. Thonssen, L., Baird, A. C., & Braden, W. W. (1970). *Speech criticism* (2nd ed.). New York, NY: Ronald Press, p. 335.

11. Loewen, J. W. (1995). *Lies my teacher told me: Everything your American history textbook got wrong* (p. 13). New York, NY: Touchstone.

12. Loewen (1995), p. 136.

13. Lyotard, J.-F. (1984). *The postmodern condition: A report on knowledge* (p. 37) (G. Bennington & B. Massumi, Trans.). Minneapolis, MN: University of Minnesota Press.

14. Fisher, W. (1984). Narration as a human communication paradigm: The case of public moral argument. *Communication Monographs, 51,* 1–22; Fisher, W. (1985). The narrative paradigm: An elaboration. *Communication Monographs, 52,* 347–367.

15. Baudrillard, J. (1988). *America* (p. 80) (C. Turner, Trans.). New York, NY: Verso.

16. President Obama quoted in Blake, A. (2015, February 6). Why Obama invoked the Crusades—and what it says about how he views terrorism. *The Washington Post*. Retrieved April 16, 2016, from https://www.washingtonpost.com/news/the-fix/wp/2015/02/06/why-obama-invoked-the-crusades -in-re-islam-and-terrorism/.

17. Jacoby, J. (2016, May 1). 'Never forget' the world said of the Holocaust. But the world is forgetting. *The Boston Globe*. Retrieved May 2, 2016, from https://www.bostonglobe.com/opinion/2016/04/30 /never-forget-world-said-holocaust-but-world-forgetting/59cUqLNFxylkW7BDuRPgNK/story.html.

18. Nakano, M. (1990). *Japanese American women: Three generations, 1890–1990* (p. xiii). Berkeley and San Francisco, CA: Mina Press and National Japanese American Historical Society.

19. Duberman, M. B. (1991). Introduction to first edition (1986). *About time: Exploring the gay past* (p. xiii). New York, NY: Penguin Books.

20. Hocquenghem, G., & Blasius, M. (1980, April). Interview. *Christopher Street, 8*(4), 40.

21. Tripp, C. A. (2005). *The intimate world of Abraham Lincoln*. New York, NY: Free Press.

22. Mohler, R. A., Jr. (2006, February 20). Was Abraham Lincoln gay? Homosexuality and history. *The Christian Post*. Retrieved May 22, 2006, from http://dc.christianpost.com/article/editorial/43 /section/was.abraham.lincoln.gay.homosexuality.and.history/1.htm.

23.  Sullivan, A. (2005, January 12). *Log cabin Republican: How gay was Lincoln?* Retrieved May 22, 2006, from http://www.andrewsullivan.com/main_article.php?artnum=20050112.

24.  Brennan, C. (2016, March 11). Joe's Crab Shack apologizes after using photo of black man's 1895 hanging as decoration. *New York Daily News.* Retrieved April 16, 2016, from: http://www.nydailynews.com/news/national/joe-crab-shack-photo-black-man-hanging-decor-article-1.2560789.

25.  Chang, I. (1997). *The rape of Nanking: The forgotten holocaust of World War II.* New York, NY: Basic Books.

26.  Tateishi, J. (1984). *And justice for all: An oral history of the Japanese American detention camps* (p. vii). New York, NY: Random House.

27.  Gilroy, P. (1993). *The Black Atlantic: Modernity and double consciousness.* New York, NY: Verso.

28.  Shome, R., & Hegde, R. (2002). Postcolonial approaches to communication: Charting the terrain, engaging the intersections. *Communication Theory, 12,* 250.

29.  Shome & Hegde (2002), p. 250.

30.  Blanchot, M. (1986). *The writing of the disaster* (A. Smock, Trans.). Lincoln: University of Nebraska Press.

31.  Houston, M. (1997). When Black women talk with White women: Why dialogues are difficult. In A. González, M. Houston, & V. Chen (Eds.), *Our voices: Essays in ethnicity, culture, and communication* (2nd ed., pp. 187–194). Los Angeles, CA: Roxbury.

32.  Kothari, G. (1995). Where are you from? In G. Hongo (Ed.), *Under Western eyes: Personal essays from Asian America* (p. 153). New York: Anchor/Doubleday.

33.  The politics of memory. (2016, April 9). *The Economist.* Retrieved April 16, 2016, from: http://www.economist.com/news/europe/21696555-poland-had-been-coming-terms-its-past-now-government-wants-bury-it-again.

34.  The politics of memory.

35.  Phillips, A. (2015, November 18). Virginia mayor cites Japanese internment camps (favorably) in making case for halting Syrian refugees. Really. *The Washington Post.* Retrieved April 16, 2016, from https://www.washingtonpost.com/news/the-fix/wp/2015/11/18/the-mayor-of-roanoke-va-cited-japanese-internment-camps-favorably-in-make-case-for-halting-syrian-refugees-really/.

36.  Bever, L. (2015, December 8). Internment camps? "I certainly hate the concept," Donald Trump says. *The Washington Post.* Retrieved May 2, 2016, from https://www.washingtonpost.com/news/post-politics/wp/2015/12/08/trump-on-internment-camps-i-certainly-hate-the-concept/.

© kristian sekulic/Getty Images RF

CHAPTER FOUR

# Identity and Intercultural Communication

## CHAPTER OUTLINE

### Understanding Identity

*Identities Are Created through Communication*
*Identities Are Created in Spurts*
*Identities Are Multiple*
*Identities Are Influenced by Society*
*Identities Are Dynamic*
*Identities Are Developed in Different Ways in Different Cultures*

### Social and Cultural Identities

*Gender Identity*
*Sexual Identity*
*Age Identity*
*Racial and Ethnic Identity*
*Physical Ability Identity*
*Religious Identity*
*Class Identity*
*National Identity*
*Regional Identity*
*Personal Identity*

### Identity Development

*Minority Identity Development*
*Majority Identity Development*
*Characteristics of Whiteness*

### Multicultural Identity

*Multiracial People*
*Global Nomads*
*Identity and Adaptation*
*Living "On the Border"*
*Post-Ethnicity*

### Summary
### Building Intercultural Skills
### Activities
### Endnotes

## STUDY OBJECTIVES

*After reading this chapter, you should be able to:*

1. Explain how identities are developed through our communicative interaction with others.

2. Identify some of the ways in which people communicate their identity.

3. Explain how the context of the larger society contributes to the formation of identity.

4. Identify some of the major social and cultural identities that are manifest in our communication.

5. Explain differences in how identities are developed for minority versus majority group members in the United States.

6. Explain identity development of multiracial people.

7. Describe the relationship between identity and language.

## KEY TERMS

age identity
class identity
constructive identity
culture shock
encapsulated identity
ethnic identity
gender identity
global nomads
hyphenated Americans
identity
intercultural personhood
majority identity development
minority identity development
multicultural identity
national identity
personal identity
physical ability identity
racial identity
regional identity
religious identity
self
sexual identity
third culture kids (TCKs)
U-curve theory
Whiteness

*We define a Canadian not by a skin colour or a language or a religion.[1]*

*—Canadian Prime Minister Justin Trudeau*

Identity plays a key role in intercultural communication, serving as a bridge between culture and communication. In his remarks in French at Toronto Pearson International Airport, Canadian Prime Minister Justin Trudeau communicated his vision about what Canadian identity means. Having flown in 163 Syrian refugees to become part of Canada, Trudeau communicated his vision of Canadian identity that is not about the color of one's skin, religion, or background, but about a set of shared values. National identities are not always free of notions of race, religion, and other aspects of identity. National identities, like other identities, are very complex and understanding that complexity is key to successful intercultural communication. Identities do not carry equal value across cultures, but they are important to communication, because it is through communication that we express or hide some of our identities from others. Knowing about our identity is particularly important in intercultural interactions.

Conflicts can arise when there are sharp differences between who we think we are and who others think we are. When Rachel Dolezal's racial identity became news, the conflict between her stated racial identity and the racial identity that others assigned her highlighted the tensions about our identities. Although Rachel Dolezal says, "I identify as black," she was born to White parents and many others identify her as "White." Her case became widely known as some felt betrayed by her presentation of her identity as Black. She says, "I don't have any regrets about how I identify. I'm still me and nothing about that has changed."[2] Are our birth identities who we "really" are? Or can we change racial identities? Do people tend to look at others and focus on who they "really" are? Is it difficult to deal with multiple identities?

In this chapter, we examine the relationship between communication and identity, and the role of identity in intercultural communication. After we define identity, we focus on the development of specific aspects of our social and cultural identity including those related to gender, age, race or ethnicity, physical ability, religion, class, and nationality. We then turn our attention to culture shock and cultural adaptation, and to multicultural identity, which refers to individuals who live on the borders between several identities and cultures. Finally, we discuss the relationship between identity, language, and communication.

## UNDERSTANDING IDENTITY

How do we come to understand who we are, our **self?** Our self is what we're born with, our gender, our physical characteristics; our **identity** is created by the

**Surf's Up!**

What does cultural identity look like? This is a difficult question to answer because we often rely on visual cues to reinforce stereotypes that we hold about certain people and groups. In a series on U.S. American images, PBS explores this question of cultural identity. For more information, go to www.pbs.org/ktca /americanphotography /features/cultural.html.

development of the "self" (our self-concept), in spurts, through communication over a long period of time. Further, we have not merely one identity but multiple identities, which are influenced by society and are dynamic. And the way identities develop depends on one's cultural background. Let's look more closely at these six aspects of identities.

### Identities Are Created through Communication

Identities emerge when communication messages are exchanged between persons; they are negotiated, cocreated, reinforced, and challenged through communication.[3] In some sense, we know who we are as a result of our communication and our relationships with others. As psychologist Kenneth J. Gergen says, "I am linked therefore I am."[4] This means that presenting our identities is not a simple process. Does everyone see you as you see yourself? Probably not. Janice, a student of ours from Canada, is proud to be Canadian and gets tired of students in the United States always assuming she is a U.S. American. Her interactions with these American students influence how she sees herself; in discussing with them her Canadian background and experiences, she has developed a stronger sense of her Canadian national identity.

Different identities are emphasized depending on whom we are communicating with and what the conversation is about. In a social conversation with someone we are attracted to, our gender or sexual orientation identity is probably more important to us than, say, our ethnic or national identities. And our communication is probably most successful when the person we are talking with confirms the identity we think is most important at the moment. For example, if you are talking with a professor about a research project, the interaction will be most successful if it confirms the relevant identities of professor and student rather than other identities—for example, those based on gender, religion, or ethnicity.

Gergen has also emphasized that recent mobile communication technologies influence our relationships and, consequently, our sense of identity. He thinks that when individuals are constantly texting and IM-ing, they avoid face-to-face encounters; their bodies may be present, but their personalities are engaged elsewhere, which can result in social isolation, the stress of always being somewhere else no matter where one might be, and a diminished sense of identity.[5]

### Identities Are Created in Spurts

Identities are created not in a smooth, orderly process but in spurts. Certain events provide insights into who we are, but these are framed by long periods during which we may not think much about ourselves or our identities. Thus, we sometimes may feel that we know exactly who we are and our place in the world and at other times may be rather confused.

Communication is crucial to the development of identity. For instance, our student Amanda felt confident of her religious identity until she married into another faith. Following long discussions with her in-laws about issues of spirituality, she began to question this aspect of her identity. As this example suggests, we may

occasionally need to take some time to think through identity issues. And during difficult times, we may internalize negative identities as we try to answer the question
of who we are. For example, Judith didn't tell any of her friends in high school that
she had an Amish background, because she was embarrassed and thought that her
friends would look down on her if they knew. Not until she became an adult would
she disclose her religious background. Similarly, our student Shawna didn't want her
friends to know that her mother was White and her father was Black, because she
was afraid it would affect the way they felt about her.

## Identities Are Multiple

It makes more sense to talk about our identities than our identity. Because we belong
to various groups, we develop multiple identities that come into play at different
times, depending on the context. Thus, in going to church or temple, we may highlight our religious identity. In going to clubs or bars, we may highlight our sexual
orientation identity. Women who join social groups exclusive to women, or men who
attend social functions just for men, are highlighting their gender identity.

## Identities Are Influenced by Society

Our identities are formed through communication with others, but societal forces
related to history, economics, and politics also have a strong influence. To grasp
this notion, think about how and why people identify with particular groups and not
others. What choices are available to them? The reality is, we are all pigeonholed
into identity categories, or contexts, even before we are born. Many parents give a
great deal of thought to a name for their unborn child, who is already part of society
through his or her relationship to the parents. Some children have a good start at
being, say, Jewish or Chicana before they are even born. It is very difficult to change
involuntary identities rooted in ethnicity, gender, or physical ability, so we cannot
ignore the ethnic, socioeconomic, or racial positions from which we start our identity
journeys.

To illustrate, imagine two children on a train that stops at a station. Each child
looks out a window and identifies his or her location. One child says that she is in
front of the door for the women's room; the other says that he is in front of the door
for the men's room. Both children see and use labels from their seating position to
describe where they are; both are on the same train but describe where they are differently. And, like the two children, where we are positioned—by our background
and by society—influences how and what we see, and, most important, what it
means.[6]

Many White students, when asked what it means to be an American, talk
about the many freedoms they experience, but members of minority groups and
international visitors may not have the same experience. As one of our Dutch students said, "I think that Americans think that being an American means having a
lot of freedom. I must disagree with that. Measuring it with my own experiences, I
found America not so free at all. There are all those little rules I don't understand
the meaning of." By "rules," she meant all those regulations that U.S. Americans

**What Do You Think?**

In her analysis of the
impact of technology
on our communication,
Sherry Turkle finds
that we are now more
connected than ever
but also more alone
than ever. While we can
text or e-mail anyone
at any time, many
people negotiate their
identities by avoiding
using the telephone, in
favor of social media
or texting because
they feel they have
more control over
their relationships
and privacy. How does
technology influence
how you present
yourself in various
media?
(Source: Turkle, S.
[2011]. *Alone together:
Why we expect more
from technology and less
from each other.* New
York, NY: Basic Books)

**Pop Culture Spotlight**

Photographer Michael Stokes has assembled a photo book of wounded U.S. military veterans. Taken as nudes or near-nudes, these photos present sexy veterans with missing limbs or other disabilities, but still communicate sexuality, confidence, and pride, and redefine disability as an identity. His book, *Always Loyal* (2015), is a large format, photography book published by the German publisher Bruno Gmünder Verlag.

accept as normal but Europeans are surprised at—for example, enforced drinking ages, leash laws, prohibitions against topless bathing on most beaches, and no-smoking ordinances.

The identities that others assign to us are socially and politically determined. But how are certain identities created by popular culture? For example, the label "heterosexual" is a relatively recent invention, less than 100 years old.[7] The word originally referred to someone who engaged in sexual activity with a person of either sex; only relatively recently has it come to mean someone who engages in sexual activity only with members of the opposite sex. And the term has had different social and political meanings over the years. In earlier times, the rules governing heterosexual behavior emphasized procreation and female submissiveness and passivity. There were even rules about when sex could happen; it was a sin for a man to "love" his wife too much. In World War II, the military devised a series of tests to determine the "true" sexuality of men, and those who failed the test were rejected from service. In this way, sex became a fixed identity, like race, with political implications.

When we think about how society or other people create ideas about our identity, we might try to resist those attempts to pigeonhole us and thus try to assign other identities to ourselves. Agusia, a Polish student of ours, counters "Polish jokes" by educating joke-tellers about the origination of the term *Polack*, which simply means "Polish man." The negative connotation came about during a period of U.S. history when there was intense hostility toward immigrants from southern and eastern Europe. By educating people about Polish immigration history, Agusia "resists" the negative, stereotypic identity that society places on her.

Similarly, people with disabilities often have the experience of being stereotyped as helpless. Many people with disabilities view themselves as public educators—determined to redefine people's perceptions concerning disabilities and resisting stereotypes. For example, they sometimes humorously refer to nondisabled persons as "TABs" (temporarily able-bodied), reminding people that no one is immune from disability, or they may redefine an assisting device, by calling a cane a "portable railing."[8]

One aspect of this education is helping nondisabled people understand when and how it is acceptable to assist a person who has a disability in opening doors, picking up something out of reach, carrying something, and so on. Nondisabled people are not always sure whether to offer assistance; and accepting assistance can make people with disabilities feel embarrassed and unnecessarily dependent. It is important to realize that disabled people, like any cultural group, do not hold one unified opinion. In one study, about 50 percent of people with disabilities surveyed said they would accept help when offered; the other half were adamant that nondisabled people should wait until their help was requested. In another study, disabled people gave five guidelines for nondisabled people who want to assist a disabled person:[9]

1. Make the request very general: "May I help you?" or "Do you need anything?"

2. Make the offer of help natural and casual, like assistance that might be given to any individual, disabled or not, rather than emphasizing the

person's dependence. "I'm going to get another drink, would you like another one also?"

3. Ask before acting . . . do not just grab the wheelchair and push.

4. Don't get your feelings hurt if the disabled person rejects the offer. As one disabled person said, "I guess ideally I'd like to have all ablebodied people in the world trained to ask the question . . . 'can I assist you or something?'" As one disabled person said, "I think offering assistance is fine as long as you don't get the feeling you are going to hurt their feelings if you say 'no' . . . don't get personally invested in the request. It may be turned down, and it is not a personal affront to you."[10]

5. Follow the instructions of the person with the disability—especially with complicated tasks like folding a wheelchair in a car or helping him or her up if fallen. Not paying attention to instructions can lead to wasted time, frustration, physical harm to the disabled person, or even breaking expensive equipment.

How do societal influences relate to intercultural communication? Basically, they establish the foundation from which the interaction occurs. Recall Sam, a Chinese American student of ours, who is occasionally asked where he is from or whether he is Chinese. The question puts him in an awkward position. He does not hold Chinese citizenship, nor has he ever lived in China. Yet the questioner probably doesn't mean to address these issues. It sometimes seems to Sam that the person who is asking the question is challenging Sam's right to his identity as an American. In this sense, the questioner seems to imply that Sam holds some negative identity.

## Identities Are Dynamic

The social forces that give rise to particular identities are always changing. For example, the identity of "woman" has changed considerably in recent years in the United States. Historically, being a woman has variously meant working outside the home to contribute to the family income or to help out the country when men were fighting wars, or staying at home and raising a family. Today, there are many different ideas about what being a woman means—from wife and mother to feminist and professional. Specific political forces can influence how identities are expressed. For example, both Caitlyn Jenner (formerly Bruce Jenner of *Keeping Up With The Kardashians* and now star of *I Am Cait*) and Laverne Cox (from *Orange Is The New Black*) have helped bring transgender issues into public discourse. Despite the acceptance of transgender identity by some people, others find it threatening to traditional notions of gender. In 2016, North Carolina passed HB 2 (the Public Facilities and Security Act) into law which, in part, makes it illegal to use the bathroom of someone's gender identity, but legal only to use the bathroom that corresponds to one's birth gender. Since the passage of this law, North Carolina has received pushback from individuals as well as businesses.[11] Similarly, the emergence of the European Union has given new meaning to the notion of being

**What Do You Think?**

Some people try to engage someone else into a relationship by creating a fictional Online persona. This behavior is called, "catfishing." Today there is an MTV show called *Catfish: The TV Show*. On the show, the hosts try to help people figure out if they are with a "catfish" and this entails navigating many different social media (e.g., Facebook, Instagram, Vine, Snapchat). How does social media make creating and revealing identities easier and more difficult? Why do people create these different Online identities? How should we approach Online identities?

"European." Some Europeans are embracing the idea of a European identity, while others are rejecting the notion; the idea is dynamic and changing. For example, some Europeans prefer to be identified as "French," "Italian," or "German," instead of "European" since "European" does not communicate their strongest feelings of identification. In the future, do you think that European may become more important than these national identities?

## Identities Are Developed in Different Ways in Different Cultures

In the United States, young people often are encouraged to develop a strong sense of identity, to "know who they are," to be independent and self-reliant. This stems from the value of individualism, discussed in Chapter 2. However, this individualistic emphasis on developing identity is not shared by all societies. In many African, Asian, and Latino/a societies, the experience of childhood and adolescence revolves around the family. In these societies, then, educational, occupational, and even marital choices are made with extensive family guidance. As Andrea, a Mexican American student, explains, "Family is the sole source behind what it means to be Hispanic. The role parents play in our lives is an ongoing process that never ends. It is the complete opposite of America where the child turns 18 and is free of restriction and authority. Family is the number-one priority and the basis of all that is to come." Thus, identity development does not occur in the same way in every society. Many African, Asian, and Latino/a societies emphasize dependency and interdependency among family members. So, in some cultural contexts, it makes more sense to speak of a familial or relational self than the self-creation of one's personal identity.[12]

However, if the dominant idea of individual identity development is presented as the only alternative, it can make members of some cultural groups in the United States feel inferior or even question their psychological health. For example, Manoj, an Indian medical student in New York, attended a lecture on adolescent development by a very well-known scholar. In his lecture, the professor said that unless a person went through a rebellious stage as an adolescent, it was impossible to achieve a healthy identity. Manoj searched within himself for any sign of rebellion he had felt against either of his parents when he was growing up in India or against any other parent figure. When he couldn't recall any such experience, he concluded that he must be abnormal.[13]

## SOCIAL AND CULTURAL IDENTITIES

People can identify with a multitude of groups based on such things as gender, age, and ethnicity, as well as on occupational interests, sports (as spectators or participants), leisure activities, and special abilities. One of our friends belongs to a special car club—all owners of 1960s and 1970s "muscle cars." All these groups help shape our identities and affect our communication to some degree. In this section, we identify those identities that most affect our cultural perceptions and influence how we communicate cross-culturally.

## Gender Identity

We often begin life with gendered identities. When newborns arrive, they may be greeted with clothes and blankets in either blue or pink. To establish a **gender identity** for a baby, visitors may ask if it's a boy or a girl. But gender is not the same as biological sex. This distinction is important in understanding how our views on biological sex influence gender identities.

We communicate our gender identity, and popular culture tells us what it means to be a man or a woman. For example, some activities are considered more masculine or more feminine. Similarly, the programs that people watch on television— reality television shows, football games, and so on—affect how they socialize with others and come to understand what it means to be a man or a woman.

As a culture changes, so do notions of what is masculine or feminine. Even the popular image of the perfect male body changes. In the 1860s, the middle-class view of the ideal male body type was lean and wiry. By the 1890s, however, the ideal male body type was bulky with well-defined muscles.[14] Today, the man bun has become popular. These popular notions of the ideal male (or female) body are largely determined by commercial interests, advertising, and other cultural forces. This is especially true for women. Advertisements in magazines and commercials on television tell us what it means, and how much it will cost, to be a beautiful woman. As one of our students explained, "I must compete with my fellow Americans for external beauty. As an American, I am expected to project a beautiful appearance. Perfection is portrayed at every stage in life—whether it is a beautiful doll little girls are given to play with or perfect-looking supermodels in fashion magazines. It is no secret what is expected and accepted." Our expression of gender identity not only communicates who we think we are but also constructs a sense of who we want to be. We learn what masculinity and femininity mean in our culture, and we negotiate how we communicate our gender identity to others.

Consider, for example, the contemporary trend against body hair on men. Today, the ideal male body type is sleek, with little body hair. Many men view their own bodies in relation to this ideal and decide to change themselves accordingly. Of course, at one time, a hairy body was considered more masculine, not less.

Or think about the controversy over whether certain actresses, like Nicole Richie, are too thin. The female models appearing in magazine advertisements and TV commercials are very thin—leading young girls to feel ashamed of any body fat. It was not always so. In the mid-1700s, a robust woman was considered attractive. Our Japanese students tell us that full lips for women, considered so desirable in the United States, are not considered very attractive in Japan. And in many societies today, in the Middle East and in Africa, full-figured women are much more desirable than thin women. This shows how the idea of gender identity is both dynamic and closely connected to culture. Society has many images of masculinity and femininity; we do not all seek to look and act according to a single ideal. At the same time, we do seek to communicate our gendered identities as part of who we are. Transgender refers to identification with a gender that differs from the biologically assigned gender at birth. Cisgender refers to identification with a gender that matches one's biological body. Like cisgendered people, transgendered people can identify with any of a number of sexual identities. Thus, if someone is transgendered, it does not mean that this person is gay or lesbian. They may identify as heterosexual or some other sexual identity. Some countries recognize transgender people; others do not. Some countries include transgender or third gender (identifying as neither male nor female) in their national census, such as India and Nepal. The U.S. Census does not include a third-gender category.

There are implications for intercultural communication as well. Gender means different things in different cultures. U.S. students who travel abroad often find that their movements are more restricted. For example, single women cannot travel freely in many Muslim countries. And gender identity for many Muslim women means that the sphere of activity and power is primarily in the home and not in public.

## Sexual Identity

Our **sexual identities** should not be confused with our gender identities. Sexual identity is complex, particularly since different cultures organize sexualities in different ways. While many cultures have similar categories for male/female and masculine/feminine, many cultures have very different definitions of sexualities. For example, in the United States today, we often think of the categories heterosexual, gay, lesbian, and bisexual; yet the development of these categories is largely a late nineteenth-century invention.[15]

The difficulty that researchers have had with sexual identity across cultures is reflected in their own difficulties categorizing and understanding other ways of organizing sexualities. Rudi Bleys has attempted to demonstrate the ways that Western researchers have attempted to understand sexualities across cultures and how those understandings have shifted over time. It is important to understand that the ways we categorize sexualities today may not be the same as other cultures in other times may have organized sexualities.[16]

The way we organize sexuality, however, is central to the development of sexual identities. If nobody identifies as "gay," then there can be no "gay rights" movement. If nobody identifies as "heterosexual," then there can be no assumption that anyone is only attracted to members of the opposite sex.

The language we use to self-identify can also complicate sexual identity. For example, someone who has not yet engaged in any sexual activities with anyone might identify as "gay," while someone else may identify as "heterosexual" but occasionally sleeps with members of the same sex. How might these categories be more complex than they first appear?

Sexual attraction, of course, makes sexual identities even less categorizable. Not only are sexual desires quite complex, but they are also influenced by attraction to those of other cultures, racial/ethnic backgrounds, ages, and cultural identities. Our language is full of terms for people who desire others who are quite different from themselves. How do these terms communicate meaning about sexual identities? How do they communicate value judgments about other sexual identities?

As you encounter people from around the world, do not assume that your framework for sexual categories is universal. Nor should you assume that the ways that sexuality is handled in public is the same as in your hometown. Sometimes people from other countries are shocked that U.S. Americans speak so openly to strangers about being in their second marriage.

## Age Identity

As we age, we tap into cultural notions of how someone our age should act, look, and behave; that is, we establish an **age identity.** The United States is an age-conscious society. One of the first things we teach children is to tell their age. Children will proudly tell their age—until about the mid-20s when people rarely mention their age. In contrast, people over 70 often brag about their age. One way of thinking about age is to consider what generation someone belongs. Different generations often have different philosophies, values, and ways of speaking. For example, recent data show that the millennium generation (or Gen Y, those born between 1982 and 2001) are more diverse and globally oriented and are more knowledgeable about computers and technology than any preceding generation. They are also more optimistic, more committed to contributing to society, and more interested in life balance between work and play than the previous Gen X group (those born between 1961 and 1981).[17]

Another way to think about age is to think about how culture shapes different age groups. For example, the development of the "adolescent" category is relatively new. In addition, scholar Jeffrey Arnett has recently argued for the creation of "emerging adulthood" as another category that describes people in their 20s. Because of changing cultural conditions in the United States, people need more education, stay in school longer, feel less pressure to get married, etc., which leads to more young adults living at home longer, changing jobs many more times, and more identity exploration before they hit age 30.[18]

Certain ages have special significance in some cultures. Latino/a families sometimes celebrate a daughter's 15th birthday with a *Quinceañera* party— marking the girl's entry into womanhood. Some Jewish families celebrate with a Bat Mitzvah ceremony for daughters and a Bar Mitzvah for sons on their 13th birthday.[19] Even as we communicate how we feel about our age to others, we receive messages from the media telling us how we should feel. Thus, as we grow older, we sometimes feel that we are either too old or too young for a certain "look." These feelings stem from an understanding of what age means and how we identify with that age.

Some people feel old at 30; others feel young at 40. There is nothing inherent in age that tells you that you are young or old. Our notions of age and youth are all based on cultural conventions—the same cultural conventions that suggest that it is inappropriate to engage in a romantic relationship with someone who is far older or younger.

Our notions of age often change as we grow older ourselves. When we are quite young, a college student seems old. But when we are in college, we do not feel so old. The relative nature of age is only one part of the age identity process; social constructions of age are another. The various meanings that our society holds for different ages is an important influence in age identity. Gender and age also work together as we age. For example, people may use the term "cougar" to describe a woman who dates a much younger man, but what term is there for a man who dates younger women? How does communication shape the ways that gender and age work together?

Age identity, however, is not simply about how you feel about your age. It is also about how others treat you based on your age. Due to the practice of discrimination against older workers, the U.S. government enacted the Age Discrimination in Employment Act of 1967, which protects people who are 40 and older from employment discrimination. Aside from employment, are there other areas in society where people are treated differently based on their age?[20]

Moreover, while in the United States old age is demeaned, in other societies it is revered. An example of this is in East Africa, where words for older persons are used endearingly to refer to any respected person in the community. These different views on aging have implications for intercultural communication. For example, in one cultural exchange program between the People's Republic of China and the United States, Chinese administrators were offended because the United States sent young adults as the first exchangees. The Chinese, wanting to include some of their best and most revered citizens, sent scholars in their 50s and 60s.

## Racial and Ethnic Identity

*Racial Identity*   In the United States today, the issue of race seems to be pervasive. It is the topic of many public discussions, from television talk shows to talk radio. Yet many people feel uncomfortable discussing racial issues. Perhaps we can better understand the contemporary issues if we look at how the notion of race has developed historically in the United States.

The roots of current debates about race can be located in the fifteenth century, when European explorers encountered people who looked different from themselves. The debates centered on the religious question of whether there was "one family of man." If so, what rights were to be accorded to those who were different? Arguments about which groups were "human" and which were "animal" pervaded popular and legal discourse and provided a rationale for slavery. Later, in the eighteenth and nineteenth centuries, the scientific community tried to establish a classification system of race based on genetics and brain size. However, these efforts were largely unsuccessful.

Most scientists now agree that there are more physical similarities than differences among so-called races and have abandoned a strict biological basis for classifying racial groups.

Recent research tracing the genetic makeup of the human race concludes that there is more genetic variation within racial groups than between them, making traditional categories of race fairly meaningless. Instead, experts now take a more social scientific approach to understanding race, emphasizing that racial categories like White and Black are constructed in social historical contexts.[21]

Several arguments have been advanced to refute the physiological basis for classifying racial groups. First, racial categories vary widely throughout the world. In general, distinctions between White and Black are fairly rigid in the United States, and many people become uneasy when they are unable to categorize individuals. By contrast, Brazil recognizes a wide variety of intermediate racial categories in addition to White and Black. This indicates a cultural, rather than a biological, basis for racial classification.

---

**What Do You Think?**

What ethnic label do you prefer for yourself? In an essay in the collection *Our Voices*, Dolores Tanno describes what the labels "Spanish," "Mexican American," "Latina," and "Chicana" mean to her. She concludes by saying that each of these terms, with its own unique meaning, describes a part of her. Which aspects of yourself do your preferred terms describe?

(Source: "Names, Narratives, and the Evolution of Ethnic Identity," by Dolores Tanno, in *Our Voices* (pp. 38–41) by A. González, M. Houston, and V. Chen (Eds.), 2004, Los Angeles: Roxbury)

Second, U.S. law uses a variety of definitions in determining racial categories. The 1982 Susie Phipps case in Louisiana reopened debates about race as socially created rather than biologically determined. When Susie Phipps applied for a passport, she discovered that under Louisiana law she was Black because she was one-thirty-second African. (Her great-grandmother had been a slave.) She then sued to be reclassified as White. Not only did she consider herself White, as she grew up among Whites and attended White schools, but she also was married to a White man. Because her children were one-sixty-fourth African, however, they were legally White. Although she lost her lawsuit, the ensuing political and popular discussions persuaded Louisiana lawmakers to change the way the state classified people racially. This legal situation does not obscure the fact that social definitions of race continue to exist.[22]

Third, as their fluid nature indicates, racial categories are socially constructed. As more and more southern Europeans immigrated to the United States in the nineteenth century, the established Anglo and German society initially tried to classify some of them (Greeks, Italians, Jews) as non-White. However, members of this group realized that according to the narrower definition they might no longer form a majority and therefore would lose some power. So the notion of who was White was expanded to include all Europeans, while non-Europeans were designated as non-White.[23]

© Rena Schild/Shutterstock RF

The Black Lives Matter movement uses the hashtag #blacklivesmatter to advance its goals. Many of its issues center on the ways that police differentially treat African Americans. As you read more about this movement, think about how racial identity can be used to devalue some groups and not others, and what role race should have in our cultural values and attitudes.

**Racial identities,** then, to some extent are based on physical characteristics, but they are also constructed in fluid social contexts. The important thing to remember is that the way people construct these identities and think about race influences how they communicate with others.

*Ethnic Identity*    One's **ethnic identity** reflects a set of ideas about one's own ethnic group membership. It typically includes several dimensions: self-identification, knowledge about the ethnic culture (traditions, customs, values, behaviors), and feelings about belonging to a particular ethnic group. Ethnic identity often involves a common sense of origin and history, which may link members of ethnic groups to distant cultures in Asia, Europe, Latin America, or other locations.[24]

Ethnic identity thus means having a sense of belonging to a particular group and knowing something about the shared experiences of group members. For example, Judith grew up in an ethnic community; her parents and relatives spoke German, and her grandparents made several trips back to Germany and often talked about their German roots. This experience contributed to her own ethnic identity.

For some Americans, ethnicity is a specific and relevant concept. These people define themselves in part in relation to their roots outside the United States—as **"hyphenated Americans"** (Mexican-American, Japanese-American, Welsh-American—although the hyphen often is dropped)—or to some region prior to its being part of the United States (Navajo, Hopi, Cherokee). For others, ethnicity is a vague concept; they see themselves as "American" and reject the notion of hyphenated Americans. (We'll discuss the issues of ethnicity for White people later in the chapter.)

The question remains, What does "American" mean? And who defines it? It is important to determine what definition is being used by those who insist that we should all just be "Americans." If one's identity is "just American," how is this identity formed, and how does it influence communication with others who see themselves as hyphenated Americans?

*Racial versus Ethnic Identity*    Scholars dispute whether racial and ethnic identities are similar or different. Some scholars emphasize ethnic identity to avoid any racism inherent in a race-centered approach; others reject this interpretation. To illustrate the complexity of the distinction, even within the United States racial and ethnic categories have varied over time. The category "Hispanic" did not appear on the U.S. Census until 1980, and then it was listed as a racial category. In the 2000 Census, "Hispanic" was categorized as an ethnicity, which one could select in addition to selecting a racial identity. Therefore, one could be "Asian" and "Hispanic," or "White" and "Hispanic." Similarly, people from India were once labeled "nonwhite Caucasians," but today are categorized with "Asian Americans" on the U.S. Census.[25] These categorizations are important because historically people have been treated quite differently based upon these categories. While racial restrictions no longer remain, we continue to live with the consequences of their past existence. For example, though slavery ended almost 150 years ago, many institutions remain racially segregated, such as many churches, schools, and other social institutions, as described in Chapter 1. On the one hand, discussions about ethnicity tend to assume a "melting pot" perspective on U.S. society. On the other hand, discussions about race as shaped by U.S. history allow for racism. If we talk not about race but only about ethnicity, we cannot fully consider the effects and influences of racism.

For most White people, it is easy to comprehend the sense of belonging in an ethnic group. Clearly, for example, being Amish means following the *Ordnung* (community rules). Growing up in a German American home, Judith's identity was characterized by seriousness and a lack of expressiveness. This identity differed from that of her Italian American friends at college, who were much more expressive.

However, what it means to belong to the dominant, White culture is more elusive. It can be difficult to identify the cultural practices that link White people together. For example, we should think of Thanksgiving and the Fourth of July as primarily White holidays. And some White people feel a sense of loss as part of their ethnic identity. In order to "join" the White race and gain White privileges, many southern and eastern European immigrants had to give up their names and their heritage. While they gained many racial privileges, they gave up certain aspects of their ethnic identities. Our student describes his feelings about this loss:

> My last name is Metz, as is my father's. However, for my father the same can't be said for his entire life. My father was born with the name Gerry Maceijczyk on his birth certificate, a Polish name pronounced Ma-chey-zyk. Granted this last name is a handful to spell and pronounce, therefore, shortly after my father's birth his parents decided to change their last name from Maceijczyk to Metz. So what does this have to do with identity? Well, now that I have had the chance to really think about this, it is my heritage that has been taken from me. I cannot relate my name to that of my ancestors, even though no blood line is lost, that line of heritage is lost through a name. I cannot say that I am in any way upset about the change because I do like my last name and at the same time it gives me and my family a chance to start a new saga of the family name Metz.

Our sense of racial or ethnic identity develops over time, in stages, and through communication with others. These stages seem to reflect phases in the development of our self-understanding. They also depend to some extent on the types of groups we belong to. For example, members of many ethnic or racial groups experience common forces of oppression and so adopt attitudes and behaviors consistent with the effort to develop a strong sense of self—and group—identity. For many groups, these strong identities have served to ensure their survival.

## Physical Ability Identity

We all have a **physical ability identity** because we all have varying degrees of physical capabilities. We are all disabled in one way or another—by our height, weight, sex, or age—and we all need to work to overcome these conditions. And our physical ability, like our age, changes over a lifetime. For example, some people experience a

**What Do You Think?**

Documentary filmmaker Whitney Dow is creating an Online documentary that asks White Americans what it means to be white. Go to http://www .whitenessproject .org to see and listen to White Americans discussing their racial identity. At the top left, you'll see that there are different series as part of this larger project. What did you learn by paying attention to the voices of these White Americans? Were you offended by any of them? Why? Were you more interested in Whiteness after watching some of these? Why or why not? What did you learn about this racial identity and how does it relate to other aspects of someone's identities?

temporary disability, such as breaking a bone or experiencing limited mobility after surgery. Others are born with disabilities, or experience incremental disability, or have a sudden-onset disability (waking up quadriplegic).

According to recent reports, about one in four Americans who are 20 years old will become disabled before they retire, and about 15 percent of the world's population (or more than a billion people) are disabled.[26] In fact, people with disabilities see themselves as a cultural group and share many perceptions and communication patterns. Part of this identity involves changing how they see themselves and how others see them. For people who become disabled, there are predictable stages in coming to grips with this new identity. The first stage involves a focus on rehabilitation and physical changes. The second stage involves adjusting to the disability and the effects that it has on relationships; some friendships will not survive the disability. The final stage is "stigma incorporation," when the individual begins to integrate being disabled into his or her own definition of self. As one woman said, "I find myself telling people that this has been the worst thing that has happened to me. It has also been one of the best things. It forced me to examine what I felt about myself. . . . [C]onfidence is grounded in me, not in other people."[27]

Communication related to issues of identity often is difficult between nondisabled people and those with disabilities. Nondisabled people may not make eye contact and otherwise restrict their communication with people with disabilities. For their part, people with disabilities struggle to convey a positive identity, to communicate that their physical ability (as is true for everyone) is only one of their many identities. As one young man said, "We need friends who won't treat us as weirdo asexual second-class children or expect us to be 'Supercrips'. . . . We want to be accepted the way we are."[28]

### Religious Identity

**Religious identity** is an important dimension of many people's identities, as well as a common source of intercultural conflict. Often, religious identity gets confused with racial/ethnic identity, which means it can be problematic to view religious identity simply in terms of belonging to a particular religion. For example, when someone says, "I am Jewish," does this mean that this person practices Judaism or views Jewishness as an ethnic identity? When someone says, "That person has a Jewish last name," does this confer a Jewish religious identity? Historically, Jews have been viewed as a racial group, an ethnic group, and a religious group. Drawing distinct lines between various identities—racial, ethnic, religious, class, national, regional—can lead to stereotyping. For example, Italians and Irish are often assumed to be Catholic, while Episcopalians are frequently seen as belonging to the upper classes.

Perhaps thinking about the various boundaries of religious identity can be helpful here. What are the criteria for being a member of a particular religion? Some religions are defined by national boundaries, as is the case for various Christian Orthodox churches (e.g., the Russian, Bulgarian, or Greek Orthodox church). Some religions are defined by biology, where one is a member by DNA (e.g., Judaism is matrilineal—passed down through the mother—or one may become a member by a special ritual of "rebirth.") Other religions define membership by lineage—where a teacher, guru, or Master can initiate devotees into a "divine" line by instruction on the path to enlightenment (e.g., Hinduism, Buddhism). Very recently, religions may be defined virtually on the Internet. Here boundaries are very permeable—one's nationality, ethnicity, and gender are all negotiable. And increasing numbers of people, particularly immigrants, are turning to cyber contexts for religious expression and support.[29] However, most religions are defined by "culture" where anyone can join if they accept the beliefs (e.g., Catholic, Protestant). However, some boundaries are stronger or weaker than others. To be either a Catholic or a Protestant in Northern Ireland is almost like being a member of an ethnic (or in another way, a national) religion—and to negotiate religious identity across religious boundaries is very challenging.[30]

When one religion is acknowledged over other religions in public places, controversy can ensue. Religion traditionally is considered a private issue, and there is a stated separation of church and state. However, as noted in some countries, religion and the state are inseparable, and religion is publicly practiced.

Intercultural communication among religious groups also can be problematic. Religious differences have been at the root of conflicts from the Middle East, to Northern Ireland, to India/Pakistan, to Bosnia-Herzegovina. In the United States as well, religious conflict forced the Mormons to migrate from New York to Ohio and Illinois and then to Utah. The traditional belief is that everyone should be free to practice whatever religion they want to, but conflict can result from the imposition of one's religious beliefs on others who may not share those beliefs.

© Robert Nickelsberg/Getty Images

Some religious communities communicate and mark their religious identities through their dress. For example, some Muslim women wear head scarves to express commitment to their religious beliefs.

Currently, the religious landscape in the United States is undergoing some changes. A 2015 Pew Research Center study on religion has found that the number of Americans who identify as Christian is on the decline. In contrast, the number of Americans who do not identify with any religion is on the increase. Unaffiliated Americans are increasing not only among young people, but also older Americans, men, women, Whites, African Americans, Latinos, as well as college graduates and those with a high school education. However, the largest movement toward being religiously unaffiliated has been among younger Americans.[31] Despite the increase in the number of Americans who do not identify with any religion, religion remains an important influence in American life and religion is certainly important in some other countries and cultures around the world.

In Hungary, Csanád Szegedi, who expressed very strong anti-Semitic remarks, was popular in the far-right Jobbik Party. However, when it was discovered that he has Jewish roots, his political career collapsed. His grandmother was a survivor of Auschwitz and Dachau.[32] In this case, Mr. Szegedi's religious identity as a Presbyterian is challenged by his Jewish heritage and his anti-Semitism.

Some religious communities communicate and mark their religious differences through their dress and other consumer practices. For example, Hassidic Jewish and Muslim women wear headscarves, and Jewish men similarly wear *yarmulkes* for religious expression. Among the Amish, the shape, color, or even size of men's hats, shirts, and trousers and the style of women's dresses or bonnets can mark subtle differences between groups. Food choices can also be religious expressions, (e.g., traditional Catholics not eating meat on Fridays; Muslims and Orthodox Jews not eating pork). Other religious expressions include clothing styles and grooming (e.g., Christians may wear jewelry with crosses) or purchase of household decorations and items like candles and ornaments that mark religious holidays.[33] In order to facilitate communication and show respect across religious groups, individuals need information about the various identity expressions. However, some religions express identities less obviously and everyday interactions may not invoke them.

Even though religious convictions (or the lack thereof) are viewed as private matters in the United States, they have implications for intercultural communication. One of our students described his experience in a discussion group made up of people of faith and those (like him) who considered themselves spiritual but had no particular religious convictions:

> It became very clear that many of the beliefs held were strong ones. It is as if two different cultures were meeting. The two groups act very differently and run their lives in very different ways. I have learned that many of the stereotypes that I have labeled religious people with are false, and I would hope that this group eliminated any stereotypes that religious people may have labeled someone like me with.

### Class Identity

We seldom think about socioeconomic class as an important part of our identity—especially those in the middle class. As with race, there is invisibility associated with this dominant or normative **class identity.** Although members of the middle class rarely think about class, those in the working class are often reminded that they do not belong to the middle class. Class plays an important role in shaping our reactions to and interpretations of culture.

In our everyday language, terms like "trailer park trash" and "White trash" mark these class differences. Given their negative associations with members of the working class, not surprisingly, many Americans identify themselves as "middle class." But many people do not like to discuss class distinctions, as these conversations can range dangerously close to discussions of money—a topic to be avoided in "polite society."

Yet class identities are an important aspect of our identities in the United States, and even more so in some other societies. People use various strategies to locate individuals in the class hierarchy, as directly asking someone may be seen as impolite and may yield inaccurate information. Certain foods, for example, are viewed as "rich folks' food": lamb, white asparagus, brie, artichokes, goose, caviar. A lack of familiarity with these foods may reveal something about one's class background. People might ask where you went to college as a clue to your class background. Other signs of your class background include the words you use, the magazines you read, and the drinks you consume.[34]

Language and communication style also reflect class status. A communication scholar describes the language challenges he experienced in attending college as a working-class student: "I vividly recall coming to college saying things such as 'I seen that,' 'I ain't worried about that,' and 'that don't mean nothing to me.' I am glad my professors and friends helped me acquire a language that allowed me to succeed in mainstream American society." And the abstract philosophical conversations expected in class were very different from the working-class communication he was used to—more focused on everyday activities and getting things done.[35]

The Occupy Wall Street movement brought renewed attention to income disparity in the United States with its slogan, "We are the 99 percent."[36] Attention to income inequality, or the disparity in income and wealth in society, has gained more attention in the public sphere due to the Great Recession. If anything, income inequality continues to widen and grow with the wealthiest gaining at much higher rates than everyone else. This new focus on income inequality has had an influence on American culture. A 2016 Pew Research Center study found that "A substantial majority of Americans—65 percent—say the economic system in this country 'unfairly favors powerful interests.' Fewer than half as many (31 percent) say the system 'is generally fair to most Americans.'"[37] The Congressional Budget Office has reported that, over nearly 30 years, incomes of the lowest 20 percent of Americans has risen less than 20 percent, while the top 20 percent has seen incomes rise by 65 percent. Yet, among the top 1 percent, incomes rose by 275 percent.[38]

Despite these stark statistics, the popular belief is in the "mobility myth"—that anyone can improve his or her status through hard work and persistence, remains a strong cultural view.. One result of this mobility myth is that when poverty persists the poor are blamed. That is, they are poor because of something they did or didn't do, or were lazy, or didn't try hard enough, or were unlucky—a classic case of "blaming the victim." The media often reinforce these notions.

Working-class individuals who aren't upwardly mobile are often portrayed on TV shows (*Shameless, The Simpsons*) and in the movies as happy but unintelligent or unwilling to do what they have to do to better their lot in life. And members of the real working class, showing up increasingly as guests on talk shows like *Jerry Springer* or *The Jeremy Kyle Show*, are urged to be contentious—verbally and sometimes even physically aggressive toward each other. Thus, the images of working-class people that are served up to the mass viewing audience are hardly positive.[39]

Race and class, and sometimes gender, identities are interrelated. For example, being born African American, poor, and female increases one's chances of remaining in poverty. At the same time, however, race and class are not synonymous; there are many poor Whites and increasing numbers of wealthy African Americans. It is important to see these multiple identities as interrelated but not identical. In any event, the lack of understanding about class differences and the stereotypes perpetuated in the media often make meaningful communication between classes difficult.

## National Identity

Among our many identities is a national identity, which should not be confused with racial or ethnic identity. **National identity,** or nationality, refers to one's legal status in relation to a nation. Many U.S. citizens trace their family history to Latin America, Asia, Europe, or Africa, but their nationality, or citizenship, is with the United States.

What does it mean to be an American? When we ask our students this question, they respond in many ways. Some mention only positive things: freedom, the ability to do what one wants (within reason), economic opportunity, entertainment, and sports. Others mention unhealthy eating habits, obsession with diets, pressure to make lots of money, media determination of what is glamorous or accepted, more tax dollars spent on prisons and sports facilities than on education, and random violence on the highway and in the neighborhoods and schools. And yet, almost every student is proud of his or her national identity.

Our national identity certainly influences how we look at the world and communicate with people of other nationalities. As one of our students observed:

> The more I do to expand my cultural horizons, the more amazed I am at the way I look at life as a result of being American. There are so many things we take for granted as the only way of doing something or thinking. Like the whole individualism thing and all the behaviors and values associated with it. And there are types of people and personalities that I just never imagined before.

National identity is often influenced by how one's country is perceived on the world stage. For example, the 2016 Olympics in Rio de Janeiro placed a lot of Brazil's political and economic issues in the world's media. The impeachment of the Brazilian president was not a positive image. Yet, hosting the Olympics was meant to create a more positive international image of Brazil. Many Pakistanis resent the image of their country as one dominated by terrorists. Koreans see their powerful neighbors, China and Japan, perceived more positively while Korea (an economic and technological powerhouse) is the "by-passed country."[40]

**What Do You Think?**

Benedict Anderson has written a book *Imagined Communities*, in which he argues that nations are fictions. That is, they are imaginary constructs not directly linked to the land that supposedly contains them. Thus, we base parts of our identities on these fictions. What parts of your identity may be based on fiction?
(Source: *Imagined Communities* by Benedict Anderson, 2006, New York: Verso)

National identity may be especially complicated when a nation's status is in doubt. For example, the Civil War erupted over the attempted secession in the mid-1800s of the Confederate States of America from the United States. More recently, bloody conflicts resulted when Eritrea tried to separate from Ethiopia, and Russia annexed Crimea from the Ukraine. Less bloody conflicts also involving nationhood led to the separation of Slovakia and the Czech Republic.

Contemporary nationhood struggles are being played out as Catalonia would like to separate from Spain, Kurdistan would like to be its own country and separate from parts of Turkey, Iraq, and Syria, and French Polynesia and New Caledonia from France. Sometimes, nations disappear from the political map but persist in the social imagination and reemerge later; examples include Korea, Poland, the Ukraine, and Norway. In all of these cases, people identify with various ways of thinking about nationality.

### Regional Identity

Closely related to national identity is the notion of **regional identity.** Many regions of the world have separate but vital and important cultural identities. For example, the Scottish Highlands region of northern Scotland is distinctly different from the Lowlands to the south, and regional identity remains strong in the Highlands.

Here in the United States, regional identities remain important. Southerners, for example, often view themselves and are viewed by others as a distinct cultural group. Texas advertises itself as "A Whole Other Country," promoting its regional identity. And people from New York are often stereotyped as brash and aggressive. These stereotypes based on regional identities often lead to difficult intercultural interactions.

Some regional identities can lead to national independence movements, but more often they are cultural identities that affirm distinctive cuisines, dress, manners, and sometimes language. These identities may become important in intercultural communication situations. For example, suppose you meet someone who is Chinese. Whether that person is from Beijing, Hong Kong, or elsewhere in China may raise important communication issues, because there are many dialects of the Chinese language, including Mandarin and Cantonese.

### Personal Identity

Many issues of identity are closely tied to one's notion of self. Each of us has a **personal identity,** but it may not be unified or coherent. While we are who we think we are, we are also who others think we are. In other words, if you think you are incredibly attractive, but others do not, are you attractive? Sometimes our personal identity is largely defined by outside forces.

At other times, how we behave and communicate to others helps construct our personal identity. If you are trustworthy and reliable, others may come to see you as trustworthy and reliable, which reinforces your personal identity.

Sometimes, however, our personal identity can come into conflict with other identities. For example, not all gay men are sharp dressers and knowledgeable about fine foods, yet they often feel as if they should be. The portrayal of Cam and

Regional identities can be important. While you may think of UFOs when you think of Roswell, NM, they are proud of their identity as a regional dairy capital. Identities can be promoted in advertising, postcards, and other formats. Who gets to define what an identity means?

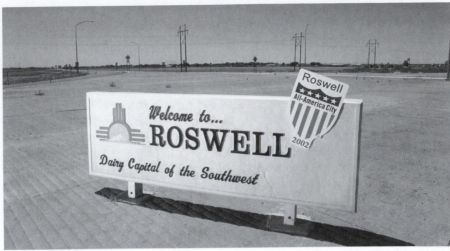

© Creatas/PunchStock RF

**What Do You Think?**

British cultural studies scholar Stuart Hall explains how he thinks of his identity and the path he has taken in life. He explains: "Instead of asking what are people's roots, we ought to think about what are their *routes*, the different points by which they have come to be now; they are, in a sense, the sum of those differences." What are the routes that you and your family have taken that explain your identities?
(Source: "A Conversation with Stuart Hall," Fall 1999, *Journal of the International Institute*, 7(1). Retrieved October 24, 2006, from http://www.umich.edu/~iinet/journal/vol7no1/Hall.htm)

Mitchell as a gay couple on *Modern Family* can often reinforce these stereotypes. As another example, some people raised in very religious families may not feel similarly about their religious identity. They may feel caught between their family's traditional religious beliefs and their own personal identities. They may feel obligated to uphold their family's traditional ways, yet not feel comfortable with those beliefs. In 2015, the Church of Jesus Christ of Latter-day Saints (more commonly known as the Mormon church) declared that "Mormons who enter into same-sex unions will be considered apostates under new church policies, and their children will be barred from blessing and baptism rituals without the permission of the faith's highest leaders."[41] This decision may force some children to choose between their religious identities, and their personal and family identities, if their parents are in a same-sex relationship.

Who we think we are is important to us, and often to those close to us, and we try to communicate that to others. We are more or less successful depending on how others respond to us. Sometimes those responses can be harsh. We use the various ways that identity is constructed to portray ourselves as we want others to see us.

## IDENTITY DEVELOPMENT

### Minority Identity Development

As mentioned previously, minority group members in the United States tend to develop a stronger sense of racial and ethnic identity than do majority group members. Whites tend to take their culture for granted; although they may develop a strong ethnic identity, they often do not really think about their racial identity.

In its four stages, **minority identity development** focuses on racial and ethnic identities but may also apply to other identities such as class, gender, or sexual orientation.[42] It is important to remember that, as with any model, this one represents the experiences of many people, but not everyone moves through these stages in exactly the same way. Some may spend more time in one stage, may experience a stage in different ways, or remain stuck in one of the early stages.

*Stage 1: Unexamined Identity*    This stage is characterized by the lack of exploration of ethnicity. Minority members may initially accept the values and attitudes of the majority culture, including negative views of their own group. They may have a strong desire to assimilate into the dominant culture, and they may express positive attitudes toward the dominant group. In this stage, their ideas about identity may come from parents or friends—if they have any interest in ethnicity.

*Stage 2: Conformity*    In this stage, individuals may have a strong desire to assimilate into the dominant culture and so internalize the values and norms of the dominant group. These individuals may have negative, self-deprecating attitudes toward themselves, as well as toward their group in general. People who criticize other members of their own group may be given negative labels such as "Uncle Toms" or "oreos" for African Americans, "bananas" for Asian Americans, "apples" for Native Americans, and "Tio Tacos" for Chicanos/as. Such labels condemn attitudes and behaviors that support the dominant White culture. This stage often continues until the person encounters a situation that causes him or her to question the dominant culture attitudes, which then starts the movement to the next stage: an ethnic identity search.

*Stage 3: Resistance and Separatism*    Many kinds of events can trigger the move to the third stage, including negative events, such as encountering discrimination or name calling. Sometimes, a growing awareness that not all the values of the dominant group are beneficial to minorities may lead to this stage. Suppose,

### Surf's Up!

While President Obama has been hailed as the first African American president of the United States, some have questioned why he has not been characterized as biracial, since his mother was white. Listen to a group of biracial Americans discuss the importance of President Obama's identity: www .npr.org/templates /story/story .php ?storyId=91375775.

© Hybrid Images/Getty Images RF

Group identities are often expressed and strengthened through communication. Which identities are expressed and affirmed by these college sorority sisters?

for example, that someone who has been denying his or her racial heritage meets another person from that racial group who exhibits a strong cultural identity. A student of ours, Amalia, recounted her experience of going to college and meeting other Chicano/a students for the first time who had strong ethnic identities and were proud to be Mexican American. She hadn't thought about her heritage very much up to that point, so this was an important experience for her. She became interested in learning about the history of Mexican Americans in the United States, and she developed a stronger sense of her own identity.

This stage may be characterized by a blanket endorsement of one's group and all the values and attitudes attributed to it. At the same time, the person may reject the values and norms associated with the dominant group. For example, at this stage, individuals may find it important to join ethnic clubs like MEChA (*Movimiento Estudiante de Chicanos d'Aztlan*), the Black Students Union, or other groups where they can discuss common interests and experiences and find support.

*Stage 4: Integration*    According to this model, the ideal outcome of the minority identity development process is the last stage, an achieved identity. People who reach this stage have a strong sense of their own group identity (based on gender, race, ethnicity, sexual orientation, and so on) and an appreciation for other cultural groups. In this stage, individuals realize that racism and other forms of oppression occur but try to redirect any anger from the previous stage in more positive ways. A Latino writer describes how he entered this stage. It happened when he shared a college apartment with students from Taipei—persons who were foreign to the United States and its prejudices and who were interested in his background. "As I spoke to them of the history of my people—something I'd always known but never before thought about—I began to internalize that history. In a sense their curiosity sparked my own. Never again could I deny it, never again would I care to."[43] The end result is a confident and secure identity for a person who wants to eliminate all forms of injustice, not just oppression aimed at his or her own group.

## Majority Identity Development

Two influential educators or scholars describe **majority identity development** for members of the dominant group. The following model differs somewhat from the minority identity model in that it is more prescriptive. That is, it doesn't represent exactly how White people's identities develop, but rather how they might move in unlearning the racism (and other "isms") that we unconsciously acquire as we grow up.[44]

*Stage 1: Unexamined Identity*    The first stage is the same as for minority individuals. People may be aware of some physical and cultural differences, but they do not fear other racial or ethnic groups or feel a sense of superiority. As our student Jenny said, "I remember in kindergarten my best friend was African American. We did everything together at school. We never even thought about the fact that we were of different races." Communication (and relationships) at this stage is not based on racial differences.

**Info Bites**

*Chicano/a* was once considered a derogatory term referring to immigrant farm workers. But due to the efforts of people like Cesar Chavez and other members of the farm workers' movement, the word has been redefined. Now, Mexican Americans use the term to help define their political struggle to participate fully in American society.

*Stage 2: Acceptance*   The second stage represents the internalization and acceptance of the basic racial inequities in society. This acceptance is largely unconscious, and individuals have no conscious identification with the dominant White culture. However, some assumptions, based on an acceptance of inequities in the larger society, are subtly racist (minority groups are culturally deprived and need help to assimilate; White culture—music, art, and literature—is "classical"; works of art by people of color are folk art or "crafts"). There is also an assumption at this stage that people of color are culturally different, whereas Whites are individuals with no group identity, culture, or shared experience of racial privilege. As a White student described it, "Where I grew up, it was all white and there was a clear sense that we were not like 'others.' Yes, we had it better, but that was because we worked harder—and the (people of color) simply did not. That was a given."[45]

At this stage, communication with minorities is either avoided or patronizing—or both. As one of our White students, Kortni, said, "I never thought about it until I took this class how I don't have any friends who aren't White. I came from a small town, and I just never really felt comfortable around people who weren't White."

Some people never move beyond this stage. If they do, it is usually the cumulative result of a number of events. Perhaps they become good friends with people of color, or they participate in a class or workshop that deals with issues of White privilege or racism. For our student Jenny, it was an undergraduate course in ethnic relations: "The professor had us read really interesting authors who talked about their experiences of growing up as people of color in the United States. I realized how little I knew about the experiences of those who aren't White." She described it as an eye-opening experience that prodded her to the next stage.

*Stage 3: Resistance*   This stage represents a major shift, from blaming minority members for their conditions to blaming the social system as the source of racial or ethnic problems. Resistance may be passive, with little behavioral change, or active—an ownership of racism. Individuals may feel embarrassed and ashamed at this stage, avoiding or minimizing their communication with other Whites and seeking out interactions with persons of color. Whites who resist are often criticized by other Whites, who may call them "race traitors" or "reverse oreos"; they may jokingly warn other Whites about dating African Americans, since "once you go Black, you never go back." This type of communication condemns attitudes and behaviors that resist dominant White culture.

*Stage 4: Redefinition and Reintegration*   In the fourth stage, as in minority identity development, people begin to refocus their energy to redefining Whiteness in nonracist terms and are finally able to integrate their Whiteness into all other facets of their identity. It is unclear why some Whites achieve this stage while others do not. Whites in this stage realize they don't have to accept the definition of White that society imposed on them. They can move beyond the connection to racism to see positive aspects of being European American and to feel more comfortable being White. They not only recognize their own identity as White but also appreciate other groups. Interestingly, at this stage there is no defensiveness about racism; individuals don't say "I'm not prejudiced." Rather, there is the recognition that prejudice and racism exist and that blame, guilt, or denial won't help solve the problem. There is also a recognition of the importance of understanding Whiteness and White identity. However, it is a big challenge to identify what White identity is for several reasons. First, because Whiteness has been the norm in U.S. society, it is often difficult to see. Next, what it means to be White in the United States is changing. As the U.S. population becomes more diverse, Whites are becoming more aware of their race and express this awareness in a variety of ways—from affinity for White supremacy groups to Wiggers (White youth adopting or co-opting Black culture) to those rejecting White privilege. These recent changes demonstrate that one single model of White identity development probably does not exist and presents a number of challenges for Whites in the United States.[46]

## Characteristics of Whiteness

What does it mean to be White in the United States? What are the characteristics of a White identity? Does some unique set of characteristics define Whiteness, just like other racial identities? For most White Americans, being White means rarely or never having to think about it. As one White student replied when asked what it is like being White:

> Whiteness to me is not having to think about being white. . . . I can make myself invisible in a majority of situations. . . . I could definitely tell my life story without mentioning race.[47]

What most Whites don't realize is that this perspective contrasts with the experiences of many people of color.

It may be difficult for most White people to describe exactly what cultural patterns are uniquely White. According to **Whiteness** experts (scholars who study inequalities among racial groups), there are at least three characteristics that many White people in the United States share: (1) an advantage of race privilege, (2) a standpoint from which White people view themselves, others, and society, and (3) a set of cultural practices, largely unrecognized by White people.[48]

### The Advantage of Race Privilege

Many white people in the United States enjoy benefits of race privilege. Some are economic, including:

- In 2010, poverty rates for Black and Hispanic were 27.4 and 26.6 percent, respectively, compared to 9.9 percent of White and 12.1 percent of Asians.[49]
- 38.2 and 35 percent of Black and Hispanic children, respectively, live in poverty, compared to 12.4 percent of White children and 13.6 percent of Asian children.[50]
- In 2011, non-Hispanic Whites continue to have the highest home ownership rates at 73.8 percent. In comparison, 58 percent of Asians, 44.9 percent of Blacks, and 46.9 of Hispanics were homeowners.[51]

Some privileges involve better health:

- White and Asian adults have the highest rates of excellent health (63 and 64 percent, respectively), while Black and American Indian/Alaska Native adults had much lower rates of excellent health (49 and 42 percent, respectively).[52]
- Hispanic children are almost twice as unlikely to have health insurance coverage compared to Black and White children (14, 6, and 6 percent, respectively).[53]

Other privileges are more social:

- Whites can wander through stores and be fairly sure that no store employees will track their movements.
- Whites are rarely asked to speak for their entire race.
- Whites see people who look like themselves most places they go.[54]

As a result of taking a Racial/Ethnic Minorities class, a White student describes her realization of some of the privileges she enjoys:

> The class is opening my eyes to the inequalities the different races possess. The inequalities affect me in all that I do, and I am only beginning to recognize them for what they entail . . . these unspoken privileges that I have been given due to my race. From the moment I wake up in the morning and listen to a white broadcaster report the white men's successes of the day, until the time I go to bed listening to a white radio broadcaster playing predominantly white music. . . . Being born in a country where white is considered normative has put me in a position where I can encounter people of my race wherever I choose to go. I will generally feel welcome and feel comfortable in most situations . . . realizations like these weren't always in my conscious thought; it wasn't until recently I came to recognize these privileges.[55]

Most Whites rarely think about these privileges. A recent study surveyed 700 students asking them to indicate how strongly they agreed or disagreed with various statements regarding the meaning of Whiteness. Students who were not White tended to agree with the following statements, whereas Whites agreed less:

- "White people have privilege in the United States."
- "When people refer to 'Americans,' it is usually Whites they have in mind."
- "White people are regarded as superior to people of other racial groups."[56]

The study shows that while Whites may not perceive their racial privilege, it is quite clearly seen by those who are not White.

At the same time, while being White in the United States is linked with privilege, the two are not synonymous. All Whites do not have power and do not have equal access to power. At times during U.S. history, some White communities were not privileged and were viewed as inferior—for example, the Irish in the early

**Pop Culture Spotlight**

In 2015, MTV aired a documentary film titled, *White People*. This film is available at HYPERLINK "http://www.lookdifferent.org/whitepeople" www.lookdifferent.org/whitepeople. It also contains additional resources and information on whiteness. Take a look at the film and some of the additional material. This film created some controversy, but it also raised some important issues. What do you think about this representation of whiteness? Is it important to talk about whiteness?

twentieth century and German Americans during World War II. There was powerful and pervasive hostility against Italians (particularly those from southern Italy) in the early twentieth century. They were stereotyped in extremely negative ways by the writers of the time:

> They are impulsive and excitable; they would rather sit and sing all day than do any work and improve their surroundings. . . .
> . . . They huddle together in the cheapest tenements, sinking in the social scale but bearing children whom we must hope to inspire for better things. . . .
> . . . They do not keep their places clean . . . they bring the district into disrepute in many ways.[57]

Discrimination and violence against Italians were common. They were prevented from employment, and even subject to lynching. However, as bad as all this was, these forms of resistance were never as violent, organized, and relentless as those directed at African Americans. Because they were considered White, Italian Americans were never prevented from owning land, marrying freely, joining unions, serving on juries, or receiving other privileges reserved for Whites.[58] There are also many poor White people now in the United States who have no economic power.

There is an emerging perception that Whiteness is not equated with privilege, particularly as demographics change in the United States and as some Whites perceive themselves to be in the minority. For example, a Chicago college professor tells the story of how her students thought that 65 percent of the population near their university was African American. They based their estimate on their observations and anecdotes. When she corrected them, they were stunned. In fact, according to the 2010 U.S. Census, the percentage of Blacks in Chicago is only 32.9 percent. How could these students be so wrong? One reason might be the growing perception among Whites that racial and ethnic minority populations are exploding in growth and that Whites will soon be the new minority. They see their own numbers decreasing and are sometimes on the defensive. This perception has caused some to be very aware of their Whiteness and to see it as somewhat of a liability: They believe they are prejudged as racist, as being held responsible for conditions they did not create, and losing out on opportunities now given unfairly to minorities.[59]

In addition, as U.S. corporations downsize and more U.S. jobs are located overseas, increasing numbers of middle-aged White men fail to achieve the economic or professional success they had hoped for. They sometimes attribute their lack of success to immigrants who will work for less or to the increasing numbers of women and minorities in the workplace. In these cases, Whiteness is not invisible; it is an important aspect of the White individuals' identities. In fact, there is probably some fear that increasing demographic power of non-White immigrants will eventually translate into political, economic, and cultural power, and then what?

> Many whites fear that the result won't be a system that is more just, but a system in which white people become the minority and could be treated as whites have long treated non-whites. This is perhaps the deepest fear that lives in the heart of

whiteness. . . . Are non-white people capable of doing to us the barbaric things we have done to them?[60]

The point is not whether these perceptions are accurate—and, indeed, many are not accurate. The reality is that most of the wealth, leadership, and power remains in the hands of Whites in the United States. Given that identities are negotiated and challenged through communication, and that people act on their perceptions and not on some external reality, perceptions related to racial identity make it difficult for Whites and Blacks to communicate effectively.

*A Standpoint from Which to View Society*    Some viewpoints are shared by many Whites, and opinion polls frequently reveal significant differences in how Whites and Blacks see many issues. According to a recent poll, 77 percent of Whites, but only 56 percent of Blacks, agreed that the position of Blacks in American society has improved in recent years. In addition, 63 percent of Whites (compared to 42 percent of Blacks) feel that Blacks who can't get ahead are mostly responsible for their own condition. The gaps on these issues have remained constant for the last decade.[61] How can the perception of race relations be so different for Whites and Blacks? Something about being White, and something about being African American, influences how people view the world and, ultimately, how they communicate.

In one research study, women were asked about their Whiteness and about White culture. Some reported that they viewed the culture as less than positive—as artificial and dominant, bland and sterile, homogeneous, and less interesting and rich than non-White culture. Others, however, viewed it as positive—as representing what was "civilized," as in classical music and fine art.[62] White identity often includes some ambivalence about being White. As these women note, there may be some elements of White culture to be proud of and others that are more problematic.

*A Set of Cultural Practices*    Is there a specific, unique "White" way of viewing the world? As noted, some views held consistently by Whites are not necessarily shared by other groups. And some cultural practices and values, such as individualism, are expressed primarily by Whites and significantly less by members of minority groups. These cultural practices are most clearly visible to those who are not White, to those groups that do not share in the privileges enjoyed by Whites.[63] For example, the celebration of Snow White's beauty—emphasizing her pure white skin—is often seen as problematic by people who are not White. Perhaps it is easier to see why Snow White is offensive if one is not White.

## MULTICULTURAL IDENTITY

Multicultural people, a group that is currently dramatically increasing in number, are those who live "on the borders" of two or more cultures. They often struggle to reconcile two very different sets of values, norms, worldviews, and lifestyles. Some have **multicultural identities** as a result of being born to parents from different racial, ethnic, religious, or national cultures, or they were adopted into families that are racially different from their own family of origin. Others are multicultural because their parents lived overseas and they grew up in cultures different from their own, or because they spent extended time in another culture as an adult or married someone from another cultural background. Let's start with those who are born into biracial or multiracial families.

## Multiracial People

According to the U.S. Census Bureau, in 2010, the United States had an estimated 9 million multiracial people—that is, people whose ancestry includes two or more races—and this number is increasing.[64] Table 4.1 shows the U.S. states with the highest percentage of multiracial people. Why might these states have the highest percentages? Which states might have the lowest percentages? The development of racial identity for multiracial children seems to be different from either majority or minority development.[65] These children learn early on that they are different from other people and that they don't fit into a neat racial category—an awareness-of-differentness stage.[66] Take our student Maureen, for example. Her mother is Korean and her father is African American. When she was 5, her family moved to a small town in northern New Mexico that was predominantly White. She recalled:

> I soon realized that I wasn't the only person who was different; the town had a large population of Hispanic and Native Americans. Yet, I also realized that I was still different from the rest of the children. It seemed that Hispanic children stayed with Hispanic children, White children with White children, Native American children with Native American children, and Asian children with Asian children. There weren't any Black children, and there definitely weren't any Black and Asian mixed children. The grouping of these children helped me realize that I was very different from all the children I went to school with. This realization left me confused and depressed.

Maureen's experience is typical of the first stage in the identity development of multiracial children.

The second stage involves a struggle for acceptance, in which these children experiment with and explore both cultures. They may feel as if they live on the cultural fringe, struggling with two sets of cultural realities and sometimes being asked to choose one racial identity over the other. This happened to Maureen. She

**TABLE 4.1   Mixed Race: States with the Highest Percentage of People Who Self-Identified as More Than One Race**

| | |
|---|---|
| 1. Hawaii (23.6%) | 6. Washington (4.7%) tie |
| 2. Alaska (7.3%) | 7. Oregon (3.8%) |
| 3. Oklahoma (5.9%) | 8. New Mexico (3.7%) |
| 4. California (4.9%) | 9. Arizona (3.4%) tie |
| 5. Nevada (4.7%) tie | 10. Colorado (3.4%) tie |

*Source:* U.S. Census Bureau. Retrieved from https://www.census.gov/prod/cen2010/briefs/c2010br-13.pdf.

was frustrated by the forms she had to fill out at school that asked her to indicate her ethnicity, because there was no space for multiracial ethnicity. She recalled, "It was explained to me that I needed to choose. I asked them if there was a possibility I could represent both, but I was firmly told that it would be a nuisance to try to identify with two different cultures for the rest of my life." As happens with some multiracial children in this stage, she chose one: "It was on this day that I officially became an African-American."

Whereas monoracial identity usually progresses toward one end state—one either resolves or doesn't resolve identity issues—biracial adolescents may resolve their identity status in several ways: they may identify with one group, both groups, or a new group (e.g., biracial people). In the final stage, self-acceptance and assertion, these children find a more secure sense of self. This exposure to more than one culture's norms and values often causes difficulty for biracial children—they may find themselves rejected alternately by both groups (not Black enough or White enough). However, most biracial children want to embrace both parents' racial/ethnic groups, as expressed by one biracial child: "I am both white and black. I ought to be able to say I'm mixed. To not say so is a lie."[67]

The family and neighborhood play a huge role in biracial children's identity development. Strong family role models and a supportive neighborhood can lead to a flexible and adaptable sense of identity—a multicultural identity. Parents play an important role in helping their biracial children develop a healthy biracial identity. They can provide supportive communication by encouraging children to embrace both minority and majority racial/ethnic backgrounds. Beth described how her mother encouraged her:

> My mom is white and she said "I love you, but the world will see you as black because you have brown skin like your dad's. Don't let that label define you. You are black but you are also part of me."

Parents can also help children cope with prejudice and discrimination they might face. Beth recalls her mother's advice:

> She said "If someone calls you the 'N' word just tell them that their use of the word shows their ignorance." She wants me to be me, and I see myself as black but I am also part of my mom who happens to be white.[68]

As you might imagine, there are many positive aspects associated with having a biracial identity. Recent studies show that the majority of biracial children embrace the cultural backgrounds of both their parents, do not find it particularly difficult to manage their competing ethnicities or races, and do not necessarily feel marginalized.[69] Table 4.2 summarizes the stages of minority, majority, and multiracial development.[70]

## Global Nomads

Individuals develop multicultural identities for other reasons. For example, **global nomads** or **third culture kids (TCKs)** grow up in many different cultural contexts because their parents move around a lot (e.g., missionaries, international business employees, or military families). According to a recent study, these children have

**TABLE 4.2  Stages in Minority, Majority, and Multiracial Identity Development**

| | STAGE | |
|---|---|---|
| *Minority* | *Majority* | *Multiracial* |
| Unexamined identity | Unexamined identity | Awareness of difference |
| Conformity | Acceptance | Struggle for acceptance |
| Resistance and separatism | Resistance | Self-acceptance and assertion |
| Integration | Redefinition and reintegration | |

unique challenges and unique opportunities. They move an average of about eight times, experience cultural rules that may be constraining (e.g., in cultures where children have less freedom), and endure periods of family separation. At the same time, they have opportunities not provided to most people—extensive travel, living in new and different places around the world. As adults they settle down and often feel the need to reconnect with other global nomads (easier now through technologies such as the Internet).[71]

President Barack Obama is a good example of a global nomad (as well as a biracial individual). His father was an African exchange student and his mother a U.S. American college student. He spent his childhood first in Hawaii and then in Indonesia when his mother and his Indonesian stepfather moved there. Like many TCKs he was separated from his family during high school when he returned to Hawaii to live with his grandparents. His stepsister credits his ability to understand people from many different backgrounds to his many intercultural experiences as a child and adolescent—like many global nomads, these experiences "gave him the ability to . . . understand people from a wide array of backgrounds. People see themselves in him . . . because he himself contains multitudes."[72]

Just like biracial children, third culture kids/global nomads often develop resilience, tolerance, and worldliness, characteristics essential for successful living in an increasingly diverse and global social and economic world.[73]

## Identity and Adaptation

People who maintain long-term romantic relationships with members of another ethnic or racial culture and children of foreign-born immigrants may also develop multicultural identities. Multicultural identities are often developed as a result of an extended stay in a foreign culture, where individuals are challenged to adapt to new ways of living. Let's examine the process of cultural adaptation.

There seem to be some common patterns of adaptation to a new culture, described as the **U-curve theory** of adaptation. In this model, migrants go through three fairly predictable phases in adapting to a new cultural situation. In the first phase, they experience excitement and anticipation, especially if they moved to the new culture voluntarily (study-abroad students, missionaries).

The second phase, culture shock (the bottom of the U-curve), happens to almost everyone in intercultural transitions. **Culture shock** is a relatively short-term feeling of disorientation, of discomfort due to the unfamiliarity of surroundings and the lack of familiar cues in the environment. However, people who are isolated from the new cultural context may experience culture shock minimally. For example, U.S. military personnel and diplomatic personnel often live in compounds overseas where they interact mainly with other Americans and have little contact with the indigenous cultures. Similarly, spouses of international students in the United States may have little contact with Americans. By contrast, corporate spouses may experience more culture shock, because they often have more contact with the host culture: placing children in schools, setting up a household, shopping, and so on.

During the culture shock phase, individuals experience disorientation and perhaps an identity crisis. Because our identities are shaped and maintained by our cultural contexts, experiences in new cultural contexts often raise questions about identities. One student in a study-abroad program in Mexico described her feelings of culture shock:

> I want to be at home—nothing feels familiar here—I'd like to be on a bus—in a theater—on a street—in a house—on the phone—ANYWHERE AND UNDERSTAND everything that's being said. I love my family and miss my friends. I'm lonely here—I'm unable to be me—conversations either elude me or make me sound like I'm 3 years old—I'm so different without my language. . . . I just ask for something simple—TO SPEAK—TO BE ME. Yet, as I think now, as I write, I see how much more than language it is—it's history— what's familiar—a lifetime—my lifetime—my home—and now I'm here—SO FAR AWAY.[74]

Notice that the challenge of language is often a big part of culture shock. The problem is the feeling that one can't really be oneself in another language—which is part of the identity crisis in cultural adaptation.

The third phase is adaptation, in which individuals gradually learn the rules and customs of the new cultural context. They may learn the language, figure out how much of themselves to change in response to the new context, and decide to change some aspects of their behavior. But they may also want to retain a sense of their previous cultural identities; each sojourner has to decide to what degree he or she wants to adapt. The student who wrote about her culture shock experiences later wrote, "Perhaps it was the rain—the downpour and the thunderstorm that preceded it. I feel good about Mexico now. The rainslick streets, the *torta Cubana* [a pastry]—the windy busride in the pitch-dark night. It's a peaceful beauty—I've regained a sense of self and space."

Although the U-curve seems to represent the experiences of many short-term sojourners, it may be too simplistic.[75] It might be more accurate to think of long-term cultural adaptation as a series of U-curves, where one alternates between feeling relatively adjusted and experiencing culture shock. Over time, the feeling of culture shock diminishes.

**Info Bites**

"The sun never set on the British Empire" because at one time Britain controlled enough colonies that it was always day somewhere in the Empire. How important is your national identity to you? Are you patriotic? Would your answer change if your nation was not a nation but a colony of another country?

**What Do You Think?**

Gloria Anzaldúa argues from what she calls the borderlands between two cultures. She also links this with racial issues involved in being *mestiza*, or of mixed heritage, as many Latinos and Latinas are. Other theorists have seized upon this notion of hybridity as something to be proud of; it also represents a rejection of years of denigration of biracial people. Do you experience living on cultural borderlands? (SOURCE: *Borderlands/La frontera: The New Mestiza* by Gloria Anzaldúa, 1987, San Francisco: Aunt Lute Books)

Culture shock occurs to almost all people who cross cultural boundaries, whether they have done so voluntarily or not. Most individuals then experience a long-term process of more or less adapting to the new culture. However, for many individuals, the long-term adaptation is not easy. Some actively resist assimilation in the short term, as is the case with many immigrants. Others resist assimilation in the long term, as is the case with religious groups like the Amish and Hutterites. Some would like to assimilate but are not welcome in the new culture, as is the case with many Latin American immigrants to the United States. And some adapt to certain aspects of the new culture but not others. In short, many people who adapt to new cultural contexts also develop multicultural identities.

### Living "On the Border"

The multicultural person is someone who comes to grips with multiple cultural realities, whether from being raised in a multiracial home or through adaptation to a new culture. This multicultural identity is defined not by a sense of belonging but by a new sense of self.[76] One of our students, Shannon, described how she has incorporated elements of Latino/a language and culture into her sense of self:

> I am white, American, raised middle class and female. All of these things make up the person I am. However, I have had the unique opportunity to be involved in numerous close relationships with people outside of my own race and ethnicity. I was engaged to a Mexican-American for nearly five years and I am also in a traditionally Latina sorority. All of my closest friends are Latino/a. As a result many of my feelings, attitudes, and my aspects of identity have changed. In particular, my language. I oftentimes use words in Spanish now because everyone around me does. For example, I'll refer to a stomach as a *panza*. This language has become a part of who I am although it does not necessarily reflect my ethnic identity.

Multicultural individuals may become "culture brokers" who facilitate intercultural interaction. However, it is important to recognize that there are stresses and tensions associated with being multicultural. These people may confuse the profound with the insignificant, lose sight of what is really important, feel fragmented, or feel a lack of authenticity.[77] Lucia, a Yaqui college student, described some of the challenges of living "on the border" between her Yaqui community and the college community:

> I get caught in the in-between. This is who I am: I'm Native American, and my belief system is to follow my Creator, walk the walk of the red road, and be aware of all things in nature around me. And then I look at the other—that is, going to school, which is geared more to the fast lane, a school of achievers. . . . When I go back to my village, I'm very special in one sense. In another sense, it makes me too smart. They still love me, but I notice I'm not like them anymore. I get sad, and it closes off communication; they don't talk to me. They think, "Now she's too intellectual."

Some people, trapped by their own multiculturalness, become "encapsulated"; others who seem to thrive on living on the border could be labeled "constructive."[78] Multicultural people with an **encapsulated identity** feel torn between different cultural identities. They have difficulty making decisions, are troubled by ambiguity, and feel pressure from both groups. They try to assimilate but never feel comfortable or "at home." As one multiracial student of ours said:

> In high school, I was the only Black student and was often left out, and when I got to college, I was thrilled that I was no longer the only Black girl, but I was different. I couldn't understand why they would want to exclude me. College has left me even more confused than elementary, junior high, or high school. I don't know if I will ever understand my culture since I am often left out of it, whatever it may be.

By contrast, multicultural people with a **constructive identity** thrive in their lives on the margins of two cultures. They see themselves, rather than others, as choice makers. They recognize the significance of being "in between," as many multicultural people do. April, a Korean American student of ours, explained:

> I still believe that I am, for lack of a better phrase, a hyphenated American because I grew up Korean in America. I am not truly Korean or American; I am somewhere in between. Yet I cannot deny that my beliefs about life stem from both my cultures. I hold many Korean notions very near my heart. Yet I am also very American.

Related to this idea of constructive identity is Communication scholar Young Yun Kim's notion of **intercultural personhood**. Kim suggests that more and more people, like April, who live on cultural borders undergo a gradual process of intercultural evolution—where one can see oneself and others as unique individuals (rather than as stereotypical categories) and at the same time as part of a larger common humanity. Furthermore, she notes that these intercultural persons are culture brokers who can "help fellow citizens see their collective 'blind spots' and to show a way of being in the world" which is much needed in today's increasingly integrated and globalized world.[79]

Even so, this identity is constantly being negotiated and explored; it is never completely easy. April went on to say, "My American selfishness fights with my Korean selflessness, my boisterous nature with my quiet contentment, my freedoms with my respect. I have had to find a way to mix those two very different cultures in my life."

## Post-Ethnicity

Recently, a new approach to racial/ethnic identity called post-ethnicity has emerged. In the post-ethnic United States, identities are very fluid and driven by personal identity preferences. As two writers for the *Washington Post* recently observed, "Post-ethnicity reflects not only a growing willingness—and ability—to cross cultures, but also the evolution of a nation in which personal identity is shaped more by cultural preferences than by skin color or ethnic heritage."[80] The freedom to cross cultures is a relatively recent phenomenon. As shown in Chapter 3, enormous social and legal barriers that prevent post-ethnicity are a part of everyday life in the United States. As these same two

**What Do You Think?**

In 1961, South Carolina placed the Confederate flag atop their capitol dome. The controversy over flying the Confederate flag and its symbolism came to a peak in 2000 when, as a compromise, it was taken down from the state capitol dome and placed in a Confederate war memorial on the capitol grounds. In 2015, in the aftermath of the murder of African American church members by Dylann Roof, the South Carolina legislature and governor agreed to remove the Confederate flag. What are some different meanings of the Confederate flag that make it controversial? What does the Confederate flag mean to you?

writers noted, however, "We aren't quite there yet."[81] What might be some reasons that we are not living in a post-ethnic society?

## SUMMARY

In this chapter, we explored some of the facets of identity and the importance of identities in intercultural communication. Identities do not develop as a smooth process and are created through communication with others. Also, they are multiple and develop in different ways in different cultures. They are dynamic and may be created for us by existing social contexts and structures and in relation to group membership. When these created identities conflict with our sense of our own identity, we need to challenge, resist, and renegotiate those identities.

We also examined how identities are multiple and reflect gender, age, race, ethnicity, physical ability, religion, class, nationality, and other aspects of our society and culture. Identities develop in several stages in relation to minority and majority group membership as well.

Finally, we discussed multicultural identities, emphasizing both the benefits and the challenges of living on the border between two or more cultural realities. It is important to try to minimize making faulty assumptions about other people's identities in intercultural interactions. We need to remember that identities are complex and subject to negotiation.

## BUILDING INTERCULTURAL SKILLS

1. Become more conscious of your own identities and how they relate to your intercultural communication. In what contexts and in which relationships do you feel most comfortable? Which aspects of your identity are most confirmed? Which identities do you most resist? Practice resisting those identities people assign to you that you're not comfortable with. Also practice communication strategies to tell people which identities are important to you and which are not.

2. Become more aware of how you assign identities to other people. What assumptions do you make about others' identities? About poor people? Older people? White people? People with disabilities? How do these assumptions influence your communication? Notice how you communicate with them based on your assumptions.

3. Practice communicating with others in ways that affirm their identities.

4. Talk about identities with your friends. Which identities are most important to them? Which identities do they resist? Which identities do they affirm?

## ACTIVITIES

1. *Stereotypes:* List some of the stereotypes that foreigners have about Americans.

   *a.* Where do you think these stereotypes come from?

   *b.* How do these stereotypes develop?

   *c.* How do these stereotypes influence communication between Americans and people from other countries?

2. *Stereotypes and prime-time TV:* Watch 4 hours of television during the next week, preferably during evening hours when there are more commercials. During the commercials, record the number of representatives from different identity groups (ethnic, racial, gender, age, class, and so on) that are included and the roles they are playing. Report on this assignment to the class, answering the following questions:

   *a.* How many different groups were represented?

   *b.* What groups were most represented? Why do you think this is so?

   *c.* What groups were least represented? Why do you think this is so?

   *d.* Were there any differences in the roles that members of the cultural groups played? Did one group play more sophisticated or glamorous roles than others?

   *e.* In how many cases were people depicted in stereotypical roles, such as African Americans as athletes or women as homemakers?

   *f.* What stereotypes were reinforced in the commercials?

   *g.* What do your findings suggest about the power of the media and their effect on identity formation and intercultural communication?

## ENDNOTES

1. CBC News. (2015, December 11). Full text of Justin Trudeau's remarks ahead of refugees' arrival. Retrieved May 10, 2016, from http://www.cbc.ca/news/canada/toronto/syrian-refugees-justin-trudeau -remarks-1.3360401.

2. Kim, E. K. (2016, April 12). Rachel Dolezal 1 year later: 'I don't have any regrets about how I identify.' *TODAY News.* Retrieved May 11, 2016, from http://www.today.com/news/rachel-dolezal-1-year-later -i-don-t-have-any-t85871.

3. Harwood, J. (2006). Communication as social identity. In G. J. Shepherd, J. St. John, & T. Striphas (Eds.), *Communication as . . . : Perspectives on theory* (pp. 84–90). Thousand Oaks, CA: Sage; Hecht, M. L. (1993). 2002—A research odyssey. *Communication Monographs, 60,* 76–82; Hecht, M. L., Warren, J. R., Jung, E., & Krieger, J. L. (2005). A communication theory of identity: Development, theoretical perspective and future directions. In W. B. Gudykunst (Ed.), *Theorizing about intercultural communication* (pp. 257–278). Thousand Oaks, CA: Sage.

4. Gergen, K. J. (1985). The social construction movement in modern psychology. *American Psychologist, 40*(3), 266–275; Gergen, K. J. (2003). Self and community in the new floating worlds. In K. Nyíri (Ed.), *Mobile democracy: Essays on society, self and politics* (pp. 103–114). Vienna: Passagen Verlag.

5. Gergen, K. J. (2002). The challenge of absent-presence. In J. Katz & M. Aakhus (Eds.), *Perpetual contact: Mobile communication, private talk, public performance* (pp. 223–227). Cambridge, UK: Cambridge University Press.

6. Lacan, J. (1977). The agency of the letter in the unconscious or reason since Freud. In *Ecrits: A selection* (A. Sheridan, Trans.) (pp. 146–178). New York, NY: Norton. (Original work published 1957).

7. Collier, M. J. (2005). Theorizing cultural identification: Critical updates and continuing evolution. In Gudykunst, pp. 235–256; Katz, J. (1995). *The invention of heterosexuality.* New York, NY: Dutton.

8. Braithwaite, D. O., & Braithwaite, C. A. (2000). Understanding communication of persons with disabilities as cultural communication. In L. A. Samovar & R. E. Porter (Eds.), *Intercultural communication: A reader* (pp. 136–145). Belmont, CA: Wadsworth.

9.  Braithwaite, D. O., & Eckstein, N. J. (2003). How people with disabilities communicatively manage assistance: Helping as instrumental social support. *Journal of Applied Communication Research, 31,* 1–26.
10. Braithwaite & Eckstein (2003), p.14.
11. Waliga, H. (2016, April 12). NC cities say they are feeling impact from HB2 backlash. *ABC 11 News.* Retrieved May 23, 2016, from http://abc11.com/politics/nc-cities-say-theyre-feeling-impact-of-hb2-backlash/1287518/.
12. Roland, A. (2003). Identity, self, and individualism in a multicultural perspective. In E. P. Salett & D. R. Koslow (Eds.), *Race, ethnicity and self: Identity in multicultural perspective* (2nd ed., pp. 3–16). Washington, DC: National MultiCultural Institute.
13. Roland (2003), p. 8. Retrieved from http://www.vindy.com/print/296810619099445.shtml.
14. Bederman, G. (1995). *Manliness and civilization: A cultural history of gender and race in the United States, 1880–1917.* Chicago, IL: University of Chicago Press.
15. Miller, N. (1995). *Out of the past: Gay and lesbian history from 1869 to the present.* New York, NY: Vintage.
16. Bleys, R. (1996). *The geography of perversion: Male-to-male sexual behavior outside the West and the ethnographic imagination, 1750–1918.* New York, NY: New York University Press.
17. Strauss, W., & Howe, N. (2006). *Millennials and the pop culture.* Great Falls, VA: LifeCourse Associates.
18. Henig, R. M. (2010, August 18). What is it about 20-somethings? Why are so many people in their 20s taking so long to grow up? *New York Times.* Retrieved September 12, 2012, from http://www.nytimes.com/2010/08/22/magazine/22Adulthood-t.html?_r=1&pagewanted=all.
19. Allen, B. J. (2004). *Difference matters: Communicating social identity.* Long Grove, IL: Waveland Press.
20. U.S. Equal Employment Opportunity Commission. (1997, January 15). Facts about age discrimination. Retrieved from http://www.eeoc.gov/facts/age.html.
21. Wells, S. (2002). *The journey of man: A genetic odyssey.* Princeton, NJ: Princeton University Press; Allen (2004).
22. Hasian, M., Jr., & Nakayama, T. K. (1999). Racial fictions and cultural identity. In J. Sloop & J. McDaniels (Eds.), *Treading judgment.* Boulder, CO: Westview Press.
23. Roediger, D. R. (2005). *Working toward Whiteness: How America's immigrants became White.* New York, NY: Basic Books.
24. Bernal, M. E., & Knight, G. (Eds.). (1993). *Ethnic identity.* Albany, NY: State University of New York Press; Spindler, G., & Spindler, L. (1990). *The American cultural dialogue.* London: Falmer Press.
25. Koshy, S. (2004). *Sexual naturalization: Asian Americans and miscegenation.* Stanford, CA: Stanford University Press.
26. Social Security Administration. (2012, July 30). Social security basic facts. Retrieved September 11, 2012, from http://www.ssa.gov/pressoffice/basicfact.htm; World Health Organization. (2011, June). Disability and health. Retrieved from http://www.who.int/mediacentre/factsheets/fs352/en/index.html.
27. Braithwaite, D. O., & Braithwaite, C. A. (2003). "Which is my good leg?" Cultural communication of persons with disabilities. In L. A. Samovar & R. Porter (Eds.), *Intercultural communication: A reader* (10th ed., pp. 165–176). Belmont, CA: Wadsworth; Braithwaite & Braithewaite (2000), p. 141.
28. Pogrebin, L. C. (1992). The same and different: Crossing boundaries of color, culture, sexual preference, disability and age. In W. B. Gudykunst & Y. Y. Kim (Eds.), *Readings on communicating with strangers* (pp. 318–332). New York, NY: McGraw-Hill.
29. Cheong, P. H., & Poon, J. (2009). Weaving webs of faith: Examining Internet use and religious communication among Chinese Protestant transmigrants. *Journal of International and Intercultural Communication, 2*(3), 189–207.
30. Barker, E. (2006). We've got to draw the boundaries somewhere: Exploration of boundaries that define locations of religious identity. *Social Compass, 53*(2), 201–213.

31. Pew Research Center. (2015, May 12). America's changing religious landscape. Retrieved May 25, 2016, from http://www.pewforum.org/files/2015/05/RLS-08-26-full-report.pdf.

32. Paterson, T. (2012, August 17). Csanad Szegedi, poster boy of Hungary's fascist right, quits after Jewish roots revealed. *The Independent*. Retrieved September 16, 2012, from http://www .independent.co.uk/news/world/europe/csanad-szegedi-poster-boy-of-hungarys-fascist-right-quits -after-jewish-roots-revealed-8054031.html.

33. Cosgel, M. M., & Minkler, L. (2004). Religious identity and consumption. *Review of Social Economy, 60*(3), 339–350.

34. Fussell, P. (1992). *Class: A guide through the American status system*. New York, NY: Touchstone Books. (Original work published 1983)

35. Engen, D. (2004). Invisible identities: Notes on class and race. In A. González, M. Houston, & V. Chen (Eds.), *Our voices: Essays in culture, ethnicity and communication* (pp. 250–255). Los Angeles, CA: Roxbury, p. 253.

36. Taylor, M. (2012, September 16). Occupy Wall Street kicks off one-year anniversary with discussions, march, and arrests. *New York Magazine*. Retrieved from http://nymag.com/daily /intel/2012/09/ows-begins-one-year-anniversary-demonstrations.html.

37. Fingerhut, H. (2016, February 10). Most Americans say U.S. economic system is unfair, but high-income Republicans disagree. Pew Research Center. Retrieved May 25, 2016, from http://www .pewresearch.org/fact-tank/2016/02/10/most-americans-say-u-s-economic-system-is-unfair-but-high -income-republicans-disagree/.

38. Eichler, A., & McAuliff, M. (2011, October 26). Income inequality reaches gilded age levels, congressional report finds. *The Huffington Post*. Retrieved September 15, 2012, from http://www .huffingtonpost.com/2011/10/26/income-inequality_n_1032632.html.

39. Moon, D. G., & Rolison, G. L. (1998). Communication of classism. In M. L. Hecht (Ed.), *Communication of prejudice* (pp. 122–135). Thousand Oaks, CA: Sage.

40. Shim, Y-j., Kim, M-S, & Martin, J. N. (2008) *Changing Korea: Understanding culture and communication*. New York, NY: Peter Lang.

41. Dobner, J. (2015, November 6). New Mormon policy makes apostates of married same-sex couples, bars children from rites. *The Salt Lake Tribune*. Retrieved May 25, 2016, from http://www.sltrib.com /home/3144035-155/new-mormon-policy-would-make-apostates.

42. Ferguson, R. (1990). Introduction: Invisible center. In R. Ferguson, M. Gever, T. M. Trinh, & C. West (Eds.), *Out there: Marginalization and contemporary cultures* (pp. 9–14). New York, NY, and Cambridge, MA: New Museum of Contemporary Art and MIT Press.

43. Manjarrez (1991), p. 61.

44. Hardiman, R. (2003). White racial identity development in the United States. In Salett & Koslow, pp. 117–136; Helms J. G. (1995). An update of the Helms White and people of color racial identity models. In J. G. Ponterotto, J. M. Casas, L. A. Suzuki, & C. M. Alexander (Eds.), *Handbook of multicultural counseling* (pp. 181–198). Thousand Oaks, CA: Sage.

45. Chesler, M. A., Peet, M., & Sevig, T. (2003). Blinded by Whiteness: The development of White college students' racial awareness. In A. W. Doane & E. Bonilla-Silva (Eds.), *White out: The continuing significance of racism* (pp. 215–230). New York, NY: Routledge, p. 223.

46. Hardiman (2003).

47. McKinney, K., & Feagin, J. R. (2003). Diverse perspectives on doing antiracism: The younger generation. In Doane & Bonilla-Silva (pp. 233–252).

48. Frankenburg, R. (1993). *White women, race matters: The social construction of Whiteness*. Minneapolis, MN: University of Minnesota Press.

49. National Poverty Center. (n.d.) Poverty in the United States: Frequently asked questions. Retrieved September 14, 2012, from http://www.npc.umich.edu/poverty/#2.

50. National Poverty Center.

51. U.S. Census Bureau Housing and Household Economic Statistics Division. (n.d.). Annual Statistics: 2011 (Including Historical Data by State and MSA), Table 22. Homeownership Rates by Race and Ethnicity of Householder: 1994 to 2011. Retrieved from http://www.census .gov/hhes/www/housing/hvs/annual11/ann11ind.html.

52. Centers for Disease Control and Prevention. (2012, January). *Summary Health Statistics for U.S. Adults: National Health Interview Survey, 2010, 10*(252): 9. Retrieved from http://www.cdc.gov/nchs/data/series/sr_10/sr10_252.pdf.

53. Centers for Disease Control and Prevention. (2011, December). *Summary Health Statistics for U.S. Children: National Health Interview Survey, 2010, 10*(250): 6. Retrieved from http://www.cdc.gov/nchs/data/series/sr_10/sr10_250.pdf.

54. For lists of White privileges, see McIntosh, P. (1995). White privilege and male privilege: A personal account of coming to see correspondences through work in Women's Studies. In M. L. Andersen & P. H. Collins (Eds.), *Race, class, and gender: An anthology* (2nd ed., pp. 76–87). Belmont, CA: Wadsworth; Kivel, P. (1996). In *Uprooting racism: How White people can work for racial justice* (pp. 28–35). Gabriola Island, BC: New Society.

55. McKinney & Feagin (2003), p. 242.

56. Bahk, C. M., & Jandt, F. E. (2004). Being White in America: Development of a scale. *Howard Journal of Communications, 15*, 57–68.

57. Guglielmo, T. A. (2003). Rethinking Whiteness historiography: The case of Italians in Chicago 1890–1945. In Doane & Bonilla-Silva, pp. 49–61.

58. Guglielmo (2003).

59. Myers, K. (2003). White fright: Reproducing white supremacy through casual discourse. In Doane & Bonilla-Silva, pp. 129–144; U.S. Census. (n.d.). *State and County Quick Facts: Chicago (city), Illinois*. Retrieved from http://quickfacts.census.gov/qfd/states/17/1714000.html.

60. Jensen, R. (2005). *The heart of Whiteness: Confronting race, racism and White privilege* (p. 5). San Francisco, CA: City Lights.

61. Allen (2004).

62. Frankenburg (1993).

63. Helms, J. (1994). *A race is a nice thing to have: A guide to being a White person*. Topeka, KS: Content Communication.

64. Humes, K. R., Jones, N. A., & Ramirez, R. R. (2011, March). *Overview of Race and Hispanic Origin: 2010*. U.S. Census Bureau, p. 4. Retrieved from http://www.census.gov/prod/cen2010/briefs/c2010br-02.pdf.

65. See Miller, R. L., Watling, J. R., Staggs, S. L., & Rotheram-Borus, M. J. (2003). Growing up biracial in the United States. In Salett & Koslow, pp. 139–167.

66. Kich, G. K. (1992). The developmental process of asserting a biracial, bicultural identity. In M. P. P. Root (Ed.), *Racially mixed people in America* (pp. 304–317). Newbury Park, CA: Sage.

67. Newsome, C. (2001). Multiple identities: The case of biracial children. In V. H. Milhouse, M. K. Asante, & P. O. Nwosu (Eds.), *Transcultural realities: Interdisciplinary perspectives on cross-cultural relations* (pp. 145–169). Thousand Oaks, CA: Sage, p. 153.

68. Newsome (2001), p. 155.

69. Miller, R. L., Watling, J. R., Staggs, S. L., & Rotheram-Borus, M. J. (2003). Growing up biracial in the United States. In Salett & Koslow, pp. 139–168; Newsome (2001).

70. Miller, Watling, Staggs, & Rotheram-Borus (2003).

71. Ender, M. G. (2002). Beyond adolescence: The experiences of adult children of military parents. In M. G. Ender (Ed.) *Military brats and other global nomads* (pp. 83–100). Westport, CT: Praeger.

72. Obama's sister talks about his childhood. (2008, February 14). CBSNews.com. Retrieved May 1, 2008, from http://www.cbsnews.com/stories/2008/02/14/politics/main3831108.shtml.

73. Ender, M. D. (1996). Recognizing healthy conflict: The postmodern self. *Global Nomad Perspectives Newsletter, 4*(1), 12–14.

74. From a student journal compiled by Jackson, R. M. (1992). *In Mexico: The autobiography of a program abroad* (p. 49). Queretaro, Mexico: Comcen Ediciones.

75. Berry, J. W. (1992). Psychology of acculturation: Understanding individuals moving between two cultures. In R. W. Brislin (Ed.), *Applied cross cultural psychology* (pp. 232–253). Newbury Park, CA: Sage.

76. Bennett, M. J. (1993). Towards ethnorelativism: A developmental model of intercultural sensitivity. In M. Paige (Ed.), *Education for the intercultural experience* (pp. 21–72). Yarmouth, ME: Intercultural Press. See also Kim, Y. Y. (2001). *Becoming intercultural*. Thousand Oaks, CA: Sage.

77. Adler, P. (1974). Beyond cultural identity: Reflections on cultural and multicultural man. *Topics in Culture Learning*, 2, 23–40.

78. Bennett, J. M. (1993). Cultural marginality: Identity issues in intercultural training. In Paige, pp. 109–136.

79. Kim, Y. Y. (2008). Intercultural personhood: Globalization and a way of being. *International Journal of Intercultural Relations*, *32*, 359–368.

80. Kotkin, J., & Tseng, T. (2003, June 16–22). All mixed up: For young Americans, old ethnic labels no longer apply. *The Washington Post National Weekly Edition*, pp. 22–23.

81. Kotkin & Tseng (2003), p. 23.

© kristian sekulic/Getty Images RF

CHAPTER FIVE

# Verbal Issues in Intercultural Communication

**STUDY OBJECTIVES**

*After reading this chapter, you should be able to:*

1. Identify and define the components of language.

2. Discuss the role that language plays within different cultures.

3. Describe ways that people deal with language and communication style differences.

4. Explain how language is related to power.

5. Discuss multilingualism and the process of moving between languages.

6. Discuss the complexities of language policies.

**KEY TERMS**

argot
back translation
bilingual
cocultural groups
code switching
communication style
equivalency
high-context communication
improvised performance
interlanguage
interpretation
language
language acquisition
language policies
low-context communication
multilingual
phonology
pragmatics
semantics
social positions
source text
syntactics
target text
third culture style
translation
verlan

*I communicate with my friends around the world—like my friends from Germany and from Venezuela—and I email, Facebook and sometimes Skype. For the most part, I feel English is such a power language, since a lot of people speak English or at least know it somewhat. So when I am speaking with my friends on Email or Facebook, they can understand me, but there are a lot of times when I talk with them, I have to use basic English because they don't understand some words, especially slang. Another thing is my friends from Venezuela are only 3 hours ahead of us but my German friends are 8 hours ahead, and they are usually online only at night (their time) after they finish their school work and dinner—which is the middle of the night for me. Here in America it seems that everyone is online all the time.*

*—Monica*

As our student Monica discovered, language is a central element in intercultural communication, whether face-to-face or online. There are often challenges, like understanding slang, and the issue of power is always present—why does Monica use English rather than German or Spanish in communicating with her friends? Online communication and other communication technologies highlight another important challenge of language—it is constantly changing. Consider the words that have become part of English (and other languages): tweet, retweet, hashtag, emoticon, troll, and sexting [*le tweet, le hashtag* (or *le mot-clic*), émoticône, and troller (to troll) in French]. In addition, social media, like twitter, makes us think carefully about language efficiency—how to communicate our idea in 140 characters (minus the usernames) or less?

In addition to these challenges, sometimes a very small misunderstanding of one simple sound or word can change the meaning in an intercultural interaction. For example, consider our student Pat's experience in his job selling motorcycles. One day he received a call from a Japanese man looking for parts for his motorcycle:

> He told me the brand, which was a Honda, and the type. He asked if we had any "changes." I then proceeded to talk about the changes to that particular motorcycle. He politely said, after I spoke for a minute without interruption, "chains." I said "motorcycle chains?" He politely said "yes." I was embarrassed but apologized. He was very receptive to my apology. I told myself that I should have asked twice since I wasn't sure. We continued our conversation and I was able to get the parts he needed.

How can we begin to understand the important role of **language** in intercultural communication? The sheer number of languages spoken in the world today, about 7,000, is staggering. The top 10 languages (Chinese, Spanish, English, Hindi-Urdu,

© Sam Diephuis/Getty Images RF

Language is an important aspect of intercultural communication, particularly when we travel internationally. People sometimes rely on universal symbols or meanings when crossing national borders.

**What Do You Think?**

• Around 175 languages in the world are spoken by fewer than 10 people.
• The language most closely related to English is Frisian (spoken in Germany and the Netherlands).
• Beware of bottles labeled "gift" in Germany. In German, *gift* means poison.
• India has 22 official languages.

*(continued)*

Arabic, Portuguese, Bengali, Russian, Japanese, and Punjabi) are spoken by nearly half the world's population[1] (see Table 5.1). Language experts estimate that 800 languages are spoken by New York City alone. How can people possibly communicate given all these different languages with more people on the move and technological connectivity to every corner of the earth? What are some of the difficulties in translating and interpreting? How can we use language to become better intercultural communicators? Is intercultural communication easier online or face-to-face? Do we use language differently online? Is it possible for two people to communicate effectively if they don't speak the same language? Should everyone learn a second or third language? These are some of the questions we explore in this chapter.

First we identify the components of language and explore the dynamic relationship between language, meaning, and perception. Next, we explore cultural variations

**TABLE 5.1  Top 10 Languages Most Commonly Spoken in the World**

| | |
|---|---|
| 1. Chinese | 6. Portuguese |
| 2. Spanish | 7. Bengali |
| 3. English | 8. Russian |
| 4. Hindi-Urdu | 9. Japanese |
| 5. Arabic | 10. Punjabi |

*Source:* https://www.alsintl.com/blog/most-common-languages/.

© Blend Images/Alamy RF

Learning another language, as some college students do, is never easy, but there are rewards. People have varying reasons for studying a language, including adapting to a new cultural context, getting a job, and traveling abroad.

of language and how people successfully communicate across these cultural variations. In the fourth section, we discuss the relationship between language and power. Finally, we examine multilingualism.

## THE STUDY OF LANGUAGE

### The Components of Language

Are there any universal aspects shared by all languages? Can the same concept be expressed in any language? Or are there ideas that can only be expressed in particular languages? For answers to these questions, we turn to the discipline of linguistics. Linguistics usually divides the study of language into four parts: phonology, semantics, syntactics, and pragmatics. Let's look at each of these components.

*Phonology*   **Phonology** is the study of the sound system of language—how words are pronounced, which units of sounds (phonemes) are meaningful for a specific language, and which sounds are universal. Because different languages use different sounds, it is often difficult for nonnative speakers to learn how to pronounce some sounds.

French, for example, has no equivalent for the voiced "th" sound (as in *mother*) or the unvoiced "th" sound (as in *think*) in English. French speakers often substitute similar sounds to pronounce English words with "th." By contrast, English speakers often have a difficult time pronouncing the French "r" (as in *la fourrure*), which is produced further back in the mouth than in English. Similarly, many English speakers have trouble "rolling the r" in Spanish, pronouncing words like *carro* (car) or *perro* (dog). English speakers also have trouble pronouncing some Japanese words

**What Do You Think? (cont.)**

- China has more English speakers than the United States.
- Which are the hardest languages to learn?
- What are some endangered languages?

To learn more about languages of the world visit http://www .allfunandgames.ca /facts/languages.shtml; http://www.bbc.co.uk /languages/guide /languages.shtml.

that contain a sound that is between the English "r" and "l" sounds—for example, the words *ramen* and *karaoke*. Also, in some African languages, sounds like "mba" and "njo" give English speakers problems because they are unfamiliar.

Languages such as Vietnamese that have tonal differences are also difficult for speakers of other languages. Vietnamese have six tones (level, high rising, low/falling, dipping-rising, high rising glottalized, and low glottalized). This means that one word (ma) can have six different meanings: ghost, check, but, tomb, horse, and rice seedling, depending on the tone.[2]

**Tones**

1. level *(không dấu)* a ă â e ê i o ô ơ u ư y ma [ mã ] = ghost
2. high rising *(dấu sắc)* á ắ ấ é ế í ó ố ớ ú ứ ý má [ má ] = cheek
3. low/falling *(dấu huyền)* à ằ ầ è ề ì ò ồ ờ ù ừ ỳ mà [ mà ] = but
4. dipping-rising *(dấu hỏi)* ả ẳ ẩ ẻ ể ỉ ỏ ổ ở ủ ử ỷ mả [ mả ] = tomb
5. high rising glottalized *(dấu ngã)* ã ẵ ẫ ẽ ễ ĩ õ ỗ ỡ ũ ữ ỹ mã [ mã' ] = horse
6. low glottalized *(dau nặng)* ạ ặ ậ ẹ ệ ị ọ ộ ợ ụ ự ỵ mạ [ mà' ] = rice seedling

**Semantics**   Semantics is the study of meaning—that is, how words communicate the meaning we intend to get across in our communication. For example, an international student ordered a cheeseburger at a fast-food restaurant, and the worker behind the counter asked him, "Is this for here or to go?" The international student understood the individual words—"for-here-or-to-go"—but not the meaning of the words strung together in that fashion.

Sometimes semantics focuses on the meaning of a single word. For example, what is a chair? Do we define a chair by its shape? Does a throne count as a chair? Do we define it by its function? If I sit on a table, does that make it a chair? Different languages have different words for the same object. Thus, the object that is called *a chair* in English is called *une chaise* in French and *la silla* in Spanish. Even different cultures that share a language, such as Great Britain and the United States, may have different words for the same object. The following list shows some differences between U.S. and British English:[3]

| *British* | *U.S.* |
|-----------|--------|
| jersey | sweater |
| pants | underwear |
| pumps | tennis shoes |
| trousers | pants |
| biscuit | cookie, cracker |
| chips | french fries |
| crisps | potato chips |
| twigs | pretzels |
| cooker | stove |
| rubber | eraser |
| loo | toilet |
| carrier bag | grocery sack |

**Surf's Up!**

Artificial languages exist around the world. Consider Elvish, pig Latin, and Klingon, to name a few. Visit www.wikihow.com/. Create-a-Language to create your own language—from devising an alphabet to coming up with your own grammar rules.

Similarly, in Mexico, a swimming pool is an *alberca,* but in Spain it is a *piscina.* Even within the United States there are semantic differences. For example, a *cabinet* in Rhode Island is often called a *milkshake* elsewhere. A *gumband* in Pittsburgh is called a *rubber band* in Phoenix.

*Syntactics*    **Syntactics** is the study of the structure of a language—the rules for combining words into meaningful sentences. One way to think of this is to consider how the order of the words in a sentence creates a particular meaning. For example, the word order in the sentence "The red car smashed into the blue car" makes a big difference in the meaning of the sentence. "The blue car smashed into the red car" means something else entirely.

In French, there is a difference between "Qu'est-ce que c'est?" and "Qu'est-ce que c'est que ça?" and "C'est quoi, ça?" Although all three questions mean "What is that?" they each emphasize something different. (Roughly translated, they mean "What's *that*?" "What *is* that?" and "That is *what*?") This illustrates that in French, meaning depends more on syntax than on the emphasis of single words in a sentence. This is often the case in English as well.

Each language has particular rules concerning the structure and expression of plurals, possessives, gender forms, subject-verb-object arrangement, and so on. For example, to express possession in English, we add an *'s* ("John's hat" or "the man's hat"). Other languages, such as Spanish, express possession through word sequence ("the hat of John" or "the hat of the man"). In English, the subject or actor is usually placed at the beginning of the sentence ("The girl ran"). By contrast, in Spanish, the subject is sometimes placed at the end of the sentence ("ran the girl"). Thus, learning a new language involves not only learning new words and their meaning but also the particular rules that govern that language. We'll give more examples of different syntactic rules in the next section.

*Pragmatics*    **Pragmatics** is the study of how language is actually used in particular contexts; the focus is on the specific purposes of language use. It is not enough to know the grammar and pronunciation of a language. We must also know how to use the language. For example, in the United States, we might ask someone, "Do you know what time it is?" A native speaker and member of that culture realizes that the correct answer is not a simple "yes."

Another example is the word "*inshallah*" (God willing) used in many Arabic-speaking cultures. Used traditionally as an expression of deep faith and a belief that all things occur (or don't occur) at God's will, the term is now used in many contexts. As one recent visitor to Egypt explained, *inshallah* is now sometimes used as a response to the question "What's your name?" The response: "Muhammad, *inshallah.*" Or in an elevator, when someone asks "Going down?" the response is "*inshallah.*" It is not enough to know the meaning and translation of the word, but a visitor would need to be familiar with the culture to know exactly how to use the word.[4]

We can employ more than one purpose for the same words. For example, if someone says "That's a lovely outfit," you might interpret it in different ways depending upon the way the speaker said it, your relationship with the speaker, and

**What Do You Think?**

One of the primary functions language serves is to communicate our feelings. Consider an experience that made you question if your words adequately express your emotions. What does this tell you about the limits of language? How might speaking many languages expand its potential to express feelings?

so on. The person might be making fun of your outfit, flirting with you, or simply giving you a compliment. So the meaning does not come from the words or the word order alone but depends on other things like nonverbal cues (facial expressions, vocal intonation), which we'll explore further in the next chapter.

## Language and Perception

Our perceptions are shaped by our language. In a way, we communicate or paint pictures with words, and this may greatly influence how we see groups of people, ourselves, or important concepts. Our language has given us a variety of pictures complete with attitudes—and much of what we hold true is actually quite incorrect. For example, we might use the word "quaint" to describe the lifestyle of people in Switzerland. However, if we visit Zurich or Berne (cities in Switzerland), we might be surprised to see gleaming glass office buildings, everyone talking on cell phones, and a bustling metropolis. This happens sometimes when we meet people from another culture and are totally surprised as to how "nice" they are. When asked, "How many of these people do you actually know?" The answer comes back "Well I've heard . . .," showing that we may have (pre)conceptions of others based only on the language we've heard (or used) to describe them.

### What Do You Think?

What you name or label something has important cultural implications. Consider the fact that on most government-sponsored forms people of Latin heritage must check "Hispanic." What power differences are revealed through institutions' use of labels? What kinds of personal power are invoked when these populations write in labels like "Latina/o, Chicana/o, Cuban American, Dominican American, Mexican American," and so forth on government forms?

*The "Power" Effects of Labels*   Another way to understand the way language and perception are intertwined is to think about how the labels we use to refer to other people and ourselves can impact perceptions. For example, in the 1960s the term "Negro" was replaced by "Black" during the civil rights movement because Black stood for racial pride, power, and rejection of the status quo. "Black is beautiful" and "Black power" became slogans during this time. In the late 1980s Black leaders proposed that "Black" be replaced with "African American," saying that this label would provide African Americans a cultural identification with their heritage and ancestral homeland.[5] The changes in these labels impact those who use and hear the terms—they have worked to strengthen group identity and facilitate the struggle for racial equality. Currently, both terms are used. Black is especially preferred by younger people, as one Black college student said, "Africa was a long time ago. Are we always going to be tethered to Africa? Spiritually I'm American. When the war starts, I'm fighting for America." Others, from the Caribbean (e.g., Jamaica, Barbados) prefer Black, or Black-Caribbean American.[6]

However, sometimes people feel trapped or misrepresented by labels, when others use labels that we don't like or that we feel inaccurately describe us. Think about how you feel when someone describes you by terms that you do not like. Many times people use labels for others without any knowledge or understanding of their meanings, origin, or even current implications, and can demonstrate prejudicial feelings.[7] For example, many descendents of Spanish-speaking people living in the United States reject the term "Hispanic" because it was a term mandated by the U.S. government and never used by the people themselves (see "What Do You Think?" on this page). In fact, in a recent survey, 71 percent said that "Hispanics" in the United States encompass many different cultures. Reflecting this notion, 51 percent said they prefer to use their family's country of origin as an ethnic label (e.g., Mexican or Cuban), and 21 percent said they use the term "American" most often.[8] Similarly, "Oriental" is a term rejected by many Asians and Asian Americans; and the word "homosexual" communicates negative characteristics about the speaker and establishes distance between the speaker and listener. Many indigenous people reject the term "Native American"—saying that it is only used by White people—preferring their more specific tribal name, or the terms American Indian or Indian. Many prefer "First Nations" people—to underscore the fact that tribes are in fact nations recognized by the U.S. government.

More recently, we can see the power of labeling when some people are labeled as "terrorists" or "freedom fighters" or "patriots." What difference does it make? What kinds of responses might someone receive from others or the government if they are labeled as a "terrorist" or a "patriot"? But if we look historically, could we call Samuel Adams a "terrorist" instead of a "patriot"? Does it depend on our perspective?

Language use is closely linked to social structure, so the messages communicated through the use of labels depend greatly on the social position of the speaker. If the speaker and listener are close friends, then the use of certain labels may not be offensive or cause a rift in the relationship. But if the speaker and listener are strangers, then these same labels might invoke anger or close the lines of communication.

*Sapir–Whorf Hypothesis*   How much of our perception is shaped by the particular language we speak? Do English speakers see the world differently from Arabic speakers? Acclaimed author Benedict Anderson asserted that a language is not simply a linguistic means of communication. It is also a way of thinking and feeling of people.[9] The idea that the particular language we speak determines our perception of reality is best represented by the Sapir–Whorf hypothesis. The hypothesis was developed by Edward Sapir and Benjamin Whorf, based on research they conducted on Native American languages. They proposed that language not only expresses ideas but also *shapes* ideas about and perceptions of the world.[10]

According to the Sapir–Whorf hypothesis, language defines our experience. For example, there are no possessives (his/her/our/your) in the Diné (Navajo) language; we might conclude, therefore, that Diné think in a particular way about the concept of possession. In contrast to English speakers, Diné may think that it's less important for individuals to own things; they may take a more communal approach to possession. The Penan people in Borneo have only one word for "he," "she," and "it," but they have six different words to express "we." This might suggest that social cooperation or collectivism is an important value for the Penan.[11]

A final example demonstrates the different ways various languages express formality and informality. English speakers do not distinguish between a formal and informal "you" (as in German, with *du* and *Sie,* and in Spanish, with *tu* and *usted*). This may mean that English speakers think about formality and informality differently than do German or Spanish speakers. And, indeed, people from outside the United States often comment on the informality of U.S. Americans, in social life, education, and business. As Geraldo, an exchange student of ours from Spain, observed, "It just amazes me how informal everyone is here—saying 'help yourself'

**What Do You Think?**

Think about how politics and social events shape our perceptions and thus the words we use. President George W. Bush, after September 11, 2001, set up Department of Homeland Security, and vowed to "protect the homeland." Some people are very uneasy about the term "homeland," find it even "creepy" and wished a different word were used.

Some say the word harkens back to dark history. Hitler very consciously used the term heimat (a German word for motherland) and converted the idea of the homeland into racial propaganda and rallying cry.

What do you think of when you hear the term "homeland"? Does the negative connotation have any meaning for you? (SOURCE: Adapted from Traub, J. (2016, April 4). The dark history of defending the "Homeland." *nytimes .com.* Retrieved

*(continued)*

**What Do You Think? (cont.)**

May 31, 2016, from http://www.nytimes.com/2016/04/10/magazine/the-dark-history-of-defending-the-homeland.html?_r=1.)

to a guest in your home and meaning it! And everyone calling each other by first names, including teachers and students. This would never happen in my country."

How close is the relationship between language and perception? Probably not as close as suggested by the Sapir–Whorf hypothesis. For example, even though cultural groups may have different words for different colors, most can identify a particular color when asked. This means that we can "see" the same colors even if we have different words to describe them. A recent study looked at the Munduruku people in rural villages in Brazil. They have no formal schooling and speak a language that has few words describing geometrical or spatial concepts, and they have no rulers, compasses, or maps. Researchers showed them diagrams with containers of various shapes and then showed them the actual containers arranged in the same way. The researchers found that the Munduruku were easily able to relate the geometrical information on the diagram to the geometrical relationships on the ground. This shows, contrary to the Sapir–Whorf hypothesis, that language is not required to think about or perceive the world in a particular way.[12] Thus, a more moderate view, in which language is a tool to communicate rather than a mirror of perception, is probably more accurate. As these examples show, however, the language we speak has a tremendous impact on what and how we communicate every day.[13] This has important implications for intercultural communication. Perhaps it's not just languages that are different; rather, it may mean that members of cultural groups really experience the world very differently and, in a sense, live in very different perceptual worlds.

## CULTURAL VARIATIONS IN LANGUAGE

Which is more important, being a good speaker or a good listener? Is it preferable to be effective at communicating verbally or nonverbally? Is it better to be direct and to the point in communicating, or is it better to take some time getting to the point? Is it more important to tell the truth or to make others feel good, even if it means being deceptive? As we'll see, different cultural groups have different answers to these questions. There are cultural variations in how language is used: differences in attitudes toward speech and silence, differences in whether meaning is more in the verbal or nonverbal communication, and differences in communication style. Let's look at each.

### Attitudes toward Speaking, Writing, and Silence

In some cultural groups, including many U.S. speech communities, speaking is highly valued. It's also important to be articulate in many contexts (interpersonal, small-group, public speaking). For example, being a good political, business, or religious leader often depends on the ability to express oneself well, or to be "quick on one's feet." In these cultural groups, a secondary, or less important, mode of communication is listening. Silence is sometimes viewed negatively. For example, people may feel bad or embarrassed if there are too many pauses or quiet moments in conversations, or they may feel that they aren't really connecting with people. Silence also can be interpreted as a sign of hostility or rejection, as when people are given "the silent treatment." It may even be interpreted as reflecting a lack of knowledge or a lack of verbal skills.[14]

By contrast, many cultural groups place a primary emphasis on silence and harmony and a secondary emphasis on speech. These groups may actually distrust speech, particularly public speech. The Amish, for example, are sometimes referred to as "the Quiet in the Land" due to their preference for silence, especially in public settings. Judith remembers being struck by the difference between her Amish friends and the non-Amish adolescents she saw in the malls in Lancaster, Pennsylvania. The non-Amish adolescents seemed so free and expressive as they roamed the malls. In fact, for some native cultures, "deeply communicative silence" is the preferred communication style and speaking is less preferred—even considered a bit risky—because it might undermine a communal "connectedness." One American Indian college student describes sitting in five hours of silence with a friend traveling in a car during an unexpected blizzard: "I don't think non-Indian people would be capable of upholding this type of silence . . . ." He goes on to say that a White person would probably give suggestions to the driver or express fear and frustration at the weather. He thought that would just distract the driver. Better to be supportive in silence. Another Indian student described feeling pressured by White instructors to speak up in class, "I'll try in every way, exams, papers but not the participation. I understand you have to live the way others do, except for that. In my culture, it's not done, it would be being boastful. I show respect where I am. It's being true to myself and who I am."[15]

Many East Asians not only distrust speech but also see the skillful use of silence as an important aspect of competent conversation; it shows the ability to read another person's mind intuitively, and it may even be a powerful way of controlling conversation. This emphasis on silence is based partly on religious teachings (Confucius rejected eloquent speaking and instead advocated hesitancy and humble talk in his philosophy of the ideal person) and partly on other cultural beliefs:

> Since ancient times, Japanese people have believed in *kotodama*, which literally means "the spirit living in words." This folk belief creates the superstition that a soul dwelling in words has a supernatural power to make anything happen simply by verbalizing it. Even in modern Japan, meaningless or careless utterance is not respected and valued.[16]

Other Asian cultures share this distrust of speech. As one of our Taiwanese students told us, "In America, sometimes students talk about half the class time. Compared to my classes in Taiwan, if a student asked too many questions or expressed his or her opinions that much, we would consider the person a show-off or insincere. Consequently, this is one of the difficulties I have experienced because of differences in culture."

Thus, it is clear that different views on silence can cause misunderstandings and even conflict in intercultural communication and that silence should be viewed as a legitimate conversational strategy. Because silence is a way of saying "no" for many cultural groups, knowing when *not* to talk in a particular cultural situation and knowing the meanings of silence is as important as knowing when and how to talk. For example, if European Americans, who think that a primary way to connect with people is through verbal communication, try to befriend Native Americans, who

© Amy Ramey/Photo Edit

In our increasingly diverse world, many languages may be represented in a given area. This sign suggests that people from many cultural backgrounds live, work, and shop in the same neighborhood.

use silence as a way to "get to know someone" and reserve talk for more intimate relationships, misunderstanding between the two groups is likely. See Table 5.2 for examples of attitudes toward speech and silence. We'll talk more about silence in the next chapter, on nonverbal communication issues.

### TABLE 5.2  Attitudes toward Speech and Silence

Often, common phrases reveal cultural attitudes toward speaking and silence. Note the following examples:

> It is what people say that gets them into trouble. (Japanese)
>
> A loud voice shows an empty head. (Finland)
>
> To be always talking is against nature. (Taoist saying)
>
> One who speaks does not know. (Taoist saying)
>
> The cat that does not mew catches rats. (Japanese)

*Source:* Non-western perspectives on human communication: implications for theory and practice by KIM, MIN-SUN. Copyright 2002. Reproduced with permission of SAGE PUBLICATIONS INC. BOOKS in the format Republish in a textbook via Copyright Clearance Center.

The relationship between writing and speaking differs across cultures. In the United States (and other Western cultures), we often emphasize writing over speaking. Having something in writing, such as a written contract, is far more powerful than a verbal promise. We often ask "Did you get that in writing?" to emphasize the importance of any agreement. Writing is clearly valued over speaking in these cultural contexts. In some cultures, however, oral communication is valued more highly than written communication. Publicly saying that you make a commitment is highly valued and seen as more significant than signing a paper. In the United States, remnants of valuing oral communication can be seen in the importance of saying "I do" when getting married, as opposed to signing a marriage license.

## Variations in Communication Style

**Communication style** combines verbal and nonverbal elements. It refers to the way people use language, and it helps listeners understand how to interpret verbal messages. Recognizing different communication styles helps us understand cultural differences that extend beyond the words we speak. There are at least three distinct dimensions of communication style: high-/low-context, direct/indirect, and elaborated/understated.

*High-/Low-Context Styles*   A primary way in which cultural groups differ in communication style is a preference for **high-context** or **low-context communication.** A high-context communication style is one in which "most of the information is either in the physical context or internalized in the person, while very little is in the coded, explicit, transmitted part of the message."[17] This style of communication emphasizes understanding messages without directly stating the meaning in verbal communication. People in long-term relationships often use this style of communication, as the meaning is assumed to be understood by the other person.

In contrast, low-context communication places the majority of meaning and information in the verbal message. This style of communication, which emphasizes being explicit, is highly valued in many cultures where they feel it is better to get to the point, be explicit, and not leave things unstated. Consider this conversation:

Robert:   What's for dinner?

Patricia:   There's a great movie playing, and Barbara told me about this new Thai restaurant that's next to the Scottsdale 24-plex.

Robert:   We could have the burritos we got the other night from Chili's.

Patricia:   Whatever.

Patricia is using a high-context communication style. In this rather indirect style, most of the information is not in the verbal message; rather, the meaning is in the context or is internalized in the speaker.[18] This style emphasizes understanding messages without direct verbal communication. Often people in long-term relationships communicate in this style. For example, one partner may send a meaningful glance across the room at a party, and the other knows that it is time to go home.

In contrast, Robert's style is low-context communication, with most of the meaning contained in the spoken word. Low-context communication emphasizes

**What Do You Think?**
We often guess where people are from in the United States based on their "accent," especially the stronger ones such as those of a Bostonian or a New Yorker. Do you think you have an accent? Do you think it is possible not to have an accent? To find out what kind of accent you have, take this quiz: http://www.gotoquiz.com/what_american_accent_do_you_have.

**Surf's Up!**
The history of the English language stretches over a great amount of time and a number of countries. Go to http://www .wordorigins.org /index.php/site /comments/a_very _brief_history_of_the _english_language3/ for a glimpse at the evolutions it has gone through and diverse influences that the English language encompasses.

explicit verbal statements ("What's for dinner?" "We could have the burritos . . ."). In most contexts in the United States, this style of communication is highly valued. For example, in business contexts, people are encouraged to value verbal communication, to make words "mean what they say."[19] Interpersonal communication textbooks often stress that we should not rely on nonverbal, contextual information. It is better to be explicit than ambiguous.

By contrast, cultural groups around the world value high-context communication. In these groups, children and adolescents are encouraged to pay close attention to contextual cues (body language, environment), and not just the words spoken in a conversation. For example, a Japanese student told us how his mother encouraged him to try to understand what a neighbor was really saying when making a comment that they (the neighbors) would be going away for a while. As the student recalled, he eventually understood that the neighbor actually was indirectly asking for help in caring for the yard while they would be away. The meaning was not in the words expressed, but in the context—the relationship between the two families, who had been neighbors for a long time.

*Direct/Indirect Styles*   The indirect/direct dimension is closely related to high- and low-context communication. A direct communication style, like Robert's, is one in which verbal messages reveal the speaker's true intentions, needs, wants, and desires; the emphasis is on low-context communication. An indirect style, like Patricia's, is one in which verbal messages may obscure or minimize the speaker's true intentions, needs, wants, and desires; the emphasis is on high-context communication. For example, Patricia didn't directly tell Robert that she preferred to go out for dinner, but the implication was evident.

Many English speakers in the United States view the direct speech style as the most appropriate in most contexts. Although "white lies" may be permitted in some situations, the preference is for honesty, openness, individualism, and forthrightness, especially in business contexts:

> White male business executives tend to be clear, specific, and direct in their verbal communication, even if it means dealing with unpleasant realities. As they like to say: "Let's lay our cards on the table, shall we?" Or, "Let's stop beating around the bush and get to the point." [They] generally do not place a high value upon indirection or ambiguity, certainly not as much as some Asian Americans. Even in personal discussion, let alone a more impersonal business conversation, directness frequently is chosen over sensitivity toward feelings.[20]

By contrast, some cultural groups prefer a more indirect style, with an emphasis on high-context communication. Preserving the harmony of relationships has a higher priority than complete honesty. A speaker might look for a "soft" way to communicate that there is a problem in the relationship, perhaps providing contextual cues. For example, three Indonesian students living in the United States were invited by their advisor to participate in a cross-cultural training workshop. They did not want to participate, nor did they have the time. But they did not want to offend their professor, whom they held in high regard. Rather than tell him that they couldn't attend, they simply didn't return his calls and didn't show up for the workshop.

Fekri, a student of ours from Tunisia, had been in the United States for several months before he realized that if one was asked directions and didn't know the location of the place, one should tell the truth instead of making up an answer. He explained that he had been taught that it was better to engage in conversation, to give a person some response, than to disappoint the person by revealing that he didn't know.

Differing communication styles are responsible for many problems that arise between men and women and between persons from different ethnic groups. Many problems are caused by different priorities with regard to truth, honesty, harmony, and conflict avoidance in relationships. Perhaps you can think of times when you tried to protect someone's feelings by communicating indirectly but that person preferred a more direct style. Or perhaps you tend to be more direct, valuing honesty over relationship harmony. For example, our student Janelle has two roommates who both preferred a more indirect style of communicating. When there are conflicts among the three, Janelle tended to "tell it like it is," even if it meant saying negative things. It took her a while to realize that her roommates were offended by her direct, low-context way of speaking. And, of course, they didn't tell her they were offended because that would have required more direct communication, which they were uncomfortable with. They eventually solved their communication problem when Janelle learned to be more indirect and began to ask them if things were going OK, and her roommates learned to be a bit more direct with Janelle. We'll talk later about the importance of flexibility and adaptability in communicating effectively across cultures.

*Elaborated/Understated Styles*   This dimension refers to the quantity of talk that people value and is related to attitudes toward speech and silence. The elaborate style involves the use of rich, expressive language in everyday conversation. For example, Arabic speakers use many metaphorical expressions in everyday speech. In this style, a simple, assertive statement means little, and the listener might believe the opposite. Thus, if my host asks me if I've had enough to eat and I simply respond, "Yes," the host may not believe me; I need to elaborate.

By contrast, in the understated style, simple assertions and silence are valued. Amish people often use this style of communication. A common refrain is, "If you can't say anything good, don't say anything at all." Free self-expression is not encouraged. Silence is especially appropriate in ambiguous situations; that is, if one is unsure of what is going on, it is better to remain silent.

In international political settings, visible differences in style can highlight these cultural variations. Two speeches concerning the Libyan conflict in the spring 2011—one by President Obama and one by Libyan leader Muammar Gaddafi—reveal striking differences. In February 2011, there was an uprising of many Libyan people against Gaddafi. Gaddafi responded by severe reprisals against the protestors. Obama made the decision to send U.S. troops along with other NATO forces to stop Gaddafi's forces, and on March 28, 2011, Obama explained U.S. plans in a speech to the U.S. people using a direct and rather understated style:

> Let me be clear, these terms are not negotiable. These terms are not subject to negotiation. If Qaddafi does not comply with the resolution, the international

**Info Bites**

Verbal communication is often the source of misunderstandings in cross-cultural encounters. However, nonverbal communication is not without its potential for misunderstandings. When ordering something to drink in a restaurant in Germany, be sure to hold up your thumb for one drink because the index finger represents the number two in most German cities.

community will impose consequences, and the resolution will be enforced through military action. . . . Our goal is focused, our cause is just, and our coalition is strong. Thank you very much. (from: https://www.whitehouse.gov/the-press-office/2011/03/18/remarks-president-situation-libya).

Gaddafi addressed *his* people in a long, 75-minute speech, full of metaphors and historical references, a more elaborated style:

> I am bigger than any Rank, I am a Revolutionary, I am the Bedouin from oasis that brought victory to enjoy it from generation to generation . . . We cannot hinder the process of this revolution from these greasy rats and cats. I am paying the price for staying here and my grandfather, Abdus Salam Bomanyar, who fell a martyr in 1911 . . . I have not yet ordered the use of force, not yet ordered one bullet to be fired . . . when I do, everything will burn. Come out of your homes, those who love Muammar Gaddafi. Women, men, girls, boys, those who side with Muammar Gaddafi and the revolution. . . . As from tomorrow, no, as from tonight, actually, people in Libyan cities and towns . . . chase [the protesters], arrest them, hand them over to the security [forces]. No sound person has taken part in these actions, they are all children. . . . Take your children back. They are drugging your children. They are making your children drunk and they're sending them to hell. Your children will die. I will not leave the country and will die as a martyr. (from: https://docs.google.com/document/d/10dy5oLJY2QL7k2VuwKonUpSgCUX-_9ATQ-134Xka9fs/edit?hl=en&pref=2&pli=1#)

While some analysts were quick to point out that Gaddafi is prone to extreme language and not held in high regard by many Arab leaders, other experts point to the particular challenges of the Arab language as it is spoken today. The classical form of the Arabic language (that based on the Qur'an), while rich and poetic, is actually nobody's mother tongue. Each Arab country/region has its own local dialect. A former British ambassador to Libya noted that Gaddafi's personal speaking style was often unintelligible to anyone who doesn't speak the Libyan dialect and clearly reflected his Bedouin background—where elaborated speech is commonplace and people talk for hours at a time; Gaddafi's speeches regularly went on for three or four hours at a stretch.[21] These different uses of language communicate different things to their culturally different audiences.

Other studies compare communication styles used by two different speech communities, like different age groups. You have probably noticed that you communicate differently from your parents and grandparents, especially online and texting. (Do your parents and grandparents know the meaning of "Netflix and chill," FOMO, Bae, ICYMI, and TBT?) (For implications of this new "language," see "What Do You Think?" on this page.) These age-related communication differences also extend to the workplace. As it turns out, Millennials (those born between 1982 and 2001) prefer digital communication at work and are not as skilled at face-to-face communication; In comparison, Gen Xers (1965–1982) tend to communicate in a more blunt and direct fashion, use e-mail as #1 digital tool and use informal

**What Do You Think?**

There are now more mobile phones than people in the world, according to a UN poll. Text messaging has different grammatical standards and many abbreviations. In many cases correct spelling is ignored and verbs are not conjugated and vowels are omitted (btwn, pls). Some people think that the text messaging language has now destroyed people's English language skills, while others say that language is not a static thing, change is the one constant in life, and changes in language simply reflect the changes in a particular society. For more details of the pros and cons of this question, go to http://englishlive.ef.com/blog/is-text-messaging-ruining-the-english-language/.

communication style. The older generation, Baby Boomers, tend to communicate in a direct but diplomatic fashion, prefer face-to-face communication but can use digital communication. These communication style differences have caused some conflicts and business experts have written extensively on how to manage multi-generational workplaces.[22]

## Influence of Interactive Media Use on Communication Style

Some experts wonder about the influence of new communication technologies on communication style. In general, e-mail, text messaging, and especially Twitter all emphasize low-context, direct, and understated communication. Do the prevalence of these social media platforms worldwide ultimately promote and lead to more direct, low-context, understated communication style regardless of our cultural background? Probably not, for several reasons. First, interactive media provides increasing opportunities to provide contextual information along with our words; we add emoticons, emojis, and stickers to our texts as well as photos and videos in order to convey more emotional meanings to our messages. Second, not everyone adopts or uses all available technologies. Business experts report that in many countries where high context, indirect communication is preferred, even though digital communication is prevalent and available (and used in marketing), business people prefer face-to-face contact or telephone (especially for initial contacts) (http://www.aperianglobal.com).

Third, people may adopt the technologies to their own style. For example, high-context communicators may use Skype and/or video teleconferencing rather than e-mail because video and audio allows for more contextual cues. We will address this further in Chapter 11 when we look at how businesses in different countries use communication technologies and virtual communication. In addition to highlighting cultural differences in language, interactive media also has an enormous impact on slang and humor, discussed in the following section.

## Variations in Slang and Humor

Another cultural variation in language use is slang, as our student Monica, in the chapter opener, discovered. Slang is generally wittier and more creative than standard language and serves an important function—it establishes a sense of community identity among its users. Slang is particularly important for youth cultures; it's almost imperative to invent slang that belongs to *each* generation, unintelligible to parents and other adults. The whole point of slang is to keep your language separate, but using social media means that one can make a video or a Vine, the link goes viral and soon 2 billion people are using the word. But the word may not endure. Social media has really "shortened the shelf life" of slang. It is not only created more quickly due to social media and technology, but goes out of style faster because once a new slang word reaches a wider audience it loses its value.[23]

International students struggle to learn slang, as well as parents and grandparents who are mystified by the language of their children. What makes it particularly

**What Do You Think?**

In the United States, we are experiencing growth in the popularity and use of personal communication technologies such as text messaging. How do technologies such as this change or expand how you understand different communication styles?

## Info Bites

Knowing another language isn't necessarily enough to communicate well. Consider all the slang used by speakers in every language. Here's some U.S. American slang from a website for students trying to learn English (and these are just the A's and B's of the alphabet):

Abs
BAE
Benjamins
To be bent on doing something
Bling
Bogus
Booty
To be broke

To see more English slang terms go to http://www .coolamericanenglish .com/american-english -slang.php.

challenging is the fact that slang is dynamic and can be fleeting. Outsiders need to use just the right amount when learning the slang of a particular culture (see "Info Bites"). Using too much slang, or in inappropriate contexts, can sound awkward to the "native" listener, like when your parents try to use your slang or when a foreign student uses lots of slang, but makes mistakes in grammar and pronunciation.

Humor can be another cultural language variation that presents challenges. Trying to use humor in a foreign language can be really challenging because the basis of humor is so often linked to particular cultural experiences (or history). For example, understanding Chinese sarcasm requires a thorough understanding of Chinese history and politics, because sarcasm is often used in a very subtle way to criticize someone (often politicians) without losing face. Thus, one way to mock present politicians is by criticizing an ancient Chinese emperor who was evil because he killed scholars and oppressed the peasants. A foreigner might not get the true humor (sarcasm) at all, but Chinese listeners would understand.

Humor in written, online communication is extremely challenging, because humor often relies on tone of voice (e.g., sarcasm), facial expressions, and other nonverbal cues that are absent in these communication media. The best advice to cultural outsiders or language learners is to use humor and slang fairly sparingly, if at all, especially in online communication.

## Variations in Contextual Rules

While recognizing that there are differences in communication styles, we need to avoid stereotyping specific groups (such as Japanese or English speakers) in terms of style. No group uses a particular communication style all the time. It is also important to realize that the particular style we use may vary from context to context. Think of the contexts in which you communicate during the day—classroom, family, work, and so on—and about how you alter your communication to suit these contexts. For example, you may be more direct in your family contexts and less direct in classroom settings.

Let's look more closely at how different communication styles vary from context to context and may reflect the values of cultural groups. For example, you may use high-context, informal communication in interaction with friends and more low-context, formal language with your professors. One of our students explained how she varies her communication from context to context:

> I have interacted with a variety of different people such as parents, sisters, friends, teachers, grandparents, and certain businesses. I have noticed with each set of different people I have altered my communication methods according to the person and the situation. For instance, with teachers I make sure to always use proper grammar and talk more professionally. On the other hand, when I am chatting with a friend online the communication is a lot more informal and I often use slang, abbreviations, and even improper grammar out of laziness since it is just my friend and it really doesn't matter. When I am writing an e-mail to my parents my wording and language is more formal than with a friend but less formal than with a business per say. If I am writing an important e-mail to a

manager, to make up for nonverbal cues such as proper attire, I may elaborate my speech more than I would in person to sound more professional.

Many research studies have examined the rules for the use of socially situated language in specific contexts. They attempt to identify contexts and then "discover" the rules that apply in these contexts for a given speech community. For example, several studies examined gender differences in the interpersonal communication "rules" of text messaging for men and women in India. It turns out that Indian women reported negative reactions from parents, extended family members, husbands, and male friends when sending or reading text messages in their presence, mostly at home.

In addition, they reported being subjected to "Eve Teasing," a form of interpersonal harassment by males who observed them text messaging in public. However, women also report the creative strategies they used to deal with these situations. They would store phone numbers of male friends under female names, some erased all text messages daily, and others communicated through SNSs (e.g., Facebook) rather than texting, so that their parents and brothers wouldn't know who they were texting. In public places, women would report the harassment, or simply not text in public. The study concludes that these differential "textiquettes" (text messaging rules) for women and men reflect the unequal power relations between men and women in India and that women texting may pose some threat to male authority figures.[24]

As we've seen, people communicate differently in different cultural communities. Thus, the context in which the communication occurs is a significant part of the meaning. And while we might communicate in one way in one culture, we might change our communication style for another culture. People who live "on the border" between two different cultures often do this with ease. It's called **code switching.** A colleague of ours can always tell whether her daughter Shaquina is talking to her African American or White friends on the phone, because she uses a different language code. Many Spanish-speaking students do the same thing, speaking "Spanglish" among themselves and then code switching to Standard English when speaking to their professors in class. Native American students who travel between their nations and university campuses may also code switch, being more direct and personal in their university context and then being more indirect and contextual at home. Understanding the dynamics of various speech communities helps us see the range of communication styles.

## COMMUNICATING ACROSS DIFFERENCES

Given all these differences in language use and communication styles, how can people successfully communicate with people from different cultures? Sometimes fear can get in our way. One of our students, Emily, described her nervousness in trying to communicate in French:

> Before leaving for France, I thought I was fully prepared for what to expect. I had, at that point, taken four years of French. When I was out to dinner with my "host" sister, one of her friends asked me in French, "What is your name?" I

**Info Bites**

English is one of the most difficult languages to learn, partly because there are a lot of homonyms (words with the same pronunciation but different meaning), homophones (words that sound alike— to, too, two) and homographs (same spelling, different pronunciation, different meanings, e.g., desert (abandon, area of land). Examples:

- The bandage was wound around the wound.
- The farm was used to produce produce.
- We must polish the Polish furniture.
- Since there is no time like the present, he thought it was time to present the present.

For more examples go to http://www .englishlearnsite.com /general/10-reason -why-english-is-weird/.

**What Do You Think?**

Are you bilingual? Multilingual? Do you or your friends ever code-switch?

A recent informal survey revealed several primary motivations for code switching:

1. *Lizard brains* take over. Sometimes people just switch to another language or accent without thinking about it. One young Japanese American woman described how she went with Japanese relatives to a popular horror house and she got so frightened, she dropped her fluent Japanese and started screaming in English (much to the amusement of staff and her relatives).

2. To fit in. People often code-switch to talk and act more like those around them. Spanish teacher in Nashville who picked up the Southern, African American English dialect of his students forgot to switch to standard

*(continued)*

was so nervous and trying so hard to understand her native accent, but I couldn't make out her sentence. After asking me multiple times, slowly, she ended up asking me in English. Needless to say, it was embarrassing because it was one of the most elementary sentences and I couldn't understand!

Even when people speak the same language, there can be differences in communication style and language use. In this situation, which style should dominate? It probably depends on the context. In situations like Emily's, a foreigner is generally expected to adapt to the language and communication style of the host country. Usually both persons try to adapt somewhat to the language and style of the other—creating together what is sometimes called a **third culture style.** That is, when two people try to adapt to each other, they sometimes end up constructing a style that is not exactly like either of their styles!

Another way of thinking about intercultural interaction is as two people putting together an **"improvised performance."** In intercultural interaction, we don't have a ready-made conversation script (like we do in our familiar cultural contexts), and we might feel like we are just making up the performance as we go. As we become more skillful at intercultural communication, we can better "sense" where one person is going, and we try to follow and adapt, like a dance or an improvised performance. As we mentioned previously, this improvisation involves being flexible and adapting to the situation.

Mary Catherine Bateson, a famous anthropologist, gives an example of an intercultural improvisation when meeting her Armenian husband's extended family for the first time. She was uncertain about whom she should and should not kiss in greeting them. She assumed she should probably kiss the mother, the brother, and the sister, so she did. But should she kiss the sister's husband? the sister's husband's brother? She wasn't sure. She describes how they improvised:

> So I kissed the sister's husband, and I could feel in the set of his shoulder muscles that I had done the wrong thing, and at least I knew better than to kiss his brother. I was only a little off in this particular improvisation and there was good will to spare.[25]

We improvise verbally in similar ways. For example, if we are speaking to someone whose native language is not English, we might follow that person's lead and speak a little slower, using less slang. We might adapt to the speaker's use of gestures and eye contact (or lack of both), which might not exactly follow our own set of cultural rules. Our student Carrie explained her strategies for communicating with her Aunt Josephina (from Mexico) while visiting here around the holidays when lots of cooking is involved:

> I ask her "can I help you with that?" rather than something longer like "would you rather I help cook or should I just wait and do the dishes after?" Second, I also find that using visual aids to support what you are saying to be helpful. In my aunt's case, and mine this usually included hand gestures such as pointing specific things out which she was usually able to put together what I was saying or asking about. And third, of course, speaking slowly and being

patient with the person you are speaking to who is not fluent in English. Showing frustration is only going to embarrass or degrade the person who you are speaking to and ultimately lead them to pull back and stop communicating altogether.

## LANGUAGE AND POWER

All language is social and powerful and complicates the view of intercultural interaction as third culture building or an improvised performance. The language that is used, the words and the meanings that are communicated, depends not only on the context but also on the social relations that are part of that interaction. For example, bosses and workers may use the same words, but the meanings that are communicated may differ. A boss and a worker may both refer to the company personnel as a "family." To the boss, this may mean "one big happy family," while to a disgruntled employee, it may mean a "dysfunctional family." To some extent, the difference is due to the power differential between boss and worker.

Language is powerful and can have tremendous implications for people's lives. For example, saying the words "I do" can influence lives dramatically. Being called names can be hurtful, despite the old adage "sticks and stones may break my bones, but words will never hurt me." In this section, we show how language is related to social position and is used by **cocultural groups**—groups that are not dominant within society's social structure.

### Language and Social Position

Just as organizations have particular structures and specific job positions within them, societies are structured so that individuals occupy **social positions**—social constructs embedded with assumptions about gender, race, class, age, sexuality, and so on. Differences in social positions are central to understanding communication. For one thing, not all positions within society are equivalent; everyone is not the same. Thus, for example, when men whistle at a woman walking by, it has a different force and meaning than if women were to whistle at a man walking by.

Power is a central element, by extension, of this focus on differences in social position. When a judge in court says what he or she thinks freedom of speech means, it carries much greater force than when your neighbor who is not a judge gives an opinion about what this phrase means. Furthermore, if the speaker is in a position of power, then he or she has potentially a greater impact. For example, when politicians deliver messages that contain racist, anti-Semitic, or other ideologies of intolerance, many people become concerned because of the influence they may have. These concerns were raised in 2016 over anti-immigrant, anti-Semitic, anti-Islam comments by many of the leaders of the growing right-wing populism in Europe (e.g., Austria's Norbert Hofer of the Freedom party; France's Marine Le Pen of the National Front; Poland's Pawel Kukiz, and others), and similar concerns have arisen over the political discourse of U. S. political leaders Donald Trump and Ted Cruz that openly and explicitly voice anti-Muslim and anti-immigrant views.

## What Do You Think? (cont.)

English when his boss asked him if he had forgot to return a book and the teacher replied, "Nah, you flaugin' bruh, I put that on your desk yesterday."

3. To get something. People in the service industry report that a Southern accent is a "surefire way to get tips" and almost everyone working in their restaurant starts using "you'all" from day one. For more reasons to code switch, see. Thompson, M. (2013, April 13). Five reasons why people code-switch. *NPR Blog—CodeSwitch: Race and Identity Remixed.* Available at http://www.npr.org/sections/codeswitch/2013/04/13/177126294/five-reasons-why-people-code-switch.)

Groups also hold different positions of power in society. Groups with the most power (Whites, men, heterosexuals)—consciously or unconsciously—use a communication system that supports their perception of the world. This means that cocultural groups (ethnic minorities, women, gays, and transgender individuals) have to function within communication systems that may not represent their lived experience. These nondominant groups find themselves in struggles: Do they try to adapt to dominant communication, or do they maintain their own styles?

There seem to be three general answers to this question of how cocultural groups can relate to the more powerful (dominant) groups. They can communicate nonassertively, assertively, or aggressively. Within each of these communication postures, cocultural individuals may emphasize assimilation—trying to become like the dominant group—or they can try to accommodate or adapt to the dominant group. They can also try to remain separate from the dominant groups as much as possible.[26] The point here is that there are both costs and benefits for cocultural members when they choose which of these strategies to use. Because language is structured in ways that do not reflect their experiences, they must adopt some strategy for dealing with the linguistic framework. For example, if Nick wants to refer to his relationship with James, does he use the word "boyfriend," "friend," "roommate," "husband," "partner," or some other word? If Nick and James are married should they each refer to their husband when they are in contexts where same sex marriage is a contentious topic? What about at work? A party? A bar? What might the consequences be in each of these situations? Let's look at how these strategies might work and the costs and the benefits of them.

These three sets of orientations result in nine types of communication strategies. Which strategy is chosen depends on many things, including the desired outcome, perceived costs and rewards, and the context. Let's look at each of these orientations; Table 5.3 gives a summary.

### Assimilation Strategies

Some cocultural individuals may use nonassertive assimilation strategies. These communication strategies emphasize trying to fit into and be accepted by the dominant group. Such strategies might be self-censoring ("I'd better be careful about what I say in this organization to make sure I don't offend those in power"), and, above all, avoid controversy ("I apologized in an attempt to diffuse the situation").

There are both costs and benefits for cocultural members who use these strategies. For example, women and members of ethnic minorities may use these strategies at work if they feel that their job success depends on not "making waves"—so they may benefit by keeping their job. For instance, they may keep quiet when they hear offensive or noninclusive remarks, such as a boss's use of "girls" to refer to female staff members. However, there are potential costs as well, for both cocultural members and the dominant group. The cocultural person may experience a lowering of self-esteem due to the feeling that he or she cannot be authentic. In addition, these kinds of strategies can foster an unhealthy communication climate that reinforces the dominant group's social and political power. For example, many African Americans have a distrust of primarily White-run medical institutions. There is a general feeling

**TABLE 5.3  Cocultural Communication Orientations**

|  | ASSIMILATION | ACCOMMODATION | SEPARATION |
|---|---|---|---|
| Nonassertive | Developing positive face | Increasing visibility | Avoiding |
|  |  | Dispelling stereotypes | Maintaining interpersonal barriers |
|  | Emphasizing commonalities |  |  |
|  | Censoring self |  |  |
|  | Averting controversy |  |  |
| Assertive | Overcompensating | Communicating self | Exemplifying strengths |
|  | Manipulating stereotypes | Intragroup networking | Embracing stereotypes |
|  | Extensive preparation | Using liaisons |  |
|  | Bargaining | Educating others |  |
| Aggressive | Distancing | Confronting | Sabotaging others |
|  | Mirroring | Gaining advantage | Attacking |
|  | Ridiculing self |  |  |

*Source:* Orbe, M., & Roberts, T. (2012). Co-cultural theorizing: Foundations, applications & extensions. *Howard Journal of Communications*, *23*(4), 295–296.

among communities of African Americans that these White institutions are not concerned with their well-being or how they feel.

Assertive assimilation strategies also seek to downplay cocultural differences and promote a convergence into existing structures. But they do so more forcefully than the nonassertive strategies, not giving priority to others' needs ("I'll try to fit in, but I have to let people know how I feel from time to time"). However, these strategies may promote an us-versus-them mentality, and many people find it difficult to sustain them for long. Eventually, the cocultural member experiences burnout.

Aggressive assimilation strategies emphasize fitting in; cocultural members using these strategies go to great lengths to prove that they are like members of the dominant group. One such strategy is self-ridiculing ("I made some self-deprecating comment that was humorous, and he finally let me go"). The benefits of these kinds of strategies are that the dominant group does not see the cocultural group members as "typical," but the costs sometimes involve ridicule from other cocultural members ("She's trying so hard to be White" or "male" or "straight"). So these individuals may find themselves constantly negotiating their position with the dominant group while being isolated from their own cocultural group.

## Accommodation Strategies

Nonassertive accommodation strategies emphasize blending in with the dominant group and also tactfully challenging the dominant structure to recognize cocultural practices. Strategies include increasing visibility and dispelling stereotypes. For

**Pop Culture Spotlight**

The crux of some of the most intense debates in the United States rests on the interpretation of words. At the heart of the gay-rights issue is the definition of marriage. Think about how opponents of gay marriage often cite the Bible as a basis for their interpretation of marriage as a union between one man and one woman. Gay marriage supporters argue that there is a difference between marriage as a religious institution and marriage as a civil union. How are other issues that affect us today framed by opposing sides?

example, an African American manager might point out that she isn't particularly good friends with the one other African American in the organization; just because both workers are minorities doesn't mean they'll be good friends. The potential benefits for both dominant and cocultural groups are obvious. In this case the cocultural member is gently educating her colleagues and helping to change stereotypes of the cocultural group.

Also, using this strategy, the cocultural member may be able to influence group decision making while still showing loyalty to larger organizational goals. For example, a female business executive who shows that she's willing to work long hours, head up committees, and travel influences decision making while showing that she doesn't fulfill the stereotype of a working mother, for whom family always comes first. However, there are costs as well. Individuals with this orientation may be criticized by others for not being more aggressive in trying to change the dominant structures. Also, these communication strategies don't really promote major change in organizations to make them more inclusive and reflective of larger society.

Assertive accommodation strategies are probably the most commonly used and involve trying to strike a balance between the concerns of cocultural and dominant group members. These strategies involve communicating self, doing intragroup networking, using liaisons, and educating others. For example, using these strategies, African Americans may share information about themselves with their coworkers and educate others about phrases that are offensive, such as "working like a slave." Or gay colleagues may educate coworkers about how they feel excluded when so much of straight people's conversation focuses on heterosexual relationships and assumes that everyone is straight.

Aggressive accommodation strategies involve becoming a part of dominant structures and then working from within to promote significant changes, no matter how high the personal cost. Cocultural members who use these types of communication strategies may be seen as confrontational and self-promoting. However, they also reflect a genuine desire to work with and not against the dominant group members. For example, a Chicana colleague of ours uses this strategy in consistently reminding our department that affirmative action goals have to be integrated into the mission of the department and not seen as a separate goal—in which case people could compartmentalize their actions and only sometimes work for affirmative action. Similarly, a colleague with a disability consistently reminds the office staff that the facilities need to be more accessible—mailboxes that can't be reached, doors that do not open automatically, bathrooms that do not accommodate wheelchairs, and so on.

Cocultural members with this orientation may periodically use assertive as well as aggressive accommodation strategies and so may be perceived as genuinely committed to the larger group's good. In this way, they reap the benefits of being perceived positively by the dominant group and also have an impact on the organization. However, cocultural members who consistently use aggressive accommodating strategies may find themselves alienated from both other cocultural members and dominant group colleagues for being too confrontational.

## Separation Strategies

Nonassertive separation strategies are employed by individuals who assume that some segregation is part of everyday life in the United States. Generally, people live, work, learn, play, and pray with people who resemble themselves. This is generally easier for the dominant group than for cocultural members. Some cocultural individuals regard segregation as a natural phenomenon but also use subtle communication practices to maintain separation from the dominant group. Perhaps the most common strategy is simply avoiding interaction with dominant group members whenever possible. Thus, gay people using this orientation may spend their social time with other gay people. Or women may prefer to use professional women's services (having a female doctor, dentist, and attorney) and socialize with other women.

Assertive separation strategies reflect a conscious choice to maintain space between dominant and cocultural group members and seem to be used much less frequently than the nonassertive strategies. One of the benefits of assertive separation strategies, like the nonassertive strategies, is that they promote cocultural unity and self-determination, for example, through cultural activities like festivals and other celebrations (see "What Do You Think?"). However, individuals might implement the strategies without having access to resources controlled by the dominant group.

Aggressive separation strategies are used by those for whom cocultural segregation is an important priority. These strategies include attacking others. Individuals using these strategies often criticize those who use assimilation or accommodation strategies. While cocultural members do not have the power base that members of the dominant group have, these strategies do enable cocultural members to confront pervasive discriminatory structures. However, they also risk retaliatory attacks by the dominant group.

It is useful to think about when it is effective to use these various strategies given that each may have some benefits and costs associated with it. For example, suppose Luis, the only minority group member, thinks that he is consistently "cut out of the loop" at work. He has just discovered that there was a meeting that impacts his projects that he was not told about. There are a number of ways that he might handle this situation. He could use an aggressive assimilation strategy and simply try as hard as he can to fit in and to be included. But this may not give him the outcome he wants and may lead to a perception that he doesn't have a strong ethnic identity. He could use an assertive accommodation strategy, reminding his coworkers that he needs to be included and explicitly pointing out when he is not included. This could produce the desired outcome and help the organization become more aware of its need for increased inclusiveness. Or he could adopt an aggressive accommodation strategy and march into the director's office, demanding to be included.

## MOVING BETWEEN LANGUAGES

### Multilingualism

People who speak two languages are considered **bilingual;** people who speak more than two languages are considered **multilingual.** Rarely, however, do bilinguals speak both languages with the same level of fluency. More commonly, they prefer to use one language over another, depending on the context and the topic.

**What Do You Think?**

Celebrations and festivals offer ways to preserve cultural diversity and in some ways reinforce separation and work against assimilation. What cultural festivals have you been to? Were there elements such as food and dancing or other cultural activities that were unique?

Sometimes, entire nations are officially bilingual or multilingual. Belgium, for example, has three national languages: Dutch, German, and French. Canada recognizes English and French. Switzerland is a multilingual nation that has four official languages: French, German, Italian, and Romansh. And the United States has a growing number of bilinguals and multilinguals. According to a recent report, the number of people who spoke a language other than English at home has more than doubled in the last three decades. (See the top non-English languages most commonly spoken at home in the United States listed in Table 5.4). Laura, a college student, describes how it feels to be bilingual:

English I learned at school was second to Spanish. Growing up, it was normal to talk English to teachers and schoolmates at school, but at home, my grandmother and family spoke Spanish, and so did I. Spanish is what I heard and learned first growing up and raised by my grandmother. I feel comfortable and happy talking in Spanish. I feel I am the Spanish words that come out of my mouth.

I am proud to be bilingual. I talk like who I am, mestiza, mixed in my blood and in my language. There are many people who grew up like me, knowing two languages. A lot of the times as we talk we mix both Spanish and English together and come up with Spanglish, un mestizo. Spanglish is not a language on its own, it is a mix of two languages, English and Spanish, like our lives. I can communicate well with my boss and English-speaking friends. I can talk to my family and friends in Spanish. I can also combine both Spanish and English languages, and still others will understand me.

On either the individual or the national level, multilinguals must engage in language negotiation. That is, they need to work out, whether explicitly or implicitly, which language to use in a given situation. These decisions are sometimes clearly embedded in power-relations. For example, French was the court language during the reign of Catherine the Great, in eighteenth century Russia. French was considered the language of culture, the language of the élite, whereas Russian was considered a vulgar language, the language of the uneducated.

Sometimes, a language is chosen as a courtesy to others. When Judith is with her bilingual friends (Spanish-English), they often speak English, because Judith's Spanish proficiency is low. Tom joined a small group going to see the fireworks display at the Eiffel Tower on Bastille Day one year. (Bastille Day is a French national holiday, celebrated on July 14, commemorating the storming of the Bastille prison

**TABLE 5.4  Top Non-English Languages Spoken in the United States**

| | |
|---|---|
| 1. Spanish | 5. French |
| 2. Chinese | 6. Korean |
| 3. Tagalog | 7. German |
| 4. Vietnamese | |

*Source:* http://2010-2014.commerce.gov/blog/2013/08/06/new-census-bureau-interactive-map-shows-languages-spoken-america.

and the beginning of the French Revolution.) One person in the group asked, "Alors, on parle français ou anglais?" ["Are we speaking French or English?"] Because one member was quite weak in English, French was chosen as the language of the evening.

Why do some people choose to learn foreign languages and others do not? Many choose to learn another language for the same reasons for studying intercultural communication that we discussed in Chapter 1. The peace imperative and conflicts in the Middle East have created a need for translators and interpreters—individuals who are fluent in Arabic, Farsi, Urdu, Punjabi, Pashto, and Dari. The demographic and economic imperatives are also especially relevant, particularly in regions of the United States where there is increasing ethnic and linguistic diversity. Our student Rowena recently moved from Michigan to Arizona, where she works with many individuals who have moved there from Mexico. She comments, "It is sometimes hard, because you want to communicate, but do not always have the words. I do not speak much Spanish, so conversations can be difficult. However, where there's a will, there's a way. My friends and I make an effort to get our meanings across, and I have met some wonderful people as a result." Learning another language is never easy, but the rewards of knowing another language are immense. While our student Katarina already speaks three languages (English, Spanish, and Serbian), she is not satisfied with this: "With an expanding world, Americans have to be more aggressive in their pursuit of cultural knowledge. I feel that learning a fourth language, specifically Chinese, would greatly benefit me in my job prospects as well as in my ability to communicate with more of the world." More personal imperatives also drive people to become bilingual. Alice Kaplan, a French professor at Duke University, notes, "Speaking a foreign language is, for me and my students, a chance for growth, for freedom, a liberation from the ugliness of our received ideas and mentalities."[27] Many people use foreign languages to escape from the history of oppression in their own languages.

Perhaps it is easier to think of language as a "prisonhouse," since all of the semantic, syntactic, pragmatic, and phonetic systems are enmeshed in a social system from which there is no escape, except through the learning of another language. Consider the case of Sam Sue, a Chinese American born and raised in Mississippi, who explained his own need to negotiate these social systems—often riddled by stigmatizing stereotypes—by changing the way he speaks:

> Northerners see a Southern accent as a signal that you're a racist, you're stupid, or you're a hick. Regardless of what your real situation is. So I reacted to that by adapting the way I speak. If you talked to my brother, you would definitely know he was from the South. But as for myself, I remember customers telling my dad, "Your son sounds like a Yankee."[28]

Among the variations in U.S. English, the southern accent unintentionally communicates many negative stereotypes. Developing another accent is, for some, the only way to escape the stereotypes. When you hear different accents, what kinds of stereotypes do these accents invoke?

Aside from accents, cocultural groups often develop **argot,** a separate way of communicating. Argot often involves creating a way of communicating that distinguishes insiders from outsiders in a group. Insiders can understand what is being said, while outsiders cannot. In many ways, it is similar to learning another language. In French, one type of argot is called **verlan.** Verlan refers to the reversing of words in order to confuse those who do not understand verlan. It most often involves reversing syllables to create different words, thus "les pourris" (the rotten guys) becomes "les ripoux." Once these words are used enough, they become familiar terms and many French-speakers may use these words without realizing that they are verlan, such as the word "beur," which is verlan from "arabe." While verlan has existed since the beginning of the French language, it has become popular among poorer youth in the French suburbs.

Global forces can sometimes produce other changes in language use, like producing a new dialect—the new *multicultural English* that is emerging among the young in Great Britain and replacing the traditional cockney.

**Language acquisition** simply refers to the process of learning another language. Language acquisition studies have shown that it is nearly impossible for someone to learn the language of a group of people they dislike. And learning another language can lead to respect for another culture. Our student Karla describes such an experience:

> As soon as I entered the seventh grade, I began to learn Spanish. It was very difficult and after speaking Spanish for many years I have a greater respect for bilingual people. (In fact, when I was little I always assumed that Mexicans were smarter than Americans because many of them spoke English and Spanish!) Once I began to advance in my Spanish classes, we learned more in depth about different cultures including Mexican and Spanish cultures. I had one teacher who realized that reading about other people was a hard way to relate to them. She designed an after-school group of teens that spoke English as their second language. As a class we would get together and talk with these students. This was a good opportunity to become friends with people I would never have met otherwise.

One interesting linguistic phenomenon that has implications for the teaching and learning of other languages is called **interlanguage.** Interlanguage refers to the type of communication that emerges when native speakers of one language are speaking in another language. The native language's linguistic structure often overlaps into the second language, which creates a third way of communicating. For example, many native English speakers might try to write in French "Je suis un Américain" in attempting to translate "I am an American." While we capitalize "American," it should not be capitalized in French. Also, the structure of the sentence reflects English grammar, as proper French would be "Je suis américain." Conversely, Sarah Turnbull, an Australian journalist, says that when she first met her French husband, Frédéric, his "English was sprinkled with wonderful expressions like 'foot finger' instead of toes."[29] The French often refer to toes as "doigts de pied" or literally "fingers of the foot" or "foot fingers." Frédéric's interlanguage caused him to overlap French structure into English, which creates a third way of communicating that is not exactly English, but certainly not French either.

Given the choice, some people, particularly in the United States, do not feel the need to learn a second language. They assume that most people they encounter either at home or abroad will be able to speak English. Or perhaps they feel they have been successful so far without learning another language, so why start now and if the need arises in a professional context, they can always hire an interpreter. Professor Christ of Demont-Heinrich disagrees. He asked English-speaking students from the United States and non-English speakers from a Danish University whether it was important to learn a second language. He found that most Danish students thought they should learn English and most American students thought they *should* learn another language but didn't really see it as necessary; a few were adamant that no American should need to know a foreign language because of the prevalence of English as a worldwide language. He concludes that the dominance of English is both a privilege and disadvantage. It's a disadvantage in that it seems to have made Americans lazy and allowed them to take their privilege for granted and the global language hierarchy forces "multilingual opportunity" on some and denies it to others.[30]

While the advantage of being an English speaker may make it easier for Americans to travel overseas, there may be some downsides. Perhaps being monolingual makes Americans less cosmopolitan and more provincial—compared to others we're competing against in the current global economy. The fact is that a person who only knows one language may be understood by others, if the language is commonly spoken (like English) as a foreign language, but can never understand what others are saying in their own languages, will always have to rely on translators, and are more likely to misunderstand what others are saying. Perhaps more importantly, they miss the opportunity to learn about a culture. As we have described, language and culture are so inextricably intertwined that to learn a new language is to gain insight on another culture and another world.

People react differently to living in a multicultural world. Some work hard to learn other languages and other ways of communicating, even if they make a number of errors along the way. Others retreat into their familiar languages and customs. The tensions that arise over different languages and different meaning systems are played out around the world. And these tensions will never disappear but will always provide new challenges for intercultural communicators.

## Translation and Interpretation

Intercultural communication scholars are also concerned with the role of translation and interpretation—that is, how people understand each other when they speak different languages. Because it is impossible to learn all of the languages in the world, we must rely on translation and interpretation—two distinct but important means of communicating across languages. The European Union (EU), for example, has a strict policy of recognizing all of the languages of its constituent members. Hence, a large number of translators and interpreters are hired to work by the EU to bridge linguistic differences.

**Translation** generally refers to the process of producing a written text that refers to something said or written in another language. The original-language text of a translation is called the **source text;** the text into which it is translated is called

### What Do You Think?

Even with Google Translate, we will still need to teach foreign languages in schools because:

1. Instant translators aren't always accurate.
2. Instant translation ignores context, so a sarcastic joke might be translated as serious or even offensive.
3. Machine translation is inconvenient—if you have to keep typing or saying every sentence into your phone?

(Source: Adapted from https://www.alsintl .com/blog/will-instant -translators-make-foreign -language-teaching -obsolete/.)

the **target text.** So, when *Gone with the Wind* is translated into Hungarian, the original text written by the author is the source text. The result of the translation, the Hungarian version, is the target text.

**Interpretation** refers to the process of verbally expressing what is said or written in another language. Interpretation can either be simultaneous, with the interpreter speaking at the same time as the original speaker, or consecutive, with the interpreter speaking only during the breaks provided by the original speaker.

Language are entire systems of meaning and consciousness that are not easily translated into other languages word for word. The ways in which different languages convey views of the world are not equivalent, as we noted earlier. Remember the dilemma regarding color? The English word *brown* might be translated as any of these French words, depending on how the word is used: *roux, brun, bistre, bis, marron, jaune,* and *gris.* For example, *brun* is used to describe brown hair, while *bis* is used to describe a brown pencil. As we noted in Chapter 1, businesses sometimes get into trouble with incorrect translations of advertising slogans (see "Info Bites").

*Issues of Equivalency and Accuracy* Some languages have tremendous flexibility in expression; others have a limited range of words. The reverse may be true, however, for some topics. This variation between languages is both aggravating and thrilling for translators and interpreters. The tradition of translation studies has tended to emphasize issues of accuracy and **equivalency**—the condition of being equal in meaning, value, quantity, and so on. That is, the focus, largely from linguistics, has been on comparing the translated meaning to the original meaning. Often, word-for-word translations that are not equivalent in meaning can yield amusing target texts, like the following signs in tourist spots around the world:[31]

- Is forbidden to steal hotel towels please. If you are not a person to do such thing is please not to read notice (Tokyo hotel).
- The lift is being fixed for the next day. During that time we regret that you will be unbearable (elevator in Bucharest, Romania).
- Please leave your values at the front desk (Paris hotel).
- Because of the impropriety of entertaining guests of the opposite sex in the bedroom, it is suggested that the lobby be used for this purpose (Zurich hotel).
- It is forbidden to enter a woman even a foreigner if dressed as a man (Bangkok temple).
- Specialist in women and other diseases (Rome doctor's office).
- The manager has personally passed all the water served here (Acapulco hotel).

In some instances (e.g., translating research questionnaires), equivalency of meaning is very important. A special **back translation** technique can improve the translation's accuracy, and is often used in small amounts of text, like a questionnaire

**Info Bites**

Translation is a complicated process, as seen in these examples:

- When McDonald's brought its big Mac to France, it translated to the name "Gros mec" which actually means "big pimp."
- Coors' "Turn it loose" campaign in Spain was translated to "You will suffer from diarrhea."
- Hunt-Wesson introduced its baked beans in French Canada as "Gros Jos" not realizing that's slang for "big breasts."
- KFC mistakenly translated its "finger lickin' good" tagline to "eat your fingers off" in Chinese.

(Source: Weinmann, K. (2011, October 17). 13 Slogans that got hilarious when they were lost in translation. Available at http://www.businessinsider.com/13-hilarious-slogans-lost-in-translation-2011-10.)

or an essay.[32] For example, Judith and Tom's colleague conducted a study comparing Japanese and U.S. students' conflict styles and used the back translation method. That is, he first developed a questionnaire in English and then translated it into Japanese. Then the translated Japanese text was translated back to English by another translator who had no prior knowledge of the text. The two texts were then compared—the original English text with the back translated text—and any discrepancies between the two versions were examined and resolved by a panel of multilingual experts. However, if the translation of the questionnaire was not acceptable, then this process (forward translation, back translation, discussion by the bilingual expert panel, etc.) would continue as many times as necessary until a satisfactory version is reached.[33]

There are some famous and very important "geopolitical" examples of bad translations creating problems. In June 1963, John F. Kennedy stood at the Berlin Wall and declared, *"Ich bin ein Berliner,"* which translates as "I am a cream bun." In December 1977, Jimmy Carter gave a speech in Poland which included the sentence, "I want to know the Polish people." When this was translated into Polish, the word "know" was mistranslated so that Carter was quoted as having said, "I want to have carnal knowledge of the Polish people."

For those interested in the intercultural communication process, the emphasis is not so much on equivalence but on the bridges that people construct to "cross" from one language to another.

Once when Tom was in Normandy, in northern France, a French police officer asked him to tell an English-speaking woman to get down from a wall that was high above the street. Tom called out to her that the officer wanted her to get down. She refused. The police officer became angry and began speaking louder and faster, repeating his request. Tom, too, began speaking louder and faster, giving the same request in English. The situation escalated until the woman hollered, "Tell him to go to hell!" At this point, Tom felt trapped, so he turned to the police officer and said, "Je ne comprends pas. Je ne parle pas français" ["I don't understand. I don't speak French"].

Tom tried to apologize and escape the situation. But the police officer interrupted him immediately and retorted, "Mais oui, tu peux parler français!" ["Oh yes, you can speak French!"] He continued barking angry commands at the woman. Throughout this situation, Tom never really expressed the nuances of the statements on either side. The officer, unless he understood English and refused to speak it, did not know the obscenities that were being hurled his way. Nor did the woman understand the demeaning familiar forms of language used by the officer, or the significance of his demands as a police officer, a position of much more authority than in the United States.

***The Role of the Translator or Interpreter***   We often assume that translators and interpreters are "invisible," that they simply render into the target language whatever they hear. The roles that they play as intermediaries, however, often regulate how they render what is said. Consider the previous example again. Because of the French police officer's position, it was nearly impossible for Tom to tell him what

**Surf's Up!**

Have you used any of
the online translation
web-based resources?
Try experimenting with
http://FreeTranslation
.com. What happens
when you attempt to
translate a phrase
such as "Don't hate me
because I'm beautiful"
from English to Spanish
and then back again?
Was the meaning
conveyed? What does
your experimenting tell
you about the nature
of communicating
to someone who is a
native speaker of a
language other than
your own?

the woman was saying—even apart from the linguistic difficulty of translating profanity.

It is important that you acknowledge the role of an interpreter if you find yourself in that situation. Tom recently met with some journalists from China, and an interpreter who spoke Chinese and English was brought along. Tom was sure to acknowledge her presence and asked her when and how he should stop speaking so she could interpret. He also ensured that she felt free to ask questions to clarify anything that might be interpreted in different ways. By doing this, the interpreter was given more flexibility and authority in interpretation, which hopefully assisted in the interpretation process.

We often assume that anyone who knows two languages can be a translator or an interpreter. Research shows, however, that a high level of fluency in two languages does not necessarily make someone a good translator or interpreter. The task obviously requires the knowledge of two languages. But that's not enough. Think about all the people you know who are native English speakers. What might explain why some of them are better writers than others? Knowing English, for example, is a necessity for writing in English, but this knowledge does not necessarily make a person a good writer. Because of the complex relationships between people, particularly in intercultural situations, translation and interpretation involve far more than linguistic equivalence, which traditionally has been the focus.

## Language Politics and Policies

Some nations have multiple official languages. Here in the United States, there is no official, legal national language, although English is the de facto national language. There were discussions about language policy during the writing of the Constitution, as a number of languages were spoken by Europeans in the Americas at that time, including English, French, German, and Spanish. Ultimately, however, the Founding Fathers decided to not say anything in the Constitution with regard to language. However, some U.S. places have also declared two official languages, such as Guam (Chamorro and English), Hawaii (English and Hawaiian), New Mexico (English and Spanish), and Samoa (English and Samoan). And recently, the U.S. Senate debated establishing English as the national language of the United States. At the time of this writing, it isn't clear what will happen to this proposal, but the attempt to establish English as the national language "does not go as far as proposals to designate English the nation's official language, which would require all government publications and business to be in English."[34] Thus, if English is the national language of the United States, it might mean something different than the official language of the United States.

Laws or customs that emerge to determine which language is to be spoken where and when are referred to as **language policies.** These policies often emerge from the politics of language use. Historically, for example, European aristocrats spoke French. Recall that in the court of Catherine the Great of Russia, one heard and spoke French, not Russian. According to the language policies of the period, speaking Russian was seen as vulgar, or as they might have said, declassé. The French language, within those language policies, was closely tied to the politics of social and economic class. To illustrate, think about how you would feel if in the United States speaking English was a sign that you were "vulgar," while speaking French was a sign of high status.

Consider the EU, which has 23 official languages and some 60 indigenous languages (e.g., Sardinian in the South, Basque in the west). The official EU policy is to protect linguistic diversity and promote knowledge of language with a goal of a Europe where everyone can speak *at least two other languages* in addition to their own native language.[35]

Of course, implementing this policy is very challenging because historical geopolitical power relations come into play. Which two or three languages should be learned? English, French, and German seem the most likely—former colonial languages and the languages of international commerce, science and technology, global knowledge, information, and entertainment. Among these three, English seems to be winning out. How can the EU protect the minority languages in Europe? What is lost if minority languages should disappear? (See "Info Bites.")

There are different motivations behind the establishment of language policies that guide the status of different languages in a place. Sometimes nations decide on a national language as part of a process of driving people to assimilate into the national culture. If the state wishes to promote assimilation, language policies that encourage everyone to speak the official language and conduct business in that language are promoted.

Sometimes nations develop language policies as a way of protecting minority languages so that these languages do not disappear. Welsh in Wales is one example, but Irish in Ireland and Frisian in Germany and the Netherlands are legally protected languages. Some language policies recognize the language rights of its citizens wherever they are in the nation. One example of this is Canada (English and French). Another is Kenya (Swahili and English). Government services are available in either language throughout the nation.

Other language policies are governed by location. In Belgium, Dutch (Flemish) is the official language in Flanders in the northern part of the country. French is the official language in Wallonia in the south, and German is the official language in the eastern Cantons bordering Germany. Thus, if you are boarding a train to go from Antwerp to Tournai, you would need to look for "Doornik" in the Antwerp train station. When you returned to the train station in Tournai to go back, you would look for the train to "Anvers." The signs would not be posted in both languages, except in the Brussels-Capital region (the only bilingual part of the nation).

Sometimes language policies are developed with language parity, but the implementation is not equal. In Cameroon, for example, English and French are both official languages, although 247 indigenous languages are also spoken. Although Germany was the initial colonizer of Cameroon, Britain and France took over in 1916—with most of the territory going to France—and these "new colonial masters then sought to impose their languages in the newly acquired

© Alex Wong/Getty Images

Languages are entire systems of meaning and con- sciousness that are not easily trans- lated into another language. This is also true for spoken language and sign language.

territory."[36] At independence in 1960, French Cameroon established French as its official language and English became the official language in the former British Cameroon areas once they joined together to form Cameroon. When united in 1961, Cameroon established both languages as official languages. Since French speakers are far more numerous than English speakers, "French has a de facto dominance over English in the areas of administration, education and the media. In fact, it is not an exaggeration to say that French influence as expressed in language, culture and political policy prevails in all domains."[37] So while Cameroon is offi- cially bilingual, French dominates in nearly all domains, as most of the people are French speakers. Thus, "What appears to be a language policy for the country is hardly clearly defined, in spite of the expressed desire to promote English–French bilingualism and protect the indigenous languages."[38] European colonialism has left its mark in this African nation, and the language policy and language realities remain to be worked out.

We can view the development of language policies as reflecting the tensions between the nation's history and its future, between the various language commu- nities, and between economic and political relations inside and outside the nation. Language policies can help resolve or exacerbate these tensions as in the case of China and the many languages spoken there (see Figure 5.1).

In Canada today, many wonder about the bilingual future of the nation. Recently, the French magazine *L'Express* asked, "Is Canada always bilingual?" Suggesting that bilingualism will not last in Canada, the answer seems to be "at least for awhile," according to the results of a recent study of bilingual Canadians.

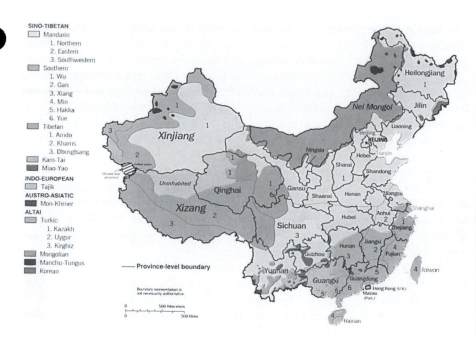

SINO-TIBETAN
- Mandarin
  - 1. Northern
  - 2. Eastern
  - 3. Southwestern
- Southern
  - 1. Wu
  - 2. Gan
  - 3. Xiang
  - 4. Min
  - 5. Hakka
  - 6. Yue
- Tibetan
  - 1. Amdo
  - 2. Khams
  - 3. Dbusgtsang
- Kam-Tai
- Miao-Yao

INDO-EUROPEAN
- Tajik

AUSTRO-ASIATIC
- Mon-Khmer

ALTAI
- Turkic
  - 1. Kazakh
  - 2. Uygur
  - 3. Kirghiz
- Mongolian
- Manchu-Tungus
- Korean

— Province-level boundary

Boundary representation is
not necessarily authoritative

0        500 Kilometers
0        500 Miles

**Figure 5.1**   Linguistic maps show where different languages are spoken. This linguistic map shows where different dialects of Chinese are spoken in China. What might a linguistic map of other parts of the world look like?

*Source:* University of Texas at Austin Library. Retrieved from http://www.lib.utexas.edu/maps/middle _east_and_asia/china_ling_90.jpg.

In 2011, 17.5 percent of Canadians reported being able to conduct a conversation in both English and French, up from 12.2 percent recorded 50 years earlier.[39] While we cannot know the future of Canada, the importance of language in Canada is not likely to go away anytime soon.

## SUMMARY

In this chapter, we explored many dimensions of language in intercultural communication. Linguists study four basic components of language as they investigate how language works: (1) phonology, the study of the sound system, (2) semantics, the study of meaning, (3) syntax, the study of structure, and (4) pragmatics, the study of the purposes and contexts of language in use.

We also discussed the Sapir–Whorf hypothesis and how the particular language we speak influences our perception. Language is powerful, but it does not totally determine our perception. The power of language can be revealed in the use of labels, with the more powerful people in a society labeling the less powerful. Individuals who occupy powerful positions in a society often don't think about the

### Info Bites

Consider that every 14 days, one of the world's nearly 7,000 languages "dies." What is lost when a language goes extinct? Linguists say that each language is a unique lens, a unique way of viewing the world. In Tuvan, spoken in the republic of Tuva in southern Siberia, for example, the past is always spoken of as ahead of one, and the future is behind one's back. It makes total sense if you think of it in a Tuvan sort of way: If the future were ahead of you, wouldn't it be in plain view? When language disappears so do significant aspects of cultural diversity. "The disappearance of a language deprives us of knowledge no less valuable than some future miracle drug that may be lost when a species goes extinct.
(Source: Rymer, R. (2012, July). Vanishing languages. *National Geographic*.)

way their positions are revealed in their communication. Languages exhibit many cultural variations, both in communication style and in the rules of context. Cultural groups may emphasize speech or silence, as well as the importance of verbal (low-context) or nonverbal (high-context) communication. Two types of communication styles are indirect/direct and elaborated/understated. We also explored the impact that interactive communication technologies may have on these cultural communication styles. The context in which the communication occurs is a significant part of the meaning. People bridge these different communication styles in intercultural interactions by together creating a "third culture style" and improvising a communication performance.

We also examined the role of power in language. Dominant groups, consciously or unconsciously, develop communication systems that require nondominant groups to use communication that doesn't fit their lived experience. We identified nine strategies that cocultural group members may use in communication with dominant group members.

Next, we discussed multilingualism. Individuals learn languages for different reasons, and the process is often a rewarding one. The complexities of moving between languages is facilitated by interpretation and translation, in which issues of equivalency and accuracy are crucial. Being a good translator or interpreter requires more than just fluency in two languages.

Finally, we looked at the situations in Belgium, Cameroon, and Canada to explore some issues surrounding language policies and intercultural communication. The issue of what language should be spoken when, to whom, and why becomes quite complex.

## BUILDING INTERCULTURAL SKILLS

1. Become more conscious of how you use language. Are you sending the messages you think you are sending? Sharpen your own skills by checking to see if people are interpreting messages the way you intend, particularly in intercultural situations. One way to do this is by asking others what they understood. If they didn't get your point, try paraphrasing.

2. Become more aware of others' verbal messages in intercultural encounters. Be aware of your own assumptions about others' language skills. For example, what kind of assumptions do you make when you hear accented English? Or a southern accent? Or an elaborated style? Or a succinct style? Practice your decoding skills. Check to see if others really meant to say what you understood. One way to do this is by asking others directly. However, remember that not everyone is comfortable with direct questions and answers. Practice other ways of trying to understand messages, such as observing or asking indirect questions.

3. Practice expanding your language repertoire in intercultural situations. When you speak with others whose first language is different from yours, speak more slowly, use easy-to-understand words and simple sentences, and avoid slang.

⬤ If English isn't your first language, practice asking questions when you don't understand. And try to vary your own language patterns. If you tend to speak a lot, try listening. If you are often quiet, try speaking up.

4. Practice being flexible and adapting to others' language style in intercultural encounters. In formal situations, use more formal language. Or if someone uses a more indirect style, try using a more indirect style.

5. Practice using labels that are preferred by group members. Gay or homosexual? African American or Black? White or Caucasian? If you aren't sure, investigate using appropriate communication strategies—after making sure that you have the kind of relationship where you can ask freely.

## ACTIVITIES

1. *Regional language variations:* Meet in small groups with other class members and discuss variations in language use in different regions of the United States (accent, vocabulary, and so on). Identify perceptions that are associated with these variations.

2. *"Foreigner" labels:* Meet in small groups with other class members, and come up with a list of general labels used to refer to people from other countries who come to the United States (such as immigrants, aliens, or foreigners). For each label, identify a general connotation (positive, negative, mixed). Discuss how the connotations of these words may influence our perceptions of people from other countries. Would it make a difference if we referred to them as *guests* or *visitors?*

## ⬤ ENDNOTES

1.  The 10 most common languages (2016, May 16). *Accredited Language Services.* Retrieved May 28, 2016, from https://www.alsintl.com/blog/most-common-languages/.
2.  Omniglot, writing systems and languages of the world. Retrieved January 29, 2009, from http://www.omniglot.com/writing/vietnamese.htm.
3.  Genzer, D. *The disorientation manual 1987–88.* (A guide for American students studying at the University of St. Andrews, Scotland). St. Andrews, Scotland: University of St. Andrews.
4.  Slackman, M. (2008, June 20). With a word, Egyptians leave it all to fate. *The New York Times,* p. A9.
5.  Smith, T. W. (1992). Changing racial labels: From "Colored" to "Negro" to "Black" to "African American." *The Public Opinion Quarterly, 56*(4), 496–514.
6.  Washington, J. (2012, February 3). Some Blacks insist, "I'm not African-American." *Foxnews.com.* Retrieved May 12, 2012, from http://nation.foxnews.com/african-american-community/2012/02/05/ap-some-blacks-insist-i-m-not-african-american.
7.  Cruz-Janzen, M. (2002). Lives on the crossfire: The struggle of multiethnic and multiracial Latinos for identity in a dichotomous and racialized world. *Race, Gender & Class, 9*(2), 47–62.
8.  Taylor, P., Lopez, M. H., Martinez, J. H., & Velasco, G. (2012). When labels don't fit: Hispanics and their views of identity. Pew Hispanic Center. Retrieved May 12, 2012, from http://www.pewhispanic.org/files/2012/04/PHC-Hispanic-Identity.pdf.
9.  Davis, W. (1999). Vanishing cultures. *National Geographic, 196,* p. 65.
10. Hoijer, H. (1994). The Sapir–Whorf hypothesis. In L. Samovar & R. E. Porter (Eds.), *Intercultural communication: A reader* (pp. 194–200). Belmont, CA: Wadsworth.

11. Davis (1999), pp. 62–89.

12. Dehaene, S., Izard, V., Pica, P., & Spelke, E. (2006). Core knowledge of geometry in an Amazonian indigene group. *Science, 311*, 381–384; Kenneally, C. (2008, April 22). When language can hold the answer. *The New York Times*, p. F1.

13. Deutscher, G. (2010). *Through the language glass: Why the world looks different in other languages*. New York: Metropolitan Books.

14. Giles, H., Coupland, N., & Wiemann, J. (1992). Talk is cheap . . . but "My word is my bond": Beliefs about talk. In K. Bolton & H. Kwok (Eds.), *Sociolinguistics today* (pp. 218–243). New York, NY: Routledge.

15. Covarrubias, P. O., & Windchief, S. R. (2009). Silences in stewardship: Some American Indian college students examples. *Howard Journal of Communications, 20*, 343.

16. Kim, M.-S. (2002). *Non-Western perspectives on human communication*. Thousand Oaks, CA: Sage, p. 135.

17. Hall, E. T. (1976). *Beyond culture*. Garden City, NY: Doubleday, p. 79.

18. Bennett, M. J. (2013). *Basic concepts in intercultural communication* (2nd ed.) Boston, MA: Nicholas Brealey.

19. Gudykunst, W. B., & Ting-Toomey, S. (1988). *Culture and interpersonal communication*. Newbury Park, CA: Sage.

20. Kikoski, J. F., & Kikoski, C. K. (1999). *Reflexive communication in the culturally diverse workplace*. Westport, CT: Praeger, p. 67.

21. Miles, O. (2011, February 24). How Gaddafi's words get lost in translation. *BBC News Africa*. Retrieved May 24, 2016, from http://www.bbc.co.uk/news/world-africa-12566277?print=true.

22. Boogaard, K. (2015, August 27). Mixing Millenials and Baby Boomers in the workplace melting pot. *officeninjas.com*. Retrieved May 27, 2016, from http://officeninjas.com/2015/08/27/mixing-millennials-and-baby-boomers-in-the-workplace-melting-pot/; Goudreau, J. How to communicate in the new multigenerational office. *forbes.com*. Retrieved May 27, 2016, from http://www.forbes.com/sites/jennagoudreau/2013/02/14/how-to-communicate-in-the-new-multigenerational-office/#f68656150d8d.

23. Social media speeds up language evolution. (2015, May). *languagemagazine.com*. Retrieved May 30, 2016, from http://languagemagazine.com/?page_id=123684.

24. Shuter, R. (2012). When Indian women text message: Culture, identity and emerging interpersonal norms of new media. In P. H. Cheong, J. N. Martin, & L. P. Macfadyen (Eds.), *New media and intercultural communication* (pp. 209–222). New York, NY: Peter Lang; Shuter, R., & Chattopadhyay, S. (2010). Emerging interpersonal norms of text messaging in India and the United States. *Journal of Intercultural Communication Research, 39*(2), 121–145.

25. Bateson, M. C. (1993). Joint performance across cultures: Improvisation in a Persian garden. *Text and Performance Quarterly, 13*, 119.

26. Camara, S. K., & Orbe, M. P. (2010). Analyzing strategic response to discriminatory acts: A co-cultural communicative investigation. *Journal of International & Intercultural Communication, 3*(2), 83–113.

27. Kaplan, A. (1993). *French lessons: A memoir*. Chicago, IL: University of Chicago Press, p. 211.

28. Sue, S. (1992). Growing up in Mississippi. In J. F. J. Lee (Ed.), *Asian Americans* (pp. 3–9). New York, NY: New Press.

29. Turnbull, S. (2002). *Almost French: Love and a new life in Paris*. New York, NY: Penguin, p. vii.

30. Demont-Heinrich, C. (2010). Linguistically privileged and cursed? American university students and the global hegemony. *World Englishes, 29*(2), 281–298.

31. Lost in translation. Retrieved May 24, 2012, from http://www.jnweb.com/funny/translation.html.

32. Brislin, R. (1986). The wording and translation of research instruments. In W. J. Lonner & J. W. Berry (Eds) *Field methods in cross-cultural research* (pp. 137–164). Newbury Park, CA: Sage.

33. Shigenobu, T. (2007). Evaluation and usability of back translation for intercultural communication. In N. Aykin (Ed.), *Usability and internationalization: Global and local user interfaces* (pp. 259–265). Berlin: Springer.

34. Hulse, C. (2006, May 19). Senate votes to set English as national language. *The New York Times*, p. A19.

35. EU Languages and Language Policy (2012, February 7). European Commission. Retrieved May 14, 2012, from http://ec.europa.eu/languages/languages-of-europe/index_en.htm.

36. Echu, G. (2003). Coping with multilingualism: Trends in the evolution of language policy in Cameroon. *PhiN, 25*, 34. Retrieved from http://web.fuberlin.de/phin/phin25/p25t2.htm#ech99b.

37. Echu (2003), p. 39.

38. Echu (2003), p. 44.

39. Demetz, J.-M. (2006, February 23). Is Canada always bilingual? *L'Express*, pp. 42–45; Lepage, J. F., & Corbeil, J. P. (2013). The evolution of English-French bilingualism in Canada from 1961 to 2011. *Statistics Canada* (Catalogue #75-006-X). Available at http://www.statcan.gc.ca/pub/75 -006-x/2013001/article/11795-eng.pdf.

© kristian sekulic/Getty Images RF

CHAPTER SIX

# Nonverbal Communication Issues

## CHAPTER OUTLINE

## STUDY OBJECTIVES

*After reading this chapter, you should be able to:*

1. Define nonverbal communication.

2. Understand the difference between verbal and nonverbal communication.

3. Describe what nonverbal behavior communicates.

4. Identify cultural differences in nonverbal behavior.

5. Understand how nonverbal communication can reinforce cultural stereotypes.

6. Define and give examples of cultural space.

7. Describe the relationship between cultural identity and cultural space.

8. Describe the dynamic nature of cultural spaces.

## KEY TERMS

adaptors
contact cultures
cultural spaces
cyberspace
deception
emblems
eye contact
facial expressions
gestures
home
illustrators
migration
MMORPGs
monochronic
neighborhood
noncontact cultures
nonverbal communication
paralinguistics
personal space
physical appearance
polychronic
regionalism
regulators
relational messages
silence
status
traveling

Nonverbal communication, just like language, can vary dramatically across cultures. These differences can sometimes lead to misunderstandings. For example, our Kenyan student Gladys describes a nonverbal misstep when she first arrived in the United States:

> Back at home women love touching and patting each other's hair as a way of admiring it. When I moved to the U.S., there was this lady who attended the same church we did. The lady was fairly friendly and even talked of inviting me to her apartment. She had long blonde hair. One day, I made the mistake of patting her hair as a way of admiring how long it was. She was so mad at me, and that occurrence strained our relationship which never recovered. Since then I became afraid of patting anyone's hair again.

Sometimes nonverbal communication can help us get our message across, when we don't understand a foreign language. For example, our student Yadira was camping with friends in Greece and wanted to ask permission to pitch their tent in a local farmer's meadow, but she didn't speak Greek. By drawing a picture of a tent and using lots of hand gestures, she was able to obtain permission. Trained nonverbal experts watching Russian diplomat's nonverbal cues led to the discovery of a bug at the State Department, and watching Saddam Hussein's body language during speeches he had given predicted his invasion of Iran. America has spent $900 million since 2007 trying to read the body language of passengers in airports.[1]

You may never be involved with law enforcement or Transportation Security Administration (TSA) officials, or be a tourist in Greece, but you certainly will find yourself in many intercultural communication situations (e.g., in a culturally diverse work situation). In this chapter, we discuss the importance of understanding nonverbal aspects of intercultural communication. We also explore specific nonverbal communication codes (personal space, gestures, facial expressions, and so on) and expressions of power in intercultural contexts. Finally, we investigate the concept of cultural space and the way people's cultural identities are shaped by the cultural spaces (home, neighborhood, and so on) as well as newer online cyber spaces they occupy. We will also consider the impact of communication encounters online or via text messaging, where nonverbal cues are often absent. Does the absence of nonverbal cues make intercultural communication easier or more difficult?

## DEFINING NONVERBAL COMMUNICATION

What is not said is often as important as what is said. **Nonverbal communication** is communication through means other than language—for example, facial expression, personal space, eye contact, use of time, and conversational silence.[2] Nonverbal communication also involves the notion of cultural space. **Cultural spaces** are the contexts that form our identity—where we grow up and where we live (not necessarily the

Understanding nonverbal communication can be a key to survival in some intercultural contexts, like Iraqis passing at this military checkpoint. Notice that the soldier's nonverbal communication is reinforced by words and international symbols on the sign in the foreground.

© Ali Al-Saadi/AFP/Getty Images

### Surf's Up!

John Bulwer was one of the first people to study nonverbal communication, way back in 1649. He is quoted as arguing that facial expressions are important to understand because "they are the neerest and immediate organs of the voluntaire or impetuous motions of the mind." Check out the website http://mambo.ucsc.edu/psl/bulwer.html to see some of Bulwer's early explorations into nonverbal *(continued)*

actual homes and neighborhoods, and online sites but the cultural meanings created in these places).

### Comparing Verbal and Nonverbal Communication

Both verbal and nonverbal communications are symbolic, both communicate meaning, and both are patterned—that is, are governed by rules that are determined by particular contexts and situations. And just as different societies have different spoken languages, so they have different nonverbal languages. However, there are some important differences between nonverbal and verbal communication in any culture. Let's look at some examples of these differences.

The following incident happened to Judith when she was teaching public speaking to a group of Japanese teachers of English. She explained how to write a speech and gave some tips for presenting the speech. The teachers seemed attentive, smiling, and occasionally nodding. But when the time came for them to present their own speeches, she realized that they had many questions about how to prepare a speech and had not really understood her explanations. What she learned was that it is customary for students in Japan to not speak up in class unless they are called upon. In Japan, a nod means that one is listening—but not necessarily that one understands. As this example illustrates, rules for nonverbal communication vary among cultures and contexts.

Let's consider another example. Two U.S. American students attending school in France were hitchhiking to the university in Grenoble for the first day of classes. A French motorist picked them up and immediately started speaking English to them. They wondered how he knew they spoke English. Later, they took a train to Germany.

The conductor walked into their compartment and scolded them in English for putting their feet on the opposite seat. Again, they wondered how he had known that they spoke English. As these examples show, nonverbal communication includes more than gestures. Even our appearance can communicate loudly; in fact, the students' very appearance no doubt was a good clue to their national identity. As these examples also show, nonverbal behavior operates at a subconscious level. We rarely think about how we stand, what hand gestures we use, what facial expressions we're using, and so on. Occasionally, someone points out such behaviors, which brings them to a conscious level.

When misunderstandings arise, we are more likely to question our verbal communication than our nonverbal communication. We can use different words to explain what we mean, or look up words in a dictionary, or ask someone to explain unfamiliar words. But it is more difficult to identify and correct nonverbal miscommunications or misperceptions.

*Learning Nonverbal Behavior*   Although we learn rules and meanings for language behavior in grammar and spelling lessons, we learn nonverbal meanings and behaviors more unconsciously. No one explains, "When you talk with someone you like, lean forward, smile, and touch the person frequently, because that will communicate

**Surf's Up! (cont.)**
communication. Do you agree that nonverbal communication reflects internal feelings? Are his ideas relevant in cross-cultural situations?

© Brand X Pictures/PunchStock RF

Tattoos and body piercing communicate different meanings to different audiences. Think about the inferences people can draw from these nonverbal communication markers about social status. For example, most of us would be shocked if the president was tattooed and pierced.

that you really care about him or her." In the United States, these behaviors often communicate positive meanings.[3] But if someone does not display these behaviors, we are likely to react quite differently.

Sometimes we learn strategies for nonverbal communication. For example, you may have been taught to shake hands firmly when you meet someone, or you may have learned that a limp handshake indicates a person with a weak character. Likewise, many young women learn to cross their legs at the ankles and to keep their legs together when they sit. In this sense, we learn nonverbal behaviors as part of being socialized about appropriate behavior.

***Coordinating Nonverbal and Verbal Behaviors*** Nonverbal behaviors can reinforce, substitute for, or contradict verbal behaviors. When we shake our heads and say "no," we are reinforcing verbal behavior. When we point instead of saying "over there," we are substituting nonverbal behavior for verbal communication. In the example of Yadira and the tent, Yadira's drawing and gestures substituted for verbal communication. When we tell a friend, "I can't wait to see you," and then don't show up at the friend's house, the nonverbal behavior is contradicting the verbal behavior.

Because nonverbal communication operates at a more subconscious level, we tend to think that people have less control over their nonverbal behavior. Therefore, we often think of nonverbal behaviors as containing the "real" message. Have you ever received a compliment from someone you thought was not being sincere? You may have thought the person insincere because her nonverbal communication contradicted the spoken words. Perhaps she did not speak very forcefully or was not smiling very much. Perhaps she was giving other nonverbal clues indicating that she did not really mean what she was saying.

## What Nonverbal Behavior Communicates

**What Do You Think?**

If you are text messaging someone you like, how would you let them know? Do you use emoticons or emojis, for conveying your emotions? Do these symbols always communicate what you are feeling? Do you think some of these are overused? How else do you convey emotion (other symbols, punctuation, and capitalization)? How does your use of signs and symbols change based on who you are texting?

Nonverbal behavior sends relational messages and communicates status and deception. Although language is effective at communicating specific information, nonverbal communication often communicates **relational messages** about how we really feel about the person, and so on. For example, when you first meet someone, he may say "Glad to meet you," but he also communicates nonverbally how he feels about you. He may smile, make direct eye contact, and mirror your body language—all very positive messages in U.S. culture. Or perhaps he does not make direct eye contact, does not smile, and does not give any other nonverbal cues that indicate enthusiasm. One difficulty is that nonverbal clues are not always easy to interpret. And it is dangerous to assume that, every time someone doesn't smile or make direct eye contact, he is communicating lack of interest. It may be that he is preoccupied, and his nonverbal message is not meant the way you interpret it. And how can we interpret someone's feelings when there are no nonverbal cues, as in text messages? Of course, emoticons (smiley faces or frowns) or abbreviations like LOL help us interpret others' verbal messages. (See "What Do You Think?")

There are three guidelines to prevent hasty interpretations of nonverbal behaviors. The first is to think about the context. What is going on in the situation that might help you interpret someone's nonverbal message? For example, if someone has her arms folded and does not make eye contact after meeting you, it may mean that she is not enthusiastic about meeting you. But it also may mean that the room is cold or that she is focusing on something else at the moment. So always remember to think about the context.

The second guideline is to consider the person's other nonverbal behaviors. Don't interpret nonverbal behaviors in isolation. If the person has her arms folded but is also smiling, making direct eye contact, and leaning toward you, then she probably is sending a positive message. So, while each message carries some relational meaning, we must be cautious about being too hasty in interpreting this message.

A third guideline is to remember to consider the verbal messages along with the nonverbal messages. If a person is talking in a pleasant voice and standing with arms folded, the overall relationship message is likely positive. On the other hand, if the person is saying negative things to you, standing with arms folded, and averting eye gaze, then it is likely that the overall message is a more negative one. Thus, you really have to read the whole message and not just part of it.[4]

Nonverbal behavior also communicates **status**—the relative position a person occupies in an organizational or social setting. For example, a supervisor may be able to touch subordinates, but it usually is unacceptable for subordinates to touch a supervisor. Expansive gestures and control over space are associated with high status; conversely, holding one's body in a tight, clenched position communicates low status.[5] For example, in meetings in most U.S. American business contexts, the people who make the grandest gestures and who take up the most space generally are the ones who have the highest status. This might be one reason women generally carry books close to their bodies and sit with their feet and legs together; by contrast, men generally carry books under their arms and tend to sprawl when sitting.

Nonverbal behavior also communicates **deception.** However, researchers have spent years trying to identify behaviors that clearly indicate deception. Some thought there were particular behaviors (e.g., avoiding eye contact or touching or rubbing the eyes), others think that deception is communicated by fairly idiosyncratic behaviors and inconsistency in an individual's behaviors. Most research reveals that it is possible but extremely time consuming to identify deceptive behaviors. Communication researcher Burgoon and her team used sophisticated computer-assisted behavioral observation tools and found that in a U.S. sample, deceivers were more redundant and less creative in their speech and used more illustrator gestures in efforts to redirect the conversation in particular ways and also used more lip adaptors (biting, pursing, crunching, or licking lips). To make it more complicated, it appears that other cultural groups may have different ways of communicating deception.[6] It is important to remember that most nonverbal communication about relational messages, status, and deception happens at a subconscious level. For this reason, it plays an important role in intercultural interactions. We may communicate messages that we aren't even aware of—as in the examples at the beginning of this section.

**Info Bites**

Roger E. Axtell, in his book *Gestures: The Do's and Taboos of Body Language Around the World,* lists some nonverbal do's and don'ts in different cultures. Did you know that in Australia it is rude to place your hands in your lap during a meal? That in Turkey it is rude to have your hands in your pocket when conversing with someone? That in Iran people rarely exhibit signs of affection in public? Or that in Pakistan you can eat only with the right hand because the left hand is used for bodily hygiene and is considered unclean? Think about the important role of nonverbal behavior in communicating across cultures and the importance of learning nonverbal meanings as well as the language of various cultures.

## CULTURAL VARIATIONS IN NONVERBAL BEHAVIOR

How do culture, ethnicity, and gender influence nonverbal communication patterns? How universal is most nonverbal communication? Do people in most countries communicate in the same way nonverbally? In this section, we look for cultural variations in nonverbal behavior that may serve as tentative guidelines to help us communicate better with others.

There is something very basic, and perhaps universal, about some of our nonverbal behaviors—particularly our **facial expressions,** facial gestures that convey emotions and attitudes. For example, smiling and laughing probably fill a universal human need for promoting social connections or bonding—an attempt to influence others, to make them feel more positive toward the sender. Researchers point out that people in all cultures use these nonverbal behaviors to influence others and that, over time, these behaviors that contributed to positive relationships were favored and eventually became automatic and nonconscious.[7] The more researchers learn about animal behavior, particularly that of nonhuman primates like chimps and gorillas, the more similarities they find between them and humans, although animal communication appears to be less complex.[8] That is, humans are capable of many more gestures and facial expressions than are animals. Apparently, there are also some nonverbal behaviors that are innate, that we don't have to learn. For example, children who are blind usually make the same facial expressions as sighted children—even though they can't see to learn how to make these expressions.[9]

There are many universal facial gestures, including the eyebrow flash (raising the eyebrow to communicate recognition), the nose wrinkle (indicating slight social distancing), and the "disgust face" (sending a strong signal of social repulsion). For many years scientists assumed that at least six basic emotions—happiness, sadness, disgust, fear, anger, and surprise—were communicated by similar facial expressions in most societies. However, these assumptions are now being questioned as the result of more research. Using more sophisticated computer-generated digital measurement, recent research found that the six basic emotions suggested earlier held true for Western Caucasians. However, East Asians showed less distinction, and more overlap between emotional categories, particularly for surprise, fear, disgust, and anger, specifically showing "signs of emotional intensity with the eyes, which are under less voluntary control than the mouth, reflecting restrained facial behaviors as predicted by the literature." So this research refutes the notion that human emotion is universally represented by the same set of six distinct facial expression signals and early research probably neglected expressions of shame, pride, or guilt, the fundamental emotions in East Asian societies.

Second, it turns out that many facial expressions do not express one emotion, but several (e.g., happily surprised and sadly disgusted). One recent project photographed 230 volunteers making faces in response to verbal cues ("you got some great unexpected news") and then analyzed the resulting 5000 images and identified 21 distinct facial expressions of emotions.[10]

However, nonverbal communication also varies in many ways from culture to culture. The evoking stimulus, or that which causes the nonverbal behavior, may vary from one culture to another. Smiling, for example, is universal. But what prompts a person to smile may be culture-specific. In some cultures, seeing a baby

**Surf's Up!**

Take a look at the Automated Face Analysis website (www.cs.cmu.edu/~face/home.htm). Do you believe that these kinds of facial expressions not only are similar across cultures but also can be accurately deciphered by a computer?

may cause people to smile; in other cultures, one is not supposed to smile a lot at babies. Judith's Diné (Navajo) friend told her that in the Navajo Nation the first person to cause a baby to smile has to throw a party for baby and family, so people don't always want to cause a baby to smile!

There are variations in the rules for nonverbal communication and the contexts in which it takes place. For example, people kiss in most cultures, but there is variation in who kisses whom and in what contexts. When French friends greet each other, they often kiss each other on both cheeks but never on the mouth. Friends in the United States usually kiss each other on greeting only after a long absence, and this is usually accompanied by a hug. The rules for kissing also vary along gender lines. In this section, we examine how nonverbal communication varies from culture to culture.

## Nonverbal Codes

*Paralinguistics*   **Paralinguistics** refer to the study of paralanguage—vocal behaviors that indicate how something is said, including speaking rate, volume, pitch, and stress, among others. Saying something very quickly in a loud tone of voice will be interpreted differently from the same words said in a quieter tone of voice at a slower rate. How would you likely respond to someone speaking in a loud voice if he or she were speaking a foreign language? There are two types of vocal behavior—voice qualities and vocalizations.

*Voice qualities* or the nontechnical term "tone of voice" includes speed, pitch, rhythm, vocal range, and articulation; these qualities make up the "music" of the human voice. We all know people whose voice qualities are widely recognized. For example, the voice of actor Fran Drescher, who starred in the TV sitcom *The Nanny*, has been frequently remarked upon. Her trademark whiny chuckle and nasal voice allow her to be recognized no matter where she is. Speakers also vary in how they articulate sounds; that is, how distinctly they pronounce individual words and sounds. We tend not to notice these paralinguistic features unless someone articulates very precisely or very imprecisely. Paralinguistics often leads people to negatively evaluate speakers in intercultural communication contexts even when they don't understand the language. For example, Chinese speakers often sound rather musical and nasal to English speakers; English speakers sound rather harsh and guttural to French speakers.

*Vocalizations* are the sounds we utter that do not have the structure of language. Tarzan's yell is one famous example. Vocalizations include vocal cues such as laughing, crying, whining, and moaning as well as the intensity or volume of one's speech. They also include sounds that aren't actual words but that serve as fillers, such as "uh-huh," "uh," "ah," and "er." The paralinguistic aspects of speech serve a variety of communicative functions. They reveal mood and emotion; they also allow us to emphasize or stress a word or idea, create a distinctive identity, and (along with gestures) regulate conversation. Paralanguage can be a confusing factor in intercultural communication. For example, Europeans interpret the loudness of Americans as aggressive behavior, while Americans might think the British are secretive because they talk quietly. The amount of silence in conversations and the speaking rate differ among cultures. For instance, the Finnish and Japanese are comfortable having pauses in their conversations, while most U.S. Americans talk rapidly and are pretty uncomfortable with silences.

*Personal Space*   **Personal space** is the "bubble" around each of us that marks the territory between ourselves and others. Are there cultural variations in how people use personal space? A recent study of personal distances in six countries did find some cultural differences as well as some universals. First, the universal norms: we tend to place ourselves further away when we are standing near to more than one stranger, we narrow down our personal space when we are in control of our own "territory" (personal space) and expand it when we arrive in someone else's territory. Now for the cultural variations, you probably know from personal experience that when someone stands too close to you or too far in conversation, you tend to feel uncomfortable and may even move to shorten or widen the space. It turns out that some cultural groups are identified as contact cultures and others as noncontact cultures.[11] These results support Edward Hall's 1966 observations about personal space.

**Contact cultures** are those in which people stand closer together while talking, make more direct eye contact, touch frequently, and speak in louder voices. Societies in South America and southern Europe are identified as contact cultures. By contrast, those in northern Europe, North America, East Asia, and the Far East are **noncontact cultures,** in which people tend to stand farther apart when conversing, maintain less eye contact, and touch less often. Jolanta, a Polish student of ours, talked about her first experience abroad, as the guest of an Italian family, and being overwhelmed by the close physical contact and intense nonverbal behavior: "Almost every aspect of this family's interactions made me anxious and insecure. This included the extreme close personal distance, touching and speaking loudly, all of which was quite overwhelming." Figure 6.1 shows the "immediacy orientations" of selected countries and regions.

Of course, many factors besides culture determine how close together or far apart people stand. Gender, age, ethnicity, the context of the interaction, and the topic of discussion all influence the use of personal space. For example, in Kenya, gender is very important in determining amounts of personal space. Our Kenyan student Mwikali tells us that touching members of the opposite sex is considered bad manners, especially in public. She describes an incident where a Kenyan young lady was taking her European boyfriend to the airport and the boyfriend turned to hug and kiss his girlfriend and cried because he was so sad to leave her. Mwikali reports that this action attracted a crowd of onlookers who were shocked at their behavior. However, it is not unusual for people of the same sex to hold hands in Kenya—it is a sign of camaraderie and has no sexual connotations. Similarly, in China (a noncontact culture) it's quite normal for girls to hold each other's hands or arms. As one of our Chinese students describes it:

It's a sign of good friendship. I did it all the time with my good female friends when I was in China. After I came to the U.S., somehow I found out that people of the same sex don't do this unless they are in a romantic relationship. So I don't

**Info Bites**

In the United States, we are concerned with making things smell pleasing to us—just think about all of the things you can buy that are scented: perfumes, colognes, candles, soaps, and even markers. According to World Watch Institute, the United States and Europe spend $12 billion a year on perfumes, when it would take $6 billion (in addition to current expenditures) to provide basic education for all people in developing nations. How do your spending habits reflect your cultural values? Do you think we have a responsibility to others in the world?
(Source: http://www .worldwatch.org/node/764)

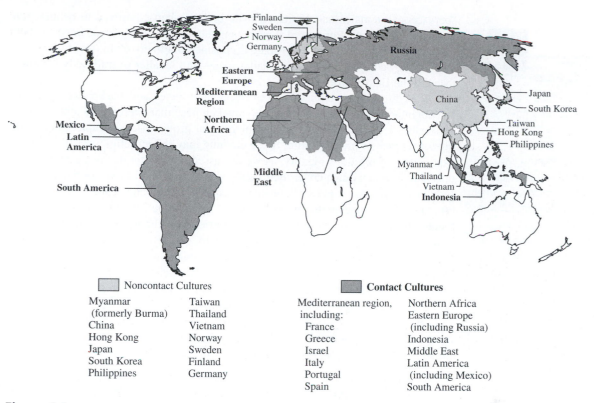

**Finland**
**Sweden**
**Norway**
**Germany**
**Russia**
**Eastern Europe**
**Mediterranean Region**
**Northern Africa**
**Mexico**
**Latin America**
**China**
**Japan**
**South Korea**
**Taiwan**
**Hong Kong**
**Philippines**
**Myanmar**
**Thailand**
**Vietnam**
**Indonesia**
**South America**
**Middle East**

| | Noncontact Cultures | | Contact Cultures | |
|---|---|---|---|---|
| Myanmar (formerly Burma) | Taiwan | Mediterranean region, including: | Northern Africa | |
| China | Thailand | France | Eastern Europe (including Russia) | |
| Hong Kong | Vietnam | Greece | Indonesia | |
| Japan | Norway | Israel | Middle East | |
| South Korea | Sweden | Italy | Latin America (including Mexico) | |
| Philippines | Finland | Portugal | South America | |
| | Germany | Spain | | |

**Figure 6.1**   Immediacy orientations of selected countries and regions.

hold other girls' hands anymore, even with my Chinese friends here. What's more interesting is that when I go back to China on vacations, I am not used to holding other girls' hands anymore!

***Physical Appearance***   **Physical appearance** is an important nonverbal code. It includes physical characteristics like height, weight, and body shape, as well as personal grooming (including body hair, clothing choices, and even the scents we apply—see "Info Bites") and personal artifacts such as jewelry, glasses, and backpacks/briefcases/purses. Of course, physical attractiveness is dynamic and variable—beauty is in the eye of the beholder, to some extent. Are there any universal measures of attractiveness? It turns out that there are two universals: (1) there is more emphasis on female attractiveness than male attractiveness, and (2) men consistently express stronger preferences for attractive mates than women.[12]

At the same time, what is considered attractive for females varies from culture to culture. For example, Japanese find smaller-bodied women more attractive than British, and in general, preferred small-headed and longer-legged women. Our Japanese students tell us that, generally, Japanese find thinner lips more attractive than do U.S. Americans. Similarly, Portuguese seem to prefer traditional,

**Info Bites**

Sometimes nonverbal choices can have dramatic impact on international politics. For example, First Lady Michelle Obama caused some controversy when she (deliberately) wore black trousers and a long patterned jacket and most importantly no head scarf when she accompanied her husband on a presidential visit to Saudi Arabia, where women must cover their hair in public and must wear *niqabs* (headscarves).

In contrast, during Iranian President Hassan Rouhani's 2016 trip to Europe where he made $18 billion worth of business deals, the Italians decided to cover some of their famous nude statues during his visits to art museums, in deference to Rouhani's strict theocratic sensibilities. They placed plywood boxes and panels around the nudes to obscure them from the president's vision or at least in photo-ops.

*(continued)*

"curvaceous" females and V-shaped male bodies when compared to people from Denmark. The Danes preferred thinner, angular shapes (with small hips) for both males and females. What type of male is considered attractive? In one study, Greek women showed a preference for smaller men—and smaller overall body weight—than did the British women.[13]

How do clothing choices and artifacts like purses and backpacks figure in? We might argue that these can be individual choices that express elements of one's personality and affiliation with particular social groups—for example, goth clothing versus jock or preppie attire. Some clothing may reflect religious affiliation and expressions of religious identity, as we discussed in Chapter 4. For example, some orthodox Jewish women cover their heads at all times with scarves or hats; some of Judith's relatives wear prayer bonnets that cover the head and "cape" dresses (modest, shirtwaist dresses with an extra layer of material designed to deemphasize the female shape); Muslim women in many countries wear the Islamic hijab (headscarf) or burqa (sheet-like covering of entire body with only eyes showing). As you might expect women have various reasons for their clothing choices, and sometimes these choices (wearing of a burqa) conflict with secular society. Several European countries have forbidden the wearing of Muslim female garb, but most U.S. Americans do not agree and suggest that values of tolerance and religious freedom should prevail, banning the burqa only in very limited contexts (schools, courts) where faces need to be seen. Communication scholar Steven M. Croucher interviewed French Muslim women about their reasons for wearing the hijab (Islamic veil/headscarf):

1. The women explained that wearing the hijab helped *integrate their multicultural identity*. They identified themselves as French and also with their country of origin (e.g., Algeria, Tunisia, and Morocco) and as Muslim women. As one woman said—growing up wearing a hijab has taught her Islamic and Algerian values in France.

2. The word for "to shield" in Arabic is *hijaba*, and many of the women talked about how the hijab provides "*a shroud of protection*," shielded from men staring at their bodies; people could then see their "real" identity—as a religious person.

3. Women also talked about how wearing the hijab made them feel closer to Muhammad—akin to a marriage relationship (similar to wearing a wedding ring). It "helps me show my virtue and be a good example for my community" (p. 207).

4. In response to the French ban, many women wear the hijab as a silent protest and an expression of unity with other Muslim women. In fact, some said that before the ban, they only saw themselves as French and Muslim but now have a stronger feeling of being Muslim and have more respect for the hijab.[14]

*Eye Contact*   **Eye contact** is often considered an element of personal space because it regulates interpersonal distance. Direct eye contact shortens the distance between two people, while a lack of eye contact increases the distance. Eye contact communicates meanings related to respect and status, and it often regulates turn taking in conversations.

Patterns of eye contact vary from culture to culture. In many societies, avoiding eye contact communicates respect and deference, although this may vary from context to context. For many Americans, maintaining eye contact communicates that one is paying attention or showing respect. But a Diné (Navajo) student told us that the hardest thing for her to learn when she left the Navajo Nation to study at Arizona State was to remember to look her professors in the eye. Her whole life, she had been taught to show respect by avoiding eye contact. A Kenyan student told us the same thing—that direct eye contact, especially with elders, is considered rude.

*Facial Expression*   As noted previously, it's important to recognize that there is variation in many aspects of facial expressions. A smile may universally indicate pleasure and happiness, and a frown may indicate sadness, but there is a lot of variation in what causes someone to smile or frown. For example, in the United States, meeting someone for the first time may call for a smile, while in other cultures, it is better to look serious. By contrast, a snake may call for a facial expression of disgust in some cultural contexts, and in others may call for a smile at the prospect of a delicious meal.

The rules that regulate facial expressions also may vary. Thus, a greeting may call for a wide smile in some cultures and a much more subdued or less expressive smile in others. Europeans often remark that U.S. Americans seem to smile too much. Some Asians make the same observation of U.S. Americans. For them, smiling is even considered somewhat "immature." In fact, someone who smiles a lot is seen as bit loony or perhaps insincere. As one of our Chinese students noted:

Most of my American colleagues and friends have very vivid facial expressions most of the time. However, in China people usually don't display that much facial expression. What's more, it is seen as being more mature and experienced if you don't disclose your inner emotions through your facial expressions (especially for men!). However, I guess that would be considered a "poker face" by most Americans.

*Gestures*   **Gestures** are simply arm and hand movements that communicate nonverbally. There are at least four different kinds of gestures: emblems, illustrators, regulators, and adaptors.[15] **Emblems** are those gestures that have a specific verbal translation. For example, when you wave your hand as someone is leaving, it means good-bye. Or when you give "the finger," it is interpreted as an insult. There are at least a hundred identifiable gestures in our culture. Of course, other cultures have their own emblems. For example, in India, a slow shaking of the head means "yes" (not "no"). You might think that there are some universal gestures or at least some universal *categories* of gestures (e.g., every culture must have an obscene gesture), but this appears not to be true. There are a number of societies (e.g., the Netherlands, Norway, Switzerland) that have no obscene gesture.[16] And in some ways, emblems are the easiest gestures to understand cross-culturally because they are easy to reproduce; when emblems have the same meaning cross-culturally, there is no problem. When people are in a foreign country and do not know the language,

**Info Bites (cont.)**

(Sources: Ridge, S. (2015, January 29). Make no mistake: Michelle Obama's Saudi Arabia headscarf snub was deliberate and brilliant. Telegraph.co.uk. Retrieved from http://www .telegraph.co.uk/women /womens-politics/11376192 /Michelle-Obamas-Saudia -Arabia-headscarf -snub-was-deliberate. html; Tharoor, I. (2016, January 26). Italy covers up nude marble statues for Iranian president's visit. washingtonpost.com. Retrieved from https:// www.washingtonpost .com/news/worldviews /wp/2016/01/26/italy -covers-up-nude-marble -statues-for-iranian -presidents-visit/.)

**What Do You Think?**

According to research, people treat those whom they consider attractive or beautiful more favorably than those whom they consider ugly or unattractive. Standards of beauty vary widely across cultures, but there is also evidence that people with the most symmetrical faces are most likely to be considered beautiful across cultures, regardless of supposed racial or cultural markers of beauty. Is beauty truly in the eye of the beholder?

they often resort to emblems. For example, our student Dave was visiting in Mexico with some friends, none of whom spoke much Spanish. They were trying to find a hotel. "We were trying to communicate that we needed somewhere to stay and the man couldn't understand us and started acting very frustrated. We started using nonverbal gestures—showing signs of sleep—and he understood and showed us a place to stay. Everything turned out okay."

However, if an emblem varies slightly from culture to culture, there can be misunderstanding. For example, in Germany and many other European cultures, the gesture for "stupid" is a finger on the forehead; the American gesture for "smart" is nearly identical, but the finger is held an inch to the side, at the temple.

Even more difficult types of gesture to understand in intercultural communication are the illustrators and regulators. **Illustrators** are all those gestures that go along with our speech. Have you ever noticed that there seems to be a "flow" to people's verbal communication—when they are talking, their gestures are usually very synchronized? For example, when emphasizing a point by shaking a finger, the speaker stops shaking the finger at the end of the sentence. And it all seems very natural. In fact, symptoms of mental illness are sometimes revealed in people's gesturing behavior; their gestures may seem "jerky" or seem not to go with their speech.

Of course, different cultural groups use different types and amounts of illustrators. Italians are often characterized as "talking a lot with their hands," or using a lot of illustrators. Another student, Marjorie, who traveled to Italy, noticed this: "In watching people in the streets, it always seemed like they must be angry at each other—all the waving of hands and gesturing." In fact, it is merely the custom there to use a lot of illustrating gestures. Other cultural groups, like the Chinese, may use fewer illustrators. Of course, the number of illustrators used may also be related to a person's family background or individual preferences. The important thing to remember is that, if you encounter someone who uses many illustrators, it doesn't mean that he's angry; and if someone uses few illustrators, it doesn't mean that she's not into the conversation.

We rarely think about it, but much of our conversation is regulated by nonverbal gestures, called **regulators.** Thus, when someone tries to interrupt while we are talking, we may put out our hand, indicating that we aren't finished speaking. Greeting and leave-taking are usually indicated by regulating gestures. For example, when we greet someone, we may shake their hands or hug them. When we get ready to leave, we often gather our stuff together. It is important to remember that each language has a somewhat unique set of regulators. For example, in Japan, turn taking is regulated more by pauses than by gestures, so that a brief pause in the conversation indicates that the next person may talk. In fact, Japanese people remark that it is sometimes difficult to jump into an American conversation because they are waiting for the regulating "pause" that never comes.

The final type of gesture is **adaptors,** which are related to managing our emotions. For example, we may tap our feet or fingers when we're nervous, or rub our eyes when we feel like crying, or clench our fists when we're angry. Again, from a cultural perspective, it's important to recognize that the adaptors we use are part of our particular cultural upbringing, and that other people may use other types of adaptors to manage or reflect their emotions.

A researcher, after studying the many variations of gestures around the world, said he was amazed by the "power, nuances, and unpredictability of cultural differences" in nonverbal behavior. On a practical note, he urged travelers to practice "gestural humility": (1) assume that the familiar gestures of our home culture will not mean the same things abroad, and (2) do not assume that we can interpret the meaning of any unfamiliar gestures we observe in other cultures.[17]

***Time Orientation***   There are many cultural variations regarding how people understand and use time. One way to understand these variations is to look at the differences between monochronic and polychronic time orientations.[18] Take

© FogStock LLC/age fotostock RF

**Surf's Up!**
Take a test to assess the degree to which you have a monochronic or polychronic approach to time at www.innovint .com/downloads/mono _poly_test.php. Think about occasions when your views on time might have created communication challenges in your encounters with others.

Holidays are often filled with nonverbal symbols that communicate important meanings to the participants. The objects in this Latino/a family's *offrenda* or altar are an important part of their "Dia de los Muertos" (All Souls Day) holiday and help them remember family members who have died. How does your family remember those who have died?

**Surf's Up!**

Explore the Handspeak website (www .handspeak.com). Take the tour and find out how to say "Hello," "Good-bye," and "Friend" in American Sign Language (ASL). How is sign language similar to and different from other forms of nonverbal communication? From other languages? Could sign language "gestures" be classified as emblems? Or another form of gestures?

the test described in "Surf's Up" to see which approach you prefer. People who have a **monochronic** concept of time, like most people in the United States, regard time as a commodity: Time can be gained, lost, spent, wasted, or saved. In this orientation, time is linear, with events happening one after another. In general, monochronic cultures value punctuality, completion of tasks, and adherence to schedules. For instance, most college staff and faculty in the United States maintain a monochronic orientation to time. Classes, meetings, and office appointments start when scheduled. Faculty members see one student at a time, hold one meeting at a time, and keep appointments except when faced with an emergency. Typical family problems are considered poor reasons for not fulfilling academic obligations—for both faculty and students.

By contrast, people with a **polychronic** orientation conceptualize time as more holistic, perhaps more circular: Many events can happen at once. U.S. American businesspeople often complain that meetings in the Middle East do not start "on time," that people socialize during meetings, and that meetings may be canceled because of personal obligations. Often, tasks are accomplished because of personal relationships, not in spite of them.

Schedules are less important than personal obligations in polychronic cultures. Sandra discovered this when she was an international student in India. She did not have a computer and had to use the university computer room. So she arrived there at 8 A.M., but the room was not open. An assistant told her to come back at 9 A.M. She went back at 9 A.M., but the room was still not open. She asked the same person and he said to return at 12 P.M.—but the room was still not open then. Later she found out that the schedule for the computer room depended on the schedule and the varying obligations of the computer lab director. It sometimes opened at 3 P.M., and other times she had to come back the next day. While this may seem inconvenient to a monochronic-oriented person, a polychronic person takes a more flexible approach and understands that keeping a strict schedule should not be the most important obligation in life.

Many international business negotiations, technical assistance projects, and team projects fail because of differences in time orientation. International students and business personnel often complain that U.S. Americans seem too busy and too tied to their schedules; they suggest that U.S. Americans do not care enough about relationships and about the personal aspects of living. An international student of ours complained, "It is so hard to get used to the fast pace of college life here. It seems that people are too busy to enjoy other people and relationships; they are just anxious and always worried about being on time and getting things done."

These differences in time orientation can be particularly consequential in contemporary work life, where technology makes it possible to be "plugged-in" 24 hours a day, seven days a week. Workers are often expected to be available to coworkers, clients, and customers at work in another time zone, even if they are off the clock.[19] This presents a challenge for many workers—how to balance personal time and work time. In Chapter 11, we'll discuss more about the important role that time orientations play in business contexts, particularly during international negotiations.

Some ethnic groups in the United States may also have a polychronic time orientation. Chicano/a college students often find that their family and social obligations, viewed as very important at home, are not as important at the university. As one student, Lucia, said, "It's hard to make sure everyone in my family is taken care of and to get my school work done at the same time. Sometimes I have to take my grandmother to the doctor, go grocery shopping with my mom, help my aunt with her Medicare problems, and still somehow find the time to attend class and get my homework done."

The implications for intercultural misunderstandings between people with these different time orientations are significant. In technical assistance projects overseas, for example, coworkers with different time orientations can become very frustrated with one another, as revealed in this summary of how monochronic Western workers and polychronic workers from Madagascar (Africa) viewed each other.[20]

| *Monochronics on Polychronics* | *Polychronics on Monochronics* |
| --- | --- |
| They never plan for the future. | They are always in a hurry. |
| They lose time and money. | They don't give priority to the art of |
| They fail to plan and so cause |    living. |
|    problems. | They are obsessed with money. |
| | They do not give priority to people. |

It takes a great deal of patience and cross-cultural understanding to work together in these situations.

*Silence*   As we noted in Chapter 5, cultural groups may vary in the relative emphasis placed on speaking and on **silence.** In most U.S. American contexts, silence is not highly valued. Particularly in developing relationships, silence communicates awkwardness and can make people feel uncomfortable. One of the major reasons for communicating verbally in initial interactions with people is to reduce uncertainty. In U.S. American contexts, people employ active uncertainty reduction strategies, such as asking questions. However, in many other cultural contexts, people reduce uncertainty by more passive strategies, such as remaining silent, observing, and perhaps asking a third party about someone's behavior. And silences can be as meaningful as language. Some of the early investigations of silence did not fully value the communicative importance of silence in many different cultures, including those in the United States. It is worthwhile for us to rethink the way we view silence, to see it not "as an absence, but, rather, as a fullness of opportunity for being and learning,"[21] particularly to understand the worlds humans create within silence. What role does silence play in your life? What does it mean when you (or your friends or family) are silent?

Communication scholar Kris Acheson acknowledges that silence in the United States has often been associated with negative, unhealthy relationships, or with disempowerment, when women and/or minorities feel their voices are not heard. However, she tells us that U.S. Americans increasingly recognize the positive and sometimes powerful uses of silence in certain contexts. For example, nurses and doctors are encouraged to honor silent patients and learn to employ silence in their ethical care; young people are advised to seek out silence in their lives for the sake of health and sanity, to even noiseproof their homes in an attempt to boost health.

In business contexts, sometimes keeping quiet is the best strategy and talking too much can kill a business deal. In education, teachers can create a space for understanding rather than counterarguments by asking for silent reflection after comments or performances. Finally, she admits that in some U.S. contexts, like politics and law, silence is still seen as completely negative; pleading the fifth equates silence with guilt and silence by politicians is often viewed as too much secrecy.[22] However, in many cultural contexts, silence is viewed rather positively. For example, silence in Japan is not simply the absence of sound or a pause in the conversation that must be filled. Silence can convey respect for the person who has spoken, or it can be a way of unifying people. Silence in Japan has been compared to the white space in brush paintings or calligraphy scrolls: "A picture is not richer, more accurate or more complete if such spaces are filled in. To do so would be to confuse and detract from what is presented."[23]

People from Finland also value silence in certain contexts. For example, researchers have described the *Asaillinen* (matter of fact) nonverbal style among Finnish people. This style involves a rather fixed and expressionless face and a belief that talkativeness is a sign of unreliability. Silence, on the other hand, for Finns reflects thoughtfulness, appropriate consideration, and intelligence—particularly in public discourse, or in educational settings, like a classroom.[24]

Some experts hypothesize that there are some underlying situational commonalities in cultures where silence is a prevalent practice. One is that silence is appropriate when the participants see the relationship or situation as ambiguous or uncertain (e.g., just getting to know someone). Another common situation that calls for silence is where there are power differences (e.g., boss–employee interaction).[25] In both these situations, whereas a Diné or Japanese response might be one of silence, an appropriate white U.S. American response might be to just "speak up" in order to reduce uncertainty.

Silence can be tricky in intercultural encounters. It can be useful when trying to sort out uncertainty in intercultural interactions because it gives one time to think through attributions. However, silence is not only a function of conversation, but an expression of culture and identity; in intercultural context, however, it may be confused with a lack of communication competence. This was the case for Japanese students studying in an Australian university. Japanese students used silence, as they would in Japan, as a strategy to save face (to avoid making mistakes when speaking English) or to be polite (to not offend the professor or other students by contradicting them). However, their silence was negatively evaluated by Australian lecturers who interpreted the silence as students' lack of engagement and a reflection on the professors' teaching expertise.[26]

A similar study shows how Chinese students' use of silence in U.S. classrooms demonstrated their Chinese cultural identities (showing politeness and respect). However, this study showed how students could, with support and encouragement from professors, reconstruct their identities and develop intercultural competence by adapting somewhat to the cultural expectations of the U.S. classroom context.[27]

## Cultural Variation or Stereotype?

As noted previously, one of the problems with identifying cultural variations in nonverbal codes is that it is tempting to overgeneralize these variations and to stereotype groups of people. Table 6.1 lists some cultural variations in nonverbal behaviors, but we must be careful not to assume that every member of that cultural group exhibits the same nonverbal behaviors, nor that we don't have to consider the context in which these nonverbal behaviors may be used.

For example, we have to be very careful when comparing Japanese and Western attitudes toward silence. Those familiar with life in Japan have observed that the television is on nonstop in many Japanese homes, and Zen gardens offer tape-recorded messages about the beauty to be seen. So, although silence might be a cultural ideal, things may differ in practice. In specific situations, such as mother–daughter relationships, there may be more emphasis on silence than in comparable U.S. American situations. Still, we should take these warnings about the dangers of overgeneralizations seriously.[28]

Cultural variations are tentative guidelines that we can use in intercultural interaction. They should serve as examples, to help us understand that there is a great deal of variation in nonverbal behavior. Even if we can't anticipate how someone's behavior may differ from our own, we can be flexible when we do encounter differences in, say, how close a person positions himself or herself, uses eye contact, or conceptualizes time.

Prejudice is often based on nonverbal aspects of behavior. That is, the negative prejudgment is triggered by physical appearances or physical behavior. Even college students' evaluations of professors' teaching may be subtly influenced by their professors' physical appearances. For example, prejudice is sometimes expressed toward Muslim women who wear the hijab, toward men from the Middle East or South Asia who wear turbans, or even toward people who appear to belong to a particular ethnic group. A recent research study showed that college students consistently rate less attractive professors as less skilled in teaching. Perhaps more interesting was that students rated both female and minority professors lower overall than their White,

### TABLE 6.1 Interesting Nonverbal Behaviors

**Brazil:** The Brazilian considers the OK sign in the United States (made with the thumb and forefinger) as obscene.

**China:** Chinese always use both hands when passing a gift or food.

**Kenya:** Pointing with an index finger is very insulting.

**Samoa:** It is rude for a person standing to sway while having a conversation.

**Fiji:** Crossed arms is a sign of respect when talking.

**Italy:** The American gesture for one (raising the index finger) means two in Italy.

**Greece and Turkey:** When saying "no," it is expressed with a small nod of the head upward.

**Japan:** Laughter may signify embarrassment instead of amusement in certain situations.

**Thailand:** Thais believe a spirit lives at the doorsill of a house, so one never pauses on the doorsill.

*Source:* From Mancini. *Selling destinations,* 5th ed. © 2010 Delmar Learning, a part of Cengage Learning, Inc. Reproduced by permission. www.cengage.com/permissions.

© Image Source/Getty Images RF

Cultures differ widely in the systems of nonverbal symbols that they use. This woman wears a tear-drop bindi. People use many other nonverbal symbols to mark their cultural identities, including attire, hair-styles, jewelry, and tattoos.

male peers. As one psychologist explained, "It just shows that white, native-speaking males are still the norm for professors in students' eyes."[29]

Teachers also may be influenced by the physical appearance of their students. Some educators suggest that decisions to place African American students in special education classes may be partially related to administrators' negative evaluations of their posture and walk. When African American high school students don't walk the typical "White walk" (erect posture and steady stride), and instead deliberately swagger with bent posture, head tilted to one side, and one foot dragging, White teachers tend to perceive them as aggressive, low achievers and potential candidates for special education programs. In fact, 21 percent of African Americans are in special education even though they represent only 16.8 percent of the U.S. public school population.[30] Similarly, immigrant Asian children and some Asian Americans are sometimes negatively evaluated and discriminated against because of their cultural practice of remaining quiet in the classroom to show respect for the teacher.[31]

A recent news report of violence toward two Mexican nationals, attacked in San Francisco because of their skin color, underscores the importance of physical appearance in prejudice. One victim was attacked by assailants yelling "White power"; he was then

> *surrounded by five men who punched and kicked him in the face, putting boots to him, while he was being held down—to the point of unconsciousness. Another man who came to his aid was similarly attacked.*[32]

As in many other instances of hate crimes, the victim's appearance was more significant than his specific cultural heritage. From these kinds of experiences with prejudice, people start to develop "a map" that tells them where they belong and where they are likely to be rejected. Victims can often spot prejudicial behavior and people with surprising accuracy. In an interesting study, Blacks were able to detect prejudiced people (identified previously by objective survey measurement) after only 20 seconds of observation, with much higher accuracy than Whites.[33] For this reason, members of minority groups may avoid places where and situations in which they do not feel welcome.

In addition to triggering prejudice, nonverbal messages also can communicate it, often in very subtle ways—like averting one's gaze, withholding a smile, or leaning one's body away. Because there is no explicit verbal expression of prejudice, the interpretation of these nonverbal behaviors is left to the person receiving the communication.

Sociologist Allan Johnson compiled the following list of nonverbal behaviors that can be interpreted as prejudicial:

- Not looking at people when we talk with them

- Not acknowledging people's presence, but making them wait as if they weren't there

- Staring as if to say "What are you doing here?" or stopping the conversation with a hush they have to wade through to be included in the smallest way

- Not listening or responding to what people say; drifting away to someone or something else

- Avoid touching their skin when giving or taking something

- Watching them closely to see what they're up to

- Avoiding someone walking down the street, giving them a wide berth when passing, or even crossing to the other side[34]

## DEFINING CULTURAL SPACE

What are cultural spaces, and what do they have to do with intercultural communication? Cultural space relates to the way communication constructs meanings of various places. For example, at the beginning of this book, we provided some background information about ourselves and the cultural places where we grew up. These particular cultural spaces are important in understanding our identities. There is nothing in the rolling hills of Delaware and Pennsylvania or the red clay of Georgia that has biologically determined who Judith and Tom are. However, our identities and our views of ourselves are formed, in part, in relation to cultural places—the mid-Atlantic region for Judith and the South for Tom. Each region has its own histories and ways of life that help us understand who we are. Our decision to tell you something about the cultural spaces we grew up in was meant to communicate something about who we think we are.

**What Do You Think?**

How we dress in large part determines how people view and feel about us. How much can a person guess about you by what you wear? For example, how does your appearance communicate your nationality? How might your appearance be viewed by people from other cultures?

The meanings of cultural spaces are dynamic and ever changing. Therefore, the Delaware that Judith left behind and the Georgia that Tom left behind are no doubt much different now. In addition, the relations between people's cultural spaces and identities are negotiated in complex ways. Thus, because someone is from India does not mean that his or her identity and communication practices are always and only "Indian." Let's look at some specific cultural spaces that we can all identify with— our homes and our neighborhoods.

### Cultural Identity and Cultural Space

*Home* Cultural spaces are important influences on how we think about ourselves and others. One of the earliest cultural spaces we experience is our **home**—the immediate cultural context for our upbringing. As noted previously, nonverbal communication involves issues of status, and the home is not exempt from issues of status. For example, the social class of an American home is often expressed nonverbally: from the way the lawn is cared for, to the kinds of cars in the driveway, to the way the television is situated, to the kinds of furniture in the home. These signs of social class are not always so obvious for all social class positions, but they often provide important clues about social class.[35]

Even if our home does not reflect the social class we wish to be in, we often identify with it strongly. We often model our own lives on the way things were done in our childhood homes. Although this is not always the case, the home can be a place of safety and security. African American writer Bell Hooks describes the "feeling of safety, of arrival, of homecoming" when as a child she would arrive at her grandmother's house, after passing through the scary white neighborhood with "those white faces on porches staring down at us with hate."[36]

"Home," of course, is not the same as the physical location it occupies, nor the building (the house) on that location. Home is variously defined as specific addresses, cities, states, regions, and even nations. Although we might have historical ties to a particular place, not everyone feels the same relationship between those places and their own identities.

Some people have feelings of fondness for the region of the country where they grew up. Another writer talks about his relationship to his hometown in South Carolina:

> Now that I no longer live there, I often think longingly of my hometown of Charleston. . . . even hearing the name casts a spell. Mirages rise up, and I am as overcome and drenched in images as a runner just come from running. I see the steeples, the streets, the lush setting.[37]

But others feel less positive about where they come from. Another writer who grew up in Texas but moved to San Francisco describes his ambivalent feelings when returning home to Texas: "Texas is home, but Texas is also a country whose citizenship I voluntarily renounced."[38] The meanings of Texas no longer "fit" this writer's sense of who he is or who he wants to be.

The relationships between various places and our identities are complex. These three writers have different feelings about their "home," which highlights the

© Alan Schein/Alamy RF

Many neighbor-hoods are marked by their ethnic and religious character. While there may have been laws that created these kinds of neighborhoods in the past, what are the advantages and disadvantages of sustaining these neighborhoods today?

complexity that exists between identity and location. Where you come from and where you grew up contributes to how you see yourself, to your current identity. Many people experience ambivalence about the regions of the country where they grew up. They may have fond memories, but they may now also see the area in a new way—as perhaps provincial, or conservative, or segregated.

*Neighborhood*   One significant type of cultural space that emerged in U.S. cities is the **neighborhood,** a living area defined by its own cultural identity, especially an ethnic or racial one. Cities typically developed segregated neighborhoods, reflecting common attitudes of prejudice and discrimination, as well as people's desire to live among people like themselves. Malcolm X, in his autobiography, tells of the strict laws that governed where his family could live after their house burned down: "My father prevailed on some friends to clothe and house us temporarily; then he moved us into another house on the outskirts of East Lansing. In those days Negroes weren't allowed after dark in East Lansing proper . . . where Michigan State University is located."[39]

The phenomenon of "Whites-only" areas has been very common in U.S. history. These types of neighborhoods are good examples of how power influences intercultural contact. The segregation of African Americans was not accidental. Beginning in 1890 until the late 1960s (the fair-housing legislation), Whites in America created thousands of Whites-only towns, commonly known as "sundown towns." This was a reference to the signs often posted at their city limits that warned, as one did in Hawthorne, California, in the 1930s: "Nigger, Don't Let The Sun Set On YOU In Hawthorne." In fact, during that 70-year period a majority of incorporated places (in the United States) kept out African Americans.[40] In these segregated neighborhoods, certain cultural groups defined who got to live where and dictated the rules by which other groups had to live. These rules were enforced through legal means and by harassment. For Malcolm X and bell hooks, these lines of segregation were clear and unmistakable. One of our older students also recalls these times:

> I lived 9 of my first 12 years in Miami, Florida, where segregation and discrimination were a way of life. Schools and housing were segregated, and "colored" people had to ride at the back of the bus. . . . When I was about 7 or 8, I saw a man get hit by a car as he was crossing the street. They called an ambulance, but when it came they wouldn't take the man to the hospital because they had sent the wrong "color" of ambulance. I don't remember if the man was Black or White; I only recall how angry I was. . . . Later we moved to California, where segregation of Whites and Blacks was accomplished covertly by "White flight"—when African Americans moved into a neighborhood, most of the Whites moved out.

In San Francisco, different racial politics constructed and isolated Chinatown. Until racial covenants were lifted in 1947, Chinese Americans were forced to live in Chinatown. The boundaries that demarcated Chinatown—the acceptable place for Chinese and Chinese Americans to live—were strictly enforced through violence. Newly arrived immigrants were sometimes stoned as they left the piers and made their way to Chinatown or those who wandered into other neighborhoods could be attacked by "young toughs" who amused themselves by beating Chinese.[41]

In contrast to Malcolm X's family being excluded from living in East Lansing, the Chinese of San Francisco were forced to live in a marked-off territory. Yet another system of segregation developed in Savannah, Georgia, around 1900. There, Chinese immigrants were advised by other Chinese Americans to live apart from each other, rather than settle in ethnic enclaves, because of the negative experiences of residents of Chinatowns in San Francisco and New York.[42] They felt that creating a Chinatown would increase anti-Chinese sentiment, as well as make them easier targets for anti-Chinese discrimination.

Historical forces and power relations have led to different settlement patterns of other cultural groups in ethnic enclaves across the U.S. landscape. Many small towns across the Midwest were settled by particular European groups—for example, in the state of Iowa, there were Germans in Amana, Dutch in Pella, and Czechs and Slovaks in Cedar Rapids. Cities, too, have their neighborhoods, based on settlement patterns. For instance, South Philadelphia is largely Italian American, South Boston is largely Irish American, and Overtown in Miami is largely African American. Although it is no longer legal to mandate that people live in particular districts or neighborhoods based on their racial or ethnic backgrounds, the continued existence of such neighborhoods underscores the importance of historical influence. Similar spaces exist in other countries as well. Remember the terrorist attacks in Paris in November 2015? A number of terrorists came from the same Brussels neighborhood, Molenbeek. There is a relationship between place and human relations, as one expert described, Molenbeek is one of the segregated suburbs, isolated from the wider Belgium society, where "there are problems with failed integration, socioeconomic problems, and crime that can be exploited for the jihadists."[43]

The relationship among identity, power, and cultural space are quite complex. Power relations influence how some cultural groups are accepted, some tolerated and others may be unacceptable. Identifying with various cultural spaces often involves negotiation. This is the case in Boyle Heights, a low-income Latino community of small shops, mariachis, and taco stands that is the last holdout to Los Angeles gentrification. The residents are fighting to keep their neighborhood from being changed by powerful outsiders. Property values are skyrocketing and posters offering cash for homes are there. The residents fear that the new money and outsiders will drive up rents, drive out residents, and erase their communal Chicano identity. They have organized their hardline tactics by harassing an opera company's performance in a park with shouts, whistles, and a brass band; masked activists stalked a group of visitors on an educational walking tour and ordered them to leave the neighborhood. Of course there is some ambivalence, as development might bring improvements, but as one said, "Make it all shiny, great. But then what? The gringos will come."[44]

***Regionalism***   Ongoing regional conflicts, expressions of nationalism, ethnic revivals, and religious strife point to the continuing struggle over who gets to define whom. Such conflicts are hardly new, though. In fact, some cultural spaces, such as Jerusalem, have been ongoing sites of struggle for many centuries. Similarly, during the twentieth century, Germany and France fought over Alsace-Lorraine, and both the Germans and the Czechs claimed the Sudetenland region. Other areas have retained their regional identities despite being engulfed by a larger nation—for example, Scotland and Wales in Britain, the Basque region in both Spain and France, Catalonia in Spain, Brittany and Corsica in France, and the Kurdish region in both Turkey and Iraq. Although regions may not always be clearly marked on maps of the world, many people identify quite strongly with particular regions.

**Regionalism**—loyalty to some area that holds cultural meaning—can take many different forms, from symbolic expressions of identification to armed conflict. Within the United States, people may identify themselves or others as southerners or midwesterners. People from Montreal might identify more strongly with the province of Quebec than with their country, Canada. Similarly, some Corsicans might feel a need to negotiate their identity with France. Sometimes people fly regional flags, wear particular kinds of clothes, celebrate regional holidays, and participate in other cultural activities to communicate their regional identification. But these expressions of regionalism are not always simply celebratory, as the violent conflicts in Kosovo, Chechnya, Eritrea, Tibet, and East Timor indicate. The idea of national borders may seem simple enough, but they often ignore or obscure conflicting regional identities. To understand how intercultural communications may be affected by national borders, we must consider how issues of history, power, identity, culture, and context come into play.

***Cyberspace***   Another set of postmodern spaces that are quite familiar are those on new media, that exist in **cyberspace.** There are **MMORPGs** (massively multiplayer online role-playing games), virtual worlds like Second Life, Onverse, Smallworlds, and Habbo, where people meet in real time and interact primarily for recreational purposes. As we discussed in Chapter 1, there are other media spaces like blogs and

**What Do You Think?**

One popular type of cultural space are blogs and social media spaces like Facebook, Instagram, Tumblr, and Pinterest, where people journal their experiences and share information about their lives as well as photos and videos. These spaces have blurred the distinction between what is seen as public and private. Often we don't even realize how many people are reading our entries or posts. How can you use these spaces to express your identity and culture? Do you make a conscious distinction between private and public information when you post information? Do you want lots of people to read your posts? How can you read others' entries as a way of learning about cultural groups different from your own? To access interesting blogs about intercultural communication, check out culturespan. blogspot.com and http://blog .englishandculture.com/.

**Info Bites**

A recent report shows some interesting similarities and differences on how racial and ethnic in the United States use cultural spaces of social media.

For example, the topics people discuss do vary.

It is interesting that White respondents were significantly less likely than their non-White counterparts to have shared any information related to topics of education or schools and crime or public safety. The reason for these differences is probably due to the persistent racial inequities in both education and the criminal justice system and why these topics are discussed more frequently by Blacks and Latinos on social media.
(Source: Zhou, L. (2015, October 5). How race influences social-media sharing. *Theatlantic .com*. Retrieved June 23, 2016, from http://www.theatlantic.com/technology/archive/2015/10/race-social-media/408889/.)

online discussion groups where people meet for fun, to gain information or experience a supportive community (e.g., heart patients, transgender people, and ethnic communities). There are also more than 2 billion people who now use social network sites such as Facebook, Instagram, and Tumbler in the United States, VK, Qzone, Renren, etc., and some scholars question the effect on relationships of so much time spent in these cultural spaces. While these sites offer opportunities for connection, learning and support, and empowerment, results of one study suggest the longer someone spends on Facebook, the worse their mood gets.[45] The reasons may be jealousy that comes from constant comparisons (my friends are having such good times, traveling to exotic places, parties I'm not invited to, etc.).

In addition, they can be hostile cultural places of harassment and exclusion. As we mentioned in Chapter 1, gay, lesbian, and transgendered individuals are much more likely to be the targets of bullying than straight individuals. Women gamers and game developers have been subjected to severe harassment by male gamers, violent threats, and rampant misogyny (#gamergate).[46] In addition, some experts suggest that the new digital divide may be between those who have and don't have access to the new "shared, collaborative, and on demand" economy, of Uber and Lyft ride sharing, Airbnb and HomeAway home sharing, and crowdfunding sites. These appear to be used mostly by the educated and urban and young (under age 45).[47] About one-quarter of Americans (28 percent) say they have not used *any* major shared or on-demand platforms, and 60 percent say they have never heard of the term "crowdfunding." We will explore social media relationships further in Chapter 9.

## Changing Cultural Space

*Traveling*    What happens when people change cultural spaces? Traveling is frequently viewed as simply a leisure activity, but it is more than that. In terms of intercultural communication, **traveling** changes cultural spaces in a way that often transforms the traveler. Changing cultural spaces means changing who you are and how you interact with others. Perhaps the old saying "When in Rome, do as the Romans do" holds true today as we cross cultural spaces more frequently than ever. However, this is not always easy to do. After traveling to Morocco, our student Jessica described the nonverbal behavior of some of the U.S. American students she was with:

> We were informed before the trip that women in Morocco dress differently, that they cover practically every inch of their bodies. We were not expected to do that, but we were told to dress appropriately, in pants or a skirt that covered our legs and a shirt with sleeves. It felt like a slap in the face when I saw two girls on the trip in cut-off jean shorts and tight tank tops that showed their midriffs. They even had the nerve to ask our tour guide why the Moroccan women were shouting "shame" and casting evil looks.

Should people alter their communication style when they encounter travelers who are not in their traditional cultural space? Do they assume that the travelers should interact in the ways prescribed by their own cultural space? Experts also caution that cyberspace may be changing the way we experience travel. Writer Frank Bruin describes his recent experience of being in Shanghai in his hotel room, watching a season of "The Wire" he had downloaded before he left home. He finally leaves his hotel room and ventures outside but "haunted by how tempting it was to stay put and to look down at our mobile devices instead of up at the world around us" and how easily we can now travel the globe in a thoroughly" "customized cocoon." He calls it "traveling without seeing."[48] Do our attachments to our mobile devices hinder us from seeing and interacting with others when we change cultural spaces? These are some of the issues that travel raises; we address these issues in Chapter 10.

*Migration*   People also change cultural spaces through **migration** from a primary cultural context to a new one. Migration, of course, involves a different kind of change in cultural spaces than traveling. With traveling, the change is temporary and, usually, desirable. It is something people seek out. By contrast, people who migrate do not always seek out this change. For example, many people were forced from their homelands of Sudan and Bosnia and had to settle elsewhere. Many immigrants leave their homelands simply to survive. But they often find it difficult to adjust to the change, especially if the language and customs of the new cultural space are unfamiliar. That is, they may suffer culture shock, as described in Chapter 4. As one recent immigrant to the United States describes it, "I myself experienced such shock after arriving in the United States. The people's language and behavior were the first aspects that made me feel insecure and disoriented. The stress I experienced caused sleeplessness and a feeling of being lost."

Even within the United States, people often find it difficult to adapt to new surroundings when they move. Tom remembers how northerners who moved to the South often were unfamiliar with the custom of banks closing early on Wednesday or with the traditional New Year's Day foods. And ridiculing or ignoring the customs of their new cultural space simply led to further intercultural communication problems.

## The Dynamic Nature of Cultural Spaces

The dynamic nature of cultural space stands in sharp contrast to more traditional Western notions of space, which promoted land ownership, surveys, borders, colonies, and territories. No passport is needed to travel in the current dynamic cultural space, because there are no border guards. The dynamic nature of current cultural spaces underscores their relationship to changing cultural needs. The space exists only as long as it is needed in its present form.

Phoenix, Arizona, for example, which became a city only in the past few decades, has no Chinatown, no Japantown, no Koreatown, no Irish district, no Polish neighborhood, and no Italian area. Instead, people of Polish descent might live anywhere in the metropolitan area but congregate for special occasions or for specific reasons. On Sundays, the Polish Catholic Mass draws worshippers from throughout Phoenix. When people want to buy Polish breads and pastries, they can go to the Polish bakery and also speak Polish there. Ethnic identity is only one of several identities important to these people. When they desire recognition and interaction based on their Polish heritage, they can fulfill these desires. When they seek other forms of identification, they may go to places where they can be, say, Phoenix Suns fans or art lovers. Ethnic identity is neither the sole factor nor necessarily the most important factor at all times in their lives. The markers of ethnic life in Phoenix are the urban sites where people congregate when they desire ethnic cultural contact. At other times, they may frequent other locations to express other aspects of their identities. In this sense, this contemporary urban space is dynamic and allows people to participate in the communication of identity in new ways.[49]

As noted earlier, the rise of the Internet has added a new dimension to the creation of cultural spaces. We can now enter (virtually) a number of spaces where we can communicate in ways that express different aspects of our cultural identities. Our physical space or location is no longer the most significant barrier to communicating with others who share our cultural identities. Because we are communicating in cyberspace, we are no longer bound by our physical bodies. We can "pass" as men or women, members of many different religious and ethnic communities, or people with different political perspectives or sexualities. Through virtual tourism, we can "travel" to exotic locales we could never afford to visit in real life.[50] While it is still difficult to communicate in languages we do not speak, the Internet even makes some rudimentary translation sites available. Many people, however, have no interest in enacting identities with which they do not identify. Why communicate about lacrosse, for example, if you would prefer to spend time communicating about your auto that reflects your identity? Cyberspace pushes the boundaries of what cultural space is, how quickly cultural spaces can shift, and how quickly we can take control over who we are and where we are, whenever we wish.[51]

### SUMMARY

In this chapter, we examined both nonverbal communication principles and cultural spaces. Nonverbal communication, which operates at a subconscious level, is learned implicitly and can reinforce, substitute for, or contradict verbal behaviors.

Nonverbal behaviors can communicate relational meaning, status, and deception. Nonverbal communication is influenced by culture, although many cultures share some nonverbal behaviors. Methods of nonverbal communication include eye contact, facial expressions, gestures, time orientation, and silence. Sometimes cultural differences in nonverbal behaviors can lead to stereotyping of other cultures.

Cultural space influences cultural identity. Cultural spaces relate to issues of power and intercultural communication. Homes, neighborhoods, regions, nations, and cyberspace are all examples of cultural spaces. Two ways of changing cultural spaces are travel and migration. Current cultural spaces are dynamic, accommodating people of different cultural identities who coexist.

**Surf's Up!**

Take the quiz at https://www.kent.ac.uk/careers/interviews/nvc.htm to learn how to manage your nonverbal communication in interviews. Think about how many of these suggestions apply only to a U.S. American context. Think about how you would manage your nonverbal interview behavior when applying for a position in a multinational corporation overseas.

## BUILDING INTERCULTURAL SKILLS

1. Become more conscious of your nonverbal behavior in intercultural encounters. Practice your encoding skills. You can do this by noting the nonverbal behaviors of others—their facial expressions, gestures, eye contact, and so on. Check to see if their nonverbal communication is telling you that they understand or misunderstand you.

2. Become more aware of others' nonverbal communication. What messages are they sending? And how do you react to those messages? Think about when you are uncomfortable in intercultural encounters. Is your discomfort due to the nonverbal messages others are sending? Are they violating the rules you're used to? Standing too close, or too far away? Touching too much, or not enough? Talking too loudly, or too softly?

3. Practice your decoding skills. Check out your perceptions of others' nonverbal behavior. Are you accurate, or do you misread their nonverbal cues? Are they misunderstanding when you think they are understanding? Are they happy when you think they are upset?

4. Expand your nonverbal communication repertoire. Practice new nonverbal behaviors. Try varying your posture, facial expressions, and eye contact.

5. Be flexible and adaptable in your nonverbal communication in intercultural encounters. Try synchronizing your behavior to that of others, which usually communicates that you feel good about your relationship. If others stand with their arms folded, do the same. If they stand closer than you're used to, don't move away. If they use more eye contact, try to do the same.

6. Become more aware of your prejudicial assumptions based on nonverbal behavior. When you have a very negative reaction to others, check out the basis for these assumptions. Is it simply because of the way they look? Give them another chance.

## ACTIVITIES

*Nonverbal rules:* Choose a cultural space that you are interested in studying. Visit this space on four different occasions to observe how people there interact. Focus on one aspect of nonverbal communication, such as eye contact or personal space. List some rules that seem to govern this aspect of nonverbal communication. For example, if you are focusing on personal space, you might describe, among other things, how far apart people tend to stand when conversing. Based on your observations, list some rules about proper (expected) nonverbal behavior in this cultural space. Share your conclusions with the class. To what extent do other students share your conclusions? Can we generalize about nonverbal rules in cultural spaces? What factors influence whether an individual follows unspoken rules of behavior?

## ENDNOTES

1. James Bond's body language. (2015, January 24). *The Economist, 414*(8922), p. 24.
2. Knapp, M. L., & Hall, J. A. (2010). *Nonverbal communication in human interaction* (7th ed.). Belmont, CA: Wadsworth/Cengage Learning.
3. Knapp & Hall (2010).
4. Jones, S. E., & LeBaron, C. D. (2002). Research on the relationship between verbal and nonverbal communication: Emerging integration. *Journal of Communication, 52*, 499–521.
5. Bente, G., Heuschner, H., Al Issa, A., & Blascovich, J. J. (2010). The others: Universal and cultural specificities in the perception of status and dominance from nonverbal behavior. *Consciousness and Cognition, 19*(3), 762–777.
6. Burgoon, J., Proudfoot, J., Schuetzler, R., & Wilson, D. (2014). Patterns of nonverbal behavior associated with truth and deception: Illustrations from three experiments. *Journal of Nonverbal Behavior, 38*(3), 325–354.
7. Montepare, J. M. (2003). Evolution and nonverbal behavior: Adaptive social interaction strategies. *Journal of Nonverbal Behavior, 27*, 141–143; Patterson, M. L. (2003). Commentary: Evolution and nonverbal behavior: Functions and mediating processes. *Journal of Behavior, 27*, 201–207.
8. Ekman, P. (2004, October 2). Happy, sad, angry, disgusted: Secrets of the face. *New Scientist, 184*(2467), 4–5. See also Galati, D., Sini, B., Schmidt, S., & Tinti, C. (2003, July). Spontaneous facial expressions in congenitally blind and sighted children aged 8–11. *Journal of Visual Impairment and Blindness, 97*, 418–428.
9. Montepare, J. M. (2003). Evolution and nonverbal behavior: Adaptive social interaction strategies. *Journal of Nonverbal Behavior, 27*, 141–143; Patterson, M. L. (2003). Commentary: Evolution and nonverbal behavior: Functions and mediating processes. *Journal of Nonverbal Behavior, 27*, 201–207.
10. Jack, R. E., Garrod, O. G. B., Yub, H., Caldarac. R, & Schyns, P. G. (2012). Facial expressions of emotion are not culturally universal. *Proceedings of the National Academy of Sciences, 109*(19), 7242; Du, S., Tao, Y, & Martinez, A. M. (2014). Compound facial expressions of emotion. *Proceedings of the National Academy of Sciences, 111*(15), 1454–1462.
11. Høgh-Olesen, H. (2008). Human spatial behaviour: The spacing of people, objects, and animals in six cross-cultural samples. *Journal of Cognition & Culture, 8*(3/4), 245–280.
12. Gottschall, J. (2008). The "beauty myth" is no myth. *Human Nature, 19*(2), 174–188; Swami, V., Furnham, A., Chamorro-Premuzic, T., Akbar, K., Gordon, N., Harris, T., Finch, J., & Tovée, M. J. (2010). More than just skin deep? Personality information influences men's ratings of the attractiveness of women's body sizes. *Journal of Social Psychology, 150*(6), 628–647.
13. Swami, V., Caprario, C., & Tovée, M. J. (2006). Female physical attractiveness in Britain and Japan: A cross-cultural study. *European Journal of Personality, 20*, 69–81; Swami, V., Smith, J., Tsiokris, A., Georgiades, C., Sangareau, Y., Tovée, M. J., & Furnham, A. (2007). Male physical attractiveness in Britain and Greece: A cross-cultural study. *Journal of Social Psychology, 147*(1), 15–26.
14. Croucher, S. M. (2008). French-Muslims and the hijab: An analysis of identity and the Islamic veil in France. *Journal of Intercultural Communication Research, 37*(3), 199–213.
15. Knapp & Hall (2010).
16. Axtell, R. E. (2007). *Essential do's and taboos: Complete guide to international business and leisure travel.* Hoboken, NJ: John Wiley & Sons, p. 20.
17. Archer (1997), p. 87.
18. Hall, E. T. (2013). The power of hidden differences. In M. J. Bennett (Ed.), *Basic concepts of intercultural communication* (pp. 165–184). Boston, MA: Nicholas Brealy.
19. Macduff, I. (2006). Your pace or mine? Culture, time, and negotiation. *Negotiation Journal, 22*(1), 31–45.
20. Dahl, O. (1993). *Malagasy meanings: An interpretive approach to intercultural communication in Madagascar.* Stavanger, Norway: Center for Intercultural Communication, p. 66.
21. Covarrubias, P. (2007). (Un)Biased in Western theory: Generative silence in American Indian communication. *Communication Monographs, 74*(2), 270.
22. Acheson, C. (2007). Silence in dispute. In C. S. Beck (Ed.), *Communication Yearbook 31* (pp. 2–59), New York, NY: Lawrence Erlbaum Associates.

23.  Condon, J. (1984). *With respect to the Japanese*. Yarmouth, ME: Intercultural Press, p. 41.
24.  Carbaugh, D., & Berry, M. (2001). Communicating history, Finnish and American discourses: An ethnographic contribution to intercultural communication inquiry. *Communication Theory, 11,* 352–366; Sajavaara, K., & Lehtonen, J. (1997). The silent Finn revisited. In Jaworski (Ed.), *Silence: Interdisciplinary perspectives* (pp. 263–283). New York, NY: Mouton de Gruyter.
25.  Braithwaite, C. A. (1990). Communicative silence: A cross-cultural study of Basso's hypothesis. In D. Carbaugh (Ed.), *Cultural communication and intercultural contact* (pp. 321–327). Hillsdale, NJ: Erlbaum.
26.  Nakane, I. (2006). Silence and politeness in intercultural communication in university seminars. *Journal of Pragmatics 38,* 1811–1835.
27.  Liu, J. (2002). Negotiating silence in American classrooms: Three Chinese cases. *Language and Intercultural Communication, 2*(1), 37–54.
28.  Mosbach, H. (1988). The importance of silence and stillness in Japanese nonverbal communication: A cross cultural approach. In F. Poyatos (Ed.), *Cross-cultural perspectives in nonverbal communication* (pp. 201–215). Lewiston, NY: Hogrefe.
29.  Montell, G. (2003, October 15). Do good looks equal good evaluations? *Chronicle of Higher Education.* Retrieved from chronicle.com/jobs/2003/10/2003101501c.htm.
30.  Neal, L. V. I., McCray, A. D., & Webb-Johnson, G. (2001). Teachers' reactions to African American students' movement styles. *Intervention in School and Clinic, 36,* 168–174.
31.  Matthews, R. (2000). Culture patterns of South Asian and S.E. Asian Americans. *Interventions in School and Clinic, 36,* 101–105.
32.  Burack, A. (2011, March 18). District Attorney George Gascón says hate crimes on the rise in San Francisco. *San Francisco Examiner Online.* Retrieved August 30, 2011, from www.sfexaminer.com /local/crime/2011/03/district-attorney-gasc-n-says-hate-crimes-rise-san-francisco.
33.  Richeson, J., & Shelton, J. N. (2005). Brief report: Thin slices of racial bias. *Journal of Nonverbal Behavior, 29,* 75–86.
34.  Johnson, A. G. (2006). *Privilege, power and difference.* (2nd ed.). New York, NY: Academic Internet Publishers.
35.  Fussell, P. (1983). *Class.* New York, NY: Summit Books.
36.  Hooks, B. (1990). *Yearning: Race, gender, and cultural politics.* Boston, MA: South End Press, p. 41.
37.  Greene, H. (1991). Charleston, South Carolina. In J. Preston (Ed.), *Hometowns: Gay men write about where they belong* (pp. 55–67). New York, NY: Dutton.
38.  Saylor, S. (1991). Amethyst, Texas. In J. Preston (Ed.), *Hometowns: Gay men write about where they belong* (pp. 119–135). New York, NY: Dutton.
39.  X, Malcolm, & Haley, A. (1964). *The autobiography of Malcolm X.* New York, NY: Grove Press, pp. 3–4.
40.  Loewen, J. (2005). *Sundown towns: A hidden dimension of American racism.* New York, NY: New Press.
41.  Nee, V. G., & Nee, B. D. B. (1974). *Longtime Californ': A documentary study of an American Chinatown.* Boston, MA: Houghton Mifflin, p. 60.
42.  Pruden, G. B., Jr. (1990). History of the Chinese in Savannah, Georgia. In J. Goldstein (Ed.), *Georgia's East Asian connection: Into the twenty-first century: Vol. 27. West Georgia College studies in the social sciences* (pp. 17–34). Carrollton, TX: West Georgia College.
43.  Robins-Early, N. (2016, March 23). Why focusing on Brussels' Molenbeek neighborhood misses the point about terrorism. *huffingtonpost.com.* Retrieved May 27, 2016, from http://www.huffingtonpost .com/entry/brussels-attack-isis_us_56f2db1ce4b02c402f6616d0.
44.  Carroll, R. (2016, April 19). "Hope everyone pukes on your artisanal treats": Fighting gentrification, LA-style. *theguardian.com.* Retrieved May 27, 2016, from http://www.theguardian.com/us -news/2016/apr/19/los-angeles-la-gentrification-resistance-boyle-heights.
45.  Kross, E., Verduyn, P., Demiralp, E., Park, J., Lee, D. S., Lin, H., Shablack, H., Jonides, J., & Ybarra, O. (2013). Facebook use predicts decline in subjective well-being in young adults. *PLOS/one, 8*(8), e69841.
46.  Dougherty, C., & Isaac, M. (2016, March 3). SCSW addresses online harassment of women in gaming. *nytimes.com.* Retrieved May 30, 2016, from http://www.nytimes.com/2016/03/14/technology /sxsw-addresses-online-harassment-of-women-in-gaming.html?_r=0.

47. Smith, A. (2016, May 19). Shared, collaborative and on demand: The new digital economy. *pewinternet.org*. Retrieved May 30, 2016, from http://www.pewinternet.org/2016/05/19/the-new -digital-economy/.

48. Bruni, F. (2013, September 2). Traveling without seeing. *nytimes.com*. Retrieved May 27, 2016, from http://www.nytimes.com/2013/09/03/opinion/bruni-traveling-without-seeing.html?_r=0.

49. Drzewiecka, J. A., & Nakayama, T. K. (1998). City sites: Postmodern urban space and the communication of identity. *Southern Communication Journal, 64,* 20–31.

50. Huang, Y-C. (2011).Virtual tourism: Identifying the factors that affect a tourist's experience and behavioral intentions in a 3D virtual world. Doctoral Dissertation. Retrieved July 3, 2012, from http://udini.proquest.com/view/virtual-tourism-identifying-the-pqid:2463907101/.

51. Strate, L., Jacobson, R. L., & Gibson, S. L. (Eds.), (2003). *Communication and cyberspace: Social interaction in an electronic environment.* Cresskill, NJ: Hampton Press.

© kristian sekulic/Getty Images RF

CHAPTER SEVEN

# Popular Culture and Intercultural Communication

**STUDY OBJECTIVES**

*After reading this chapter, you should be able to:*

1. Define popular culture.

2. Identify some types of popular culture.

3. Describe characteristics of popular culture.

4. Explain why it is important to understand popular culture in intercultural communication.

5. Discuss why people consume or resist specific cultural texts.

6. Understand how cultural texts influence cultural identities.

7. Discuss how cultural group portrayals in popular culture forms influence intercultural communication.

8. Suggest effects of the global domination of U.S. popular culture.

**KEY TERMS**

cultural identities
cultural imperialism
cultural texts
culture industries
electronic colonialism

folk culture
media imperialism
popular culture
reader profiles

*My parents were quite worried when I told them that I wanted to study in the United States. They had seen a lot of violence in the U.S., especially gun shootings, and were concerned about my safety. Although they had not been to the U.S., their image of the country was very influenced by television images in Ireland. I too had an image of everyone in the U.S. carrying guns.*

*—Seán*

As Seán discovered, the impact of television images can influence how people view everyday life in various cultures around the world. While popular culture can be an important influence in how we make decisions about traveling to other places, these images also have to be connected to our experiences as well. These are complex relationships that highlight the importance of thinking about this kind of culture when we think about intercultural communication.

Culture is central to intercultural communication, but we often overlook some of the meanings of culture in everyday life. One kind of culture that is often overlooked by intercultural communication scholars is popular culture. But popular culture plays a very important role in how we understand the world, helping us reinforce our sense of who we are and confirming our worldviews.

Neither Tom nor Judith has ever been to Cuba, Kenya, Nigeria, India, Russia, or Argentina. Yet all of these places, and many more, evoke images of what it is "really" like to be there. We derive images about these places from the news, movies, television shows, advertisements, and other kinds of popular culture. Sometimes we feel as if we've been somewhere when we watch the Travel Channel. And when people actually visit Paris, or Honolulu, or Tokyo, they might exclaim that it looks just like it does on television! Obviously, not all of this "information" in popular culture is up-to-date and accurate. Some popular culture images reinforce stereotypes of other cultures, while other images challenge those stereotypes. In this chapter, we examine the role that popular culture plays in building bridges in, as well as barriers to, intercultural communication.

## VIEWING OTHERS THROUGH POPULAR CULTURE

We can experience new places by traveling and by migrating. But there will always be places around the world that we have not visited and where we have not lived. Most of us do not even make it around the globe.

So what do we know about places we have never been, and how do we acquire this "knowledge"? Much of what we know about these places probably comes from popular culture—the media outlets of television, music, videos, and magazines that most of us know and share. And how does this experience of places traveled to only through popular culture affect intercultural communication?

The complexity of popular culture is often overlooked in our society. People express concerns about the social effects of popular culture—for example, the effects of television violence on children or the relationship between heterosexual pornography and violence against women. Yet most people look down on the study of popular culture, as if there is nothing of significance to learn there. This attitude can make it difficult to investigate and discuss popular culture.

As U.S. Americans, we are in a unique position in relationship to popular culture. Products of U.S. popular culture are well known and widely circulated around the globe. Many U.S. film, music, and television stars, such as Beyoncé, Brad Pitt, Angelina Jolie, Ryan Gosling, and Jennifer Lopez, are also popular outside the United States, creating an uneven flow of **cultural texts**—cultural artifacts that convey norms, values, and beliefs—between the United States and other nations. Scholars Elihu Katz and Tamar Liebes note the "apparent ease with which American television programs cross cultural and linguistic frontiers. Indeed, the phenomenon is so taken for granted that hardly any systematic research has been done to explain the reasons why these programs are so successful."[1]

By contrast, U.S. Americans are rarely exposed to popular culture from outside the United States. Exceptions to this largely one-way movement of popular culture include foreign performers who sing in English, such as ABBA, Björk, Shakira, Golden Earring, and Celine Dion. Not only do many non-English speakers sing in English, but many of them and other English speakers from around the world sing in American English. Andy Gibson, a researcher at the Auckland University of Technology in New Zealand, has studied vowel pronunciation in New Zealand singers when speaking and singing. He says, "The American-influenced accent is automatic in the context of singing pop music, and it is used by people from all around the world."[2] The dominance of American English and U.S. popular culture makes U.S. Americans more dependent on an American-centric popular culture which can also lead to cultural imperialism, a topic we will discuss later in this chapter.

The study of popular culture has become increasingly important in the communication field. Although intercultural communication scholars traditionally have overlooked popular culture, we believe that these forms of culture are significant influences in intercultural interaction. In this chapter, we explore some of these influences.

## WHAT IS "POPULAR CULTURE"?

Sometimes it may seem obvious what constitutes **popular culture** and what does not. For example, we often consider soap operas, reality television shows, and romance novels to be popular culture, while symphonies, operas, and the ballet are not. Popular culture often is seen as populist, in that it includes forms of contemporary culture that are made popular by and for the people through their mass consumption of these products. As John Fiske, professor of communication arts, observes:

> To be made into popular culture, a commodity must also bear the interests of the people. Popular culture is not consumption, it is culture—the active process of

**What Do You Think?**

The ongoing development of new technologies and products means that many more people can easily access international television programming and movies than ever before. For example, KORTV has developed an app that can be used with Apple products, such as Apple TV, and iPad, to watch South Korean television and movies. DramaFever (www.dramafever.com) offers Korean and Latin American television shows and movies through its website. Despite the technological advances, not all programming around the world is available everywhere else. Licensing agreements and other legal barriers can prevent people in some countries from watching content from other countries. What might be some reasons that some countries and corporations block content from some other countries?

Pop stars, like Rihanna, often enjoy worldwide popularity. Although she is from Barbados, she moved to the United States, and the popularity of U.S. popular culture products can launch many careers. This has important implications for both individuals and cultures worldwide.

© Kevin Mazur/WireImage/Getty Images

generating and circulating meanings and pleasures within a social system: culture, however industrialized, can never be adequately described in terms of the buying and selling of commodities.[3]

In his study of popular Mexican American music in Los Angeles, ethnic studies professor George Lipsitz highlights the ways that marginalized social groups are able to express themselves in innovative, nonmainstream ways. In this study, he demonstrates how the "popular" can arise from a mixing and borrowing from other cultures. He suggests that "the ability of musicians to learn from other cultures played a key role in their success as rock-and-roll artists."[4] Here, as elsewhere, the popular speaks to—and resonates with—the people, but it speaks to them through many cultural voices.

Intercultural contact and intercultural communication play a central role in the creation and maintenance of popular culture. Yet, as Lipsitz also points out, the popular is political and pleasurable, which opens new arenas for complicating the ways we might think about popular culture.

Thus, popular culture can be said to have four significant characteristics: (1) It is produced by culture industries, (2) it is different from **folk culture,** (3) it is everywhere, and (4) it fills a social function. As Fiske points out, popular culture is nearly always produced by what are called **culture industries** within a capitalist system that sees the products of popular culture as commodities to be sold for profit. The Disney Corporation is a noteworthy example of a culture industry because it produces amusement parks, movies, cartoons, and a plethora of associated merchandise. As shown in Table 7.1, culture products can be imported from other countries.

Folk culture refers to the traditional rituals and traditions that maintain cultural group identity. Unlike popular culture, folk culture is typically not controlled by any industry and is not driven by a profit motive. For examples, pow-wows across North

**TABLE 7.1  U.S. Television Shows Imported from Other Countries**

While many television shows from the United States are popular in other countries, sometimes U.S. television shows borrow ideas from other countries. Here are some examples:

*Who Wants to be a Millionaire*—Great Britain

*The Voice*—the Netherlands

*Survivor*—Sweden

*America's Funniest Home Videos*—Japan

America are laden with traditions. UNESCO has begun identifying important folk culture through its "Masterpieces of the Oral and Intangible Heritage of Humanity" list. While these rituals may be open to outsiders, they express and confirm cultural identity and group membership.

More recently, communication scholars Joshua Gunn and Barry Brummett have challenged the notion that there is an important difference between folk culture and popular culture. They note that scholars "write as if there is a fundamental difference between a mass-produced and mass-marketed culture and a more authentic 'folk' culture or subculture. Such a binary is dissolving into a globally marketed culture. A few remaining pockets of folk culture remain here and there: on the Sea Islands, in Amish country, in departments of English. The rest of folk culture is now 50% off at Wal–Mart."[5] In the new context of globalization, whatever happened to folk traditions and artifacts? Have they been unable to escape being mass-produced and marketed around the globe?

Popular culture also is ubiquitous. We are bombarded with it, every day and everywhere. On average, U.S. Americans watch more than 40 hours of television per week. Movie theaters beckon us with the latest multimillion-dollar extravaganzas, nearly all U.S.-made. Radio stations and TV music stations blast us with the hottest music groups performing their latest hits. And we are inundated with a staggering number of advertisements and commercials daily. Much of this consumption of popular culture happens on smartphones and tablets today, rather than exclusively on radios and televisions, as it once was.

It is difficult to avoid popular culture. Not only is it ubiquitous, but it also serves an important social function. How many times have friends and family members asked about your reactions to recent movies or television programs? What kind of reaction would you get if you said, "I don't watch television"? Communication scholars Horace Newcomb and Paul Hirsch suggest that television serves as a cultural forum for discussing and working out our ideas on a variety of topics, including those that emerge from television programs.[6] We see how others feel about various issues—from gay marriage to immigration to school shootings—and how we feel about them as they are discussed on television. These forums include daytime and late-night talk shows, news programs, and situation comedies, among many others. Television, then, has a powerful social function: to serve as a forum for social issues.

In their study on the early tweets after Michael Brown was shot and killed by Officer Darren Wilson in Ferguson, Missouri, Sarah Jackson and Brooke

**Info Bites**

Scholar Raymond Williams argued that popular culture is important to study because in one week we are exposed to more stories and dramas in the media than Europeans a thousand years ago would have been exposed to in their entire lives.

Foucault Welles studied how Twitter and the hashtag #Ferguson shaped discussion on race, policing, and social justice. In analyzing the tweets, they identified @AyoMissDarkSkin as the most influential after the shooting, as she was in the neighborhood at the time. Jackson and Foucault Welles contrast her tweet with the tweet from the *St. Louis Post Dispatch:*

> The discourse of this tweet immediately frames Brown as the innocent ('unarmed' 'boy') victim of extreme violence ('executed' 'Shot him 10 times') and communicates an effective response ('smh'—Shaking My Head—generally used to indicate disgust or incredulousness). This discursive work stands in sharp contrast to a tweet sent two hours later by the only media outlet to achieve crowd-sourced elite status on day one, local mainstream newspaper the St. Louis Post Dispatch (@stltoday). @stltoday reported: 'Fatal shooting by Ferguson police prompts mob reaction'.[7]

The use of Twitter to provide and produce a counter discourse to the elite discourse of the newspaper opens an arena for various publics to come to understand what happened in Ferguson and what it means. Popular culture offers differing interpretations which are particularly important for marginalized cultures and communities.

In contrast, not all popular culture serves to open forums for public deliberation. In his study of the "Pro Football and the American Spirit" exhibit, communication scholar Michael Butterworth examined this exhibit at the Pro Football Hall of Fame in Canton, Ohio, which connects football with militarism.[8] By connecting various wars with the role of the NFL, it highlights the sacrifices of veterans affiliated with football, including Pat Tillman. But it also shuts down public deliberation about militarism and war. Rather than challenging the history and role of military conflicts, the exhibit ends up accepting war and celebrating militarism, rather than peace. In this analysis, popular culture reduces the arena of contemporary democratic deliberation.

The ways in which people negotiate their relationships to popular culture are complex. It is this complexity that makes understanding the role of popular culture in intercultural communication so difficult. Clearly, we are not passive receivers of this deluge of popular culture. We are, in fact, quite active in our consumption of or resistance to popular culture, a notion that we turn to next.

## U.S. POPULAR CULTURE AND POWER

*Whenever I go to China, people always ask me, "Is America like what we see on TV?" They want to know if everyone owns a gun, if we eat at McDonald's everyday, and if it's as wild and free as it's portrayed in cinema. For those who have never traveled to America, all they have to base their perception on was what they see through media. I politely laugh and tell them they can't believe everything they read and see.*

*—Shanyu*

One of the dynamics of intercultural communication that we have highlighted through-out this text is power. In considering popular culture, we need to think about not only the ways that people interpret and consume popular culture but also the ways that these popular culture texts represent particular groups in specific ways. If people largely view other cultural groups through the lens of popular culture, then we need to think about the power relations that are embedded in these popular culture dynamics.

## Global Circulation of Images/Commodities

As noted previously, much of U.S. popular culture is circulated worldwide. For example, U.S.-made films are widely distributed by a culture industry that is backed by consider-able financial resources. Some media scholars have noted that the U.S. film industry earns far more money outside the United States than from domestic box-office sales.[9] This situation ensures that Hollywood will continue to market its films overseas and that it will have the financial resources to do so. For example, the 2015 film, *Jurassic World*, earned 61 percent of its revenues from overseas and 39 percent from U.S. audiences.[10]

© AP Photo/Saleh Rifai

McDonald's has adapted to differ-ent cultures. For example, women in Dhahran, Saudi Arabia, must wait for their orders at the single women's counter. Cultural adaptation is an important phenom-enon in the exporta-tion of U.S. popular culture.

Many other U.S. media are widely available outside the United States, including television and newspapers. Cable News Network (CNN) is widely available around the world. MTV also broadcasts internationally. And the *International New York Times*, published in conjunction with the *New York Times*, is available in many parts of the world. The implications of the dominance by U.S. media and popular culture have yet to be determined, although you might imagine the consequences.

Recently, however, the emergence of Aljazeera, the news channel based in Qatar, has begun to offer a different voice in international news. Given the recent focus on the Arabic-speaking world, Aljazeera's perspective has taken a particularly significant place. As they describe themselves: "With more than 30 bureaus and dozens of correspondents covering the four corners of the world Aljazeera has given millions of people a refreshing new perspective on global events."[11] The French have launched a CNN-type news channel (FRANCE 24) that is focused on presenting an alternative view to the BBC, CNN, and Aljazeera. The goals of the network are to promote French views and values as stated on its webpage: FRANCE 24's "mission is to cover international current events from a French perspective and to convey French values throughout the world."[12] Aside from broadcasting from a French perspective, FRANCE 24 aims to expand on the web: "The Internet is central to FRANCE 24 and the channel aims to make FRANCE24.com the leading video site for international news."[13]

### Popular Culture from Other Cultures

Although U.S. popular culture tends to dominate the world market, the power of popular culture from outside the United States can also make important impacts in the world we live in. For example, the James Bond books and movies have roots in Britain but have been exported to the international market. In his study of James Bond, for example, film scholar James Chapman places images of James Bond in changing political and cultural contexts to understand this popular culture phenomenon.[14] The appropriation of the British character into U.S. ideological and economic terrain complicates arguments about the dominance of U.S. popular culture products.

The popularity of Japanese animé or cartoons reflects another non-U.S. popular culture phenomenon. Animé clubs have emerged across the United States and around the world. The fascination with animé highlights the ability of non-U.S. popular culture to become popular internationally. Although many people think of animé as children's cartoons, "most animé tells sophisticated stories with complex characters aimed at adults."[15] Yet, "like so many cultural phenomena, animé is not just about animé itself, but about a subculture that's grown up enough to find some mainstream acceptance but is often still misunderstood."[16] The way that Japanese popular culture is imported into the United States is reflected in the development of animé clubs, websites, meetings, and other social activities.

More recently, the worldwide controversy over the protest and trial of Pussy Riot, a Russian punk band, highlights the ways that U.S. popular culture can influence political and cultural movements in other countries. It also highlights ways that others can resist these popular culture influences. In February 2012, the three

**Pop Culture Spotlight**

Did you like the last Tom Cruise movie? How about his last three? What about the films of Leonardo DiCaprio? Stars can be as important as the films themselves because they help sell movies internationally. So which non-U.S. movie stars can you name other than Jackie Chan?

members of Pussy Riot performed a punk prayer in a church as a protest against President Vladimir Putin. In August 2012, they were convicted of hooliganism and sentenced to two years in prison.

U.S. popular culture figures, including Madonna, Chloë Sevigny, and the Red Hot Chili Peppers have spoken out against the court's sentence and in favor of free speech. Musicians from around the world have also expressed support for Pussy Riot, including Björk (Iceland) and Paul McCartney and Sting (among others from the United Kingdom). Protests were staged in a number of cities around the world, including New York, Toronto, and Paris.[17]

In her concert in St. Petersburg, Russia, Madonna included a segment where she spoke in favor of Pussy Riot and wore a balaclava (a key piece of head covering used by Pussy Riot) along with the band's name on her back. She also spoke in favor of gay rights. In order to resist her influence, some Russians have sued Madonna for about $10 million for supporting gay rights.[18] Pressing for gay rights and free speech might be considered a type of cultural imperialism. What do you think? This is a topic that we turn to next.

## Cultural Imperialism

It is difficult to measure the impact of the U.S. and Western media and popular culture on the rest of the world. But we do know that we cannot ignore this dynamic. The U.S. government in the 1920s believed that having American movies on foreign screens would boost the sales of U.S. goods. The U.S. government worked closely with the Hays Office (officially, the Motion Picture Producers and Distributors of America) to break into foreign markets, most notably in the United Kingdom.[19]

The discussions about **media imperialism** (domination or control through the media), **electronic colonialism** (domination or exploitation utilizing technological forms), and **cultural imperialism** (domination through the spread of cultural products), which began in the 1920s, continue today. These are three of the terms that are often used to discuss the larger phenomenon of one culture dominating another, typically through economic domination and the infusion of cultural products that change the cultural values of the recipient culture. While media imperialism emphasizes this domination through media systems, electronic colonialism draws attention to the technological means of domination. Table 7.2 shows the 10 top-grossing movies worldwide, but note how many of them are U.S.-made. The interrelationships among economics, nationalism, and culture make it difficult to determine how significant cultural imperialism might be. The issue of cultural imperialism is complex because the phenomenon of cultural imperialism is complex. In his survey of the cultural imperialism debates, scholar John Tomlinson identified five different ways of thinking about cultural imperialism: (1) as cultural domination, (2) as media imperialism, (3) as nationalist discourse, (4) as a critique of global capitalism, and (5) as a critique of modernity.[20] Tomlinson's analysis underscores the interrelatedness of issues of ethnicity, culture, and nationalism in the context of economics, technology, and capitalism. Because economic, technological, and financial resources are not equally distributed around the world, some ethnic, cultural, and national groups face more difficulty in maintaining their identities and traditions. To understand the concerns

**What Do You Think?**

What do the entertainment rating systems mean to you? Can you identify the differences between a teen-rated (13+) and a mature (17+) video game? Log onto www.esrb.org and you can search games by rating, platform, and content to better understand how rating systems work.

**What Do You Think?**

Bob Jones University, located in Greenville, South Carolina, is a private, Christian institution. The *Student Handbook* highlights concerns about the use of popular culture and its effects. The university "encourages students to honor the Lord in how they spend their time and to carefully consider the desensitizing effects of excessive exposure to popular entertainment, even if the content itself is not objectionable." The *Student Handbook* outlines more specifically what this means in a number of popular culture venues. It bans listening to or using "Rock, Pop, Country, Jazz, Electronic/Techno, Rap/ Hip Hop or the fusion of any of these genres" and "because of the sensual nature of many of its forms, dancing is not permitted." Students are not allowed to watch movies on campus but, in private homes, *(continued)*

**TABLE 7.2  Top 10 Grossing Movies Worldwide**

1. *Avatar* (2009)
2. *Titanic* (1997)
3. *Star Wars: The Force Awakens* (2015)
4. *Jurassic World* (2015)
5. *The Avengers* (2012)
6. *Furious 7* (2015)
7. *Avengers: Age of Ultron* (2015)
8. *Harry Potter and the Deathly Hallows: Part 2* (2011)
9. *Frozen* (2013)
10. *Iron Man 3* (2013)

*Source:* http://www.boxofficemojo.com/alltime/world/. Last updated July 18, 2016.

about cultural imperialism, therefore, it is necessary to consider the impact of U.S. American popular culture. There is no easy way to measure the impact of popular culture, but we should be sensitive to its influences on intercultural communication.

Many cultural groups around the world worry about the impact of cultural imperialism. The government of Quebec, for example, is very concerned about the effects of English-language media on French Canadian language and culture. The French have also expressed concern about the dominance of U.S. popular culture and its impact on French society. Yet the popularity of U.S. popular culture products, such as *Law & Order, CSI,* and Lady Gaga's music, outside the United States reinforces particular notions of romance, masculinity, friendship, and happiness and promotes often idealized images of where U.S. Americans live and what kinds of commodities they purchase.

Yet, we must also remember that viewers are active agents and it is not always clear that they are dominated by imported images. In a recent study on this tension between global networks and local networks, Jonathan Cohen examines the situation in Israel. He examines Israel's 99 channels and identifies six different ways that these channels function in the global and local environment. He then notes: "Foreign television is often thought to be harmful because it separates people from their national communities,"[21] but he warns that we should not so easily view foreign television in this way. He doesn't think it is yet clear that watching U.S. television shows "like *Sex and the City* or *The Apprentice,* weakens viewers' connections to Israeli culture or strengthens them by providing a stark contrast to viewers' lives."[22] Cohen is emphasizing that we cannot assume that people who watch certain shows are passive viewers. The influence of media is more complex than a simple imposition of meaning from abroad.

Popular culture plays an enormous role in relations among nations worldwide. It is through popular culture that we try to understand the dynamics of other cultures and nations. Although these representations are problematic, we also rely on popular culture to understand many kinds of issues: the future of the euro and the European Union,

© William Ryal 2010 RF

Although this sign from Quebec is in French, you can probably recognize a lot of the food being sold, with the exception of "poutine" which is a regional dish. French speakers in Quebec sometimes worry about the dominance of English all around them. Do they have reason to worry?

the preparations for the 2016 Olympics in Rio de Janeiro, the tensions and conflicts in the Middle East, as well as the war in Afghanistan. For many of us, the world exists through popular culture.

## CONSUMING AND RESISTING POPULAR CULTURE

We navigate our ways through the numerous popular culture choices. After all, as Australian scholar Nadine Dolby notes, "Popular culture [. . .] is a key site for the formation of identities, for the ways in which we make sense of the world, and locate ourselves within it."[23] In order to maintain our identities, as well as to reshape them, we often turn to popular culture. At times, we seek out cultural texts; at other times, we try to avoid certain texts.

### Consuming Popular Culture

Faced with such an onslaught of cultural texts, people navigate their ways through popular culture in quite different ways. Popular culture texts do not have to win over the majority of people to be "popular." In fact, people often seek out or avoid specific forms of popular culture. For example, romance novels are the best-selling form of literature, but many people are not interested in reading these novels. Likewise, whereas you may enjoy watching soap operas or professional wrestling, many people find no pleasure in those forms of popular culture. We are bombarded every day with myriad popular

**What Do You Think? (cont.)**

students are permitted to watch G-rated movies. Similarly, television viewing is not allowed on campus, including shows, movies, or sports broadcasts. The policy also bans some kinds of periodicals, "such as *Esquire, GQ, People, Entertainment, Yahoo Magazine, Men's Fitness* and *ESPN.*" You can read more about these guidelines and others in the

*(continued)*

culture texts. We actively seek out and choose those texts that serve our needs. Often people in our social groups participate in particular forms of popular culture, and so we feel that we should participate as well.

Although there is unpredictability in the ways in which people navigate popular culture, certain patterns are evident. Advertising departments of popular magazines even make their **reader profiles** available to potential advertisers. These portrayals of readership demographics indicate what the magazine believes its readership "looks" like. Although reader profiles do not follow a set format, they generally give the average age, gender, individual and household incomes, and other pertinent data about their readers. For example, the reader profiles of *BusinessWeek, GQ, Cosmopolitan,* and *Maxim* should not look alike, as they are targeting different groups.

Other popular culture industries likewise attempt to market their products to particular audiences. The advertisements you see during the Super Bowl are not

*Keeping Up with the Kardashians* is one of the longest running reality television shows. Although it has often been criticized, why is it so popular? How does the show influence how we understand gender, transgender, and U.S. culture? Do you think this show might influence how others view the United States?

© 123RF

always the same ones you will see on MTV or during beauty pageants. While demographic information alone will not predict which forms of popular culture a particular person will consume, certain trends in popular culture consumption usually can be identified. For example, the type of consumers who might be interested in *Blue's Room,* as opposed to MTV's *The Challenge,* should be fairly evident.

The recent rise of reality television shows has again sparked debates about the consumption of these cultural texts and the type of cultural identity they reinforce. The enormous popularity of some of these shows, including *American Idol, The Bachelor, Survivor,* and *Dancing with the Stars,* point to their importance in our society. But what is it about these shows that we enjoy? Why do we consume them? A writer for *Time* magazine asks, "Isn't there something simply wrong with people who enjoy entertainment that depends on ordinary people getting their heart broken, being told they can't sing or getting played for fools?"[24] There are no easy answers, of course, and we do not know what meanings people are drawing from reality TV. But perhaps we do enjoy a critique of our mainstream cultural values: "Companies value team spirit; *Survivor* says the team will screw you in the end. The cult of self-esteem says everybody is talented; *American Idol*'s Simon Cowell says to sit down and shut your pie hole. Romance and feminism say a man's money shouldn't matter; *Joe Millionaire* waged $50 million that they're wrong."[25] The popularity of these shows points to some cultural needs that are being fulfilled. Why do you think so many reality TV shows are popular? What kind of cultural identity might be served by these shows?

The important point here is that popular culture serves important cultural functions that are connected to our **cultural identities**—our view of ourselves in relation to the cultures we belong to. We participate in those cultural texts that address issues that are relevant to our cultural groups, for example, by offering information and points of view that are unavailable in other cultural forums. They also tend to affirm, by their very existence, these other cultural identities that sometimes are invisible or are silenced in the mainstream culture. Some cultural texts focus on issues relevant to people in particular religious, ethnic, regional, political, and other contexts.

Readers actively negotiate their way through cultural texts such as magazines, consuming those that fulfill important personal and social needs. Sometimes popular culture can also be an arena where people consume these products but as a way to empower their identities rather than simply affirm them. For example, in Iran, there has been much discussion about the ban on women attending sporting events. In 2015, Iranian authorities arrested Ghonchen Ghavami, a British Iranian woman who protested the ban on women watching a men's volleyball match between Iran and Italy. After five months in jail, the deputy minister of sports announced that the ban would be eased on some sports. He reported: "This proposal is designed according to our cultural, social, and religious sensibilities and for certain sports which are exclusive to men."[26] Because of the work of activists, Iranian culture may be changing. In this case, sports is used to reconfigure how Iranian culture considers gender in everyday life. Think about the various television programs, movies, mass market paperbacks, and tabloids that flood the cultural landscape. The reasons that people enjoy some over others cannot easily be determined.

**What Do You Think?**

Reality television programs continue to draw strong audience ratings. This popularity is reflected in *Keeping Up with the Kardashians,* one of the longest running reality television shows. It has been criticized for focusing on being famous, and fabricated situations, but it also has received very high audience ratings. How "real" is this reality show? Do you watch this show? Why or why not? What draws you or repels you from this show?

**Pop Culture
Spotlight**

In 2016, Mattel, the maker of Barbie dolls, came out with new shapes and skin colors that marked a departure from the stick-thin traditional models. Barbie has long been a site of contestation in American culture, as some people see the doll as impacting girls in a negative way. These new dolls are constructed to give more realistic expectations about women's bodies and these new dolls are part of a multiyear move by Mattel to recreate the image promoted by Barbie. How powerful are these dolls in shaping how girls view gender? Go to www.barbie.com and explore the messages on the site? Does Barbie empower or disempower females?

## Resisting Popular Culture

At times, people actively seek out particular popular culture texts to consume. At other times, they resist cultural texts. People often resist particular forms of popular culture by refusing to engage in them. For example, some people feel the need to avoid television completely; some even decide not to own televisions. Some people refuse to go to movies that contain violence because they do not find pleasure in such films. These kinds of conscious decisions are often based on concerns about the cultural politics at work.

In a recent study on media consumption practices among members of the Church of Jesus Christ of Latter-day Saints (Mormons), there was significant resistance to Hollywood and television texts. Three media practices were identified in this study: "resistant readings of media texts that focus on the immoral nature of Hollywood and television personalities; a demarcation of the sanctity of the home and the media as an outside threat to their religiosity; and finally practices of program avoidance or resistance in some instances."[27] By resisting the messages of popular culture, their religious identity can be reaffirmed. For example, those who did watch some *Jerry Springer* shows felt the shows served as "a lens into the outside world of those who do not practice family values."[28] Some church members simply avoided certain shows once they were seen as threatening to their religious identity.

Recently, the Playmobil Pirate was criticized for what some consumers and organizations saw as a racist toy within the box. Many people do not see slavery as appropriate for children's toys and resist this type of cultural product. In this case, a "Playmobil toy pirate ship equipped with what appears to be a shackled slave figurine has sparked outrage after a California woman stumbled upon instructions telling her to slap a chain around its neck."[29] While this woman was offended by the reproduction of slavery in a children's toy, the toy company saw the pirate as a former slave and pointed to the historical accuracy of the toy. What impact do images of slavery have on children? What role should historical accuracy play?

One artist, Margaux Lange, takes Barbie dolls and cuts them up in various ways. She then uses these Barbie parts to make jewelry. As you might guess, "Some Barbie fans, however, find her jewelry off-putting."

Additionally, people resist popular culture because of the impact that outside cultural influences might have on a nation. For example, recently, "Iran's prosecutor general railed on Sunday against the invasion of Barbie, Batman, Spider-Man, and Harry Potter and demanded that the country's young be protected against them."[30] In 2012, a national commission in charge of public morality in the Ukraine determined that SpongeBob Squarepants was unacceptable as it is too gay and a threat to children. SpongeBob's relationship with his "friend" Patrick (the starfish) is an issue.[31] Protecting children is often used in discussions about the impact of popular culture. In this case, resistance can be on a national level, rather than an individual level.

Resistance to popular culture can be related to a number of other identities; unlike members of the Church of Jesus Christ of Latter-day Saints, however, the motivation behind this resistance emerges more from how others might view their group. For example, consider the show *Trading Spouses: Meet Your New Mommy,* which often brings mothers from wealthy families into the homes of less fortunate families and vice versa. This type of home switching raises many questions about how those in differing socioeconomic classes are represented in popular culture. Sometimes other social differences are emphasized, such as religious differences, on this television show. Concerns about the stereotyping and images that would occur from media images have motivated resistance. People resist popular culture in many ways, and organizations have emerged to monitor media images and coverage. For example, Media Action Network for Asian Americans (MANAA) monitors anti-Asian images in the media and organizes resistance to them. Gay and Lesbian Alliance Against Defamation (GLAAD) serves a similar function by focusing on gay and lesbian media images. Both groups also praise positive and accurate depictions of their social identities. There are many other groups serving similar functions. Resistance, then, can happen on an individual level or a social level. You may choose not to watch a particular television show, or you may work with others to picket studios, boycott advertisers' products, or resist particular media images in more public ways.

## REPRESENTING CULTURAL GROUPS

*A White student pointed out that his difficulty in answering questions about Latino culture was due to lack of knowledge. Growing up in an all-White town, he had never had any contact with Latinos. Based on what he knew from TV, he had negative feelings about their culture. This all changed when he came to college and had his own experiences. I thought this was interesting because I didn't think an all-White place existed in America.*

—*Adam*

As noted at the beginning of this chapter, people often are introduced to other cultures through the lens of popular culture. And these introductions can be quite intimate. For example, through movies, the audience sees and enters the private lives of people they do not know, in ways they never could as tourists.

Yet, we must also think about how these cultural groups are portrayed through that lens of popular culture. Not everyone sees the portrayal in the same way. For example, you may not think that the TV show *The Real Housewives of Orange County* represents quintessential U.S. American values and lifestyles. But some viewers may see it as their entree into the ways that European Americans live.

Because some groups are not portrayed as often in popular culture, it is easier to stereotype them. Conversely, some groups are portrayed so often in popular culture that it is difficult to stereotype them. For example, White Americans are portrayed as heroes and villains, as good people and bad people, as responsible and irresponsible, as hardworking and lazy, as honest and dishonest.

To understand other cultures and groups, and their experiences, we can investigate their representations in popular culture. For example, U.S. Americans seldom learn about the Navajo code talkers, who played an important role in World War II. Serving as Marines during the war, the Navajo code talkers utilized the Navajo language to devise an unbreakable code. And by creating a GI Joe doll, called "Navajo

**Surf's Up!**

Many people's stereotypes of other cultural groups are used when they visit dating websites. Because little information about other people are given on these websites, many people invoke stereotypes to fill in the missing information. While some may feel that strong racial preferences in dating are personal preferences, many others see their connections to racist attitudes and stereotypes. Some stereotypes about overweight people or people who do not perform more rigid gender stereotypes are also often topics of concern. Two of the many websites devoted to concern about this are www .douchebagsofgrindr .com and www .douchebagsoftinder .tumblr.com. As you surf the web and see the ways that stereotypes are used when people are dating or hooking up with

*(continued)*

The Barbie doll, a popular cultural product, is displayed at her 50th birthday celebration in 2009. Some people embrace her and some reject her. What are some of the ways that people resist this image of female beauty?

© Toru Yamanaka/APF/Getty Images

**Surf's Up! (cont.)**

each other, what role should stereotypes play? Does the Internet make it more difficult to judge people as individuals, rather than members of groups?

GI Joe," the culture industry ensured that this history would not be forgotten. In this way, popular culture representations can increase a group's visibility in society.

## Migrants' Perceptions of Mainstream Culture

Ethnographers and other scholars have crossed international and cultural boundaries to examine the influence of popular culture. In an early study, Elihu Katz and Tamar Liebes set up focus groups to see how different cultural groups viewed the TV show *Dallas:* "There were ten groups each of Israelis, Arabs, new immigrants to Israel from Russia, first and second generation immigrants from Morocco, and kibbutz members. Taking these groups as a microcosm of the worldwide audience of *Dallas,* we are comparing their readings of the program with [those of] ten groups of matched Americans in Los Angeles."[32]

Katz and Liebes found that the U.S. Americans in Los Angeles were much less likely to perceive *Dallas* as portraying actual life in the United States. By contrast, the Israelis, the Arabs, and the array of immigrants were much more inclined to believe that this television show was indeed all about life in the United States. Katz and Liebes note: "What seems clear from the analysis, even at this stage, is that the non-Americans consider the story more real than the Americans. The non-Americans have little doubt that the story is about 'America'; the Americans are less sure."[33] The results of this study are not surprising, but we should not overlook what we can learn about the intercultural communication process. We can see that these popular culture images are often influential in constructing particular ways of understanding cultural groups other than our own.

Another study that focused on immigrants to the United States found similar results.[34] Researchers asked female Korean immigrants why they preferred watching

Korean TV shows (which they had to rent at the video store) to U.S. American TV shows. The women pointed out that, because of the cultural differences, the Korean TV shows were more appealing. Yet, as one respondent noted,

> I like to watch American programs. Actors and actresses are glamorous, and the pictures are sleek. But the ideas are still American. How many Korean women are that independent? And how many men commit incest? I think American programs are about American people. They are not the same as watching the Korean programs. But I watch them for fun. And I learn the American way of living by watching them.[35]

Here, both consumption of and resistance to U.S. American popular culture are evident. This woman uses U.S. American television to learn about the "American" way of living, but she prefers to watch Korean shows because they relate to her cultural identity.

The use of popular culture to learn about another culture should not be surprising. After all, many teachers encourage their students to use popular culture in this manner, not only to improve their language skills but also to help them learn many of the nuances of another culture.

## Popular Culture and Stereotyping

*Intercultural communication still has a long way to go in this country. With so many different races being American, why do we still only picture white skin/blond hair/blue eyes as American?*

— Cindy

In what ways does reliance on popular culture create and reinforce stereotypes of different cultures? As noted at the outset of this chapter, neither Judith nor Tom has had the opportunity to travel all over the world. Our knowledge about other places, even places we have visited, is largely influenced by popular culture. For people who do not travel and interact in relatively homogeneous social circles, the impact of popular culture may be even greater.

There are many familiar stereotypes of ethnic groups represented in the media. Scholar Jack Shaheen, who is of Lebanese descent, went in search of "real" Arabs after tiring of the way Lebanese and other Arabs were portrayed in the media—as oil billionaires, mad bombers, and sexy belly dancers. According to Shaheen, "Television tends to perpetuate four basic myths about Arabs: they are all fabulously wealthy; they are barbaric and uncultured; they are sex maniacs with a penchant for white slavery; and they revel in acts of terrorism."[36] Shaheen describes other common untruths—for example, that all Iranians are Arabs and that all Arabs are Muslims.

Communication scholar Lisa Flores describes the portrayal in television documentaries of Mexicans responding to natural disasters. According to Flores, news programs often show Mexicans as resilient, patient, faithful, and rather passive—and therefore as somehow acceptable. Yet we are also encouraged to feel pity for them; the inference is that they need White America's assistance to cope with these natural disasters. In turn, this feeds into the stereotype that Mexicans are not sufficiently

**What Do You Think?**

Twitter, like any tool, can be used for many different purposes, from weather and traffic alerts to political opinions. In a recent study, communication scholars J. David Cisneros and Thomas Nakayama studied the twitter explosion that occurred after Miss New York (Nina Davuluri) was crowned Miss America in 2012. Many tweets claimed that she was a terrorist, a Muslim, not American, and so on, as she was not White and her parents had immigrated from India. In the face of these racist tweets, how can social media enhance rather than decimate intercultural communication? Does social media make racism more obvious and public? What is the proper response to the explosion of racist tweets? (SOURCE: Cisneros, J. D., & Nakayama, T. K. (2015). New media, old racisms: Twitter,

*(continued)*

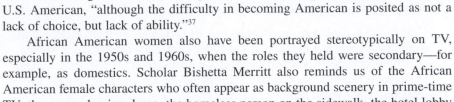

**What Do You Think? (cont.)**

Miss America, and the cultural logics of race. *Journal of International and Intercultural Communication, 8*(2), 108–127.)

**Info Bites**

In 2011, the number of homes in the United States with a television fell for the first time in 20 years. As more people move toward watching television shows on various platforms (Netflix, Hulu Plus, Amazon, etc.), traditional television viewing is losing ground. Some internet sites are developing their own programming. At the same time, more opportunities for interactive media have opened up with apps for some television shows, polls, voting on various issue, and so on. How will these changes influence intercultural communication? Stereotyping?

*(continued)*

hardworking, honest, or driven to become "Americans." In her study, Flores connects these images of Mexicans to portrayals of Mexican Americans as not quite U.S. American, "although the difficulty in becoming American is posited as not a lack of choice, but lack of ability."[37]

African American women also have been portrayed stereotypically on TV, especially in the 1950s and 1960s, when the roles they held were secondary—for example, as domestics. Scholar Bishetta Merritt also reminds us of the African American female characters who often appear as background scenery in prime-time TV: the person buying drugs, the homeless person on the sidewalk, the hotel lobby prostitute. Merritt points out that these women still project images, even if they aren't the focus.[38]

> In her study of ten reality television programs, scholar Tia Tyree found that African American participants were shown as "stereotypical character[s], including the angry black woman, hoochi.e, hood rat, homo thug, sambo, and coon." She argues that reality television is not "real" but constructed. These stereotypical images continue to be reproduced and circulated on contemporary television.[39] Why is it difficult to create and show other images of African Americans?

What about those ethnic groups that simply don't appear except as infrequent stereotypes: Native Americans and Asian Americans? In her study of the usage of "squaw" in popular culture, communication scholar Debra Merskin found that this racialized and sexualized term creates "ethnostress" on Native American women and affects their everyday lives. In underscoring the power of stereotypes, she urges us all to recognize the ethics of these stereotypes. In her study of U.S. television shows, communication scholar Celeste Lacroix identified the emergence of a new threatening stereotype, the "casino Indian." In the current context of tribal casinos and debates about them, this image reinforces the older image of American Indians as a threat.[40] In his study of stereotypes of Asian Americans, Qin Zhang found four predominant stereotypes: (1) academically successful, (2) nerds, (3) excluded from their peers, and (4) least likely to be chosen as friends. Asian Americans, then, may be socially left out of social activities and friendships, but expected to perform well in school.[41]

What can we learn from these studies? Stereotypes are powerful ways that we organize our perception of the world and the society we live in. They help guide us throughout everyday lives, but they can also constrain and affect how others interact and see us. Sensitivity to stereotyping is an important part of intercultural interaction and conflict. Let's look at the controversy that ensued after a music video was released.

In February 2016, Beyoncé released a new music video and song, "Formation," shortly before she was to perform in the Super Bowl halftime show. She also performed this song at Super Bowl 50 during the halftime show. After its release, the ensuing discussion about her video underscored the various ways that stereotypes about African Americans were used by viewers to serve very different ends. The video itself is:

Bookended by the flooding of the city of New Orleans after 2005's Hurricane Katrina—and by which the city's black residents were disproportionately affected—and a black child in a hoodie dancing opposite a police line and a quick cut to graffiti words "stop shooting us," Beyoncé morphs into several archetypical southern black women.[42]

The imagery reminded viewers of the racialized experience of Hurricane Katrina, the Black Lives Matter movement, and more about blackness and black politics. This video created quite a reaction as "she is one of those stars of color who until now has been beyond race for the mainstream audience."[43] Some celebrated and embraced Beyoncé's video, while others were upset by it. *Saturday Night Live* created a short piece, "The Day Beyoncé Turned Black," that showed White people panicking when they realize that Beyoncé is Black and unable to understand her music.

The response to the video was not limited to the realm of popular culture. For example, "U.S. Representative Peter King (R-Long Island) released a statement which referred to Beyoncé as 'a gifted entertainer' but took issue with her 'pro-Black Panther and anti-cop video.'"[44] Javier Ortiz, the president of the Miami Fraternal Order of Police declared that "The fact that Beyoncé used this year's Super Bowl to divide Americans by promoting the Black Panthers and her antipolice message shows how she does not support law enforcement."[45] This police organization called for a nationwide boycott of her shows. A number of police unions discussed boycotting off-duty security work during her concerts, including Tampa, Nashville, and Raleigh. While not all thought that was the right approach to communicating their unhappiness with the video, a group called "Proud of the Blues" sent out a call for a protest at the NFL headquarters in New York City to express their unhappiness that they allowed Beyoncé to perform during the Super Bowl. On the day and time of the protest, only "a handful of Beyoncé supporters gathered in Manhattan to fend off an anti-Beyoncé protest that never happened."[46]

The visibility of the Super Bowl, coupled with the attention given to her video by *Saturday Night Live* and other venues, boosted "Beyoncé's new 'Formation' single zoomed straight to No. 1 on the real-time Billboard + Twitter Trending 140 chart shortly after its release on Feb 6"[47] and earned her "over $100 million in ticket sales"[48] for her concerts. This visibility means that the issues raised by her video reach a very large audience with very different interpretations of it, as audiences see different stereotypes being invoked for very different ends. The video brings a number of cultural tensions into public discussions on the Internet, newspapers, magazine, and other outlets. These stereotypes guide us through our everyday lives which are played out in popular culture.

**Info Bites (cont.)**

(Source: Bernstein, P. "Who Needs to Watch TV?" *Adweek*, April 10, 2012. Retrieved from http://www.adweek .com/sa-article /who-needs-tv -watch-tv-139687.)

**Pop Culture Spotlight**

Consider controversies over sport mascots such as the NCAA's or the National Baseball Association's use of American Indian symbols and imagery. What do these symbols reveal about the ways cultures are represented in popular culture? Sports such as basketball and baseball serve as hallmarks of great American pastimes and as such are relevant to examine for the ways American pop culture fosters static images of what other cultures "look" like.

## SUMMARY

In this chapter, we focused on popular culture, one of the primary modes of intercultural experience. The images produced by culture industries such as film and television enable us to "travel" to many places. We rely heavily on popular culture as a forum for the development of our ideas about other places. For example, many people who have never been to China or studied much about the Chinese economic system have very strong ideas about the country and its economy based on news reports, films, documentaries, and so on.

It is significant that much of our popular culture is dominated by U.S.-based cultural industries, considering how we use popular culture as a form of intercultural communication. Not all popular culture emerges from the United States, but the bulk of it does. And it contributes to a power dynamic—cultural imperialism—that affects intercultural communication everywhere.

Popular culture has four important characteristics: it is produced by culture industries; it is distinct from folk culture; it is ubiquitous; and it serves social functions. Individuals and groups can determine the extent to which they are influenced by popular culture. That is, we may choose to consume or resist the messages of popular culture. Our cultural identities play a significant role as we navigate our way through popular culture. Popular culture also helps us understand other cultural groups. We tend to rely more heavily on media images of cultural groups we have little or no personal experience with, but stereotyping can be a problem here.

A great deal of popular culture is produced in the United States and circulated globally. The imbalance in the exchange of American popular culture and other popular culture texts has raised concerns about cultural imperialism.

## BUILDING INTERCULTURAL SKILLS

1. Be a reflective consumer of popular culture. Be conscious of the decisions you make about which popular culture texts you choose. Think about why you choose certain television shows, magazines, and other cultural texts. Try reading magazines or watching films or TV shows that you normally would not to expand your intercultural communication repertoire.

2. Be aware of how popular culture influences the formation of your cultural identity and worldviews. Be conscious of how popular culture images create or reinforce your views about other places and other people, as well as yourself and your immediate environment.

3. Be aware of how media portrayal of different cultural groups might influence your intercultural interactions with those groups. How might others see you?

4. Think about how you might resist popular culture and when you should do so. Do you talk back to the TV when news is framed in a particular way? Do you notice who gets to speak and who is interviewed, as well as who is not allowed to speak?

5. Think about how you might be an advocate for those whose voices are not heard in popular culture. How might you help challenge imbalances in popular culture?

## ACTIVITIES

1. *Popular culture:* Meet with other students in small groups, and answer the following questions:

   a. Which popular culture texts (magazines, TV shows, and so on) do you watch/buy, and why?

   b. Which popular culture texts do you not like and not watch/buy, and why? Discuss why we like certain products and not others. For example, do some products reinforce or support our worldviews? Do they empower us in some way? Enlighten us?

2. *Ethnic representation in popular culture:* Keep a log of your favorite TV shows for one week. Answer the following questions for each show, and discuss your answers in small groups.

   a. How many different ethnic groups were portrayed?

   b. What roles did members of these ethnic groups have?

   c. What ethnic groups were represented in the major roles?

   d. What ethnic groups were represented in the minor roles?

   e. What ethnic groups were represented in the positive roles?

   f. What ethnic groups were represented in the negative roles?

   g. What types of roles did women have?

   h. What kinds of intercultural interactions occurred?

   i. What were the outcomes?

   j. How do the roles and interactions support or refute common stereotypes of the ethnic groups involved?

## ENDNOTES

1. Katz, E., & Liebes, T. (1987). Decoding *Dallas:* Notes from a cross-cultural study. In H. Newcomb (Ed.), *Television: The critical view* (4th ed., pp. 419–432). New York, NY: Oxford University Press.

2. Quoted in Alleyne, R. (2010, August 2). Rock 'n' roll best sung in American accents. *The Telegraph.* Retrieved July 17, 2016, from http://www.telegraph.co.uk/news/science/science-news/7922639/Rock-n-roll-best-sung-in-American-accents.html.

3. Fiske, J. (1989). *Understanding popular culture.* New York, NY: Routledge, p. 23.

4. Lipsitz, G. (1990). *Time passages: Collective memory and American popular culture.* Minneapolis, MN: University of Minnesota Press, p. 140.

5. Gunn, J., & Brummett, B. (2004). Popular culture after globalization. *Journal of Communication, 54,* 707.

6. Newcomb, H., & Hirsch, P. M. (1987). Television as a cultural forum. In Newcomb.

7. Jackson, S. J., & Foucault Welles, B. (2016). Ferguson is everywhere: Initiators in emerging counterpublic networks. *Information, Communication & Society, 19*(3), 397–418. doi: 10.1080/1369118X.2015.1106571.

8. Butterworth, M. L. (2012). Militarism and memorializing at the Pro Football Hall of Fame. *Communication and Critical/Cultural Studies, 9*(3), 241–258.

9.   Guback, T. (1969). *The international film industry: Western Europe and America since 1945.* Bloomington, IL: Indiana University Press. See also Guback, T., & Varis, T. (1982). *Transnational communication and cultural industries.* Paris: UNESCO.

10.  See http://www.boxofficemojo.com/alltime/world/.

11.  About Aljazeera. (2003). *Aljazeera.* Retrieved from http://english.aljazeera.net/NR/exeres /5D7F956E-6B52-46D9-8D17-448856D01CDB.htm.

12.  France 24, International 24/7. (n.d.) *France 24.* Retrieved September 7, 2012, from http://www .france24.com/en/about-france-24.

13.  France 24 in the world. (n.d.). France 24. Retrieved from http://www.france24.com/en/about -france-24.

14.  Chapman, J. (2007). *Licence to thrill: A cultural history of the James Bond films.* New York, NY: Palgrave Macmillan.

15.  Hung, M. (2001, August 2). Tooned into anime. *Houston Press.* Retrieved from http://www .houstonpress.com/issues/2001-08-02/feature.html/1/index.html.

16.  Hung (2001, August 2).

17.  Rucker, J. (2012, August 12). Before Pussy Riot verdict, artists and activists show support for the incarcerated Russian punk band. *The New York Observer.* Retrieved August 20, 2012, from http:// observer.com/2012/08/before-pussy-riot-verdict-and-new-york-day-of-action-artists-and-activists -show-support-of-the-incarcerated-russian-punk-band/; Williams, C. J. (2012, August 17). Russian punk band's plight galvanizes artists, rights groups, leaders. *Los Angeles Times.* Retrieved August 17, 2012, from http://latimesblogs.latimes.com/world_now/2012/08/plight-of-russian-pussy-riot -rockers-galvanizes-artists-rights-groups-world-leaders.html.

18.  Herszenhorn, D. M. (2012, August 7). In Russia, Madonna defends a band's anti-Putin stunt. *New York Times.* Retrieved August 20, 2012 from http://www.nytimes.com/2012/08/08/world /europe/madonna-defends-pussy-riot-at-moscow-concert.html; Madonna sued in Russia for supporting gays. (2012, August 20). *USA Today.* Retrieved August 20, 2012, from http://www .usatoday.com/life/people/story/2012-08-19/madonna-russia-lawsuit/57136198/1.

19.  Nakayama, T. K., & Vachon, L. A. (1991). Imperialist victory in peacetime: State functions and the British cinema industry. *Current Research in Film, 5,* 161–174.

20.  Tomlinson, J. (1991). *Cultural imperialism.* Baltimore, MD: Johns Hopkins University Press, pp. 19–23.

21.  Cohen, J. (2005). Global and local viewing experiences in the age of multichannel television: The Israeli experience. *Communication Theory, 15,* 451.

22.  Cohen (2005), p. 451.

23.  Dolby, N. (1999). Youth and the global popular: The politics and practices of race in South Africa. *European Journal of Cultural Studies, 2*(3), 296.

24.  Poniewozik, J. (2003, February 17). Why reality TV is good for us. *Time*, p. 67.

25.  Poniewozik (2003, February 17), pp. 66–67.

26.  Dehghan, S. K. (2015, April 4). Iran's deputy minister for sports: Yes, women can go watch big matches. *The Guardian.* Retrieved July 19, 2016, from https://www.theguardian.com/world/2015 /apr/04/iran-national-security-council-women-watch-big-sports-matches.

27.  Scott, D. (2003). Mormon "family values" versus television: An analysis of the discourse of Mormon couples regarding television and popular media culture. *Critical Studies in Media Communication, 20*(3), 325.

28.  Scott (2003), p. 328.

29.  Chan, M. (2015, October 8). Playmobil toy pirate ship with slave dolls sparks outrage: "Slavery is not a game." *New York Daily News.* Retrieved July 18, 2016, from http://www.nydailynews.com/news /national/playmobil-toy-pirate-ship-slave-figurine-sparks-outrage-article-1.2390336.

30.  van Gelder, L. (2008, April 28). Iran versus Barbie. *New York Times.* Retrieved January 30, 2009, from: http://www.nytimes.com/2008/04/28/arts/28arts-IRANVERSUSBA_BRF.html? scp=7&sq=barbie&st=cse.

31.  Vives, M. (2012, August 21). Ukraine: jugé trop gay, Bob l'éponge est "une menace pour les enfants". *Têtu.* Retrieved August 21, 2012, from http://www.tetu.com/actualites/international /ukraine-juge-trop-gay-bob-leponge-est-une-menace-pour-les-enfants-22072.

32.  Katz & Liebes (1987), pp. 419–432.
33.  Katz & Liebes (1987), p. 421.
34.  Lee, M., & Cho, C. H. (1990, January). Women watching together: An ethnographic study of Korean soap opera fans in the U.S. *Cultural Studies, 4*(1), 30–44.
35.  Lee & Cho (1990), p. 43.
36.  Shaheen, J. G. (1984). *The TV Arab.* Bowling Green, OH: Bowling Green State University Press, p. 4.
37.  Flores, L. (1994). *Shifting visions: Intersections of rhetorical and Chicana feminist theory in the analysis of mass media.* Unpublished dissertation, University of Georgia, p. 16.
38.  Merritt B. D. (2000). Illusive reflections: African American women on primetime television. In A. González, M. Houston, & V. Chen (Eds.), *Our voices* (3rd ed., pp. 47–53). Los Angeles, CA: Roxbury.
39.  Tyree, T. (2011). African American stereotypes in reality television. *Howard Journal of Communications, 22*(4): 394–413.
40.  Merskin, D. (2010). The S-word: Discourse, stereotypes, and the American Indian woman. *Howard Journal of Communications, 21*(4): 345–366; Lacroix, C. C. (2011). High stakes stereotypes: The emergence of the "casino Indian" trope in television depictions of contemporary Native Americans. *Howard Journal of Communications, 22*(1): 1–25.
41.  Zhang, Q. (2010). Asian Americans beyond the model minority stereotype: The nerdy and the left out. *Journal of International and Intercultural Communication, 3*(1): 20–37.
42.  McFadden, S. (2016, February 8). Beyoncé's Formation reclaims black America's narrative from the margins. *The Guardian.* Retrieved June 10, 2016, from http://www.theguardian.com /commentisfree/2016/feb/08/beyonce-formation-black-american-narrative-the-margins.
43.  France, L. R. (2016, February 24). Why the Beyoncé controversy is bigger than you think. *CNN.* Retrieved June 10, 2016, from http://www.cnn.com/2016/02/23/entertainment/beyonce -controversy-feat/.
44.  Ex, K. (2016, February 10). Why are people suddenly afraid of Beyoncé's black pride? *Billboard.* Retrieved June 13, 2016, from http://www.billboard.com/articles/columns/pop/6873899/beyonce -formation-essay.
45.  Quoted in Chokshi, N. (2016, February 19). Boycott Beyoncé's "Formation" tour, police union urges. *The Washington Post.* Retrieved June 13, 2016, from https://www.washingtonpost.com/news /post-nation/wp/2016/02/19/boycott-beyonces-formation-world-tour-police-union-urges/?utm _term=.8d088db2e086.
46.  Bonesteel, M. (2016, February 16). No one showed up to the anti-Beyoncé rally at NFL headquarters. *The Washington Post.* Retrieved June 13, 2016, from https://www.washingtonpost.com/news/early -lead/wp/2016/02/16/no-one-showed-up-to-the-anti-beyonce-rally-at-nfl-headquarters/?tid=a_inl.
47.  Caulfield, K. (2016, February 6). Beyoncé's "Formation" hits no. 1 on Billboard + Twitter Trending 140 chart. *Billboard.* Retrieved June 13, 2016, from http://www.billboard.com/articles/columns /chart-beat/6867196/beyonce-formation-number-1-billboard-twitter-trending-140.
48.  *Ibid.,* 43.

© kristian sekulic/Getty Images RF

CHAPTER EIGHT

# Culture, Communication, and Conflict

## STUDY OBJECTIVES

*After reading this chapter, you should be able to:*

1. Identify and describe the characteristics of intercultural conflict.

2. Define interpersonal conflict and its characteristics.

3. Identify five different types of conflict.

4. List the basic principles of nonviolence.

5. Suggest some ways in which cultures differ in their views toward conflict.

6. Understand how people come by their conflict strategies.

7. Identify and describe four styles for dealing with intercultural conflict.

8. Discuss the relationship between ethnicity, gender, and conflict communication.

9. Define social movements.

10. Explain why it is important to understand the role of the social and historical contexts in intercultural conflicts.

11. Discuss some suggestions for dealing with intercultural conflicts.

## KEY TERMS

accommodating style
anti-Americanism
conflict
direct approach
discussion style
dynamic style
emotionally expressive style
engagement style
facework
facilitated intergroup dialogue
incompatibility
indirect approach
intercultural conflict
interdependent
intermediary
international conflict
interpersonal conflict
mediation
pacifism
peacebuilding
political conflict
religious conflict
restraint style
social conflict
social movements

One thing we can be sure of is that conflict is unavoidable. Conflicts are happening all around the world, as they always have, and at many different levels. For example, conflicts can happen on the interpersonal level, called **interpersonal conflict,** which was the case for our student Joy, who described a recent conflict with her boyfriend. Joy is from a midwestern, third-generation Scotch-Irish family. Her boyfriend's family is first-generation Filipino/a. Cultural differences between the groups often cause conflict and misunderstanding. The most recent conflict occurred when Joy's family discovered that her step-grandmother was very sick with cancer. Joy described her boyfriend's reaction when she told him this news on the telephone:

> He really said nothing. His first reaction was "Oh," and then he went on with whatever he was doing at the time. I was shocked. I couldn't believe that he had been so insensitive to me and my family. I was furious, but he saw nothing wrong in what he had done. . . . We managed the conflict by arguing and talking . . . [and then] discussed what we were both angry about . . . and then agreed to try to be more aware of the differences we both have in regards to certain situations and to meet each other halfway, not just blame each other.

Interpersonal conflicts can also be intergenerational. You may disagree with your parents about where to attend college, or what you spend your money on, or where to live in the summer. These conflicts can have varying outcomes. Intergenerational conflicts can occur in the workplace. For example, experts say that baby boomers and Generation Y in particular have characteristics and different sets of work-life values that can clash. While boomers tend to be work-obsessed, millennials are demanding flexible schedules that allow them to pursue an active life away from the office. Boomers tend to like autonomy, while millennials want more direction and enjoy collaboration.[1] These conflicts can make the workplace uncomfortable and challenging. Intergenerational conflicts can have more serious outcomes. Kenji, a Japanese American student from Alabama, had conflicts with her dad—with more serious consequences. When he found out she was gay, he threw her out of the house and still refuses to see her.[2]

Conflicts can also happen on a societal level, known as **political conflict.** For example, various groups in the United States engage in conflict based on deeply held value differences; some feel that health care is a right that should be provided to everyone for the good of the society in general, and others feel that it is an individual privilege that each person is responsible to obtain. There are also strong feelings that lead to societal conflict around immigration issues. Some U.S. Americans believe that children of undocumented immigrants should not have access to educational opportunities (e.g., scholarships, internships) that are typically reserved for U.S. citizens—that doing so only rewards the illegal actions of their parents. Others believe that these children and young people should not be denied opportunities because of the actions of their parents.

**What Do You Think?**

What types of conflict do you find to be the most difficult to negotiate? Do you approach conflicts with your partner, your coworkers, friends, and parents in different ways? Are there patterns in the ways you deal with conflict? If conflicts are inevitable, why do we sometimes avoid them with certain people in our lives?

Some conflicts are managed by mediators, who help disputants resolve their differences. Mediators may be used informally, as in auto accidents, or more formally, as when lawyers are consulted in divorce or real estate disputes.

© Bonnie Kamin/Photo Edit

An example of **international conflict** has been seen tensions between the United States, Russia, and their allies being played out in the proxy war in Syria. While the war in Syria began as a civilian protest against the repressive Assad government in 2011, it quickly escalated into a proxy war with international, competing interests fighting their battles in Syria. The Assad regime retaliated against civilians, with material and military support from Iran and another long-time powerful ally, Russia—which has interest in weakening the anti-government Islamist groups whom it has fought on its own soil in Chechnya. On its part, the United States, along with Saudi Arabia and Turkey, resolved to prevent Russia, a long-time adversary, from determining the fate of this important region. Another nuance is that Turkey is conflicted in its support because the United States is using Kurdish fighters—a group Turkey has viewed as terrorists for many years. As discussed earlier, the human consequences of this complicated conflict have been devastating, with hundreds of thousands of lives lost and millions displaced.[3]

Conflicts in one country can spill over into another, as we have discussed—the thousands of refugees from Syria (and Iraq and Afghanistan) fleeing to nearby and even distant countries, often encountering violence and conflict in their new country. These conflicts have even reached the United States, as individuals supporting the various Middle East factions have attacked civilians here, at the Boston Marathon in 2013, at a social agency holiday party in San Bernardino in 2015, and at a gay nightclub in Orlando, Florida in 2016.

As you can see from these examples, conflict is not simply a matter of disagreement. Conflict among cultural groups can escalate into tragedies that stretch across generations and continents. Russia and the United States, Afghanistan and Pakistan, Iran and Saudi Arabia, all have complicated historical relationships. Conflicts are often complicated and layered. One conflict may have interpersonal, political, and international dimensions, dramatically seen, for example, in clashes between migrants and residents in many European locales in 2015. How can people overcome conflict and put it behind them? How can families and individuals restore relationships after hurtful interpersonal conflict? There are no easy answers to these questions, but we must consider them as part of our understanding of intercultural conflict.

In this chapter, we identify characteristics of intercultural conflict, as well as different types of conflict and conflict styles. We also examine how cultural background can influence conflict management and discuss guidelines for engaging in intercultural conflict. Finally, we look at societal forces that influence intercultural conflict.

As you think about intercultural conflict, consider the role of communication in these situations. While communication differences can sometimes be the cause of intercultural conflict, particularly in interpersonal situations, communication is often not the clear cause of conflicts on international or societal levels. International conflicts can be ignited by struggles over resources, such as oil, food, or water. Yet, communication can often play important roles in how the conflict is played out. Communication can exacerbate the conflicts or help reduce the conflicts.

For example, social media can exacerbate conflict at all levels, from nasty tweets to sophisticated ISIS recruitment, in which citizens in any country can be radicalized through the Internet. For example, Yemeni American al Qaeda leader Anwar al-Awlaki has been described as the "bin Laden of the Internet" with a blog, a Facebook page, the al-Qaeda magazine *Inspire*, and many YouTube videos. Even though he was killed in 2011, his lectures, sermons, and other video messages are still easily found and have been noted as influencing a number of terrorist attackers in the United States including Dzhokhar and Tamerlan Tsarnaev of the 2013 Boston Marathon bombing and two of the Paris *Charlie Hebdo* attackers.[4] On the other hand, some experts suggest that online communication can help resolve conflict (see "Info Bites" on this page).

## CHARACTERISTICS OF INTERCULTURAL CONFLICT

**Conflict** is usually defined as involving a perceived or real **incompatibility** of goals, values, expectations, processes, or outcomes between two or more **interdependent** individuals or groups.[5] A good example of intercultural conflict can be seen in the *maquiladoras*—sorting or assembly plants along the Mexican–U.S. border. Because Mexicans and U.S. Americans work alongside one another, intercultural conflict inevitably occurs.[6] For example, some Mexican managers think that the U.S. American managers are rude in their dealings with each other and with the workers. While both Mexican and U.S. American managers have common goals, they also have some different expectations and values, which leads to conflict. The Mexican managers expect the U.S. American managers to be more polite and to value harmony in their relationships. The U.S. American managers expect the Mexicans to be more direct and honest and to not worry so much about the "face" and feelings of other managers and workers. These conflicts have roots in the history of U.S.–Mexican relations, a history characterized by

**Info Bites**

Communication expert Yair Amichai-Hamburger thinks that the Internet can play a useful role in de-escalating or resolving intercultural conflict for discordant groups. First, Internet contact is cheaper and easier to organize. Second, the Internet is a great status leveler. If the online contact does not involve visual cues, it's impossible to know whether the other is wearing a Rolex watch or is 20 years younger than you and/or much better looking! Third, Internet contact can mean less anxiety—often a factor in conflict situations, allowing people to meet from a place where they feel comfortable, possibly from their own living room.
(Sources: Amichai-Hamburger, Y. How we can use the Internet to resolve intergroup conflict. June 6, 2013, *psychologytoday.com*. Retrieved from https://www.psychologytoday.com/blog/the-social-net/201306/how-we-can-use-the-internet-resolve-intergroup-conflict.)

economic and military domination on the part of the United States and by hostility and resentment on the part of Mexico.

What are characteristics of **intercultural conflict?** How does intercultural conflict differ from other kinds of conflict? One unique characteristic is that intercultural conflicts tend to be more ambiguous than intracultural conflict. Other characteristics involve language issues and contradictory conflict styles.

## Ambiguity

There is often some ambiguity in intercultural conflicts. We may be unsure of how to handle the conflict or of whether the conflict is seen in the same way by the other person. And the other person may not even think there is a conflict. In Joy's case presented at the beginning of the chapter, she and her boyfriend both admitted the conflict; that was the first step in resolving it.

However, often when we encounter ambiguity, we quickly resort to our default style of handling conflict—the style we learned in our family. If your preferred way of handling conflict is to deal with it immediately but you are in a conflict with someone who prefers to avoid it, the conflict may become exacerbated as you both retreat to your preferred styles. Thus, the confronting person becomes increasingly confrontational, while the avoider retreats further.

## Language Issues

The issues surrounding language may be important ones. Language can sometimes lead to intercultural conflict, and it can also be the primary vehicle for solving intercultural conflict. This was true for Jodi, a student of ours, who described a recent conflict she had with some fellow workers:

> I work in a restaurant where the kitchen employees are mostly of Mexican descent. Some of the men would make inappropriate comments in Spanish. I chose to ignore it, but my method of resolving the conflict was not beneficial. It just resulted in my feeling uncomfortable. Finally, I decided to take the initiative. I used my Spanish speaking skills to let the employees know I could understand them—somewhat. Then I decided to make an effort to greet them whenever I came into contact with them. I found that they are much more friendly. This was the best approach to take, and it yielded good results.

However, when you don't know the language well, it is very difficult to handle conflict effectively. At the same time, some silence is not necessarily a bad thing. Sometimes it provides a "cooling off" period during which the participants can calm down and gather their thoughts. This was our student Dotty's experience with her host family in France. Initially, she was experiencing culture shock and was not getting along with her host "brother." So she told her host family to go out without her because she wasn't feeling well. She recalls: "I spent the afternoon and evening walking along the beach and exploring the forest. This allowed relations to continue, but it gave time to work things out. I felt good about the time out. It all turned out well, but it required some time and patience."

### Contradictory Conflict Styles

Intercultural conflict also may be characterized by contradictory conflict styles. In the *maquiladoras*, the biggest difference between U.S. Americans and Mexicans seems to be in the way U.S. Americans express disagreement at management meetings. The Mexican managers tend to be more indirect and more polite in conflict situations, whereas the U.S. American managers prefer to confront conflict directly and openly. These very different styles in handling conflict cause problems in the workplace and sometimes lead to more conflict.

## CONFLICT TYPES AND CONTEXTS

Perhaps if everyone agreed on the best way to view conflict, there would be less of it. The reality is that different approaches to conflict may result in more conflict. In this section, we identify five different types of conflict and some strategies for resolving them.

### Types of Conflict

Common categories of conflict include affective conflict, conflict of interest, value conflict, cognitive conflict, and goal conflict.[7] Affective conflict occurs when individuals become aware that their feelings and emotions are incompatible. For example, suppose someone finds out that his or her romantic feelings for a close friend are not reciprocated. Their different levels of affection may lead to conflict.

A conflict of interest describes a situation in which people have incompatible preferences for a course of action or plan to pursue. For example, one student of ours

© AP Photo/Max Becherer

Nonviolent confrontation provides an opportunity for social change. People who protest peacefully can highlight injustices and lend credibility to social movements.

**Surf's Up!**
Consider the implications that stereotypes about women drivers, the elderly, Arab Americans, and Asian Americans might have for conflicts occurring while driving. Go to the website http://roadragers.com/ and take a survey to analyze your driving style.

described an ongoing conflict with an ex-girlfriend: "The conflicts always seem to be a jealousy issue or a controlling issue, where even though we are not going out anymore, both of us still try to control the other's life to some degree. You could probably say that this is a conflict of interest."

Value conflict, a more serious type, occurs when people have differing ideologies. For example, suppose that Ruben and Laura have been married for several months and are starting to argue frequently about their views on when to start their family and how to raise their children. Laura believes strongly that one parent should stay at home with the children when they are small, so she would like to wait until they have saved enough money and she can stop working for a few years. Ruben wants to have children immediately but does not want Laura to stop working; he thinks their children will do fine in day care. This situation illustrates value conflict.

Cognitive conflict describes a situation in which two or more people become aware that their thought processes or perceptions are in conflict. For example, suppose that Marissa and Derek argue frequently about whether Marissa's friend Bob is paying too much attention to her. Derek suspects that Bob wants to have sex with Marissa, but Marissa doesn't agree. Their different perceptions of the situation constitute cognitive conflict.

Goal conflict occurs when people disagree about a preferred outcome or end state. For instance, consider the decision that Rodrigo and Jason had to make when Rodrigo was offered an upper management position in a state over 1,500 miles away from their home. Moving meant that Jason had to give up his job and move away from his family, but it also meant that Rodrigo would have the position he wanted and they would be living in the city they had always hoped for.

### The Importance of Context

How we choose to manage conflict may depend on the particular context or situation. For example, we may choose to use discussion style when arguing with a close friend about serious relational issues in a quiet movie theater. By contrast, we may feel freer to use a more confrontational style at a political rally.

Nikki, a student with a part-time job at a restaurant, described an experience she had in serving a large group of German tourists. The tourists argued with her about the bill, claiming that they had been overcharged. Nikki explained that a 15 percent service charge had been added. The Germans thought that she had added the tip because they were tourists; they hadn't realized it was the policy when serving large groups. Nikki explained that she was much more conciliatory when dealing with this group in the restaurant than she would have been in a more social context. She thought the Germans were rude, but she practiced good listening skills and took a more problem-solving approach than she would have otherwise.

One of our students, Courtney, recounted a conflict she had when one of her friends made the college football team. She told him he had "natural talent," and he thought she was being racist because he was Black. Even though Courtney didn't mean to be racist, we can only understand the conflict within the historical context of White–Black relations in the United States; as he told her, he gets these kinds of comments a lot. Thus, the conflict context can be viewed in two ways: (1) in terms of the actual situation in which the conflict happens and (2) as a larger societal context. We'll discuss the larger societal context of conflict later in the chapter.

## INFLUENCES ON CONFLICT MANAGEMENT

A key question is this: Is open conflict good or bad? That is, should conflict be welcomed because it provides opportunities to strengthen relationships? Or should it be avoided because it can only lead to problems for relationships and groups? Another key question is this: What is the best way to handle conflict when it arises? Should individuals talk about it directly, deal with it indirectly, or avoid it? Should emotions be part of the conflict resolution? Are expressions of emotions viewed as showing commitment to resolving the conflict at hand? Or is it better to be restrained and solve problems by rational logic rather than emotional expressiveness? Also consider the following questions: How do we learn how to deal with conflict? Who teaches us how to solve conflicts when they arise? How we answer all of these questions depends in large part on our cultural background and the way we were raised.

### Cultural Values Influences

How do cultural values influence conflict management? One way to answer this question is to look at cultural variations in facework. **Facework** refers to specific communication strategies we use to "save" our own or another person's face and is a universal concept; how we "do" facework varies from culture to culture and influences conflict styles. For example, people from individualistic societies tend to be more concerned with saving their own face than another person's, so they tend to use more direct conflict management styles. In contrast, people from collectivistic societies tend to be more concerned with preserving group harmony and with saving the other person's face (and dignity) during conflict. They may use a less direct conversational style; protecting the other person's face and making him or her look good is considered a skillful facework style. We will revisit this concept later in Chapter 11 to explore how differences in facework affect intercultural business communication. But now, let's look more closely at other influences on conflict management.

### Family Influences

The ways in which people respond to conflict may be influenced by their cultural background. More specifically, most people deal with conflict in the way they learned while growing up—their default style. Conflict resolution strategies usually relate to how people manage their self-image in relationships. For example, they may prefer to preserve their own self-esteem rather than help the other person "save face." Or they may prefer to sacrifice their own self-esteem in order to preserve the relationship.

We tend to prefer a particular conflict style in our interactions for many reasons. A primary influence is our family background; some families prefer a particular

### What Do You Think?

People often don't see a conflict situation in the same way. Consider the 2016 Orlando nightclub massacre:

Some saw it as a hate crime—caused by the gunman's anti-gay prejudice. Or as a clash of cultures and religions—U.S. (Christianity) and Islam—rejecting the anti-gay element. Others saw it as an attack on freedom of all individuals. Still others saw it as the actions of a deranged individual. The proposed solutions to the conflict—more gun control, more protection/rights for gay Americans, stricter immigration policies—depended on one's view of the cause. What do you think? Do we need agreement on the causes of intercultural conflict? Is it possible to resolve intercultural conflict without this agreement?
(SOURCE: Healey, P. *After Massacre at Orlando Gay Club, an Array of Opinion about Motive*

*(continued)*

**What Do You Think? (cont.)**

and Meaning. June 16, 2013. Retrieved from http://www.nytimes.com /2016/06/14/us/politics /shooting-reaction. html?_r=0.)

conflict style, and children come to accept this style as normal. For example, the family may have settled conflict in a direct, confrontational manner, with the person having the strongest argument (or the biggest muscle) getting his or her way.

Sometimes people try very hard to reject the conflict styles they saw their parents using. For example, suppose that Maria's parents avoided open conflict and never discussed what was bothering them. Their children learned to avoid conflict and become very uncomfortable when people around them use a more expressive style of conflict management. Maria has vowed she will never deal with conflict that way with her own children and has tried very hard to use other ways of dealing with conflicts when they do arise in her family. It is important to realize that people deal with conflict in a variety of ways and may not have the same reasons for choosing a certain style.

Family conflict can also arise from generational differences in immigrant families that reflect intercultural differences. In Europe, the focus is sometimes on "Muslim girls who are harassed or punished for being too Western. Latifa Ahmed, 25, arrived in the Netherlands from Morocco when she was 8. As she grew up near Amsterdam, her family turned against her because she preferred to be with her Dutch classmates.

"They were bad, they were infidels, I was told," she said. "My parents and my brothers started hitting me." Latifa, who lived at home until she was 23, said, "I was going crazy from all the fights and the lies, but I was afraid to run away and lose my family."[8]

Other immigrant families may have conflicts over arranged marriages, dating, and other cultural expectations that may highlight differences between the country of origin and the new homeland.

## Two Approaches to Conflict

There are at least two primary ways that you can approach conflict. You can be either direct or indirect, and you can be either emotionally expressive or restrained.[9] The way you approach conflict probably depends on your cultural background and the way you were raised. Let's look at each of these two dimensions more closely.

*Direct and Indirect Conflict Approaches*   This **direct/indirect approach** to conflict is similar to the direct/indirect language dimension we discussed in Chapter 5. There it was applied specifically to language use, whereas here it represents a broader conflict resolution approach. Some cultural groups think that conflict is fundamentally a good thing; these groups feel that it is best to approach conflict very directly, because working through conflicts constructively results in stronger, healthier, and more satisfying relationships. Similarly, groups that work through conflict can gain new information about members or about other groups, defuse more serious conflict, and increase group cohesiveness.[10]

People who take this approach concentrate on using very precise language. While they may not always feel comfortable with face-to-face conflict, they think that it's important to "say what's on your mind" in a conflict situation. The goal in this approach is to articulate the issues carefully and select the "best" solution based on an agreed-upon set of criteria.

However, many cultural groups view conflict as ultimately destructive for relationships. For example, many Asian cultures, reflecting the influence of Confucianism and Taoism, and some religious groups in the United States see conflict as disturbing the peace. For instance, most Amish think of conflict not as an opportunity for personal growth, but as a threat to interpersonal and community harmony. When conflict does arise, the strong spiritual value of **pacifism** dictates a nonresistant response—often avoidance or dealing with conflict very indirectly.[11] We will talk more about nonviolent responses to conflict later in the chapter.

Also, these groups think that when members disagree they should adhere to the consensus of the group rather than engage in conflict. In fact, members who threaten group harmony may be sanctioned. One writer gives an example of a man from the Maori culture in New Zealand who was swearing and using inappropriate language in a public meeting:

> A woman went up to him, laying her hand on his arm and speaking softly. He shook her off and continued. The crowd now moved back from him as far as possible, and as if by general agreement, the listeners dropped their gaze to their toes until all he could see was the tops of their heads. The speaker slowed, faltered, was reduced to silence, and then sat down.[12]

These people tend to approach conflict rather indirectly. They concentrate on the meaning that is "outside" the verbal message and tend to be very careful to protect the "face" of the person with whom they disagree. They may emphasize vagueness and ambiguity in language and often rely on third parties to help resolve disagreements. The goal in this approach is to make sure that the relationship stays intact during the disagreement. For example, they may emphasize the past history of the disputants and try to build a deeper relationship that involves increased obligation toward each other.

*Emotional Expressiveness/Restraint Conflict Style*    A second broad approach to conflict concerns the role of emotion in conflict. People who value intense and overt displays of emotions during discussion of disagreement rely on the **emotionally expressive style.** They think it is better to show emotion during disagreement than to hide or suppress feelings; that is, they show emotion through expressive nonverbal behavior and vocalization. They also think that this outward display of emotions means that one really cares and is committed to resolving the conflict. In fact, one's credibility is based on the ability to be expressive.

On the other hand, people who believe in the **restraint style** think that disagreements are best discussed in an emotionally calm manner. For these people, it's important to control and internalize one's feelings during conflict and to avoid nonverbal emotion. They are uncomfortable with emotional expression and think that such expressions may hurt others. People who use this approach think that relationships are made stronger by keeping one's emotions in check and protecting the

## Pop Culture Spotlight

*Babel* (2006) is a movie that shows an interlocking story involving four different families, all converging at the end to reveal a complex and tragic story. In Morocco, an American couple is on vacation trying to work out their differences; meanwhile, a Moroccan herder buys a rifle for his sons so they can keep the jackals away, and a deaf/mute girl in Japan is dealing with the death of her mother and the emotional distance from her father. The American couple's Mexican nanny takes their children to her son's wedding in Mexico.

This film shows how all these families and individuals are interconnected: although all are too far apart to imagine each other, their lives collide in rather tragic ways. It shows the modern world, and the propensity for conflict among people separated by cultural, religious, and political differences.
(Source: http://www .imdb.com/title /tt0449467/)

"face" or honor of the other person. Credibility is demonstrated by maintaining tight control over one's emotions.

These two approaches to conflict resolution reflect different underlying cultural values involving identity and preserving self-esteem. In the more individualistic approach that sees conflict as good, the concern is with individuals preserving their own dignity. The more communal approach espoused by both Amish and Asian cultures and by many other collectivist groups is more concerned with maintaining harmony in interpersonal relations and preserving the dignity of others. For example, in classic Chinese thought, social harmony is the goal of human society at all levels—individual, family, village, and nation.[13]

### Intercultural Conflict Styles

**Surf's Up!**

Do you know the style of conflict negotiation that best describes you? Access www. personalitytest.net/ and find out more about how personality type and conflict negotiation coincide. (SOURCE: Personality Test Center © 2000–2005)

It is possible to combine the four dimensions discussed and come up with four different conflict resolution styles that seem to be connected to various cultural groups: the discussion style, the engagement style, the accommodating style, and the dynamic style.[14] For information about discovering your own particular conflict style preferences, see "Surf's Up" on this page.

The **discussion style** combines the direct and emotionally restrained dimensions and emphasizes a verbally direct approach for dealing with disagreements—to "say what you mean and mean what you say." People who use this style are comfortable expressing disagreements directly but prefer to be emotionally restrained. This style is often identified as the predominant style preferred by many White Americans, as well as Europeans, Australians, and New Zealanders. This approach is expressed by the Irish saying, "What is nearest the heart is nearest the mouth."

The **engagement style** emphasizes a verbally direct and confrontational approach to dealing with conflict. This style views intense verbal and nonverbal expression of emotion as demonstrating sincerity and willingness to engage intensely to resolve conflict. It has been linked to some African Americans and Southern Europeans (France, Greece, Italy, Spain), as well as to some people from Russia and the Middle East (Israel). This approach is captured in the Russian proverb, "After a storm, fair weather; after sorrow, joy."

The **accommodating style** emphasizes an indirect approach for dealing with conflict and a more emotionally restrained manner. People who use this style may be ambiguous and indirect in expressing their views, thinking that this is a way to ensure that the conflict "doesn't get out of control." This style is often preferred by American Indians, Latin Americans (Mexicans, Costa Ricans), and Asians. This style may best be expressed by the Swahili proverb, "Silence produces peace, and peace produces safety," or by the Chinese proverb, "The first to raise their voice loses the argument."

In this style, silence and avoidance may be used to manage conflict. For example, the Amish would prefer to lose face or money rather than escalate a conflict, and Amish children are instructed to turn the other cheek in any conflict situation, even if it means getting beat up by the neighborhood bully.

Individuals from these groups also use an **intermediary**—a friend or colleague who acts on their behalf in dealing with conflict.[15] For example, a Taiwanese student at a U.S. university was offended by the People's Republic of China flag that her roommate displayed in their room. The Taiwanese student went to the international student advisor and asked him to talk to the U.S. American student about the flag. People who think that interpersonal conflict provides opportunities to strengthen relationships also use **mediation,** but mainly in formal settings. For instance, people retain lawyers to mediate disputes, hire real estate agents to negotiate commercial transactions, and engage counselors or therapists to resolve or manage interpersonal conflicts.

What are the basic principles of nonviolence applied to interpersonal relations? In fact, nonviolence is not the absence of conflict, and it is not a simple refusal to fight. Rather, it involves peacemaking—a difficult, and sometimes very risky, approach to interpersonal relationships. Individuals who take the peacemaking approach (1) strongly value the other person and encourage his or her growth, (2) attempt to de-escalate conflicts or keep them from escalating once they start, and (3) attempt to find creative negotiation to resolve conflicts when they arise.[16]

It is often difficult for people who are taught to use the discussion or engaging style to see the value in the accommodating style or in nonviolent approaches. They see indirectness and avoidance as a sign of weakness. However, millions of people view conflict as primarily "dysfunctional, interpersonally embarrassing, distressing and as a forum for potential humiliation and loss of face."[17] With this view of conflict, it makes much more sense to avoid direct confrontation and work toward saving face for the other person.

The **dynamic style** uses an indirect style of communicating along with a more emotionally intense expressiveness. People who use this style may use strong language, stories, metaphors, and use of third-party intermediaries. They are comfortable with more emotionally confrontational talk and view credibility of the other person grounded in their degree of emotional expressiveness. This style may be preferred by Arabs in the Middle East.

*Cautions about Stereotyping*   As with any generalization, however, it must be remembered that all conflict resolution styles can be found in any one cultural group, and while cultural groups tend to prefer one style over another, we must be careful not to stereotype. Also, these cultural differences may depend on a number of factors, including (1) whether regions have been historically homogeneous and isolated from other cultures, (2) the influence of colonization, and (3) the immigration history of different cultural groups. For example, there is much more African influence in the Caribbean (compared to Central and Latin America), resulting in a more direct and emotionally expressive approach (engagement style) than in Mexico—which has maintained a more indirect and emotionally restrained approach (accommodation style). And there is a great variety of cultures within the African continent, accounting for tremendous variation in conflict resolution styles.

It is also important to recognize that people deal with conflict in a variety of ways for a variety of reasons. We should not think of preferred styles as static and set in stone. For example, people may use a discussion style at work and accommodating style at home, or they may use an accommodating style at work and engagement style at home.

And they may use different styles with different partners. Kaori, a Japanese student, told us about a conflict she had with her U.S. American friend, Mara, when the two were working together on a sorority project. Mara seemed to take a very competitive, individualistic approach to the project, saying things like, "I did this on the project," or referring to it as "my project." Kaori became increasingly irritated and less motivated to work on the project. She finally said to Mara, "Is this your project or our project?" Mara seemed surprised, tried to defend herself, and eventually apologized; the two women continued to work on the project and put the conflict behind them. This illustrates that not all Japanese use indirect or accommodating styles in all conflict encounters. Young Japanese especially may use an engagement style in encounters with friends.[18]

In addition, our styles often change over the course of a conflict and over the life span. For example, individuals who tend to avoid and accommodate may learn the benefits of engaging and working through conflicts.

## Gender, Ethnicity, and Conflict

Our gender and ethnicity may influence how we handle conflict. Some research shows that men and women do tend to behave in stereotypical ways in some contexts—men use a more engagement conflict style, whereas women use a more accommodating style.[19] This may reflect the fact that in many cultures, women are socialized to focus on relationships and to be more accommodating and indirect in their interaction, while men are socialized to be more competitive.

Ethnicity may also influence conflict style. At least one study showed that Asian and Latino Americans tended to use accommodating and third-party conflict styles more than African Americans, and Asian Americans also tended to use more accommodating conflict tactics than European Americans.[20]

In their study of African American and European American women's views on workplace conflict, communication scholars Lynn Turner and Robert Shuter found that African American women viewed workplace conflict more negatively, more passively, and with less optimism about a positive resolution than European American women.[21]

In any case, it is important to remember that, while ethnicity and gender may be related to ways of dealing with conflict, it is inappropriate and inaccurate to assume that any one person will behave in a particular way because of his or her ethnicity or gender.

## Religion and Conflict

Religious differences also can be an important source of conflict. Religious beliefs are often a source of very strongly held views that can cause **religious conflict** with others who may not share those views. For example, in 2015 an evangelical Christian baker in Colorado argued that he should not have to provide services to same-sex couples (e.g., bake a wedding cake); however, the court rejected this argument, saying that religious beliefs cannot be used as an excuse to discriminate.[22] More recently, a preacher in the Verity Sacramento Baptist church praised the attack on an Orlando nightclub that left

**What Do You Think?**

The recent discovery that former CIA technical assistant Edward Snowden made public massive amounts of sensitive information including classified U.S. surveillance programs has fueled a lot of public discussion about what is considered public and private information. Snowden handed over the documents to *The Guardian*, a British newspaper, which then published some of the information. This situation has also fueled a discussion about what is protected speech in times of domestic and international crisis. What sorts of information should be protected? When, if at all, does the state have the right to be listening?

49 people dead in June 2016. He reportedly said in a sermon that he thought Orlando, Florida was a little safer now because of the deaths of 49 "pedophiles." Some felt that these types of remarks promote prejudice and even violence against members of the lesbian, gay, bisexual, and transgender (LGBT) community.[23] In these cases, religious differences are the source of the conflict. While not all people read the Bible in the same way, these religious differences can influence how people view their civic responsibilities and how to appropriately respond.

A little farther west, in Utah, conflicts between Mormons and non-Mormons are not uncommon. The *Salt Lake Tribune* noted that "It is nothing new for protesters to loiter near the LDS Conference Center and Salt Lake Temple." Protests and conflicts with Mormons surfaced during the 2012 presidential campaign of Mitt Romney, a devout Mormon. Some Protestants declare Mormon religion as not truly Christian. Other conflicts center on the anti-gay stance of the Mormon church and its financial support that helped pass the 2008 Proposition 8 in California that banned gay marriages.[24] Within a historical context, the anti-Mormon views of Latter-day Saints (LDS) by other Christian groups are nothing new. Pressured to leave New York, Ohio, Missouri, and later Illinois before settling in Utah, Mormon history points to many anti-Mormon incidents, including the murder of the founder, Joseph Smith, in Illinois. The semiannual LDS General Conference in Salt Lake City continues to draw protesters, including "a small coterie of self-described Christian preachers." Some of their protests included displaying "in disrespectful and vulgar ways, some of the intimate, sacred temple garments worn by LDS women." This kind of conflict may provoke the LDS members into responding, which may escalate the conflict.[25]

## MANAGING INTERCULTURAL CONFLICT

### Productive versus Destructive Conflict

Given all the variations in how people deal with conflicts, what happens when there is conflict in intercultural relationships? One option involves distinguishing between productive and destructive conflict in at least four ways.[26] First, in productive conflict, individuals or groups try to identify the specific problem; in destructive conflict, they make sweeping generalizations and have negative attitudes. For example, in an argument, one shouldn't say, "You never do the dishes," or "You always put me down in front of my friends." Rather, one should state the specific example of being put down: "Last evening when you criticized me in front of our friends, I felt bad."

Second, in productive conflict, individuals or groups focus on the original issue; in destructive conflict, they escalate the conflict from the original issues and anything in the relationship is open for reexamination. For example, guests on talk shows discussing extramarital affairs might start by citing a specific affair and then expand the conflict to include any number of prior arguments. The more productive approach would be to talk only about the specific affair.

Third, in productive conflict, individuals or groups direct the discussion toward cooperative problem solving ("How can we work this out?"); in destructive conflict, they try to seize power and use threats, coercion, and deception ("Either you do what I want, or . . .").

**What Do You Think?**

Writing in 2001 about contemporary global wars, Arundhati Roy expresses: "People rarely win wars; governments rarely lose them. People get killed. Governments molt and regroup, hydra-headed" (p. 126). Is this true? Can you think of contemporary conflicts where her statement holds true?
(Source: Roy, A. (2001). *Power politics.* Cambridge, MA: South End Press.)

The "Truth and Reconciliation" hearings in South Africa were founded on a notion of forgiving—but not forgetting. The hearings provided a forum for South Africans to recount and admit to the injustices and violence of apartheid and move toward national healing.

© AP Photo/Mike Hutchings

Finally, in productive conflict, individuals or groups value leadership that stresses mutually satisfactory outcomes; in destructive conflict, they polarize behind single-minded and militant leadership. In many political conflicts, such as those in the Middle East, people seem to have fallen into this trap, with leaders unwilling to work toward mutually satisfactory outcomes.

### Competitive versus Cooperative Conflict

As you can see, the general theme in destructive conflict is competitive escalation. Conflict often spirals into long-term negativity, with the conflicting parties establishing a self-perpetuating, mutually confirming expectation. As one writer notes, "Each is treating the other badly because it feels that the other deserves to be treated badly because the other treats it badly and so on."[27]

How can individuals and groups promote cooperative communication in conflict situations? According to Morton Deutsch, the general tone of a relationship will promote certain processes and acts.[28] For example, a competitive atmosphere will promote coercion, deception, suspicion, rigidity, and poor communication; a cooperative atmosphere will promote perceived similarity, trust, flexibility, and open communication. The key here is that this atmosphere needs to be established in the beginning stages of the relationship or group interaction. It is much more difficult to turn a competitive relationship into a cooperative one once the conflict has started to escalate. Our colleague Moira remembered a potential conflict during her first week at a new job and how she tried a cooperative approach:

One of the staff members, Florence, seemed very cool to me. All the other staff members welcomed me to the organization; Florence never said a word. Then we had a misunderstanding about a project we were working on together, and it looked as if things could escalate into a big conflict. I decided that I really didn't want to get off on the wrong foot with her. So I took a deep breath, took a step back, and tried to get things off on a better foot. She had remarked that she was worried about her son, who was having problems in school. We talked and found out that we had a lot in common. She wasn't aware that she was being cool; she was just worried about a lot of family problems. We got the work thing cleared up, and we're actually pretty good friends now. I'm really glad I didn't let things escalate.

Exploration is essential in developing a cooperative atmosphere. Exploration may be done in various ways in different cultures, but it has several basic steps: (1) the issue is put on hold, (2) both parties explore other options, or (3) they delegate the problem to a third party. Blaming is suspended, so it's possible to come up with new ideas or positions. "If all conflicting parties are committed to the process, there is a sense of joint ownership of the recommended solution. . . . [M]oving toward enemies as if they were friends exerts a paradoxical force on them and can bring transcendence."[29]

## UNDERSTANDING CONFLICT AND SOCIETY

To fully understand intercultural conflict, we need to look beyond individuals who may be in conflict. Many intercultural conflicts can be better understood by looking at the social, economic, historical, and political forces. Figure 8.1 shows the location of many armed conflicts around the world.

### Social and Economic Forces

**Social conflict** arises from unequal or unjust social relationships. Remember the conflict we described in Chapter 1, the recurring rioting in French cities in 2005, 2007, and 2012 and the riots in London in 2011? Let's look more closely at these conflicts.

Some experts say it's just hooliganism—young undisciplined looters lashing out against society. And some point out the religious element, describing the conflict as rooted in Islamic discontent with the West, particularly in France, because many of the rioters come from Islamic backgrounds. And in both France and England, many of the rioters were ethnic and racial minorities. In France, it was primarily the children and grandchildren of North African immigrants; in London, many were from families originally migrated from former British colonies in the Caribbean—Jamaica, Bahamas, Barbados. However, we need to look beyond religious or ethnic differences to economic, political, and even historical contexts and emphasize the point that conflicts are often more complicated than they first appear.

As we suggested in Chapter 1, the rioting in both England and France started with those economically marginalized in society, those living in poor neighborhoods.

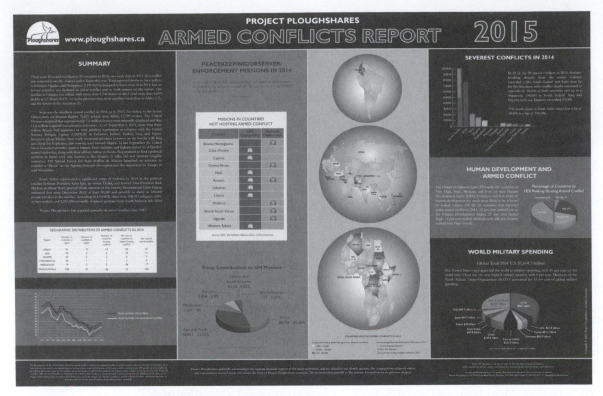

**Figure 8.1** Hot spots of conflict in 2015. There are currently many countries that have conflicts. Conflicts are not unusual, but common around the world.

*Source:* http://ploughshares.ca/programs/armed-conflict/armed-conflicts-report/

Some experts said that it was more a lack of jobs than religious fanaticism that motivated the riots and may have even contributed to the 2015 terrorist attacks in Paris. On the other hand, to exclude other explanations is to insult the poor people who didn't riot (i.e., most of them).

In addition to economic marginalization, many ethnic and racial minorities who rioted feel excluded from French and English society. Unlike the United States and Canada, where there is a belief (not always realized) that anyone can become American or Canadian, immigrants in France, particularly of African heritage, can never really become French; they remain forever on the margins. There is no such concept as *Algerian French*. In fact, they are systematically referred to not as French, or even Algerian French or Moroccan French but always with a religious label "Muslim"—a label that has some consequence. In contrast, one can be Chinese Canadian or Japanese American and still be considered a full citizen.[30] For these reasons, even terrorist attacks may be rooted in deep social and cultural conflict. British and French officials had warned of tensions in many neighborhoods, and as long as these cultural groups remain marginalized, alienated, and largely unemployed, these cultural conflicts are likely to continue.

Similar conflicts can be seen in the United States as the disparity between the wealthy and the poor steadily increases. The Occupy Wall Street protests in 2011 and 2012 drew attention to the "greed and corruption" of the top 1 percent of the U.S. population that controls almost 50 percent of the country's wealth. More recently the election of Donald Trump reflected discontent on part of working class whites and the Black Lives Matter movement drew attention to conflicts between police and communities of color.[31]

Some believe protests and even violence are ways that society can be forced to confront social inequalities and begin the long process of improving the situation. While there are no easy solutions to these conflicts, there have been some attempts to change the economic and cultural conditions underlying the social conflict in England and France, including renovating neglected neighborhoods and trying to connect with local Muslim leaders. U.S. FBI agents are also engaging with community and religious leaders (*imams*) in Muslim neighborhoods like Dearborn Michigan to decrease chances of disaffected youth from becoming radicalized and to send messages of acceptance and inclusion. However, there are other forces at work. After several terrorist attacks in 2015, the French government extended emergency powers, outlawed public demonstrations, made more than a thousand raids, detained many people, and even surveilled Muslims who were not terrorists. Likewise, some in the United States are calling for restricting the civil liberties of U.S. Muslims (e.g., tracking, surveillance).[32] The point here is that there is no reason to seek a single source for conflict. Rather, you can see how these various forces—economic, social, political, religious—may all play different roles simultaneously.

## Historical and Political Forces

Although as children we may have learned that "Sticks and stones may break my bones, but names will never hurt me," we know that derogatory words can be a source of intercultural conflicts. Many derogatory words gain power from their historical usage and the legacy of oppression that they reference. As noted in Chapter 3, much of our identity has historical roots. It is only through understanding the past that we can understand what it means to be a member of a particular cultural group. For example, understanding the history of Ireland helps us understand the meaning of Irish identity.

Other examples of historical and political forces can be seen in international conflicts over border disputes. For example, longstanding disputes continue between Japan and three neighboring countries—Russia, China, and South Korea—over islands north of Japan. The conflict over these islands flared up again in 2014, a result of rising nationalism and political tensions in the region. While largely uninhabited, the islands do represent strategic military positions and substantial fishing and mineral resources—and represent unresolved conflicts dating back centuries (in the conflict between Japan and China, to the fifteenth century!). Experts think that while these conflicts will probably not turn into a military confrontation, neither are the chances that any of them will be resolved peacefully in the near future.[33] The historical reasons for such conflicts help us understand the claims of both sides.

Sometimes ongoing tensions between groups is not limited to those groups and draws in others. For example, the conflict between the Israelis and the

**Info Bites**

Sometimes intercultural conflicts center on environmental issues, e.g. like air pollution from large China and the U.S. which cause catastrophic impact in many other countries (e.g., rising sea levels, severe droughts). Attempts to establish regulations on polluting nations were finally successful December 2015 (a landmark accord signed by 195 countries) and reached partly because of improved relations between China and the United States—the world's two largest polluters. Other conflicts have more immediate tragic outcomes. In 2015 there were—185 reported deaths across 16 countries, e.g., indigenous people defending their land from mining, logging, and agricultural businesses. In Peru, police killed four and injured 15 people protesting a Chinese-run mining company.

*(continued)*

**Info Bites (cont.)**

(Sources: Davenport, C. (2015, December 12). Nations approve landmark climate accord in Paris. Retrieved from http://www.nytimes.com/2015/12/13/world/europe/climate-change-accord-paris.html?_r=0; https://uk.news.yahoo.com/report-2015-deadliest-environmental-activism-173626876.html.)

Palestinians is not limited to those two groups. The history of this part of the world, the role of religious differences, and the contemporary issues fueling the conflict all work together to ensure that the conflict draws in others.

On May 31, 2010, a Turkish flotilla carrying humanitarian aid was on its way to Gaza, in spite of an Israeli naval blockade, when Israeli commandos boarded one of the boats, the Mavi Marmara; a fight ensued and the commandos opened fire, killing eight Turks and one Turkish American. The news went viral due to the seeming brutality of the Israeli attack. Relations between the two countries, already strained, broke down completely and remained so until recently. Historically, however, Turkey and Israel have been allies. They have had strong trade ties and even when diplomatic relations were nonexistent, 2014 saw one of the highest ever volume of Turkish-Israeli trade—$5.44 billion dollars.[34]

In addition to mutual trade interests, Turkey has played a mediator role in the Middle East in the past and in the recent war in Syria called for realigning of political powers. After Israeli Prime Minister Binyamin Netanyahu apologized to Turkey's Prime Minister Tayyip Erdoğan for the Mavi Marmara incident in 2013, Erdoğan seemed willing to normalize relations and resume his shuttle diplomacy between Israel and the Palestinian Hamas. But there are a few sticking points. First, Turkey demanded that Israel lift its blockade on Hamas-ruled Gaza (Israel considers the Gaza blockade a national security), and also compensation for those killed on the Mavi Marmara: "Erdoğan sees much to be gained to getting into the Gaza Strip and helping with the reconstruction there, but has stressed that the families of those who were killed on the Mavi Marmara must be compensated before hands are shaken and photoshoots are staged . . . [but] Syria's civil war is making all regional players look at restoring relations with old foes, regardless of how much pride has to be swallowed."[35] These conflicts did not emerge from interpersonal conflicts among the current inhabitants; rather, in large part, they represent reenactments of conflicts grounded in the history of conflicts in the Middle East between Arabs and Israeli. The contemporary participants are caught in a historical web pitting cultural identities against one another. In fact, these dynamics are at work all around the world. Historical antagonisms become part of cultural identities and cultural practices that place people in positions of conflict. Whether in the Middle East, Northern Ireland, Rwanda, Uganda, Nigeria, Sri Lanka, East Timor, Kosovo, or Chechnya, we can see these historical antagonisms lead to various forms of conflict.

Another type of political influence on intercultural conflict is **anti-Americanism.** Anti-Americanism refers to the ideas, feelings, and sometimes actions against the United States—most often against the U.S. government, although it can also refer to the culture and people. Anti-Americanism has a very long history and it is complicated by the economic, military, and political differences between the United States and other nations around the world. Anti-Americanism can affect intercultural interaction on many levels—from the interpersonal to the social—and you may want to reflect on the potential for conflict that may arise. How well do you understand anti-Americanism and what is the best way to deal with it?

Anti-Americanism is complex because it is a unifying perspective that crosses many cultures in ways that many cultural values do not: Foreign policy decisions

© Ozan Kose/AFP/Getty Images

Turkish demonstrators in 2016, marking the sixth anniversary of the Mavi Marmara incident, when Israeli naval commandos boarded the Turkish ship, the Mavi Marmara—which was delivering humanitarian aid to Gaza—and killed 10 Turkish individuals. The implications of this international conflict incident can only be understood in terms of the long history of relations between Turkey and Israel.

by the U.S. government, like U.S. and NATO presence in the Middle East and unmanned drone attacks on civilians in Pakistan and Afghanistan, have resulted in anti-American sentiments in many parts of the world.[36]

Whatever you may feel about U.S. foreign policy, think about how these policies impact other people around the world. While it may not be easy to avoid the kinds of conflict that arise due to anti-Americanism, ignorance of how U.S. foreign policy impacts others around the globe is not a helpful place to start understanding the perspective of others. Whether you agree or disagree with some of the overseas activities of the U.S. government, your own personal beliefs may not always matter in avoiding anti-Americanism.

When people witness conflict, they often assume that it is caused by personal issues between individuals. When we reduce conflict to the level of interpersonal interaction, we lose sight of the larger social and political forces that contextualize these conflicts. People are in conflicts for reasons that extend far beyond personal communication styles.

So how do we escape the historical, political, and social forces that entrap us in conflict and work toward a more peaceful society and world? Earlier in the chapter we outlined some strategies for dealing with interpersonal conflict. Let's now turn our attention to several other responses to conflict situations.

## Societal Responses to Conflict

Some conflict may be motivated by a desire to bring about social change. In **social movements**, individuals work together to bring about social change. They often use confrontation as a strategy to highlight the injustices of the present system. So, for example, when African American students in Greensboro, North Carolina, sat down at white-only lunch counters in the 1960s, they were pointing out the injustices of segregation. Although the students were nonviolent, their actions drew a violent reaction that, for many people, legitimized the claims of injustice. The women's suffrage movement of the early twentieth century is another example of a social movement, a mass effort to win women the right to vote in the United States. Indeed, many contemporary social movements involve conflicts, including movements against racism, sexism, and homophobia; movements to protect animal rights, the environment, free speech, civil rights; and, recently, the Black Lives Matter movement.

College campuses are likely locations for much activism and a 2016 survey found that the number of students who said there was a "very good chance" they would participate in a protest while in college rose to 8.5 percent (up from 5.6 percent in 2014). Among black students, the number rose from 10.5 percent to 16 percent. These numbers were the highest ever recorded since the survey began in 1967! The report goes on to say that in more than 50 schools "student protesters made demands to right what they see as historic wrongs—demands for greater faculty diversity, new courses, public apologies, administrators' ousting." The tactics included hunger strikes, boycotts, walkouts, marches, occupying administrative offices, as well as social media strategies. Much of the protests focused on racist incidents including fraternity parties where members are invited to dress up and "go back to da hood," offensive statues (and building names) on campus, honoring nineteenth-century White supremacists and pro-slavery graduates/benefactors.[37]

There is, of course, no comprehensive list of existing social movements. They can arise and fall apart, depending on the opposition they provoke, the media attention they attract, and the strategies they use. To stimulate social change, social movements need confrontation to highlight whatever perceived injustice is being done and to open the way for social change to halt the continuation of this injustice.

Confrontation, then, can be seen as an opportunity for social change, and social movements have also used violent forms of confrontation. Groups such as *Action Directe* in France; the Irish Republican Army; the environmental group Earth First!; and independence movements in Corsica, Algeria, Kosovo, and Chechnya have all been accused of using violence, which tends to result in their being labeled as terrorists rather than simply protesters.

However, confrontation does not necessarily mean violence. Nonviolent sanctions like strikes and boycotts confront and undermine the status quo. For example, in the resistance to apartheid in South Africa, widespread boycotts and strikes put pressure on white business owners, employers and government officials.  When the regime reacted with open force, "repression . . . cost the regime any chance of avoiding economic punishment by the international community. Nonviolent power did not by itself bring down the curtain on white rule, but it discredited the regime's authority and undermined its strategy for shielding apartheid from the many forces arrayed against it."[38]

Although nonviolence is not the only form of confrontation employed by social movements, it has a long history—from Mahatma Gandhi's struggle for India to gain independence from Britain, to the civil rights struggle in the United States, to the struggle against apartheid in South Africa. And images of the violent confrontations with nonviolent protesters tended to legitimize the social movements and delegitimize the existing social system. For example, the televised images of police dogs attacking schoolchildren and riot squads turning fire hoses on protesters in Birmingham, Alabama, in the 1950s and 1960s swung public sentiment in favor of the civil rights movement.

Even the suggestion of violence can be threatening to people. For example, in 1964, Malcolm X spoke in favor of civil rights: "The question tonight, as I understand it, is 'The Negro Revolt and Where Do We Go from Here?' or 'What Next?' In my little humble way of understanding it, it points toward either the ballot or the bullet."[39] Malcolm X's rhetoric terrified many U.S. Americans, who then refused to give legitimacy to his movement. To understand communication practices such as these, it is important to study the social context in which the movement operated.

## Peacebuilding

Some of the conflicts described in this chapter involve long-standing and violent intergroup conflicts that have lasted for decades, often between ethnic or religious groups within the same geographic area (e.g., Palestinians and Israelis, Sunni and Shia Muslims in Iraq and other countries, Hindus and Muslims in India, Serbs and Croats in former Yugoslavia, Greeks and Turks in Cyprus). These conflicts—where neighbor or sometimes members of the same family are on different sides—are particularly horrific and have devastating psychological effects, often enduring for generations.

Experts stress that these types of conflicts require special communication processes and a reframing of the problem and the enemy. For example, communication scholar Don Ellis suggests that the other side should not be considered as an enemy, that needs to be destroyed but as an adversary that needs to be engaged. In addition, both sides need to reframe the problems such that solutions require interdependence and engagement in "reasonable and skilled disagreement."[40] Thus, communication is essential (see "Info Bites" on this page) and needs to take place at all levels, from informal intercultural community dialogue groups to high-level government negotiation and diplomacy.

After years of working with these types of conflicts, communication scholar Benjamin Broome has developed a particularly effective type of dialogue group—**facilitated intergroup dialogue.**[41] Dialogue differs from conversation in that it focuses on the *power* of speaking and being understood; it involves listening and speaking, not to persuade, but to clarify—even to clarify and truly understand an opposing viewpoint.

Intergroup dialogue is one of several strategies of **peacebuilding** (working toward equilibrium and stability in a society so that new disputes do not escalate into violence and war). The idea behind facilitated intergroup dialogue, and peacebuilding, is that government leaders alone cannot negotiate a true peace in these types of conflict. Rather, the general population and civic leaders must also be involved. Broome has conducted countless dialogue workshops and programs in the United States and all over the world—particularly on the small island of Cyprus, where Cypriot Turks and Greeks

**Info Bites**

Communication scholar Don Ellis emphasizes the important role of communication in resolving longstanding intercultural conflicts:

• Individuals and groups in conflict strategize, discuss, and manipulate symbols, all in an effort to control others and define themselves.

• Individuals argue, persuade, inform, and develop relations that accumulate into cultural forces that can reduce prejudice and discrimination.

• Simplistic communication processes cannot resolve longstanding conflicts, only interaction: diplomacy, dialogue, negotiation, that reach across cultural divides and provide the mechanisms by which conflicts are processed and may be reduced or even resolved.

These processes are not naive or soft, they

*(continued)*

**Info Bites (cont.)**

are the requirements of problem solving.
(Source: Ellis, D.G. (2015, January 21). "Devoted" conflict actors are not "rational" actors. Retrieved from https://peaceandconflictpolitics.com/page/2/.)

have been in (often violent) conflict for years. Broome and colleague stress that it is important the dialogue groups take place within larger strategies of community engagement/meetings wherein participant groups have the opportunity to present their ideas and have the potential to develop intercultural alliances with each other.[42]

The facilitated intergroup dialogue process usually begins with bringing together members from the two sides—persons, often community leaders, who are interested in working toward peace. Sometimes, presentations are made by each party describing their view of the conflict. Then a three-phase systematic dialogue—an exchange of ideas and perceptions—is conducted, facilitated by an impartial, third-party expert, like Ben Broome. The first step involves analyzing the current situation that affects peacebuilding efforts, the second is building a collective vision for the future, and the final step is developing a specific action plan to achieve peaceful collaboration. Each phase is carefully facilitated with the goal that each side really listens to and tries to understand the opposing side's views. As you can imagine, achieving a vision and plan that everyone agrees to in situations where both sides feel tremendously hurt and victimized by the other is not easy!

Broome has identified some of the challenges that a third-party facilitator faces when conducting peacebuilding efforts. He stresses the importance of earning the trust of parties in both sides of the conflict, which involves a great deal of time and effort. He spent two years in Cyprus, first learning about the problems there and building relationships across the ethnic divide. A facilitator also needs to be seen as impartial. Broome had to overcome some initial perceptions that, because he was American, he would favor the Greek side. Facilitators also need to deal with cultural differences (1) between the two groups (e.g., Greek Cypriots tend to be more expressive than Turks and so, monopolized some of the early dialogue sessions) and (2) between the facilitator's own cultural orientation and the culture orientation of those involved in the discussion.[43] They also note that it's very important for facilitators to acknowledge the power relations and relative privilege or lack thereof of each group and also the role strong emotion plays in conflict situations. In spite of these challenges, Broome and others who use this peacebuilding approach have seen success in reducing intergroup conflict in many conflict contexts.[43]

### Forgiveness

Today, forgiveness is the strategy being used around the world to break the trap of conflict. This means letting go of—not forgetting—feelings of revenge. It often includes an acknowledgement of feelings of hurt and anger and a need for healing. Perhaps the most fundamental aspect of forgiveness is trying to let go of hostile feelings and desire for revenge and retribution.[44] Yet forgiveness is often complicated, as we can see in the case of Michael Lapsely, an anti-apartheid chaplain who was targeted with a letter bomb in 1990 which took both hands, an eye, and both eardrums. "For the first three months I was as helpless as a newborn baby. I realized soon after that if I was filled with hatred and desire for revenge, I'd be a victim forever." He found that he was able to move beyond these feelings. However, for him and other survivors of the brutal apartheid reign, compensation and/or some measure of restorative justice is important in preventing violent revenge and encouraging forgiveness:

> I believe in restorative justice and I believe in reparation. So my attitude to the perpetrator is this: I'll forgive them, but since I'll never get my hands back, and will therefore always need someone to help me, they should pay that person's wages. Not as a condition of forgiveness, but as part of reparation and restitution.[45]

He developed "Healing of Memories" workshops to support those, like him, who suffered physical and psychological scars of apartheid. Similarly, South African government's Truth and Reconciliation Commission was formed in 1996 after the abolition of apartheid in 1994 to investigate and facilitate the healing of racial wounds as a result of apartheid—seen as essential in progressing as a nation past this terrible era (see photo of these hearings on page 240). As you can see, it isn't always easy to move on from conflict, but it can help avoid future conflicts and future pain for others who follow.

## SUMMARY

In this chapter, we identified several characteristics of intercultural conflict: ambiguity, language issues, and contradictory conflict styles. There are different types of conflict relating to interests, values, and goals, and to cognitive and affective factors. We also emphasized the importance of context in understanding and dealing with conflict. We then described various influences on conflict management (cultural values and family influences) and outline four different conflict styles, including discussion style which is direct and emotionally restrained, the engagement style which is direct and confrontational, the accommodating style which is indirect and emotionally restrained, and the dynamic style which is indirect and emotionally intense. Some cultural groups use intermediaries to resolve conflict.

For example, people from individualistic cultures may tend to use discussion style, whereas people from collectivist cultures may prefer the accommodating or dynamic style. However, the type of conflict and the relationship of the disputants also influence these tendencies. Gender, and may also influence conflict style but it is important not to assume that any one individual will behave in a particular way due to their gender or ethnicity. We also discussed ways in which religious differences can be a source of intercultural conflict.

We then highlighted productive versus destructive and cooperative versus competitive approaches to conflict and discussed the importance of social, economic, historical, and political forces in understanding conflict and society. Conflicts arise against the backdrop of existing social movements—for example, in reaction to racism, sexism, and homophobia. Some social movements use nonviolent means of dealing with these conflicts; others confront conflict with violence.

Finally, we described other societal responses to conflict, particularly those involving peacebuilding efforts, such as the facilitated intergroup dialogue that has been implemented in Cyprus and other conflict areas. We concluded by emphasizing the importance of forgiveness, not easy, but one way to stop the cycle of conflict.

**Info Bites**

Active listening is a three-step process suggested by interpersonal communication scholars to help reduce conflict. It includes paraphrasing the other person's ideas, expressing understanding of them, and then asking questions about them. From an intercultural perspective, why would this process be helpful?

## BUILDING INTERCULTURAL SKILLS

1. Stay centered and do not polarize. This means moving beyond traditional stereotypes and either-or thinking. It is important, though difficult, to avoid explaining the other person's motives as simple while seeing your own as complex. Try to see both sides, and be open to a third, centered perspective that may bring a new synthesis into view. It's OK to get angry, but it's important to move past the anger—to refrain from acting out feelings.

2. Maintain contact. This does not mean that you have to stay in the conflict situation. Sometimes we need to walk away for a while. However, do not cut off the relationship. Attempt a dialogue rather than isolating yourself from or fighting with your opponent. Unlike normal conversation, dialogue is slow, careful, full of feeling, respectful, and attentive. Dialogue offers an important opportunity for coming to a richer understanding of your own intercultural conflicts and experiences.

3. Recognize the existence of different styles. Conflict is often exacerbated because of the unwillingness of partners to recognize style differences, which often have cultural origins. Failure to recognize cultural differences can lead to negative evaluations of partners.

4. Identify your preferred style. Although we may change our way of dealing with conflict, based on the situation and the type of conflict, most of us tend to use the same style in most situations. It is also important to recognize which conflict styles "push your conflict button." Some styles are more or less compatible, and it's important to know which styles are congruent with your own.

5. Be creative and expand your repertoire. If a particular way of dealing with conflict is not working, be willing to try a different style. In most intercultural communication, adaptability and flexibility serve us well, and conflict communication is no exception. This means that there is no so-called objective way to deal with conflict. Recognizing this condition may promote conflict resolution.

6. Recognize the importance of context. It is important to understand that larger social, political, and historical contexts give meaning to many types of conflict. Conflict arises for many reasons, and it would be misleading to think that all conflict can be understood solely within the interpersonal context. And once you understand the contexts that frame the conflict, whether cultural, social, historical, or political, you will be in a better position to conceive of possibilities for resolution.

7. Be willing to forgive. This means letting go of—not forgetting—feelings of revenge. This may be particularly useful in intercultural conflict.

## ACTIVITY

*Cultures in conflict:* In groups of four, select two countries or cultural groups that are currently or have historically been in conflict. Divide each group of four into pairs, and have each pair research the conflict from the perspective of one of the two cultural groups. Using online and library resources, including interviews with cultural members, outline the major issues and arguments of the assigned culture. Explore the role of cultural values, political contexts, and historical contexts in the conflict. Be prepared to present an oral or written report of your research.

## ENDNOTES

1. Koeppel , D. (2011, November 11). Workplace conflict heats up. *thefiscaltimes.com*. Retrieved April 28, 2016, from http://www.thefiscaltimes.com/Articles/2011/11/11/Gen-Y-vs-Boomers-Workplace-Conflict-Heats-Up.

2. Kramer, S. (2011, May 20). "Coming out": Gay teenagers, in their own words. *The New York Times online*. Retrieved September 7, 2012, from http://www.nytimes.com/2011/05/23/us/23out.html?_r=1.

3. al-Masri, A. (2015, March 14), Syria: Proxy war, not civil war. *Middleeastmonitor.com*. Retrieved June 13, 2016, from https://www.middleeastmonitor.com/20150314-syria-proxy-war-not-civil-war/.

4. Madhani, A. (2010, August 24). Cleric al-Awlaki dubbed 'bin Laden of the Internet'. *Usatoday.com*. Retrieved June 13, 2016, from http://usatoday30.usatoday.com/news/nation/2010-08-25-1A_Awlaki25_CV_N.htm; Berger, P. (2015, January 12). The American who inspires terror from Paris to the U.S. *cnn.com*. Retrieved June 13, 2016, from http://www.cnn.com/2015/01/11/opinion/bergen-american-terrorism-leader-paris-attack/index.html

5. See Wilmot, W., & Hocking, J. (2013). *Interpersonal conflict* (9th ed.). New York, NY: McGraw-Hill.

6. Lindsley, S. L., & Braithwaite, C. A. (1996). You should "wear a mask": Facework norms in cultural and intercultural conflict in *maquiladoras*. *International Journal of Intercultural Relations, 20,* 199–225.

7. Cole, M. (1996). *Interpersonal conflict communication in Japanese cultural contexts*. Unpublished dissertation, Arizona State University, Tempe, AZ.

8. Simons, M. (2005, December 29). Muslim women in Europe claim rights and keep faith. *New York Times*, p. A3.

9. Hammer, M. R. (2005). The Intercultural Conflict Style Inventory: A conceptual framework and measure of intercultural conflict approaches. *International Journal of Intercultural Relations 29*(6).

10. Filley, A. C. (1975). *Interpersonal conflict resolution*. Glenview, IL: Scott, Foresman.

11. Kraybill, D. (2001). *The riddle of Amish culture*. Baltimore, MD: Johns Hopkins University Press.

12. Augsburger, D. (1992). *Conflict mediation across cultures*. Louisville, KY: Westminster/John Knox Press, p. 80.

13. Ting-Toomey, S. (2010). Applying dimensional values in understanding intercultural communication. *Communication Monographs, 77*(2), 169–180; Ma, R. (2011). Social relations (*guanxi*): Chinese approach to interpersonal relations. *China Media Research, 7*(4), 25–33.

14. Hammer, M. R. (2005). The Intercultural Conflict Style Inventory: A conceptual framework and measure of intercultural conflict approaches. *International Journal of Intercultural Relations, 29,* 675–695.

15. Ting-Toomey, S., Yee-Jung, K. K., Shapiro, R. B., Garcia, W., Wright, T. J., & Oetzel, J. G. (2000). Ethnic/cultural identity salience and conflict styles in four U.S. ethnic groups. *International Journal of Intercultural Relations, 24,* 47–81.

16. Hocker, J. L., & Wilmot, W. W. (1991). *Interpersonal conflict* (3rd ed.). Dubuque, IA: Brown.

17. Kim, M-S. (2002). *Non-Western perspectives on human communication*. Thousand Oaks, CA: Sage, p. 63.

18. Cole, M. (1996). *Interpersonal conflict communication in Japanese cultural contexts.* Unpublished dissertation, Arizona State University, Tempe, AZ.

19. Brewer, N., Mitchell, P., & Weber, N. (2002). Gender role, organizational status, and conflict management styles. *International Journal of Conflict Management, 13*(1), 78–94; Davis, M., Capobianco, S., & Kraus, L. (2010). Gender differences in responding to conflict in the workplace: Evidence from a large sample of working adults. *Sex Roles, 63*(7/8), 500–514.

20. Ting-Toomey et al. (2000); Cai, D. A., & Fink, E. L. (2002). Conflict style differences between individualists and collectivists. *Communication Monographs, 69,* 67–87.

21. Turner, L. H., & Shuter, R. (2004). African American and European American women's visions of workplace conflict: A metaphorical analysis. *Howard Journal of Communications, 15,* 169–193.

22. Gershman, J., & Audi, T. (2015, Aug 13). Court rules baker can't refuse to make wedding cake for gay couple. *wsj.com.* Retrieved April 28, 2016, from http://www.wsj.com/articles/court-rules-baker-cant-refuse-to-make-wedding-cake-for-gay-couple-1439506296.

23. Fierce controversy over pastor's remarks. (2016, June 14). *cbsnews.com.* Retrieved June 15, 2016, from http://www.cbsnews.com/news/mass-shooting-orlando-gay-club-pulse-fierce-controversy-over-pastors-remarks-about-orlando-attack/.

24. McKinley, J., & Johnson, K. (2008, November 14). Mormons tipped scale in ban on gay marriage. *New York Times.* Retrieved September 7, 2012, from http://www.nytimes.com/2008/11/15/us/politics/15marriage.html?pagewanted=all.

25. The other cheek. (2003, October 19). *The Salt Lake Tribune,* p. AA1.

26. Augsburger (1992), p. 47.

27. Deutsch, M. (1987). A theoretical perspective on conflict and conflict resolution. In D. Sandole & I. Sandole-Staroste (Eds.), *Conflict management and problem solving.* New York, NY: New York University Press, p. 41.

28. Deutsch, M. (1973). *The resolution of conflict: Constructive and destructive processes.* New Haven, CT: Yale University Press.

29. Hocker & Wilmot (1991), p. 191.

30. Smith, T. (2005, November 8). French nationalism and the Paris riots. *SimplyPut.blogspot.com.* Retrieved September 7, 2012, from http://simply-put.blogspot.com/2005/11/french-nationalism-and-paris-riots.html; Ting-Toomey, S. (2010). Applying dimensional values in understanding intercultural communication. *Communication Monographs, 77*(2), 169–180; Ma, R. (2011). Social relations (*guanxi*): Chinese approach to interpersonal relations, *China Media Research, 7*(4), 25–33.

31. www.ocuppywallst.org.

32. After the riots: The knees jerk. (2011, August 20). *The Economist, 400*(8747), 13–14. Chan, S. (2015, November 29). France uses sweeping powers to curb climate protests but clashes erupt. *nytimes.com.* Retrieved June 22, 2016, from http://www.nytimes.com/2015/11/30/world/europe/france-uses-sweeping-powers-to-curb-climate-protests-but-clashes-erupt.html.

33. Shifts in Asia fuel flare-ups over islands (2012, August 24). *Wall Street Journal,* p. A12. Chan, S. (2015, November 29). France uses sweeping powers to curb climate protests but clashes erupt. *nytimes.com.* Retrieved June 22, 2016, from http://www.nytimes.com/2015/11/30/world/europe/france-uses-sweeping-powers-to-curb-climate-protests-but-clashes-erupt.html.

34. Arbell, A. (2015, February 19) Turkey-Israel relations: a political low point and an economic high point. *brookings.edu.* Retrieved June 24, 2016, from http://www.brookings.edu/blogs/markaz/posts/2015/02/19-israel-turkey-trade-business-economy.

35. Jay, M. (2016, January 16). Israel-Turkey relations: Keep your friends close, but your enemies closer. *akademikperspektif.com.* Retrieved June 24, 2016, from http://en.akademikperspektif.com/2016/01/16/israel-turkey-relations-keep-your-friends-close-but-your-enemies-closer/; Turkey announces 'progress' in restoring ties with Israel (2016, April 8). *dw.com.* Retrieved June 24, 2016, from http://www.dw.com/en/turkey-announces-progress-in-restoring-ties-with-israel/a-19174004.

36. Murder in Libya. (2012, September 15). *Economist.com.* Retrieved September 20, 2012, from http://www.economist.com/node/21562914. See also Spiegel, A. M. (2012, September 19). The real reason behind Anti-American protests. *The Huffington Post.* Retrieved September 20, 2012, from http://www.huffingtonpost.com/avi-spiegel/the-real-reason-behind-an_b_1891839.html.

37.  Dickey, J. (2015, May 31). The revolution on America's campuses. *time.com*. Retrieved June 23, 2016, from http://time.com/4347099/college-campus-protests/; Spinella, S. (2015, November 19). Protests against racism on campuses spread nationally. *Dailycampus.com*. Retrieved on June 24, 2016, from http://dailycampus.com/stories/2015/11/18/protests-against-racism-on-college-campuses-extend -nationally.

38.  Ackerman, P. & Duvall, J. (2000). *A force more powerful: A century of nonviolent conflict*. London: Palgrave McMillan, p. 367.

39.  X, Malcolm. (1984). The ballot or the bullet. In J. C. Albert & S. E. Albert (Eds.), *The sixties papers: Documents of a rebellious decade* (pp. 126–132). New York, NY: Praeger. (Original work published in 1965.)

40.  Ellis, D. G. (2015). *Fierce entanglements: Communication and ethnopolitical conflict*. New York, NY: Peter Lang, p. xi; Ellis, D. G. (2010). Intergroup conflict. In C.R. Berger, M.E. Roloff, & D.R. Roskso-Ewoldsen (Eds.), *Handbook of communication science* (pp. 291–308). Thousand Oaks, CA: Sage.

41.  Broome, B. J. (2004). Reaching across the dividing line: Building a collective vision for peace in Cyprus. *International Journal of Peace Research*, *41*(2), 191–209.

42.  Broome, B. J., & Hatay, J. (2006). Building peace in divided societies: The role of intergroup dialogue. In J. Oetzel and S. Ting-Toomey (Eds.), *Handbook of conflict communication* (pp. 627–662). Thousand Oaks, CA: Sage; Broome, B. J., & Collier, M. J. (2012) Culture, communication, and peacebuilding: A reflexive multi-dimensional contextual framework. *Journal of International and Intercultural Communication, 5*(4), 245–269.

43.  Broome, B. J., & Hatay, J. (2006). Building peace in divided societies: The role of intergroup dialogue. In J. Oetzel and S. Ting-Toomey (Eds.), *Handbook of conflict communication* (pp. 627–662); Ellis, D. G. (2010). Intergroup conflict. In C. R. Berger, M. E. Roloff, & D. R. Roskso-Ewoldsen (Eds.), *Handbook of communication science*, (pp. 291–308). Thousand Oaks, CA: Sage.

44.  Waldron, V. R., & Kelley, D. L. (2008). *Communicating forgiveness*. Thousand Oaks, CA: Sage.

45.  Lapsley, M. (2010, March 29). The forgiveness project. Retrieved June 24, 2016, from http:// theforgivenessproject.com/stories/michael-lapsley-south-africa/.

© kristian sekulic/Getty Images RF

CHAPTER NINE

# Intercultural Relationships in Everyday Life

**STUDY OBJECTIVES**

*After reading this chapter, you should be able to:*

1. Identify and describe the benefits and challenges of intercultural relationships.

2. Understand the role that similarities and differences play in intercultural relationships.

3. Identify cultural differences in relational communication.

4. Identify and describe issues in intercultural friendships, intercultural romantic relationships, and gay relationships.

5. Describe how computer-mediated communication (CMC) can both facilitate and hinder intercultural relationships.

6. Understand how society influences intercultural relationships.

**KEY TERMS**

complementarity
compromise style
consensus style
contact hypothesis
friendships
gay relationships
intercultural dating
intercultural relationships
intimacy
obliteration style
physical attraction
romantic relationships
similarity principle
submission style
transgender relationships

Mathias and Liam are an international couple living in Brussels. Mathias is from Flanders and speaks English, Dutch, French, and German. Liam is from Ireland and only speaks English. The overwhelming majority of people in Brussels speak French, but Liam says:

> Although I've lived in Brussels for three years now, I haven't needed to learn French as Mathias does all of the speaking when necessary. Many other times, other people can speak English. I'm a little embarrassed that I haven't learned French, but I like living in Brussels and I've learned a lot without speaking French.

While Liam could learn Dutch as well, he hasn't been pushed into learning any other language because he can navigate his way in English. Instead, he has learned a lot about Flemish and Walloon cultures, as well as experienced a variety of foods, festivals, traditions, and more. International relationships can teach you a lot about your own culture and other cultures as you discover cultural things that influence your experiences.

Think about your friends, classmates, and coworkers, all of whom may differ from you in terms of age, physical ability, ethnicity, religion, class, or sexual orientation. How did you get to know them? Maybe you met and developed a relationship online. Do your intercultural relationships differ from those characterized by cultural similarity? How do intercultural relationships form? Do intercultural relationships online develop differently from offline relationships? How are these relationships influenced by society? Are they supported or discouraged by local institutions like schools, churches, and synagogues? What are some strategies you can use to build better intercultural relationships—at school, at work, and at play?

In this chapter, we explore the benefits and challenges of intercultural relationships. We then discuss different kinds of intercultural relationships, including friendships and romantic relationships. We also examine the role society plays in intercultural relationships. Finally, we talk about strategies to build solid intercultural relationships and alliances.

## BENEFITS OF INTERCULTURAL RELATIONSHIPS

Most people have a variety of **intercultural relationships** that span differences in age, physical ability, gender, ethnicity, class, religion, race, and nationality. Take Maria, for example, a student who works part time in a resort as a bartender. Her coworkers are ethnically diverse—Latinos/as, Whites, and African Americans. The clientele is international—Europeans, Asians, and South Americans who come to the resort to play golf and relax. One of her good friends is an older woman, Linda, a neighbor who is disabled with severe emphysema. Maria and Linda watch TV and fix meals together. Maria's Black friend Shawna is dating Jurgen, an international student from Germany, and all three enjoy rollerblading and hiking together. Maria's family is Catholic, but her sister married Jay, who is Jewish.

### Info Bites

Did you know that in 1966 National Broadcasting Company (NBC) shocked audiences when *Star Trek* episode 67, "Plato's Stepchildren," aired. In this episode, Captain Kirk, a White man, and Lieutenant Uhura, a Black woman, kissed each other, creating what now is considered the first interracial kiss in television history. In the 2016 film, *Star Trek Beyond*, Sulu is revealed to be a gay man. How does this development in his character influence, how you see the film, and the Star Trek series? Did they choose the right character to be gay?

Maria's parents had difficulty accepting Jay at first, but eventually they became more accepting, especially after the grandchildren were born.

As this example shows, intercultural relationships can encompass many kinds of cultural differences and offer many rewards and opportunities. The key to these relationships is often an interesting balance of differences and similarities. While Maria's friends are diverse, she has many things in common with each one—roller-blading with Shawna and Jurgen, watching TV and preparing gourmet meals with Linda, and building ties with her sister's family. Through all these relationships, Maria and her friends and acquaintances learn about each other's different worlds.

The benefits of such relationships include (1) learning about the world, (2) breaking stereotypes, and (3) acquiring new skills. In intercultural relationships, we often learn specific information about unfamiliar cultural patterns and language. For example, Anneliese, a graduate student who lived in Guatemala, explained that she learned a new way of looking at time, that "meeting at nine o'clock" might mean 9:30 or 10:00, not because someone forgot or wasn't "on time," but because there was a completely different definition for "9:00." She also learned a different language than the Spanish she had learned in the university setting.

We may also learn more about what it really means to belong to a different culture. For example, recall how Susie learned something about what it meant to grow up in a different class and ethnic environment through her relationship with her boyfriend. A romance or close intercultural friendship may be a way to bring abstractions like "culture" or "race" to life.

We may learn something about history. Another one of our students, Jennifer, told us how she learned more about the Holocaust from her Jewish friends and about the "Middle Passage" from her African American friends. This is a kind of "relational learning," learning that comes from a particular relationship but generalizes to other contexts. While Jennifer learned something specific about Jewish and African American history, she also learned the importance of different ethnic histories and is now more curious to learn about the histories of other ethnic groups. Relational learning is often much more compelling than knowledge gained from books.

Finally, the Internet can also be an important influence in helping new arrivals establish friendships in their new country. A recent study of children who immigrated from the former Soviet Union to Israel found that the Internet helped the children to integrate into Israeli life. The Internet helped these children bridge the gap between their former lives and friends and helped them learn new language skills as well as make new friends in Israel. One 16-year-old said, "It is outstanding that we have the Internet. Thanks to whoever created it—it helps me survive."[1]

We also often learn how to do new things in intercultural relationships. For example, through her friendships with students in the United States and abroad, Judith has learned to make paella (a Spanish dish) and *nopalitos con puerca* (a cactus-and-pork stew), to play bridge in French, and to downhill ski. Through intercultural relationships, newcomers to the society can acquire important skills.

In short, intercultural communication can lead to a sense of connection with others and can establish a lifelong pattern of communicating to bridge differences.

**Info Bites**

In April 2011, the United Nations officially recognised July 30 as International Friendship Day to promote peace and build bridges between communities, cultures, and peoples. Does your community, city, or nation celebrate or mark this day in any way? How might international friendships be promoted?

© Corbis RF

Relationships often are formed because of proximity. That is, we are attracted to people who live near us and who work, study, and worship with us. How many friends do you have who are culturally different from you?

For example, yet another student, Jessica, recounts how an encounter with an international exchange student led to a lifetime interest in intercultural relations. It all began when she was a first-year high school student.

> My best friend's older sister had just gotten back from Germany and brought home an exchange student. My one memory of my first encounter with Edith, the exchange student, happened at breakfast one morning after a sleep-over party. We were going to make waffles, and Edith didn't know what waffles were. I loved explaining them to her and telling her about different syrups and then learning about the different foods she ate in Germany. It was so fun to talk to her.

Three years later, Jessica went on the same exchange program to New Zealand:

> What an amazing experience. Not only did I get to stay with a family that had three girls, one my age, but I also learned about the Maoris, the first people to inhabit New Zealand. I developed a lifelong relationship with my host family and relished learning the differences and similarities between our cultures. I have fond memories of sitting up late at night drinking tea, not coffee, with my New Zealand mother. We would talk for hours. This was a powerful learning experience.

This led to still more intercultural experiences and relationships:

> My exchange sister came home with me, and the other seventeen delegates in the program also brought their exchange sisters or brothers home from all over the world. Talk about a salad mix of cultures. We took various trips for six weeks. It was so exhilarating.

**What Do You Think?**

The Friendship Force International website (www.friendshipforce .org/) says, "Friendship Force International is a non-profit organization dedicated to the principle that each person can make a contribution to global goodwill. Home hospitality—the heart of a Friendship Force exchange—provides the opportunity for people of different countries and

*(continued)*

**What Do You Think? (cont.)**

cultures to connect at a personal level." How important are intercultural friendships in today's world? Do you agree they are the key to global goodwill and world peace?

Although my experiences have for the most part been overseas, I feel they have opened a window for me. My worldview has gone from just me to phenomenally huge. I see things from other people's point of view; I actually try to see things in a different light. I have my experiences with people from other cultures to thank.

In some parts of the world, intercultural relationships are not unusual. In fact, it might be unusual not to engage in them. Lauren, a student of ours, explains:

Having grown up in a multiracial household and in Singapore, a very diverse country, I view having intercultural relationships as something very natural and normal. However, since I have been in the United States, I realized that intercultural relationships are not always the norm, and some people explicitly do not look for intercultural relationships. This struck me as odd because ever since I can remember, intercultural relationships were completely normal and it was not something that people would explicitly point out or try to avoid.

## CHALLENGES IN INTERCULTURAL RELATIONSHIPS

While intercultural relationships can enrich our lives and provide tremendous benefits, they can also present several challenges, including motivation; differences in communication styles, values, and perceptions; negative stereotypes; anxiety; affirming another's cultural identity; and the need for explanations. Let's look at each of these in turn.

### Motivation

Perhaps the most fundamental challenge in intercultural relationships is motivation. In order to build relationships across cultural boundaries, there has to be a desire. There are increasing opportunities to meet people from other cultures through the Internet, and increasing cultural diversity in many schools and workplaces, and yet a recent survey shows that today's first-year college students have less interest in meeting people who are different from them.[2] In surveys, young people repeatedly say that they are open to intercultural romantic relationships and yet for some groups, the rate of intercultural dating is approximately the same as it was 20 years ago.[3] What do you think motivates people to pursue (or not pursue) intercultural relationships?

### Differences in Communication Styles, Values, and Perceptions

A second challenge is that intercultural relationships, by definition, are often characterized by cultural differences in communication styles, values, and perceptions. These dissimilarities probably are most noticeable in the early stages of the relationship, before people get to know each other on a more personal, individual level. For example, an American couple was a bit offended when some of their Chinese friends—whom they had met only recently—asked them how much they paid for their car or their house. They didn't realize that these are commonly expected questions in China, and if you don't want to answer them, you can just change the topic. One of our Chinese students noticed this cultural difference in communication "rules":

> I recently bought a car, and when I mentioned it to my Chinese friends, all of them asked how much it cost and told me whether or not they thought it was a good deal. However, when I told my American friends about my car, they asked about the make, the model, the year, everything except the price!

However, once some commonality is established, these cultural differences may have less effect because all relationships become more individualized as they move to more intimate stages. For example, when Agusia first met Angelina in a class project, all they knew about each other was that Angelina was a Latina and that Agusia grew up in Poland. But as they got to know each other, they found out they both had small daughters, were active in their Catholic churches, and were social work majors. As they got to be good friends and learned about what they shared and how they differed, the cultural differences became less important.

As Angelina and Agusia found out, there is an interplay of both differences and similarities in intercultural relationships. The differences may be more obvious but the challenge is to discover and build on the similarities in intercultural relationships. These similarities may consist of common interests and activities, common beliefs, or common goals.

## Negative Stereotypes

A third challenge in intercultural relationships is negative stereotyping. As discussed in Chapter 2, stereotypes are a way of categorizing and processing information, but they are particularly detrimental when they are negative and held rigidly. These mainstream ideas and stereotypes can be powerful and persistent. Sometimes it takes conscious effort to detect the stereotypes we hold in everyday life and to find information that counteracts them.

One suggestion is to detect when you are "thinking under the influence" (TUI) of prejudices or stereotypes. Notice when you feel surprised by someone "different," because this can often signify a negative assumption or stereotype. A communication colleague, Brenda Allen, gives two examples of TUI "aha" moments.

> A panelist on a program I attended was a wheelchair user who also was hearing impaired. When she made several witty comments, I noticed that her sense of humor amazed me. As I questioned my feelings, I realized that I assumed she would have a gloomy outlook on life because of her disabilities. Aha! I was TUI of the prejudicial notion that disability is a state of being doomed. . . .
>
> Recently an elderly man slowly boarded a bus I was riding on. After he sat down, he began to talk with another older man. As I eavesdropped on their conversation, I was impressed with how articulate they were, especially after the first man said he was 90 years old. I had assumed that both men would have limited communication competence. Aha! I was TUI of a stereotype of aging as decline.

**Info Bites**

Yasuko Kanno, in her book *Negotiating Bilingual and Bicultural Identities: Japanese Returnees Betwixt Two Worlds* (Erlbaum, 2003), describes bilingual and bicultural identities: "bilingual individuals position themselves between two languages and two (or more) cultures, and incorporate these languages and cultures into their sense of who they are." In the United States, the number of bicultural or bilingual people is rapidly increasing. Some experts believe that these people can play a key role in facilitating intercultural communication in many contexts.

Allen goes on to wonder if other people write these men off as "over the hill" and how many of us miss rich opportunities to interact with someone "different" because of TUI.[4]

### Anxiety

A fourth challenge in intercultural relationships involves overcoming the increased anxiety commonly found in the early stages of the relationship. (Some anxiety always exists in the early stages of any relationship.) This anxiety stems from fears about possible negative consequences of our actions. We may be afraid that we will look stupid or will offend someone because we're unfamiliar with that person's language or culture. For example, our student Sam has a lot of friends who speak Spanish at home, and he has studied Spanish for five years in high school and college. But when he visits with his friends' families, he's often anxious about speaking Spanish with them. He's afraid he'll say something stupid or reveal his ignorance in some way.

Differences of age are not usually cause for discomfort, but relationships that span differences in physical ability, class, or race may engender more anxiety. Caterina described for us the last meeting of an interracial discussion group.

> We really did make great connections and friendships in our time together, based on intelligence and honor. It was great to see that some of the girls who initially spoke of their discomfort around others who are different from them spoke out and informed us they were not as scared anymore. They gave up their fear and took a great step forward, one that I hope they will remember always.

As this statement suggests, people face a kind of "hurdle" in developing intercultural relationships, and once they pass that hurdle, it's much easier to develop other intercultural relationships.[5]

The level of anxiety may be even higher if people have negative expectations based on previous interactions or on stereotypes.[6] For example, some White and African American students seem to have more difficulty discussing intercultural issues with each other than they do with international students, perhaps because of negative stereotypes held by both groups. By contrast, intercultural interactions in which there are few negative expectations and no history of negative contact probably have less anxiety associated with them. For example, one student tells of traveling to New Zealand as an 18-year-old on a sports team. He had no negative preconceptions about New Zealanders and no real language barrier. While he experienced a little anxiety at the beginning, he quickly found similarity with people he met, and it was "truly an unforgettable experience."

### Affirming Another Person's Cultural Identity

A fifth challenge in intercultural relationships is affirming the other person's cultural identity. This means that we need not only to recognize that the other person might have different beliefs, perceptions, and attitudes, but also to accept those characteristics as an important part of the other's identity.[7]

However, this is often difficult, especially for majority group individuals. There is often a tendency for members of the majority culture to assume their attitudes, beliefs, and behaviors are the norm and that the minority member should adapt to them.[8] For example, a college student, Andrea, had a good friend Sherry who is Filipina and tended to have a collectivistic approach to friendship. When the two friends went to Europe, Sherry had a last-minute emergency and needed to borrow $600 from Andrea. From Sherry's perspective, lending money was a natural thing for friends to do and was not that unusual. But Andrea had a tough time getting over the fact that Sherry took it so matter of factly, did not thank Andrea profusely, and did not repay it immediately. This aspect of Sherry's identity was a difficult thing for Andrea to accept and is still a barrier in their friendship.

## The Need for Explanations

Finally, intercultural relationships often present the challenge of having to explain things. Intercultural relationships can be more work than in-group relationships and can require more "care and feeding" than do those relationships between people who are very similar. A lot of the work has to do with explaining—explaining to themselves, to each other, and to their respective communities.[9]

First, in some way, consciously or unconsciously, we ask ourselves what it means to be friends with someone who is not like us. Do we become friends out of necessity, or for our job, or because everyone around us is different in some way? Do we become friends because we want to gain an entree into this group for personal benefit or because we feel guilty?

Second, we explain things to each other. This process of mutual clarification is one of the healthiest characteristics of intercultural relationships. Judith recalls her Algerian friends explaining that they really thought their sisters and mothers were treated better in some ways than women are treated in the United States. For example, they explained that no woman would be expected to raise children by herself in Algeria, as is commonly practiced in the United States. They felt sorry for single mothers in the United States who often struggle on their own to raise children. Judith grew to understand that situations can be viewed in very different ways and to realize that others can interpret things very differently.

Note that usually the biggest obstacles to boundary-crossing friendships come not from minority communities but from majority communities. This is because those in the majority, such as Whites, have the most to gain by maintaining social inequality and are less likely to initiate boundary-crossing friendships. By contrast, minority groups have more to gain. Developing intercultural relationships can help them survive and succeed, particularly economically and professionally.

In intercultural relationships, individuals recognize and respect the differences. In these relationships, we often have to remind ourselves that we can never know exactly what it is to walk in another person's shoes. Furthermore, those in the majority group tend to know less about those in minority groups than vice versa. As one of our White students told us, thanks to intercultural relationships with other students, she "was able to hear several examples of true stories of discrimination that Hispanic people go through on a daily basis. I never really thought any of that existed anymore. I don't know why, but their stories really impacted me, and made me much more aware of

**Info Bites**

The divorce rate in Russia is the highest in the world, while the United States is the sixth highest. Some countries have very low divorce rates, such as Australia and Japan. India has the lowest divorce rate in the world. How might cultural differences explain these different divorce rates? (SOURCE: www.divorcerate .org)

© Author's Image/PunchStock RF

Intercultural relationships present both opportunities for and challenges to communication. They can also reflect an interesting balance of similarities and differences. In what ways might these young women be similar, and in what ways might they be different?

### Pop Culture Spotlight

A 2013 Cheerios ad featuring a Black father, White mother, and biracial child created a storm on social media by people who were upset with the interracial family. In 2016, an Old Navy *(continued)*

the hardships that minorities have to go through. It was a real learning opportunity." Overall, intercultural friendships, while challenging, add a special richness to our lives. To be successful, they require "mutual respect, acceptance, tolerance for the faux pas and the occasional closed door, open discussion and patient mutual education; all this gives crossing friendships—when they work at all—a special kind of depth."[10]

## FOUNDATIONS OF INTERCULTURAL RELATIONSHIPS

How do we come to know people who are different from ourselves? Some relationships develop simply because of circumstances—for example, when students work together on a course project. Some relationships develop because people come into contact with each other on a frequent basis: for example, neighbors in dorms or apartments. Others develop because of a strong **physical attraction** or because of similar interests, attitudes, or personality traits. And sometimes relationships develop between dissimilar people simply because they are different. Paradoxically, there seems to be some truth to both "Birds of a feather flock together" and "Opposites attract."

### Similarities and Differences

An awareness of the importance of both similarities and differences is at the heart of understanding intercultural relationships. According to the **similarity principle,** we tend to be attracted to people whom we perceive to hold attitudes similar to ours in terms of politics, religion, personality, and so on.[11] And there is evidence that this principle holds for many cultural groups.[12] Finding people who agree with our own beliefs confirms those beliefs. After all, if we like ourselves, we should like others who share our views. Thus, individuals may explicitly seek partners who hold the same beliefs and values due to deep spiritual, moral, or religious convictions. For example, our student Christine, who is Greek Orthodox, has decided that she'll seek a marriage partner who shares her religious beliefs and values. Also, if we're friends with people who are like us, we can better predict their behavior than if they are different from us.

In addition, the similarity principle seems to reinforce itself. Not only do we like people we think are similar to us, but we also may think that people we like are more similar to us than they actually are. Similarity is based not on whether people actually are similar, but on the perceived (though not necessarily real) recognition or discovery of a similar trait. This process of discovery is crucial in developing relationships. In fact, when people think they're similar, they have higher expectations about future interactions.[13]

But we may also seek out people who have different personality traits and therefore provide balance, or **complementarity**, in the relationship. For example, an introverted individual may seek a more outgoing partner, or a spendthrift may be attracted to an individual who is more careful with money.

Some individuals are attracted to people simply because they have different cultural backgrounds. Intercultural relationships present intriguing opportunities to have new experiences and to learn new ways of looking at the world. And whether (and when) we seek out people who are different from or similar to ourselves may be due partly to our own experiences. For example, when Judith was in college, she wanted to socialize with international students because she was intrigued by their backgrounds and experiences. Growing up, Judith had had little opportunity to be with people who were different from her. By contrast, Tom sought out other Asian Americans when he was in college because he had had little prior opportunity to be around Asian Americans.

U.S. Americans tend to accept some relationships of complementarity more than others. For example, it's more acceptable to date international students than to date across class lines. So, intercultural relationships are characterized by both similarities and differences. Although we may be attracted initially by differences, some common ground or similarity must be established if the relationship is to develop, flourish, and be mutually satisfying over time.[14]

**TABLE 9.1  Some Interesting Cultural Variables in Relationships**

**Brazil:** To be invited to a Brazilian's home is an honor. Guests are expected to stay for many hours rather than stop for a brief visit.

**China:** Face-saving is extremely important in China. Chinese always avoid embarrassing situations and help one another save face and retain self-respect.

**France:** When the French greet people, they tend to be formal. Titles such as Monsieur, Madame, and Mademoiselle are often used. If they know the person, they may give the traditional kiss by the cheek/air.

**Spain:** The Spanish often invite guests to their home out of courtesy. One should wait until the host insists to accept the invitation.

**Germany:** Germans tend to be formal. They do not use first names unless they know the person very well.

**Egypt:** Always use titles such as Doctor or Professor to address people.

**Kenya:** The Kenyans socialize at the end of the meal, not before the meal.

**Greece:** Avoid overpraising any item in a Greek home because the host may feel obligated to present it as a gift later.

*Source:* From Mancini, M. (2010). *Selling destinations* (5th ed.) © 2010 Delmar Learning, a part of Cengage Learning, Inc. Reproduced by permission. www.cengage.com/permissions.

**What Do You Think?**

How would (or did) your family respond to your being in an intercultural romantic relationship? If you are the product of an intercultural relationship, do you think that would make your family more or less accepting?

## Cultural Differences in Relationships

*Friendships*   How are **friendships**—personal, nonromantic relationships with culture-specific overtones—formed? What are the characteristics of a friend? How do these notions vary across cultures? For some people, a friend is someone to see or talk with occasionally and someone to socialize with—go to lunch or a movie, discuss interests, and maybe share problems. These casual friendships may not last if one person moves away. But other people view friendship much more seriously. For these people, friendships take a long time to develop, include many obligations (perhaps lending money or doing favors), and last a lifetime. Some differences in relationship expectations can be seen in Table 9.1.

The term *friend* may have different meanings for different cultural groups. For example, in the United States, the term applies to many different kinds of relationships. In contrast, in India and in many other countries, the concept is defined more narrowly. Shyam, a student from India, described the difference between friendship in the United States and friendship in India:

> [Americans] try to have a lot of friends; they don't meet the same people again and again all the time. . . . In India close friends are together most of the time, day after day after day hanging out together. My impression is, Americans probably don't do that; they try to meet different people.[15]

What most people in the world consider simply a friend is what U.S. Americans would consider a "close friend." A German student explained that in Germany one can hardly call somebody a friend even if he or she has known that person for over a year. Only if one has a "special emotional relationship" can he or she view that person as a friend.[16] For most U.S. Americans, the special emotional relationship would be reserved for a close friend.

Europeans are often amazed at the openness and informality of Americans and how quickly they can form friendships. In contrast, Europeans are not so quick to invite people into their home and do not necessarily introduce their friends to other friends. While in America, a friend of a friend is practically your own friend, Europeans see friendship as much more of an exclusive club.[17]

The upshot is that Americans often come across as forward, intrusive, and overbearing. They sometimes embarrass their European acquaintances by their openness and by how quickly they reveal things about themselves. As one Polish man visiting the United States observed:

> I discover I am learning many intimate details of the personal lives of the people I have just met. I find myself a bit embarrassed, but I doubt that they are. They become my friends so quickly, and as quickly they begin to share their problems with me. . . . In America, when one meets someone, he or she immediately becomes a friend.[18]

It's possible that this American informality and openness may drive Europeans to be even more reserved and distant. It might be better for Americans to give their European acquaintances more time to open up and initiate **intimacy,** and they should be careful not to interpret European reserve as lack of warmth.

Sometimes this openness and informality can be interpreted negatively. For example, international students in the United States often remark that U.S. American students seem superficial. That is, they welcome interactions with strangers and share information of a superficial nature—for example, when chatting at a party. When some international students experience these types of interactions, they assume that they have become "close" friends. But then they discover that the U.S. American students consider them to be merely acquaintances. A student from Singapore described her relationships with American students:

> I learned in the first couple months that people are warm yet cold. For example, I would find people saying "Hi" to me when I'm walking on campus or asking me how I am doing. It used to make me feel slighted that even as I made my greeting back to them, they are already a mile away. Then when real interaction occurs, for example, in class, somehow I sense that people tend to be very superficial and false. Yet they disclose a lot of information, for example, talking about personal relationships, which I wasn't comfortable with. I used to think that because of such self-disclosure, you would share a special relationship with the other person, but it's not so because the same person who was telling you about her personal relationship yesterday has no idea who you are today. Now I have learned to not be offended or feel slighted by such incidents.

The differences in the openness and informality of Americans compared to Europeans may have something to do with the different histories and geography. Early Americans had to reach out to people they didn't know, whether they wanted to or

**What Do You Think?**

Although polygamy is legal in a number of countries worldwide, it is not legal in the United States. And in some countries, such as Australia and Germany, same-sex couples cannot get married, but they can register for domestic partnerships. The United States Citizenship and Immigration Services does not recognize polygamous marriages, nor domestic partnerships, even if they are legal in the country where they occurred. Should the United States recognize these relationships, if they were legal in the country where the people were married or engaged in a domestic partnership?

**Pop Culture Spotlight**

Have you seen either the movie or the television show *The Odd Couple*? How does the friendship between Felix, the neat freak, and Oscar, the slob, resemble an intercultural friendship?

**Pop Culture Spotlight**

In the 2015 movie, *Brooklyn*, Eilis Lacey is a young Irish woman who comes to the United States to work and finds herself caught between a life in the United States and a life in Ireland. In the United States, she meets a young man, Tony Fiorello, whom she marries before returning to Ireland, where she meets a well-to-do bachelor who offers her a life in Ireland that wasn't available earlier. How do her family and romantic relationships influence her connections to Ireland and

*(continued)*

not; when people move to a new place, they don't have the luxury of keeping distant. For Europeans, whose populations are much denser and who have a history of invasions and wars from close neighbors, a certain caution and formality seems understandable.[19]

There are also both similarities and differences between Japanese and U.S. American students with regard to friendships.[20] In general, young people in both countries seem to be attracted to people who are similar to them in some way, and they use the same words to describe characteristics of a friend: trust, respect, understanding, and sincerity. However, they give these characteristics different priority. For Japanese students, togetherness, trust, and warmth are the top characteristics; for U.S. American students, understanding, respect, and sincerity are most important. These preferences may reflect different cultural values: The Japanese value relational harmony and collectivism, whereas the U.S. Americans value honesty and individuality. For many U.S. Americans, relationships are based on and strengthened by honesty, even if the truth sometimes hurts. In general, Japanese college students seem to disclose less about themselves to friends than do Americans.[21]

Hispanic, Asian American, African American, and Anglo American students hold similar notions about two important characteristics of close friendship: trust and acceptance. However, whereas Latino/a, Asian American, and African American students report that it takes, on average, about a year to develop a close friendship, Anglo Americans report that it takes only a few months. And each group may emphasize a slightly different aspect of friendship. For example, Latinos/as emphasize relational support; Asian Americans emphasize a caring, positive exchange of ideas; African Americans emphasize respect and acceptance; and Anglo Americans emphasize recognizing the needs of individuals.[22]

*Romantic Relationships*   There are also similarities and differences in how **romantic relationships** are viewed in different cultures. In general, most cultures stress the importance of some degree of openness, involvement, shared nonverbal meanings, and relationship assessment in romantic relationships. However, there are some differences. In general, U.S. American students emphasize the importance of physical attraction, passion, love, and autonomy, reflecting a more individualistic orientation. Thus, togetherness is important as long as it doesn't interfere too much with one's own freedom. Practicing openness, talking things out, and retaining a strong sense of self are strategies for maintaining a healthy intimate relationship.

But many other cultural groups emphasize the acceptance of the potential partner by family members as more important than romantic or passionate love, reflecting a more collectivist orientation.[23] For example, our student Mark described the experience of meeting his fiancée Elea's Greek American parents for the first time:

It was the inevitable "meeting the parents" that posed the greatest conflict in this relationship. At home, they spoke Greek, ate only Greek food, went to a Greek Orthodox church, and lived under traditional, conservative, old-country rules. In this meeting, what ended up causing difficulties for me was a cultural handicap in interpreting their messages. I could listen politely and answer respectfully, yet I could not understand their stories and how they related to me. I sensed they were

© PhotoAlto/PunchStock/RF

Intercultural relationships can provide a window into different ways of living and thinking. They can also lead to a sense of connection with others and help establish a lifelong pattern of communication across differences.

probing for some key to my values and integrity. They asked questions about my intentions toward their daughter, my goals in life, and my family's background. I sensed that there were "right" and "wrong" answers, and I grew anxious without their cultural answer key.

Mark went on to say that he was still learning about their culture and values: "Years into this relationship, I am continually developing a sense of the values, philosophies, and methods that drive the culture, the questions, and the stories of my parents-in-law."

The U.S. American emphasis on individual autonomy in relationships can be problematic. Trying to balance the needs of two "separate" individuals is not easy, and extreme individualism makes it difficult for either partner to justify sacrificing or giving more than he or she is receiving. All this leads to fundamental conflicts as partners try to reconcile the need for personal freedom with marital obligations. In fact, one study indicated that people with extremely individualistic orientations may experience

**Pop Culture Spotlight (cont.)**

The United States? How do your relationships impact your connections to various cultures?

less love, care, trust, and physical attraction with their partners in romantic relation-ships. These problems are less common in more collectively oriented societies.[24]

Also, not all cultures are as open to intercultural marriages as others. The role of the family and parents can be an important influence in selecting marriage partners. Our student, Kamilla, explains:

> When I came to the United States, I found how interesting intercultural rela-tionships are, both romantic and friendships. This was something exotic and cool for me, as in Kazakhstan we don't have a lot of international people. I realized that my outlook is very different from others and it is really hard to change it. However, I think that in my country, the most important problem are parents; they would never allow us to marry an international person. Here it is not like this.

It is important to keep in mind the role of the family, parents, and culture when develop-ing intercultural relationships. These differences can impact your relationship experience.

***Gender, Sexuality, and Relationships***    We have far more information about het-erosexual friendships and romantic relationships than about **gay relationships,** and even less about **transgender relationships.** But we do know that homosexuality has existed in every society and in every era. And while we in the United States tend to have fairly rigid categories ("heterosexual," "bisexual," "homosexual," and so on), cross-cultural and historical studies show a great deal of variety in how intimate human relations are carried on. For example, although sexual relations among the ancient Greeks occurred between persons of the same gender, there is no evidence that they were systematically differentiated from others or made into a uniform cat-egory. For another example, traditional Mojave Indians recognize gay individuals as being unique, "two spirit persons." A special ceremony in late childhood marks a transition into the third-gender role. The child is then recognized as a two spirit person, usually accepted by the parents who supported him. This acceptance of homosexuality was the product of a long cultural history that involved myth and ceremonial initiation.[25] Here you can see how these terms—gay, homosexual, trans-gender, third gender, etc.—can get conflated, as the categories are not always clear or mutually exclusive.

In many cultures, people engage in activities that would be considered homo-sexual in the contemporary United States, but are not regarded as such in their culture. They may regard themselves as "straights" or just "human beings" who on occasion participate in gay encounters. They simply might be unwilling to identify themselves with a category term such as *homosexual.*

Gay relationships may be intracultural or intercultural. Although there are many similarities between gay and straight relationships, they also differ in at least four ways: their views on intimacy, the role of sexuality, conflict management strategies, and the importance of close friendships. First, U.S. gay males tend to seek emotional support from same-sex friendships, whereas straight males, socialized toward less self-expression and emotional intimacy, turn to women for emotional support—often a wife or female romantic partner, rather than a same-sex friend.

This was not always the case in the United States. And in many countries today, male friendships are similar to romantic love relationships in that men feel free to reveal to their male friends their deepest feelings and may show physical affection by holding hands. In this instance, same-sex friendships and romantic love relationships may involve expectations of undying loyalty, devotion, and intense emotional gratification.[26] This seems to be true for men in gay relationships; they tend to seek emotional support from same-sex friendships.[27] But this does not seem to apply for straight women and lesbians. That is, both gay and straight women seek intimate friendships with women more than with men.

Second, the role of sexuality also may differ in heterosexual relationships and in gay friendships. In heterosexual relationships, friendship and sexual involvement typically are mutually exclusive; the sex thing always seems to "get in the way." Friendships between straight men and women can be ambiguous because of the sex thing. This ambiguity does not hold in gay relationships. Gay friendships often start with sexual attraction and involvement but persist even after sexual involvement is terminated.

Third, while relationship satisfaction is about the same for both straight and gay couples, there seem to be some differences in the area of conflict management. Overall, gay and lesbian couples seem to manage conflict better than straight couples. They use more affection and humor and fewer hostile emotional tactics during conflict, and they are more positive after a disagreement. They tend to emphasize power-sharing and fairness; their partners' positive comments have more impact on feeling good, while their negative comments are *less* likely to produce hurt feelings.[28]

Finally, close friendships may be more important for gay people than for straight people. Gay people often suffer discrimination and hostility from the straight world.[29] In addition, they often have strained relationships with their families. For these reasons, the social support they receive from friends in the gay community can play a special role.

Research on transgender friendships is beginning to be undertaken. In a recent study on friendships between transgender and non-transgender people, both benefits and barriers were identified. For some transgender people, acceptance by others helped to normalize their lives and feel accepted. They also offer the opportunity to help educate about transgender issues and create allies. Some of the barriers were the inability of non-transgender people to understand the issues, insensitivity to language issues, and creating a sense of discomfort.[30] More research on transgender friendships will likely add to our understanding of these kinds of friendships.

In *Obergefell v. Hodges,* the U.S. Supreme Court ruled that, under the Fourteenth Amendment to the U.S. Constitution, all states had to allow and recognize same-sex marriages.[31] By the time the United States legalized same-sex marriage nationwide, about 20 countries had already done so, including Argentina, Belgium, Brazil, Canada, France, the Netherlands, South Africa, Spain, and Uruguay.[32] In countries where same-sex marriage is not legal, some offer other kinds of recognition, including "domestic partnerships" and "civil unions." For example, Germany does not allow same-sex marriages, but offers an alternative type of legal recognition of these relationships.[33] The development of same-sex relationships is very much influenced by the legal and social contexts in which they occur.

**What Do You Think?**

When North Carolina governor Pat McCrory signed House Bill 2 (Public Facilities Privacy and Security Act) into law in 2016, it eliminated all anti-discrimination laws protecting gay, lesbian, transgender, intersex, and other sexual minorities. It also mandated that people use the bathroom corresponding to their gender at birth, rather than their current gender identity. This law has led to legal battles, but the law has also been widely condemned by a number of politicians, corporations, celebrities, and others. Why do you think this law was passed? How does it impact gay, lesbian, and transgender friendships and relationships?

**Surf's Up!**

Erving Goffman argues that we present ourselves in terms of social roles, much like the roles an actor plays. We have different roles for different situations, and Goffman says that trying to keep them straight involves "impression management." Go to this website to learn more about Goffman's ideas: http://en .wikipedia.org/wiki /Impression_ management. Do you ever have trouble keeping your different roles straight?

A recent study from the Williams Institute at UCLA has found that same-sex couples are less likely to divorce than opposite-sex couples. The report observed: "The average divorce rate for same-sex couples was just 1.1 percent annually, compared to an annual average of 2 percent divorce rate for heterosexual couples. When data sets were expanded to include dissolutions by same-sex couples in any type of legally recognized relationship (including civil unions and domestic partnerships), the rate increased to 1.6 percent annually—still lower than the average rate of heterosexual divorces."[34] This study did not explain why same-sex couples divorced less frequently than heterosexual couples; it focused on compiling the quantitative data.

We should also note that in some countries, there are strong negative attitudes about gay and lesbian relationships, making these relationships very difficult.

In Cameroon, homosexuality is a crime, and there have been a number of arrests of gay men. In that country, gay men risk a prison term of five years, as same-sex activities are unlawful.[34] Even more repressive than Cameroon is ISIS which has reportedly killed more than 25 men suspected of being gay. Reports from the Syrian Observatory for Human Rights has reported: "Six have been stoned to death, three killed from direct shooting to the head and 16 thrown from high-rise buildings. Those that survived the fall, the group added, were then stoned on the streets below by scores of bystanders. Two of those killed were under 18."[35] Under these conditions, same-sex relationships are undertaken with great risk, because the anti-gay attitudes are institutionalized under the law. Regardless of one's position on the desirability of gay and lesbian marriage, it is important to understand how society can influence same-sex relationships.

## RELATIONSHIPS ACROSS DIFFERENCES

### Communicating in Intercultural Relationships

Intercultural relationships among people from different cultures may be similar to intracultural relationships in many ways. But some unique themes related to issues of competence, similarity, involvement, and turning points can guide our thinking about communicating in these relationships.[36]

*Competence*   It is important to have language skills in intercultural interactions. Even when people speak the same language, they sometimes have language difficulties that can prevent the relationship from flourishing. There are four levels of intercultural communication competence: (1) unconscious incompetence, (2) conscious incompetence, (3) conscious competence, and (4) unconscious competence.[37]

Unconscious incompetence reflects a "be yourself" approach in which an individual is not conscious of cultural differences and does not see a need to act in any particular way. Sometimes this works. However, being ourselves works best in interactions with people who are very similar to us. In intercultural contexts, being ourselves often means that we're not very effective and we don't realize our ineptness. For example, a few years ago, high-ranking government officials from

**Surf's Up!**

Visit the website of the National Association for the Advancement of Colored People (NAACP) (www.naacp .org) and read about its history, mission, and goals. This organization is almost 100 years old and is dedicated to "ensuring the political, educational, social, and economical equality of rights of *all* persons and eliminating *(continued)*

© Digital Vision/Getty Images RF

Sharing a common goal or working on a common task, as these workers are doing, can help facilitate intercultural relationships. Sometimes intercultural alliances are formed when people share common interests, beliefs, and goals.

Rwanda visited an American university to participate in an agricultural project. The Americans dressed informally for the meeting and did not pay attention to the seating arrangement. In Rwanda, however, the seating arrangements in meetings indicate rank and are very important. Thus, the Rwandans were insulted by what they perceived to be rudeness on the part of the Americans, although they said nothing. The Americans, by "being themselves" and being oblivious to Rwandan cultural preferences, were unconsciously incompetent.

At the level of conscious incompetence, we realize that things may not be going very well in the interaction, but we're not sure why. Most of us have experienced intercultural interactions in which we felt that something wasn't quite right but we couldn't figure out what it was.

As instructors of intercultural communication, we teach at a conscious, intentional level. Our instruction focuses on analytic thinking and learning. This describes the level of conscious competence. Reaching this level is a necessary part of the process of becoming a competent communicator. However, reaching this level is necessary but not sufficient.

Unconscious competence is the level at which communication goes smoothly but is not a conscious process. You've probably heard of marathon runners "hitting the wall," or reaching the seeming limits of their endurance, and then, inexplicably, continuing to run past this point. Communication at the level of unconscious competence is like this. We cannot reach this level by consciously trying; rather, we achieve it when the analytic (conscious, rational) and holistic (unconscious, intuitive) parts of our brains are functioning together. When we concentrate too hard or get too analytic, things don't always go easier.

**Surf's Up! (cont.)**
racial hatred and racial discrimination." Think about how the work of organizations like this can improve intercultural relationships.

You've also probably had the experience of trying unsuccessfully to recall something, letting go of it, and then remembering it as soon as you're thinking about something else. This is what unconscious competence involves—being well prepared cognitively and attitudinally, but knowing when to "let go" and rely on your holistic cognitive processing.

*Similarity*   While dissimilarity may account for an initial attraction between two people, it is very important to find and develop some similarity that transcends the cultural differences. For example, shared religious beliefs can help establish common bonds, as can shared interests in sports or other activities, or similar physical appearances, lifestyles, or attitudes.[38] When our student Jaclyn was 15, her family hosted a student from France for the summer. She automatically assumed that they wouldn't have anything in common and that the French student would be "uncool." However, Jaclyn was wrong, and they got to be good friends: "It turned out that we both liked the same music and the same groups. We both learned a lot about each other and each other's cultures. I even decided to start learning French. To this day we keep in touch through e-mail."

*Involvement*   All relationships take time to develop, but it is especially important to make time in intercultural relationships. This is one aspect of involvement. Intimacy of interaction is another element of involvement, as are shared friendship networks. Sharing the same friends is often more important for international students than the host country students because they have left their friends behind. Our student Dotty recalled introducing her friend Sung Rim to her other friends:

> I actually felt a little nervous about introducing my friends to her. I wasn't sure how well they would communicate with her. It was fine, though, and I think she felt at ease. She mostly just listened to the conversation. I could tell she was listening and trying to understand. We would try to talk slower so she could feel comfortable to participate and we made some plans to get together after finals. I would like to continue to really get to know her.

*Turning Points*   There are often significant events that relate to perceived changes in the relationship—turning points that move the relationship forward or backward. For example, asking a friend to do a favor or to share an activity might be a turning point. And if the other person refuses, the relationship may not develop beyond that point. Likewise, self-disclosure may reveal similarities and move a relationship to a new level. For example, in conversation, two professors found that they had similar ideas about communicating and teaching in the classroom. They also discovered that they both came from working-class families and that religion played a strong role in their childhood. But a turning point in their relationship came when one professor revealed that she was gay. Her friend recalled, "As a heterosexual I had never before given much thought to sexual orientation or gays 'coming out of the closet.' Thanks to Anna, I have become far more sensitive and enlightened."[39]

## Pop Culture Spotlight

When *The Hunger Games* was released as a movie in the spring of 2012, it quickly rose to the top of the box office. However, a flurry of racist tweets were posted about the casting of some of the characters with non-White actors. Casting Magnus with an Asian actor and having Rue, Thresh, and Cinna portrayed by Black actors created a negative reaction among some viewers. Damien Scott assembled what he felt were the "25 most racist tweets about *The Hunger Games*" at http://www.complex.com/tech/2012/03/the-25-most-racist-tweets-about-the-hunger-games#1, and "Hunger Game Tweets" was set up to discuss and analyze the racist tweets: http://hungergamestweets.tumblr.com/.

The process of dealing with differences, becoming involved by finding similarities, and moving beyond prejudice was summed up by a U.S. American student talking about her relationship with a Singaporean friend:

> We just had different expectations, different attitudes in the beginning, but at the end we were so close that we didn't have to talk about it. . . . After we erased all prejudices, that we thought the other person has to be different, after we erased that by talking, we just understood each other.[40]

## Intercultural Dating

**Intercultural dating** involves the pursuit of an intercultural romantic relationship. Why do some people date interculturally and others not? The reasons people give for dating within and outside their own ethnic group are very similar: They are attracted to the other person, physically or sexually. However, the reasons people give for not dating someone within or outside their own ethnic group are often very different. One reason given for not dating someone within the ethnic group is lack of attraction; reasons given for not dating outside the ethnic group include not having an opportunity and not having thought about it.[41]

In one survey, a majority of 18- to 29-year-olds (61 percent) said that people of different races being romantically linked is a change for the better for society.[42] This survey showed that attitudes are more tolerant, but do people's behaviors match their attitudes? The answer to this seems to depend on at least five different factors: gender, ethnicity, diversity of social environment, diversity of friendship network, and diversity of parents' friendships. First, most studies show that men are more likely than women to date interculturally—reflecting their greater power and ability to choose romantic partners. Males may also be less inclined to heed parents' disapproval. Second, people of color are more likely to date interethnically than Whites. Whites are the least likely to date outside their ethnic/racial group and Latinos/as are the most dated ethnic group. This probably reflects family and societal disapproval of Black-White relationships and higher tolerance for other pairings (White–Latino/a, Latino/a–Black, Black–Asian, etc.).[43]

Third, people are more likely to date someone from another cultural group if they have contact with people from different cultures—if their neighborhood, schools, and churches are culturally diverse.[44] However, even more important is the diversity of friendship network, a fourth influence. That is, it isn't enough just to *be around* people who are culturally different—one must form friendships in order to develop romantic relationships. Friends may introduce you to potential romantic partners, and having their approval probably helps sustain the intercultural relationship. Having a diverse set of friends, then, is more important than being in a diverse environment in general.[45]

Having a diverse set of friends and romantic relationships may be difficult in some instances. Most people, by the time they reach adolescence, have been taught that it is better to date within one's own ethnic and racial group. This seems to be especially true for Whites and Blacks. A very recent national survey found that young White and Black students who dated interracially were likely to encounter

**Info Bites**

Did you know that until June 12, 1967, it was illegal in Virginia (and 13 other states) for Whites and Blacks to marry? The ban against miscegenation (interracial sexual relationships) was enforced in 30 U.S. states until the 1950s. It was challenged in Virginia by Mildred and Richard Loving who had been married in 1958 in Washington, DC, where interracial marriages were permitted. Upon their return to Virginia a group of police officers invaded their home in hopes of finding them in the act of sex. They were charged and sentenced to prison time, which would be suspended if they agreed to leave the state. They moved to Washington, DC, and in 1963 the ACLU filed a motion on their behalf. Finally, in 1967 the Supreme Court declared that Virginia's anti-miscegenation law was unconstitutional, thereby ending all race-based legal

*(continued)*

disapproval, ranging from very subtle to overt hostility from their peers—often from students of the same race. Whites and Blacks who dated Asian Americans and Latinos did not encounter such disapproval.[46]

Parents play an important role in whether their children date interculturally.[47] A fifth influence on the decision to date interculturally is the ethnic diversity of parents' friends. It's possible that the initial decision to date interculturally may depend on one's friends. However, the decision to *continue* dating probably depends on the attitudes and, more important, on the *behavior* of one's parents. In other words, the deciding influence isn't whether parents are parents accept intercultural dating, but whether they have diverse friendships. It's not what the parents say that is influential, but what they do.[48]

On the other hand, parents can pass on their negative attitudes about intercultural dating to their children. Women are particularly prone to pressure from parents. As one Latina woman said, "It would be hard to date interethnically because my parents wouldn't agree with it and neither would my [H]ispanic friends." A White woman expressed similar feelings: "It would be difficult for me to date someone of another ethnicity. Not because of any prejudices I have but because I come from a family that doesn't approve of that. My grandparents (on both sides) look down on dating other races and my father isn't too crazy about it."[49] The parents often reflect the general societal sentiment. And, indeed, a major reason people give (especially Whites) for not dating interethnically is negative social pressure.[50] Later in the chapter, we'll discuss the impact of societal influence on intercultural relationships.

## Intercultural Marriage

There has been a steady increase in the number of intercultural marriages over the past 20 years, and the opposition to such marriages seems to be in a continuing decline, so much so that one scholar refers to it as a "love revolution."[51] In fact, more than one-fifth of all American adults say they have a close relative who married someone of a different race.[52] According to the Pew Research Center, in 2013, 12% of marriages were interracial marriages with American Indians (58%) marrying outside their racial group, followed by Asians (28%), blacks (19%) and whites (7%). However, gender also makes a difference as black men (25%) are more likely than black women (12%) to marry a non-black spouse. The reverse is true of Asians as more Asian women (37%) marry outside than Asian men (16%).[53] However, not all intercultural marriages are accepted. While there seems to be little opposition to a German American marrying an Italian American, there is still some resistance to interreligious marriages. Some Jewish, Christian, and Muslim parents object to their children marrying outside their faith. Religion often plays an important role in decisions about intercultural dating and marriage. For example, studies have shown that more religious Christians tend to favor dating and marrying within one's own racial group.[54] Similarly, many Muslim Americans feel the same, although it can be the source of conflict sometimes between first-generation and second-generation Muslim immigrants, as interracial marriages among second-generation Muslims are becoming increasingly common. As one young Muslim, Nora, describes it:

It's so hard to marry [someone] of your same race. We're in America, we go to school with . . . different people our entire lives. And then parents . . . say . . . "I don't care if you've been friends with white, black, red, whatever, brown [Muslims]. Those are not people that you can fall in love with."[55]

However, the real division seems to lie in crossing racial lines. There is increasing acceptance of interracial marriages, but Whites continue to be the least accepting with 84 percent approving, compared with 96 percent of Blacks who approve of interracial marriage.[56]

Robyn Preston-McGee, who is White, recounts her family's reaction to her marrying her husband who is African American:

> When my husband and I finally decided to take the plunge after dating for four years, we eloped. I think deep down we were worried about the "if anyone here can show just cause" part. My father's side of the family was horrified, my mother's tolerant, but not overjoyed. When my grandmother showed our wedding photo to a family member, they asked, "What nationality is he?" Perhaps they were hoping she would respond with the more exotic-sounding "Nigerian" or "Haitian." Nope. Just plain ol' African-American. My marriage and the subsequent birth of my daughter solidified my father's "disownership" of me. . . . All of this is not to whine about the opposition I've faced for marrying the person I married. . . . But when my white students, for example, joyously remark that "racism is a thing of the past," I ask them to consider how their own parents would react if they brought home a black person to marry. A flash of awareness comes across their faces . . . and I already know their answer.[57]

What are the major concerns of couples who marry interculturally? Their concerns, like those of dating couples, often involve dealing with pressures from their families and from society. In addition, intercultural couples face the issue of raising children. Sometimes these concerns are closely related. Although many couples are concerned with raising children and dealing with family pressures, those in intercultural marriages must deal with these issues to a greater extent. They are more likely to disagree about how to raise the children and to encounter opposition and resistance from their families about the marriage. They are also more likely to have problems related to values, eating and drinking habits, gender roles, and attitudes regarding time, religion, place of residence, stress, and ethnocentrism.[58]

Of course, every husband and wife develop their own idiosyncratic way of relating to each other, but intercultural marriage poses consistent challenges. Most couples have their own systems for working out the power balance in their relationships, for deciding who gives and who takes. As shown in Table 9.2, there are four common styles of interaction in intercultural marriages: submission, compromise, obliteration, and consensus. Couples may adopt different styles depending on the context.

**Info Bites (cont.)**

restrictions on marriage in the United States. (SOURCE: http://www .msnbc.msn.com/id /18090277/)

**Info Bites**

In 2016, a Mississippi couple were forced to move out of an RV park because they were in an interracial marriage. Erica Dunahoo who is Hispanic and Native American is married to Stanley Hoskins who is African American. She recounts what happened in Tupelo, a small city in the northeastern part of the state:

> "He was real nice," she said. "He invited me to church and gave me a hug. I bragged on him to my family."
>
> The next day, she said, Baker telephoned her and said, "Hey, you didn't tell me you

*(continued)*

**Info Bites (cont.)**

*was married to no black man."*

*She said she replied that she didn't realize it was a problem.*

*"Oh, it's a big problem with the members of my church, my community and my mother-in-law," she quoted him as saying. "They don't allow that black and white shacking."*

*"We're not shacking. We're married," she replied.*

*"Oh, it's the same thing," she quoted him as replying.*

When he was asked if he would rent the RV space to another interracial couple, Gene Baker, the owner of the park said, "I'm closing it down, and that solves the problem."
(Source: Mitchell, J. (2016, April 5). Mississippi RV park owner evicts interracial couple. *The Clarion-Ledger.* Retrieved July 19, 2016, from http://www.clarionledger.com/story/news/2016/04/02/mississippi-rv-park-owner-evicts-interracial-couple/82469086/.)

**TABLE 9.2  Four Styles of Interaction in Intercultural Marriages**

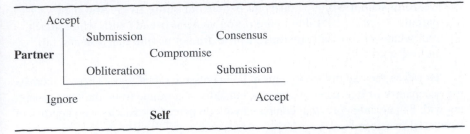

*Source:* From Romano, D. (1997). *Intercultural marriage: Promises and pitfalls* (2nd ed). Nicholas Brealey Publishing. Reprinted by permission.

The **submission style,** the most common style, occurs when one partner accepts the culture of the other partner, abandoning or denying his or her own. The submission may occur only in public; in their private life, the relationship may be more balanced. But this style rarely works in the long run. People cannot erase their core cultural background, even though they may try.

With the **compromise style,** each partner gives up some parts of his or her culturally bound habits and beliefs to accommodate the other. Although this may seem fair, it really means that both people sacrifice important aspects of their life. For example, the Christian who gives up celebrating Christmas for the sake of a Jewish spouse may eventually come to resent the sacrifice.

With the **obliteration style,** both partners deal with differences by attempting to erase their individual cultures. They may form a new culture, with new beliefs and habits, especially if they live in a country that is home to neither of them. In fact, this might seem to be the only way for couples whose backgrounds are completely unreconcilable to survive. However, because it's difficult to be completely cut off from one's own cultural background, obliteration is not a particularly good long-term solution.

The style that is the most desirable, not surprisingly, is the **consensus style,** one based on agreement and negotiation. It is related to compromise in that both partners give and take, but it is not a tradeoff. It is a win–win proposition. Consensus may incorporate elements of the other models. Thus, on occasion, one spouse might temporarily "submit" to the other's culture. One of our Navajo (Diné) students described how she adapts somewhat to her husband's more traditional culture when his mother comes to visit by letting his mother cook breakfast.

I am half Native American and half Irish. Though I was raised on the reservation, I attended school in town and was taught to try to adapt to the "outside" world. Because of this I was often accused of trying too hard to "be white."

I never realized how drastic these differences were until after I got married. My husband, who is full Native American, grew up on an isolated reservation and in a home where his mother woke up at 6 each morning to make breakfast for the family.

© 123RF

Although interra-
cial marriages have
been legal in the
United States since
1967, controversies
emerge when inter-
racial couples are
featured in adver-
tisements, such as
Cheerios and Old
Navy, as noted
in this chapter.
What might help
U.S. Americans to
accept such rela-
tionships now and in
the future?

My husband got used to me not doing this and seemed OK with it, but the first time his parents came to visit, boy did I hear about it! His mom was so upset with me. We explained my point of view to her but it didn't really help. Whenever she comes over now, she gets up early and makes breakfast.

True consensus requires flexibility and negotiation.

The challenges can be especially difficult for the spouse who is living in the foreign country. The one who is speaking the other language may be put in a weaker position, especially during times of conflict.[59] A Belgian wife describes her frustration during times of conflict with her Finnish spouse:

> I get very angry and frustrated when I am trying to explain something and he doesn't understand me, or misunderstands me. Then I feel: how can you be so stupid. However, I know very well that the fault is in me, because I just can't say it so well, but still it makes me so furious that he doesn't understand me.[60]

This wife felt welcomed and excluded at the same time living in the home country of her spouse. It had an important impact on her self-concept and identity:

> In the beginning I felt accepted; people spoiled me and invited me with open arms. However, I have my frustrations to find my identity here. I often think back at what kind of person I had become if I would've stayed there. . . . I experience myself as an international person, as a citizen of the world. I don't really belong here, if I go back I don't belong there, but I belong enough here and enough there to be actually happy.[61]

**What Do You Think?**

Nowadays, with the development of Internet and online chatting tools, people can form intercultural friendships or romantic relationships via the Internet. Some people argue that it is impossible to establish a meaningful relationship with somebody you only meet online, whereas others believe that online relationships are not that different and it is easier for you to "be yourself" online. What do you think?

Couples who are considering permanent intercultural relationships should prepare carefully for the commitment by living together, spending extended time with the partner's family, learning the partner's language, studying the partner's religion, and learning the partner's cuisine. For example, a student named Vicki dated and eventually married Hassan, a graduate student from Morocco. Before marrying, they spent time in Morocco with his family; Vicki even lived with his family for six months while Hassan was still in the States. They knew it was important for her to get to know his family and cultural background, as he had learned about her and the American culture. Couples who marry interculturally should also consider legal issues like citizenship, children's citizenship, finances and taxation, ownership of property, women's rights, divorce, and issues regarding death.

A recent study of intercultural marriages, some based on religious and some on ethnic/racial differences, found that these differences did indeed lead to conflict, but that communication played an important role in the success of these relationships. That is, open communication about the differences helped promote relationship growth. If partners were able to understand, appreciate, and integrate each other's similarities and differences, they would be able to use these in an enriching manner.[62]

### Online Relationships

As we noted in Chapter 1, more and more people are using new technologies to communicate. The most important impact of new communication technologies, particularly for young people, is the opportunities they provide for developing and maintaining relationships. Through social networking sites (SNSs) like Facebook, e-mail, instant messaging (IM), and Twitter, we can stay in touch with old friends, maintain almost constant contact with current friends, and find new friends.

These new media technologies present us with enormous opportunities to communicate and develop relationships with people who are very different from us. We can communicate with people in other countries as easily as talking to our next-door neighbors. One of our students, Mariana, described her experience of getting to know Charlotte, a Finnish student, during a virtual team project in one of her classes:

> Although we're separated by oceans and many miles, we share the same daily activities and understand each other quite well. What I enjoyed most about this experience was that even after this project Charlotte and I will be friends. We've already contacted each other on *Facebook* and sent messages. Besides focusing on the course project, I've gotten to know a lot about my partner's studies in school and her personal life.

Social media and social networking sites like Facebook and Twitter are a worldwide phenomenon. Facebook reports that "approximately 84.2 percent of our daily active users are outside the U.S. and Canada."[63] See the top Facebook countries by number of users (see Table 9.3). Keep in mind that some countries have severely restricted Facebook, such as China. Facebook, of course, is only one of many SNS. Whatever the particular audience, they present endless opportunities to develop and maintain intercultural relationships.

**TABLE 9.3  Top 10 Countries by Number of Facebook Users (in millions)**

1. India (195)
2. United States (191)
3. Brazil (90)
4. Indonesia (77.6)
5. China (52.9)
6. Mexico (46)
7. Philippines (39.8)
8. Germany (36.8)
9. United Kingdom (36.4)
10. Turkey (33)

*Source:* http://www.statista.com/statistics/268136/top-15-countries-based-on-number-of-facebook-users/.

In addition, it appears that communication technologies like the Internet and social media both facilitate and inhibit the development of intercultural relationships.[64] For example, some online communication (e-mail, instant messages, text messages) facilitates intercultural encounters in that it filters out much of the information we base first impressions on—physical attractiveness, gender, age, and race. While we may find it helpful to have information about people's characteristics, this information also sometimes causes prejudice and discrimination. Thus, some of our new media interactions may be freer of the tendency to stereotype or discriminate against someone based on those physical characteristics, and online relationships can flourish if they are based on honest self-disclosure, good communication, and established solid commonality—just like any offline relationship.[65]

Another way that intercultural communication may be facilitated online—the asynchronicity of some new media formats (e-mail, text messaging, Twitter)—allows nonnative speakers more time to compose a message and to decode and respond than is true to face-to-face interaction. However, at the same time, language differences can lead to possible misunderstanding of specific words and phrases, and humor online can often be misunderstood—thus inhibiting intercultural communication.

Understanding humor in a language often requires a sophisticated understanding of subtle nuances: irony, sarcasm, and cynicism in online communication across cultures should be approached with great caution.[66] And when humor is misunderstood, it often takes complicated explanations to clarify, as one communication professor discovered:

> One of the students in my online course made a remark meant to be slightly sarcastic and humorous, about one of the group projects he was involved in for our course. However, the remark was perceived by some of the international members of his group to be in poor taste. Some thought it very rude and insulting.

Others just found it childish. It took almost half the semester to figure out what had gone wrong, why the remark was misunderstood and to get things back on a good footing. I can't imagine it would have taken even half that long if the inter- action had been face to face instead of on the Internet.

Sometimes problems caused by language differences are exacerbated because one or both interactants may not be aware of the problem, since confusion or mis- understanding is generally shown nonverbally—by a quizzical look or a raised eyebrow. Online communicators may have to work a little harder to make sure they understand each other and to give the other some leeway in expressing different cultural values and communication styles.

One CEO responsible for virtual teams reported misunderstandings between Israelis and U.S. Americans during e-mail exchanges. Americans thought the Israelis a bit rude and Israelis thought the Americans a bit superficial. As it turns out, Israelis, whose speaking style is often characterized as very direct and low-context, found it odd that the Americans would add "niceties" to their e-mails like "Thanking you in advance for . . . ." The Israelis responded "What are they thanking me for? I haven't done anything yet." After this was brought to their attention, all team members agreed to be more tolerant and to accept this small cultural difference in e-mail etiquette.[67]

Dating websites continue to flourish; according to one survey, 37 percent of single American Internet users who are looking for a romantic partner have gone to a dating website.[68] Some focus on bringing people together from specific religious backgrounds (e.g., JDate.com, for Jewish singles, CatholicMingle.com, christianmingle.com) or specific ethnic/racial groups (e.g., InterracialSingles.net, BlackSingles.com, LatinSinglesConnection.com). Sites like lavalifePRIME.com, ourtime.com, and silversingles.com are among those offering social networking for older singles. In one study, the fastest growing group of online dating sites is people over 60, probably because it is relatively difficult for people of this age group to find a romantic partner using more traditional strategies.[69] As noted earlier, there are advantages to online relationships: you can meet more people, and first impres- sions are not based solely on physical attributes. But there are still some dangers— the user puts personal information in a relatively public place, and because of characteristics of the Internet—anonymity and filtering of cues—people can pres- ent false information about themselves (e.g., marital status, age, and even gender).[70]

## SOCIETY AND INTERCULTURAL RELATIONSHIPS

Finally, it is important to consider how society views and influences interpersonal relationships. Why do some people marry outside their racial or ethnic group more than others? For example, 61 percent of American Indian females and 54 percent of American Indian males marry outside of their group, while only 7 percent of Whites do.[71] Of course, people marry outside of their group for love, but this "love" is always in a larger context of racial attitudes and stereotypes. Despite what those in the marriage think, society will tend to view them as unequal, as the stereotypes and attitudes are not equal. This phenomenon is reflected in who marries whom.

For example, in 2013, Black men were much more likely than Black women to marry outside their group with 25 percent of Black men marrying outside versus 12 percent of Black women. In contrast, 37 percent of Asian women married a non-Asian, while only 16 percent of Asian men did so.[72]

These statistics reflect a great deal of frustration for African American women and Asian American men. The statistics also beg the question of why this is the case. Why do so few African American women and Asian men marry outside their racial group? One answer might be that society, the media, and individuals reinforce a negative image of both groups.

One young Taiwanese American who attended a dinner/discussion event, "Mating and Dating in the Asian American Community," said, "we're at the bottom of the pile, right along with black women." Lakshmi Chaudhry, an Indian American who attended the dinner, recounts:

> The rage among the men in that room was palpable as they spoke of a lifetime of sexual invisibility in a culture that constructs them as either effeminate or repulsive. . . . The sexual marketplace is a minefield for people of color. Our choice of bed partners is defined by a racial hierarchy that places Anglos squarely at the top. They determine who's hot and who's not. . . . Asian men, unfortunately don't cut it.[73]

And we can see how Hollywood movies reinforce this negative image by consistently pairing Asian women with Anglo men rather than Asian men. For example, in *Shanghai Knights,* actress Fann Wong is paired up with Owen Wilson instead of Jackie Chan, who is conveniently cast as her brother. As Chaudhry describes it, "Hollywood's message is unmistakable: No women for the Asian guy." Asian women have a better shot at connecting with Anglos, but it comes at a price. They are often stereotyped as exotic and expected to be deferring and serve White men. One of our Japanese graduate students recounted her experience in dating a White American:

> Everything went fine at the beginning. My English was not good, so he would help me with different things, and I thought that he was very nice and good to me. . . . When I didn't speak English well, he had the control in our relationship and he could manipulate information around me, for example, if his friends said something he didn't want me to understand, he didn't translate it for me and kept it secret from me. . . . [A]fter I started understanding English and American culture more, I gained more power and he lost his power. When we were fighting, we were actually negotiating our power relation, and when it changed so significantly that the relationship was no longer worth it for either of us, our relationship was over.

Chaudhry summed up her feelings on the issue:

> A chirpy white woman I once met at an airport lounge said to me, "I don't care about race when it comes to dating. It's all about chemistry." Smug in her liberal credentials, she didn't understand that color-blind attraction is a racial privilege. . . . [I]n a world still defined by racial division, there is no such thing as just plain old chemistry.

It is important to consider intercultural relationships within the society in which they develop. Because of societal pressures, interracial couples especially find that they have to develop strategies for dealing with the outside world. If they have internalized the negative images of the other group, they may feel like they're "sleeping with the enemy" or feel cut off from their own ethnic group. They may develop ways of ignoring those who see every problem as racial, and they may turn to each other for support and strength—seeing their home as a refuge from an often hostile society.[74]

How can society promote satisfying relationships between people from different cultures? Just putting people together is not the answer. Policies based on this notion, like busing to desegregate schools, have not resulted in desired outcomes. Another answer is the **contact hypothesis,** the notion that only under very specific conditions do intercultural contacts result in positive and tolerant attitudes toward the other groups.[75] While this contact hypothesis can be applied to intercultural contact in general, it is very useful in explaining patterns of interethnic dating and marriage. In the dating and marriage context, the contact hypothesis asserts that the chance for members of different groups to intermarry depends mainly on their opportunities to meet and interact socially—in cooperative (not competitive) situations, where members of both groups have equal status and hold common goals. In addition, knowing just one individual from another group as an acquaintance is not sufficient. Interracial tolerance occurs only when Blacks and Whites of equal status share a wide variety of contacts; when the contact is intimate, personal and friendly, and ideally involves several individuals of the other group. In other words, intercultural friendships and relationships occur when the conditions of encounter promote friendly interaction.

As a society, which institutions or contexts promote these types of opportunities for interracial contact? Neighborhoods? Educational institutions? Churches, synagogues, and other places of worship? The workplace? From very recent research, it appears that *integrated* religious institutions and educational institutions provide the best opportunities for intercultural friendships and the best environment to improve attitudes about interracial marriage.[76] For example, a study of six California State University campuses found that the students on these campuses interacted equally, in interracial and intraracial encounters.[77] These campuses are very diverse; no one ethnic or racial group is a majority. On the other hand, neighborhoods and workplaces do not seem to provide opportunities for the *kind* of contact (intimate, friendly, equal status interaction) that clearly facilitates intercultural friendships.[78]

## SUMMARY

In this chapter, we discussed intercultural communication in relationships with people who are both similar to and different from ourselves. Through intercultural relationships, we can acquire specific and general knowledge beyond our local communities, break stereotypes, and acquire new skills. But developing relationships with people who are different from ourselves requires us to be motivated; to deal with differences in communication styles, values, and perceptions; to avoid the tendency to stereotype; to cope with the anxiety that sometimes accompanies these relationships; to try to confirm the other's cultural identity; and to explain to ourselves and others.

We also discussed the foundations of intercultural relationships and the cultural variations in how relationships develop. Two principles—similarities and differences—seem to operate for most people in most cultures, in that individuals are simultaneously drawn to the similarities and the differences of other people. Gay relationships are similar in many ways to heterosexual relationships, but they differ in some aspects. In gay relationships, friendship and sexual involvement are not mutually exclusive, as they tend to be for heterosexuals. Gay men seem to seek more emotional support from same-sex friends than heterosexual men do. Gay couples seem to manage conflict better than straight couples. Friendships may play a special role in gay relationships because the individuals often experience strained relationships with their families.

Finally, we described how communication in intercultural relationships involves issues of competence, involvement, and similarity and hinges on turning points. Intercultural dating and marriage, particularly in the United States, are still not very common and are often disapproved of by family and society. Computer-mediated communication can both facilitate and hinder intercultural relationships. Society can influence our relationships in important ways, helping or hindering us in exploring and developing intercultural relationships.

## BUILDING INTERCULTURAL SKILLS

1. Be aware of the complexities of communicating across cultures and of power issues. The goal is to find a way in which we can work toward unity based on "conscious coalition, of affinity, of political kinship," in which we all win.[79]

   Intercultural friends recognize and try to understand how ethnic, gender, and class differences lead to power differentials, and to manage these power issues. They also recognize that history is seen as more or less important by those who are more and those who are less powerful. Finally, they value differences and affirm others as members of culturally different groups.

2. Recognize the value of building coalitions. Coalitions can develop from the multiple identities of gender, sexual orientation, race, physical ability, region, religion, age, social class, and so on. Become involved in whatever way you can in your immediate spheres—of friendships and activities—and cultivate emotional interdependence with others.

3. Look to role models for how to be an effective agent of change. Perhaps you can find these role models in the lives of those around you or in literature or those who have gone before us. Be aware that it's easy to get overwhelmed and feel a sense of despair or powerlessness in working to improve things. Identify your strengths, and use them. Thus, if you're a parent, talk to your children about intercultural issues and building bridges and coalitions between cultural groups. If you have a job, talk to your coworkers. If you are an extrovert, use your people

skills to gather others together for dialogues on cross-cultural awareness and understanding. If you are an employer, identify who is missing from your workforce. What are you doing about it?

## ACTIVITY

1. *Intercultural relationships:* Think about all your friends, and make a list of those to whom you feel close. Identify any friends on the list who are from other cultures. Then answer the following questions, and discuss your answers with other class members.

   *a.* Do people generally have more friends from their own culture or from other cultures? Why?

   *b.* What are some of the benefits of forming intercultural friendships?

   *c.* In what ways are intercultural friendships different from or similar to friendships with people from the same culture?

   *d.* What are some reasons people might have for not forming intercultural friendships?

## ENDNOTES

1. Elias, N., & Lemish, D. (2009). Spinning the web of identity: The roles of the Internet in the lives of immigrant adolescents. *New Media & Society, 11*(4), 533–551. doi: 10.1177/1461444809102959.

2. Farrell, E. (2005, February 4). More students plan to work to help pay for college. *The Chronicle of Higher Education,* pp. A1, A34.

3. Clark-Ibanez, M. K., & Felmlee, D. (2004). Interethnic relationships: The role of social network diversity. *Journal of Marriage and Family, 66,* 229–245.

4. Allen, B. J. (2004). *Difference matters: Communicating social identity.* Long Grove, IL: Waveland Press.

5. Brislin, R. W. (1983). The benefits of close intercultural relationships. In S. H. Irvine & J. W. Berry (Eds.), *Human assessment and cultural factors* (pp. 521–538). New York, NY: Plenum Press.

6. Stephan, W. G. (1999). *Reducing prejudice and stereotyping in schools.* New York, NY: Teachers College Press.

7. Collier, M. J., & Bornman, E. (1999). Core symbols in South African intercultural friendships. *International Journal of Intercultural Relations, 23,* 133–156.

8. Chen, L. (2002). Communication in intercultural relationships. In W. B. Gudykunst & B. Mody (Eds.), *Handbook of international and intercultural communication* (2nd ed., pp. 241–257). Thousand Oaks, CA: Sage.

9. Pogrebin, L. C. (1992). The same and different: Crossing boundaries of color, culture, sexual preference, disability, and age. In W. B. Gudykunst & Y. Y. Kim (Eds.), *Readings on communicating with strangers* (pp. 318–336). New York, NY: McGraw-Hill.

10. Pogrebin (1992), p. 318.

11. Byrne, D. (1971). *The attraction paradigm.* New York, NY: Academic Press. See also Byrne, D., & Blaylock, B. (1963). Similarity and assumed similarity of attitudes between husbands and wives. *Journal of Abnormal and Social Psychology, 67,* 636–640.

12. Osbeck, L. M., & Moghaddam, F. M. (1997). Similarity and attraction among majority and minority groups in a multicultural context. *International Journal of Intercultural Relations, 21,* 113–123. See also Tan, D., & Singh, R. (1995). Attitudes and attraction. *Personality and Social Psychology Bulletin, 21,* 975–986.

13. Duck, S., & Barnes, M. K. (1992). Disagreeing about agreement: Reconciling differences about similarity. *Communication Monographs, 59,* 199–208. See also LaGaipa, J. J. (1987). Friendship

expectations. In R. Burnett, P. McGee, & D. Clarke (Eds.), *Accounting for relationships* (pp. 134–157). London: Methuen.

14. Hatfield, E., & Rapson, R. L. (1992). Similarity and attraction in close relationships. *Communication Monographs, 59,* 209–212.

15. Gareis, E. (1995). *Intercultural friendship: A qualitative study.* Lanham, MD: University Press of America, p. 96.

16. Gareis (1995), p. 128.

17. Storti, C. (2001). *Old world, new world: Bridging cultural differences: Britain, France, Germany and the U.S.* Yarmouth, ME: Intercultural Press.

18. Storti (2001), p. 68

19. Storti (2001).

20. Barnlund, D. S. (1989). *Communication styles of Japanese and Americans: Images and reality.* Belmont, CA: Wadsworth.

21. Kito, M. (2005). Self-disclosure in romantic relationships and friendships among American Japanese college students. *Journal of Social Psychology, 14,* 127–140.

22. Collier, M. J. (1991). Conflict competence within African, Mexican and Anglo American friendships. In S. Ting-Toomey & F. Korzenny (Eds.), *Cross-cultural interpersonal communication* (pp. 132–154). Newbury Park, CA: Sage. See also Collier, M. J. (1996). Communication competence problematics in ethnic friendships. *Communication Monographs, 63,* 314–346.

23. Gao, G. (1991). Stability of romantic relationships in China and the United States. In Ting-Toomey & Korzenny, pp. 99–115. See also Sprecher, S., Aron, A., Hatfield, E., Cortese, A., Potapova, E., & Levitskaya, A. (1994). Love: American style, Russian style, and Japanese style. *Personal Relationships, 1,* 349–369. And see Kito (2005).

24. Dion, K. K., & Dion, K. L. (1991). Psychological individualism and romantic love. *Journal of Social Behavior and Personality, 6,* 17–33. See also Dion, K. K., & Dion, K. L. (1993). Individualistic and collectivistic perspectives on gender and the cultural context of love and intimacy. *Journal of Social Issues, 49,* 53–59.

25. Herdt, G. (1997). *Same sex, different cultures: Exploring gay and lesbian lives.* Boulder, CO: Westview Press.

26. Hammond, D., & Jablow, A. (1987). Gilgamesh and the Sundance Kid: The myth of male friendship. In H. Brod (Ed.), *The making of masculinities: The new men's studies* (pp. 241–258). Boston, MA: Allen & Unwin.

27. Nardi, P. (1999). *Gay men's friendships: Invincible communities.* Thousand Oaks, CA: Sage.

28. Gottman, J., & Levenson, R. (2004). 12-year study of gay & lesbian couples. Retrieved January 29, 2009, from http://www.gottman.com/research/gaylesbian/12yearstudy.

29. Nakayama, T. K. (1998). Communication of heterosexism. In M. L. Hecht (Ed.), *Communication of prejudice* (pp. 112–121). Thousand Oaks, CA: Sage.

30. Galupo, M. P., Bauerband, L. A., Gonzalez, K. A., Hagen, D. B., Hether, S. D., & Krum, T. E. (2014). Transgender friendships experiences: Benefits and barriers of friendships across gender identity and sexual orientation. *Feminism & Psychology, 24*(2), 193–215. doi: 10.1177/0959353514526218.

31. Yoshino, K. (2015). A new birth of freedom?: Obergefell v. Hodges. *Harvard Law Review, 129,* 147–179.

32. Gay marriage around the world. (2015, June 26). *Pew Research Center.* Retrieved July 19, 2016, from http://www.pewforum.org/2015/06/26/gay-marriage-around-the-world-2013/.

33. Dick, W. (2015, July 24). In Germany, marriage remains out of reach for gays. *Deutsche Welle.* Retrieved July 21, 2016, from http://www.dw.com/en/in-germany-marriage-remains-out-of-reach-for-gays/a-18606682.

34. Brydum, S. (2004, December 13). Report: Same-sex couples less likely to divorce. *The Advocate.* Retrieved July 19, 2016, from http://www.advocate.com/politics/marriage-equality/2014/12/13/report-same-sex-couples-less-likely-divorce.

35. Cowburn, A. (2016, January 5). ISIS has killed at least 25 men in Syria suspected of being gay, group claims. *Independent.* Retrieved July 19, 2016, from http://www.independent.co.uk/news/world/middle-east/isis-has-killed-at-least-25-men-in-syria-suspected-of-being-gay-group-claims-a6797636.html.

36. Sudweeks, S., Gudykunst, W. B., Ting-Toomey, S., & Nishida, T. (1990). Developmental themes in Japanese–North American relationships. *International Journal of Intercultural Relations, 14,* 207–233.

37. Howell, W. S. (1982). *The empathic communicator.* Belmont, CA: Wadsworth.

38. Graham, M. A., Moeai, J., & Shizuru, L. S. (1985). Intercultural marriages: An intrareligious perspective. *International Journal of Intercultural Relations, 9,* 427–434.

39. Allen, B. J. (2004). Sapphire and Sappho: Allies in authenticity. In A. González, M. Houston, & V. Chen (Eds.), *Our voices: Essays in culture, ethnicity and communication* (4th ed., pp. 198–202). Los Angeles, CA: Roxbury.

40. Quoted in Gareis (1995), p. 136.

41. Martin, J. N., Bradford, L. J., Drzewiecka, J. A., & Chitgopekar, A. S. (2003). Intercultural dating patterns among young white U.S. Americans: Have they changed in the past 20 years? *Howard Journal of Communications, 14,* 53–73.

42. Taylor, P. (2012, February 16). *The rise of intermarriage.* Pew Internet & American Life. Retrieved August 24, 2012, from http://www.pewsocialtrends.org/files/2012/02/SDT-Intermarriage-II.pdf.

43. Clark-Ibanez & Felmlee (2004); Moore, R. M. (2000). An exploratory study of interracial dating on a small college campus. *Sociological Viewpoints, 16,* 46–64.

44. Martin et al. (2003).

45. Clark-Ibanez & Felmlee (2004).

46. Kreager (2008).

47. Mills, J. K., Daly, J., Longmore, A., & Kilbride, G. (1995). A note on family acceptance involving interracial friendships and romantic relationships. *Journal of Psychology, 129,* 349–351; Moore (2000).

48. Clark-Ibanez & Felmlee (2004).

49. Clark-Ibanez & Felmlee (2004), p. 300.

50. Clark-Ibanez & Felmlee (2004).

51. Root, M. P. P. (2001). *Love's revolution: Interracial marriage.* Philadelphia, PA: Temple University Press.

52. Lee, S. M., & Edmonston, B. (2005). New marriages, new families: U.S. racial and Hispanic intermarriage. *Population Bulletin, 60*(2).

53. Wang, W. (2015, June 12). Interracial marriage: Who is 'marrying out'? Pew Research Center. Retrieved November 4, 2016 from: http://www.pewresearch.org/fact-tank/2015/06/12/interracial-marriage-who -is-marrying-out/

54. Yancey, G. (2008). Homogamy over the net: Using internet advertisements to discover who interracially dates. *Journal of Social and Personal Relationships, 24*(6), 913–940.

55. Grewal, Z. A. (2009). Marriage in colour: race, religion and spouse selection in four American mosques. *Ethnic and Racial Studies, 32*(2), 323–345.

56. Newport, F. (2013, July 25). In U.S., 87% approve of black-white marriage, vs. 4% in 1958. *Gallup.* Retrieved July 20, 2016, from http://www.gallup.com/poll/163697/approve-marriage-blacks-whites .aspx.

57. Preston-McGee, R. (2008, September 30). Interracial marriage: Yes, it's still hard. Retrieved January 30, 2009, from http://www.alternet.org/sex/100981/interracial_marriage:_yes,_it's_still_hard/.

58. Romano, D. (1997). *Intercultural marriage: Promises and pitfalls* (2nd ed.). Yarmouth, ME: Intercultural Press.

59. Cools, C. A. (2006). Relational communication in intercultural couples. *Language and Intercultural Communication, 6*(3&4), 262–274.

60. Cools (2006).

61. Cools (2006).

62. Reiter, M. J., & Gee, C. B. (2009). Open communication and partner support in intercultural and interfaith romantic relationship: A relational maintenance approach. *Journal of Social and Personal Relationships. 25*(4), 539–599.

63. Facebook. (2016). Newsroom. Retrieved July 20, 2016, from http://newsroom.fb.com/company -info/.

64. Yang, P. (2012). Who am I in virtual space? A dialectical approach to students' online identity expression. In P. H. Cheong, J. N. Martin, & L. P. Macfadyen (Eds.), *New media and intercultural communication: Identity, community and politics.* (pp. 109–122). New York, NY: Peter Lang.

65. McKenna, K. Y. A., Green, A. S., & Gleason, M. E. J. (2002). Relationship formation on the Internet: What's the big attraction? *Journal of Social Issues, 58,* 9–31.

66. St. Amant, K. (2002). When cultures and computers collide: Rethinking computer-mediated communication according to international and intercultural communication expectations. *Journal of Business and Technical Communication, 16,* 196–214.

67. Snyder, B. (2003, May). Teams that span time zones face new work rules. *Stanford Business.* Stanford Graduate School of Business website. Retrieved from http://www.gsb.stanford.edu /news/bmag/sbsm0305/feature_virtual_teams.shtml.

68. Online dating statistics (2012, June 20). Retrieved August 24, 2012, from http://www .statisticbrain.com/online-dating-statistics/.

69. Adams, S. (2012, February 13). Silver surfer daters "more honest." *The Telegraph.* Retrieved August 24, 2012, from http://www.telegraph.co.uk/health/healthnews/9080057/Silver-surfer -daters-more-honest.html.

70. Hegarty, J. (2012, May 7). How to avoid online dating scams. Retrieved August 24, 2012, from http://www.omaha.com/article/20120517/MONEY/705179962.

71. Wang, W. (2015, June 12). Interracial marriage: Who is "marrying out"? *Pew Research Center.* Washington, DC. Retrieved July 20, 2016, from http://www.pewresearch.org/fact-tank/2015/06/12 /interracial-marriage-who-is-marrying-out/.

72. Wang (2015).

73. Chaudhry, L. (2003, February 3). Chemistry isn't color-blind. *AlterNet.org.* Retrieved from http:// www.alternet.org/story.html?StoryID=15090.

74. Foeman, A., & Nance, T. (2002). Building new cultures, reframing old images: Success strategies of interracial couples. *Howard Journal of Communications, 13,* 237–249.

75. Pettigrew, T. F. (1998). Intergroup contact theory. *Annual Review of Psychology, 49,* 65–85.

76. Johnson & Jacobson (2005).

77. Cowan, G. (2005). Interracial interactions of racially diverse university campuses. *Journal of Social Psychology, 14,* 49–63.

78. Johnson & Jacobson (2005).

79. Kivel, P. (1996). *Uprooting racism; How White people can work for racial justice.* Gabriola Island, British Columbia: New Society, pp. 204–205.

© kristian sekulic/Getty Images RF

CHAPTER TEN

# Intercultural Communication in Tourism Contexts

**STUDY OBJECTIVES**

*After reading this chapter, you should be able to:*

1. Identify and describe characteristics of tourist–host encounters.

2. Understand how social and political contexts influence tourism encounters.

3. Describe variations in host attitudes toward tourists.

4. Describe the language challenges that tourists might face.

5. Identify cross-cultural differences in social norms and expectations encountered by tourists.

6. Understand the role culture shock might play in a tourism experience.

7. Describe the tourist challenges of the search for authenticity.

8. Describe ways in which tourists can learn about the cultures they visit.

9. Describe the role of social media in intercultural tourism.

10. Understand the various environmental and political impacts on tourism.

**KEY TERMS**

adventure tourism
authenticity
boundary maintenance
cultural tourism
ecotourism
host
medical tourism
resistance
retreatism
revitalization
socially responsible tourism
staged authenticity
tourist
volunteer tourism (voluntourism)

Since the beginning of time, humans have been traveling in ever-widening patterns about the Earth. From the days of early explorers, who traveled on foot and by boat, to modern roamers, who travel by car and plane, there has been an increase in travel and tourism. The World Tourism Organization (WTO) estimates that more than a billion people cross international borders every year—almost 3 million a day. In fact, travel and tourism is one of the world's largest industries. In 2015, international tourism receipts reached a record of $1,232 billion—the sixth consecutive year of above average growth.[1] (See the world's top 10 tourism destinations in Table 10.1). In addition, many people engage in tourism within their own country. Experts estimate that U.S. Americans make 1.7 billion person-trips a year for leisure purposes.[2]

Almost all of us have been tourists or will be someday. Being a **tourist** may involve travel to another region of the United States, like visiting the annual Diné (Navajo) Nation Fair in Window Rock, Arizona, or taking a trip to famous civil war battlefields like Gettysburg, Pennsylvania, or embarking on an international trip like those taken by many college students. It may involve a bus trip through Europe with a high school choir, an organized trip with a sport team to compete in a basketball tournament in Canada, or a family trip to visit ancestral sites in Japan or Ukraine. (See "Did You Know" for the most common types of tourism.) In any case, tourism contexts provide rich opportunities for intercultural encounters.

These encounters may be positive, as was our student Sarah's experience when she traveled to Italy with her senior class. She gained a great appreciation for the art and history of Italy and an admiration for the bilingual Italians she met. It was the first time she had been out of the country and didn't know what to expect:

> I remember getting off the plane and being in awe of my surroundings. During our two-week stay, we traveled to Rome, Venice, Assisi, and the Padua. I learned a lot about the Italian culture during those two weeks, but the one thing that stood out in my mind was that most of the Italians we met spoke English, while hardly any of us could speak Italian.

**TABLE 10.1  World's Top 10 Tourism Destinations in 2015**

| 1. | France | 6. | Turkey |
|----|--------|----|--------|
| 2. | United States | 7. | Germany |
| 3. | Spain | 8. | United Kingdom |
| 4. | China | 9. | Russia |
| 5. | Italy | 10. | Mexico |

*Source:* World's Top 10 Tourism Destinations 2015, Tourism Highlights, 2015 edition. World Tourism Organization. Reprinted by permission.

There are many different types of tourist experiences that offer opportunities for intercultural encounters. Some of the most common are listed here. Which of these have you experienced or would you like to experience?

- **Adventure tourism** involves travel to remote or exotic destinations for the purpose of engaging in rugged outdoor activities.
- **Ecotourism** emphasizes unspoiled destinations and travel with minimal impact on the natural environment.
- **Cultural tourism** emphasizes learning the history, language, and/or unique cultural aspects of a destination.
- **Medical tourism** involves travel for purpose of acquiring medical procedures, most often elective plastic surgery.

*(continued)*

© John Neubauer/Photo Edit

Some cultural groups desire only limited contact with the outside world, often restricted to business transactions. This is the case for many Mennonites and Amish. Here, a Mennonite girl sells cheese in Chihuahua, Mexico.

**Did You Know? (cont.)**

• Volunteer tourism or "voluntourism" combines vacation travel with participation in service projects, often in underserved world regions.

In contrast to Sarah's experience, some tourist encounters have more negative outcomes, often due to power differentials. For example, Rahe, a middle class U.S. American student, visited Mexico with his family and was unprepared to deal with the poverty he encountered: "It was not a positive experience and influences my views on cultures of economically poor regions. Due to that experience, I have no desire to ever visit similar regions, even if they do have beautiful scenery."

All of this has implications for intercultural communication. What are typical intercultural encounters in tourist contexts? How do cultural differences influence communication in these contexts? How do societal structures influence tourist encounters? How do politics and economic events impact tourist encounters? How can communication be improved in these contexts? These are some of the questions we'll be tackling in this chapter. First, we describe the characteristics of host–tourist encounters and the larger contexts (historical, political) in which these encounters occur. Then we discuss the communication challenges in tourist contexts, and how tourism encounters can lead to culture learning. Finally, we discuss the role of social media and the political and environmental impacts on tourism, and then identify skills that can help us communicate better in tourist contexts.

# INTERCULTURAL COMMUNICATION AND TOURISM

## Characteristics of Tourist–Host Encounters

Let's now turn our focus to the tourist–**host** encounter. How do these encounters differ from many of our daily interactions? Experts suggest at least four fairly unique characteristics: they are short-term and transitory, commercialized, and often involve unbalanced power dynamics.[3] For example, consider Sena's tourist experience in Manipur, India. When she returned, she talked with her friends about the treatment of women in Manipur. She said that the women she met were more similar to Western women—in the clothing they wore and the jobs they had—compared with women in other parts of India. Her experiences with Manipuri women were, however, only surface level. If she had stayed longer and learned more about the culture, she might have discovered that although Manipuri women have some freedom socioeconomically and educationally, when it comes to decision making, an important responsibility, a woman's domain is confined to the domestic sphere.

As Sena's experience illustrates, most tourism encounters, by definition, are short-term and transitory. Tourists rarely stay in one place for long and often have very little interaction with people in the host country. In fact, one writer observes that tourists on tour buses rolling through a country are really watching a silent movie, with the tour guide supplying the soundtrack.[4] This means that most contact between tourists and hosts or service providers will be quite brief, as in the preceding example. Since many tourists are in the host country for a limited time, they lack both knowledge of local customs and the motivation to gain a deep understanding of the culture. Therefore, their impressions are based on superficial knowledge and have the potential to perpetuate stereotypes or misperceptions.[5]

Second, most host–tourist interactions are commercialized. This commercializing of interpersonal relationships has had dramatic effect in some developing countries where generous hospitality is the norm; people often invite visitors, even strangers, for meals and to participate in community life. They may even offer gifts as part of the hospitality. With the development of a tourism industry, these goods and services that used to be part of people's personal and social lives are commercialized and offered as products to be bought by tourists. So these brief, superficial interactions are predictable and ritualistic and offer few opportunities for tourists to engage in genuine social interactions with local people.

The final characteristic of tourist–host communication is the unbalanced nature of the interaction. First, host and tourist have very different views on the meaning of tourism. For tourists, "tourism" means playtime, a break from the normal work routine, a quest for novelty, and an escape from the mundane life at home. However, for many of the hosts whose jobs rely on tourism it can mean exhausting menial work, family stress, and the commercialization of their culture. Also, tourists, hosts, and service providers often have different socioeconomic backgrounds, with the tourists more economically and socially privileged than those with whom they interact. While the tourists may be disadvantaged in not knowing the local language, in general, they are in the privileged position of "buying" the hosts' services. Depending

**What Do You Think?**

According to the U.S. Passport Service Guide, there were more than 15 million U.S. passports issued in 2015 (http://www.us-passport-service-guide.com/passport-statistics.html). However, Americans are often criticized for having little knowledge of other countries and limited travel experiences. Consider the following: (1) If you had the chance to give a short presentation about another country, which would you select? (2) What information about that country and people do you think would be important to highlight? (3) What does this scenario tell you about your understanding of nations outside the United States?

on the strength of the local economy, the locals' very survival may depend on the tourists' purchases.

How does this imbalance affect communication between host and tourist? For one thing, those with less power in general often feel they have to accommodate to the more powerful. For example, hosts must learn the tourists' language(s) or risk losing out on economic benefits; they might feel pressure to deliver the most desirable products and services. But perhaps most important, they may experience a feeling of being patronized, of not being recognized as on the same level with tourists—in all aspects of the tourist encounter, from the language they speak to the way they are treated in the commercial transactions involving souvenirs, lodging, and other goods and services. The pressure to provide for family in an economically poor region, combined with the perception that tourists have a lot of money can also lead to overcharging, as a Kenyan student explains:

> We view most tourists as old and rich Caucasians. They have a lot of money to spend and people overcharge them and sell them stuff (which they convince them are original and made in the country). These tourists are considered ignorant about African culture.

The end result then of power imbalances can lead tourists to be suspicious of locals and feelings of resentment at possibly being taken advantage of. However, many factors influence the imbalance between tourist and host. An interaction between a middle-class English businessperson on holiday in Spain with a local restaurant manager does not represent a huge power differential. However, the relationship is still unbalanced due to the commercial nature of the interaction.

## Social, Historical, and Economic Contexts of Tourism

As tourists, we may be stepping, unaware, into a situation where past or current social and political events influence the interactions we'll have with members of host culture. Let's look briefly at some of these. For example, some of the tourist–host imbalances we discussed earlier stem from political history. The extremes of these imbalanced relationships are represented in tourism in developing countries, or in previously colonized countries where the legacy of colonialism still lingers. For example, Kenyans have been complaining on social media about poor treatment they receive in popular Nairobi restaurants, cafes, and hotels—where locals are subject to racial profiling while white foreigners receive top-notch treatment. One Kenyan customer lamented, "When black Africans come in, no one sits them down and the waiters take time to bring menus. When *mzungus* (foreigners) come in, waiters trip over each other to show them where to sit and with menus in hand. I don't know when black waiters in Nairobi restaurants will understand that not all *mzungus* have more money than blacks."[6]

So tourism encounters occur in complex social and economic contexts. On the one hand, tourism can bring benefits to host communities: local businesses prosper because of tourism, and interaction with tourists can promote a sense of cultural pride and provide a window to the outside world for local residents. However, there can be negative impacts as well, especially in small, less economically developed communities. Tourism can result in increased crime, traffic problems, disruption of family life, alcohol and drug problems, crime, and sexual promiscuity.

The United Nations has focused on tourism as one way to address the severe economic imbalances in some developing countries (2.5 billion people live on less than U.S.$2 a day). One of the projects outlined in the United Nations "2030 Agenda for Sustainable Development" is the Small Island Development States (SIDS), focusing on 52 islands in the Caribbean, the Pacific, the Mediterranean, the Indian Ocean, and South China Sea, where tourism accounts for 40 to 50 percent of annual gross domestic product (GDP) and the number of international tourists visiting SIDS reaches more than 40 million a year. While these islands contribute less than 1 percent to total greenhouse gas emissions, they are among the first to experience adverse impact of climate change (rising oceans, destruction of rain forests, etc.). The United Nations is working with local governments and organizations to create jobs, promote local culture and products, and improve access to transport, electricity, water, and sanitation while at the same time minimize environmental impacts as well as social and cultural changes in SIDS communities (i.e., tourists' behavior and life styles are sometimes not in harmony with local cultures).[7]

However, some UN experts are less optimistic about the potential of tourism to boost economies in poor countries. They estimate that only a fraction of the tourist money spent actually stays in the local community. In fact, some estimate that for every $100 spent on a vacation tour by a tourist from a developed country, only around $5 actually stays in a developing country destination's economy. There are several reasons for this "leakage."

One is that many of the tour operators and hotel chains are foreign owned, so money stays with the foreign companies. Another is that tourists often demand standards of equipment, food, drinks, and other products that a poor host country cannot provide, so they have to be imported, and income leaves once again. A third reason is that increasing numbers of tourist destinations are "enclave" experiences (e.g., Sandals resorts in the Caribbean) or "all-inclusive" vacation packages: "When tourists remain for their entire stay at the same cruise ship or resort, which provides everything they need and where they will make all their expenditures, not much opportunity is left for local people to profit from tourism." One report concluded that all-inclusive locations imported more and employed fewer people per dollar of revenue than other hotels.[8]

The result of these complex social, economic, and historical contexts can influence attitudes of host toward tourists, our next topic.

## Attitudes of Hosts toward Tourists

Given the social and political contexts described earlier, and the unequal power relations between hosts and tourists, coping with tourists can be a complex process for people in some host countries. The attitudes of residents may range from retreatism, to resistance, to boundary maintenance, to revitalization and adoption.[9] Some communities that are not enthusiastic about tourism may simply practice **retreatism,** or avoiding contact with tourists. This may occur especially in places where the economy has become dependent

Several Western tourists were arrested in Malaysia for allegedly taking naked pictures on a mountaintop considered sacred by locals. Is it ever acceptable to engage in behavior considered improper by locals? Should you always follow the adage "When in Rome, do as the Romans do?"

© Europics/Newscom

on tourism but the community feels invaded by tourists. The downside of tourism can include crowded streets, transportation, and shops. High demand during tourist season results in high prices of food and other items and can lead to overcharging of locals and tourists alike. Scarce resources like water and sanitation systems may come under pressure, and tourists may unknowingly insult local sensibilities. For example, locals in small Mediterranean villages and Africans in many tourist locations are often shocked and feel violated by the scantily clad tourists who walk the streets of their conservative villages or go topless on their beaches: "We perceive tourists as people who are spoiled . . . the way they dress and/or hang around—kissing in public, nude in beaches and sun bathing—is somewhat of a risk to our cultural values." Some behaviors such as the recent fad of tourists' undressing and taking nude photos of themselves at famous tourist sites can even result in arrests. (See photo on this page.)

Another example of retreatism happens in many small villages in touristy regions of Europe where residents complain that tourists feel free to walk into their yards and peer into their "quaint" houses. Similar situations occur when U.S. tourists visit American Indian reservations. They sometimes violate the pueblo residents' boundaries for personal space by touching them, or picking up residents' babies without permission. When people feel so invaded, they may resort to forms of **resistance** to tourist intrusions. Resistance may take fairly passive forms like grumbling and gossiping about tourists or creating denigrating stereotypes about difficult tourists. For example, stereotypes about arrogant Germans, complaining Dutch, and stingy Swedes abound in many Mediterranean tourist locales.

Resistance can also include more assertive forms, as when Mexican resort staff occasionally pretend not to speak English to rude tourists or in mild harassment of female tourists. When locals feel pushed beyond their limit by tourism, they may even resort to organized protest or even violence. In one incident, a furious Navajo (Diné) man shot out the tires of a tourist's car when the tourist barged into his hogan to photograph his family eating there.[10]

**Boundary maintenance** to regulate the interaction between hosts and tourists is a common response among certain cultures within the United States, like the Amish, Hutterites, or Mennonites, that do not really desire a lot of interaction with tourists. The Amish in these communities may interact with tourists on a limited level, but they maintain a distance from outsiders and often will turn their backs to cameras, believing they are following the second commandment in the Bible (Exodus 20:12: "Thou shalt not make unto thee any graven image . . ."). They ignore or endure the tourists' gaze and the insulting photography, and go on with their lives.[11]

In Lancaster County, Pennsylvania, where many Amish and Mennonites live, there are several commercial simulated cultural experiences, like "Amish Village" or "Amish Farm and Home," in which actors play Amish characters and educate tourists about Amish culture. In this way, a boundary is retained between the real Amish and the tourists. However, due to escalating land prices, fewer Amish can afford to farm and now depend more and more on tourism and interact more directly with tourists—turning their homes into bed and breakfast inns and selling quilts, crafts, and Amish food.

A final response of host to tourists is **revitalization** and adoption. Some communities have been revitalized economically by embracing tourism—like colonial Williamsburg and many towns in New England that feature colonial architecture. Communities may decide to actively invest money to draw tourists or may be more passive, accepting the tourism but maintaining boundaries. Other communities wholeheartedly embrace tourism and welcome interaction with tourists, accepting tourism as part of their social and cultural fabric. For example, there are communities in Africa with flourishing Homestay economies. One Kenyan farm, close to national parks, has coffee and tea plantings, a vegetable garden, as well as cattle and chickens. This farm hosts more than 60 visitors a year, yielding a good income. Here, in addition to lodging, visitors can learn about local practices, including how to milk a cow or pick coffee and tea, how to cook local dishes, and also gain knowledge about African hairstyles and traditional sports such as archery.[12]

By marketing their culture, local residents sometimes rediscover their own history and traditions and begin to realize their own worth. They may establish museums for tourists, and they learn about their own traditions. Or they may set up heritage parks, festivals, and handcraft markets that lead to preservation of the local culture. In some poor areas with declining populations, tourism can have the effect of revitalizing the area and halting the depopulation. However, residents often do not share equally in the profits from revitalization and marketing of culture.

Of course, there can be a variety of responses within the same community. There may be some residents who prefer to retreat and limit their interaction with tourists, while others may embrace tourism and welcome the visitors. This can cause conflicts in communication among community members.

**What Do You Think?**

James Clifford, in the essay "Traveling Cultures" (in *Cultural Studies*, Routledge, 1992), argues that when we travel we are involved in many more relationships than we might think—with maids, bellhops, guides, and so on. If you have traveled to other countries for vacations, what different kinds of people did you depend on that you were perhaps unaware of?

**What Do You Think?**

When we speak of vacationing or traveling, we often think of going out of the country, or at least to some resort location. Have you thought about what you can do in and around your state? The U.S. government has collected all of the states' tourism pages and put them in one location. Check it out at https://www.usa.gov /recreation-and-travel.

## COMMUNICATION CHALLENGES IN TOURISM CONTEXTS

Being a student of intercultural communication in tourism contexts provides many interesting communication challenges, including (1) rising to the challenges of a foreign language, (2) following social norms and expectations, (3) dealing with culture shock, and (4) searching for authenticity.

Let's examine each of these challenges in turn.

### Language Challenges

Language is often the first challenge encountered by tourists. One cannot learn all the languages of the cultures where one might visit in a lifetime, and it can be frustrating not to be able to understand what is being said. It is often part of culture shock. Language challenges can even occur when visiting countries where people speak the same language you do. For example, our student Genevieve described her experience of visiting Australia with her family as a teenager:

> The different slang in Australia was, by far, the hardest part about the trip. Even though they speak English, some of the slang or sayings that they used in Australia made absolutely no sense to me! My family and I even bought a book of sayings to try to help us understand some of the things that we were hearing.

The expectations of various host cultures regarding language also may differ. Sometimes tourists are expected to get along using the host language, but other cultures provide more language assistance for travelers. Our student April was 16 when she took a trip to France with a group from her high school, while a group of French students visited her hometown. She recalled the experience:

> The first day we arrived, everyone spoke in English. We got to our hotel, and everything there had English writing. Since none of us spoke fluent French, an English speaker accompanied us, happily translating for us. I thought it was a wonderful trip.

However, when she got back home, she discovered that the French students had had quite a different experience:

> They were expected to know English, so nobody from my school district bothered to get an interpreter. They had to rely on the fluent English speakers of their own group to do even the most simple things like ride the bus. At the dinner my town hosted, the English-speaking French students had to interrupt their meal to translate to the other students. I am sure when they returned they could not have had many good things to say about my town.

Translator apps for mobile phones (e.g., Google Translate, iTranslate) can make navigating foreign languages easier for tourists and business travelers, but as we discussed in Chapter 5, there are challenges of using machine translators. If you know nothing of the foreign language you'll have to depend completely on the app translation and we know that machine translation is still no match for human

**Info Bites**

Don't speak the language of the foreign country(ies) you're visiting? Want to be able to take photos of signage and get immediate translation? Try a mobile phone translator app. Consider:

- Cost: Some are free, but then you see ads.
- Compatibility with your mobile device: Some are for iPhones, some for android, etc.
- Range of languages: Range from a few to more than 100.
- Text vs. speech: Some work with written text, others record your voice and then translate.

(Source: Adapted from Kotenko, J. (2016, January 12). *The best translator apps for travel in 2016*. Retrieved from http://www.dailydot .com/irl/best-translator -apps-travel-2016/.)

translators (or native language proficiency). Also, you might be able to get the program to translate a question (e.g., "where are the rest rooms?"), but you might not be able to understand the answer. We've also heard that some people are reluctant to engage with the tourist's phone (speak directly into the mic) and this can present another challenge. For more information about using mobile phone translation apps, see "Info Bites" on preceding page.

## Social Norms and Expectations

There are many cultural norms that have implications for intercultural communication between tourists and hosts. Some of the most relevant are norms about public social behavior and shopping.

***Comportment in Public***   As we saw in Chapter 6, norms regarding nonverbal behavior vary dramatically from culture to culture. And expectations about public behavior are no exception, ranging from very informal, as in the United States, to more formal, as in many countries. Sometimes the norms are related to religious beliefs and traditions, as with Muslims, Amish, and others whose religion dictates one's appearance (see Info Bites).

In some cultures, strangers are expected to greet each other and interact in the streets. For example, in Egypt and many North African countries, there is a great deal of interaction in the streets, with shopkeepers greeting everyone and children interacting with strangers, especially tourists. In the United States, strangers may interact in some public contexts, such as in a line at a checkout counter, on an airplane, or at a sporting event. And people may smile at strangers. However, in some countries, such as those in Europe, there is much less smiling at strangers. In Japan, there is very little interaction, verbal or nonverbal, among strangers in public.[13]

Restaurant etiquette can present another communication challenge—from ordering in a foreign language to using utensils appropriately. Our student Matthew discovered a difference in dining etiquette in Paris:

> I am accustomed to eating foods such as hamburgers or pizza with just my hands and maybe a napkin if one is available. In Paris it would be considered inappropriate to use your hands when eating meals such as these. It was an interesting change because I consider these foods to be finger foods and naturally assumed everyone thought the same.

Another student (who is left-handed) was stationed in Okinawa, Japan, and stopped for lunch in a small village:

> We ordered our meal and as we dined I noticed that we were being stared at. At first I thought it was because I was Caucasian but that was not the case. As I started to eat, this elderly very tiny Okinawan woman came over to me and promptly took the chop sticks out of my left hand and placed them into my right hand. I was quite shocked and nodded, then put chop sticks back into my left hand after she left. This went on for three more times; each time I tried to be polite. Finally, I discovered

**Info Bites**

Travelers visiting famous churches in Italy, like the Sistine Chapel in Rome or the Duomo in Florence, are required to dress in a certain way. Women must put on a dress, and men must wear pants. Guidebooks suggest that women carry around a lightweight dress in a backpack that they can quickly slip on over their more casual clothes.

that eating with your left hand was the sign of evil spirits and that it was a bad thing to do. (I learned to eat with chop sticks with my right hand.)

Of course, the type of interaction that occurs in public depends on many things, including the size of the town and cultural expectations for male–female interaction. Our student Shannon described an experience she had when she and her mother were visiting Mexico:

> As we were walking along the streets, window shopping, several groups of men were whistling and shouting things at us. We were both extremely offended. As we were eating lunch, we asked our waiter about this. We wanted to know if they were being rude or making fun of us. He informed us that it was actually a compliment. The way we reacted was not productive, and we realized that we were just not accustomed to this.

This same kind of interaction is expected in many other cultures that value open appreciation of (mainly) women's appearance. French women comment that they feel invisible in the United States, that no one notices them, unlike in France, where appreciation is expressed more openly.

*Shopping*   Communication norms involved in shopping also vary from culture to culture. One shopping norm has to do with touching merchandise. In the United States, shoppers are expected to touch the merchandise and try on clothing before making a purchase. However, in many cultures, one does not touch merchandise and tries on clothing only if one is almost certain to buy. This is true in most countries in Europe. Similarly, in Japan, the relationship between customers and shop clerks is very businesslike. People speak only when necessary. Shop clerks say only "thank you" and customers don't talk with clerks except when ordering. However, in the United States, shop clerks are expected to talk with customers, starting with "How are you?" and "Did you find everything?" and so on. Sometimes customers even talk about their private lives with cashiers at grocery stores, which never happens in Japan.

A second shopping norm has to do with bargaining. Expectations about bargaining also vary from culture to culture. In most transactions in the United States, for example, the price for the merchandise is set and is not negotiated. However, in many countries, shoppers are expected to bargain; through the act of bargaining, people are connected. Some tourists find this very challenging and, given the differences in resources between tourist and host, confusing. Should one enter into the bargaining process as part of adapting to local customs, or should one simply pay the stated price, given the fact that the tourist often has more resources? A student visiting Mexico described this dilemma after she was approached by street vendors who seemed tired of what they were doing: "Their voices are weary of the effort to persuade. I feel uncomfortable and out of place in this environment. The uneasiness and suspicions concerning business relationships vie with my feelings about humanity. This lingers on with me and I am left confused."[14] We feel uncomfortable with our First World status only when we are confronted with another's poverty, which highlights the economic disparity between tourists and hosts.

© Bonnie Kamin/Photo Edit

Many tourist groups depend on a tour guide while exploring unfamiliar lands. The tour guide becomes the "culture broker" for the group, interpreting the language, history, and cultural traditions of the host country.

## Culture Shock

As we discussed in Chapter 4, being in a new cultural context can often lead to culture shock—feelings of disorientation and distress. Language challenges and differing social norms can trigger these feelings, of course, but sometimes seemingly mundane challenges like dining norms can also do it. One of our students Leticia, who visited an Indonesian island on a side trip from Singapore, recounts her experience of culture shock:

> I was 19 years old and thought I had a grasp on how the world worked. As soon as we got off the ferry at Batam Center I knew I was in a completely different world. The first place we went was a fast food restaurant in a small mall. I was amazed by the language they were speaking. . . . I didn't recognize any of the food, so just pointed at a menu item and ordered otak-otak and teh manis (tea). Had no idea what I was eating!

Of course, sometimes tourists have so little contact with the host culture that there is little opportunity for culture shock. The degree of culture shock may also depend on how different the host culture is from the tourist's home culture. For example, when our student Jordan visited Canada with his grandparents, he experienced very little culture shock because the language was the same (they visited English-speaking areas of Canada). He experienced very little culture shock when he visited Austria with his church choir as well. The little sightseeing he did was by bus with other members of the choir and with an English-speaking tour guide. The group ate all its meals together and stayed in the same hotel. So he actually had very few intercultural encounters.

### Pop Culture Spotlight

A "slum tour" is based on the 2008 film *Slumdog Millionaire* which tells the story of an orphan growing up in one of the world's poorest and most densely populated neighborhoods and eventually succeeds on *Who Wants to Be a Millionaire*. These organized tours—popular with foreign visitors—visit the shantytown in India where the orphan boy lived. But people in India criticize these tours as "poverty

(*continued*)

**Pop Culture Spotlight (cont.)**

tourism." Do you think that these tours come out of genuine desire to learn Or more of a spectacle, with inhabitants on display like in a zoo?

By contrast, when he visited Vietnam with his father, who had been there during the war, he experienced quite a big culture shock: "It was so hot, I couldn't understand a word that was said, and the food was strange. I thought it would be easier, since I had already been abroad before, but it was hard." Indeed, the physiological aspects of traveling can be troublesome for tourists. On short-term trips, one's body doesn't have the time to adjust to new climate conditions or new foods or eating customs. And feeling fatigued or under the weather often can affect communication with others.

Keep in mind that it is the tourist who is experiencing the culture shock; the problem is not the culture itself. However, tourists who experience culture shock often take it out on the host community. For example, they may get angry with servers for not serving food fast enough, or complain about the smells or sights, or take a prejudicial or patronizing attitude toward the local culture. This behavior also presents a challenge for members of the host culture. When presented with rude behavior, it is difficult for them to remember that the tourist who is complaining about the service actually may be expressing general frustration, may be suffering from culture shock, or may simply be fatigued.

Perhaps it is not just the tourist who experiences culture shock, for the host population can suffer the same shock. The encounters might be stressful for both

Some tourist experiences represent a prepackaged version of national or regional history, such as this reenactment of these eighteenth-century colonial activities—lace-making in Independence Mall in Philadelphia. How might colonial history be presented differently from the viewpoints of American Indians or slaves?

© Thomas K. Nakayama

because both tourist and host are being confronted with new values and behaviors and uncertainty. They are both required to accommodate, to some extent, the other group. Both hosts and tourists probably experience more shock when they have limited previous intercultural experience.[15]

### The Search for Authenticity

The issue of **authenticity** is often a challenge in tourist–host encounters, particularly for those engaged in cultural or heritage tourism. Many tourists feel it is important that they experience the "real" cultural traditions of a visited community—not a simulated or a "Disneyfied" experience. They want a unique experience: something very different from their own mundane cultural life. Host communities, then, sometimes feel they have to present the tourists with experiences that are exotic and appeal to tourists—sometimes requiring that they alter the reality of their everyday cultural life.[16]

The challenge for host communities, especially those involved in cultural tourism, is to maintain a balance between presenting their cultural traditions in a way that maintains their value for the community, while still appealing to tourist tastes. Tourists can mistakenly believe that they have seen the authentic culture—when in fact the locals have altered their cultural traditions in order to please tourists—presenting what some scholars call **staged authenticity.**[17] For example, consider the American Indians who perform their dances in traditional dress at tourist centers in the Midwest and Southwest. Tourists assume they are seeing how the Indians "really live." While the dances may be somewhat authentic, they are only a small part of the American Indian experience and the dress is worn only on special days and tourists end up with a very incomplete, and rather stereotypical, notion of the everyday lives of local Indians.

Unknowingly, the tourist's search for authenticity can create the very conditions that he or she was trying to avoid—an "inauthentic" cultural experience. So as a tourist, you might remind yourself that *all* societies evolve and change; no group (including your own) stays the same, and it is rather ethnocentric to prefer that others in less developed communities remain in a less technologically advanced and primitive state.[18] Another reminder is that local hosts are people just like you, meeting the challenges of everyday living and not historical objects, whose cultural life exists only for the tourists' pleasure and purchase.

### CULTURAL LEARNING AND TOURISM

Some tourist–host encounters do go beyond the superficial confines of the tourist role, and learning something about cultures is a goal of many tourists. This may happen unexpectedly when sharing food, holding a long conversation, or simply participating in a meaningful slice of the local culture. Letitia, the student we talked about earlier in the Culture Shock section, described how her experience in Singapore and Indonesia became a learning experience of a lifetime—once her culture shock diminished:

> At first it was a negative experience . . . but once I let my guard down it became an experience of a lifetime. The music, food, the interesting architechure and the surroundings, etc. were something that I still think about today . . . . I learned that

**What Do You Think?**

Consider the challenges of traveling for pleasure to places that are not safe for lesbian, transgender, and gay tourists. For example, the Russian government passed antigay legislation in 2013 and soon after, two gunman opened fire at a gay club in Moscow and Dutch tourists, were jailed under this legislation. How can travel be made safer for all? The British government has a website for  lesbian, gay, bisexual, and transgender (LGBT) citizens who travel abroad, offering the embassy staff's help if LGBT British tourists encounter problems overseas and also monitor and record antigay incidents. (Sources: Sieczkowski, C. (2013, July 22). http://www.huffingtonpost.com/2013/07/22/dutch-tourists-jailed-russia-gay_n_3635803.html; Lesbian, gay, bisexual, and transgender foreign travel advice (n.d). *gov.uk.* https://www.gov.uk/guidance/lesbian-gay-bisexual-and-transgender-foreign-travel-advice.)

my little bubble and world was NOT as big as I thought it was. We took a cable car and at the top I could see the whole city and Malaysia beyond and I think it was at this moment I had a respect for the world and realized that each culture is just as important as any other. It helped me understand that my personal culture was not the only one that mattered . . . .

And one can learn something about the local culture even in a short time, by using many of the communication guidelines you have learned so far in this textbook: being observant, being more conscious of your own and others' communication, and being flexible and open to other ways of living. One of our students, Michaela, visited London with her grandparents while in high school. She recounted something of what she learned about the cultural practices there:

In London people often spend time during the day at restaurants and having tea and often spend much longer time at these restaurants than you typically see in America. They tend to appreciate their time and leisure a little bit more, not always in such a hurry or seem so stressed. I feel that if Americans could slow down a little bit they would be surprised at how enjoyable life could be sometimes.

She concludes, "Regardless of how little or big the difference is, it feels good and is a positive experience when you feel that you can learn about another person's culture and are able to adapt. It's exciting and almost empowering."

Given the impact of social, political, and historic context and the often economic imbalance of so many tourist encounters, when is contact between locals and tourists likely to result in more positive feeling, good communication between hosts and tourists, and culture learning? When is the outcome more likely to be negative? As you might expect, when tourists are friendly and respectful and demonstrate interest in a country and culture (beyond an interest in the beaches and recreational sites), local residents perceive tourists to be more like guests, develop pride in their culture, and are more likely to welcome interaction with tourists. Also, when tourists take opportunities for more extensive interaction with locals, there is the possibility of mutual understanding, culture learning, and even lasting friendships.

On the other hand, when tourists visit historically unfriendly places (like U.S. Americans visiting the Middle East), have little prior knowledge of the culture, and have only superficial encounters with hosts, outcomes of tourist–host encounters are likely to result in negative attitudes and reinforced stereotypes. In addition, as mentioned earlier, when wealthy first world tourists visit developing countries and display little regard for their hosts, their attitudes and behavior can lead to resentment on the part of hosts, and tourists then learn less about the host culture than they might have otherwise.

A type of tourism that fits nicely with culture learning and ethical intercultural communication and that emphasizes positive economic, social, cultural, and environmental impacts in the tourist industry is called **socially responsible tourism** (see Table 10.2 and "What Do You Think?"). Many tourists support this move; in addition to simply enjoying travel, they want to learn more about the host country, meet local people, and reduce the environmental and social impact of their visit.[19]

**TABLE 10.2  Goals of Socially Responsible Tourism**

- Generates greater economic benefits for local people and enhances the well-being of host communities; improves working conditions and access to the industry.
- Involves local people in decisions that affect their lives and life chances.
- Makes positive contributions to the conservation of natural and cultural heritage and to the maintenance of the world's diversity.
- Provides more enjoyable experiences for tourists through more meaningful connections with local people and a greater understanding of local cultural, social, and environmental issues.
- Minimizes negative economic, environmental, and social impacts.
- Is culturally sensitive, engenders respect between tourists and hosts, and builds local pride and confidence.

*Source: Responsible Travel Handbook 2006.* Published by Travel Learning Connections, Ronan, MT 59864-0159. Retrieved July 27, 2012, from http://page.travelearning.com/content/RT_Handbook.pdf.

## TOURISM, INTERCULTURAL COMMUNICATION, AND SOCIAL MEDIA

What is the role of social media in intercultural tourist encounters? We can think of at least three answers to this question; social media can be used (1) in gathering pre-departure information, (2) in tourism marketing, and (3) during the tourism experience.

First, tourists can be much better prepared for intercultural encounters with the vast amount of online information, especially produced for tourism marketing campaigns. For example, the Chamber of Commerce Facebook page of the small seaside community of Ocean City, New Jersey, has more than 100,000 likes—some with "fun in the sun" photos. This Facebook page is one social media strategy for increasing tourism revenue—targeting especially millennials and young families. "It's how people get all their information today," a local said, "It's the easiest outlet. Pretty much everyone has some sort of social media presence." Another strategy was an "InstaMeet" day—a meetup of prominent Instagram users who toured the area and shared their photos with thousands of their followers.[20]

Social media and the Internet make travel preparation easy and efficient, with useful info and recommendations about currency, lodging, language, transportation, and what to expect in terms of food and local cultural customs. However, we also need to think about how destinations are "packaged" and marketed. Are people/cultures represented in realistic ways or in more stereotypical images? Does the particular audience or market result in tour operators presenting country inhabitants as caricatures or stereotypes? For example, African governments and tour operators sometimes market their cultures at the extreme, as "exotic." Tour operators in Thailand, where there is a huge market for "sex tourism," portray Thai women as exotic, passive, and promiscuous, eager to please Western tourists. Similarly, Brazilian tourism has focused on Brazilian women as promiscuous,[21]

**What Do You Think?**

Proponents of socially responsible tourism give the following suggestions for travelers who care about people and the planet:

- Be an informed consumer. Ask questions. Is the hotel locally owned? If so, your tourism dollars can benefit the local economy. If it's foreign-owned, ask if they give back or profit share to the local community? Do they employ locals?
- Choose a locally owned place when eating out.
- When buying souvenirs and gifts, visit local vendors and artists.
- Even when going on a "fun in the sun" resort vacation, try to find a locally owned beach property.

Do you think tourists have an ethical mandate to follow socially responsible travel principles? Why or why not?

*(continued)*

**What Do You Think? (cont.)**

(Source: Adapted from http://www .independenttraveler.com /blog/index.php/2016 /03/29/socially -responsible-travel-a -qa-with-malia-everette/.)

and Iceland's tourism industry has shifted from a focus on the amazing natural geological wonders (geysers, glacial fields, hot springs) to Icelandic women, portrayed as beautiful and sexually promiscuous (interesting in a country known for gender equality).[22] The question for intercultural communication students should be: How do these images distributed globally through social media influence interactions when tourists and Icelandic, Brazilian, and Thai (especially women) nationals meet?

A third consideration is how tourists use social media while visiting other countries and cultures. As mentioned, social media, especially mobile technology, offer enormous assistance in finding lodging and restaurants and gaining useful destination information. You can also stay connected with family and friends through Facebook and Twitter, post photos as you travel, and keep a blog—not just to stay connected but to offer helpful travel tips to others.[23] A colleague of ours traveled around the world with his family for a sabbatical research trip, and family members took turns contributing to their family travel blog, recording their interesting intercultural experiences in Uganda, India, China, Vietnam, and many other countries.

However, some tourists may use social media to such an extent that they have little interaction with host-country nationals. A student recounted the following experience during her study abroad in Germany:

> During a vacation, I took a train through the Alps—the Glacier Express—with a group of international students. A group of young American students were also on the same train. I noticed that most of the time they were on their phones, texting, some taking photos, but mostly not paying much attention to the immediate experience.

It is worth noting that some study-abroad administrators limit the time that students abroad can be engaged with social media—partly to ensure that students interact with the local cultures and don't spend all their time being connected to folks back home.[24]

## POLITICAL AND ENVIRONMENTAL IMPACTS ON TOURISM

We also need to consider the political, health, and environmental impacts on tourism. We have seen how political events can impact the tourism industry dramatically. In the past few years terrorists have targeted specific locations that can do maximum damage to world travel, including the 2016 attacks in the busy and important Brussels and Istanbul airports. In addition, there have been attacks on upscale restaurants in Paris and Brussels, resorts in French and Tunisian beachside cities, cafés in Bangladesh and Indonesia, and other locations in many countries where expats and tourists gather. Terrorist attacks and political instability can have devastating consequences for tourism. For example, Turkey has been a very popular tourist destination for Western tourists and Istanbul—one of the best travel destinations in the world (see Table 10.1). However, the 2016 attacks on busiest airport and other Turkish sites severely damaged the tourism industry there—already suffering from the impact of the Syrian war on its border. A recent report showed that net daily bookings from the

United States to Istanbul were down 58 percent in Spring 2016 and several cruises already cancelled stops in Turkey.[25]

Likewise, tourism in the North African countries of Egypt and Tunisia has also been hit hard and has seen sharp decline in tourists. Egypt experienced the passenger jet loaded with a bomb in the beach resort of Sharm el-Sheikh. Gunmen opened fire at holidaymakers in Sousse, Tunisia; and in another incident, terrorists killed 22 people at the Bardo museum in Tunis.[26]

However, experts note that the effect of terrorist attacks on tourism depends on several factors, including the stability of the country, whether the attack was aimed at tourists, and the government response. As one tourism expert explains, "The recent terrorist incidents are predominantly regional—they are isolated incidents that impact the region in which it has happened, but do not impact travel and tourism on a macro-economic level. One of the reactions we see from travelers is that they change destinations, but they do not tend to stop traveling as a whole." And tourism statistics seem to confirm this. Months after terrorist attacks in Paris and Brussels, travel to Europe overall was strong, an almost 10 percent increase in 2016 summer travel—except for Istanbul and Brussels (down 30.4 percent). But other cities, considered safer destinations, recorded increased tourism revenues, including Dublin and Shannon in Ireland, Athens in Greece, as well as Lisbon in Portugal and Amsterdam in the Netherlands.[27] However, not coincidentally, purchase of travel insurance has increased.[28]

Sometimes, tourism can exacerbate or create political tensions. Take Mount Kilimanjaro, for example. It's officially on Tanzanian soil, but the more spectacular views are from the Kenyan countryside. In addition, there is a Kenyan belief that Kilimanjaro originally belonged to Kenya, but was "given" away by Queen Victoria during the colonial era. Now Tanzanian and Kenyan tour operators are in fierce competition for tourist dollars, sometimes accusing the other country's tour operators of deceptive practices (e.g., Tanzanian brochures that sell entry or climbing expeditions with beautiful images of the mountain taken from Kenya viewpoints). This conflict only fuels other ongoing conflicts over access to various game preserves and tourist opportunities in borderlands between the two countries.[29]

Pandemics, a global disease outbreak, can also wreak havoc on tourism. The 2014 Ebola outbreak in Central Africa is estimated to have cost the countries of Sierra Leone, Liberia, and Guinea around $32 billion and even affected travel to Africa in general. Similarly, the spread of the Zika virus adversely affected tourism-dependent Caribbean nations and also Brazil (host of the 2016 Summer Olympic Games), according to the World Bank.[30]

We also need to mention the enormous effect of natural disasters on travel and tourism. In addition to devastating loss of life and human suffering, the 2016 earthquake in Nepal and the extensive flooding in Chennai, India caused widespread economic distress. The triple earthquake, tsunami, and nuclear disaster in Japan in spring 2011 resulted in the biggest annual drop in overseas tourists to Japan since records were established almost 60 years ago.[31] Similarly, many favorite Japanese tourist destinations (Hawaii, Thailand, Guam, Korea, Indonesia) also suffered economically as Japanese curtailed pleasure trips abroad.[32]

**Surf's Up!**

Safety and accessibility are two issues in the tourism industry. Safety: Visit the U.S. State Department website (https://travel.state.gov/content/travel/en.html) which publishes detailed safety protocols and tip sheets including current travel "alerts" and "warnings" for specific countries. Accessibility: According to the United Nations, everyone, regardless of physical ability, should be able to experience tourism. People with disabilities represent 15 percent of the world population and represent economic opportunities for the tourism sector. For more information, visit the UN World Tourism Organization's *Accessible Tourism for All* (http://www.e-unwto.org/doi/pdf/10.18111/9789284417919)

Experts have estimated the relative impact of various disasters on tourism. In general, it takes approximately 13 months for a place to recover from a terrorist attack, according to research from the World Trade and Tourism Council (WTTC). While this may seem long, comparable to other crises, tourism takes even longer to recover from diseases (21 months), an environmental disaster (24 months), and political unrest (27 months). Terrorism also has the lowest impact on recovery time and overall visitor numbers,though the number of incidents are a factor and each destination should be assessed individually.[33]

While the travel industry concentrates primarily on the economic impacts of the industry, we should also explore the many implications for intercultural communication. These political, environmental, health, and economic events can lead to an atmosphere of fear of each other and fear of traveling to certain areas of the world, which can lead to a lack of opportunity for understanding and empathy for others.

## SUMMARY

In this chapter, we addressed the intercultural communication issues that are relevant in tourist contexts. It's important to learn more about communication aspects of cross-cultural tourism encounters, especially given the increase in travel and the enormous amount of money spent on tourism each year.

We first described the characteristics of most tourist–host encounters—transitory, commercialized, and involving imbalance of power—and some of the implications of social, historical, and economic contexts of tourism, as well as attitudes of host cultures toward tourists. Host communities may resist tourist encounters, retreat from them, maintain some boundaries, or actively seek them out.

We then identified some of the communication challenges in these encounters, including dealing with language issues, differing social norms, culture shock on the part of the tourist, and the search for authenticity. We also provided some suggestions for culture learning through the tourism experience and the role of social media in intercultural tourism. Finally, we explored some of the political, health, and environmental impacts on tourism like terrorism, political unrest, Ebola virus, Zika virus, and environmental disasters including tsunami, earthquakes, and floods.

## BUILDING INTERCULTURAL SKILLS

1. Gather knowledge about the culture that you would like to visit, even if you would be there for only a short time. Having some information about the places you are visiting communicates respect for the local culture and customs.

2. Learn a few words of the language—again, even if you visit for only a short time. Locals tend to respect the traveler who tries to communicate something in the local language. At least learn how to say "Please" and "Thank you."

3. Learn something about the local customs that may affect your communication. What are the local religious holidays? For example, Ramadhan, celebrated in many Muslim countries, falls on different days each year and is a time of fasting

by day and feasting at night. In many Muslim countries, it is considered very impolite to eat in public during the day. Learn something about the social norms for public dress, behavior, and comportment.

4. Observe. Perhaps this is the primary skill to practice, especially for many Americans who are used to acting or speaking first when presented with ambiguous or unfamiliar situations. There's a piece of advice for travelers to Africa that could apply anywhere: "Keep quiet. Listen and observe behavior before offering an opinion." As a Swahili proverb says, "Travel with open eyes and you will become a scholar."[34] This underscores the importance of observation before speaking. If you're not sure of appropriate behavior, observe others.

5. Practice staying flexible and tolerating ambiguity. In traveling, the cardinal rule is to be flexible. You often don't know exactly how things are going to turn out. Your communication in encounters with local people and service providers will always be more effective and enjoyable if you remain flexible.

6. Be reflective. If you take the time to learn about the cultural practices of the host community, you will also likely learn much about yourself and your culture. With this greater awareness of different and similar approaches to time, family, work, play, and interpersonal relationships, you are in a better position to interpret tourist encounters. Self-reflexivity also allows you to recognize the importance of your own "location" in the historical, geopolitical tourist context.

## ACTIVITIES

1. *Tourist websites:* Go to various tourist websites (e.g., http://www.govisithawaii .com/ or www.visitmississippi.org or www.state.nj.us/travel). Analyze these sites for cultural aspects of their marketing strategies. For example, which cultural groups are they targeting? How many and which languages are available on these websites?

2. *Online newspaper travel sections:* Go to the travel section in an online newspaper. Read some of the travel advice or articles about other places. What kind of cultural information is presented? Who is the intended audience of the articles? How are the host communities portrayed? As welcoming tourists? As retreating from tourists? As maintaining boundaries?

## ENDNOTES

1. *UNTWO tourism highlights 2015 edition.* Retrieved July 5, 2016, from http://cf.cdn.unwto .org/sites/all/files/pdf/annual_report_2015_lr.pdf; exports from international tourism rise 4% in 2015 (2016, May 6) (UNWTO Press Release). Retrieved July 5, 2016, from http://media.unwto.org/press -release/2016-05-03/exports-international-tourism-rise-4-2015.

2. *U.S. travel answer sheet.* Retrieved July 5, 2016, from https://www.ustravel.org/system/files/Media %20Root/Document/US_Travel_AnswerSheet_2015.pdf.

3. Bean, S. R., & Martin, J. N. (2006). Touring culture(s): Intercultural communication principles and international tourism. In M. B. Hinner (Ed.), *Freiberger Beiträge zur interkulturellen und Wirtschaftskommunikation, Band 2* (A Forum for General and Intercultural Business Communication). Frankfurt am Main, Germany: Peter Lang.

4.  Leclerc, D. (personal communication, 2005). Clinical professor of cross-cultural communication, Thunderbird School of Global Management, Glendale, AZ.

5.  Ooi, C.-S. (2002). *Cultural tourism and tourism cultures: The business of mediating experiences in Copenhagen & Singapore.* Herndon, VA: Copenhagen Business School Press.

6.  Kenyans demand fair treatment in leading hotels as they celebrate Christmas holiday (2015, December 25). *Nation.co.ke.* Retrieved July 5, 2016, from http://www.nation.co.ke/news/Kenyans -demand-fair-treatment-in-top-hotels/-/1056/3008950/-/u3qg20/-/index.html.

7.  Challenges and opportunities for tourism development in Small Island Developing States SIDS). (2012). *UNWTO publication.* Retrieved July 5, 2016, from http://www2.unwto.org/en/publication /challenges-and-opportunities-tourism-development-small-island-developing-states-0; *Sustainable development knowledge platform.* (2014, August 28). United Nations Department of Economic and SocialAffairs Publication. Retrieved July 5, 2016, from https://sustainabledevelopment.un.org/?page =view&nr=221&type=230&menu=2059#sthash.3yliGHTD.DTXJlyXK.dpuf.

8.  Negative economic impacts of tourism. (n.d.). *United Nations Environment Program (UNEP) publica- tion.* Retrieved July 8, 2016, from http://www.unep.org/resourceefficiency/Business/SectoralActivities /Tourism/FactsandFiguresaboutTourism/ImpactsofTourism/EconomicImpactsofTourism /NegativeEconomicImpactsofTourism/tabid/78784/Default.aspx.

9.  Boissevain, J. (1996). Introduction. In J. Boissevain (Ed.), *Coping with tourists: European reactions to mass tourism* (pp. 1–26). Providence, RI: Berghahn Books.

10.  Boissevain (1996), p. 21.

11.  Denlinger, M. (1993). *Real people: Amish and Mennonites in Lancaster County, Pennsylvania* (4th ed.). Scottdale, PA: Herald Press.

12.  Weru, G. (2014, February 12). 'Homestay' deal opens new doors to tourism cash. *Nation.co.ke.* Retrieved July 5, 2016, from http://www.nation.co.ke/business/Homestay-Nyeri-County-Tourism/-/996/2704446 /-/lhm543z/-/index.html.

13.  Duronto, P. M., & Nakayama, S. (2005). Japanese communication: Avoidance, anxiety, and uncer- tainty during initial encounters, *NOAG 177/178*, 101–115. Retrieved August 19, 2012, from http:// www.uni-hamburg.de/Japanologie/noag/noag2005_5.pdf.

14.  From a student journal compiled by Jackson, R. M. (1992). *In Mexico: The autobiography of a program abroad.* Queretaro, Mexico: Comcen Ediciones, p. 73.

15.  Reisinger, Y., & Turner, L. W. (2003). *Cross-cultural behavior in tourism.* Oxford, UK: Butterworth.

16.  Boissevain (1996), p. 15.

17.  MacCannell, D. (1973). Staged authenticity: Arrangements of social space in tourist settings. *American Journal of Sociology, 79*(3), 589–603.

18.  Sheperd, R. (2002). Commodification, culture, and tourism. *Tourist Studies, 2*(2), 183–201.

19.  Bean & Martin (2006).

20.  Rotondo, C. (2015, March 28). Social media plays large role in tourism marketing campaigns. *washingtontimes.com.* Retrieved July 9, 2016, from http://www.washingtontimes.com/news/2015 /mar/28/social-media-plays-large-role-in-tourism-marketing/.

21.  Bandyopadhyay, R., & Nascimento, K. (2010). "Where fantasy becomes reality": How tourism forces made Brazil asexual playground. *Journal of Sustainable Tourism, 18*(8), 933–949.

22.  Alessio, D., & Jóhannsdóttir, A. L. (2011). Geysers and "girls": Gender, power and colonialism in Icelandic tourist imagery. *European Journal of Women's Studies, 18*(1), 35–50.

23.  Using social media while traveling. (2012, January 30). *Retargeter blog.* Retrieved July 27, 2012, from http://www.retargeter.com/general/using-social-media-while-traveling.

24.  Mikal, J. P., & Grace, K. (2012). Against abstinence-only education abroad: Viewing Internet use during study abroad as a possible experience enhancement. *Journal of Studies in International Education, 16*(3), 287–306.

25.  Trejos, N. (2016, June 29). Airport attack another blow for Turkey's tourism industry. usatoday.com. Retrieved July 5, 2016, from http://www.ktvb.com/news/nation-now/airport-attack-another-blow-for -turkeys-tourism-industry/259579769.

26.  Terror dampens vital tourism to parts of North Africa. (2016, January). *bbcnews.com.* Retrieved July 7, 2016, from http://www.bbc.com/news/world-africa-35342281.

27. LaGrave, K. (2016, March 31). How terrorism affects tourism. *Conde-nast.* Retrieved July 7, 2016, from http://www.cntraveler.com/stories/2016-03-31/how-terrorism-affects-tourism.

28. Leposa, A. (2016, May 23). Europe and terrorism: Mixed signs ahead for travel and tourism. *Travelagentcentral.com.* Retrieved July 7, 2016, from http://www.travelagentcentral.com/europe/europe-and-terrorism-mixed-signs-ahead-travel-and-tourism-56519.

29. Wachira, P. (2011, August 13). Tale of Kenya's ride in Tanzanian mountain. *Standard on Saturday,* p. 131.

30. Ebola's impact on West African tourism industry. (2014, October 17). *bbc.com.* Retrieved July 7, 2016, from http://www.bbc.com/news/business-29656707; Goodman, J. (2016, February 19). The Zika effect. Retrieved July 7, 2016, from http://www.nashuatelegraph.com/business/1077296-464/the-zika-effect.html.

31. Demetriou, D. (2012, January 19). Japan suffers biggest decline in tourism since 1950. *The Telegraph.* Retrieved July 23, 2012, from http://www.telegraph.co.uk/news/worldnews/asia/japan/9024997/Japan-suffers-biggest-decline-in-tourism-since-1950.html.

32. Kate, D. T. (2011, March 18). Tourism drop in Japan leaves Asian hotels counting on Chinese for business. *Bloomberg.com.* Retrieved July 25, 2012, from http://www.bloomberg.com/news/2011-03-18/japan-tourism-drop-leaves-chinese-to-fill-asia-s-empty-rooms.html.

33. LaGrave, K. (2016, March 31). How terrorism affects tourism. *cntraveler.com.* Retrieved July 23, 2016, from http://www.cntraveler.com/stories/2016-03-31/how-terrorism-affects-tourism.

34. Richmond, Y., & Gestrin, P. (2009). *Into Africa: A guide to Sub-Saharan culture and diversity* (2nd ed.). Boston, MA: Nicholas Brealey, p. 199.

© kristian sekulic/Getty Images RF

CHAPTER ELEVEN

# Intercultural Communication and Business

## STUDY OBJECTIVES

*After reading this chapter, you should be able to:*

1. Describe how demographic changes influence intercultural communication in business contexts.

2. Identify and describe the role of power in intercultural business contexts.

3. Identify the primary work-related values.

4. Discuss how work-related values influence intercultural business encounters.

5. Discuss the role of language and communication style (in both virtual and face-to-face encounters) in intercultural business.

6. Give an example of how rules for business etiquette vary from culture to culture.

7. Understand how diversity, prejudice, and discrimination play out in various domestic and global business contexts.

8. Describe the role and goals of cross-cultural and diversity training in business contexts.

9. Describe the impact of social and political events on business encounters.

## KEY TERMS

affirmative action (AA)
Americans with Disabilities Act (ADA)
collectivist
cross-cultural training
diversity training
equal employment opportunity (EEO)
international negotiations
mentoring
multinational

It is possible that for many people, particularly in the United States, the workplace presents the most opportunities for intercultural encounters. Indeed, the business context presents many opportunities and challenges for intercultural communication. Often the challenges are introduced by language differences. One of our students works in a bilingual (Spanish/English) company that recently changed health care providers. As a result, the many benefits changes (physician networks, copays, and so on) had to be communicated accurately to both English- and Spanish-speaking employees. Our student recounted the frustration of trying to ensure that all technical terms were communicated properly in both languages.

Sometimes cultural differences surface in the form of lack of knowledge and stereotyping, as Kaori, one of our graduate students, experienced when she worked for a Japanese American boss at a small company in the United States. Her boss was born and raised in the United States and never lived in Japan.

> One day, we had very important clients from Japan. As we got seated around the table, my boss offered them beer. Yes, beer, during the business meeting! They politely declined his offer, but he insisted that we had beer, saying he knows that Japanese people drink alcohol when they do business. I had no idea where he got that information from, but the Japanese businessmen didn't want beer, so we did not drink during the meeting.

Many of us actually have experience in dealing with cultural differences in a business context—perhaps from working in a restaurant with a multicultural kitchen and serving staff, or perhaps in a business that exports or communicates frequently with overseas clients and consumers. In this chapter, we address intercultural communication issues that arise in both domestic and international cultural settings.

## THE DOMESTIC AND GLOBAL ECONOMY

### Domestic Growth

As we noted in Chapter 1, there is increasing demographic diversity in the United States, and the workforce, business ownership, and consumer trends are becoming increasingly diverse as well. Business employees today are older, more likely to be female, include a growing number of disabled employees, and more ethnically diverse than in the past. According to recent reports, the number of businesses owned by minorities increased dramatically in the past 10 years. Latino-owned businesses recorded the largest increase—a 46 percent increase. Black or African American-owned firms increased by 35 percent and Asian American–owned firms recorded an increase of 24 percent.[1] Women are also playing a larger role in the marketplace. There were more than 10 million women-owned businesses in the United States in 2016, generating over $1.6 trillion. The number of businesses owned by women of color in the United States has increased even more dramatically, growing by 215.7 percent and increasing revenues by 193 percent.[2] In addition, immigrants continue to make significant contributions to the economy; about a third of venture-backed companies that went public between 2006 and 2012 had at least one immigrant founder.[3]

Consumer trends are also increasingly diverse. African Americans, Latinos, Asian Americans, and Native Americans have a collective buying power of $2 trillion, more than doubling in the past 15 years. Asian Americans, the most affluent ethnic group, recorded a 180 percent increase in buying power from 2000.[4] The buying power for Hispanics is $1.3 trillion, a 155 percent increase since 2000 and for Native Americans, a 149 percent increase during the same time period. African Americans' buying power is currently at $1.1 trillion, an increase of almost 90 percent since 2000.[5] Women also have more buying power than ever before. Eighty-five percent of all consumer purchases in the United States are made by women and this number is probably higher when it comes to online shopping. Experts estimate that women will control two-thirds of the consumer wealth in the United States over the next 10 years.[6]

Businesses also realize the enormous buying power of people with disabilities. The U.S. Census estimates that about 13 percent of all Americans are disabled—and steadily rising with the return of wounded military veterans. This group has an estimated $200 billion in discretionary spending—not including their extended families and support networks—and means an enormous number of potential customers for businesses that are accessible to people with disabilities.[7] One other minority group with increasing buying power is the lesbian, gay, bisexual, and transgender (LGBT) community. Regardless of attitudes toward same-sex marriage, many states in the United States are poised to profit from wedding revenues. One study in the state of Georgia estimated that the total spending by gay couples on wedding arrangements and tourism would add almost $80 million to the state economy over the course of three years.[8]

Marketing specialists have to be intercultural specialists—they have to figure out how to make Internet sites more accessible to those with disabilities (bigger font for visually impaired, audio enabled for hearing impaired) and understand the intricacies of marketing to diverse heterogeneous Latino groups (Mexican, Guatemalan, Peruvian) with varying purchasing priorities and preferences.

This increasing diversification in both the workplace and the consumer market has tremendous implications for intercultural communication—from the supervisors who manage diverse workers, to employees who work with diverse coworkers and customers, to marketing and advertising specialists who craft meaningful messages encouraging diverse customers to purchase products.

### Global Growth

As shown in Table 11.1, global markets (importers, exporters) are now more connected than ever. While the U.S. economy has recovered somewhat from the devastating recession, its trade deficit is now the highest since the financial crisis 10 years ago. That is, it buys far more products than it sells to the rest of the world. The economy in many

**TABLE 11.1  The Top Five Importer/Exporter Countries to the United States in 2015**

International trade is very important to the U.S. economy. Note the countries to which the United States exports most of its goods and the countries from which it imports most of its goods.

| EXPORTS TO: | IMPORTS FROM: |
|---|---|
| 1. Canada | 1. China |
| 2. Mexico | 2. Canada |
| 3. China | 3. Mexico |
| 4. Japan | 4. Germany |
| 5. United Kingdom | 5. Japan |

*Source:* http://atlas.media.mit.edu/en/profile/country/usa/.

countries continues to be sluggish, but emerging markets and developing economies in Asia and Africa are still doing relatively well, for example, China, the Philippines, Nigeria, Kenya, India, and Indonesia. In contrast, many European countries are dealing with the economic impacts of the influx of immigrants, the impending departure of Great Britain from the European Union (EU), as well as fragile economies in several member countries (e.g., Greece).[9]

© Thomas K. Nakayama

This abandoned customs building on the France–Belgium border shows how moving goods across borders has become easier due to the creation of the EU.

As discussed in Chapter 1, a lot of debate exists about the pros and cons of rampant globalization. Americans seem increasingly skeptical about the benefits of globalization, free trade, and the common practice of outsourcing. They argue that workers displaced by foreigners and left unemployed or in lower paid jobs have less income to spend and fewer retirement savings to invest—ultimately hurting the economy and a lose-lose situation for American employees, American businesses, and the American government.[10] However, one thing is certain: The economies of the world are now connected more than ever. One only has to look at the U.S. economy, where the stock market rises and falls with breaking news of the latest economic crisis in Europe or the political instability in the Middle East. And in both domestic and international settings, intercultural encounters occur.

## POWER ISSUES IN INTERCULTURAL BUSINESS ENCOUNTERS

Intercultural communication occurs in many different types of business settings, including domestic contexts with multicultural workforces and international contexts. Elements of power exist in almost every business encounter. Some power comes from political and economic strength. Consider the common practice of outsourcing American jobs to India. While we often see the benefits in cheaper products for U.S. Americans (along with the loss of jobs), we rarely consider the effects of this practice on Indian culture. And yet, as one of our Indian students explains, the pressure to meet expectations of powerful American **multinational** corporations has led some Indians to change their language and cultural practices:

> Any time you talk to a customer service representative in the United States, there are good chances you are talking to someone in India. As a result, people have started to put their kids in English schools rather than just native language schools. So many people now "proudly" say their kids don't read/write their native language but they read/write English, American English.

He worries about the effect of these economic opportunities (and pressures), how they might change the cultures and languages of India:

> I worry about how my heritage will be carried on once everyone becomes "Americanized." There are nearly 118 languages and many dialects now spoken in India. I ponder how we will pass on a culture once we lose complete knowledge of it.

Intercultural communication occurs in encounters with superiors, subordinates, and peers, and with customers and clients. Power is also evident in these encounters. Although customers and workers come from diverse cultures, management ranks and boardrooms remain almost exclusively white male enclaves and there is some indication that diversity is actually decreasing—and the "heyday" of diversity in U.S. business leadership has come and gone. These numbers reflect the relative power

**Info Bites**

Which tech companies do you think have the most diverse work forces? Recent reports from these companies confirmed what many suspected: White and Asian American men dominate. Everyone else—women, Blacks, and Hispanics are notably absent. *Fortune.com* compiled the stats and also calculated an overall diversity score for each (e.g., gender diversity overall, in leadership, and among technical workers; ethnic/racial diversity overall, in leadership, etc.). Here are the least diverse (in order). Read

*(continued)*

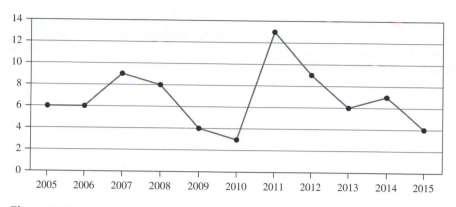

**Figure 11.1**   Total number of "New CEOs" during 2005 to 2015

*Source:* Zweigenhaft, R. (2016). The rise and fall of diversity at the top: The appointments of *Fortune* 500 CEOs from 2005 through 2015. Retrieved from http://www2.ucsc.edu/whorulesamerica/power/rise_and_fall_of_diversity.html.

of these particular racial, ethnic, and gender groups. As shown in Figure 11.1, over the past four years, there has been a dramatic decline in the appointments of "New CEOs" (women, African Americans, Latinos, and Asian Americans) in Fortune 500 companies. For example, at one time there were as many as 12 Black CEOs in the Fortune 500, in 2015 there were just five.

The diverse appointments that have been made go mostly to White women and recent South Asian immigrants rather than to African Americans, Latinos, or those from traditional Asian American backgrounds (China, Japan, or Korea). In terms of gender and social class backgrounds, men still outnumber women by a ratio of about 17 to 1 (almost 90 percent of the CEOs in 2015 were White men) and the large majority of the new CEOs come from privileged economic backgrounds. Perhaps the most dramatic CEO announcement of the decade came in 2014 from a White male who was already a CEO when Tim Cook, the CEO of Apple, announced he was gay.[11]

Studies show that diversity is good for business, so what explains this decrease? Ronald C. Parker, the CEO of the Executive Leadership Council, gives several reasons. One is the common unconscious biases against people who don't look like a "typical" (aka White male) leader; that is, most people, including leaders are often subconsciously more comfortable working with people like themselves. Parker explains that the White men at the top "are comfortable with their network of the people that they know, therefore the people that get those opportunities tend to look like them." In addition, some companies committed to diversity haven't quite figured out how to effectively recruit, cultivate, and retain women and minority talent. Finally, and ironically perhaps, an increase in diversity doesn't seem to promote more diversity but rather a feeling of "well that's taken care of," which actually leads to less attention to diversity and fewer diverse hires.[12]

**What Do You Think?**

Have you ever been told to respect and value independent behavior? Most Americans accept—in fact, celebrate— nonconformity. But, in Japan, there is a saying, "The nail that sticks up will be hammered down." In other words, people in Japan like conformity and try to restrain or avoid people who are unconventional and attract attention. The Japanese try to stay as similar to others as possible and are afraid to attract attention from others. This is one of the major national characteristics of the Japanese people. Do you think that the different values that American and Japanese cultures give to conformity versus nonconformity will create problems for American business associates in Japan who believe that success in business involves sticking out?

However, business experts suggest that truly effective leaders realize that in order to be more successful in a diverse global marketplace, power needs to be shared. The same experts see a potential for renewed pressure to diversify which calls for individuals who are culturally "flexible," multicultural and maybe multilingual, in both domestic and international businesses. Rather than trying to hire a certain number of African Americans or Hispanics and then encouraging these groups to blend together and conceal their differences, the best leaders are trying to tap into the differences to capture new business and increase the bottom line. There's evidence that this diversity can pay off in profits. For example, Schlotsky's, known for its meat-laden sandwiches, was inspired by a native of India to develop new vegetarian menu items to capture the world's ever-growing vegetarian market. Similar inspirations resulted in Frito-Lay's guacamole-flavored Dorito chips and wasabi-flavored snacks.[13] AT&T sees that marketing to diverse racial and ethnic groups is important enough to have an executive position (vice president of diverse markets) devoted entirely to such campaigns. Harley Davidson started marketing to women by creating classes to teach women to ride.[14]

Power relations can also play out on a more interpersonal level. For example, Francine, a student of ours, described an intercultural encounter with the manager, who happened to be from Syria, of the health club where she worked: "He was very rude and disrespectful to me. He humiliated me in front of other members and refused to give me any information in order to contact the corporate office." She described how she tried to resolve the conflict, but she felt very dominated by the manager. She speculated that the root of the conflict might lie in cultural differences in communication style. He had a forceful, expressive way of speaking, and she interpreted this very negatively, although it may have been perfectly appropriate conduct in his culture.

Communication across power divides can be very difficult, particularly when there is a cultural difference in how power is viewed or how power distance, as explained in Chapter 2, is expressed. Cultural groups that believe in high power distance feel that an organization functions best when differences in power are clearly marked. That is, bosses act like bosses and workers act like workers, and there is no confusion about which is which. For example, in Kenya, "A good employee is one who knows his work and respects his/her boss. Respect and humility are very important virtues an employee should have. If you keep on challenging your boss, it is taken negatively as a sign of disrespect. So sometimes keeping quiet is better than speaking your mind." Francine may have been in a similar situation. Her boss may have been emphasizing the power difference between himself and Francine, expecting the same kind of deference from her.

By contrast, cultural groups that believe in low power distance (as in most U.S. contexts) feel that power differences, though very real, should be minimized and that an egalitarian view is best. In intercultural business situations, varying values concerning power dynamics and different behavioral expectations can result in communication challenges for bosses and subordinates alike.

## COMMUNICATION CHALLENGES IN BUSINESS CONTEXTS

There is a lot of discussion recently whether rampant globalization is resulting in a global business culture where national cultural differences do not matter as much as they used to. Most experts conclude that this is not happening, that there are very few instances where culture does not matter at all.[15] In fact, communication challenges in business contexts can reflect cultural differences in work-related values, language issues, communication styles, and business etiquette, as well as issues related to diversity, prejudice, and discrimination.

### Work-Related Values

*Individualism versus Collectivism*   As discussed in Chapter 2, many cultures (such as most U.S. cultures) are individualistic, while others (such as many cultures in Asia and in Central and South America) are **collectivist**—that is, they place more importance on the individual in relation to groups. How does this difference play out in work situations?

In countries with individualistic views, workers are expected to perform certain functions with clearly defined responsibilities; a clear boundary exists between their job and another person's job. In collectivist countries like Japan, the opposite is true. That is, Japanese organizations do not necessarily define the precise job responsibilities assigned to each individual; rather, it's the job of a work unit, a section, or a department. The same is true for many Latin American and southern European cultures, as well as many Asian countries, like China and India, in which people are much more apt to help one another at work and to see less rigid lines between tasks.[16] These cultural differences in values can present challenges to workers and management. For example, Roberto, a manager from Colombia, has a high collectivist work and communication style. He encourages his subordinates to fill in for each other when they can, he tries to preserve the harmony of the work team, and he is careful not to criticize workers in front of their peers. This style sometimes clashes with that of other managers, who have a more individualistic orientation. They think he is too lenient with his staff and sticks up for them too much.

There are some cultural groups, like the Greeks, for whom individualism in the workplace may be even more developed than in the United States. Thus, most Greeks strongly prefer not to work for a large company. Greeks are not accustomed to working in teams—unless the team happens to be the family. Indeed, the concept of family often extends to the workplace. As one observer noted, "Greek managers sometimes use the term *nikokyris* to describe their job, which means that they see themselves as the head of the family, the one who takes care of family matters."[17]

These value differences are not always hard and fast; international business experts acknowledge that, with globalization, many of these differences are blurred. For example, young business workers in Asia and other parts of the world are

**Surf's Up!**

Have you ever thought of owning your own business? This can be difficult for some. In particular, many women face challenges in getting key investors to take their ideas seriously. Woman Owned is an online resource and community that assists women in working through all of the steps of starting and owning a business. Check it out at www .womanowned.com.

© Yuri Arcurs/Cutcaster RF

Working on projects in groups is very common in business settings. Although this diverse project group may have more cultural gaps to work through than a more homogeneous group, the potential benefits of diverse viewpoints are significant. What do the nonverbal cues tell you about this group's communication?

blending traditionally collectivist practices with more individualistic beliefs.[18] As we have stressed throughout this book, it is important to always remember that cultures are complex and heterogeneous and that our cultural generalizations should always be open to change.

***Work and Material Gain***   Most Americans think that hard work is a virtue that will eventually pay off. To the people of many other cultures, however, work is a necessary burden. Most Mexicans consider work a necessary evil, needed to earn enough money to live and, if possible, to have enough left over to enjoy the really important things in life: family and friends.[19] And some Europeans share the Mexican attitude toward work. A business consultant describes one Italian worker's impressions of Germans:

> He liked Germany, but found the Germans very *lineare,* meaning direct, purposeful, and efficient. "*Lineare*" is not a compliment. It characterizes a one-dimensional person, while Italians feel it is important to develop the whole person, not just the work side. I said I thought the Americans were probably

just as bad as the Germans, but he shook his head and grinned. "Worse," he said, "much worse."[20]

Cultural groups that see work as having a low priority believe that, because work is necessary and takes up most of the daylight hours, ways should be found to make it more agreeable by creating a convivial workplace.

The different attitudes toward work can lead to intercultural communication conflicts in the workplace. This was the case when U.S. Americans, Japanese, and Saudi Arabians experienced terrible conflict when working together on a project in Tokyo:

> The Saudis stood too close, made intense eye contact and touched the Japanese. On top of that, the Saudis were enjoying Tokyo's sights. Their leisurely approach clashed with the Japanese work ethic—the Japanese concluded they weren't serious about the project. The tension escalated until Americans became the buffers between the Saudis and Japanese.[21]

***Quality versus Efficiency***    Another conflict in work-related values is based on the relative value placed on quality versus efficiency and practicality. For most Americans, efficiency and getting the job done for the lowest cost are the ultimate goals. However, people in many different cultures hold different views. For example, the French are more interested in designing. There is a notion among the French that in business one should not worry so much about whether a product is competitive as long as it is well designed. They feel that if the product is well designed and elegant, it will be competitive.

© Yann Layma/The Image Bank/Getty Images

Cultural norms regarding space and privacy in business contexts vary from culture to culture. How might this business space be set up differently if it were in the United States?

Germans insist on quality, as both producers and consumers. Quality may come at a high price, but the German view is that people will pay for the best quality and that as a worker it's important to do the best job on principle. In German and American work settings, conflict can arise when Americans would rather produce something expediently than elegantly (or exquisitely).

One might explain these U.S. business values partly by the fact that the United States is a young country and that we have less appreciation for history and time. We feel pressured by time, because we don't think we have much of it, whereas for European businesses, five years is not long, and many European businesses routinely plan 10 and 20 years ahead. Also, U.S. Americans historically have placed more emphasis on the practical aspects of products. In the history of the European settlers, things had to be done expediently, and there was little time to tinker with perfection.[22]

*Task versus Relationship Priority*   A related value has to do with whether the highest priority is placed on relationships or on task completion. In most work contexts in the United States, the most important thing is to accomplish the task. It is not necessary to like the people one works with. However, in many cultures, work gets done because of relationships. This seems to be the case in China where personal relationships are vital for business success. The importance of personal relationships is such that there is a special term, *guanxi,* which means a personal bond or connection that goes beyond social and cultural connections. The Chinese do not differentiate business from friendship, so in order to be successful in business, personal relationships (*guanxi*) must be developed.[23] Cultural differences in task versus relationship priorities can cause much frustration in international work settings.

For example, as one of the top salespeople at his U.S. firm, Tom was asked to head up a presentation to a Latin American company. He arrived, ready to explain his objectives to the marketing rep sent to meet him at the airport. But the rep was continually changing the subject and asking personal questions about his family and his interests.

> [Tom] was informed that the meeting was arranged for several days later . . . During the next few days, Tom noticed that though they had said they wanted to discuss details of his presentation, they seemed to spend an inordinate amount of time on inconsequentials [and socializing]. This began to annoy Tom as he thought that the deal could have been closed several days earlier.[24]

This was a classic case of culture clash. Tom's top priority was to accomplish the task; his counterparts' top priority was to establish a good relationship so that the work could get accomplished. These different priorities also show up in the multicultural workplaces of the United States. Some people work better if they have a good relationship; others merely want to get the task done. Our student Karla observed this in her job:

> Currently, I work in a restaurant with many people who are from Mexico. After working with them, I have come to realize that they have very different attitudes about work from what I am used to. While teamwork is always stressed at my

job, these workers actually do look out for the best interests of one another. It is a great learning experience for me to work side by side with them and to learn about their work ethics.

## Language Issues

Language issues can come into play in various ways in business contexts. One of our students, Robert, who worked for a cellular telephone company, described a language problem he experienced one day when he had two customers who spoke only Spanish:

> I couldn't tell the exact problem they were having with their phone and ended up getting our Spanish customer service rep on the phone to help bridge the communication gap between us. I was glad in the end that I could help, but was also very frustrated and it was a very uneasy feeling: to stand face-to-face with someone and have no idea what they are talking about and not being able to communicate with them.

International business is sometimes conducted in English even when none of the participants speak English as a first language. For example, a recent study identified communication challenges faced by Icelandic companies doing business in Spain, France, and India.[25] The Icelanders conducted business in all three countries in English and each country's setting presented particular language challenges. In India, accent was a problem. Even though both Icelanders and Indians spoke English fluently, Icelanders have a Scandinavian accent and the Indians have different accents depending on their first language. (There are 22 official languages in India.)[26] Communicating with the Spanish and the French posed different challenges. Icelanders are less reticent about using English than their French and Spanish counterparts, because of the almost universal practice of studying foreign language in Icelandic schools. They found that their French and Spanish counterparts were often reluctant to explicitly discuss misunderstandings or problems that arose. If they did not understand something the Icelanders said, they would not immediately ask for clarification, but would carry on with the work (in some cases even avoiding the Icelanders); the language problem only became evident later, when projects were not completed on time or other difficulties arose. The Icelanders weren't sure if this reticence to speak up was because of their discomfort with speaking English, or because of a preference for a more indirect or high-context communication style. This example also points to a common problem in intercultural communication—one cannot always be sure of the cause of the problem! Increasingly, international business travelers have to deal with a medley of languages.

The same can be true in domestic business situations. With the growing cultural diversity in the workplace comes linguistic diversity. To make working with a multilinguistic workforce easier, don't assume that, just because people are speaking a language other than English, they are talking about you. This may be a common reaction when those around us are speaking a language we don't understand, but it's egocentric and erroneous. Generally, people speak the language they feel most comfortable with. Laura, one of our students, experienced this firsthand:

**What Do You Think?**

In 1993, the U.S. National Basketball Association (NBA) included just five non-U.S. players. However, there are now more than 100 players from 37 different countries and a record was set when 15 international players were among the first 30 picks in the June 2016 NBA draft. How many of these players can you name? Taking into consideration the ways in which new technology allows for greater access to U.S. media, why might the NBA be reaching out to international players?

Many cultures emphasize the importance of building strong relationships in effective business endeavors. What do the nonverbal gestures and facial cues tell you about the relationships among these four businessmen?

© Digital Vision/Getty Images RF

When I was working in a restaurant, I was constantly hearing my name being spoken in Spanish conversations. When I asked one of my coworkers why people were always talking about me, he gave me a blank look. I told him one of the staff had just said my name. He laughed and said, "No, no, they said '*La hora*'" (per hour). We both had a good laugh, and now I know that wages, not me, are a popular subject.

A second suggestion in working with a multilinguistic workforce is to speak simple, but not simpleminded, English. A non-native speaker can better understand language that is spoken slowly and clearly, and that includes no big words. For example, use "letter" instead of "communication" and "soon" instead of "momentarily." However, don't be condescending in tone and don't raise your voice. In addition, don't crowd too much into one sentence, and pause between sentences. A third suggestion is to avoid slang and jargon and be careful with jokes. Many times humor is based on puns and word play, which seldom translate into another language; what one culture considers funny, another might consider not funny, or even rude or crude. Finally, be culturally sensitive. The more you know about the cultures of others, the easier it will be for you to speak with a foreigner who knows only a little of your language. For example, just knowing that most Asians value formality and hierarchy would help you in interacting with Japanese or Chinese people, even if you only know a few words of their language.[27]

Another potential language issue involves communication between deaf and hearing people. For example, Linda, a sales associate, is deaf in one ear. When customers ask her for assistance, she may not hear them, and they sometimes interpret her behavior negatively.

## Communication Styles

Several elements of communication style, as introduced in Chapter 5, are especially relevant in business contexts. These include indirect versus direct, high versus low context, and honesty versus harmony.

***Indirect versus Direct***   Exchange of information is important in many work settings, especially when a problem exists and information is needed to solve it. People with a direct communication style simply ask for information from the appropriate person. However, a person with an indirect style might not feel comfortable giving the information, particularly when a problem exists and there is a need to save face. How do you obtain information when no one is speaking up? One way is to watch how others who are respected get information from one another and how they get it from you. Observe how subordinates, supervisors, and colleagues give and obtain information, since the approach may vary with an individual's status or relationship.[28]

In general, to have good intercultural business communication, people need to slow down and "sneak up" on information. Many Europeans don't get right to the point. For example, even at a business meeting in a restaurant, the French want to enjoy their dinner. Many Africans, too, are suspicious of U.S. American directness. In fact, in African business settings, intermediaries often are used to smooth business dealings. One foreign worker was puzzled when a Kenyan coworker complained to him at length about the behavior of someone outside the office. At first, the foreigner couldn't understand why his colleague was complaining so much about an outsider's behavior, but he eventually realized that the Kenyan was trying to explain indirectly what he should be doing.[29]

***High/low context communication***   Closely related to indirect/direct communication is the notion of high- and low-context style. As discussed in Chapter 5, low-context communicators (most U.S. Americans) prefer to make information very explicit—expressed in words. On the other hand, high-context communicators (many Asians and Africans) prefer to communicate more of the message *nonverbally* or *contextually*. This difference can result in challenging business encounters. Remember our earlier example of the Icelandic company with subsidiaries in France, Spain, and India? The Icelanders (mostly low-context communicators) ran into problems in communicating with the French, Spanish, and Indians. For example, the majority of the conversations between Icelandic and French employees were by phone which excludes most of the nonverbal (high-context) communication cues, such as hand gestures, facial expressions, and body movements. This lack of nonverbal cues was very challenging for the French, who prefer a high-context communication style. Moreover, most French people, like other high-context communicators, prefer to communicate face-to-face, believing that it is the best way to build a trusting relationship with people. In the Icelandic-French business venture, there were a lot of sensitive issues being dealt with (e.g., having to lay off employees, adopting a new computer system, and entering new markets) that required cooperation between the two cultural groups. The French found it difficult to build effective, trusting relationships with the Icelanders because of the lack of opportunities to communicate face-to-face.[30]

***Honesty versus Harmony***   Honesty is not always the best policy in intercultural business contexts, as noted in Chapter 5; relational harmony is more important in many countries in Asia and, in fact, sets the standard for communicators. Communication scholar Wen Jia describes how effective communication is defined in China:

> The kind of communication behavior best at creating and sustaining harmony is regarded as the most effective and most competent communication in Chinese culture.[31]

The focus here is not on truth, per se, but on achieving harmony. Achieving relational harmony in China and many other Asian countries includes the notion of facework, especially the importance of saving another's face. U.S. Americans tend to focus on saving their own face—maintaining self-pride, reputation, and credibility. However, for many Asians, the concept of saving face is more about interdependence, achieving mutual honor and respect, not focused just for the individual but for the larger group, the family, or organization.[32] In a business context, this may mean allowing other persons room to maneuver, and not saying the unvarnished truth.

As one experienced businessman said, "Everywhere you go, except in Europe and Australia, people will tell you what they think you want to hear." This means that if you ask people for directions and they don't know the way, they will give you directions anyway simply to make you happy. In addition, you need to listen carefully to understand when a "yes" really means "no." According to Korean specialists, Koreans may say "yes" but actually mean "no" when they

- Pause and suck in air through their teeth.
- Say, "Yes, but. . . ."
- Express opinions or qualify their "yes" with such phrases as "it may be difficult."
- Seem to be avoiding a definitive answer, giving an indirect or vague response.[33]

Thus, in these contexts, you need to ask questions in such a way that the other person can't really figure out what you want to hear. Even better, you need to engage the other person in a conversation such that the information you need simply "falls out."

There are also cultural variations in how truth is defined. In many businesses in Asia, there are a number of behaviors that would be considered acceptable in everyday practices, whereas in the United States they would be regarded as deceptive, perhaps even unethical. For example, many Chinese consider the contents of

## Pop Culture Spotlight

Hollywood has always functioned as a transnational institution, reflecting and promoting America's international relationships with other countries. Many Hollywood films have focused on European settings—for example, *The Bourne Ultimatum* (2007), *Taken* (2009), *Bridge of Spies* (2015)—reflecting America's close political and business ties with Europe. But other movies—*Mao's Last Dancer* (2010), *Battleship* (2012), *Bourne Legacy* (2012), and *Shanghai Calling* (2012) set in Asia and *Blood Diamond* (2006), *Invictus* (2009), and *Timbuktu* (2015) in Africa—reflect other business and political partners with America. To what extent do you think this increase in Asian and African presence in American cinema reflects the increase in their presence in America's business/political relations and

*(continued)*

a contract to be non binding, more like guidelines, and assume that strong business relationships can simply change contract details that most American business people would consider binding.[34]

**Pop Culture Spotlight (cont.)**
vice versa? How do these Hollywood priorities shape U.S. Americans' views of other countries and cultures?

## Business Etiquette

Business etiquette varies from culture to culture and is related to the differences in values and communication styles discussed previously. In general, most cultural groups tend to be more formal in business contexts than Americans are. For instance, most Europeans greet each other formally with a verbal greeting and a handshake. In fact, in Germany, as many as 20 minutes daily may be devoted to shaking hands, at the beginning of the day and again at the end.

Similarly, Latin Americans attach great importance to courtesy. A well-mannered person is described as *muy educado* in Mexico, and a prescribed set of behaviors is expected in business settings, including ritual handshaking with and greeting of staff members each morning. The same is true in many African countries. There, high-level officials and business executives expect to be treated with the solemnity and respect due their position. Protocol must be observed; in many countries, at official dinners, no one eats or drinks until the higher-ranking people do, and no one leaves before the highest-ranking guests do so. Protocol may involve serving beverages. One of our students worked in a company located in a heavily Asian community (particularly Chinese): "We regularly kept room temperature water and went through a great deal of tea, as beverages were a standard part of every customer interaction."

In general, when conducting business in most cultures, one should be very careful to avoid excessive familiarity, especially in initial meetings; this means no slouching, putting one's feet up on a desk, or lounging in general.[35] This emphasis on formality can extend to language use. For example, the formal form of "you" (*Usted*) is always used in business contexts in Spanish-speaking Central and South America, except with personal friends. And it is considered proper to address a person by his or her title. The French also do not like informality, the use of first names, or anything that smacks of familiarity or lack of respect. This is also true in business settings in Francophone Africa, where language is more formal and flowery, and titles are necessary—for example, *Monsieur Ministre* or *Conseiller,* or *Monsieur le Directeur* or *Monsieur le Président*.[36]

Etiquette is a traditional value that pervades French society, and business etiquette is symbolized by properly engraved business cards, giving a professional title and academic credentials. But the Japanese may have perfected business card etiquette. When people present cards to a Japanese business professional, they hold the card with both hands so that the other person can read it, and then bow and give their name. If they are presenting cards to several people, they start with the highest ranking. Similarly, in the People's Republic of China, when people receive someone else's card, they should use both hands, bowing and thanking the person for the opportunity to meet him or her. It is considered rude to put the card away immediately.[37] Business cards also are important in most African business settings, and the more elaborate the better; the fancy cards indicate that you want to stay in touch.[38]

## Virtual Communication

As more and more business interaction occurs online, it is worth considering intercultural communication issues that may arise in virtual communication.

First, there are access issues. As we discussed in Chapter 1, the telecommunication infrastructure varies widely around the world, from very high Internet and mobile technology access in North America, Europe, and the highly industrialized Asian countries, to less coverage in South America and little coverage in most of Africa (except South Africa). Workers in countries with limited access may communicate less virtually or they may send very concise or infrequent messages—which may be misinterpreted by their business colleagues who don't experience these challenges.

A second issue concerns the language used in e-mails or in videoconferencing/Skype communication. In general, the guidelines given earlier also work virtually (e.g., using simple language, avoiding jargon and jokes), whether written or video. Additionally, communicating by e-mail, rather than video may be preferred when there are language challenges, because it allows non-native speakers the time to craft their messages and eliminates misunderstandings due to accent or other paralinguistic cues.[39]

A third issue is the unique impact of values on virtual messages. For example, in many countries where high-context communication is preferred and relationships are highly valued, businesspeople may actually prefer face-to-face meetings over virtual contact—especially for initial meetings. In fact, China experts caution that technology should not be used there as a substitute for interpersonal communication; that businesspeople are likely to get limited responses if technology is used as the sole mode of communicating, partly because the Chinese are reluctant to reply to messages from people they do not know. Once a relationship is firmly established, doing business over the phone or by e-mail is acceptable.[40]

A fourth issue concerns the impact of communication style in virtual encounters. For example, when communicating virtually with people who prefer indirect communication, and value harmony over honesty, virtual discussions (including e-mail exchanges) should avoid direct mention of issues that might cause loss of face for anyone involved. As one experienced virtual team member said, "In general, I've found when I have something positive to say, I send it immediately and when I have something negative I sometimes give myself some time to mull it over. I am usually glad I did." In many Asian countries, it is also useful to allow for some silence so all participants feel they can contribute, especially non-native speakers.[41]

Finally, it is always preferable to be a bit more formal (yet personable) and not too casual in any virtual communication context. And one more note: There may be generational and urban/rural difference in technology preference and use. Almost anywhere in the world, younger, urban youth are more comfortable with communication technologies, including social media, than those who are older and those living in rural areas.

**Info Bites**

A report of a recent survey of more than 1000 global businesses in 80 countries include these suggestions for global virtual teams:

- **Set ground rules from day 1** concerning communication frequency, technology usage, and knowledge access. Predictability and timely response build trust.
- **Overcommunicate** to reduce misunderstandings. Solicit opinions, poll participants, ask questions frequently, request clarification and provide meeting agendas, etc.
- **Meet face to face** *if* at all possible, especially at the beginning of a project, to establish trust and loyalty—later, for completing ambiguous tasks, making difficult decisions, resolving conflicts, or negotiating.
- **Give the benefit of the doubt**. Forgive each other

*(continued)*

### International Negotiations

What happens when people from different national and ethnic cultures engage in business negotiations? Negotiating is a special communication task that occurs when business groups have both common interests in working together and conflicting interests which may prevent them from working together. Negotiation is the process of resolving the conflicts to a mutually satisfactory end. There is abundant evidence that the cultural differences identified earlier (differences in work-related values, communication styles, and even business etiquette) have an impact on negotiation processes and outcomes. However, there are no comprehensive lists that identify all cultural patterns, and negotiators often find themselves relying on stereotypes and preliminary data. Here are some of the basic dimensions of **international negotiations** that may be affected by cultural differences.[42]

Cultural groups may differ in their view of *the basic concept of the negotiation process.* Some cultural groups may view negotiation as one party gaining at the expense of the other, while others see it as a process where parties place different values on each of the issue being negotiated and can then find effective trade-offs with each other. For example, Chinese and Turks tend to see the negotiation process as a win-lose situation. Other countries, like the United States and Scandinavian countries, view it as a process of effective compromises.[43]

Cultural groups may differ in the *task or relationship priority:* either a focus on the specific project at hand, where negotiators spend most time exchanging information regarding various alternatives (relationship is considered unrelated to task), or a focus on the relationship between the two parties. Many cultural groups have the second priority—that good relationships between the parties are essential. Remember our earlier discussion of *guanxi*—the Chinese notion of connection or relationship-building? One of the foremost Western experts on Chinese negotiating style, Lucian Pye (1992), noted early on the importance of relationships in negotiations with the Chinese: "The driving purpose behind much of Chinese negotiating tactics is the goal of creating a relationship, characterized as friendship, in which the American partner will feel strong and imprecisely limited bonds of obligation."[44] Once a business relationship is established, Chinese believe that the relationship is "on" even when negotiation isn't active. They are also thrown off sometimes by the North American practice of using lower-level people for preliminary discussion and then sending in top-level people to sign the contract.[45] This exaggerated sense of friendship obligations can be confusing and frustrating to U.S. American negotiators.

However, it may be that U.S. American negotiators are recognizing how important relationships are to some cultural groups. In a recent study, researchers selected negotiators from four countries representing four major regions of the world (United States, Mexico, Finland, Turkey) and asked them about their priorities in international negotiations.[46] They found that negotiators from all four countries, including the United States, agreed that it was important to build trust and friendship with members of the other team. Both Turks and U.S. Americans thought it was also important to focus on task, while Finns were highly focused on building relationships.

There may be a *difference in the basis of trust*. One side may believe that the other party will fulfill obligations because of a signed contract (trust is external to relationship), or because of the relationship between the two parties (trust is internal to relationship). In the study mentioned above, both U.S. and Mexican negotiators thought that relationships were the basis for building trust. Again, the researchers suggest that this may reflect a growing emphasis in U.S. businesses on developing and maintaining long-term relationships with suppliers and customers.

Moreover, there may be cultural differences in the *preferred form of agreement*. One side may prefer agreement based on formal written contracts while the other side may prefer an informal agreement based on the historical and social context of the relationships. Finally, all countries expect and depend on written agreements— so, one implication of the study findings is that negotiators should realize that the goals of a signed contract and of building a relationship are not necessarily mutually exclusive.

## Intercultural Relationship Building

As we have seen, so many cultures emphasize the importance of relationships in effective business endeavors that a general guideline for intercultural business success might be: learn how to develop good relationships.[47] What are some suggestions for developing good communication and business relationships? A recent study asked this question of business managers in different countries around the world and found some interesting results.[48] The managers all reported that relationships were important, though individualists (e.g., Europeans, New Zealanders, South Africans) tended to see relationships as central to achieving business goals, whereas collectivists (e.g., Chinese, Indians) saw relationships as more worthy just in themselves. They gave many suggestions for building relationships—getting to know colleagues and clients in one-on-one or larger meetings. They emphasized two important general processes, building trust and reciprocal behavior, which varied along cultural lines. For example, New Zealander and South African managers take an egalitarian, informal, direct approach ("old-mate" networking system) to developing business contacts and then follow up, keeping in touch in more impersonal public meetings. They use a direct but flexible communication style, founded on a win-win approach. This direct, informal style to relationship building is also embraced by many North American business people.

On the other hand, Chinese managers emphasized the need for building *guanxi,* offering assistance often in indirect ways through a third party, and then building the relationship to a friendship—always on an interpersonal one-to-one basis. This more indirect, interpersonal style is embraced by business people from many Asian and Latin/South American countries. They prefer building relationships one-on-one, and are always careful to respect hierarchy. In most intercultural business relationships, it's important to pay attention to people's places in the hierarchy and to recognize and respect symbols of authority, to know whose views may carry more weight and whose opinions must be asked before decisions are made. A senior manager in Japan, for example, is not considered just a manager by a new recruit. The new recruit looks up to the senior manager as his teacher. Similarly, German managers have enormous power—they are in charge of their departments, and employees generally accept the authority and don't argue. These examples show how specific strategies may vary from culture to culture, but the fundamental value of strong relationships is seen as crucial to effective business encounters the world over.

## Diversity, Prejudice, and Discrimination

You may never have the occasion to hand out business cards in a multinational context overseas, or engage in international business negotiation, but you still may have to address issues of diversity in the U.S. workplace. It may be interesting to identify cultural differences in workplace communication styles and values, but the real challenge is knowing how to work with these differences in a productive way. Unfortunately, not all differences are seen as "equal," and certain communication styles often are viewed negatively and can lead to prejudice and discrimination.

As discussed in Chapter 5, the language and communication style of those holding the most power is often the desired form of communication, and business contexts are no exception. Until recently, in most U.S. organizations, there was one dominant culture with a corresponding style of communication—White, Anglo Germanic, mostly Protestant, and male. In terms of communication and values, this means it was individualistic and emphasized directness, honesty over harmony, and task completion over relationship building. Individuals who held other values and used different communication styles often didn't fit in—or worse, were not hired or promoted.

Sometimes prejudice and discrimination are based on personal characteristics like names. The discrimination may begin even before one is hired. For example, employers may be more likely to interview job applicants with names like Smith and Jones than Mohamed or Farrah. As discussed in Chapter 6, some discrimination is based on physical appearance. For example, Muslim American women have reported discrimination based on their wearing of head covering—an expression of their belief in the importance of modesty and a conscious expression of their commitment to the teachings of the Qurán. However, this practice has led to prejudice and discrimination. For example, a Muslim woman was sent home from her job as a security guard when her supervisor told her to remove her head covering, as it was not part of her uniform—which she was not told during her employment interview. Orthodox Jews share a similar belief and a similar practice, but have not faced as much discrimination. The difference in the treatment between U.S. American Jews and Muslims shows how political and historical factors influence communication in business contexts—discussed later in the chapter.

Discrimination may also be based on skin color. There are few cases of blatant discrimination in the workplace today; rather (less explicit), discrimination based on race and gender now exists more at higher levels of organizations where criteria for advancement are more subjective—where it depends more on who you know than on your specific job skills.[49]

This discrimination may be one explanation for the problem of retention of minority workers in high-level jobs. In a study of a law firm where 100 percent of African American lawyers left the firm to seek employment elsewhere, an

**Info Bites**

Here are a few snippets on international business:

- eBay got completely destroyed by local competitor *Taobao* in China. *Taobao* understood that Chinese like talking, and even haggling with sellers and building relationships with them, and, unlike eBay, it had a chat feature.
- In Brazil, international businesses failed to notice that people liked to shop as a family group; turns out that the aisles of the shops were too narrow to accommodate the standard family parties.

(Source: http://sukalpa-ib.blogspot.com/2010/11/interesting-facts-cross-cultural.html; https://www.techinasia.com/3-biggest-reasons-foreign-companies-fail-china)

investigation found that there was a consistent pattern of very subtle marginalization and alienation from White colleagues. The African American lawyers all recounted being ignored by White lawyers who were too busy to advise them, but not too busy to assist other White junior colleagues. The African American lawyers were also not invited to professional or social engagements with White colleagues.

What is interesting is that while the African American lawyers saw the pattern of discrimination from their vantage point, none of the White lawyers did—each just saw his or her individual action as a minor lack of courtesy. The White lawyers became defensive when asked to explain their lack of interest and missed appointments with the Black attorneys—and recited their credentials as "good" White people who "belong to the ACLU" and who have a Black friend or even a distant relative "who is married to one."[50] It is these types of small, seemingly unimportant actions (from the Whites' point of view) that help maintain the structural inequality in the workplace. The resulting discrimination and prejudice have led, among other things, to diversity training (described in the next section) and **affirmative action (AA)** policies—statutes that direct companies to hire a certain percentage of women and minorities.

Most organizations define diversity as having the right racial composition and think that if they get the right racial composition, then everything is fine. Experts say that diversity should be much more than that. Diversity should be used as a resource to be more effective as a business.[51] In order to achieve this, diversity expert R. Roosevelt Thomas Jr. says corporations must do two things. First, they have to discard the assimilation myth—the idea that everyone should share the same cultural practices. Rather, organizations should learn to leverage the differences—develop an environment where employees are able to serve customers different from themselves, and also where employees aren't afraid to share perspectives that are unique to them.

Second, management (and workers) need to separate job requirements from personal preference and simply ask this question of job applicants: *Do they meet the requirements?* Can I work with people who are qualified that are not like me? Thomas explains what this means:

> As a rule, I tell people to practice "foxhole diversity." Let's pretend the enemy is active all around and I've got to find people to be in the foxhole with me. I don't have to ask too many questions. I don't care where they went to school, their religion or their sexual preference. Can they do the job? If you're on a basketball team and you only pass to someone of your own race, then there's going to be a problem.[52]

Some minorities and women are grateful for the emphasis on diversity and the implementation of affirmative action policies. But other women and minorities, while grateful for a chance to compete, are troubled by the question of whether they are viewed as having been given advantages.[53] Anna, a successful businesswoman, observes:

> I have worked in corporate management for 11 years. We were deciding promotional moves when the director asked where we were in terms of affirmative action for a particular department. I was floored. We had ranked potential

candidates based on productivity and results. I started to doubt my own self-worth. Even though I have won awards and received recognition for my accomplishments, I still had to wonder if that was truly the only variable in their decision to promote me.

Anna describes her struggles in dealing with affirmative action issues in her position as manager:

> I have struggled with how to balance this idea of affirmative action when picking my candidates. I don't want to be perceived as someone who gives special privileges to minorities. And I don't want to be perceived as a minority who ignores affirmative action policies. I only want to try to make a difference.

Companies have many reasons for addressing affirmative action and diversity issues. There may be moral grounds—a need to address the long history of racism, sexism, and conflictual intergroup relations in the United States. There may be a feeling that it is the responsibility of those who have benefited from this historical pattern to begin to "level the playing field." However, more often it is legal and social pressures—in the form of **equal employment opportunity (EEO)** laws (see "What Do You Think?" on the preceding page), affirmative action (AA), and the **Americans with Disabilities Act (ADA)**—that cause companies to address affirmative action issues. For example, the ADA requires employers to make "reasonable" accommodations for employees and potential employees with disabilities. It also requires that public accommodations, buildings, transportation, and telecommunications be accessible to people with disabilities. One area of ADA noncompliance is in cyber accessibility, where customers sued companies such as Charles Schwab (brokerage firm) because their websites were not navigable by blind and low-vision clients, and banks because their ATMs were not voice-activated.[54]

Finally, companies may address issues of multiculturalism and diversity because they think it will have an impact on their bottom line—profit. And this does seem to be the case. For example, when Arizona proposed legislation (SB 1062—Arizona's Religious Freedom Restoration Act) allowing businesses and churches to refuse to serve LGBT individuals, the business community reacted quickly, worried about potential boycotts and the loss of jobs (e.g., 2017 Super Bowl) and urged the governor to withdraw support for the bill. Similarly, Paypal cancelled $3.6 million investment in North Carolina after the state passed similar legislation. A number of studies show that companies that value, encourage, and ultimately include the full contributions of all members of society have a much better chance of succeeding—and profiting.[55]

## INTERCULTURAL COMMUNICATION TRAINING IN BUSINESS

How do businesses respond to the challenges we've outlined so far—cultural differences in communication style, values, and issues of discrimination and prejudice in business contexts? The answer is that they often employ intercultural professionals,

**Pop Culture Spotlight**

*Mad Men*, the 1960s-era workplace drama set in a New York advertising agency, depicts the typical office environment in the 1960s. Thankfully, the blatant sexism, the managers' lack of decency, and the constant smoking and drinking in the office are less prevalent today. But, there still are many recurring themes that can be seen in today's offices here and in many countries, like Nepotism—favoritism granted to relatives regardless of merit—is still acceptable, even seen as desirable in many workplaces around the world. (Source: http://www.forbes.com/sites/work-in-progress/2012/03/28/can-you-spot-these-mad-men-behaviors-in-your-office/#113679c958d7) experts in an applied field of intercultural communication called **cross-cultural training** or **diversity training**.[56]

Cross-cultural trainers tend to focus on cultural differences that affect business effectiveness in international business settings. They conduct training sessions to help employees understand how value and communication style differences—say, between Japanese and German workers (like those we've identified)—can affect their working relationships and productivity. They also provide guidance and suggestions for managing these differences and using the differences to improve working relationships and even bottom-line profits.

Diversity trainers tend to focus more on racial/ethnic/gender differences and on power issues in domestic business contexts (i.e., in U.S. locations). They tackle issues of prejudice and discrimination, showing how these issues sometimes operate at an unconscious level and how workers sometimes unintentionally express prejudice and discrimination (as we've described in earlier chapters). A first step for these trainers is to help employees identify some of the negative behaviors and develop an awareness of the issues; they then show the devastating effect these attitudes and behaviors can have on a workforce (conflict, absenteeism, etc.). They also provide suggestions for improving relationships and productivity among culturally different employees.

However, recently, diversity experts caution that traditional training efforts often fail for many reasons, including lack of buy-in/commitment from the entire organization (especially upper management), lack of clear focus on how diversity goals fit with strategic long-term organizational goals, resistance from the existing workforce, emphasis on race, ethnicity, and gender to exclusion of other diversity demographics, and lack of clear evidence of the value of diversity training. They stress that diversity training needs to be well integrated into broader, long-term business goals with buy-in from all stakeholders.[57]

One response to these cultural differences and communication challenges that is related to broad organizational strategies is a **mentoring** program (see "Did You Know?").

## SOCIAL AND POLITICAL CONTEXTS OF BUSINESS

It is important to consider the social and political contexts of business and to think about how social and political events can affect business encounters. For example, terrorist attacks, both physical and in cyberspace, can have a tremendous effect on business encounters, both domestically and internationally. These acts can trigger a loss of confidence, and result in lost opportunities for intercultural contact, fear of contact, and suspicion about particular cultural groups. Recently, people who simply appear to be Middle Eastern have been denied service in businesses and denied boarding on airplanes. During the Ebola scare in 2015 some people refused to interact with or sit close to people who appeared to be from Africa: "Children were teased in high school, adults were the butt of jokes at work, . . . resulting in stress and hardships for these populations . . . Some felt they had to hide their ethnicity in an effort to avoid the stigma."[58] Similarly, during the

**Did You Know?**

Many businesses are implementing mentoring programs as a way to assist new employees to be successful in a new work-culture environment. These programs link up a more experienced worker (mentor) who assists another (mentoree) in developing specific skills and knowledge.

These programs can be particularly effective in multicultural organizations where new employees may be culturally different from other employees and need to adapt to new work norms and practices.

*(continued)*

2003 SARS scare business declined in Chinatowns and incidents of harassment were reported.

We might also consider how the current discussion on immigration affects intercultural communication. Many economists have argued that the net impact of immigration is often positive, particularly in the United States and Britain. One economist calls immigration in these countries a "trillion-dollar bill lying on the sidewalk." They reason that immigrants here boost economies by purchasing goods and services, pay local (sales and property) taxes, and ultimately reduce cost of government services. However, the reality is that many native-born—those who feel left behind by global economy, with stagnating wages, many not even in areas where jobs have been lost to immigration—are taking out their anxiety on immigrants. For example, the net immigration from Mexico to the United States has been zero for several years and yet negative attitudes toward Mexican immigrants remain quite prevalent. As described in Chapter 1, these challenges are not unique to the United States as many European countries and also Australia are also experiencing challenges of anti-immigrant attitudes.[59] In sum, it is clear that immigration issues affect intercultural business relations between immigrants and native-born citizens. Increased anti-immigrant feelings may lead to increased discrimination in the workplace.

Another political issue impacting intercultural communication in business contexts is the legislation related to same-sex marriage and policies related to transgender individuals, leading to suspicion, anxiety, and uneasy encounters between LGBT individuals and others in business contexts.[60] Thus, it is important to remember that each intercultural encounter occurs in a social and political contexts that goes beyond the few individuals involved.

## SUMMARY

In this chapter, we looked at some of the communication issues in intercultural business settings. Intercultural communication is becoming increasingly important in business due to increasing domestic diversity and the expansion of global markets.

We also described the various kinds of intercultural encounters that occur in various business settings. Intercultural encounters can occur between subordinates and superiors or among peers. Power differentials often complicate intercultural work encounters.

We then addressed several communication challenges in business contexts: cultural differences in work-related values and communication style, in language use, and in norms of business etiquette and in virtual communication practices. These cultural differences can also influence important business processes—such as international negotiation and relationship-building. These differences can also lead to prejudice and discrimination if only one dominant style is accepted in an organization. Some companies respond to these challenges by hiring cross-cultural or diversity trainers to improve their workplace effectiveness. Finally, we described how political and economic contexts can affect intercultural business encounters.

**Did You Know? (cont.)**

(SOURCES: Samdahl, E. (2010, March 16). Mentoring programs prove effective, but can anyone prove it? http://www.i4cp.com/productivity-blog/2010/03/16/mentoring-programs-prove-effective-but-can-anyone-prove-it.)

## BUILDING INTERCULTURAL SKILLS

1. Try to identify the ways in which your workplace is diverse. Are there differences in race, ethnicity, gender, age, and physical ability? Are there different values and communication styles (in face-to-face and virtual contexts) that accompany this diversity?

2. Try to identify the different cultural values in your workplace. What are the dominant values that are expressed in your workplace? Are these similar to those values you were raised with? Or are they in conflict with your own values? Or in conflict with values of other employees? Are there communication style differences (in face-to-face and virtual contexts) in your workplace?

3. If you are dealing with a multilingual workforce, remember to practice good language skills: Speak slowly, use everyday language, and avoid jargon and humor. Also try paraphrasing. Apply these same strategies when communicating virtually—sending e-mails, text messaging, videoconferencing, etc.

4. Be flexible; try to see other people's point of view. Practice being patient. Sometimes a diverse workplace requires more empathy and understanding than a monocultural setting, and this takes time to achieve.

5. Be an advocate for people who are not being treated fairly in your workplace. Are the legal standards (EEO and ADA laws) being met?

## ACTIVITIES

1. *Newsworthy businesses:* Watch the news for international coverage of business events. What kinds of businesses are newsworthy? What kinds of business events are considered important? Which countries' economies are considered most interesting? Are we more interested in learning about business etiquette in England or Japan than in Kenya or Egypt?

2. *Business media:* View/read online business news sites such as *Wall Street Journal* (wsj.com) or *Forbes* (forbes.com). How much focus is there on diversity issues in American businesses? How much of the coverage is on the dominant culture values and communication style? How many stories are there about women and minorities in the business world, here and overseas?

3. *State websites:* Look at a state website (such as www.yesvirginia.org). Analyze the site for cultural benefits for locating in Virginia. To which cultural groups are the appeals pitched? Is any attention given to attracting a diverse workforce?

## ENDNOTES

1. Number of minority- and women-owned firms each increase by more than 2 million nationally. (2015, December 15). *census.gov.* Retrieved July 10, 2016, from https://www.census.gov/newsroom /press-releases/2015/cb15-209.html; Women-owned and minority-owned businesses in the rise in the U.S. (2015, June 2). *imdiversity.com.* Retrieved July 11, 2016, from http://imdiversity.com /diversity-news/women-owned-and-minority-owned-businesses-on-the-rise-in-the-u-s/.

2. The 2016 state of women-owned business report: A summary of important trends 2007–2016. (2016 April). *americanexpress.com.* Retrieved July 11, 2016, from http://about.americanexpress

.com/news/docs/2016x/2016SWOB.pdf; Women-owned and minority-owned businesses in the rise in the U.S. (2015, June 2). *imdiversity.com*. Retrieved July 11, 2016, from http://imdiversity.com /diversity-news/women-owned-and-minority-owned-businesses-on-the-rise-in-the-u-s/.

3. Harrison, J. D. (2013, July 11). The Foreign 500: American brands, built by immigrant entre- preneurs. *washingtonpost.com*. Retrieved July 11, 2016, from https://www.washingtonpost.com /business/on-small-business/the-foreign-500-american-brands-built-by-immigrant-entrepreneurs /2013/07/11/84aa424c-ea41-11e2-a301-ea5a8116d211_story.html; Overly, S. (2013, June 25). Study: Venture-backed companies with immigrant founders contribute to economy. *washingtonpost .com*. Retrieved July 11, 2016, from https://www.washingtonpost.com/business/capitalbusiness /study-venture-backed-companies-with-immigrant-founders-contribute-to-economy/2013/06/25 /b3689ac6-dce4-11e2-85de-c03ca84cb4ef_story.html?tid=a_inl.

4. Asian-Americans: culturally diverse and expanding their footprint. (2016, May 19). Retrieved July 10, 2016, from http://www.nielsen.com/us/en/insights/reports/2016/asian-americans-culturally -diverse-and-expanding-their-footprint.html.

5. Tanna, K. (2014, October 28). Buying power of minorities in U.S. economy growing at 'exponen- tial rate.' *redandblack.com*. Retrieved July 11, 2016, from http://www.redandblack.com/uganews /buying-power-of-minorities-in-us-economy-growing-at-exponential/article_9833a37c-5e1b-11e4 -910d-0017a43b2370.html.

6. The purchasing power of women (2013). Retrieved July 11, 2016, from https://www.fona.com/sites /default/files/Purchasing%20Power%20of%20Women_1114_0.pdf; http://www.thefemalefactor .com/statistics/statistics_about_women.html.

7. Erickson, W., Lee, C., & von Schrader, S. (2015). 2013 *Disability status report: United States*. Ithaca, NY: Cornell University Employment and Disability Institute (EDI). Retrieved from http:// www.disabilitystatistics.org/StatusReports/2013-PDF/2013-StatusReport_US.pdf; Diverse perspec- tives: People with disabilities fulfilling your business goals. (n.d.). U.S. Department of Labor Office of Disability Employment Policy. *dol.gov*. Retrieved July 11, 2016, from https://www.dol.gov/odep /pubs/fact/diverse.htm.

8. Viera, M. (2014, September 15), Legalizing same-sex marriage would add $78.8 million to Georgia economy, study finds. *www.cnbc.com*. Retrieved July 11, 2016, from http://www.cnbc .com/2015/07/21/same-sex-marriage-is-good-for-economy-ubs.html.

9. Nordrum, A. (2015, May 6). U.S. economy 2015. *Ibtimes.com*. Retrieved July 11, 2016, from http://www.ibtimes.com/us-economy-2015-check-out-top-imports-exports-every-us-state-1910766; Robinson, J. (2015, February 25). The 20 fastest-growing economies this year. Bloomberg.com. Retrieved July 11, 2016, from http://www.bloomberg.com/news/articles/2015-02-25/the-20-fastest -growing-economies-this-year; Global economy faltering from too slow growth for too long (2016, April 22). *Imf.com*. Retrieved July 11, 2016, from http://www.imf.org/external/pubs/ft/survey /so/2016/NEW041216A.htm.

10. Roberts, P. G. (2016, March 13). The offshore outsourcing of American jobs: A greater threat than terrorism. Retrieved July 11, 2016, from http://www.globalresearch.ca/the-offshore-outsourcing-of -american-jobs-a-greater-threat-than-terrorism/18725.

11. Zweigenhaft, R. (2016). The rise and fall of diversity at the top: The appointments of *Fortune* 500 CEOs from 2005 through 2015. Retrieved July 11, 2016, from http://www2.ucsc.edu /whorulesamerica/power/rise_and_fall_of_diversity.html.

12. Soon, not even 1 percent of Fortune 500 companies will have black CEOs. (2015, January 29). *huffingtonpost.com*. Retrieved July 11, 2016, from http://www.huffingtonpost.com/2015/01/29 /black-ceos-fortune-500_n_6572074.html; Zweigenhaft, R. (2016).

13. Fletcher, J. (2011, May). Leveraging franchisee diversity. *QSR Magazine*. Retrieved August 21, 2012, from http://www.qsrmagazine.com/franchising/leveraging-franchisee-diversity; Chozick, A. (2005, November 14). Beyond the numbers. *Wall Street Journal,* p. R4.

14. Diversity marketing. (n.d.). Retrieved July 11, 2016, from http://www.marketing-schools.org/types-of -marketing/diversity-marketing.html.

15. Kanungo, R. P. (2006). Cross culture and business practice: Are they coterminous or cross-verging? *Cross Cultural Management: An International Journal, 13*(1), 23–31; Leung, K., Bhaga, R. S., Buchan, N. R., Erez, M., & Gibson, C. B. (2005). Culture and international business: recent

advances and their implications for future research. *Journal of International Business Studies, 36,* 357–378.

16. Bhasin, B. B. (2007). Succeeding in China: Cultural adjustments for Indian businesses. *Cross Cultural Management: An International Journal, 14*(1), 43–53.

17. Broome, B. J. (1996). *Exploring the Greek mosaic: A guide to intercultural communication in Greece.* Yarmouth, ME: Intercultural Press, p. 86.

18. Bhasin (2007); Negi, V. S. (2007, October 30). Cultural challenges in cross border mediation. Law and technology resources for legal professionals. Retrieved October 8, 2008, from http://www.llrx .com/features/crossbordermediation.htm; Shim, Y-J., Kim, M-S., & Martin, J. N. (2008) *Changing Korea: Understanding culture and communication.* New York, NY: Peter Lang.

19. Kras, E. S. (1989). *Management in two cultures: Bridging the gap between U.S. and Mexican managers.* Yarmouth, ME: Intercultural Press, p. 46.

20. Copeland, L., & Griggs, L. (1985). *Going international: How to make friends and deal effectively in the global marketplace.* New York, NY: Random House, p. 13.

21. Copeland & Griggs (1985), p. 112.

22. Varner, I., & Beamer, L. (2011). *Intercultural communication in the global workplace* (5th ed.). Boston, MA: McGraw-Hill.

23. Bhasin (2007); Zhu, Y., Nel, P., & Bhat, R. (2006). A cross cultural study of communication strategies for building business relationships. *International Journal of Cross Cultural Management, 6*(3), 319–341; Ma, R. (2011). Social relations (Guanxi). *China Media Research, 7*(4), 25–33.

24. Brislin, R. W., Cushner, K., Cherrie, C., & Yong, H. (1986). *Intercultural interactions: A practical guide.* Beverly Hills, CA: Sage, p. 154.

25. Kristjánsdóttir, E. S., & Martin, J. N. (2010). *A case study in intercultural management communication: Icelandic managers and French, Spanish and Indian employees.* In M. Hinner (Ed.), Freiberger Beiträge zur interkultrellen und Wirtschaftskommunikation (Vol 7). Frankfurt am Main, Germany: Peter Lang.

26. Storti, C. (2007). *Speaking of India: Bridging the communication gap when working with Indians.* Boston, MA: Nicholas Brealey Publishing.

27. Varner & Beamer (2011).

28. Varner & Beamer (2011).

29. Richmond, Y., & Gestrin, P. (2009). *Info Africa: A guide to Sub-Saharan culture & diversity* (2nd ed.). Boston, MA: Nicholas Brealey, p. 115.

30. Kristjánsdóttir & Martin (2010).

31. Jia, W. (2008). Chinese perspective on harmony: An evaluation of the harmony and the peace paradigms, *China Media Research, 4*(4), p. 25.

32. Jia, W. (1997–98). Facework as a Chinese conflict-preventive mechanism: A culture/discourse analysis. *Intercultural Communication Studies, 7*(1), 43–61; Ting-Toomey, S., & Oetzel, J. G. (2002). Cross-cultural face concerns and conflict styles: Current status and future directions. In W. B. Gudykunst & B. Mody (Eds.), *Handbook of international and intercultural communication* (pp. 143–164). Thousand Oaks, CA: Sage.

33. Shim, T., Kim, M-S., & Martin, J. N. (2008). *Changing Korea: Understanding communication and culture.* New York, NY: Peter Lang.

34. Varner & Beamer (2011).

35. Varner & Beamer (2011).

36. Richmond & Gestrin (2009).

37. Varner & Beamer (2011).

38. St. Amant, K. (2002). When cultures and computers collide: Rethinking computer-mediated communication according to international and intercultural communication expectations. *Journal of Business and Technical Communication, 16,* 196–214.

39. Osman, G., & Herring, S. (2007). Interaction, facilitation, and deep learning in cross-cultural chat: A case study. *Internet and Higher Education, 10,* 125–141; Thompson, L., & Ku, H-Y. (2005). Chinese graduate students' experiences and attitudes toward online learning. *Educational Media International, 42*(1), 33–47.

40. China: Communicating effectively, *Globesmart.* Retrieved August 21, 2012, from http://www .aperianglobal.com/web/globesmart/locale/?locale=CN.

41. Varner & Beamer (2011); Berry, P. (2014, October 30). Communication tips for global virtual teams. *HBR.org*. Retrieved July 23, 2016, from https://hbr.org/2014/10/communication-tips-for -global-virtual-teams.

42. Metcalf, L. E., Bird, A., Peterson, M. F., Shankarmahesh, M., & Lituchy, T. R. (2007). Cultural influences in negotiations: A four country comparative analysis. *International Journal of Cross Cultural Management, 7*(2): 147–168.

43. Metcalf, Bird, Peterson, Shankarmahesh, & Lituchy (2007); Negi, S. (2007, October 30).

44. Pye, L. W. (1992). *Chinese negotiating style: Commercial approaches and cultural principles.* New York, NY: Quorum, p. 103.

45. Varner & Beamer (2011).

46. Metcalf, Bird, Peterson, Shankarmahesh, & Lituchy (2007).

47. Hinner, M. B. (2005). General Introduction: Can quality communication improve business relation- ships? In M. B. Hinner (Ed.), *Freiberger Beiträge zur interkultrellen und Wirtschafts kommunikation* (Vol 1; pp. 15–40). Frankfurt am Main, Germany: Peter Lang.

48. Zhu, Nel, & Bhat (2006).

49. Preciphs, J. (2005, November 14). Moving ahead but slowly. *Wall Street Journal,* p. R4.

50. Pierce, J. L. (2003). "Racing for innocence": Whiteness, corporate culture, and the backlash against affirmative action. In A. W. Doane & E. Bonilla-Silva (Eds.), *White out: The continuing signifi- cance of racism* (pp. 199–230). New York, NY: Routledge, p. 213.

51. Chozick (2005, November 14).

52. Chozick (2005, November 14), p. R4.

53. Riley, J. L. (2012, May 7). Affirmative action's stigma. *Wall Street Journal (online)*. Retrieved August 1, 2012, from http://online.wsj.com/article/SB10001424052702304451104577389812043 031028.html.

54. Orlick, M. H. (2012, May 3). Cyber accessibility. *Global Hospitality Group*. Retrieved August 21, 2012, from http://hotellaw.jmbm.com/2012/05/cyber_accessibility_litigation_explosion.html.

55. Toye, S. (2011, December 13). Diversity in workplace enhances bottom line. *PHYS.org*. Retrieved August 21, 2012, from http://phys.org/news/2011-12-diversity-workplace-bottom-line.html; Clift, E. (2014, February 25). From anti-gay to no way. *Yahoo.com*. Retrieved July 15, 2016, from https:// www.yahoo.com/news/anti-gay-no-way-104500661–politics.html?ref=gs; Katz, J. M. & Eckholm, E. (2016, April 5). Anti-gay laws bring backlash in Mississippi and North Carolina. *nytimes.com*. Retrieved July 15, 2016, from http://www.nytimes.com/2016/04/06/us/gay-rights-mississippi-north -carolina.html.

56. Landis, D., Bennett, J. M., & Bennett, M. J. (Eds.). (2004). *Handbook of intercultural training* (3rd ed.). Thousand Oaks, CA: Sage

57. Davidson, M. N. (2011). *The end of diversity as we know it: Why diversity efforts fail and how leveraging difference can succeed.* San Francisco, CA: Berrett-Koehler Publishers.

58. Fuller, D. (2015, November 2). How the Ebola scare stigmatized African immigrants in the US. *ScienceDaily.com*. Retrieved July 14, 2016, from www.sciencedaily.com/releases/2015 /11/151102131515.htm.

59. Taub, A. (2016, June 26). A lesson from "Brexit": On immigration, feelings Trump facts. *nytimes.com* Retrieved July 13, 2016, from http://www.nytimes.com/2016/06/27/world/europe /brexit-economy-immigration-britain-european-union-democracy.html?_r=0; Anderson, S. (2016). Immigration and the economy. *Cobank Outlook: Economic Data and Commentary, 13*(4). Retrieved July 13, 2016, from http://www.cobank.com/Newsroom-financials/~/media/Files/Searchable%20 PDF%20Files/Newsroom%20Financials/Outlook/Outlook%202016/Outlook_0416.pdf.

60. Discrimination against transgender workers. (n.d.). *Human Rights Campaign*. Retrieved July 15, 2016, from http://www.hrc.org/resources/discrimination-against-transgender-workers.

© kristian sekulic/Getty Images RF

# CHAPTER TWELVE

# Intercultural Communication and Education

**STUDY OBJECTIVES**

*After reading this chapter, you should be able to:*

1. Understand the role of culture in setting educational goals. Note how colonization influences educational goals and curricula. Explain how colonization might influence study-abroad programs.

2. Understand the ways that different cultural groups were educated and the purposes of those different experiences. Be able to identify the educational goals of different types of minority-serving institutions and women's institutions.

3. Explain how different cultural role expectations can influence classroom communication. Note that different cultures may use different grading systems.

4. Explain how power differences can influence communication in educational contexts.

5. Describe the complexities of affirmative action and reverse discrimination.

6. Understand how cultural identities are formed in the educational process.

7. Be able to describe some social issues that arise in education.

**KEY TERMS**

Afrocentric
Alaska Native and Native Hawaiian-Serving Institution
Asian American Native American Pacific Islander-Serving Institution
bullying
colonial educational system
Eurocentric
HBCUs
Hispanic-Serving Institutions
international students
learning styles
Minority-Serving Institution
Native American-Serving Nontribal Institution
reverse discrimination
study-abroad programs
teaching styles
Tribal Colleges or Universities

*When I was going to school in Spain, I noticed a few differences in
their educational system compared to the U.S. The teachers valued
work inside the classroom more than work outside the classroom.
For example, less homework was given than the amount given in the
U.S. In the U.S., work outside the classroom is valued tremendously
and a lot of homework is given to students every day. One teacher in
Spain compared the two systems and said that if it were up to him,
he also wouldn't give us exams; instead, he would take us to the field
to learn. He felt that the U.S. viewed exams as the only way to prove
that students were learning. He disagreed with it.*

—*Susan*

**Surf's Up!**

The Fulbright
Scholarship is
an international
educational exchange
program sponsored
by the Bureau of
Educational and
Cultural Affairs of
the U.S. Department
of State. Since its
inception in 1945,
more than 310,000
participants have taken
the opportunity to
observe one another's
political, cultural, and
economic institutions.
Participants in this
program include
scholars, professionals,
graduate students, and
teachers from other
countries who come to
the United States, and
those from the United
States who go to
foreign countries. For
further information,
check their website at
http://www.cies.org
/about-us/.

As Susan learned from her international education experience, cultural differences can influence how different cultures conceptualize education and how students learn. Her international education experience revealed different ways of thinking about learning and changed how she thinks about education. If an important goal of education is to make a change in the lives of students, then international education is one of the most successful experiences where this can happen. Education can play a key role in developing culturally competent, global citizens; however, simply studying another culture does not necessarily develop intercultural competence.

One common approach to studying other cultures has been to focus on studying the language and literature of another culture. In studying French, Judith and Tom both learned the grammar and vocabulary of French and read many classic French works of literature, such as Albert Camus' *L'Étranger* (*The Stranger*), Émile Zola's *Germinal*, as well as some of the short stories of Guy de Maupassant. While it may seem outdated to study French today, it is predicted to become "the world's most commonly spoken language by the year 2050,"[1] largely due to the rise of Francophone Africa. While this approach to French language and culture was followed by many students, and can form the foundation for future intercultural experiences, both Judith and Tom found that the intercultural competence they developed to cross between U.S. and French cultures did not occur in those classrooms.

In their work on intercultural education, Janet Bennett and Riika Salonen note that "being global citizens—seeing ourselves as members of a world community, as well as participants in our local contexts, knowing that we share the future with others—requires powerful forms of intercultural competence."[2] But the intercultural competence to learn how to communicate effectively with others who have very different experiences—in our society and around the globe—is not easily taught. We do not often learn to listen to the voices of others in our own society, much less those from around the world. We may sit next to others in class who have very different experiences, but how much do we really understand these differences?

Education is an important context for intercultural communication, since students and teachers come from a variety of cultural backgrounds and bring a variety of expectations to the classroom. Educational institutions may be structured differently within different cultures, but they remain one of the most important social institutions for advancement in any society. If educators and students communicate in ways that are not sensitive to cultural differences in the educational institution, these same institutions may end up reproducing the social inequality of U.S. society. As reported by the National Center for Education Statistics, "The percentage of American college students who are Hispanic, Asian/Pacific Islander, Black, and American Indian/Alaska Native has been increasing. From 1976 to 2013, the percentage of Hispanic students rose from 4 percent to 16 percent, the percentage of Asian/Pacific Islander students rose from 2 percent to 6 percent, the percentage of Black students rose from 10 percent to 15 percent, and the percentage of American Indian/Alaska Native students rose from 0.7 to 0.8 percent. During the same period, the percentage of White students fell from 84 percent to 59 percent."[3] Despite the reduction in barriers to college admissions based upon race, minority enrollments are decreasing. Improved intercultural communication practices can only help alleviate this problem. Further, many students are **international students,** meaning that they come to the United States or go abroad to study. In this chapter, we explore intercultural communication issues in the educational context.

## EDUCATIONAL GOALS

What is the purpose of education? As noted earlier, education is widely perceived to be an important avenue for advancement in society. After all, if you cannot read or write, it is difficult to succeed in this society. Yet, beyond the basic skills of reading, writing, and arithmetic, we need to think about the educational goals that various cultures establish. For example, what kinds of knowledge does an Italian need to acquire to succeed in Italian society? What kinds of things should a South Korean student study to prosper in South Korean society? How might these things differ from what U.S. American students need to study to advance in their society?

There is no universal curriculum that all students follow. Thus, clearly, it's more important for Brazilians to know the history of Brazil than it is for Indonesians. Not surprisingly, educational goals for different cultural groups are largely driven by members' need to know about themselves and their society. For example, students in France study French geography and learn that "La Manche" separates France from Britain; students in Britain study their island's geography and learn that the "English Channel" separates Britain from France. We are all taught to look at the world through our own culture's framework. Thus, in the United States, we call that body of water the "English Channel," just as the British do, because of our common language and historical ties. Our education necessarily frames our worldviews and our particular ways of knowing.

**What Do You Think?**

The Institute for the International Education of Students surveyed people who studied abroad from 1950 to 1999, and included more than 3400 respondents, and found that studying abroad was a life-changing experience for them. Not only did the study abroad experience change them personally, but it also influenced their professional careers. The impact of the study abroad experience was profound even many years later; it was often a life-changing experience. Despite all of the evidence of the benefits of study abroad, most U.S. American students do not study internationally. Why do you think most students prefer to stay in the United States? How can they be persuaded to go to another country? (Source: http://www.iesabroad.org/study-abroad/news/benefits-study-abroad#sthash.ZLhMCctf.dpbs)

© Stuart Cohen/The Image Works

Many universities attract students from all over the world and so are common sites for intercultural inter-action. Thus, many U.S. American students study abroad, just as many international students come to the United States to study. Cultural differences can impact what happens in the classroom.

Education, however, is not driven simply by the desire to teach and learn about ourselves. In colonial contexts, for example, the colonial power often imposed its own educational goals and system upon the colonized. In so doing, this **colonial educational system** served educational goals that differed from what the colonized might have valued. Thus, "in colonial and neocolonial historical situations, a hier-archy of cultural importance and value is imposed by the colonising power, both on the conquered indigenous societies and on the white agents of colonial oppres-sion themselves."[4] Within educational institutions, this meant that students were expected to study Bach, Beethoven, and Debussy rather than their own culture's music; to read Chaucer, Shakespeare, and Milton instead of their native literature; and so on. This displacement of educational goals had a tremendous impact upon the ways that these former colonial societies were formed. The path to success involved embracing and understanding the colonizer's culture, history, literature, and society rather than the native one.

You might be surprised to learn that your educational experience reflects America's colonial legacy. Despite the popular claim that we are a multicultural society with immigrants from all over the world, we tend to value European writers, artists, and histories more than, say, Asian writers, artists, and histories. For example, you learned more about the medieval period than the Heian period. The United States began as 13 colonies, and the reverberations of this colonial history persist in our educational goals today—to the benefit of some people and the detriment of others.

## STUDYING ABROAD

We encounter cultural differences in education in a variety of contexts. While you may be most familiar with the traditional U.S. classroom setting, this is not the only educational context. Many students become "international students" by studying in another country. You may have encountered international students in your classes (see Table 12.1), and you may know American students who have gone abroad to study and to experience another culture. In fact, many universities offer **study-abroad programs** to give their students international experiences. However, study-abroad opportunities are not equally available or taken advantage of by all students. Most are White, as shown in Table 12.2. Because the cultural norms in different educational settings vary widely, international students engage directly in issues relevant to intercultural communication.

History plays an important role in these students' experiences, as do the educational systems they enter. Many students from former European colonies study at institutions in the former colonizing nation. For example, Indonesian students may study in the Netherlands, Indian students may study in Britain, and Lebanese students may study in France. Belgians sometimes point out that the second largest Congolese city in Belgium is Louvain-la-Neuve, where the Francophone (French-speaking) Université Catholique de Louvain is located. When Tom asked students from the Congo why they came to Belgium, which once colonized the Congo, to study, they pointed out that the Belgian educational system is structured similarly to their own and that they learn French in school. Therefore, they can move easily between institutions in the two nations. Because of the history of Belgium's colonization of the Congo, these intercultural connections remain vibrant. Notably, fewer students from the Congo attend the Katholieke Universiteit Leuven in Belgium; this university is located across the Belgian linguistic border in Leuven, where Flemish, not French, is spoken. Again, history is very important in understanding intercultural relations and intercultural communication.

As the global economy changes, where students go to study and which languages they choose to study also changes. As you can see from Table 12.3, China is the fifth most popular country for U.S. students to go to study. Yet, the United Kingdom, where English is spoken, remains the most popular destination. As China grows economically, the importance of understanding Chinese culture and language becomes increasingly vital. This phenomenon is not limited to the United States, as

**Surf's Up!**

The U.S. Department of State has a webpage set up to give information about studying in the United States for non-U.S. Americans and U.S. Americans: http://www.educationusa.state.gov/. Check out this webpage and see what kinds of information are provided. What more should be added? How helpful is this information?

**TABLE 12.1  Top 25 Places of Origin of International Students, 2013/2014 to 2014/2015**

| Rank | Place of Origin | 2013/2014 | 2014/2015 | % of Total | % Change |
|---|---|---|---|---|---|
| | **WORLD TOTAL** | **886,052** | **974,926** | **100.0** | **10.0** |
| 1 | China | 274,439 | 304,040 | 31.2 | 10.8 |
| 2 | India | 102,673 | 132,888 | 13.6 | 29.4 |
| 3 | South Korea | 68,047 | 63,710 | 6.5 | −6.4 |
| 4 | Saudi Arabia | 53,919 | 59,945 | 6.1 | 11.2 |
| 5 | Canada | 28,304 | 27,240 | 2.8 | −3.8 |
| 6 | Brazil | 13,286 | 23,675 | 2.4 | 78.2 |
| 7 | Taiwan | 21,266 | 20,993 | 2.2 | −1.3 |
| 8 | Japan | 19,334 | 19,064 | 2.0 | −1.4 |
| 9 | Vietnam | 16,579 | 18,722 | 1.9 | 12.9 |
| 10 | Mexico | 14,779 | 17,052 | 1.7 | 15.4 |
| 11 | Iran | 10,194 | 11,338 | 1.2 | 11.2 |
| 12 | United Kingdom | 10,191 | 10,743 | 1.1 | 5.4 |
| 13 | Turkey | 10,821 | 10,724 | 1.1 | −0.9 |
| 14 | Germany | 10,160 | 10,193 | 1.0 | 0.3 |
| 15 | Nigeria | 7,921 | 9,494 | 1.0 | 19.9 |
| 16 | Kuwait | 7,288 | 9,034 | 0.9 | 24.0 |
| 17 | France | 8,302 | 8,743 | 0.9 | 5.3 |
| 18 | Indonesia | 7,920 | 8,188 | 0.8 | 3.4 |
| 19 | Nepal | 8,155 | 8,158 | 0.8 | 0.0 |
| 20 | Hong Kong | 8,104 | 8,012 | 0.8 | −1.1 |
| 21 | Venezuela | 7,022 | 7,890 | 0.8 | 12.4 |
| 22 | Malaysia | 6,822 | 7,231 | 0.7 | 6.0 |
| 23 | Thailand | 7,341 | 7,217 | 0.7 | −1.7 |
| 24 | Colombia | 7,083 | 7,169 | 0.7 | 1.2 |
| 25 | Spain | 5,350 | 6,143 | 0.6 | 14.8 |

*Source:* Institute of International Education. (2015). Top 25 places of origin of international students, 2013/14–2014/15." *Open Doors Report on International Educational Exchange.* Retrieved from http://www.iie.org/Research-and-Publications/Open-Doors/Data/International-Students/Leading-Places-of-Origin/2013-15.

European students are also turning to Chinese. "In France, 12,000 secondary students are now studying it. Ten years ago, there were only 2,500."[5] As the market for those with knowledge of Chinese culture and language grows, those with additional skills (e.g., engineering, business) may be highly in demand. Studying abroad can help you learn so much more than you could ever learn in a classroom in your home institution that many students are taking the opportunity to go abroad.

**What Do You Think?**

As you can see from Table 12.2, women make up about two-thirds of the U.S. students who study abroad. Why do you think there is such a disparity between women and men? Given the increasingly global environment we live in and work in, wouldn't males benefit from international experiences as much as females? How can more male students be persuaded to go abroad for part of their educational experiences?

**TABLE 12.2  Sex and Ethnicity of U.S. Students Who Studied Abroad, 2003/2004 to 2013/2014**

| Characteristic | 2003/2004 | 2013/2014 |
|---|---|---|
| *Gender* | | |
| Women | 65.6 | 65.3 |
| Male | 34.4 | 34.7 |
| *Race/Ethnicity* | | |
| White | 83.7 | 74.3 |
| Hispanic or Latino(a) | 5.0 | 8.3 |
| Asian, Native Hawaiian, or Other Pacific Islander | 6.1 | 7.7 |
| Black or African American | 3.4 | 5.6 |
| Multiracial | 1.3 | 3.6 |
| American Indian or Alaska Native | 0.5 | 0.5 |
| **TOTAL** | **191,231** | **304,467** |

*Source:* Institute of International Education. (2015). Profile of U.S. study abroad students, 2003/04–2013/14. *Open Doors Report on International Educational Exchange.* Retrieved from http://www.iie.org/Research-and-Publications/Open-Doors/Data/US-Study-Abroad/Student-Profile/2003-14.

This photo of the segregated Monroe School in Topeka, Kansas, was taken in 1949. In 1954, in *Brown v. Board of Education of Topeka*, the Supreme Court declared such segregation to be unconstitutional. How do you think integration changes the educational process? As you look around your classroom, how integrated is your educational experience?

© Carl Iwasaki/The LIFE Images Collection/Getty Images

**TABLE 12.3  Top 25 Destinations of U.S. Study Abroad Students, 2012/2013 to 2013/2014**

| Rank | Destination | 2012/2013 | 2013/2014 | % of Total | Change |
|---|---|---|---|---|---|
| | **WORLD TOTAL** | **289,408** | **304,467** | **100.0** | **5.2** |
| 1 | United Kingdom | 36,210 | 38,250 | 12.6 | 5.6 |
| 2 | Italy | 29,848 | 31,166 | 10.2 | 4.4 |
| 3 | Spain | 26,281 | 26,949 | 8.9 | 2.5 |
| 4 | France | 17,210 | 17,597 | 5.8 | 2.2 |
| 5 | China | 14,413 | 13,763 | 4.5 | −4.5 |
| 6 | Germany | 9,544 | 10,377 | 3.4 | 8.7 |
| 7 | Ireland | 8,084 | 8,823 | 2.9 | 9.1 |
| 8 | Costa Rica | 8,497 | 8,578 | 2.8 | 1.0 |
| 9 | Australia | 8,320 | 8,369 | 2.7 | 0.6 |
| 10 | Japan | 5,758 | 5,978 | 2.0 | 3.8 |
| 11 | South Africa | 5,337 | 4,968 | 1.6 | −6.9 |
| 12 | India | 4,377 | 4,583 | 1.5 | 4.7 |
| 13 | Mexico | 3,730 | 4,445 | 1.5 | 19.2 |
| 14 | Argentina | 4,549 | 4,301 | 1.4 | −5.5 |
| 15 | Brazil | 4,223 | 4,226 | 1.4 | 0.1 |
| 16 | Ecuador | 3,438 | 3,699 | 1.2 | 7.6 |
| 17 | Czech Republic | 3,552 | 3,572 | 1.2 | 0.6 |
| 18 | Denmark | 3,302 | 3,545 | 1.2 | 7.4 |
| 19 | Peru | 2,956 | 3,396 | 1.1 | 14.9 |
| 20 | Chile | 2,879 | 3,333 | 1.1 | 15.8 |
| 21 | South Korea | 3,042 | 3,219 | 1.1 | 5.8 |
| 22 | Greece | 2,394 | 3,066 | 1.0 | 28.1 |
| 23 | New Zealand | 2,793 | 3,021 | 1.0 | 8.2 |
| 24 | Israel | 2,798 | 2,876 | 0.9 | 2.8 |
| 25 | Austria | 2,673 | 2,744 | 0.9 | 2.7 |

*Source:* Institute of International Education. (2015). Top 25 destinations of U.S. study abroad students, 2012/13–2013/14. *Open Doors Report on International Educational Exchange.* Retrieved from http://www.iie.org/Research-and-Publications/Open-Doors/Data/US-Study-Abroad/Leading-Destinations/2012-14.

When the University of Southern California decided to stop teaching German, many people were alarmed at the trend that may be forming over which languages should be prioritized. Howard Gillman, dean of USC's College of Letters, Arts and Sciences, is quoted as saying, "There was a time when, because of world events, the study of German and Russian and a few other languages and cultures struck us as really central. We now have a much broader perspective in the world." In this new world that we now live, the university should also shift its attention to this "broader perspective."[6]

Part of this broader view means that the university "wanted to shift resources away from European languages to Asian languages like Chinese and Japanese. The decision was made in view of the growing importance of Asia for the American economy generally and the economy in Los Angeles specifically."[7] Not only are universities responding to our changing global environment, students are also shifting their language studies. Today, however, the situation continues to change. After increasing enrollments in foreign language courses since 1995, enrollments have begun to drop in the United States from 2009 to 2013; enrollments fell for Spanish, French, German, Italian, Japanese, Arabic, Russian, and Hebrew, but continued to rise in Chinese, Korean, and Portuguese.[8] As you watch the world changing, which languages do you think will become more important in the future? Which languages will become less important?

Although we cannot predict the future, especially what kinds of international relations may or may not develop, China looks to be a powerhouse in the future. What other languages may become important? What will happen with Russia? Will it become an economic powerhouse? Or will capitalism falter there? Should you study Arabic? Will the Middle East become even more important in the future as oil becomes scarce? Or will alternative fuels decrease our relationships there? How might you best position yourself to work in this new global environment?

## CULTURALLY SPECIFIC EDUCATION

The development of **Minority-Serving Institutions** (MSIs) is also relevant to intercultural communication, as their history and mission can be quite different from other institutions. The U.S. Department of Education has classified MSIs into different categories which are listed at https://www2.ed.gov/about/offices/list/ocr/edlite-minorityinst.html. For example, the Morrill Act of 1890 established what are today known as **HBCUs,** or historically Black colleges and universities. Alabama State, Delaware State, South Carolina State, Tennessee State, Grambling State, and Howard are all examples of HBCUs. Debates over the purpose of these educational institutions reflect the cultural attitudes inherent in education. For example, rather than being routes for empowering African Americans, some critics charged that these educational institutions focused on creating subservient Black workers in a White-dominated society. A century ago, for example, the famous Black educator Booker T. Washington pushed for the study of industrial arts and vocation training, as "no race can prosper till it learns that there is as much dignity in tilling a field as in writing a poem."[9] After all, one writer noted, "Black colleges, which in many cases were little more than secondary schools, received unequal funding from state or, under land-grant provisions, federal sources."[10] And this inequality only served to perpetuate the historical inequality between Whites and Blacks—a sad legacy that persists to this day. At the same time, it is important to remember that many universities were not open to African American students, for example, University of Alabama, and HBCUs often offered the only opportunity for those students.

Other types of MSIs include **Hispanic-Serving Institutions** (HSIs), which must have at least 25 percent Hispanic students and include institutions such as California State University, Bakersfield, and Texas State University; **Tribal Colleges or Universities,** which are typically controlled by a federally recognized tribe or otherwise categorized as such under federal law, such as Diné College, which is run by the Navajo Nation; **Native American-Serving Nontribal Institutions,** which are higher education institutions not run by a tribe but with at least 10 percent Native American enrollment, such as Montana State University-Northern and Northeastern Oklahoma A & M College; **Alaska Native and Native Hawaiian Serving Institutions** (ANSIs and NHSIs), which are institutions with at least 20 percent Alaska Native students or at least 10 percent Native Hawaiian students, such as the University of Alaska Southeast at Sitka and Chaminade University of Honolulu; **Asian American and Native American Pacific Islander-Serving Institutions** (AANAPISIs), which must have at least 10 percent Asian American or Native American Pacific Islander student enrollment and at least 50 percent of students are economically disadvantaged, such as the University of Guam and the University of Hawai'i at Hilo.

Although not MSIs, the development of women's colleges also reflected a need to connect cultural needs of White women to higher education. Examples include Mississippi University for Women (MUW) and Texas Woman's University (TWU), which were both founded as public institutions for women's education. Chartered in 1884, the Mississippi University for Women was "the first state-supported college for women in America." Almost a hundred years later, it changed its policies and began to admit both women and men. Today, MUW's mission statement reflects its traditional emphasis: "Admitting men since 1982, MUW still provides a high quality liberal arts education with a distinct emphasis on professional development and leadership opportunities for women."[11]

And, although TWU now admits men, "Texas Woman's University is the nation's largest university primarily for women."[12] But gender and culture can influence how people perceive education for women. As one of our female students from Qatar noted, "Traditionally in Qatar, the importance, especially for women, is marriage, kids, and being able to take care of the household. Therefore, women who finish college do not feel a need to go beyond a college degree; some do not even feel a need to go beyond a high school degree, as they achieved all they needed and it is time to be married, have babies, and that is what "life" is all about."

The educational experiences of minority and majority students in these institutions are not necessarily the same as those of students in institutions that were initially established for White males, such as Georgia Tech. Georgia Tech has long since departed from its original charter as the university's website boasts: "Women students were admitted in 1952, and in 1961 Georgia Tech became the first university in the Deep South to admit African American students without a court order."[13] The student experiences at these different kinds of institutions reflect these different histories, different student composition, and different social contexts, as well as institutional goals.

There are many other kinds of educational institutions that no longer exist but whose reverberations are still felt. For example, "Indian schools" were established to assimilate Native American children to White American society by educating them off

**Info Bites**

Historically, American Indians were placed in many boarding schools across the country for cultural assimilation into White society. White people thought forced assimilation in boarding schools would be the best solution to American Indian problems. This forced cultural assimilation caused many cultural struggles for both teachers and students. Boarding schools served as a site for both cultural loss and cultural persistence of the Native American people. Check this website for more information about these schools: http://xroads.virginia.edu/~HYPER/INCORP/Native/school.html.

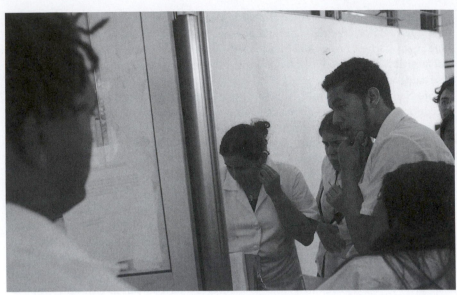

These students are viewing their grades publicly posted on a bulletin board in a glass case outside their classroom. In the United States, grades are considered private information. Do you think grades should be public or private?

© Joe Raedle/Getty Images

reservation in boarding schools. In Phoenix today, there is a main artery called "Indian School Road," along which the Phoenix Indian School once sat. In writing about an Indian school in Oklahoma, K. Tsianina Lomawaima tells us that "although Chilocco was closed in 1980, it persists as a social reality today in many communities across Oklahoma,"[14] in that many alumni continue to gather regularly. Indeed, because in these schools "acculturation and assimilation into the dominant White society remained the explicit goal of policy and practice,"[15] it is hardly surprising that the education that these students received after being separated from their families and communities "had a tremendous impact on language use and retention, religious conservatism and conversion, attitudes toward education and feelings of self-esteem, to name but a few influences."[16]

The effects of education reverberate across generations because once languages, customs, traditions, and religions are lost it is difficult, if not impossible, for subsequent generations to recover them. Education is very influential in maintaining or irreparably altering various cultural communities.

In addition to the many cultural communities that already exist in the United States, immigrants bring new challenges to the education system. In 2001, the DREAM Act was first introduced into the U.S. Senate. Also known as the Development, Relief, and Education for Alien Minors, this act would allow immigrants who were brought to the United States as children a pathway to permanent residency by either attending a higher education institution or serving in the U.S. military for at least two years and receiving an honorable discharge without any criminal activities.[17] Since 2001, the DREAM Act has been reintroduced a number of times, but it has not passed Congress.

Because there has been no federal action on the DREAM Act, children brought to the United States without documentation are treated very differently in higher education depending upon the state they live in. Different states have taken different actions on these undocumented immigrants who grew up in the United States. For example, in California, "tuition and financial aid policies encourage undocumented students to enroll at public colleges and help them afford it," whereas Georgia "has some of the most restrictive rules in the nation for undocumented students, even banning them from attending some public universities."[18] Which approach is the best for building a better society? Why are educational institutions placed at the forefront of this immigration battle?

Another issue that stems from immigration is the issue of bilingual education. Again, different states have taken different paths to working with students who do not speak English. In Crete, Nebraska, for example, a meatpacking plant has drawn many immigrant workers and their families. This influx of new residents has changed the school, but also brought in more state aid to help hire bilingual teachers: "While the percentage of minority students rose from 5 percent to 35 percent in 10 years, Crete school superintendent John Fero said state aid covered the additional costs for bilingual teachers and other expenses."[19] In contrast to that approach, other places, such as Arizona, forbid the teacher explaining words or concepts—even if the teacher does know the word in another language, since "By state law, their teacher cannot teach in any language but English."[20] In 2000, Arizona voters passed Proposition 203, "the most restrictive English-only education law in the country and prohibited textbooks, materials, bulletin boards, or teaching in any language but English."[21] Debates continue to focus on the best approach to help non-native English speakers in the educational system. There are no easy answers, but these issues confronted U.S. Americans in the past and the way that they handled those issues continues to reverberate today. How will the decisions made today impact us in the future?

Religious educational institutions are another site where cultural values can influence the educational experience. At Stonehill College, a private Catholic institution in Massachusetts, Katie Freitas, a student, decided to make condoms available to students. She and some classmates made boxes of condoms available in the dormitories on campus. The college removed them because it was against college policy to distribute birth control on campus. The college's spokesman, Martin McGovern, said, "We make no secret of our religious affiliation, and our belief system is fairly straightforward. We don't expect everyone on campus to agree with our beliefs, but we would ask people, and students in particular, to respect them."[22] Some people have sided with the students and their interest in promoting safe sex practices. Some people have sided with the institution because the students chose to attend a Catholic college.

Some religious groups have established educational institutions to further their values in the educational context. Like gender and race, religion can also shape the educational experiences of students.

## INTERCULTURAL COMMUNICATION IN EDUCATIONAL SETTINGS

Much of our communication behavior in the classroom is not interpreted in the way we intend it by people from different cultural backgrounds. Education is deeply embedded in culture, and our expectations for the educational process are a part of our culture. The

**Info Bites**

It wasn't until 1934 that discussions of Native American culture were permitted in schools sponsored by the Bureau of Indian Affairs. Previously, the policy of the federal government had been "to acculturate and assimilate Indian people by eradicating their tribal culture." (Source: http://www.bia .gov/WhatWeDo /ServiceOverview /IndianEducation/index .htm) roles that we enact in the classroom are very much a part of the cultural influences on education. Let's look at how these roles can differ.

### Roles for Teachers and Students

When Tom taught at a Francophone university in Belgium, another professor gave him a helpful cultural tip: "In Belgium, students don't answer the professor's questions, even if they know the answer. In the United States, American students answer the professor's questions, even if they don't know the answer." This cultural generalization was helpful to Tom as he navigated the role of professor in this different context. Although he did ask questions throughout the term, the lack of discussion in the classroom was understandable. Because he was concerned about imposing his own cultural framework on the Belgian students, Tom did not push them to participate in discussions, nor did he demand that they answer his questions. As the term progressed, some of the students began to speak more in class, even as Tom felt that he was moving toward more of a lecture format. The classroom became a site for negotiation of these cultural differences.

These kinds of cultural differences can create confusion in the classroom for students and teachers. Note the following example from the Netherlands:

> When Setiyo Hadi Waluyo came from his native Indonesia to study at Wageningen Agricultural University here, he was shocked by what he saw. Time and again a professor would ask a question, a student would answer, and the professor would say, "You're absolutely right!"
>
> "I felt: What's going on here?" recalls Mr. Waluyo. "The students know more than the professors?"[23]

The culture clash over **learning styles** (the different ways that students learn in different cultures) and **teaching styles** (the styles that instructors use to teach) is common as students increasingly travel to study in other cultures. Often we are unaware of our cultural assumptions about education until we are confronted with different ways of learning. In a recent study focusing on Chinese students who were studying at a university in New Zealand, scholar Prue Holmes found that the Chinese students learned to adapt to the New Zealand classroom communication styles which included interrupting, asking, and challenging the material. They found much guidance from other international students who helped them adapt, but they still found it difficult to engage in intercultural communication with New Zealand students.[24] Think about the assumptions you have concerning how your instructors should behave. Perhaps you think that instructors should set time aside in class for discussion of the material, or that students should be allowed to say what they think about the readings, or that grading should be done "on a curve." In many universities, for example, students are assigned books to read before the end of the term and take one exam at the end of the term, rather than getting a structured reading list and assignments along the way.

### Grading and Power

When Tom taught at a Francophone Belgian university, he was surprised when the instructors posted the exam grades in a large glass case in the main hall of the building.

The exam scores were posted by name, alphabetically. The students would crowd around the list and some would exclaim in joy at their scores, while others would be comforted by their friends when they saw their scores. In the United States, posting grades in this manner would be a violation of the Family Educational Rights and Privacy Act of 1974, also known as the Buckley Amendment. Students' grades are considered private information.

When you think about grades, how important are they? Should grades be private or public information? Different cultures feel differently about grades and you should not assume that everywhere is the same. How important are grades? What do they mean in our culture? What do your grades communicate to others?

As in any other social setting, the classroom is embedded with cultural expectations about power relations. While there may always be a power difference in the communication between instructors and students, this difference can be greater or lesser in various cultures. In the United States, for example, the relationships between instructor and students tend to be less formal than in other cultures. Michael, a student of ours, recalled the following intercultural conflict, which reflects this power difference:

> While on a study-abroad program in Malaysia, I received what I thought was an unfair grade on a paper. As I discussed my unhappiness in his office, the teacher became increasingly angry that I was commenting about his grading in his office. In the heat of the argument, I was threatening to report him to the school's governing board, and he was threatening to get me kicked out of the school! Obviously, this conflict spiraled way out of control. . . . Several red flags were telling me that intercultural differences were at play. . . . In his culture, students are disrespectful when they question teachers' decisions. In my culture, questions show that you are paying attention. I chose to explain my actions to the teacher, and we were able to put out the fire. We refocused on communication behaviors and ended in a win/win situation: I got a better grade, and he received more respect.

Michael's experience highlights the role that culture plays in the educational process. The relationship between instructor and student is not uniform around the world. Michael's decision to discuss these cultural differences openly with his instructor in Malaysia was helpful in resolving this situation. Cultural differences often cause intercultural conflicts simply because the individuals involved fail to confront those differences.

Notions of "fair" and "unfair" are culturally embedded as well. Our grading system is far from universal. Different cultures use different ways of evaluating student work. When Tom taught in Francophone Belgium, he was familiar with the grading system, as it is the same grading system used in French universities, where the highest grade (which is almost never given) is 20. In most U.S. colleges and universities, the highest grade, which is expected to be given to a number of students in every class, is an A.

Grading scales differ around the world and it is not always easy to know what a particular grade means. In South Africa, in grades 4–6, students are graded on a

**What Do You Think?**

What are the major issues that international students face in a different educational system? Many U.S. American students want to go to England or Ireland where they may not encounter language barriers. Do you think language is the biggest barrier to studying abroad? What are the benefits of living in a place where a non-English language is spoken? Find more information at the website www .studentsabroad.com. Think about what kind of experiences would be the most valuable to studying abroad and what kind of things need to be taken care of living abroad?

scale of 1 to 4, and 4 is the highest grade. But in grades 7–9, students are graded on a scale of 1 to 7, and 7 is the highest grade.[25] There are no easy ways to understand different grading systems, but the World Education Service's website has a converter that lends insight into different systems at www.wes.org/gradeconversionguide. You can see that a "1" would be a very good grade in Germany, but a very poor grade in Switzerland. Do not assume that all grading scales are the same, nor that the highest grades are always given in a class. In some cultures, there is no grading "on a curve."

### Admissions, Affirmative Action, and Standardized Tests

Debates over university admissions are not new. Because university resources are expensive and limited, admissions to universities are competitive. The University of Bristol in the United Kingdom faces such competition, receiving "about 39,000 applicants for 3,300 undergraduate places each year."[26] Bristol has denied discrimination against Welsh as a language equivalent to French or German, in making admissions decisions.

Because of the economic importance of university degrees, admissions are important in empowering and disempowering cultural groups. Thus, many people struggled to break down barriers to university admissions that were based on nonacademic factors such as race. Florida State University, for example, reflects many of these tensions, as "The first black student enrolled in 1962, and the first black Ph.D. candidate graduated in 1970."[27] Those explicit barriers to admission have long been dismantled. Today, universities do not deny admission based on race. Today, most universities do not discriminate based upon race, and many other characteristics. For example, the University of Illinois "will not engage in discrimination or harassment against any person because of race, color, religion, sex, national origin, ancestry, age, order of protection status, genetic information, marital status, disability, sexual orientation including gender identity, unfavorable discharge from the military or status as a protected veteran and will comply with all federal and state nondiscrimination, equal opportunity and affirmative action laws, orders, and regulations."[28]

In order to overcome some of the historical as well as contemporary reasons that have led to student bodies that do not reflect the demographic profiles of society at large, the civil rights movement led to the establishment of affirmative action policies. These policies encouraged institutions to act affirmatively to ensure a more representative student body. As a part of this movement, questions were raised about the ability of institutions to measure "merit," particularly on standardized tests. How do we know who is more qualified to be admitted? "A growing number of schools—about 850 and counting—no longer require applicants to submit their scores"[29] due to concerns about cultural bias of these standardized tests. Recently, questions have been raised about the ways that equal opportunity is thwarted by privileging children of alumni in the admissions process. Given the historical barriers that prevented some cultural groups from attending some colleges and universities, how might the children of alumni not reflect society at large?

Across the Atlantic, the prestigious *Institut d'études politiques* in Paris has established what some have called a French affirmative action program and what the French refer to as *zone d'éducation prioritaire,* or ZEP. Students from disadvantaged backgrounds are "offered counseling, special courses, and visits to Sciences Po's campus."[30] This way of acting affirmatively has recently withstood a court challenge. The court did not question the principle of the program but has instructed the institution to modify and to clarify some of its regulations. According to government commissioner Jean-Pierre Demouveaux, however, there was no opposition from the court to creating "a path for access to high school students from socially disadvantaged backgrounds."[31] The principle behind ZEP is to integrate all sectors of society into French society.

More recently, concern over admissions policies also have shifted to the admissions criteria themselves and the ways that they favor some cultural groups over others in admissions. The emergence of the notion of **reverse discrimination,** or policies that disadvantage Whites and/or males, has become a rhetorical strategy to argue for more spaces for those dominant groups. In 2016, the U.S. Supreme Court ruled in *Fisher v. University of Texas* that consideration of the applicant's race is constitutional in the narrow way that the university used race.

In contrast to the current downplaying of the importance of standardized tests in the U.S. college admissions, China places even greater emphasis on tests. For those in China, "no car may honk, nor lorry rumble near secondary schools on the two days... when students are taking their university entrance exams, known as *gaokao*. Teenagers have been cramming for years for these tests which they believe (with justification) will determine their entire future."[32] This emphasis on these exams has tended to tilt college admissions in favor of those students from more elite backgrounds. As Susan noted at the outset of this chapter, different cultures think about education and learning in different ways. In Spain, exams are much less central than they are in China.

More recently, changes in the student body profile have led some admissions officers to give preference to men over women. Preferential admissions are not only about racial differences. As the dean of admissions at Kenyon College in Gambier, Ohio, noted in reviewing one woman's application, "Had she been a male applicant, there would have been little, if any, hesitation to admit. The reality is that because young men are rarer, they're more valued applicants. Today, two-thirds of colleges and universities report that they get more female than male applicants, and more than 56 percent of undergraduates nationwide are women."[33] Given these demographics, some admissions officers have chosen to give preference to male applicants. While this dean acknowledges this preferential treatment, she also notes, "I admire the brilliant successes of our daughters. To parents and the students getting thin envelopes, I apologize for the demographic realities."[34] What do you think about this kind of preferential treatment? How do admissions officers judge the merits of any applicant? How should colleges admit students? There are no easy answers to this question, but whatever decisions are made are likely to impact how our culture develops and the kinds of intercultural interaction that will ensue.

In 2016, Judge Aaron Persky sentenced Brock Turner, a former Stanford University swimmer, to six months in jail for three counts of sexual assault. This sentence created a public uproar: "Instead of sentencing him to the minimum of two years in state prison prescribed by law, Persky made an exception for Turner, determining that his case was 'unusual' and that prison would have a 'severe impact' on him. After the victim's impact statement went viral, the judge's controversial sentencing decision, which will result in Turner spending three months in jail, received international scorn." This sentence came under additional criticism after the same judge sentenced a Latino man to three years in state prison, which "provides a sharp contrast to the outcome for Turner, a white 20-year-old former Stanford swimmer."[35] Under Title IX, no one should be treated differentially based on his or her sex. The Stanford case, among many others, raises the issue of how universities handle cases of sexual assault and how it impacts women's access to higher education.

Complicating matters, there was a letter from the U.S. Department of Education's Office for Civil Rights that "directed university administrators to judge allegations according to the lowest burden of proof available: the preponderance of the evidence, a mere 50.01 percent certainty that whatever the accuser claimed actually happened. It also highly discouraged cross-examinations, suggesting they might violate federal anti-discrimination law."[36] This means that sometimes basic fairness is overlooked. For example, "a student sued the University of Southern California for suspending him for a year—not for sexually assaulting his accuser, but for failing to intervene quickly enough when someone else slapped her on the bottom. The school did this despite a complete lack of evidence that the student knew the slap was coming or could have done anything to prevent it."[37] Universities have been placed in a difficult situation in creating an atmosphere where everyone can have access to education without regard to gender. There are no easy answers, as it is difficult to ensure that everyone is treated fairly and equally in both university adjudications and criminal justice systems.

## COMMUNICATION, EDUCATION, AND CULTURAL IDENTITY

*A Navajo student shared a cultural myth/experience that people from her tribe are all familiar with. Apparently, people in her tribe have encountered "beings" called skin chasers. They are beings that have the face of a human but the body of an animal. They appear in the evening, but not to everyone. She received feedback from her teacher, who said in so many words that it couldn't be true. The Navajo student was really upset that [the teacher] could pass judgment and in her eyes ridicule something that was so sacred to her tribe and cultural background.*

*—Mona*

Mona's story strikes at the heart of the debates over cultural identity, education, and the role of communication in reinforcing or challenging identities. Education itself is an important context for socialization and empowerment. Education professor Ann Locke Davidson observes:

Library of Contress Prints and Photographs Division LC-USZC4-4700

This photo of a class-room at the Carlisle Indian Industrial School in Carlisle, Pennsylvania, was taken about 1902. Carlisle was one of many "Indian schools" that attempted to "civilize" their students by eradicating tribal identities, languages, and religions. What ramifications might this educational process have for contemporary Native Americans?

Education is popularly conceptualized as one factor integral to achieving the economic parity and geographic dispersal presumed basic to integrating diverse citizens into American society. Yet, while it is clear that education improves individual chances for social mobility, it is equally apparent that schools work less well for impoverished African American and Latino school children.[38]

Similarly, Mona's story about her Navajo (Diné) friend demonstrates the alienation that students from other cultures may experience in the classroom.

We often like to think that education provides equal opportunities for all students, but inequities in the paths that students follow reflect differing patterns of treatment. These experiences are powerful forces in the shaping of their identities, and students are very attuned to these forces. One Mexican American high school student, Sonia, notes about her White teachers:

> It's probably in the way they look at you, the way they talk, . . . like when they talk about the people who are going to drop out. And then Mr. Kula, when he's talking about teenage pregnancy or something like that, he turns around and looked at us. It's like, he tries to look around the whole room so we won't notice, but like he mostly tries to get it through our heads. . . . Sometimes I think he's prejudiced.[39]

Sonia, like other students, develops her identity within this educational context. Because her experience is shared by other students who are also of Mexican descent, it is a shared cultural experience that shapes a cultural identity. It is not simply an individual identity.

**What Do You Think?**

Texas is a large buyer of school textbooks and, therefore, what Texas wants in its textbooks has an enormous impact on the textbook market beyond Texas. It also affects the education of millions of students in Texas. In 2010, the Texas Board of Education approved new guidelines that highlight Republican historical contributions, as well as conservative philosophies. Because history and other social studies are never "neutral," how should decisions be made about what to include and exclude? Given the increasing use and importance of the Internet, will students seek out other histories and other views? Or will they stick with the information in the school textbooks?

Even teachers who are not overtly racist may not have received the kind of education necessary to incorporate materials into the curriculum that reflect the diversity of their students. Nor have they been able to develop this curriculum. Education professor Henry Giroux tells us that "despite the growing diversity of students in both public schools and higher education, there are few examples of curriculum sensitivity to the multiplicity of economic, social and cultural factors bearing on a student's educational life."[40]

Think about your own education. How much did you learn about the history of other cultural groups in the United States or elsewhere? How much literature did you read that was written by authors from a range of cultural backgrounds? How much art and music were you exposed to that came from non-Western cultures?

This issue about the key role of education in creating our identities was highlighted by James Loewen's best-selling book *Lies My Teacher Told Me*.[41] In this book, Loewen underscores the ways that U.S. students are taught about the past by reviewing U.S. history textbooks for high schools. He points out the misinformation, as well as blind patriotism, in recounting many historical events. Although this approach to U.S. history may encourage U.S. students to be loyal citizens, it does little to help them understand the importance of history to their identities, as well as the real importance of understanding the past.

The United States is not alone in shaping history to build particular cultural identities. In 2005, "anti-Japanese demonstrations in China—over Japanese school textbooks allegedly glossing over wartime atrocities—spark heated press comment in both countries."[42] Japan has come under critique for the content of its history textbooks as well, particularly by South Korea and China. Both of these nations experienced Japan's militarism prior to Japan's pacifism after World War II. Yet, Chinese, Koreans, and Japanese all recognize the key importance of education and what is taught in building national identities: "Their students learn history through government-approved textbooks that are, especially with nationalism rising in all three countries, useful tools in shaping national identities. Since the textbooks require the central government's imprimatur, they are taken as a reflection of the views of the current leaders."[43] Yet, these countries are not the only ones that teach history to their students.

After the attacks on September 11, 2001, Saudi Arabia came under attack for its educational content, as a number of the terrorists came from that nation. In light of that background, "the government has faced significant pressure from both inside and outside the country to change its schools."[44] Yet a review of these textbooks released in 2006 found that "a sample of official Saudi textbooks for Islamic studies used during the current academic year reveals that, despite the Saudi government's statements to the contrary, an ideology of hatred toward Christians and Jews and Muslims who do not follow Wahhabi doctrine remains in this area of the public school system. This indoctrination begins in a first-grade text and is reinforced and expanded each year, culminating in a 12th-grade text instructing students that their religious obligation includes waging jihad against the infidel to 'spread the faith.'"[45] If you are interested in reading more about the report from Freedom House, see the web page at www.freedomhouse.org/religion/.

While we have looked only at the United States, Japan, and Saudi Arabia, many of these trends in history education are probably not unique to these three countries. Think about what you were taught in school and how that might influence how you see the world. How might the education that others have received shaped their worldviews in ways that might create intercultural barriers as you encounter others from around the world? Since we cannot agree about the past, you can see how it would be impossible to create history textbooks that could be used around the world. This is an educational issue that is likely to continue to impact intercultural relations.

## SOCIAL ISSUES AND EDUCATION

Many social issues are played out in the educational context and can influence the educational experiences of students. Schools and colleges are never outside of the societies and social attitudes in which they exist. Here, we want to highlight a few of these social issues, but there are many more and you should continue to be aware of the many social issues that will emerge in the coming years.

Although **bullying** is not necessarily an intercultural interaction, it can be exacerbated by cultural differences. The U.S. Department of Health and Human Services has defined bullying as "unwanted, aggressive behavior among school aged children that involves a real or perceived power imbalance. The behavior is repeated, or has the potential to be repeated, over time."[46] Bullying can include verbal, nonverbal, and cyber communication. This definition emphasizes school-aged children, but bullying has also been applied to college students.

In May 2016, Emilie Olsen, a Fairfield, Ohio teenager, killed herself after what her parents say "was precipitated by cruel, relentless bullying," including being told "Go kill yourself Emilie."[47] Adopted from China, Emilie was the target of racist bullying, as well as accused of being gay. Her parents have filed a lawsuit against the school district and the case is scheduled to be heard in 2018.

Many other students have experienced bullying and some have gone on to commit suicide. Because school attendance is compulsory, the bullied students are required to see their bullies day after day. Should the bullies be tried in criminal court? Or is there a different way to teach students how to handle differences?

Racial intolerance is another important area where social issues arise can affect the educational experiences of international students. While much of the scholarly literature on international students has focused on adaptation issues, some of the encounters can be difficult because of the intolerance of the host culture. Recently, the Chinese embassy in Australia issued two warning for Chinese travelers in Australia; then in April 2012, two international students from China were attacked on a train in Sydney. One of the students said, "They attacked us with glass and burnt us with lit cigarettes. My face is burnt and totally disfigured! Worst of all, I really hated their racist comments."[48] Social media, as well as traditional media, made this incident widely known in China and elsewhere. In 2014, a gang attack on an Indian student in Melbourne, Australia left the student in critical condition in a hospital. This attack reminded people in India of "A spate of attacks on Indian

**What Do You Think?**

"OSU Haters" is a website that has been set up to post racist (and other forms of intolerance) tweets from Ohio State University students. The purpose of the website is to work toward erasing racism and other forms of intolerance from Ohio State. Take a look at the website and read some of the tweets and the responses at http://osuhaters.tumblr.com/. What do you think? How are student educational experiences shaped by issues of race, racism, and racial difference, as well as homophobia, transphobia, etc? Is this website an effective way to use social media to work on creating a more tolerant educational climate?

students in 2009 and 2010, and the stabbing to death of student Nitin Garg led to a big Melbourne rally by concerned students and taxi drivers, which made front-page news in India. [...] the safety concerns contributed to a 70 per cent drop in the number of students traveling from India."[49] These kinds of incidents create difficult contexts for international students and make it difficult to foster international exchanges.

In contrast, China has set a "goal of bringing half a million foreign students to its shores by 2020" by "pouring money into colleges to establish programs friendly to Americans and other international students."[50] As China increases its international student population, will China face the same kinds of social issues as other countries? Or different ones?

In the United States, the challenges of tolerance and intolerance can be an issue as well. In her rant against Asian students, Alexandra Wallace, who was at UCLA, posted a YouTube video that went viral. Entitled, "Asians in the Library," this video drew a strong reaction that highlighted the volatility of race, as well as the power of social media. In February 2016, Michael Young, the president of Texas A&M University, apologized to African American high school students who were visiting the campus. The high school students were approached by a White woman who pointed out her Confederate flag earrings and "then other students aimed racial slurs at members of the group of about 60, including the N-word and 'go back where you came from.'"[51] If you visited campuses before deciding where to attend college, how would such an experience influence your decision to attend that institution? While universities strive to create learning environments that enhance the experience of all students, not all students experience that ideal.

As the world grows smaller, it is important to strive to become a global citizen by profiting from your interactions with others who are different. Education is one crucial site where this can happen.

As noted earlier, the development of educational institutions, as well as the educational process itself, is deeply embedded in any culture. As students and instructors meet in the classroom, cultural differences can lead to misunderstandings in communication. There is, of course, no way to escape the history of education and the ways this history has created cultural expectations about what should happen in the educational process. Nor is this a call to find a way to escape education. After all, you are pursuing education in an educational institution, and as authors of this book, we also have a role in the educational institution. In any case, there are some social issues that we should consider as they bear upon intercultural communication.

First, it is important to recognize that the educational process reflects cultural power. The things we study (and do not study), the way we communicate in the classroom, the relationships between students and instructors all involve issues of power. How do we determine what gets studied and what does not in various courses? Whose communication style sets the tone in the classroom? Why are interactions between students and instructors always embedded in a hierarchical relationship? The answers to these questions all have to do with power issues, and it is important to recognize that everyone's culture is not treated the same in the curriculum.

© Ryan McVay/Getty Images RF

Thanksgiving is an important U.S. holiday. The educational process is important in instilling a sense of the significance of this holiday. Thanksgiving is not seen as a "White" holiday in the way that Kwanzaa, Lunar New Year, and other holidays are seen as ethnically specific. Why do you think it is important for us to view Thanksgiving as a national holiday instead of a holiday for Whites?

Second, it is important to recognize that the structure of educational institutions, as opposed to the people in them, often plays a significant role in the way that power functions. Thus, we need to understand how the educational system empowers some over others—and how this happens because of the way the system is set up. For example, some colleges require history or literature courses, but the history and literature that they teach might be **Eurocentric,** focusing on European or Western views of history and literature. By taking a Eurocentric approach, these courses reinforce a particular worldview that challenges some student identities more than others. As noted earlier in the book, we are often taught the history of our state or nation. Clearly, however, this approach to education can create barriers to intercultural communication.

One response to this problem is to teach **Afrocentric** history,[52] which centers on the African rather than the European experience and exposes African American students to an entirely different view of the world and their place in it. Of course, as sociologist James Loewen notes, "To be sure, the answer to Eurocentric textbooks is not one-sided Afrocentric history, the kind that has Africans inventing everything good and whites inventing slavery and oppression."[53] These curriculum innovations are vital to the self-esteem, cultural identity, and empowerment of all students, but schools don't seem to know how to teach in ways that are more inclusive and that are fair to all cultural groups. As James Loewen says about U.S. history, "Students will start learning history when they see the point of doing so, when it seems interesting and important to them, and when they believe history might relate to their lives and futures. Students will start finding history interesting when their teachers and textbooks stop lying to them."[54]

Finally, as education professor William Tierney suggests, "Our colleges and universities need to be noisier—in the sense that honest dialogue that confronts differences is good. To be sure, we must not drown out other voices. . . . We must work harder at developing dialogues of respect."[55] To accomplish this, we must be willing to point out cultural differences that are creating problems in the educational process. It is only by addressing these cultural differences and the reasons for the differences that we can begin to change the educational process. We have to create an environment in which cultural differences are assumed to exist and are discussed. We need to move away from an environment in which culture is assumed to be irrelevant since everyone shares the same culture.

In her study of racism in higher education, communication professor Jennifer Simpson concludes, "'Racism is not a theory.' It is not an easy lesson for white people to learn. It is also a difficult lesson for groups of people in higher education to learn, as we cling to safe and predictable routes to knowledge. Changes in the classroom and in higher education are not easy either. They will come only with costs, heavy at times."[56] Whether or not we are ready to undertake the difficult work ahead of us to ensure that education is for everyone, whatever their background, remains to be seen. It is important to be aware that not everyone shares the same culture and has the same orientation to learning and teaching.

## SUMMARY

In this chapter, we looked at some of the challenges that cultural differences bring to the educational process. Because education is a process of socialization and enculturation, it is relevant to intercultural communication. Different cultures have different educational goals. The curricula in some nations do not reflect their own cultures, but instead focus on the European cultures of their former colonizers. Some culturally specific educational institutions may have different educational goals from other institutions. Both teachers and students enact cultural roles in the educational setting. Even grading is cultural, in that all educational systems do not use the same grading system. And varying admissions policies, sometimes discriminatory, have important historical and contemporary implications for intercultural relations. Standardized tests, part of the admission procedures, have sometimes contained implicit cultural biases.

We also examined the ways that communication in education can influence the cultural identities and self-esteem of students. Some instructors may knowingly or unknowingly communicate their cultural biases in the classroom. Finally, the issue of Eurocentric versus Afrocentric approaches to history and the need for more dialogue in the classroom highlight the social relevance of education.

## BUILDING INTERCULTURAL SKILLS

1. Be more sensitive to the ways that your educational curriculum reinforces or challenges your culture and cultural identity. Think about how it might not function in the same way for other students. How is the education you receive targeted toward the majority of students at your college? How is bias reflected in the history you are taught, the literature you are assigned, the music and art you experience, and the social issues you study?

2. Be aware of the cultural nature of the expectations you have for educational roles. If you sense that someone is not acting as a "student" should or as an "instructor" should, how much of this feeling is due to cultural differences?

## ACTIVITIES

1. *Maps and worldviews:* Look at a map of the world. Unless you are looking at a "Peters Projection" map, you will notice that the equator is not in the middle of the map, even if it does run around the middle of the world. Why is the equator not in the middle of the map, and what kinds of worldview might this map be projecting?

2. *Culture and the curriculum:* Find an old college catalog from your school or another one. Look for courses that were taught then but that are less important or nonexistent today. Were there courses in home economics? Whom were these for? What assumptions did such courses make about socialization? How about industrial arts? What languages were taught then, and which ones are taught today? What cultural needs did education fulfill?

## ENDNOTES

1. Palet, S. C. (2014, May 31). Is French the language of the future? *USA Today.* Retrieved July 27, 2016, from http://www.usatoday.com/story/news/world/2014/05/31/ozy-french-language/9781569/.

2. Bennett, J. M., & Salonen, R. (2007, March/April). Intercultural communication and the new American campus. *Change,* pp. 46–50.

3. Judy, R. W., & D'Amico, C. (1997). *Workforce 2020: Work and workers in the 21st century.* Indianapolis: Hudson Institute, p. 116.

4. Docker, J. (1995). The neocolonial assumption in university teaching of English. In B. Ashcroft, G. Griffiths, & H. Tiffin (Eds.), *The post-colonial studies reader* (pp. 443–446). New York, NY: Routledge.

5. Hennebelle, I. (2006, April 20). Mon avenir, c'est…du chinois! *L'Express,* p. 80. (In France, 12,000 secondary students are now studying it. Ten years ago, there were only 2,500.)

6. Das Ende for German at USC. (2008, April 11). *Inside Higher Education.* Retrieved March 7, 2009, from http://www.insidehighered.com/news/2008/04/11/german.

7. Brockmann, S. (2009, March 6). The study of foreign languages should not be a zero-sum game. *The Chronicle of Higher Education.* Retrieved March 3, 2009, from http://chronicle.com/weekly/v55/i26/26a03301.htm.

8. Flaherty, C. (2015, February 11). Not a small world after all. *Inside Higher Ed.* Retrieved July 28, 2016, from https://www.insidehighered.com/news/2015/02/11/mla-report-shows-declines-enrollment-most-foreign-languages.

9. Washington, B. T. (1971). The Atlanta Exposition address, September 1895. In A. Meier et al. (Eds.), *Black protest thought in the twentieth century* (2nd ed., pp. 3–8). Indianapolis, IN: Bobbs-Merrill, p. 5.

10. Goodenow, R. K. (1989). Education, Black. In C. R. Wilson & W. Ferris (Eds.), *Encyclopedia of southern culture* (Vol. 1). New York, NY: Anchor Books, p. 253.

11. Our history. (n.d.) Mississippi University for Women. Retrieved from http://www.muw.edu/about-muw/our-history.

12. About TWU. (2015, November 1). Texas Woman's University. Retrieved from http://www.twu.edu/about-twu/.

13. History and Traditions. (n.d.). Georgia Tech. Retrieved from http://www.gatech.edu/about/history-and-traditions.

14. Lomawaima, K. T. (1994). *They called it Prairie Light: The story of Chilocco Indian School.* Lincoln, NE: University of Nebraska Press, p. 160.

15. Lomawaima (1994), p. 3.

16. Lomawaima (1994), p. xv.

17. Miranda, L. (2010, December 1). Get the facts on the DREAM Act. *White House.* Retrieved July 17, 2016, from https://www.whitehouse.gov/blog/2010/12/01/get-facts-dream-act.

18. Gordon, L. (2016, April 7). Some states by pass Congress, create their own version of the DREAM Act. *PBS Newshour.* Retrieved July 27, 2016, from http://www.pbs.org/newshour/rundown/some-states-bypass-congress-create-their-own-versions-of-the-dream-act/.

19. Bauer, S. (2006, May 31). Nebraskans show immigration frustration. *The Washington Post.* Retrieved June 1, 2006, from http://www.washingtonpost.com/wp-dyn/content/article/2006/05/31/AR2006053100335.html.

20. Bland, K. (2006, February 26). State struggles to help English-learners achieve. *The Arizona Republic.* Retrieved June 1, 2006, from http://www.azcentral.com/specials/special24/articles/0226ellday1blomo0226.html.

21. Kossan, P. (2006, February 28). English-only immersion debated for schools. *The Arizona Republic.* Retrieved June 1, 2006, from http://www.azcentral.com/specials/special24/articles/0228ellprimer0228.html.

22. Schworm, P. (2009, March 5). Catholic college bars student's free condoms. *The Boston Globe.* Retrieved March 7, 2009, from http://www.boston.com/news/local/massachusetts/articles/2009/03/05/catholic_college_bars_students_free_condoms/.

23. Burton, B. (2000, February 25). Preventing culture clashes: Learning styles, food, and dorm life challenge foreign students in Holland. *The Chronicle of Higher Education,* p. A56.

24. Holmes, P. (2005). Ethnic Chinese students' communication with cultural others in a New Zealand university. *Communication Education, 54,* 289–311.

25. National policy on assessment and qualifications for schools in the general education and training band. (n.d.) Department of Education, Republic of South Africa. Retrieved on March 7, 2009, from http://www.education.gov.za/Curriculum/GET/doc/ANatioanalPolicy.pdf.

26. Bristol denies admissions bias. (2003, February 26). *BBC News.* Retrieved from http://news.bbc.co.uk/2/hi/uk_news/education/2798507.stm.

27. About Florida State: History. (n.d.). Florida State University. Retrieved from http://www.fsu.edu/about/history.html.

28. Policy Council. (2010, June 24). University of Illinois Nondiscrimination Statement. Retrieved from https://nessie.uihr.uillinois.edu/pdf/eeo/ndispost.pdf.

29. Lobosco, K. (2015, September 8). Here's what happened when these colleges ditched SAT scores. *CNN Money.* Retrieved July 28, 2016, from http://money.cnn.com/2015/09/08/pf/college/sat-college-diversity/.

30. Bollag, B. (2003, November 7). French court upholds landmark program of affirmative action in college admissions. *The Chronicle of Higher Education.* Retrieved from http://chronicle.com/prm/daily/2003/11/2003110703n.htm.

31. Laronche, M. (2003, November 7). Sciences-Po condemned to review the method of its ZEP conventions. *Le Monde.* Retrieved from http://www.lemonde.fr/web/recherche_articleweb/1,13-0,36-341087,0.html?query=sciences+po&query2=&booleen=et&num_page=1&auteur=&dans=dansarticle&periode=30&ordre=pertinence&G_NBARCHIVES=796331&nbpages=2&artparpage=10&nb_art=11.

32. The class ceiling. (2016, June 4–10). *The Economist,* p. 39.

33. Britz, J. D. (2006, March 23). To all the girls I've rejected. *New York Times,* p. A25.

34.  Britz (2006, March 23), p. A25.

35.  Levin, S. (2016, June 27). Stanford trial judge overseeing much harsher sentence for similar assault case. *The Guardian*. Retrieved July 28, 2016, from https://www.theguardian.com/us-news/2016 /jun/27/stanford-sexual-assault-trial-judge-persky.

36.  Dillon, J., & Kaiser, M. (2016, April 21). Absurdity reigns in campus sexual assault trials. *Los Angeles Times*. Retrieved July 29, 2016, from http://www.latimes.com/opinion/op-ed/la-oe -0421-dillon-kaiser-campus-sex-assault-20160421-story.html.

37.  Dillon & Kaiser (2016).

38.  Davidson, A. L. (1996). *Making and molding identity in schools: Student narratives on race, gender, and academic empowerment.* Albany, NY: State University of New York, p. 22.

39.  Davidson (1996), p. 128.

40.  Giroux, H. A. (1996). Is there a place for cultural studies in colleges of education? In H. A. Giroux, C. Lankshear, P. McLaren, & M. Peters (Eds.), *Counternarratives: Cultural studies and critical pedagogies in postmodern spaces.* New York, NY: Routledge, p. 50.

41.  Loewen, J. W. (1995). *Lies my teacher told me: Everything your American history textbook got wrong.* New York, NY: New Press.

42.  China, Japan eye textbook tension. (2005, April 11). *BBC News*. Retrieved May 23, 2006, from http://news.bbc.co.uk/2/hi/asia-pacific/4432535.stm.

43.  Onishi, N. (2005, April 17). In Japan's new texts, lessons in rising nationalism. *New York Times*. Retrieved May 23, 2006, from http://www.nytimes.com/2005/04/17/weekinreview/17onishi .html?ex=1271390400&en=60e4a68bc70713c4&ei=5090&partner=rssuserland&emc=rss.

44.  Fattah, H. (2006, May 24). Don't be friends with Christians or Jews, Saudi texts say. *New York Times,* p. A10.

45.  Shea, N. (2006, May 21). This is a Saudi textbook. (After the intolerance was removed.) *The Washington Post,* p. B1.

46.  U.S. Department of Health and Human Services. (n.d.) Bullying definition. *Stopbullying.gov.* Retrieved September 2, 2012, from http://www.stopbullying.gov/what-is-bullying/definition/index .html.

47.  Wang, Y. (2016, May 23). After years of alleged bullying, an Ohio teen killed herself. Is her school district responsible? *The Washington Post*. Retrieved July 27, 2016, from https://www.washingtonpost. com/news/morning-mix/wp/2016/05/23/after-years-of-alleged-bullying-an-ohio-teen-killed-herself-is -her-school-district-responsible/.

48.  Cai, P. (2012, April 24). "This city is so dangerous": Outrage in China over Sydney train assault. *The Sydney Morning Herald*. Retrieved September 2, 2012, from http://www.smh.com .au/national/this-city-is-so-dangerous-outrage-in-china-over-sydney-train-assault-20120424-1xiv4 .html#ixzz25P2pQeHv.

49.  Whinnett, E., & Hussain, T. (2014, January 5). Indian student numbers plunge after fresh attack. *Herald Sun*. Retrieved July 27, 2016, from http://www.heraldsun.com.au/news/law-order/indian-student -numbers-plunge-after-fresh-attack/story-fni0fee2-1226795039267.

50.  Hennock, M. (2012, August 17). China rolls out welcome mat for foreign students. *The Chronicle of Higher Education*, p. A13.

51.  Dart, T. (2016, February 19). Texas A&M rife with racial tension after another incident of campus racism. *The Guardian*. Retrieved July 27, 2016, from https://www.theguardian.com/world/2016/feb/19 /texas-am-high-school-students-harassed-racism-on-campus.

52.  Loewen (1995), p. 302.

53.  Loewen (1995), p. 302.

54.  Loewen (1995), p. 311.

55.  Tierney, W. G. (1997). *Academic outlaws: Queer theory and cultural studies in the academy.* Thousand Oaks, CA: Sage.

56.  Simpson, J. (2003). *I have been waiting: Race and U.S. higher education.* Toronto: University of Toronto Press, p. 196.

© kristian sekulic/Getty Images RF

CHAPTER THIRTEEN

# Intercultural Communication and Health Care

## STUDY OBJECTIVES

*After reading this chapter, you should be able to:*

1. Understand the importance of communication in health care delivery. Describe some of the ways that communication can be overlooked and how this might impact the delivery of medical services.

2. Explain some of the intercultural barriers to effective health care. Explain the ways that some cultural groups have been or continue to be treated in the health care system. Describe how prejudicial attitudes can influence health care delivery.

3. Explain how religious or spiritual beliefs may be important in effective health care delivery. Describe some of the ways that health care professionals can deal with religious and spiritual beliefs. Discuss the ethical implications of some of the ways that health care professionals deal with religious or spiritual beliefs.

4. Explain how power differences can influence health communication.

5. Identify the four frameworks that physicians might use in communicating about a patient's health.

6. Describe the role of ethics committees. Describe some of the complex issues to be dealt with in making ethical health care decisions.

## KEY TERMS

AIDS
benevolent deception
complementary and integrative medicine
contractual honesty
ethics committees
euthanasia
Fat Acceptance Movement
health care professionals
HIPAA
HIV
medical jargon
medical miscommunication
medical terminology
prejudicial ideologies
religious freedom
religious history
strict paternalism
Tuskegee Syphilis Project
unmitigated honesty

*The longer I stay in the U.S., the more differences I find between American and Chinese health care practices. For instance, some elderly people spend the rest of their lives in nursing homes even if they have children, and that seems to be commonly acceptable. However, in China, children have the responsibility to take care of their elder parents. Sending one's parents to nursing homes, although not illegal, is considered by the general public as a very bad practice. Another difference I found is that, in the U.S., abortion is a very controversial topic; however, in China, it's commonly considered just as a medical practice, and is not associated with moral judgments in general.*

—*Lan*

*My cousin is an American who moved to China a few years ago. When she was pregnant, she decided to come back to America to have her baby after realizing all of the differences in healthcare over there. In China, they refuse to tell you the sex of your baby, and have you deliver your baby in the same room as other women in labor which are practices that are not standard in the U.S.*

—*Shanyu*

In comparing health care in China and the United States, both Lan and Shanyu highlight the ways that cultural differences are reflected in health care. Their insights are helpful in how we might think about health care more generally. While we may often think of health care as a scientific or medical issue, health care and communication are also deeply embedded in culture.

What you have learned about intercultural communication has important applications in the health communication context. As the U.S. population ages and new medical technologies are developed, health care will become even more significant in our lives. Health care has also become increasingly controversial as more and more managed care corporations have entered the market. Within this changing context, as the U.S. population becomes increasingly diverse, U.S. Americans are beginning to seek out health care from a variety of sources—from traditional Western practitioners to more "exotic" Eastern practices.

In this chapter, we discuss some of the reasons communication about health has become more important and some of the ways you might navigate this communication context. Not only patients, but **health care professionals**—including physicians, nurses, physical and occupational therapists, and medical technicians—can come

**Info Bites**

The National Institutes of Health houses the National Center for Complementary and Integrative Health (NCCIH). The NCCIH, in part, researches complementary and integrative health practices that are not considered part of conventional, or Western, medicine. "Complementary health approaches" refer to non-mainstream health practices and products, while "integrative health" refers to the incorporation of those complementary health approaches into mainstream, conventional medical and health care. Over a third of adults use complementary and integrative health approaches. For more information, see https://nccih.nih.gov /health/integrative -health.

**TABLE 13.1  Home Countries of Foreign Doctors**

Many physicians earned their medical degrees at institutions outside the United States. These International Medical Graduates (IMGs) come from many different countries. How might intercultural communication be important here? The top 10 providers of IMGs are:

1. India—19.9% (47,581)
2. Philippines—8.7% (20,861)
3. Mexico—5.8% (13,929)
4. Pakistan—4.8% (11,330)
5. Dominican Republic—3.3% (7,892)
6. former U.S.S.R.—2.5% (6,039)
7. Grenada—2.4% (5,708)
8. Egypt—2.2% (5,202)
9. Korea—2.1% (4,982)
10. Italy—2.1% (4,978)

*Source:* "IMGs by country of origin," American Medical Association, 2007. Retrieved from http://www.ama-assn.org/ama/pub/about-ama/our-people/member-groups-sections/international-medical-graduates/imgs-in-united-states/imgs-country-origin.page.

from a variety of cultural backgrounds. Intercultural communication and misunderstandings in health communication arise daily in this context.

## THE IMPORTANCE OF COMMUNICATION IN HEALTH CARE

Intercultural communication is increasingly relevant in the health communication context for a number of reasons. First, as our population becomes increasingly diverse, complexities arise in communicating about health issues. Not only are health care professionals communicating with people from differing cultural backgrounds, but these same patients are communicating with nurses, doctors, and other health care professionals from differing cultural backgrounds. Table 13.1 shows some of the diversity of cultural backgrounds of U.S. physicians. And in some cultures, there may be certain stigmas associated with communicating about health issues, making it difficult to discuss these concerns. For example, in some cultures, subjects such as mental illness, AIDS, sexually transmitted diseases (STDs), impotence, and abortion are not easily broached.

Second, health care professionals and patients may not realize the importance of communication. This oversight may seem incidental to medical training and treatment, but the reality is, much medical practice, particularly diagnosis, relies heavily on patient communication. In many ways, this shortcoming in health care reflects a Western cultural phenomenon, "due partly to the belief that the biomedical model of health care—the predominant model in Western societies—is based on a range of predominantly physical procedures (physical examination, physical manipulation, injections, etc.) rather than communication between two parties."[1] In other words, Western physicians tend to rely heavily on physical symptoms to evaluate illness, rather than communicating with patients about what they are experiencing.

However, good communication is crucial to quality health care. Health care providers ask questions to diagnose problems, to help patients understand the treatment,

**Surf's Up!**

Did you know that you can major in health communication? Health communication covers a variety of issues such as patient–physician communication, health communication in organizations, social support, and health promotion. In a culturally diverse setting, how should we approach these issues?

and so on. And patients come to health professionals to seek treatment and ask questions. But even native English speakers complain about the use of **medical jargon**—potentially confusing or difficult-to-understand medical terminology—by physicians.

Kathleen B. Kennedy, dean of the College of Pharmacy at Xavier University in New Orleans, developed a communication model called LEARN to help with interactions with patients.

- Listen to the patient's perception of the problem.
- Explain your point of view.
- Acknowledge and discuss the differences and disparities in perceptions of the problem.
- Recommend treatment.
- Negotiate treatment.[2]

It is also important to be constantly working on increasing your knowledge about other cultures and their values and beliefs, especially in relation to health issues. There is no easy way to do this, but learning about other cultures is a lifelong, ongoing process.

If English speakers have trouble with common medical terms, health care professionals need to be especially careful using these terms. For those patients who are communicating in a second language, **medical terminology**—scientific language used by doctors to describe specific medical conditions—can be particularly confusing. If you have ever studied a foreign language, how many medical terms did you learn in class? How well could you speak to a medical professional in that language? And when cultural misunderstandings arise, it can lead to inadequate treatment. This misunderstanding is sometimes called **medical miscommunication**. This type of miscommunication can result in medical mistakes, problems with patient use of medication, and other problems. A study of medical miscommunication in Japan also shows that there can be significant financial costs that result as well. In cases where there was no medical error, 64.4 percent of the problems were due to miscommunication between medical providers and patients (and families).[3]

Third, and probably the most obvious barrier to health services, are language barriers. Some health care providers ask their bilingual employees to serve as interpreters to patients who do not speak English. In a case cited in New York City, for example, when a "Spanish-speaking hospital receptionist refused to interpret during her lunch hour, doctors at St. Vincent's Staten Island Hospital turned to a 7-year-old child to tell their patient, an injured construction worker, that he needed an emergency amputation."[4] Language issues can create problems in health care, not only in hospitals, but also in pharmacies. A study done by pediatricians in the Bronx section of New York City found that "pharmacies often used computer programs to translate prescriptions. Only one pharmacy employed a Spanish-speaking pharmacist that could check the translations."[5] This raises even more issues with language barriers in health care. As the authors of this study noted, "we visited one of the large chain pharmacies, and discovered that the computer could not translate some commonly used terms, such as *dropperful,* or *for thirty days.*"[6] Many hospitals rely on their workers or bilingual children of patients to help translate. At one California hospital, "there have often been no Hmong-speaking employees of any kind present in the hospital at night. . . . Sometimes not even a child is available. Doctors on the late shift in the emergency room have often had no way of taking a patient's medical history. . . . I asked one doctor what he did in such cases. He said, 'Practice veterinary medicine.' "[7] It is also important to remember that Title VI of the 1964 Civil Rights Acts requires that institutions receiving federal funding make accommodations for those who have limited English proficiency. Because many patients rely on federal assistance (e.g., Medicare, Medicaid, Veterans benefits), accommodation must be made for those with limited English language skills. There are no easy answers to many of these concerns, given the numerous languages spoken in the United States and around the world, but awareness of these issues may lead to innovative ways of dealing with language differences.

Fourth, health care providers and patients alike may operate out of an ethnocentric framework without realizing it. Assumptions about health care often have cultural roots. Consider the following example: Setsuko, a Japanese woman now living in the United States, had to spend several months in the hospital for a chronic illness. She became extremely depressed, to the point of feeling suicidal. Whenever the staff would ask her how she was doing, Setsuko would answer that she was fine. Based on this lack of communication, the nursing and medical staff were unaware of her depression for weeks. It was not until she began to exhibit physical signs of depression that she was offered a psychiatric consultation. The problem was that Setsuko was culturally conditioned to be a good patient by not making a fuss or drawing attention to herself or embarrassing her family with complaints about being depressed, so she always reported that she was fine. Although the psychiatrist tried to explain that in this context a "good patient" was expected to discuss and report any and all problems or symptoms, Setsuko still had to work to redefine her cultural role as a good patient in order to receive better health care. In this case, both the health care providers and the patient struggled to negotiate a more effective communication framework to ensure better treatment.

Fifth, treating patients is not always a matter of communication between the physician and the patient. While one-to-one communication generally works well in Western cultures, which are more oriented to individualism, other cultures may focus more on the family's role in health care. Thus, communication between the physician and the patient is only one element in the communication process. Unfortunately, most health communication research has limited itself to the physician–patient relationship. Laurel Northouse, a nursing professor, and Peter Northouse, a communication professor, note: "This lack of systematic study of professional-family interaction is symptomatic of the lack of importance that health professionals have traditionally attributed to this relationship in health care."[8]

For example, a recent study on patients from Togo, a former French colony in Africa, found that 42 percent of Togolese prefer that if there is bad news the physician must inform the relatives only, and not the patient. Thirty-three percent preferred the physician telling the relatives the complete news, but less information to the patient.[9] In the United States, disclosure of health information is guided by a federal law known

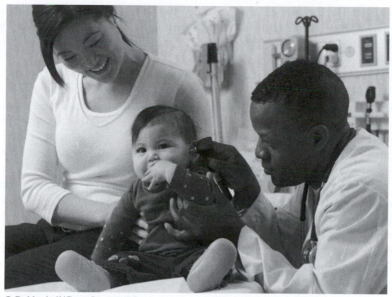
© Rubberball/Getty Images RF

Patients and health care providers come from a variety of cultural backgrounds with differing assumptions about health care and the proper roles of doctors and nurses. These cultural differences can influence the health care patients receive. Health care providers need to be sensitive to these cultural differences in providing health services.

as the Health Insurance Portability and Accountability Act (**HIPAA**). HIPAA includes a strict privacy rule that restricts communicating health information to anyone other than the patient and those who may need to know, for example, other physicians, nurses, and health insurance companies for billing purposes. There are limited cases where health care providers can share information with family and friends,[10] but culturally the United States is much more centered on the individual than Togo.

This cultural bias in thinking about the role of the family in health care can lead to problems. Consider the case of the Samoan man hospitalized with a gunshot wound. Throughout the day, more and more family members gathered in the waiting room. Because there were so many extended family members, hospital personnel asked them to wait in the main lobby. The family members became increasingly irate because they wanted to see the patient as a large group, but the hospital had a policy of only three visitors at a time. Tensions between the family and the staff continued to escalate until a hospital administrator, sensitive to cultural differences, made a special exception and allowed large groups of family members to visit the patient.

A similar cultural pattern occurs in Iranian culture, where families may be seen as ignoring or violating hospital visiting hours, which can create conflict with the hospital staff. This cultural pattern emerges from a cultural duty to be there for the patient:

> Iranians are very sociable, and hospital visits to friends or relatives are considered a moral duty. Visitors come in large number, bring sweets, flowers, and gifts. It is a time to socialize and to keep the patient company, and most hospitalized Iranians enjoy having large numbers of noisy visitors. In Iranian culture it is considered shameful to leave a loved one alone in the hospital without visitors.[11]

If hospital staff understand this cultural difference in health care, it might help avoid cultural conflicts with the patient's family. Given the importance of the family in the overall health care of the patient, cultural accommodation might be seen as one way of nursing the patient to better health.

Families, of course, can provide very important support to a patient as she or he recovers. Their role is even more important after the patient returns home. But this means that the family must receive adequate information about the patient's condition. In turn, this means that health care professionals must be sensitive to cultural differences and must adapt their communication accordingly.

Finally, some work has begun to show the importance of community involvement in health care. In their work on community-based health communication, communication scholars Leigh Arden Ford and Gust Yep found that a community-oriented approach often works much better than a focus on individuals. Part of this effectiveness emerges when community health workers "become catalysts for change. Through their public health and communication network role enactments, they promote community organizing efforts and enable individual empowerment. Significantly, community health workers empower themselves as they become a means to empowerment for individuals, families, neighborhoods, and communities."[12] This community-based approach seems to work in Haiti, where Dr. Paul Farmer of Partners in Health focused on "community-based solutions to its health problems. That meant, for example, training local residents as doctors, technicians, and outreach workers who could diagnose and treat their neighbors."[13] A focus on community as a foundation for health care is quite different from a more traditional focus on the individual, but it seems to work.

## INTERCULTURAL BARRIERS TO EFFECTIVE HEALTH CARE

In Chapter 3, we discussed the importance of history in intercultural communication. Let's look at some of these historical dynamics as they influence health care today. This is important because the history of medicine guides how different cultural communities may relate to health care.

### Historical Treatments of Cultural Groups

First, historically, widespread ideologies about different cultures have fostered differential treatment for some groups, especially racial and ethnic minorities, by medical professionals. This created a tension between sameness and difference in medicine. For example, on the one hand, medical professionals viewed African American bodies as the same as White bodies and used them as cadavers in medical schools, such as the one in Augusta, Georgia (now known as the Medical College of Georgia, a part of Augusta University). In the nineteenth and twentieth centuries, the college used the bodies of recently buried African Americans for medical research and instruction by White males without the consent of the deceased or their families.[14] On the other hand, White bodies would not be dug up for instructional use without permission. So while

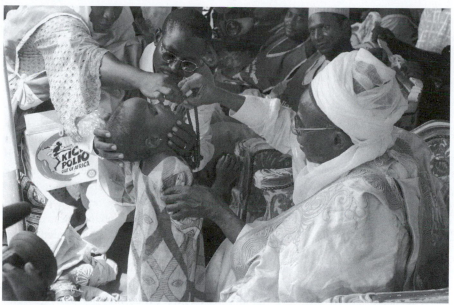

© Jean-Marc Giboux/Getty Images

These doctors are vaccinating children against polio, despite rumors in some countries that polio vaccines were a conspiracy to sterilize children. What might have happened in the past to lead to such fears?

African American bodies were seen as the same as White bodies, they were not treated the same. As sociologist Chris Shilling writes, "Historically, the negative construction of Black bodies has made them targets for a variety of moral panics surrounding health and disease."[15] In the past, medical conclusions about alleged racial difference have justified a number of deplorable social practices, from slavery, to colonization, to immigration restrictions.[16]

This differential treatment has caused some cultural groups to be justifiably suspicious of contemporary health care. For example, the infamous **Tuskegee Syphilis Project,** conducted by the U.S. Public Health Service on unsuspecting African Americans in Tuskegee, Alabama, over a 40-year period, spurred some of these concerns.[17] In this study, Black patients who sought out medical care for syphilis were instead given placebos (sugar pills), but were not told that they were part of a study, simply to establish an experimental control group. The purpose of the study was to explore how syphilis spreads in a patient's body and how it spreads in a population. Periodic reports were published in medical journals, but the Centers for Disease Control and Prevention (CDC) received only one letter from a physician raising ethical concerns. The study was finally halted, not by the medical community, but only after a public denouncement by Senator Edward Kennedy in Congress. Unfortunately, it's hardly surprising that such a study was not conducted on wealthy White Americans in Beverly Hills.

The Tuskegee Syphilis Project, among other studies and projects, has reinforced suspicion about the medical community from many marginalized communities. This "mistrust of the medical system by some African Americans has been identified as a barrier to optimal health care and participation in clinical trials."[18] In a recent study on perceptions of trust in medical care, differences in trust emerged between White and Black respondents. These researchers found that "African Americans have been shown to have greater awareness of the documented history of racial discrimination in the health care system than white Americans, and this greater awareness of historical discrimination has been associated with less trust of clinical and research institutions. This is consistent with our finding of greater concern among African Americans about the potential for harmful experiments being performed in hospitals."[19] Given this horrible history, how might health care providers work with African Americans to gain their trust? Given the "alarming inequities in health outcomes between different racial and ethnic groups in the United States," it is important that we focus on "the development of strategic, adaptive, and sensitive health communication across a range of communication channels and media" to enhance the health of all of us.[20] In a recent study on life expectancies across race and educational differences in the United States, researchers found that these disparities are continuing to grow. For example, college-educated White men tended to live 14.2 years longer than Black men with less than a high school diploma. The differential life spans are growing, rather than shrinking, which has a tremendous impact on the very different worlds that we live in.[21]

The rise of **AIDS** (acquired immune deficiency syndrome) and **HIV** (human immunodeficiency virus) in the late twentieth century provoked new fears among gays and minorities that the medical community would again provide differential treatment. As Jeffrey Levi, an AIDS and health policy consultant, argues:

> Homophobia was not introduced into the health-care system with the AIDS epidemic. Rather, its long-standing legacy of discrimination and exclusion has resulted in the creation of a separate health-care system within the gay community, a health-care system that responded to this new crisis immediately, saving countless gay lives—and heterosexual lives as well—while the government-sponsored system floundered, unable to find the will or the funds to operate.[22]

The slow response to the AIDS epidemic by the federal government has been widely discussed and critiqued. In his analysis of public discourses about AIDS, Larry Gross, a communication professor, concludes that "AIDS thus taught two lessons. First, a disease that strikes gay people (and people of color, and drug users, and poor people) will not receive adequate attention. Second, people will begin to pay attention when famous and important people are involved."[23] Thus, the HIV/AIDS epidemic highlighted the traditional lack of trust between the health care system and minority communities.

### Prejudicial Ideologies

Second, **prejudicial ideologies**—sets of ideas based on stereotypes—about various cultural groups affect both health care professionals and patients. These attitudes can present significant barriers to intercultural communication. Consider the following case: A social worker in one of the nursing units was recording information on a patient's chart when she overheard staff members discussing a patient who had recently been admitted to the unit. They were not certain if the patient was Chinese, Taiwanese, or Vietnamese. The head nurse called the supervisor of international services, who helped clarify that the patient was Taiwanese and so needed a Taiwanese-speaking interpreter. As they continued to discuss the patient, one staff member said, "So she doesn't speak any English at all? How does she get along in this country if she can't speak English?" Another staff member responded, "She doesn't need to get along here. They are all on welfare."[24] Given our concern with the kinds of health care received by members of nonmainstream cultural groups, these comments take on even more significance than simply being prejudicial. Such attitudes may influence the quality of health care that patients receive. And health care professionals are hardly immune to prejudice. Attending nursing school or medical school does not purge feelings of homophobia, racism, sexism, and other kinds of prejudice.

Patients, too, often enter the health care system with prejudicial attitudes. Tom's brother-in-law, for example, a physician in North Carolina, often encounters patients who prefer not to be treated by doctors who are "Yankees." He is frequently asked, Where are you from?" which suggests that regional differences remain barriers. Because he is from California, these patients consent to his treatment; after all, he is not a "damn Yankee." Regional identities can influence whether people trust medical professionals.

Because of this mistrust, many people prefer to obtain a significant amount of their medical information from their own communities. For example, in the case of AIDS, many gay men turned to the gay community for information on the latest experimental drugs and treatments. In the South, some low-income Whites believe that Prozac is addicting despite scientific evidence to the contrary. However, because Prozac is seen as addictive within this community, patients often refuse to take the drug when it is prescribed. The point here is that people may turn to their own communities out of mistrust of medical professionals. Sometimes these communities can provide significant integrative health care, as in the case of gay men and AIDS; other communities, however, can provide misinformation.

Although there is no cure for polio, an inexpensive and widely available vaccine to prevent polio has been available for over half a century. Despite having come close to eradicating polio worldwide, in 2014, the World Health Organization (WHO) "declared polio a global health emergency" as immunization services in many countries have been "severely compromised." Vaccination programs came under tremendous pressure after it was revealed that the Central Intelligence Agency (CIA) was using these programs to infiltrate other countries. It has been reported that "as many as 60 polio vaccinators have been killed in Pakistan since December 2012."[25] In January 2013, the deans of a number of medical schools wrote to President Obama to point out the damage caused by the CIA infiltration of vaccination programs and requested that it be stopped. In May 2014, Lisa Monaco, Assistant to the President for Homeland Security and Counterterrorism, wrote back to tell them that the director of the CIA has decided "that the Agency make no operational use of vaccination programs, which includes vaccination workers."[26] Despite the announcement that the CIA is no longer using vaccination programs to infiltrate other countries, how long will it take for people to see these programs as public health campaigns again,

**Info Bites**

Did you know that December 1 is World AIDS Day? Do you know what the international symbol of AIDS awareness is? Do you know what you can do to support World AIDS Day? To learn more, explore the website at www.avert .org/worldaid.htm.

rather than as potential CIA operations? How can these vaccination programs regain their credibility among people overseas? What kind of communication campaign can they undertake?

In July 2016, the first cases of Zika virus acquired in the United States were identified in Miami, Florida. Because of the impact on the fetus, pregnant women (or women who may become pregnant) have been an important audience for communication about the virus. Although the Zika virus was first discovered over 70 years ago, it has drawn little attention in the United States until now. Today, the CDC has put up a webpage at http://www.cdc.gov/zika/index.html which has information on the virus, how to prevent acquiring it as no vaccine exists, travel warnings to certain parts of the world, and other information. This webpage includes the CDC's communication plan for informing the public about Zika. Take a look at the information and the communication strategies employed. What do you think about the CDC response? Besides the CDC, what other organizations need to be communicating about Zika?

## RELIGION AND HEALTH CARE

Even when they are not facing serious illness or death, many people turn to religion or spirituality to help them try to understand the complexities of life.[27] When they are ill, however, some people are driven to seek answers to questions that science cannot always answer. While some people turn to spiritual healing, others prefer to combine their spiritual beliefs with traditional medical care. Sometimes spirituality and/or religion can be helpful in the healing process; other times, it may be helpful in facing death.

The role of religion and spirituality in health care is still a controversial topic, but today "more than half of the med schools in the country" offer courses in religion and spirituality, "up from just three a decade ago."[28] Yet the role of religion and spirituality in health care raises a number of issues about ethical ways to approach the topic of incorporating health practices into existing beliefs and helping patients avoid any pressure they may feel about their beliefs. It is also important for health care professionals to avoid imposing their beliefs on patients. One example of such an error is when a "doctor told his patient that 'if she was right with God, she wouldn't be depressed.'"[29] Needless to say, health care professionals should not assume that all patients share their beliefs, as people around the world hold a wide range of spiritual views.

Yet, accommodating for religious differences can be an important part of effective health care. Consider the following example:

> Dr. Susan Strangl, a family-medicine doctor at UCLA, [had] a Muslim patient who needed medication but was observing Ramadan and couldn't drink or eat during the day. After taking a **religious history**—routine for all hospitalized patients at UCLA—Strangl chose a once-a-day medication that could be taken after sundown. "If we hadn't talked about it, I would have written him a prescription for four times a day and he would not have taken it," she says.[30]

**What Do You Think?**

Should hospitals provide interpreters for their patients who do not speak English? If so, for all languages or only a few? If you were vacationing in, say, Italy and had to go to the hospital, would you expect someone at the hospital to speak English? What about Mongolia, which gets very few English-speaking tourists?

While religious and spiritual beliefs vary widely, Drs. Koenig, McCullough, and Larson attempted to survey the studies available in this area and compiled the *Handbook of Religion and Health Care.* Our understanding of the role of religion and spirituality in health still leaves us with many unanswered questions, but they do recommend seven specific strategies for physicians and other health care professionals in dealing with patients:[31]

- Take a religious history.
- Support or encourage religious beliefs.
- Ensure access to religious resources.
- Respect visits by clergy.
- View chaplains as part of the health care team.
- Be ready to step in when clergy are unavailable.
- Use advanced spiritual interventions cautiously.

Some of these suggestions may be difficult for health care professionals to follow, particularly when they are followers of different religions, hold different spiritual beliefs, or are atheists or agnostics. Patients also may not want to discuss such topics. One physician, "Dr. Jim Martin, head of the American Academy of Family Physicians, teaches residents to take spiritual histories, but 'if a patient flinches, we don't go there.' And if a patient says faith or spiritual beliefs are not important, 'we check that box and move on.' "[32]

Some physicians, however, argue against some of the previously suggested guidelines. For example, Dr. Richard P. Sloan of the Columbia-Presbyterian Medical Center cautions against praying with patients: "It confuses the relationship. It may encourage patients to think a prayer is going to somehow improve their well-being. It certainly will improve their spiritual well-being but there's no evidence it's going to improve their health." His biggest concern about health care professionals engaging in religious issues is "Manipulation of **religious freedom.** Restriction of religious freedom. Invasion of privacy. And causing harm. It's bad enough to be sick, it's worse still to be gravely ill, but to add to that the burden of remorse and guilt for some supposed failure of religious devotion is unconscionable."[33] While some health care professionals may believe that spiritual beliefs or religious beliefs can help patients be healthier, Dr. Sloan notes, "The question is if religion is demonstrably efficacious, if it really influences longevity, morbidity and mortality, and the quality of life, why don't the insurance companies get in on it?"[34] The point here is that there is no easy list of ways to deal with cultural differences and religious differences in health care. Issues of ethics, however, should always be at the forefront of considerations. Communication about these issues can be key to unraveling the ethical issues at hand.

Many health care professionals may not be aware of the diversity of religious and spiritual beliefs around the world. How can studying religious and cultural differences be helpful to health care professionals? How can health care professionals communicate respect for others' religious or spiritual beliefs without compromising their own beliefs? How assertive should patients be about asking health care professionals to accommodate their religious or spiritual beliefs? Health care professionals

**What Do You Think?**

Currently, obesity is measured according to Body Mass Index (BMI), which is calculated by dividing weight by height in inches squared. What is your BMI? Is this a fair measure or are there other factors that should be considered? Using BMI statistics, the National Center for Health Statistics estimates that of U.S. adults 20 years and older 32.7 percent are overweight, 34.3 percent are obese, and 5.9 percent are extremely obese. What would other cultures think of the use of BMI as a measure of overall health?

should also be aware that some patients may fear getting inferior care if they do not share the dominant religious beliefs. How might patients and health care professionals assure each other in this context? All of these questions are at the forefront of the debate about the role of religious or spiritual beliefs in health care.

## Cultural Influences on Approaches to Medicine

Different cultures bring different perspectives on our health—how we stay healthy, as well as how we fall ill. You may have heard many cultural stories in your own home about staying healthy or ways to avoid illness. Some people are told that wearing a hat in cold weather is important because the head loses an enormous amount of heat, when in reality, any exposed parts of your body are places where heat is lost. If you wear a swimsuit in cold weather, for example, the exposed parts of your body will release heat at the same rate as the head. Some people are told to eat chicken soup when they are ill, because chicken soup is a cure. For others, boiling citrus in water is a drink to help cure various illnesses.

There are also many cultural differences about what might be considered something that needs medical attention. Increasingly, in the United States, for example, the loss of hair on men is seen as something that may require medicines, such as Rogaine (minoxidil) to help correct this "problem." The television show, *Atlanta Plastic,* highlights the use of medicine to solve other "problems" that may not be considered health care problems in other cultures. For example, is the need for breast augmentation a cultural issue? Or a health issue? Or both?

Lots of attention has been focused on obesity in the United States. Cultural attitudes about weight have changed over the years in the United States, as well as in cultures around the world. Once seen as a sign of wealth, today obesity is seen as a sign of medical disorder in need of medical treatment. The CDC has focused on the obesity epidemic in the United States and has communicated the health problems associated with obesity, including diabetes, some types of cancer, high blood pressure, and other health problems. The United States has one of the highest, but not the highest, obesity rates in the world. The CDC notes that obesity rates vary among cultural groups: "Non-Hispanic blacks have the highest age-adjusted rates of obesity (47.8 percent) followed by Hispanics (42.5 percent), non-Hispanic whites (32.6 percent), and non-Hispanic Asians (10.8 percent)."[35] States also vary in obesity rates with Arkansas, Mississippi, and West Virginia having the highest obesity rates. California, Colorado, District of Columbia, Hawaii, Massachusetts, and Vermont have the lowest obesity rates.[36] The CDC has additional information on other correlations with obesity, but it isn't clear what kinds of cultural changes need to occur to change the increasing rates of obesity. Two physicians, Dr. Jody Zylke and Dr. Howard Bauchner, note: "The obesity epidemic in the United States is now three decades old, and huge investments have been made in research, clinical care, and development of various programs to counteract obesity. However, few data suggest the epidemic is diminishing."[37] What kinds of communication strategies and communication campaigns might get U.S. Americans to change their culture to respond to this public health problem?

The debates over weight and what should be acceptable have been at the forefront of the **Fat Acceptance Movement,** a social movement that works to end discrimination against overweight people and the assumption that they are necessarily unhealthy or in need of medical treatment. A recent study from Liverpool University in Britain reports that discrimination and shaming overweight and obese people can cause people to eat to ease the hurt that comes from that kind of communication. Instead, "we now have some solid evidence to support the idea that fat acceptance and body love are inherently linked to shaping a more healthy and positive lifestyle."[38] Although we live in a culture flooded with images of beautiful people with thin bodies and overweight people are treated differently, once people come to accept their bodies and feel free from discrimination, they can and do turn to healthier lifestyles.

In the United States and many other westernized nations, the dominant model of medicine is based on biomedical science. All other approaches fall under the term, **complementary and integrative medicine**. There is no comprehensive list of all of the other ways that cultures around the world think about health care and medical care, but some of the major approaches to complementary health approaches include homeopathy, naturopathy, and traditional Chinese medicine. Acupuncture is one approach used in traditional Chinese medicine, and many patients report that it does work for them. The use of herbs is another aspect of traditional Chinese medicine. There are many other approaches that developed in China and are widely accepted in many Asian cultures.

There are too many other approaches to medicine that would fall under complementary medicine than we can list here, but they are also seen as equally valid approaches to health care. These other approaches are sometimes referred to as "complementary and integrative medicine." Currently, the National Institute of Health has a unit called the National Center for Complementary and Integrative Medicine that is focused on other approaches to health. See the Info Bites earlier in this chapter for more information. Some health care providers are more open than others to integrating these other approaches to health care into more conventional, Western, medicine. If you are interested in integrating some other approaches into your health care, it is important to communicate that desire with your physician and relevant health care providers.

## POWER IN COMMUNICATION ABOUT HEALTH CARE

There is often an imbalance of power in health communication situations. We examined the role of power in Chapter 2, but let's take a look at how it might function in communication in the health care context.

### Imbalances of Power in Health Communication

Communication between physician and patient is often marked by an imbalance in power with regard to medical knowledge and access to treatment. Patients, for example, may not have access to drugs without a written prescription from a physician. In order to get that prescription, the patient must rely on the physician,

**What Do You Think?**

Much of the communication about the Zika virus has focused on the need for pregnant women (or women who might become pregnant) to avoid getting the virus by not traveling to certain areas, using mosquito sprays and other strategies. One part of the strategy has been to avoid getting pregnant. As you watch the media coverage of the Zika virus, does it place more of the burden of dealing with Zika on women than men? Can men play a role in helping women avoid pregnancy?

Physician-patient communication reflects the power imbalance built into the health care structure in the United States. Physicians' power over patients includes medical knowledge and access to treatment, prescriptions, and tests.

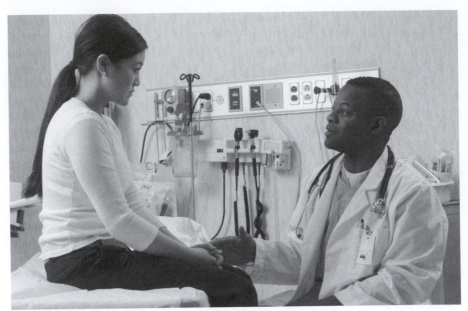

© Rubberball/age fotostock RF

who has the power to prescribe drugs. Physicians in health maintenance organizations (HMOs), which are increasingly common in the United States, can elect to refer or not refer patients to specialists. Physicians have power over patients in other ways as well. For example, they can recommend certain treatments (and not others), order medical tests, and otherwise determine what kind of treatment the patient receives.

This power imbalance is built into the health care structure in the United States, but physician–patient communication also reflects these power differences. For example, if Judith goes to see a physician for the first time, the physician may introduce herself by saying, "Hi Judith, my name is Doctor Tyndall." What would happen if Judith were to respond, "Hi Lisa, my name is Doctor Martin"? Some physicians would be amused, but others would be irritated by the perceived effort to challenge the power imbalance.

Note also the potential confusion of patients when they meet Dr. Tyndall. Who is Dr. Tyndall? Is she an intern? A staff physician? What role does she play in providing health care? And how many other health care professionals will the patient see today? Because patients may encounter many health care workers in a single day, cultural differences in communication may be exacerbated. The process of negotiating cultural differences may be especially difficult for the patient because each communication interaction may be brief.

### Health Care as a Business

It is important to remember that the health care industry in the United States is a huge business. The implications for patients have been the subject of heated public debates over the allocation of health care resources. One controversial issue is whether HMOs ration health care resources; obtaining such resources often is not easy or automatic.

Rising health care costs have had a huge impact on how we think about medical resources and their distribution. Health care systems around the world differ widely in how they are financed and what kinds of financial burdens are placed on patients and their families. In the United States, most people get health insurance from their employers, yet the costs are increasing for employers and employees. In this context, "Seven in 10 workers report their medical costs have gone up in the past two years, and the vast majority says the additional expenses are significant enough to force them to save less for retirement."[39] At the same time, medical debt is increasing as a factor in decisions to declare personal bankruptcy. Medical debt is often referred to collection agencies far faster than other types of debt.[40]

In response to growing costs and concerns about the U.S. health care system, President Obama signed the Patient Protection and Affordable Care Act into law on March 23, 2010. Although sometimes derided as "Obamacare," this act marks a major change in health coverage. It aims to reduce the number of uninsured (or under-insured) Americans and decreasing the rapid rise of health care costs overall. Many of these changes will take place over a number of years, and the U.S. Department of Health and Human Services has set up a website to explain all of the changes: www.healthcare.gov.

Patients from countries where health care is provided by the government may be confused by the private health care system in the United States. U.S. Americans, too, can become lost in the maze of rules and regulations governing the access to specialists and special treatments. Because there is a power imbalance at work here, patients need to recognize that HMOs and health insurance companies and other providers are businesses. It may not be enough simply to ask for many medical services, particularly higher-priced treatments.

Many people from other countries do not understand why the United States sees health care as a profitable business, as opposed to a civil right. One of our students, Katrina, says, "The healthcare system in America upsets me. People go bankrupt or put their families through bankruptcy just to survive while fighting painful, strenuous diseases, and illnesses. It is beyond ridiculous that insurance companies and healthcare companies make such big profits. Do they really care about the patients or making money? The healthcare system needs reform in a major way for society to truly be just." Another student from Sweden had a health issue and says that "despite the long wait and pain that I went through, we did not end up paying a dime. I realize now that if that happened to me while I was living in the U.S., my parents would have ended up paying a fortune, even if it was only for one night at the hospital." Our international students are often shocked by the high costs of health care in the United States and the U.S. cultural view that health care should be a capitalist enterprise, a big business. The consequences of this health care system are described by a student from Singapore: "I have heard a lot of stories about how bad the healthcare system is in the United States, and it is strange to think that people try to avoid going to clinics or hospitals in order to

## Pop Culture Spotlight

There are a number of television shows that feature medical settings, including *Private Practice, Royal Pains,* and *Chicago Med.* Medical settings have long been favorite settings for television shows, such as *General Hospital, Dr. Welby, MD,* and *M\*A\*S\*H.* What is our cultural fascination with this type of work setting? What kinds of cultural issues arise in these shows in the depictions of illness, death, birth, and families? How many of the encounters involve intercultural issues, and how are they handled?

avoid paying huge bills." Because health care in Singapore is heavily subsidized by the government, the idea of people going bankrupt because of health needs seems unthinkable, culturally incomprehensible, to her.

In June 2016, the worst mass shooting in U.S. history took place at the Pulse nightclub in Orlando, Florida. Because the shooting took place in the United States and in Florida, a state that has not expanded Medicaid coverage, the medical costs for the victims became an issue quickly and websites were set up to help defray these costs almost immediately. While it is impossible to know the complete medical costs for this mass shooting, estimates run into the millions of dollars. Mario Perez who was shot and taken to Orlando Regional Medical Center emergency room received a bill of $20,000 from the emergency department (which does not include the costs of specialists, x-rays, or other tests). He had no health insurance and, therefore, no money for follow-up care. His GoFundMe page has "only raised about $600." The Orlando Regional Medical Center "received 44 of the shooting victims. A hospital spokeswoman says some patients have insurance coverage, some don't. The hospital is going to look for payment sources from the community or the state, such as victim funds that are raising money across the country. But she says the hospital expects unreimbursed costs of more than $5 million."[41] On top of the many issues that survivors and their families will have to deal with in the coming years, the medical costs will be a part of that journey.

## Intercultural Ethics and Health Issues

What are the ethics of health care communication? In the physician–patient relationship, the physician has far more information than the patient, and the ethics are complicated, particularly in intercultural situations. With regard to communication ethics in health care, physicians can give information about the patient's health within four general frameworks: (1) strict paternalism, (2) benevolent deception, (3) contractual honesty, and (4) unmitigated honesty.[42]

**Strict paternalism** reflects a physician's decision to provide misinformation to the patient when the physician believes it is in the best interests of the patient. If a patient has terminal cancer, for example, the physician may not feel it would be helpful to tell the patient that he or she has high blood pressure as well. **Benevolent deception** occurs when the physician chooses to communicate only a part of a patient's diagnosis. For example, a patient might be told that she or he has cancer and that treatments are available, but not be told that the prognosis is very poor. **Contractual honesty** refers to the practice of telling the patient only what she or he wants to hear or to know. For example, if a patient says, "I only want to hear about the treatments available to me, but not my chances of survival," a physician may choose to follow the patient's wishes. Finally, **unmitigated honesty** refers to when a physician chooses to communicate the entire diagnosis to a patient. Some health care professionals prefer this communication route as a protection against lawsuits. However, some patients are put off by the bluntness of this approach. For instance, if a physician told

© 123RF

After a mass shooting that resulted in many dead and wounded, we sometimes overlook the healthcare costs that will follow. After the shooting at the Pulse nightclub in Orlando, the victims and the hospital faced enormous medical bills. The way that the U.S. health care system functions is not the same around the world. What is the best way to cover these medical bills?

a patient that some very expensive and painful treatments were available but the patient probably wouldn't survive anyway, that patient might be justifiably upset.

The fear of malpractice suits guides many decisions related to ethics. Sometimes health care organizations use **ethics committees**—often staffed by health care professionals, religious leaders, and social workers—to help make decisions about ethics.[43] In the intercultural context, these decisions can be complex. In some cultures, the family is intimately involved in the health care and medical treatment of its members. In other cultures, medical information is confidential and is given only to the patient, unless he or she is incapacitated or incapable of understanding. Knowing the appropriate way to communicate with patient and family is not easy. For example, some patients may not want their families involved in their care if they have a miscarriage, are suffering from colon-rectal cancer, or are depressed. And many medical procedures are very controversial, even among members of the same culture.

In early 2014, Brittany Maynard was diagnosed with "stage 4 malignant brain tumor" and, after researching her options, she and her husband "moved from California to Oregon to gain access to the state's death-with-dignity law. Oregon is one of five states with such legal protections."[44] In the remaining months of her life, she became an advocate for the right to die. As her condition deteriorated, she made the decision to end her life. In November 2014, she said her goodbyes and took the medication and died peacefully. Aside from some states in the United States, euthanasia is legal in a number of countries, including Belgium, the Netherlands,

## Info Bites

In 2015, Martin Shkreli, CEO of Turing Pharmaceuticals, raised the price of Daraprim (a drug used for toxoplasmosis which can be fatal to HIV patients) from $13.50 per pill to $750. Outrage over the price increase led to a Congressional Hearing in which Shkreli refused to answer questions. In the United States, there is nothing illegal about pharmaceutical companies raising prices

*(continued)*

Albania, Japan, Colombia, and Canada. The debate over euthanasia and the ethical issues involved will likely continue to be contested in a number of other U.S. states and countries around the world.

In some religious systems, **euthanasia,** which involves ending the life of a terminally ill patient, is seen as suicide and therefore is unacceptable. In other religions, euthanasia is acceptable for terminally ill patients. Key issues include how much control a patient should have in this situation, how much power a physician should have if his or her ethical framework differs from the patient's, and how much power the state should have in making laws preventing or permitting euthanasia.

## SUMMARY

In this chapter, we examined a number of issues relevant to intercultural communication and health care. Intercultural communication is becoming more important in health care as the population becomes more culturally diverse. Communication is vitally important to the functioning of health services, and this communication is not simply between patient and physician.

We also looked at barriers to effective health care. The history of differential medical treatment and medical studies has created mistrust among some cultural groups. The Tuskegee Syphilis Project and the AIDS epidemic are two examples of how and why groups can come to mistrust the health care system. Many health care providers and patients also hold prejudicial ideologies that can create barriers to effective treatment and to the provision of health care resources. In addition, religious beliefs can also present communication and health care challenges.

Finally, we turned to the issue of power in health communication. There is an imbalance of power between physician and patient, as well as an imbalance of power between patients and the health maintenance organizations. Four ethical approaches to health issues are strict paternalism, benevolent deception, contractual honesty, and unmitigated honesty.

## BUILDING INTERCULTURAL SKILLS

1. Reflect on the history of your own family and traditional health care. Do you have many family members who are health care professionals? Did you grow up going to the doctor frequently? How much trust do you have in physicians?

2. Think about how you communicate to others in health care situations. As a patient, do you realize the importance of your communication to the physician or nurse in the diagnosis and treatments you receive? How might you better communicate your health situation to health care professionals? What kinds of cultural attitudes about various health issues do you hold that could be barriers to more effective communication? For example, have you been raised to be ashamed to ask questions about certain parts of your body?

3. Think about how health care professionals communicate with you. If you have a serious illness that may require much interaction with a physician, for example, is this someone whom you can trust?

4. Think about how health care professionals might encourage more open communication from patients so that they can receive better health care.

## ACTIVITIES

1. *The media and health care:* Watch the news media for coverage of health issues as they relate to the most affected cultural groups. For example, is AIDS still framed as a "gay disease"? Is the Ebola virus portrayed as an African illness? In what ways does the conflation of the cultural group with the disease create misunderstandings?

2. *Communication about health care:* Talk to a health care professional about his or her experiences with cultural differences in communication. What were the main problems in the communication process? What suggestions might you make to avoid these problems in the future?

## ENDNOTES

1. Pauwels, A. (1995). *Cross-cultural communication in the health sciences.* South Melbourne, Australia: Macmillan Education Australia, p. 3.

2. Quoted in Edlin, M. (2012). Cultural competency means better patience service. *Drug Topics, 156*(6), 18.

3. Aoki, N., Uda, K., Ohta, S., Kiuchi, T., & Fukui, T. (2008). Impact of miscommunication in medical dispute cases in Japan. *International Journal for Quality in Health Care, 20*(5), 358–362.

4. Bernstein, N. (2005, April 21). Language barrier called health hazard in E.R. *New York Times,* p. B8.

5. Sharif, I., Lo, S., & Ozuah, P. O. (2006). Availability of Spanish prescription labels. *Journal of Health Care for the Poor and Underserved, 17*(1), 67.

6. Sharif et al. (2006), p. 67.

7. Fadiman, A. (1997). *The spirit catches you and you fall down: A Hmong child, her American doctors, and the collision of two cultures.* New York, NY: Farrar, Straus and Giroux.

8. Northouse, L. L., & Northouse, P. G. (1998). *Health communication: Strategies for health professionals.* Stamford, CT: Appleton & Lange, p. 103.

9. Kpanake, L., Sorum, P. C., & Mullet, E. (2016). Breaking bad news to Togolese patients. *Health Communication, 31*(11), 1311–1317.

10. U.S. Department of Health and Human Services. (n.d.). HIPAA for individuals: Family members and friends. Retrieved from http://www.hhs.gov/hipaa/for-individuals/family-members-friends/index.html.

11. Bahjati-Sabet, A., & Chambers, N. A. (2005). People of Iranian descent. In N. Waxler-Morrison, J. M. Anderson, E. Richardson, & N. A. Chambers (Eds.), *Cross-cultural caring: A handbook for health professionals* (2nd ed., pp. 127–161). Vancouver, BC: University of British Columbia Press.

12. Ford, L. A., & Yep, G. A. (2003). Working along the margins: Developing community-based strategies for communicating about health with marginalized groups. In T. L. Thompson, A. M. Dorsey, K. I. Miller, & R. Parrott (Eds.), *Handbook of health communication* (pp. 241–261). Mahwah, NJ: Erlbaum, p. 253.

13. Arnst, C. (2006, May 29). Health as a birthright. *BusinessWeek,* p. 20.

14. Lovejoy, B. (2014, May 6). Meet Grandison Harris, the grave robber enslaved (and then employed) by the Georgia medical college. *Smithsonian Magazine*. Retrieved July 30, 2016, from http://www.smithsonianmag.com/history/meet-grandison-harris-grave-robber-enslaved-and-then-employed-georgia-college-medicine-180951344/?no-ist.

15. Shilling, C. (1993). *The body and social theory*. Newbury Park, CA: Sage, p. 58.

16. See, for example, Gilman, S. L. (1985). *Difference and pathology: Stereotypes of sexuality, race and madness*. Ithaca, NY: Cornell University Press; Gilman, S. L. (1988). *Disease and representation: Images of illness from madness to AIDS*. Ithaca, NY: Cornell University Press; Harding, S. G. (Ed.). (1993). The *"racial" economy of science: Toward a democratic future*. Bloomington, IL: Indiana University Press; Harding, S. G. (1998). *Is science multicultural? Postcolonialism, feminisms, and epistemologies*. Bloomington, IL: Indiana University Press; Mondimore, F. M. (1996). *A natural history of homosexuality*. Baltimore, MD: Johns Hopkins University Press; Stoler, A. L. (1995). *Race and the education of desire*. Durham, NC: Duke University Press.

17. Solomon, M. (1985). The rhetoric of dehumanization: An analysis of medical reports of the Tuskegee Syphilis Project. *Western Journal of Speech Communication*, *49*, 233–247.

18. Scherer, C. W., & Juanillo, N. K., Jr. (2003). The continuing challenge of community health risk management and communication. In Thompson, Dorsey, Miller, & Parrott, p. 228.

19. Boulware, L. E., Cooper, L. A., Ratner, L. E., LaVeist, T. A., & Powe, N. R. (2003, July–August). Race and trust in the health care system. *Public Health Reports*, *118*, 363–364.

20. Kreps, G. L. (2006). Communication and racial inequalities in health care. *American Behavioral Scientist*, *49*, 1–15.

21. Olshansky, S. J., et al. (2012). Differences in life expectancy due to race and educational differences are widening, and many may not catch up. *Health Affairs*, *31*(8), 1803–1813.

22. Levi, J. (1992). Homophobia and AIDS public policy. In W. J. Blumenfeld (Ed.), *Homophobia: How we all pay the price* (pp. 217–232). Boston, MA: Beacon Press, p. 217.

23. Gross, L. (1993). *Contested closets: The politics and ethics of outing*. Minneapolis, MN: University of Minnesota Press, p. 34.

24. Northouse & Northouse (1998), pp. 288–289.

25. Robison, P. (2014, May 14). The CIA stops fake vaccinations as real polio rebounds. *Bloomberg Businessweek*. Retrieved July 30, 2016, from http://www.bloomberg.com/news/articles/2014-05-21/the-cia-stops-fake-vaccinations-as-real-polio-rebounds.

26. Sun, L. H. (2014, May 19). CIA: No more vaccination campaigns in spy operations. *The Washington Post*. Retrieved July 30, 2016, from https://www.washingtonpost.com/world/national-security/cia-no-more-vaccination-campaigns-in-spy-operations/2014/05/19/406c4f3e-df88-11e3-8dcc-d6b7fede081a_story.html?tid=pm_pop.

27. Aldridge, D. (2000). *Spirituality, healing and medicine: Return to the silence*. Philadelphia, PA: Jessica Kingsley.

28. Kalb, C. (2003, November 10). Faith & healing. *Newsweek*, p. 44.

29. Kalb (2003, November 10), pp. 55–56.

30. Kalb (2003, November 10), p. 54.

31. Koenig, H. G., McCullough, M. E., & Larson, D. B. (2001). *Handbook of religion and health*. Oxford: Oxford University Press.

32. Kalb (2003, November 10), p. 54.

33. Sloan, R. P. (2003, November 10). 'Religion is a private matter.' Interview with C. Kalb. *Newsweek*, p. 50.

34. Sloan, R. P. (2000, January/February). Religion, spirituality and medicine. *Freethought Today*. Retrieved from http://www.ffrf.org/fttoday/jan_feb00/sloan.html.

35. Centers for Disease Control and Prevention. (2015, September 21). Adult obesity facts. Retrieved July 30, 2016, from https://www.cdc.gov/obesity/data/adult.html.

36. Centers for Disease Control and Prevention. (2016, July 1). Obesity prevalence maps. Retrieved July 30, 2016, from https://www.cdc.gov/obesity/data/prevalence-maps.html.

37. Quoted in Fox, M. (2016, June 7). America's obesity epidemic hits a new high. *CNBC*. Retrieved July 30, 2016, from http://www.cnbc.com/2016/06/07/americas-obesity-epidemic-hits-a-new-high.html.

38.  Hayden, F. (2015, August 5). Finally, a study that confirms what I knew all along: Far acceptance is good for our health. *The Independent*. Retrieved July 30, 2016, from http://www.independent .co.uk/voices/finally-a-study-that-confirms-what-i-knew-all-along-fat-acceptance-is-good-for-our -health-10440615.html.

39.  Kadlec, D. (2016, April 13). How rising health care costs are wrecking retirement savings. *Time*. Retrieved July 30, 2016, from http://time.com/money/4287323/health-care-costs-wreck-retirement -savings/.

40.  Carrins, A. (2011, August 18). Medical debt cited more often in bankruptcies. *New York Times*. Retrieved September 5, 2012, from http://bucks.blogs.nytimes.com/2011/08/18/medical-debt -cited-more-often-in-bankruptcies/.

41.  Aboraya, A. (2016, July 30). The costs of the Pulse nightclub shooting. *NPR*. Retrieved July 30, 2016, from http://www.npr.org/sections/health-shots/2016/07/30/486491527/the-costs-of-the -pulse-nightclub-shooting.

42.  Pauwels (1995), p. 272.

43.  Kreps, G. L., & Kunimoto, E. N. (1994). *Effective communication in multicultural health care settings*. Thousand Oaks, CA: Sage, pp. 67–69.

44.  Bever, L. (2014, November 2). Brittany Maynard, as promised, ends her life at 29. *The Washington Post*. Retrieved July 30, 2016, from https://www.washingtonpost.com/news/morning -mix/wp/2014/11/02/brittany-maynard-as-promised-ends-her-life-at-29/.

# Glossary

**accommodating style** Emphasizes an indirect approach for dealing with conflict and a more emotionally restrained manner.

**adaptors** Gestures related to managing our emotions.

**adventure tourism** Involves travel remote or exotic destinations for the purpose of engaging in a rugged outdoor activities.

**affirmative action (AA)** Statutes that attempt to stop discrimination by encouraging the hiring of minorities and women.

**Afrocentric** An orientation toward African or African American cultural standards, including beliefs and values, as the criteria for interpreting behaviors and attitudes.

**age identity** The identification with the cultural conventions of how we should act, look, and behave according to our age.

**AIDS** Acquired immune deficiency syndrome; a disease caused by a virus, HIV, transmitted through sexual or blood contact, that attacks the immune system. (See **HIV.**)

**Alaska Native and Native Hawaiian—Serving Institution** Higher education institution designated by U.S. Department of Education and has at least 20 percent Alaska Native or 10 percent Native Hawaiian enrollments.

**Americans with Disabilities Act (ADA)** A law requiring that places of business make "reasonable" accommodations for employees with physical disabilities.

**anti-Americanism** Negative ideas, feelings, and sometimes actions against the United States, most often the U.S. government.

**argot** A nonstandard way of communicating that separates insiders from outsiders of a coculture.

**Asian American and Native American Pacific Islander—Serving Institution** Higher education institution with at least 10 percent Asian American or Native Pacific Islander enrollment and at least 50 percent of the students are economically disadvantaged.

**assimilable** The degree of participation in a type of cultural adaptation in which an individual gives up his or her own cultural heritage and adopts the mainstream cultural identity.

**authenticity** In tourism, the search for "real" cultural experiences very different from the tourist's everyday life.

**back translation** The process of translating a document that has already been translated into a foreign language back to the original language—preferably by an independent translator.

**benevolent deception** Withholding information from a patient, ostensibly for his or her own good.

**bilingual** Able to speak two languages fluently or at least competently.

**blog** Web log; website, like a journal, maintained by an individual with regular entries of commentary, descriptions of events or other material such as graphics or video.

**boundary maintenance** The regulation of interaction between hosts and tourists.

**bullying** Repeated or potentially repeated unwanted, aggressive behavior among school children involving power imbalances.

**class identity** A sense of belonging to a group that shares similar economic, occupational, or social status.

**class structure** The economic organization of income levels in a society; the structure that defines upper, middle, lower, and other social classes.

**cocultural group** Nondominant cultural groups that exist in a national culture—for example, African American or Chinese American.

**code switching** Changing from one language or communication style to another.

**collectivism** The tendency to focus on the goals, needs, and views of the ingroup rather than individuals' own goals, needs, and views. (Compare with **individualism.**)

**colonial education system** Schools established by colonial powers in colonized regions. They often forbade the use of native languages and discussion of native cultures.

**colonial histories** The histories that legitimate international invasions and annexations.

**communication** A symbolic process whereby reality is produced, maintained, repaired, and transformed.

**communication style** The metamessage that contextualizes how listeners are expected to accept and interpret verbal messages.

**complementarity** A principle of relational attraction suggesting that sometimes we are attracted to people who are different from us.

**complementary and integrative medicine** Health and medical care that are not based on Western, or conventional, medicine. Complementary medicine is used in place of conventional medical approaches, while integrative medicine is incorporated into conventional medical approaches.

**compromise style** A style of interaction for an intercultural couple in which both partners give up some part of their own cultural habits and beliefs to minimize cross-cultural differences. (Compare with **consensus style, obliteration style,** and **submission style.**)

**conflict** The interference between two or more interdependent individuals or groups of people who perceive incompatible goals, values, or expectations in attaining those ends.

**consensus style** A style of interaction for an intercultural couple in which partners deal with cross-cultural differences by negotiating their relationship. (Compare with **compromise style, obliteration style,** and **submission style.**)

**constructive identity** An identity that is actively negotiated from various cultures in contact and that often creates feelings of a new multicultural identity.

**contact cultures** Cultural groups in which people tend to stand close together and touch frequently when they interact—for example, cultural groups in South America, the Middle East, and southern Europe. (See **noncontact cultures.**)

**contact hypothesis** Intercultural contacts can result in more positive and tolerant attitudes toward other cultural groups, but only under very specific conditions.

**context** The physical or social situation in which communication occurs.

**contractual honesty** Telling a patient only what he or she wants to know.

**cosmopolitans** People who view themselves as citizens of the world and are responsible to each other.

**cross-cultural training** Workshops that teach the knowledge, skill and motivation to communicate effectively and appropriately in a variety of cultural, usually international, contexts.

**cross-cultural trainers** Trainers who teach people to become familiar with other cultural norms and to improve their interactions with people of different cultures.

**cultural contact** When two or more cultures come together, sometimes on an individual basis, but often through larger social migrations, wars, and other displacements.

**cultural group histories** The history of each cultural group within a nation that includes, for example, the history of where the group originated, why the people migrated, and how they came to develop and maintain their cultural traits.

**cultural identities** Who we are as influenced by the cultures to which we belong.

**cultural imperialism** Domination through the spread of cultural products.

**cultural space** The particular configuration of the communication that constructs meanings of various places.

**cultural texts** Cultural artifacts (magazines, TV programs, movies, and so on) that convey cultural norms, values, and beliefs.

**culture** Learned patterns of behavior and attitudes shared by a group of people.

**culture industries** Industries that produce and sell popular culture as commodities.

**culture shock** A relatively short-term feeling of disorientation and discomfort due to the lack of familiar cues in the environment.

**cultural tourism** A type of tourism that emphasizes learning the history, language, and/or unique cultural aspects of a destination.

**deception** The act of making someone believe what is not true.

**demographics** The characteristics of a population, especially as classified by age, sex, and income.

**diaspora** A massive migration, often caused by war or famine or persecution, that results in the dispersal of a unified group.

**diasporic histories** The histories of the ways in which international cultural groups were created through transnational migrations, slavery, religious crusades, or other historical forces.

**direct approach** Emphasizes that conflict is fundamentally a good thing and should be approached head on.

**discrimination** Behaviors resulting from stereotypes or prejudice that cause some people to be denied equal participation or rights based on cultural group membership (such as race).

**discussion style** Combines the direct and emotionally restrained dimensions and emphasizes a verbally direct approach for dealing with disagreements.

**diversity training** Workshops that teach knowledge, skill and motivation for working effectively across cultural (e.g., racial, ethnic, gender, sexual orientation, physical abilities) and power differences, usually in domestic (U.S.) contexts.

**dynamic style** Uses an indirect style of communicating along with a more emotionally intense expressiveness.

**ecotourism** Tourism of sites of environmental or natural interest.

**electronic colonialism** Domination or exploitation utilizing technological forms.

**emblems** Gestures that have a specific verbal translation.

**embodied ethnocentrism** Feeling comfortable and familiar in the spaces, behaviors, and actions of others in our own cultural surroundings.

**emotionally expressive style** Conflict style where intense and overt displays of emotions are valued during discussion of disagreements.

**encapsulated identity** An identity that is torn between different cultural identities and that often creates feelings of ambiguity.

**enclaves** Regions that are surrounded by another country's territory; cultural minority groups that live within a larger cultural group's territory.

**engagement style** Emphasizes a verbally direct and confrontational approach to dealing with conflict.

**equal employment opportunity (EEO)** Laws against discrimination in the workplace.

**equivalency** An issue in translation, the condition of being equal in meaning, value, quantity, and so on.

**ethics** Principles of conduct that help govern behaviors of individuals and groups.

**ethics committees** Groups that provide guidance in making health care decisions; usually composed of health care professionals, administrators, lawyers, social workers, members of the religious community, and patient representatives.

**ethnic histories** The histories of ethnic groups.

**ethnic identity** A set of ideas about one's own ethnic group membership; a sense of belonging to a particular group and knowing something about the shared experience of the group.

**ethnocentrism** An orientation toward one's own ethnic group; often a tendency to elevate one's own culture above others.

**Eurocentric** The assumption of the centrality or superiority of European culture.

**euthanasia** The ending of the life of a terminally ill patient.

**eye contact** A nonverbal code that communicates meanings about respect and status and often regulates turn taking during interactions.

**facework** Specific communication strategies used to maintain our own face or other people's faces.

**facial expressions** Facial gestures that convey emotions and attitudes.

**facilitated intergroup dialogue** A peace-building approach developed by Benjamin Broome that involves listening and speaking, not to persuade, but to clarify. It is built on the premise that government officials cannot alone negotiate a true piece in situations of long-standing conflict but rather civic leaders and the general public must also be involved.

**family histories** The body of knowledge shared by family members and the customs, rituals, and stories passed from one generation to another within a family.

**Fat Acceptance Movement** A social movement that works to end discrimination against overweight people and the assumption that they are necessarily unhealthy or in need of medical treatment.

**folk culture** Traditional culture that is not practiced for financial profit.

**friendships** Personal, nonromantic relationships that have culture-specific definitions.

**gay relationships** Same-sex romantic relationships.

**gender histories** The histories of how cultural conventions of men and women are created, maintained, and/or altered.

**gender identity** The identification with the cultural notions of masculinity and femininity and what it means to be a man or a woman.

**gestures** Nonverbal communication involving hand and arm movements.

**global nomads (third culture kids)** People who grow up in many different cultural contexts because their parents relocated.

**globalization** The increasing tendency toward international connections in media, business, and culture.

**grand narrative** A unified history and view of humankind.

**HBCUs** Historically Black colleges and universities.

**health care professionals** Physicians, nurses, and all the other medical staff with whom patients in the health care system come into contact.

**heterogeneity** Consisting of different or dissimilar elements.

**hidden histories** The histories that are hidden from or forgotten by the mainstream representations of past events.

**high-context communication** A style of communication in which much of the information is contained in the contexts and nonverbal cues rather than expressed explicitly in words. (Compare with **low-context communication.**)

**HIPAA** Health Insurance Portability and Accountability Act that includes, among other federal guidelines, strict privacy rules regarding patient health information.

**Hispanic-serving institution** One type of Minority-Serving Institution and must have 25 percent Hispanic student enrollment, among other criteria.

**HIV** Human immunodeficiency virus. (See **AIDS.**)

**home** The immediate cultural context for our upbringing; where we have lived.

*Homo narrans* A Latin term used to describe the story-telling tendencies of human beings.

**host** Residents of a tourist region.

**hyphenated Americans** Americans who identify not only with being American citizens but also with being members of ethnic groups.

**identity** The concept of who we are. Characteristics of identity may be understood differently depending on the perspectives that people take (e.g., social psychological, communication, or critical perspectives).

**illustrators** Gestures that go along with and refer to speech.

**immigration** Movement to a new country, region, or environment to settle more or less permanently.

**improvised performance** A way of thinking about intercultural interaction in which two people are making up a performance as they go along.

**incompatibility** A state of incongruity in goals, values, or expectations between two or more individuals.

**indirect approach** Emphasizes that conflict should be avoided.

**individualism** The tendency to emphasize individual identities, beliefs, needs, goals, and views rather than those of the group. (Compare with **collectivism.**)

**indulgence** The cultural tendency to allow relatively free gratification of needs related to enjoying life and having fun; value freedom of speech over maintaining order.

**intellectual histories** Written histories that focus on the development of ideas.

**intercultural communication** The interaction between people from different cultural backgrounds.

**intercultural conflict** The perceived or real incompatibility of goals, values, or expectations between two parties from different cultures.

**intercultural dating** The pursuit of a romantic intercultural relationship.

**intercultural relationships** Relationships that are formed between individuals from different cultures.

**interdependent** A state of mutual influence; the action or behavior of one individual affecting the other person in a relationship.

**interlanguage** The form of language that emerges when a nonnative speaker overlaps his or her native grammar or structure onto another language.

**intermediary** In a formal setting, a professional third party, such as a lawyer, real estate agent, or counselor, who intervenes when two parties are in conflict. Informal intermediaries may be friends or colleagues who intervene.

**international conflict** Conflict that occurs on the international level, often between nations.

**international negotiations** The process of two national groups (who have common and conflicting interests) resolving conflicts to a mutually satisfactory end.

**international students** Students attending high school or college in another country. (See **study-abroad programs.**)

**interpersonal allies** People, often friends, who work for better interpersonal and intergroup relations.

**interpersonal conflict** Conflict that occurs between individuals rather than groups or nations.

**interpretation** The process of verbally expressing what is said or written in another language.

**intimacy** The extent of emotional closeness.

**language** A means of communication using shared symbols.

**language acquisition** The process of learning language.

**language policies** Laws or customs that determine which language will be spoken when and where.

**learning styles** The different ways students learn in different cultures.

**low-context communication** A style of communication in which much of the information is conveyed in words rather than in nonverbal cues and contexts. (Compare with **high-context communication.**)

**macrocontexts** The political, social, and historical situations, backgrounds, and environments that influence communication.

**majority identity development** The development of a sense of belonging to a dominant group.

*maquiladoras* A Mexican term indicating assembly plants or factories (mainly of U.S. companies) established on the U.S.–Mexico border and using mainly Mexican labor.

*masculinity/femininity value* A cultural variability dimension that concerns the degree of being feminine—valuing fluid gender roles, quality of life, service, relationships, and interdependence—and the degree of being masculine—emphasizing distinctive gender roles, ambition, materialism, and independence.

**media imperialism** Domination or control through media.

**mediation** The act of resolving conflict by having someone intervene between two parties.

**medical jargon** Medical terminology, especially that which is confusing or difficult for the layperson to understand.

**medical miscommunication** Misunderstandings that arise in the medical context due to communication problems.

**medical terminology** A set of scientific words and phrases used by doctors to precisely describe illness.

**melting pot** A metaphor that assumes that immigrants and cultural minorities will be assimilated into the U.S. majority culture, losing their original cultures.

**mentoring** A partnership where one person shares knowledge, skills, information, and perspective to foster the personal and professional growth of someone else.

**migrating** When an individual leaves the primary cultural context in which he or she was raised and moves to a new cultural context for an extended period of time.

**minority identity development** The development of a sense of belonging to a nondominant group.

**Minority-Serving Institution** Refers to higher education institutions recognized by the U.S. Department of Education as having a history and mission of serving minority students.

**MMORPGs** (Massively Text-based Multiplayer Online Games) Participants interact with environments, objects, and other participants.

**mobility** The state of moving from place to place.

**monochronic** An orientation to time that assumes it is linear and is a commodity that can be lost or gained.

**multicultural identity** A sense of in-betweenness that develops as a result of frequent or multiple cultural border crossings.

**multilingual** The ability to speak more than two languages fluently or at least competently.

**multinational** Companies that have operations in two or more nations.

**multiracial and multicultural people** People whose heritage draws from more than one racial or cultural group.

**national histories** Bodies of knowledge based on past events that influenced countries' development.

**national identity** National citizenship.

**Native American–Serving Nontribal Institution** Unlike Tribal Colleges or Universities, these higher education institutions are not controlled by any tribe and have at least 10 percent Native American enrollment.

**neighborhood** Living area defined by its cultural identity, especially an ethnic or racial one.

**noncontact cultures** Cultural groups in which people tend to maintain more space and touch less often than people do in contact cultures. Great Britain and Japan tend to have noncontact cultures. (See **contact cultures.**)

**nonverbal codes** Systems for understanding the meanings of nonverbal behavior, including personal space, eye contact, facial expressions, gestures, time orientation, and silence.

**nonverbal communication** Communication through means other than language—for example, facial expressions and clothing.

**obliteration style** A style of interaction for an intercultural couple in which both partners attempt to erase their individual cultures in dealing with cultural differences. (Compare with **compromise style, consensus style,** and **submission style.**)

**pacifism** Opposition to the use of force under any circumstances.

**peacebuilding** A process of working toward equilibrium and stability in a society so that new disputes do not escalate into violence and war.

**perception** The process by which we select, organize, and interpret external and internal stimuli to create our view of the world.

**personal identity** A person's notions of self.

**personal space** The immediate area around a person, invasion of which may provoke discomfort or offense.

**phonology** The study of speech sounds.

**physical ability identity** A knowledge of self based on characteristics related to the body, either more permanent or temporary—for example, sight, hearing, and weight.

**physical appearance** An important nonverbal code that includes physical characteristics like height, weight, and body shape, as well as personal grooming.

**physical attraction** Sexual desire based on the appearance of another.

**political conflict** Conflict that happens at the societal level over political issues.

**political histories** Written histories that focus on political events.

**polychronic** An orientation to time that sees it as circular and more holistic.

**popular culture** Forms of contemporary culture that are made popular by and for the people through their mass consumption of these products. Those systems or artifacts that most people share and that most people know about, including television, music, videos, and popular magazines.

**postcolonialism** An intellectual, political, and cultural movement that calls for the independence of once colonized states and also liberation from colonialist ways of thinking.

**power** A state of differential levels of societal and structural privilege.

**power distance** A cultural variability dimension that concerns the extent to which people accept an unequal distribution of power.

**pragmatics** The study of how meaning is constructed in relation to receivers and how language is actually used in particular contexts in language communities.

**prejudice** An attitude (usually negative) toward a cultural group based on little or no evidence.

**prejudicial ideologies** Sets of ideas that rely on stereotypes.

**racial and ethnic identity** Identifying with a particular racial or ethnic group. Although in the past racial groups were classified on the basis of biological characteristics, most scientists now recognize that race is constructed in fluid social and historical contexts.

**racial histories** The histories of nonmainstream racial groups.

**reader profiles** Portrayals of readership demographics prepared by magazines.

**regionalism** Loyalty to a particular region that holds significant cultural meaning for that person.

**regulators** Gestures used to guide the flow of a conversation, especially for turn taking.

**relational messages** Messages (verbal and nonverbal) that express how we feel about others.

**relativist position** The view that the particular language we speak, especially the structure of the language, shapes our perception of reality and cultural patterns. (Compare with **nominalist position** and **qualified relativist position.**)

**religious conflicts** Conflicts that arise from strongly held views and religious beliefs.

**religious freedom** The ability to practice one's religion without fear; a concern among health care professionals who worry about engaging in religious issues.

**religious histories** Bodies of knowledge containing the items of faith and that faith's prescriptions for action that have been important for a cultural group.

**religious identity** A sense of belonging to a religious group.

**resistance** Avoiding intrusions; may take fairly passive forms or more assertive forms.

**restraint** The cultural tendency to suppress gratification of needs and regulate it by strict social norms; value maintaining order over freedom of speech.

**restraint style** Conflict style where disagreements are best discussed in an emotionally calm manner.

**retreatism** The avoidance of tourists by hosts.

**revitalization** The economic benefits associated with tourism in certain areas.

**romantic relationships** Intimate relationships that comprise love, involvement, sharing, openness, connectedness, and so on.

**self-awareness** Related to intercultural communication competence; the quality of knowing how you are perceived as a communicator, as well as your strengths and weaknesses.

**self-reflexivity** A process of learning to understand ourselves and our own position in society.

**semantics** The study of words and meanings.

**sexual orientation histories** The historical experiences of gays and lesbians.

**silence** The absence of verbal messages.

**similarity principle** A principle of relational attraction suggesting that we tend to be attracted to people whom we perceive to be similar to ourselves.

**social conflict** Conflict that arises from unequal or unjust social relationships between groups.

**social histories** Written histories that focus on everyday life experiences of various groups in the past.

**social movements** Organized activities in which individuals work together to bring about social change.

**social positions** The places from which we speak that are socially constructed, and thus embedded with assumptions about gender, race, class, age, social roles, sexuality, and so on.

**social roles** Roles we enact that are learned in a culture—for example, mother, big brother, and community leader.

**socially responsible tourism** Tourism that emphasizes positive economic, social, cultural, and environmental impacts from the tourism industry.

**socioeconomic class histories** Bodies of knowledge relating to a group's relationship to social class and economic forces.

**source text** The original language text of a translation. (See also **target text.**)

**staged authenticity** When local people alter their cultural performances to meet tourist expectations, the resulting representation of the local culture is not authentic.

**status** The relative position an individual holds in social or organizational settings.

**stereotypes** Widely held beliefs about a group of people.

**stereotyping** The use of stereotypes.

**strict paternalism** A physician's provision of misinformation for the supposed benefit of the patient.

**study-abroad programs** University-sponsored programs that give course credit for study in other countries.

**submission style** A style of interaction for an intercultural couple in which one partner yields to the other partner's cultural patterns, abandoning or denying his or her own culture. (Compare with **compromise style, consensus style,** and **obliteration style.**)

**syntactics** The study of the structure, or grammar, of a language.

**target text** The new language text into which the original language text is translated. (See also **source text.**)

**teaching styles** The different ways teachers teach in different cultures.

**third culture style** A new communication style that results from two people trying to adapt to each other's styles.

**third culture kids (TCKs)** Children who develop multicultural identities because they grow up in many different cultural contexts.

**tourists** Visitors to another country or region.

**transgender relationships** Refers to relationships with transgender people whether among themselves or with non-transgender people.

**translation** The process of producing a written text that refers to something said or written in another language.

**traveling** The changing of cultural spaces through locomotion.

**Tribal College or University** Higher education institution typically controlled by a federally recognized tribe or categorized in this definition under federal law.

**Tuskegee Syphilis Project** A government-sponsored study of syphilis in which treatment of the disease was withheld from African American males for the purpose of establishing an experimental control group.

**U-curve theory** A theory of cultural adaptation positing that migrants go through fairly predictable phases (excitement/anticipation, shock/disorientation, and adaptation) in adapting to a new cultural situation.

**uncertainty avoidance** A cultural variability dimension that concerns the extent to which uncertainty, ambiguity, and deviant ideas and behaviors are avoided.

**universalist position** An ethical approach that emphasizes the similarity of beliefs across cultures—for example, killing within the group or treason.

**unmitigated honesty** A physician's communication of the entirety of a medical diagnosis to a patient.

**values** A system for viewing certain ideas as more important than others.

**verlan** A French form of argot in which the syllables in words or the words are often reversed.

**volunteer tourism (Voluntourism)** A type of tourism that combines vacation travel with participation in service projects, often in underserved world regions.

**Whiteness** The associations having to do with the identities of White people.

**worldview** Underlying assumptions about the nature of reality and human behavior.

# Index